www.wadsworth.com

wadsworth.com is the World Wide Web site for Wadsworth/Thomson Learning and is your direct source to dozens of online resources.

At *wadsworth.com* you can find out about supplements, demonstration software, and student resources. You can also send e-mail to many of our authors and preview new publications and exciting new technologies.

wadsworth.com
Changing the way the world learns®

LISTENING TO
MUSIC

3rd Edition

CRAIG WRIGHT

Yale University

Australia • Canada • Mexico • Singapore • Spain • United Kingdom • United States

Music Publisher: *Clark Baxter*

Development Editor: *Sharon Adams Poore*

Assistant Editor: *Cherie Hackelburg*

Editorial Assistant: *Melissa Gleason*

Marketing Manager: *Pamela Shaffer*

Marketing Assistant: *Cara Durr*

Print Buyer: *Stacey Weinberger*

Permissions Editor: *Susan Walters*

Production Service: *Johnstone Associates*

Text and Cover Designer: *Diane Beasley*

Photo Researcher: *Susan Friedman*

Cover Image: *"Liszt at the Grand Piano" by Josef Danhauser, 1840 (Bildarchiv Preussischer Kulturbesitz, Berlin)*.

Compositor: *Thompson Type*

Printer: *Transcontinental Printing, Inc.*

Printed in Canada

2 3 4 5 6 7 03 02 01 00

For permission to use material from this text, contact us by
Web: http://www.thomsonrights.com
Fax: 1-800-730-2215
Phone: 1-800-730-2214

For more information, contact
Wadsworth/Thomson Learning
10 Davis Drive
Belmont, CA 94002-3098
USA
http://www.wadsworth.com

International Headquarters
Thomson Learning
International Division
290 Harbor Drive, 2nd Floor
Stamford, CT 06902-7477
USA

UK/Europe/Middle East/South Africa
Thomson Learning
Berkshire House
168-173 High Holborn
London WC1V 7AA
United Kingdom

Asia
Thomson Learning
60 Albert Street, #15-01
Albert Complex
Singapore 189969

Canada
Nelson Thomson Learning
1120 Birchmount Road
Toronto, Ontario M1K 5G4
Canada

Library of Congress Cataloging-in-Publication Data
Wright, Craig M.
    Listening to music / Craig Wright.—3rd ed.
      p. cm.
    Includes index.
    ISBN 0-534-51733-1
      1. Music appreciation. I. Title.
MT6.W94 L6 2000
781.1'7—dc21
                          99-052933

CONTENTS

CHAPTER 3

MUSICAL COLOR, TEXTURE, AND FORM 37

CHAPTER 4

MEDIEVAL MUSIC 65

CHAPTER 5

RENAISSANCE 80

CHAPTER 6

EARLY BAROQUE MUSIC 95

CHAPTER 7

LATE BAROQUE MUSIC: BACH AND HANDEL 121

CHAPTER 8

CLASSICAL IDEALS: THE WORLD OF HAYDN AND MOZART 149

CHAPTER 9

CLASSICAL FORMS 164

CHAPTER 10

CLASSICAL GENRES 185

CHAPTER 11

THE BRIDGE TO ROMANTICISM: LUDWIG VAN BEETHOVEN 209

CHAPTER 12

THE ROMANTIC SPIRIT (1820–1900) 230

CHAPTER 13

THE EARLY ROMANTICS 246

CHAPTER 14

ROMANTIC OPERA 248

CHAPTER 15

LATE ROMANTICISM 299

CHAPTER 16

FROM ROMANTIC TO MODERN:
IMPRESSIONISM 320

CHAPTER 17

THE TWENTIETH CENTURY   333

CHAPTER 18

AMERICAN POPULAR MUSIC: BLUES, JAZZ, BROADWAY, AND ROCK 377

CHAPTER 19

CONTRASTS: WESTERN MUSIC AND NON-WESTERN MUSIC 400

LISTENING EXERCISES

BOXES

PREFACE

 The painting that serves as the cover for this book is a fascinating artifact. Indeed, one could write a book about it alone. Executed in 1840 by a minor Austrian painter, Josef Danhauser, it is a fanciful depiction of a gathering of some of the greatest artistic luminaries of the nineteenth century. Engaged at the piano is the imposing figure of Franz Liszt, perhaps the most formidable pianist who ever lived. Standing immediately behind him are Gioachino Rossini, the famous opera composer, and Niccolò Paganini, a violin virtuoso whose playing was so extraordinary that he was widely thought to be in league with the devil. With arm on chair, book in hand, is the French nineteenth-century lion of letters, Victor Hugo. Below him, cigar in hand, is Aurore Dudevant, the prototype of the nineteenth-century feminist and a novelist of more than two dozen volumes under her pen name George Sand. Reclining under the sway of the music is Marie d'Agoult, herself a novelist, playwright, and historian of distinction. Finally, radiating the very spirit of music from Olympian heights, a bust of the great Beethoven sits atop the piano—Beethoven the law-giver surrounded by his apostles. Although most of the listeners are poets, playwrights, and novelists, it is the art of music that dominates the scene. From the faces of the guests we can see that they are profoundly affected by what they hear. Music touches their emotions. They are transfixed by its power.

PEDAGOGICAL GOALS

The aim of this textbook is to help the student of today discover and be moved by the great expressive power of music, as in the painting by Danhauser. As this scene suggests, music can be the most compelling of the arts. Yet ironically, most beginning students feel more comfortable with the visual arts than with music. The reason for this is not difficult to fathom: Painting, sculpture, and architecture have an immediate appeal to our visual senses. But music cannot be seen or held. It is intangible, ephemeral, and more mysterious. Because of this, our ways of thinking and talking about music are different from those used to address the visual arts. A new and separate set of concepts and vocabulary is needed. The notion of scales, chords, meters, and rhythms, for example, involves a technical understanding that can be intimidating to the beginning student. This book aims to present these concepts in simple, straightforward terms so as to remove this technical barrier. Pursuing the same desire for clarity, it will also use the language of the visual arts whenever possible to explain musical concepts. With this third edition the number of color illustrations has been increased to more than three hundred. Their purpose is to help transfer concepts already understood in the visual arts to the art of music.

A course in music should be a very different experience from that which the student has elsewhere in the university. It should involve feelings, imagination, notions of beauty, and personal taste, not precise formulas, equations, figures, or dates. Students will be moved by the beauty of music, and they should be encouraged to think about, and express, why and how this is so. In this way they will begin to judge this art more critically. But most textbooks of this sort treat music not as an expressive art, but more as a history of that art. The student is required to learn something of the technical workings of music (what a tonic chord is, for example) and specific facts (how many symphonies Beethoven wrote) but is not asked to become personally engaged in the act of listening to music. What listening there is is passive, not active and participatory.

PEDAGOGICAL AIDS

Listening Exercises

Listening to Music is the only music appreciation text on the market to include Listening Exercises *within* the book. For the Third Edition, forty wholly new or refashioned exercises have been prepared. By means of these, the student will embrace hundreds of specific passages of music and make critical decisions about them. The exercises begin by developing basic listening skills—recognizing rhythmic patterns, distinguishing major keys from minor, and differentiating various kinds of textures. The exercises then move on to entire pieces in which the student is required to become a participant in an artistic exchange, the composer communicating with the listener, and the listener reacting over a long span of time. Ultimately, equipped with these newly developed listening skills, the student will move comfortably to the concert hall, listening to classical and popular music with greater confidence and enjoyment.

The Listening Exercises are the most novel and important part of this text, and the student should be assigned at least two of them each week. Many instructors make the Listening Exercises and tests the backbone of the course. The exercises are all calibrated on a scale of ten and can be quickly corrected. Duplicate copies are contained in the excellent Study Guide prepared by Professor Timothy Roden of Ohio Wesleyan University. (Many students will benefit from the additional drills, self-tests, lists of Internet sites, and suggestions for further listening and reading contained in Professor Roden's Study Guide.)

Listening Guides

In addition to the Listening Exercises, more than eighty Listening Guides appear regularly throughout the text to help the novice enjoy extended musical compositions. Within each guide is a "time log" that allows the listener to follow along as the piece unfolds. The compact disc makes this especially easy, since all that is required is a glance at the minute and second counter to know how far the piece has progressed. The discussion in the text, the Listening Exercises, and the Listening Guides have been carefully coordinated, minute by minute, second by second, with the CDs.

Introductory CD

By now all students own inexpensive CD players. Thus the Third Edition does away with tapes. More important, CDs are much easier for the student to use because the counter times do not vary from one machine to the next. Here the Introductory CD, which comes wrapped with the book, contains the music for the first part of the course, specifically Chapters 1 to 3.

Building a Symphony

Perhaps the most significant addition to the Third Edition is the section "Building a Symphony" (Chapter 3). Experience shows that Britten's *Young Person's Guide to the Orchestra* does not provide enough material for beginning students to master instrumental sounds and textures. To offer more, we engaged a professional-quality symphony orchestra and had the performers take apart and reassemble a significant section of Beethoven's "Eroica" Symphony. Now all of the primary orchestral instruments can be heard in solos, soprano can be distinguished from bass, melody from accompaniment, harmony from counterpoint, and the three basic string techniques (vibrato, tremolo, and pizzicato) heard and understood. This music appears on the Introductory CD that is bound with the book.

Selected Web Resources

This Third Edition contains a new appendix, Selected Web Resources, page 413. Links to websites are organized by topic, and are accompanied by descriptions of each site's offerings. Students can use these websites as supplements to their course work, and as stepping stones to further research. These selected web links will also be available on the website for *Listening to Music*, accessible through Wadsworth's Music Lounge (*http://music.wadsworth.com*).

Musical Terminology and the Glossary

As with every specialized discipline—be it medicine, architecture, or the art of painting—music has its own vocabulary to express concepts unique to the experience of composing and listening. To engage in a lively dialogue about music, we must all understand and be conversant with this musical vocabulary. All musical terms used in this book are defined in the Glossary (beginning on page 423). They appear in the text with an asterisk to remind the reader that definitions can be found in this Glossary. They also are set in boldface type, usually at their first appearance in the text, and are included in the appropriate list of Key Words found at the ends of chapters.

✵ REPERTOIRE

Every book about music aims to present the very best musical repertoire, but some musical works make better teaching pieces than others, which only becomes apparent with time. Moreover, instructors need variety: Teaching the same compositions, no matter how great, year after year can take the joy out of music. Thus movements from Bach's Brandenburg Concerto No. 5, Mozart's Piano Concerto in G (K. 453), Beethoven's "Eroica" Symphony, and Brahms's *A German Requiem*, among others, are new to this Third Edition.

Students need to know that not all music worth hearing was composed by "dead white men." To that end the coverage of four women composers—namely Hildegard of Bingen, the Countess of Dia, Clara Schumann, and Ellen Taaffe

Zwilich—has been expanded. So too has the role of woman as patrons and performers. Finally, the most recent treads of rock and pop music are explored, drawing on the expertise of Mark Spicer, himself a professional rock musician.

ANCILLARIES

CD Sets

All of the music in the book is found on a 6-CD set. A smaller, core repertoire also appears on a 2-CD set. A few Listening Exercises involve works not on the 2-CD set, but students can access these pieces by means of copies of the 6-CD set placed in a music library or listening center. To request complimentary copies of the 6-CD set for such purposes, the instructor should contact the local Wadsworth sales representative (see *http://www.wadsworth.com*).

Instructor's Manual

Dr. Timothy J. Roden, of Ohio Wesleyan University, has prepared an imaginative Instructor's Manual that includes core material for lectures as well as Listening Guides and Listening Exercises not found in the text.

Study Guide

Professor Roden has also written an extraordinary study guide that includes key words for each chapter, biographical descriptions of composers, key facts about important compositions, web links, study questions, self-tests, and suggestions for further listening and reading.

CD-ROM

Dr. Tom Smialek, of Pennsylvania State University, Hazleton, has developed multi-platform listening software to accompany the major pieces discussed in the text and found on the Introductory CD and the 2-CD set.

Acetates

The acetate package featuring Listening Guides and important images from the text is available to adopters.

Wadsworth's Music Lounge

Visit the Wadsworth music website at *http://music.wadsworth.com* to find online activities for students and information for instructors. In the Music Lounge, you can also explore links to other great music websites, select a favorite tune from the jukebox, order a text, or contact the Wadsworth Music Editor.

ACKNOWLEDGMENTS

Part of the fun of teaching music appreciation comes from discussing with colleagues how to introduce classical music to students who know little about music. What can students be reasonably expected to hear? What is the best terminology to use? Profs. Keith Polk (University of New Hampshire) and Tilden Russell (Southern Connecticut State University) have gently taken me to task for using the term "ternary form" where "rounded binary" is more correct; they are right, yet for fear of overloading the beginning student with too many new formal concepts, here I simplify and call both rounded binary and ternary forms just ternary. I am, nevertheless, grateful for their continuing support and attention to matters of detail. So too I am indebted to Profs. Anne Robertson and Robert Kendrick of the University of Chicago for help in many overt and covert ways. Two former students, Prof. Marica Tacconi (Pennsylvania State University) and Prof. Laura Nash (Fairfield University) continue to provide me with valuable criticisms and suggestions. Earlier editions of the book benefitted greatly from the careful eyes of Prof. James Ladewig (University of Rhode Island), Prof. William E. Hettrick (Hofstra University), and Prof. Edmund Goehring (University of Notre Dame). Finally, Prof. Timothy Roden (Ohio Wesleyan University), the author of the Study Guide and Instructor's Manual, provided a steady stream of good ideas.

The following reviewers also evaluated material or provided helpful information during the writing of this book:

D. E. Bussinaeau-King
University of the Incarnate Word

Andrew Byrne
Columbia University

Ann B. Caldwell
Georgia College and State University

Cheong L. Chuah
Cerro Cosso Community College

Hollie Duvall
Westmoreland County Community College

Harry Faulk
Fairmont State College

Fenton G. Fly
Alabama State University

Benjamin K. Gish
Walla Walla College

Patricia L. Hales
Purdue University, Calumet

Marymal L. Holmes
Bowie State Univerity

David Lee Jackson
Baylor University

Walter Kreiszig
Univerisity of Saskatchewan

Charles S. Larkowski
Wright State University

Gary Lewis
Midwestern State University

Bernard C. Lemoine
Mary Washington College

Ed Macan
College of the Redwoods

Laura Nash
Fairfield University

Sharon H. Nelson
Wright State University

Laurie H. Ongley
Southern Connecticut State University

Diane M. Paige
University of California, Santa Barbara

Linda Pohly
Ball State University

Thomas C. Polett
Culver-Stockton College

Ronald Rabin
University of Michigan

Daniel Ratelle
San Diego Mesa College

Laurie A. Reese
Lebanon Community College

Steven Roberson
Butler University

Karl Schmidt
Towson University

Chirstine Larson Seitz
Indiana University South Bend

John Sinclair
Rollins College

Richard Shillea
Fairfield University

Jayme Stayer
Owens Community College

Gary R. Sudano
Purdue University

Timothy P. Urban
Rutgers University

Melva Villard
*Louisiana State University at
Alexandria*

Susan Weiss
Johns Hopkins University

Cynthia Wong
Columbia University

Annette H. Zalanowski
*Pennsylvania State University,
Altoona*

Ray H. Ziegler
Salisbury State University

I owe a debt of gratitude to several colleagues at Yale, including Profs. Leon Plantinga, Ellen Rosand, Ramon Satyendra, and Kathryn Alexander. A number of graduate students helped in diverse ways, namely Harris Crist and Mark Spicer with ideas, Michael Puri with musical performances, Kay Tidwell with editorial suggestions and proofreading, and especially Edward Latham, who carefully prepared the musical examples. In addition, I benefitted greatly from the help and good will of the staff of the Yale Music Library: Ken Crilly, librarian, and Helen Bartlett, Richard Boursey, Suzanne Eggleston, Eva Heater, and Kathy Manzi. Karl Schrom, record librarian at Yale, gave frequent good advice regarding the availability and quality of recordings. Dr. Shinik Hahm graciously agreed to take the Yale Symphony Orchestra under his deft baton to help construct Building a Symphony. Gene Kimball skillfully recorded and/or edited all of the new audio material. Within my own family, my wife Sherry, sons Andrew and Evan, daughter Stephanie, daughter-in-law Melanie, and esteemed brother-in-law Sterling Murray (West Chester University) provided many good ideas and a noisy counterpoint to my own. As always, it has been a privilege to work with my editor, Clark Baxter, and his staff at Wadsworth—specifically copyeditor and production manager Judy Johnstone, editorial assistant Melissa Gleason, photo researcher Susan Friedman, and project editor Hal Humphrey—as well as audio manager Wayne Olsen at Universal Records. A special thanks to Diane Beasley for her scintillating design of each and every page.

LISTENING
TO MUSIC

1

"It is perhaps in music that the dignity of art is most eminently apparent, for it elevates and ennobles everything that it expresses."
Johann Wolfgang von Goethe (1749–1832)

"It don't mean a thing if it ain't got that swing."
Edward Kennedy "Duke" Ellington (1899–1974)

 Why do we listen to music? Because it gives us pleasure. Why does it give us pleasure? We don't know, though psychologists have spent a great deal of time trying to find out. By some inexplicable means, music has the power to intensify and deepen our feelings, to calm our jangled nerves, to make us sad or cheerful, to incite us to dance, and even, perhaps, to march proudly off to war. Long ago, the ancient Greeks recognized the powers of music; indeed, Plato thought exposure to the proper sort of music would encourage the young men of Athens to study diligently and avoid the eternal temptations of wine and women. We in the modern world have made music an indispensable part of our most important religious, social, and artistic activities. Music adds to the solemnity of our ceremonies, arts, and entertainments, and thus "moves" (heightens the feelings) of all who watch and participate. If you doubt this, try looking at a motion picture without listening to the musical score, or imagine a parade, a wedding, or a funeral without music and think how empty these events would be.

When we listen to music, physically speaking, we are reacting to an organized disturbance of our environment (Fig. 1–1). A voice or an instrument emits energized sounds that set the air in motion, creating waves that carry the sound to our ears. In the inner ear, these vibrations are transformed into electrochemical impulses that, in turn, are transferred to the brain. What happens there is not certain, but it appears that the impulses are sorted and recognized as patterns and shapes, perhaps not unlike visual patterns or geometric shapes. In the end, the way we perceive a musical composition may not be much different from our perception of a harmonious work of architecture, the colorful relationships within a tapestry, or the gently moving contours of a lovely landscape. We respond emotionally to, and are moved by, musical relationships that are pleasing, novel, or even disturbing. Responding to the endless patterns of music—by tapping our feet, moving our bodies, or humming along—is an experience common to us all.

BECOMING A GOOD LISTENER

Listening to music is an art, and like all the arts it requires preparation and discipline. Part of the preparation involves learning what to listen for and what to expect in music. For this, we must have some knowledge of how music works. How do melodies unfold? How do musical phrases work together to mark the

✿ FIGURE 1–1

A musical instrument produces regular waves of sound that pass through the ear. The listener sorts and tries to make sense of the sound patterns.

progress of a piece? How does a composer get from one section to the next, and how does he or she signal that the conclusion is near? One of the aims of this book is to give you an understanding of what these common musical processes are, so that you can make sense out of what you hear and can even anticipate what may come next. In this way, knowledge will increase your enjoyment.

Along with learning how music works comes the development of good listening skills. We should be able to recognize which instruments are playing, sort out the melody from the harmony, identify how many distinctive layers or lines there are in the musical texture, feel the meter and the rhythm of the piece, and sense where we are in the formal design of the work. This will require *active, not passive, listening*. But once such skills have been mastered, they can be applied equally well to both classical and popular music. Hearing a bass line in a tune of R.E.M., for example, is not much different from hearing one in a symphony by Beethoven.

Focus Solely on the Music

The first step toward improving your listening skills is to focus solely on the music. Most of us use music as a backdrop for other activities. You may be in the habit of listening to the radio or a CD while doing your class assignments. Some music, specifically the "easy listening" music that floods the FM airwaves, is in fact designed *not* to be heard, or at least not to be the object of any heavy thinking. But, for more serious music, this sort of background listening won't do. Similarly, the superficial hearing we give to most popular music is anything but deep and penetrating. We respond emotionally with our hearts (and bodies, if we wish to dance), but not with our minds. Classical music and jazz require that we engage our intellect and think critically about what we hear. We have to recognize specific musical events, retain these in our memory, and relate them to one another over a span of time. For this, we must devote our full attention to the music.

Improve Your Memory

Memory is essential to good listening. Unlike the visual arts, music passes through time. When we look at a painting, for example, it stands still before us, to be taken in all at once. If we relate this painting to anything, it is to other, similar paintings that we know. Our approach to a musical composition, however, is much different. We are not given the entire object at once. Rather, it comes to us gradually, bit by bit, as the seconds and minutes go by. To make sense of what we hear *now*, we have to remember what we heard *before*. Trying to remember and relate sounds that seem to pass by all too quickly is the greatest challenge for the beginning listener. How do we deal with this rush of music? Simply said, the listener must learn to seize upon a few key events and hold them firmly in mind. The Listening Exercises in this book are designed to improve your capacity to remember sounds. And, like most physical and mental exercises, the more you use your musical memory, the better it becomes.

Grasp the Important Sounds

Unless we happen to have a talent like Mozart's, our minds cannot retain all that our ears hear. The music passes too quickly, no matter how hard we concentrate or how good our memory is. But composers have main themes they wish to communicate, and they also have moments of preparation, transition, and just plain filler. Some parts of the music should be strongly locked in our consciousness and other parts we can let go. Being able to differentiate between the important and the unimportant in music is thus the listener's first task. The Listening Guides in this book are designed to sharpen your critical faculties by showing you what the author thinks is important. The Listening Exercises at the end of the chapters, however, are intended to get you actively involved in the decisionmaking process. Later, you yourself will make all the critical judgments about music when you buy a new CD, hear a new piece on the radio, or attend a concert.

seize the important ideas

A violinist records music in a studio.

Incoming analog sound is sampled 44,100 times a second.

A digital version of the sound is created, by converting music into numerical "words" of 16 bits each. The encoded sound is then stored as digital data along an extremely narrow (1/100th the thickness of a human hair) spiral track. The track, if uncoiled, would extend for three miles.

 FIGURE 1–2

A violinist sets sound waves in motion in a recording studio.

The finished CD is coated with aluminum to give it a reflective surface and covered with ultraviolet lacquer.

Finally, a digital analog converter within the CD player changes numbers to electrical impulses that can be amplified and pushed through audio speakers.

CD player and speakers.

CLASSICAL MUSIC–POPULAR MUSIC

There is an astonishing variety of music in the world, both good and bad. Most of the music that will be discussed in this book is what we refer to as "classical" music. It is also called "art" music or "serious" music. Someone said that classical music is music that was written by "dead white men." That's not entirely accurate: no small amount of it has been written by women, and many classical composers, of both sexes, are very much alive and well today. But in truth, most of what we hear in the way of classical music—the music of Bach, Handel, Mozart, Haydn, Beethoven, Schubert, and Tchaikovsky, for example—was written by composers working in Europe or Russia between 1700 and 1900, and thus was created at least a century ago. Indeed, one thing that makes a cultural artifact a "classic" is that it possesses certain qualities of expression, proportion, and balance that are timeless in their appeal.

a classic has a timeless appeal

Popular music embraces the sounds that most people want to hear. Pop and rock CDs outsell those of classical music by about nine to one. Popular music can be just as artful and just as serious as classical music, and often the musicians who perform it are just as talented and skilled as classical musicians. But popular music, unlike classical, rarely contains multiple levels of musical activity, and for this reason does not require, and does not reward, intensely active listening. What we hear the first time is (more or less) what we get. Perhaps this inability to reward repeated hearings or to allow for a different interpretation each time we listen is why the listening public quickly tires of particular popular songs and moves on to new ones. Only when a popular song does give pleasure to more than one generation, over a span of twenty or thirty years do we say that that tune has become a "classic."

Popular music can be useful in learning good listening skills. When trying to hear how and when chords change in a piece by Bach, for example, it can be helpful to listen first to a rock tune, say one by R.E.M., in which the chords are uncomplicated, the chords change at regular time intervals, and the bass, which carries the chords, is very loud and thus easy to hear. What we learn in one style can easily be transferred to another.

FIGURE 1–3
Trumpeter Wynton Marsalis can record a collection of Vivaldi trumpet concertos one week and an album of Dixieland jazz the next. He has won eight Grammy awards, six for various jazz categories and two for classical discs.

ATTENDING A CONCERT OF CLASSICAL MUSIC

Compared to pop or rock concerts, a performance of classical music may seem strange indeed. People dress up, not down. They sit quietly, saying nothing to friends or performers. No one sways or dances to the music. Only at the very end of each composition does the audience express itself, by respectfully clapping.

But classical concerts weren't always so formal. In the eighteenth century the audience talked during the performance and yelled words of encouragement to the players. People clapped at the

FIGURE 1–4

Symphony Hall in Boston, Massachusetts. The best seats for hearing the music are not up front, but at the back, in the middle of the balcony.

end of each movement of a symphony and often in the middle of the movement as well. After an exceptionally pleasing performance, the audience would demand that the piece be repeated immediately (an **encore**). But if the audience didn't like what it heard, it would show displeasure by throwing fruit and other debris toward the stage. Our modern, more dignified classical concert was a creation of the nineteenth century (see page 235).

Attending a classical concert requires forethought. Get familiar with the pieces in advance. Go to a music library and listen to a CD of the pieces that will be performed. Read the liner notes that accompany the CD to learn something about the history and cultural context of the works. Having heard a professional-quality recording, you will be prepared to judge the merits of a live (perhaps student) performance.

preparation for a concert

Choosing the right seat is also important. What is best for seeing may not be best for hearing. In some concert halls the sound sails immediately over those seated in the front rows and coalesces at the back (Fig. 1–4). Often the optimal place for sound (the best in terms of acoustics) is at the back of the hall, in the first balcony. Sitting closer, of course, allows you to enjoy watching the interplay of the performers on stage. If you attend a concert of a symphony orchestra, follow the gestures of the conductor to the various soloists and sections of the orchestra. The conductor is communicating not only to the players but also to the audience the essential lines and themes of the music.

where to sit?

VISUALIZING CLASSICAL MUSIC

Many people feel more comfortable looking at the visual arts than listening to classical music. They prefer to visit an art museum rather than attend a classical concert. But why is music thought more inaccessible? Probably because we cannot see or touch it. Music is difficult to measure and quantify. It wafts through the air and works its magic in mysterious ways. Our inability to hold on to music makes it just a little bit intimidating. To get to the heart of classical music, an entirely new vocabulary—that of music theory—has to be learned; this is what music majors study in universities. But for the beginning listener there is a simpler, more immediately satisfying way: visualizing the music. We can picture—make a mental image—of the music as it passes. Here in this text we will do so by means of listening exercises and visual aids. This book contains more than 300 color illustrations. Most of these amplify themes discussed in the text. Many, however, offer visual illustrations of phenomena that occur in music. They show the workings of music by drawing analogies to identical practices in architecture, painting, and design. "Analogies decide nothing that is true," Sigmund Freud (1856–1939) said, "but they can make one feel more at home." Let us begin to feel more at home with classical music by listening to a work composed with the aim of capturing in sound the emotions present in a series of paintings.

make a mental image of the music

PICTURES AT AN EXHIBITION (1874), MODEST MUSORGSKY

In February 1874 an exhibition of the works of designer and architect Victor Hartmann (1833–1873) was held at the Academy of Artists in St. Petersburg, Russia. Hartmann had died unexpectedly of a stroke the previous year, and a group of his friends organized this show to honor his memory. One of Hartmann's closest colleagues, the Russian composer Modest Musorgsky, paid further homage to the artist in 1874 by transforming ten of his pictures into a musical work. The classic that Musorgsky created, his *Pictures at an Exhibition,* has perpetuated not only the fame of Musorgsky but also the name of Hartmann, whose art otherwise would likely be forgotten.

Modest Musorgsky (1839–1881) was born into a land-rich, aristocratic family near St. Petersburg. As a youth he showed great musical talent, performing a piano concerto at the age of nine. But the life of a professional musician was not deemed an appropriate vocation for a member of the aristocracy, and so he trained half-heartedly to be a military officer, receiving a commission in 1856. When Czar Alexander II emancipated the serfs in 1859, the Russian leader simultaneously separated the Musorgsky family from the source of its wealth. Having resigned his commission in the army and finding himself suddenly penniless, Musorgsky took a job as a clerk in the forestry department to put food on the table. But his real love—indeed obsession—remained music, and he composed during all of his spare moments.

Support for his music came to Musorgsky from a group of other young composers then active in St. Petersburg. Contemporaries dubbed this musical club "The Mighty Handful" or, less grandiosely, **The Russian Five.** It included Alexander Borodin (1833–1887), César Cui (1835–1918), Mily Balakirev

🌿 FIGURE 1–5
Modest Musorgsky.

🌿 FIGURE 1–6
Still from motion picture *Wizard of Oz* (1939) in black and white.

(1837–1910), Nikolai Rimsky-Korsakov (1844–1908), and Musorgsky himself. Sadly, Musorgsky's brief, chaotic life was marked by increasing poverty, depression, and alcoholism. Still he managed to create a small but impressive list of works that includes a boldly inventive symphonic poem, *Night on Bald Mountain* (1867) and an operatic masterpiece, *Boris Godunov* (1874). Musorgsky is best remembered today, however, for his *Pictures at an Exhibition*.

Musorgsky created his musical response to Hartmann's art at the piano, to be performed on the piano. Yet, there are times in the history of music when a densely packed composition written at the keyboard cries out for a more elaborate presentation by an orchestra. Musorgsky's inventive *Pictures at an Exhibition* was one work that demanded an instrumental presentation to reach its fullest potential. When music conceived at the keyboard is allocated to the various instruments of the orchestra, an **orchestration** results. The most successful orchestration of *Pictures at an Exhibition* was effected in 1922 by French composer Maurice Ravel (on Ravel, see page 329). To the usual symphony orchestra, Ravel added a saxophone and novel percussion instruments for special effects. The result is astonishing. Just as the addition of color radically alters the impact of a motion picture filmed in black and white (see Figs. 1–6 and 1–7), so Ravel's orches-

🌿 FIGURE 1–7
Still from motion picture *Wizard of Oz*, color-enhanced version. Just as color can enrich the art of film, so a full orchestra can add color to a musical score created at the piano.

tration intensifies Musorgsky's originally monochromatic music. The effect of Ravel's orchestration is to make Musorgsky's musical pictures both more powerful and more vivid. Let us begin our visit to the Musorgsky-Ravel musical museum.

PROMENADE Here the composer portrays himself (and by extension us, the listeners) as wandering through an exhibition of Hartmann's paintings. The first piece, *Promenade,* later returns between pictures to create the sense of moving through a gallery from one painting to the next. Immediately, we are transported musically into a world of purely Russian art. *Promenade* is marked "Fast but resolute, in the Russian manner" (*Allegro giusto, nel modo russico*). This is an indication of the **tempo,** the speed at which the beat of a piece is to proceed. The music unfolds in purposeful, evenly spaced sounds as the viewer marches resolutely up to each picture. Let us call this marching melody the Promenade theme. The musical notation for it is given in the Listening Guide. This notation may seem alien to you, but don't panic—musical notation will be explained fully in Chapter 2. For the moment, simply put on the CD and follow the music as it unfolds according to the minute and second counter on your CD player.

a world of Russian art

LISTENING GUIDE

Modest Musorgsky
Promenade from *Pictures at an Exhibition* (1874)
(orchestrated by Maurice Ravel, 1922)

Intro CD/1

0:00	Solo trumpet begins Promenade theme
0:07	Full brasses respond
0:15	Trumpet and full brass continue to alternate
0:30	Full strings and then woodwinds and brass enter
1:22	Brasses briefly restate Promenade theme

PICTURE 4 Now we stand before a painting in the exhibition. Alas, this particular tableau, called *Polish Ox-Cart,* has not survived, so we will have to picture it in our mind's eye. Imagine an overloaded wagon pulled by oxen, lumbering down a dirt road in rural Russia. The rocking of the cart is suggested by a bass that alternates, back and forth, between just two notes (down-up-down-up-down-up). A rhythm, melody, or harmony that repeats over and over in this fashion is called an **ostinato** (from the Italian word meaning "obstinate" or "stubborn"). Here the ostinato helps create a sense of motion. Thus a musical composition has the capacity to project a feeling of movement in a way that a painting cannot. The viewer stands stationary as the cart appears **pianissimo** (very softly), hence in the distance; it moves closer and closer by means of a **crescendo** (a gradual increase in the volume of sound). Now the cart shakes the earth **fortissimo** (very loud) as it rumbles past, and then it slowly disappears as the orchestra effects a **diminuendo** (a gradual reduction of the volume of sound).

dynamics create distance

Creating this sense of motion (coming and going) required a knowledge of the physics of music. Musorgsky knew that larger sound waves (those of the lower pitches) travel farther than shorter waves (higher pitches). In other words, sounds made by low instruments go farther than those made by high ones. We have all experienced this law of musical acoustics: when listening to a marching band approaching from the distance we hear the sounds of the bass drum and tubas long before the higher ones of the trumpets and clarinets. Thus, in

Polish Ox-Cart, Musorgsky begins and ends with the very lowest sounds (orchestrated by Ravel with tuba and double basses), to give the impression that the sound comes from a distance and then disappears again into the distance. By changing musical dynamics (soft to loud to soft) and by shifting ranges of sound (low to high to low), Musorgsky makes the ox-cart move before our eyes.

LISTENING GUIDE

Modest Musorgsky
Pictures at an Exhibition
Polish Ox-Cart

Intro CD/2

0:00   Solo tuba plays Ox-Cart melody against backdrop of a two-note ostinato
0:51   Strings, and soon full orchestra, join in
1:33   Full orchestra plays Ox-Cart theme (rattle of tambourine suggests cart shaking the earth)
1:54   Tuba returns with Ox-Cart theme
2:24   Diminuendo and fadeout

PICTURE 6 Let's walk now to the next picture, *Samuel Goldenberg and Schmuyle: Two Jews, Rich and Poor.* As the title suggests, we are looking here at a pair of drawings, both of which survive (Figs. 1–8 and 1–9). One Jew stares out confidently; the other displays an attitude of despair. They might just as well be two Christians or two Moslems—what counts here is social status. We can be sure, however, that the two come from Eastern Europe because the music has an oriental quality to it; Musorgsky is drawing on melodies found in Eastern European folk music. First we see Goldenberg, haughty and imperious. His music sounds domineering because it is loud and because all the instruments join forces on a single musical line. When instruments or voices play or sing together on one pitch in this fashion they do so in musical **unison.** The sound is assured and self-confident. The music of the Poor Jew, on the other hand, is fragmented between woodwinds and a trumpet. The trumpet is played with a **mute,** a mechanical device placed on or into an instrument to soften sound. Schmuyle cringes meekly in rapidly quivering notes that steadily fall down. We can almost see his teeth chattering and his body trembling. A confrontation between Goldenberg and Schmuyle follows, as the musics of the two characters sound simultaneously. Musorgsky not only makes the characters come alive in music but also causes them to interact in a way portrait paintings cannot. As you listen, ask yourself who has the last word in this musical encounter.

🌸 FIGURE 1–9
Victor Hartmann. Pencil and watercolor, *A Poor Jew.* The subject sits downcast, a sack containing all his worldly possessions placed to his left.

🌸 FIGURE 1–8
Victor Hartmann. Pencil drawing, *A Rich Jew.* The subject wears a comfortable fur skull cap, the symbol of his religion.

LISTENING GUIDE

Modest Musorgsky
Pictures at an Exhibition
Goldenberg and Schmuyle: Two Jews, Rich and Poor

Intro CD/3

0:00   Strings in unison play imposing music of Goldenberg

0:45   Trumpet (with mute), accompanied by woodwinds, play trembling music of Schmuyle
1:23   Strings loudly interject the music of Goldenberg
1:51   The music of Schmuyle slithers away in the strings

❀ FIGURE 1–10

Victor Hartmann's vision *The Great Gate of Kiev,* which inspired the last of the musical painting in Musorgsky's *Pictures at an Exhibition.* Note the bells in the tower, a motif that is featured prominently at the very end of Musorgsky's musical evocation of this design.

PICTURE 10   Finally, we arrive at the last painting in this musical exhibition, *The Great Gate of Kiev.* The stimulus for the majestic conclusion to *Pictures at an Exhibition* was Victor Hartmann's design for a new and grandiose gate to the ancient Ukrainian city of Kiev, then part of Russia (Fig. 1–10). The gate, which was designed by Hartmann but never constructed, was to celebrate an event in the life of Czar Alexander II. It was to be the Russian equivalent of the triumphal arch that the victorious Emperor Napoleon I had constructed in Paris and which Hartmann had seen in his travels to France (Fig. 1–11). This vision of a great triumphal arch accounts for the grand and majestic sound of the music.

Musorgsky disposes his musical material to give the impression of a parade passing beneath the giant gate. The music of the gate itself (music **A**) alternates with religious music for a procession of Russian pilgrims (music **B**), and even the composer-viewer walks beneath the gate as the Promenade theme (music **C**) appears, before a final return to a panoramic view of the gate **(A),** now with Hartmann's bells ringing triumphantly. Taken in sum, the events in *The Great Gate of Kiev* constitute a pleasing musical form **(ABABXCA)** in which a refrain **(A)** provides unity and coherence. Here in this final tableau, the full orchestra is able to create a strong feeling of the local color and, at the same time, of the great power of old Russia.

❀ FIGURE 1–11

The Arch of Triumph in Paris, built by Emperor Napoleon to celebrate his victories over the Prussians and Austrians (1811) during the Napoleonic Wars. It served as inspiration for Victor Hartmann's design for Kiev.

LISTENING GUIDE

Modest Musorgsky
Pictures at an Exhibition
The Great Gate of Kiev

0:00	A	Gate theme in full brass
1:05	B	Pilgrims' hymn sounds in woodwind choir
1:35	A	Gate theme in brasses, with running scales in strings
2:10	B	Pilgrims' hymn returns in woodwinds
2:42	X	Strange, exotic sounds
3:21	C	Promenade theme returns in trumpet
3:59	A	Gate theme in full glory, with Russian bells added toward the end

Musorgsky's *Pictures at an Exhibition* has remained popular with audiences down to the present day—with those who attend "pops" as well as classical concerts. In addition, the rock group Emerson, Lake, and Palmer has fashioned a version aimed at pleasing more modern listeners (*Pictures at an Exhibition*, Rhino Records R2 72225). If you have occasion to hear this rock rendering of *Pictures at an Exhibition*, you may enjoy the more "with-it" version of the orchestration. On the other hand, you may come away with a new-found respect for the ingenuity of both Musorgsky and Ravel, as well as the power and beauty of classical music generally.

a rock version

LISTENING EXERCISE

Modest Musorgsky
Pictures at an Exhibition (1874)
(orchestrated by Maurice Ravel, 1922)

Intro CD/1–4

Be sure that you have read the discussion of this work in the text (pages 6–11) and listened to it following the Listening Guides (pages 8–11). Now listen to it once again and answer the following questions. They are intended to sharpen your capacity to recognize the instruments of the orchestra. Should you have difficulties, CD technology allows you to move quickly back and forth to rehear passages as many times as you wish. This first exercise is designed to be user-friendly—the questions are not too difficult.

Promenade Intro CD/1
1. (0:00–0:07) What brass instrument(s) opens the work?
   a. a solo trumpet   b. a group of trumpets   c. trumpets and trombones
2. (0:08–0:31) Which statement is true regarding this next passage?
   a. Other brass instruments enter and the trumpet stops playing.
   b. Other brass instruments enter and the trumpet continues playing.
3. The sound of the trumpet can be said to be
   a. at the top of the sound of the brass family
   b. in the middle of the sound of the brass family
   c. at the bottom of the sound of the brass family
4. (1:31–1:37) At the end of the movement, do the strings join with the brasses in playing the Promenade theme? _____

Polish Ox-Cart Intro CD/2

5. (0:00–0:50) How many parts, or musical lines, do you hear here?
   a. two: trumpet and supporting harmony in the bass
   b. two: tuba and supporting harmony in the bass
   c. three: trumpet on top, tuba in middle, supporting bass underneath
6. (0:00–0:50) Focus now on the bass, which is played by the large string double basses (Fig. 3–6). Which of the following statements is true?
   a. The double basses alternately play sounds that are long and short.
   b. The double basses alternately play sounds that are short and long.
   c. The double basses constantly play sounds of the same duration.

Goldenberg and Schmuyle: Two Jews, Rich and Poor Intro CD/3

7. (0:45–1:14) The character of Schmuyle is depicted in music by means of a fluttering trumpet (played with a softening mute) supported by members of the woodwind family. The woodwinds play notes moving
   a. more rapidly than those of the trumpet
   b. more slowly than those of the trumpet
   c. at the same speed as those of the trumpet
8. (2:10–2:12) Which character ultimately has the last word, Goldenberg (loud, unison writing for the string family) or Schmuyle (fluttering trumpet)?
   _____

The Great Gate of Kiev Intro CD/4

9. The Gate theme is heard in full three times in this movement (at 0:00, 1:36, and 3:35). When it appears the second time (1:36–2:09) the texture is enriched by means of running scales in the strings. Which of the following is true?
   a. High strings play racing scales while the Gate theme sounds in the low brasses. Then at 1:51 the roles are reversed. Low strings play racing scales while the Gate theme sounds in the high brasses.
   b. Low strings play racing scales while the Gate theme sounds in the high brasses. Then at 1:51 the roles are reversed. High strings play racing scales while the Gate theme sounds in the low brasses.
10. The Gate theme is briefly recalled toward the very end, and it sounds very grand indeed! Circle four ways in which the composer creates a sense of majesty and gives a feeling of finality to the work.
    a. The Gate theme moves at half its usual tempo.
    b. Percussion (drums and cymbals and bells) are added for emphasis.
    c. All of the orchestra is playing, and doing so *fortissimo*.
    d. The last chords are very drawn out.
    e. A piano plays loudly at the end.

 KEY WORDS

crescendo	mute	the Russian Five
diminuendo	orchestration	tempo
encore	ostinato	unison
fortissimo	*pianissimo*	

RHYTHM, MELODY, AND HARMONY

 Music can be defined as sound that moves through time in some organized fashion. Sounds and silences can be shaped, given a profile, as they pass through time. Durations can be organized in patterns to form rhythms. And musical pitches can be placed one after the other in a purposeful way to form a melody. When more than one pitch sounds at a time, the potential exists for musical harmony. Rhythm, melody, and harmony, then, are the most basic musical elements. They are the building blocks of music, and how they are arranged determines the color, texture, and form of every musical composition.

In discussing rhythm, melody, and harmony, we depend greatly on a terminology that has grown up around the practice of notating music. Musical notation is simply music put down on paper by means of special signs or symbols. The horizontal axis (left to right) specifies the element of time, while the vertical one (top to bottom) indicates pitch, high to low. By recording a piece in musical notation, we, in effect, "freeze dry" the musical work so that it can be exactly reproduced by performers at some later date. In addition, musical notation allows us to stop at any point, to look at a composition as it is standing still, talk about its various parts, and learn something about how it is put together. You do not have to know musical notation to derive great pleasure from listening to music, nor will you have to read it to be highly successful in using this book. But the enjoyment of music can be enhanced if we understand how music works, and to explain this we need to know something of the technical language of music.

RHYTHM

Rhythm is arguably the most fundamental element of music. When asked to sing a favorite song, most of us will recall the rhythm better than the melody. Similarly, when hearing a piece of music for the first time, we are more likely to be struck by, and remember, a catchy rhythm than a catchy tune. We have a direct, even physical, response to rhythm.

Rhythm, in its broadest definition, is the organization of time in music. It divides up long spans of time into smaller, more easily comprehended units. It gives a shape, or profile, to the melody or tune. Basic to rhythm is the principle of the beat. The **beat** is an even pulse that divides the passing of time into equal segments. It may be strongly felt, as in a waltz or a straight-ahead rock 'n' roll tune, or it may be only dimly heard (because no instrument plays it strongly),

❊ FIGURE 2–1
Performers of traditional New Orleans jazz often play simultaneously in different rhythms.

as in much of the Impressionistic music of the late nineteenth century (Chapter 16). But whether immediately or distantly heard, almost all music has a beat to it. When we tap our foot to music, we are reacting to such a beat.

The beat in music is most often carried by a unit of measurement called the quarter note (♩), a basic duration in music. Normally, the quarter note will move along roughly at the rate of the average person's heartbeat, sometimes faster, sometimes slower. As you might suspect from its name, the quarter note is shorter in length than the half and the whole note, but longer than the eighth and the sixteenth note. These other note values account for durations that are longer or shorter than the beat. Here are the symbols for the most-used musical notes and an indication of how they relate to one another in length:

EXAMPLE 2–1

(whole note) 𝅝	=	𝅗𝅥 𝅗𝅥	(2 half notes)
(half note) 𝅗𝅥	=	♩ ♩	(2 quarter notes)
(quarter note) ♩	=	♪ ♪	(2 eighth notes)
(eighth note) ♪	=	𝅘𝅥𝅯 𝅘𝅥𝅯	(2 sixteenth notes)

To help the performer keep the beat when playing or singing, the smaller note values, specifically, those with flags on the vertical stem, are beamed, or joined together, in groups of two or four:

EXAMPLE 2–2

becomes

In vocal music, however, the beaming is broken when a syllable of text is placed below a note:

EXAMPLE 2–3

♪ ♪ ♩ ♪ ♪ ♩ ♪ ♪ ♪ ♪ ♩

Jin-gle bells, jin-gle bells,   jin-gle all the way

In addition to notes that signify the duration of sound, there are other signs, called rests, that indicate silence. For each note there is a corresponding rest of the same value:

EXAMPLE 2–4

𝅝 whole note	▬ whole rest
𝅗𝅥 half note	▬ half rest
♩ quarter note	𝄽 quarter rest
♪ eighth note	𝄾 eighth rest
𝅘𝅥𝅯 sixteenth note	𝄿 sixteenth rest

You will have noticed that, in their basic form, adjacent note values (and rests) in music all have a 2:1 ratio to one another: One half note equals two quarter notes, and so on. But triple relationships can and do exist, and these are created by means of the addition of a dot after a note, which increases the duration of the note to one and one-half its original value:

EXAMPLE 2–5

Let's take a look at how the various note values can reflect the rhythm of an actual piece of music. For this we choose a simple, well-known tune, *Yankee Doodle*. First the text is given to refresh your memory as to how the song goes, next the rhythm of the tune indicated by horizontal lines of different lengths to show how long each pitch lasts, then the rhythm in musical notation, and finally the position of the beat in *Yankee Doodle* as indicated by quarter notes:

EXAMPLE 2–6

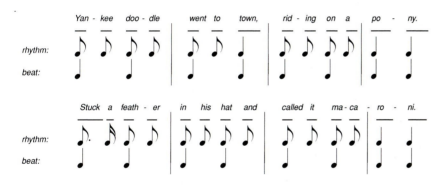

Here's the patriotic song *America* (first known in England and Canada as *God Save the King—*or *Queen*) arranged the same way:

EXAMPLE 2–7

� FIGURE 2–2
Rhythm of a Russian Dance (1918) by Theo van Doesburg. Rhythm in music is the rational organization of time into longer and shorter durations. The same process can be at work in the visual arts. Here the painter places units of color of different lengths to form complementary patterns.

Listening Exercise 2a at the end of the chapter will help you to focus on the many musical rhythms you already have in your ear.

Meter

Notice how in the preceding examples vertical lines divide the music into groups of two beats, in the case of *Yankee Doodle*, and into groups of three beats in *America*. These strokes are called measure lines, or bar lines. A **measure,** or bar, is a group of beats. Usually, there are two or three, sometimes four or more beats per measure. The gathering of beats into regular groups produces **meter.** Instead of having a steady stream of undifferentiated beats, we instinctively stress some more than others in a regular and repeating fashion. If we stress every other beat—ONE two, ONE two, ONE two—we have two beats per measure and therefore duple meter. The stressed beats are called strong beats and the unstressed beats weak beats. Similarly, if we emphasize every third beat—ONE two three, ONE two three, ONE two three—we have three beats per measure and thus triple meter. Triple meter has one strong beat and two weak beats per bar. In addition, there are other meters with four or six beats per measure. Here is a familiar folk song in the more common quadruple meter (four beats per measure):

duple and triple meter

EXAMPLE 2–8

And here is an equally well-known tune in sextuple meter:

EXAMPLE 2–9

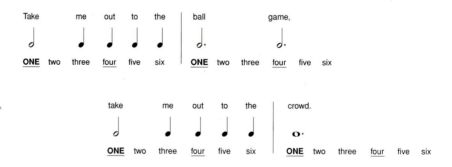

Most music, however, is written in duple ($\frac{2}{4}$), triple ($\frac{3}{4}$), or quadruple ($\frac{4}{4}$) meter.

Meter in music is indicated by a **time signature,** two numbers, one on top of the other, placed at the beginning of the music to tell the performer how the beats of the music are to be grouped. The top number of the signature indicates how many beats there are per measure; the bottom number tells what note value is the beat. Since, as we have said, the quarter note most often carries the beat, most time signatures have a "4" on the bottom. The three most frequently encountered time signatures are given here:

time signatures

EXAMPLE 2–10

Having a time signature at the beginning of the music may be of great value to the performer, but it doesn't help the listener, unless he or she happens to be following along with the musical notation—following the **score,** as musicians call it. Without a score, the listener must of necessity hear and feel the meter. Most music, as we have said, is written in $\frac{2}{4}$, $\frac{3}{4}$, or $\frac{4}{4}$. Since $\frac{4}{4}$ is in most (but not all) ways merely a multiple or extension of $\frac{2}{4}$, there are really only two meters that the beginning listener should be aware of: duple meter ($\frac{2}{4}$) and triple meter ($\frac{3}{4}$). But how do we hear these and differentiate between them?

Hearing Meters

One way you can more easily come to hear a given meter is to establish some sort of physical response to the music: Obvious as it seems, start tapping the beat with your foot and moving with the music in a way that groups beats into measures of two or three. Perhaps the most graceful way to move with the music is to adopt the same patterns of motion that conductors use to lead symphony orchestras and other musical ensembles. These are patterns cut in the air with the right hand (a baton is optional!). Here are the patterns that conductors use to show $\frac{2}{4}$ and $\frac{3}{4}$ meter:

EXAMPLE 2–11

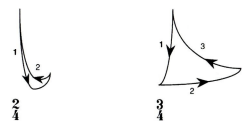

conducting duple and triple meter

Notice that in both of these patterns, and indeed in all conducting patterns, the first beat is indicated by a downward movement of the hand. This is called the **downbeat.** It is always the first and by far the strongest beat in the measure. In $\frac{2}{4}$ the downbeat is stronger, or more accented, than the **upbeat** (the beat signaled by an upward motion); in $\frac{3}{4}$ it is more accented than either the middle beat (2) or the upbeat (3). When listening to a piece of music, then, tap the

feel the downbeat

Is It in $\frac{2}{4}$ or $\frac{3}{4}$?

In most music it is easy to tell whether the meter is duple or triple. But occasionally even famous musicians can be fooled, as this heated exchange between the opera composer Giacomo Meyerbeer (1791–1864) and the great pianist-composer Frédéric Chopin (1810–1849) suggests.

"That's in $\frac{2}{4}$," said Meyerbeer. The music was repeated while Chopin, pencil in hand, beat time on the piano, his eyes blazing. "$\frac{2}{4}$," Meyerbeer calmly repeated . . .

"It's in $\frac{3}{4}$," Chopin almost yelled, he who never normally raised his voice above a murmur. He went to the piano and *three times* played the piece, counting aloud and stamping out the beat with his foot. He was beside himself! Meyerbeer still held his own and they parted on bad terms. (Tad Szulc, *Chopin in Paris*, p. 77)

Chopin, it turns out, was right: The piece in question was one of his own compositions!

---

beat with your foot, listen for the downbeat, and try to get your conducting pattern synchronized with the music. If you hear only one weak beat between each strong beat, the music is in duple meter and you should be conducting in $\frac{2}{4}$ time. If you hear two weak beats between each downbeat, on the other hand, you are listening to a piece in triple meter and should be using the $\frac{3}{4}$ pattern. Try conducting *Yankee Doodle* and *America* in $\frac{2}{4}$ and $\frac{3}{4}$, respectively.

EXAMPLE 2–12

| Yan - kee | doo - dle | went to | town | rid - ing | on a | po - | ny. |
| **ONE** | two | **ONE** | two | **ONE** | two | **ONE** | two |

| My | coun - try | 'tis | of thee, | sweet | land of | lib | - er-ty | of | thee | I | sing. |
| **ONE** two three | **ONE** two three | **ONE** two three | **ONE** two three | **ONE** two three | **ONE** two three |

One final observation about meters and conducting patterns: Almost all music that we hear, and especially dance music, has a clearly identifiable meter and a strong downbeat. But not all music *starts* with the downbeat. Often a piece will begin with an upbeat. An upbeat at the very beginning of a piece is called a pickup. The **pickup** is usually only a note or two, but it gives a little momentum or extra push into the first downbeat, as can be seen in the following two patriotic songs.

pickup to the downbeat

EXAMPLE 2–13

| Oh | beau- | ti- | ful | for | spa- | cious | skies |
| two | **ONE** | two | **ONE** | two | **ONE** | two | **ONE** | two |

| Oh | say | can | you | see | by | the | dawn's | ear - | ly | light |
| three | **ONE** | two | three | **ONE** | two | three | **ONE** | two | three | **ONE** | two |

Turn now to the end of the chapter and complete Listening Exercise 2b. Then go on to Listening Exercise 3, which asks you to identify the meter of several musical works and gives you a chance to practice conducting in $\frac{2}{4}$ and $\frac{3}{4}$ time.

Syncopation

One of the ways to add variety and excitement to music is by the use of syncopation. In most music the **accent,** or musical stress, falls on the beat, with the downbeat getting the greatest accent of all. **Syncopation** places the accent either on a weak beat or between the beats. The note that is syncopated sounds accented because it is played louder or held longer than the surrounding notes. A good example of syncopation is found at the end of the first phrase of Stephen Foster's *Camptown Races*, where the "dah" of "doo-dah" is syncopated.

EXAMPLE 2–14

Syncopation gives an unexpected bounce or lift to the music and is a prominent feature in jazz. Indeed, part of the fun of playing jazz is to obscure the beat by means of syncopation and thereby to tease or tantalize the listener.

Tempo

If meter is the grouping of beats, and rhythm the durational patterns superimposed on the meter, tempo is the speed at which the beats occur. Obviously, the tempo, or speed, of the beat can be fast or slow, but it usually falls somewhere in the neighborhood of 60 to 100 beats per minute. Tempo is indicated to the performer by means of tempo markings placed at the beginning of the piece. Because they were first used in Italy in the seventeenth century, at the beginning of the Baroque period in music, tempo markings are most often written in Italian. The following are a few of the most common tempo indications, arranged from slow to fast:

tempo: the speed of the beat

grave (grave)	very slow
largo (broad)	
lento (slow)	slow
adagio (slow)	
andante (moving)	moderate
andantino (slightly faster than *andante*)	
moderato (moderate)	
allegretto (moderately fast)	fast
allegro (fast)	
vivace (fast and lively)	very fast
presto (very fast)	
prestissimo (as fast as possible)	

Naturally, general terms such as these allow for a good deal of interpretive freedom. Conductors like Leonard Bernstein (1918–1990), Arturo Toscanini (1867–1957), and Seiji Ozawa (b. 1935), for example, have had different notions of just how fast a movement of Beethoven marked *allegro* (fast) should really go. In addition, composers often call for fluctuations in tempo within a piece by placing commands such as *accelerando* (getting faster) and *ritardando* (getting slower) in the score. One particularly colorful term is *rubato* (robbed), meaning that the performer is given license to steal some additional time for the passage of music in question and thus to slow it down. Frequent changes in

✵ FIGURE 2–3
Leonard Bernstein (1918–1990), one of the most forceful, and flamboyant, conductors of the twentieth century.

tempo make it more difficult for the listener to follow the beat, but they add much in the way of expression and feeling to the music.

MELODY

A **melody** is a series of notes arranged in order to form a recognizable unit. The more beautiful the melody, the more we are drawn to the music. When supported by its companions, rhythm and harmony, melody can produce an overwhelming emotional experience. Yet one of the wonders of music is that we are hard pressed to explain in precise terms why this is so. What is it about the shape of a melody, its balance and contour, that makes one so moving and another so very forgettable? The pursuit of this question, however, would carry us off into the realm of aesthetic theory. Instead, let us simply describe how melodies are put together so that we can more readily grasp them.

Pitch

Just as a grammatical sentence is made up of building blocks we call words, so a melody is composed of individual units called pitches. **Pitch** is the relative position, high or low, of a musical sound. When sound comes in regular vibrations, it produces a musical **tone.** If it occurs in irregular vibrations, then it is merely noise of the sort generated by a crashing plate or a barking dog. Musical tones are usually produced when a string or a column of air is set in motion on a musical instrument, and this motion, in turn, creates vibrating airwaves that reach the ear at equal time intervals. The faster a string vibrates, for example, the higher the pitch. Normally, humans will hear sounds produced in a range between a low of about 20 vibrations (or cycles) per second to a high of about 16,000. (Some animals can hear sounds twice this high.) In theory, pitch can occur anywhere on this wide band of sound—think of a fire siren starting low, rising, and then falling back down. But when making music, we take this broad spectrum of sound and divide it into individual steps or degrees of pitch. We then string these units together in time to produce a melody.

faster vibrations produce a higher pitch

EXAMPLE 2–15

Some-where o-ver the rain-bow, way up high

Take me out to the ball game, take me out to the crowd

The Octave

One of the remarkable qualities of pitch is that, when singing or playing a succession of tones up or down, a performer often comes to a tone that sounds like an exact duplication of an earlier pitch, but at a higher or lower level. For a reason that will become clear shortly, the duplicating pitch is called an **octave.**

Pitches an octave apart sound similar because the frequency of vibration of the higher pitch, or note, is precisely twice that of the lower. Middle C on the piano, for example, vibrates at 256 cycles per second, while the C an octave above does so at 512 cycles. When men and women sing a song or hymn together without harmony, they invariably sing at the octave; it sounds as if they are all singing the same notes, but, in fact, the men are an octave below the women. Almost all musical cultures, Western and non-Western, make use of the principle of octave duplication in their melodies. But not all cultures agree as to how the octave should be divided, that is, how many notes there should be within an octave. In many traditional Chinese melodies, the octave is divided into five separate pitches. Some Arabic and Turkish melodies, however, make use of fourteen. Judging from our earliest written music, which dates back more than a thousand years, we in the West have always preferred melodies that were built on seven pitches within the octave. The eighth pitch duplicated, or doubled, the sound of the first, and thus it was called the octave.

octave duplication used in all musical cultures

dividing the octave

At first, the seven notes within the octave corresponded to the white keys of the keyboard. Eventually, five additional notes were inserted within the span of the octave, and these correspond to the black keys.

EXAMPLE 2–16

To get the sound of the octave in your ear, try singing *Over the Rainbow* and *Take Me Out to the Ball Game*. Both begin with a leap up an octave no matter on what pitch you choose to start.

Notating Melodies

The type of notation used for the two tunes in Ex. 2–15 is useful if you merely need to be reminded of how a melody goes, but it is not precise enough to allow a singer to produce the tune if he or she didn't know it already. When the melody goes up, how *far* up does it go? More precision for musical notation began to appear in the West as early as the eleventh century, when notes came to be situated on lines and spaces so that the exact distance between pitches could be judged immediately. This gridwork of lines and spaces came to be called a **staff.** The higher on the staff the note is placed, the higher the pitch.

EXAMPLE 2–17

The staff is always provided with a **clef sign** to indicate the range of pitch in which the melody is to be played or sung. One clef, called the **treble clef,** designates the upper range and is appropriate for high instruments like the trumpet and the violin, and a woman's voice. A second clef, called the **bass clef,** covers

treble and bass clefs

the lower range and is used for lower instruments like the trombone and the cello, and a man's voice.

EXAMPLE 2–18

For a single vocal part or a single instrument, a melody could easily be placed on either one of these two clefs. But for two-hand keyboard music with greater range, both clefs are used, one on top of the other. The performer looks at this combination of clefs, called the **great staff,** and relates the notes to the keys beneath the fingers. The space between the two clefs is filled in by a short, temporary line called a ledger line. On the keyboard it indicates middle C (the middle-most C key on the piano).

EXAMPLE 2–19

🌱 FIGURE 2–4
G Clef (1935) by Josef Albers (1888–1976).

Each musical pitch can be referred to by a letter name, like C, as well as represented by a note placed on the great staff. Only seven letter names (A, B, C, D, E, F, and G) are used because, as we have said, melodies were originally made up of only seven pitches within each octave—corresponding to the seven white notes of the keyboard. When the pitch is duplicated at the octave, the letter name repeats (see Ex. 2–19). But gradually, the spaces between the white keys were divided and additional (black) keys inserted. This increased the number of pitches within the octave from seven to twelve. Since they were not originally part of the staff, the five additional pitches were not represented by a line or space, nor were they given a separate letter name. Instead, they came to be indicated by a symbol, either a sharp or a flat, applied to one of the existing notes. A **sharp (♯)** raises the note to the key immediately above, usually a black one, whereas a **flat (♭)** lowers it to the next key below, again usually a black one. A **natural (♮),** on the other hand, cancels either of the two previous signs. Here, as an example of musical notation on the great staff, is a well-known melody as it might be notated for a chorus of male and female voices, the women an octave higher than the men. To keep things simple, the melody is notated in equal whole notes (without rhythm).

names of the notes

EXAMPLE 2–20

Tonality, Keys, and Scales

Melodies have a central pitch, called the **tonic,** around which they gravitate and on which they usually end. The organization of music around this central tone, the tonic, is called **tonality.** In the case of *Twinkle, Twinkle,* C is the tonic—the tune not only ends on C but happens to begin on C as well. A melody may, in fact, have C or D or F♯, or any other of the twelve notes within the octave, as the tonic. In addition, we say that *Twinkle, Twinkle* is written in the tonality, or key, of C major, meaning that it has the tonic C, but also that it makes use of a C major scale. A **key,** then, is a tonal center built on a tonic note and making use of a scale.

But what is a scale? A **scale** is an arrangement of pitches that ascends and descends in a fixed and unvarying pattern. Almost all Western melodies are written in one of two types of scales—one called major, the other called minor. To understand the difference between the major and minor scale, it's necessary to look at a keyboard for a moment (see Ex. 2–19). Notice that there are no black keys between B and C and between E and F. All the adjacent white notes of the keyboard are not the same distance apart. The difference, or distance, in sound between B and C is only half of that between C and D. B to C is the interval of a half step, while C to D is the interval of a whole step. The major and minor scales, in turn, are built on two distinctly different patterns of whole and half steps, each starting on a tonic note. The **major scale** has a succession of whole and half steps that proceeds 1–1–½–1–1–1–½. The **minor scale** goes 1–½–1–1–½–1–1. Every scale uses only seven of the available twelve pitches within each octave; and once the octave is reached, the pattern can start over again. A major or minor scale may begin on any of the twelve notes within the octave, and thus there are twelve major and twelve minor scales and keys. Here are the notes of the major and minor scales as they start on C and then on A. Next time you pass by a piano, try playing these to get the sound of major and minor in your ear.

🌼 FIGURE 2–5
Contrasting Sounds (1924) by Wassily Kandinsky (1866–1944).

major and minor scales

EXAMPLE 2–21

A major scale built on C uses only the white notes of the keyboard, as does a minor scale constructed on A. When begun on a note other than C (for the major scale) or A (for the minor scale), however, sharps and flats are needed so that the pattern of whole and half steps does not vary. For example, a major scale may begin on A and ascend up the octave; but to keep the major scale pattern intact, the notes C, F, and G must be sharped (see Ex. 2–21). Similarly, starting the minor scale pattern on C will require that E be lowered to E♭, A to A♭, and B to B♭ (see Ex. 2–21).

key signatures   Composing a piece in A major would require writing out many sharps, just as one in C minor would require writing many flats. To avoid this labor, musicians have developed the custom of "preplacing" the sharps and flats at the beginning of the staff. The sharps and flats are then active throughout the piece. Preplaced sharps or flats are called a **key signature.**

EXAMPLE 2–22

Key signatures indicate to the performer the key in which a piece is written; that is, they show what scale is about to be employed and what the tonic note is.

MODULATION **Modulation** is the change from one key to another. Most short pieces—folk songs, hymns, and the like—don't modulate; they stay in one key. But longer pieces need to modulate or the listener is soon bored. Modulation gives a dynamic sense of movement to music. As the composer Arnold

Schoenberg (1874–1951) said, "Modulation is like a change of scenery." The beginning listener will find modulations difficult to hear. You may not recognize precisely when they occur, but you will sense, however subconsciously, that the music is changing from one key to another.

HEARING MAJOR AND MINOR Scales are like colors on an artist's palette. A composer will choose what he or she believes is the right scale to achieve the desired musical mood or feeling for the composition. The differences in mood or color within each of the two principal melodic types, major and minor, are small and are not commonly agreed on even by professional musicians. Some say D major is a bright key, F major comfortable and restful, D♭ major dark and rich. But what may seem rich to one listener may sound bright to the next. Taste in music, as in the other arts, is a very personal matter.

One thing we can all agree on, however, is that a melody in a major key sounds decidedly different from one in a minor. Major melodies seem bright, cheery, optimistic, while minor ones are dark, somber, even sinister. Try singing the beginning of the following familiar major and minor songs to establish firmly in your mind's ear the difference between major and minor:

EXAMPLE 2–23

Music theorists since the sixteenth century have noticed the distinctly different moods associated with major and minor. Positive emotions (joy, confidence, triumph, tranquility, love, etc.) have traditionally been expressed in major, while negative feelings (fear, anxiety, sorrow, despair, etc.) have usually been played out in minor. Major and minor scales are constructed according to two distinctly different patterns of whole and half steps (see Ex. 2–21), and this is why they affect us in different ways. The change from a major key to a minor one with the same tonic (C major to C minor, for example), or from minor to major (F minor to F major, for example) is called a change of **mode.** Lest there be any doubt that a change in mode can change how you feel about a melody, listen to the following familiar tunes (your instructor will play them for you). The mode in each has been changed from major to minor by inserting a flat

changing the mode

into the scale near the tonic note (C). Notice here how all the happiness, joy, and sunshine have disappeared from these formerly major tunes. Such shifts create the subtle emotional language of music.

EXAMPLE 2–24

Now turn to Listening Exercise 4, which asks you to distinguish between melodies in the major and minor mode.

DIATONIC VERSUS CHROMATIC Most of the melodies we know are what we call **diatonic** melodies, meaning that they are written in either the major or the minor scale and use only the seven notes of each, the so-called diatonic notes. A scale using all twelve notes within the octave, however, is called a **chromatic** scale. In a chromatic scale all twelve pitches are a half step apart.

EXAMPLE 2–25

Chromatic (from the Greek *chroma*, "color") is a good word for this scale because the additional five pitches do indeed add color and richness to a melody. Here is a popular tune that begins by using a chromatic scale.

EXAMPLE 2–26

In general, chromatic melodies sound more intense, tight, and angular than diatonic ones.

Melodic Structure

Difficult as it is to say why some melodies are so pleasing and others so dull, all good melodies seem to have a few essential qualities: a strong tonic note, forward motion, a goal or climax, and ultimately a feeling of repose or completion.

These qualities are all found in abundance in the *Ode to Joy* by Ludwig van Beethoven (1770–1827). Beethoven originally composed this music for the last movement of his Symphony No. 9 (1824), but in more recent times the melody has been used as a Christmas carol, a hymn for the United Nations, a movie score (*Die Hard*), and as background music in countless TV commercials. Here the melody is notated in the bass clef in D major, the key in which Beethoven composed it.

EXAMPLE 2–27

Praise to Joy the God de-scend-ed, Daugh-ter of E - ly - si - um.

Ray of mirth and rap-ture blend-ed, God-dess, to thy shrine wel-come.

By thy ma-gic is u - nit-ed what stern cus-tom part-ed wide. All

man-kind are broth-ers plight-ed where thy gen-tle wings a-bide.

🌸 FIGURE 2–6
A portrait of Ludwig van Beethoven painted in 1818–1819 by Ferdinand Schimon (1797–1852).

We can make a few general observations about Beethoven's melody: First, notice that it moves mainly by **step,** from one letter name of the scale to the next (D to E, for example), and rarely moves by **leap,** a jump of one or more letter names (D to F♯, or D to G, for example). Melodies that move predominantly by step are called **conjunct** melodies, while those that move mainly by leap are called **disjunct** ones. *Ode to Joy* may be the most conjunct melody ever written! The only leaps of any importance are the two at the end of phrase **c** (measure 12). Clearly, Beethoven wanted to keep this melody simple so that all the world could sing it.

Next, notice that there are, in fact, four melodic phrases here. A **phrase** in music functions much like a dependent phrase or clause within a grammatical sentence. It constitutes a dependent idea within a melody. Here four four-measure phrases form a complete sixteen-bar melody. Let's concentrate for a moment on the first two phrases. The opening phrase (**a**) begins on the third step of the D major scale, F♯, and ends on the second step, E. If you try to sing, hum, or whistle this first phrase, you will notice that when you get to the end ("Elysium"), the music doesn't sound complete or finished—it wants to go on. By the end of the second phrase (**b**), however, you arrive on the tonic note ("welcome") and now do have a feeling of arrival and completion. Many melodies begin this way: The initial phrase opens the melody and ends on some note *other* than the tonic; the second phrase answers this idea and returns the melody to the tonic. Two phrases that work in tandem this way are called **antecedent** and **consequent** phrases. Both end with a cadence. A **cadence** is the concluding part of a

antecedent and consequent phrases

musical phrase. The cadence at the end of Beethoven's antecedent phrase does not sound final, and therefore is called a **half cadence;** the one at the end of his consequent phrase, because it ends on the tonic, does sound complete and is called **full cadence.** A half cadence functions like a comma, a full cadence like a period.

Ode to Joy then pushes off in a new direction (**c**). The music gains momentum by means of a repeating rhythm in measures 10–11 and reaches a musical climax in measure 12 with the two leaps. The fourth and final phrase is an almost exact repeat of the second phrase (**b**), with the exception of one interesting detail (see * in Ex. 2–27). Beethoven brings the return of this phrase in one beat early—a bit of rhythmic syncopation*—thereby giving an unexpected lift to the melody.

The melodic structure of Beethoven's *Ode to Joy*—balanced groups of four-bar phrases arranged antecedent–consequent–extension–consequent—is found frequently in music, from the works of Haydn, Mozart, and Beethoven in the eighteenth and early nineteenth centuries to popular songs of nineteenth- and twentieth-century America. You may have been singing antecedent–consequent phrases and using full and half cadences all your life and not been aware of it. To prove the point, sing the following two well-known tunes:

The Saints Go Marching In (traditional)
"Oh when the saints, go marching in, oh when the saints go marching in"   (half cadence)
(antecedent phrase)
"Oh how I want to be in that number, when the saints go marching in."   (full cadence)
(consequent phrase)

Oh Suzanna (Stephen Foster)
"Oh I come from Alabama with my banjo on my knee"   (half cadence)
(antecedent phrase)
"I'm bound for Louisiana my true love for to see."   (full cadence)
(consequent phrase)

Now do Listening Exercise 5, which invites you to become more familiar with the melodic structure of Beethoven's famous *Ode to Joy.*

Hearing Melodies

Hearing melodies may be the single most important part of listening to music. Melodies contain the main musical ideas the composer wishes to communicate. Once a composer has hit on a good melody, he or she is likely to repeat or elaborate on it several times in the course of a composition. Beethoven, for example, brings back his *Ode to Joy* in various guises at least a half-dozen times in his Symphony No. 9. Indeed, by reintroducing a melody at certain important moments in a work, the composer reveals the form, or structure, of the musical creation. It is important, therefore, that the listener be able to seize on the melody, to remember it over a span of time, and to recognize its return, as if welcoming an old friend.

How do we improve our ability to hear melodies and recognize their return? The best way is perhaps not to try to take in an entire melody, or even a full phrase, at once. A melody can move by rapidly, and the beginning listener can expect to absorb only three to four seconds of it at a time. Instead of trying to grasp everything at once, grab hold of some small part of the melody. Find a distinctive rhythmic figure of three or four notes, or a salient melodic motive. A

melodic motives

motive in music is a short, distinctive melodic figure that stands by itself. Concentrate on this one figure and lock it into your mind by asking: What is it doing? Does it drop down rapidly? If so, by a lot or just a little? Does it move up by steps? Does it repeat a note in some distinctive way? Does it end on the same pitch as it began? To do this it is helpful to visualize, even draw a picture of (see Ex. 2–15), the melodic motive that you seize on.

✸ HARMONY

Melody provides a lyrical voice for music, rhythm gives vitality and definition to that voice, while harmony adds depth and richness to it, just as the dimension of depth in painting adds a rich backdrop to that art. Although melody can and sometimes does stand by itself, most often it is closely bound to, and, indeed, grows out of, the harmony. The two work gracefully in tandem, the harmony supporting and amplifying the melody. Sometimes, however, discord arises—as when a folksinger strumming a guitar fails to change the chord to make it agree with the melody—and the result can be startling. The melody and harmony now clash: They are out of harmony. The double sense of this last statement shows that the term **harmony** has several meanings. Broadly speaking, harmony means the peaceful cohabitation of diverse elements; the ancient Greeks, for example, spoke of the unheard harmony of the planets and of the soul. When applied specifically to music, harmony is said to be the sounds that provide a support and enrichment—an accompaniment—for melody. Finally, we often speak of harmony as if it was a specific musical event, as when we say the harmony changes, meaning that one chord in the accompaniment changes to another. Thus, we say that the cowboy ballad *The Streets of Laredo* is a harmonious piece, harmonized in the key of F major, and that the harmony changes fifteen times:

✸ FIGURE 2–7

A mixed chorus sings in a harmonious fashion. Some voices sing the melody while others supply the harmony.

EXAMPLE 2–28

Building Harmony

Chords are the building blocks of harmony. A **chord** is simply a group of two or more pitches that sound at the same time. When we learn to play guitar or jazz piano, we first learn mainly how to construct chords. The basic chord in music is the **triad,** so called because it consists of three pitches arranged in a very specific way. Here is a C major triad:

EXAMPLE 2–29

Note that it comprises the first, third, and fifth notes of the C major scale. The distance between each of these notes is called an **interval.** C to E, spanning three letter names (C,D,E) is the interval of a third. E to G, again spanning three letter names (E,F,G) is another third. Triads always consist of two intervals of a third placed one on top of the other. Here are triads built on every note of the C major scale:

EXAMPLE 2–30

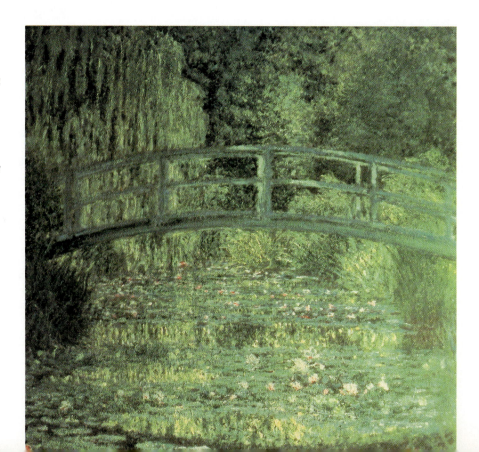

✿ FIGURE 2–8

Harmony in Green by Claude Monet. In this painting of water lilies in his pond at Giverny, France, Claude Monet (1840–1926) shows the harmonious relationship of colors, dominated by green. It was during the Impressionist period (see Chapter 16) that painters began to borrow musical terms such as "harmony" and "symphony" to identify their works.

These triads provide all the basic chords necessary to harmonize a melody in C major.

Notice that each of the chords is given a Roman numeral, indicating on which note of the scale the triad is built, and that the triads built on I, IV, and V are called the tonic, subdominant, and dominant chords. We have already met the tonic note in our discussion of melody—it is the pitch around which a tune gravitates and on which it ends. Similarly, the tonic chord, or triad, is the "home" chord of the harmony. It is the most stable and the one toward which the other chords move. The **dominant** triad, always built on the fifth note of the scale, is next in importance. Note in *The Streets of Laredo* how most of the melody is harmonized simply by changing back and forth between tonic and dominant triads. Dominant triads are especially likely to move to tonic triads at the ends of musical phrases, where such a movement (V–I) helps create the strong effect of a full cadence*. The **subdominant** triad is built on the note below the dominant, and it frequently moves to the dominant, which, in turn, moves to the tonic (IV–V–I). A movement of chords in a purposeful fashion like this is called a **chord progression.** The separate chords in a chord progression pull one to the next, all gravitating toward the powerful tonic. The end of *The Streets of Laredo* is marked by a subdominant–dominant–tonic chord progression (IV–V–I), one that is heard frequently in music and, perhaps for that reason, gives a solid, reliable feeling to the harmony.

chord progressions

The notes of a triad need not always enter together but can be spaced out over time. Such a broken, or staggered, triad is called an **arpeggio.** Arpeggios can appear either as part of the melody or in the harmony that supports a melody. An arpeggio used in an accompaniment usually gives the listener the sense that the harmony has more substance than it really does. In Ex. 2–31, the beginning of *The Streets of Laredo* is harmonized with the triads spaced out as arpeggios (beneath the brackets). The supporting triads are the same as in Ex. 2–28, but now the accompaniment seems more active because one note of the triad is sounding on every beat:

EXAMPLE 2–31

Consonance and Dissonance

You have undoubtedly noticed, when pressing the keys of the piano at one time or another, that some combinations of keys produce a harsh, jarring sound, while others are pleasing and harmonious. The former chords are characterized by **dissonance** (pitches sounding disagreeable and unstable) and the latter by **consonance** (pitches sounding agreeable and stable). Generally speaking, chords that contain pitches that are very close together, just a half or a whole step apart, sound dissonant. On the other hand, chords that involve a third, a somewhat larger interval, are usually consonant. Each of the triads built on the notes of the major scale (see Ex. 2–30), for example, contains two intervals of a third

FIGURE 2–9

Henri Matisse, *Violinist at the Window* (1918). In his writings on art, Matisse often spoke of the "consonance and dissonance of color."

and therefore is consonant. Dissonant chords add a feeling of tension and anxiety to music; consonant ones produce a sense of rest and stability. Composers have traditionally used dissonant chords sparingly, like a hot spice. They prepare them carefully in a bed of consonance and then immediately resolve them—move them—back to a consonance. Our musical psyche demands this constant ebb and flow between the tension of dissonance and the stability of consonance.

Hearing the Harmony Change

Chords move from consonance to consonance, from consonance to dissonance, from dissonance to consonance, and sometimes, in modern music, from dissonance to dissonance. The rate of change may be rapid or slow, regular or irregular. In *The Streets of Laredo* (Ex. 2–28), the rate of harmonic change is moderately fast and regular. There are three beats for each chord and then a new chord appears, without exception, at the beginning of each group of three (each new measure). Composers can alter the rate at which new chords appear in order to achieve particular effects. A rapid rate of change communicates to the listener a feeling of movement and perhaps tension. A deceleration in the speed with which chords change from one to the next can convey a sense of slowing down and relaxation, even though the tempo of the piece (the real speed at which it is moving) remains the same. Handel (1685–1759) and Beethoven (1770–1827) were especially fond of slowing down the rate of harmonic change toward the end of a piece in order to give it a feeling of conclusion, to tell the listener that the piece, in fact, is at an end.

listen to the bass

The first step to listening to harmony is to focus your attention on the bass, separating it from the higher melody line. Chords are often built upon the bass note, and a change in the bass from one pitch to another may signal a change in chord. Concentrating on the bass at first will not be easy. Most of us have always thought that listening to music is listening to melody. Certainly, hearing melody is crucial. But the bass is next in importance, and it rules supreme in a sort of subterranean world. It carries the chords and determines where the harmony is going, more so than the higher melody. Baroque music (1600–1750) usually has a clear, driving bass line, and hard rock music perhaps even more so. Next time you listen to a piece of rock, follow the bass guitar line instead of the melody and lyrics. See if you don't begin to sense when the chords are changing and when you have reached a chord that feels like the home key (the tonic triad). Listening Exercise 6 helps you to focus on the bass and begin to recognize when the harmony changes from one chord to the next.

  LISTENING EXERCISES

  Identification of Rhythm

In this exercise you are asked to recall and listen to rhythms that are already in your musical memory. Following are the opening text and rhythm of several well-known songs. Place the correct note values above the unnotated portion of the text in order to complete the rhythm for the entire phrase. For example:

Row, row, row your boat gent-ly down the stream

Row, row, row your boat gent-ly down the stream

(If you are unfamiliar with one or more of these tunes, feel free to substitute your own. Simply write out the text and then try to indicate the musical rhythm above it by writing in the note values.)

Three blind mice, three blind mice, see how they run, see how they run

My coun-try 'tis of thee, sweet land of lib - er-ty, of thee I sing.

Bah, bah, black sheep, have you an-y wool? Yes Sir, Yes Sir,

Mar - y had a lit - tle lamb, lit - tle lamb, lit - tle lamb

Oh what a beau-ti-ful mor - nin', Oh what a beau-ti-ful day.

Jin - gle bells, jin - gle bells, jin - gle all the way

Lon - don bridge is fal - ling down, fal - ling down, fal - ling down

I've been work - ing on the rail - road, all the live long day.

Now that you have read about meters and time signatures (pages 16–18), complete this exercise by inserting the bar lines and beats (1 2 or 1 2 3) for each of the preceding examples. The meter for each example is either $\frac{2}{4}$ or $\frac{3}{4}$, and each begins with a downbeat, not a pickup. For example:

Example:

Are you sleep-ing, are you sleep-ing, broth-er John, broth-er John

becomes

Are you sleep-ing, are you sleep-ing, broth-er John, broth-er John
1 2   1 2   1 2   1 2   1 2   1 2   1 2   1 2

Hearing Meters

On your Introduction to Listening CD, track 5, you have ten short musical excerpts, each played once. (You can replay each as many times in rapid succession using the "reverse" control on your CD machine.) Identify the meter of each excerpt. To do this, you should listen for the beat, count 1–2 or 1–2–3, and get your conductor's beat pattern in synchrony with the music (downbeat of the hand with the downbeat of the music). If you have done it correctly, the completion of each full conductor's pattern will equal one measure. All the pieces are in duple ($\frac{2}{4}$) or triple ($\frac{3}{4}$) meter. Most begin with a downbeat, some with a pickup.[†]

Track 5

1. (0:00) Meter _____ Mouret, *Rondeau* from *Suite de symphonies*[†]
2. (0:28) Meter _____ Musorgsky, *Pictures at an Exhibition, Polish Ox-Cart*
3. (0:55) Meter _____ Beethoven, *Variations on God Save the King*
4. (1:11) Meter _____ Haydn, Symphony No. 94, 3rd movement[†]
5. (1:43) Meter _____ Mozart, Symphony No. 40, 1st movement[†]
6. (2:03) Meter _____ Brahms, *Wiegenlied (Lullaby)*[†]
7. (2:27) Meter _____ Mozart, *The Marriage of Figaro*, "You ladies who know"
8. (3:12) Meter _____ Mozart, *A Little Night Music*, Trio[†]
9. (3:37) Meter _____ Bach, Brandenburg Concerto No. 5, 1st movement
10. (4:01) Meter _____ Clara Schumann, Romance for Violin and Piano

 Hearing Major and Minor

On your Introduction to Listening CD, track 6, you will find ten musical excerpts that will help you begin to differentiate a piece in a major key from one in a minor key. For most listeners, melodies in major are bright, cheerful, sometimes bland, whereas those in minor tend to be darker, more somber, sometimes exotic, even oriental, in sound. In the blanks below indicate whether each piece is in major or minor.

Track 6

1. (0:00) Key _____ Musorgsky, *Pictures at an Exhibition, Polish Ox-Cart*
2. (0:26) Key _____ Musorgsky, *Pictures at an Exhibition, Goldenberg and Schmuyle*

[†]Excerpt begins with a pickup.

6   Hearing Chord Changes in the Harmony
Listening to Music Blues

The following exercise encourages you to focus on the bass line and the chords that support a melody, rather than the melody itself. The music you hear (Introduction to Listening CD, track 8) consists of three improvisations on a standard blues chord progression. The rate at which the chords of the harmony change is slow to moderately slow. It is also irregular, meaning that a chord is held sometimes for many beats and sometimes only for a few. In this performance the left hand of the electronic keyboard player holds one chord until it is time to move on to the next. Each time it stops holding and moves elsewhere, we have a new chord. Below you are asked to fill in a time log for the chord changes in this repeating blues harmony. Record the minute and second that each chord changes. A few of the correct times are already filled in to make your task easier.

There are several traditional blues harmonies. The one employed here is an old standard that uses the repeating chord progression tonic (I), subdominant (IV), tonic (I), dominant (V), subdominant (IV), tonic (I) to carry the blues tune. The blues and its history are discussed in Chapter 18, but for now let's just concentrate on the harmony.

1. 0:00   ____   ____   ____   ____   ____
      I   IV   I   V   IV   I
2. 0:25   ____   ____   ____   ____   ____
      I   IV   I   V   IV   I
3. 0:50   ____   ____   ____   ____   1:10
      I   IV   I   V   IV   I

KEY WORDS

arpeggio	harmony	octave
bass clef	key	pickup
beat	key signature	rhythm
cadence	major scale	subdominant chord
chord	measure	syncopation
chord progression	melody	time signature
chromatic	meter	tonality
diatonic	minor scale	tonic
dominant chord	mode	treble clef
downbeat	modulation	triad
great staff	motive	upbeat

3. (1:05) Key _____ Musorgsky, *Pictures at an Exhibition, The Great Gate of Kiev*
4. (1:34) Key _____ Vivaldi, Violin Concerto, "The Spring," 1st movement
5. (2:08) Key _____ Vivaldi, Violin Concerto, "The Spring," 1st movement
6. (2:19) Key _____ Tchaikovsky, Symphonic poem, *Romeo and Juliet*
7. (2:50) Key _____ Mouret, *Rondeau* from *Suite de symphonies*
8. (3:19) Key _____ Robert Schumann, *Scenes from Childhood, Of Foreign Lands and People*
9. (3:37) Key _____ Mozart, Overture to *Don Giovanni*
10. (4:23) Key _____ Handel, *Water Music*, Minuet

· ·

Hearing Melodic Structure
Ludwig van Beethoven, *Ode to Joy* from Symphony No. 9 (1824)

On your Introduction to Listening CD, track 7, you have an excerpt from the last movement of Beethoven's Symphony No. 9, in which his famous *Ode to Joy* can be heard. You are probably familiar with the tune already, but look at it again as it is given on page 27. Try to get the antecedent (**a**), consequent (**b**), and extension (**c**) phrases firmly in your ear. Now listen to the music on your CD. The melody is actually heard four times, first played softly by the low string instruments, then more loudly by the higher strings, then louder still by yet higher strings, and finally loudest of all by the trumpets and full orchestra.

Your task is to prepare a listening guide that shows when each phrase occurs. Indicate in the blanks the minute and second when each phrase is heard. (Notice that Beethoven actually repeats the extension (**c**) and consequent (**b**) phrases at the end of each of the four presentations of the melody.) Some of the timings have already been inserted to help you along.

After you have filled in the blanks, go back and treat yourself to one final hearing in which you listen unencumbered to the growing power of Beethoven's melody.

Playing Number:	1	2	3	4
	Low strings (double basses)	Higher strings (2nd violins)	Higher strings (1st violins)	Trumpets with full orchestra
Antecedent	**a** 0:00	**a** 0:49	**a** 1:40	**a** 2:30
Consequent	**b** 0:08	**b** _:_	**b** _:_	**b** _:_
Extension	**c** _:_	**c** _:_	**c** _:_	**c** _:_
Consequent	**b** _:_	**b** _:_	**b** _:_	**b** _:_
	(repeat)	(repeat)	(repeat)	(repeat)
Extension	**c** 0:32	**c** 1:23	**c** 2:13	**c** 3:03
Consequent	**b** _:_	**b** _:_	**b** _:_	**b** _:_

Hearing Meters

On your Introduction to Listening CD, track 5, you have ten short musical excerpts, each played once. (You can replay each as many times in rapid succession using the "reverse" control on your CD machine.) Identify the meter of each excerpt. To do this, you should listen for the beat, count 1–2 or 1–2–3, and get your conductor's beat pattern in synchrony with the music (downbeat of the hand with the downbeat of the music). If you have done it correctly, the completion of each full conductor's pattern will equal one measure. All the pieces are in duple ($\frac{2}{4}$) or triple ($\frac{3}{4}$) meter. Most begin with a downbeat, some with a pickup.[†]

Track 5

1. (0:00) Meter _____ Mouret, *Rondeau* from *Suite de symphonies*[†]
2. (0:28) Meter _____ Musorgsky, *Pictures at an Exhibition*, *Polish Ox-Cart*
3. (0:55) Meter _____ Beethoven, *Variations on God Save the King*
4. (1:11) Meter _____ Haydn, Symphony No. 94, 3rd movement[†]
5. (1:43) Meter _____ Mozart, Symphony No. 40, 1st movement[†]
6. (2:03) Meter _____ Brahms, *Wiegenlied (Lullaby)*[†]
7. (2:27) Meter _____ Mozart, *The Marriage of Figaro*, "You ladies who know"
8. (3:12) Meter _____ Mozart, *A Little Night Music*, Trio[†]
9. (3:37) Meter _____ Bach, Brandenburg Concerto No. 5, 1st movement
10. (4:01) Meter _____ Clara Schumann, Romance for Violin and Piano

 Hearing Major and Minor

On your Introduction to Listening CD, track 6, you will find ten musical excerpts that will help you begin to differentiate a piece in a major key from one in a minor key. For most listeners, melodies in major are bright, cheerful, sometimes bland, whereas those in minor tend to be darker, more somber, sometimes exotic, even oriental, in sound. In the blanks below indicate whether each piece is in major or minor.

Track 6

1. (0:00) Key _____ Musorgsky, *Pictures at an Exhibition*, *Polish Ox-Cart*
2. (0:26) Key _____ Musorgsky, *Pictures at an Exhibition*, *Goldenberg and Schmuyle*

[†]Excerpt begins with a pickup.

Example:
Row, row, row your boat gent - ly down the stream   (2/4)

becomes
Row, row, row your boat gent - ly down the stream   (2/4)

(If you are unfamiliar with one or more of these tunes, feel free to substitute your own. Simply write out the text and then try to indicate the musical rhythm above it by writing in the note values.)

Three blind mice, three blind mice, see how they run, see how they run   (2/4)

My coun-try 'tis of thee, sweet land of lib - er-ty, of thee I sing.   (3/4)

Bah, bah, black sheep, have you an-y wool? Yes Sir, Yes Sir,   (2/4)

Mar - y had a lit - tle lamb, lit - tle lamb, lit - tle lamb   (2/4)

Oh what a beau-ti-ful mor - nin', Oh what a beau-ti-ful day.   (3/4)

Jin - gle bells, jin - gle bells, jin - gle all the way   (2/4)

Lon - don bridge is fal - ling down, fal - ling down, fal - ling down   (2/4)

I've been work - ing on the rail - road, all the live long day.   (2/4)

2b

Now that you have read about meters and time signatures (pages 16–18), complete this exercise by inserting the bar lines and beats (1 2 or 1 2 3) for each of the preceding examples. The meter for each example is either $\frac{2}{4}$ or $\frac{3}{4}$, and each begins with a downbeat, not a pickup. For example:

Example:
Are you sleep - ing, are you sleep-ing, broth-er John, broth-er John

becomes
Are you sleep - ing, are you sleep-ing, broth-er John, broth-er John
1 2   1 2   1 2   1 2   1 2   1 2   1 2   1 2

MUSICAL COLOR, TEXTURE, AND FORM

3

 Every musical composition is made up of a number of elements, just as every painting has a number of components to it. Color, texture, and form are important in both these arts. They are the broad, general qualities of a work that help give it its meaning and structure. Form in music is the general shape of a composition as perceived by the listener. It becomes apparent only gradually as the work progresses from beginning to end. Color and texture, on the other hand, are qualities that may be obvious to the listener immediately. We may be struck by a particular melody, not so much because of its pitches or rhythm, but because it is played on a brilliant-sounding instrument like the trumpet. Or we may be captivated by a musical climax, not because the melody at that point is particularly original, but because the full sound of a large orchestra is heard for the first time—the musical texture has gained impressive substance. Color and texture, then, are less musical ideas in themselves and more ways of expressing ideas.

COLOR

Simply said, **color** in music is the tone quality of any sound produced by a voice or an instrument. **Timbre** is another term for the tone quality of musical sound. Instruments produce sounds of different colors, or timbres, because they are constructed in different ways and of different materials. We need not go into the acoustical reasons why this is so—instinctively, we all recognize that the sound of a flute has a different tone quality from that of a trombone. Similarly, the voice of pop singer Michael Jackson has a different timbre to it than that of opera star Luciano Pavarotti (Fig. 3–2), even when the two produce the same pitches. Since the human voice was probably the first "instrument" to make music, let's start our investigation of musical color with it.

The Voice

The human voice is an instrument of a very special sort that naturally generates sound without the aid of any kind of mechanical contrivance. It is highly expressive, in part because it can produce an enormously wide range of sounds.

When we sing we force air up through our vocal cords (two folds of mucous membrane within the throat), causing them to vibrate. Men's vocal cords are longer and thicker than women's, and for that reason the sound of the mature male voice is lower. (This principle is also at work with the string instruments:

the longer and thicker the string, the lower the pitch.) Voices are classified by range into four principal parts. The two women's vocal parts are the **soprano** and the **alto,** and the two men's parts the **tenor** and the **bass.** The soprano is the highest voice and the bass the lowest. When many voices join together, they form a **chorus;** the soprano, alto, tenor, and bass constitute the four standard choral parts. In addition, the area of pitch shared by the soprano and alto is sometimes designated as a separate vocal range called the **mezzo-soprano,** just as the notes adjoining the tenor and bass are said to be encompassed by the **baritone** voice.

high   soprano
                         (mezzo-soprano)
                         alto
                         tenor
                         (baritone)
low   bass

The voice is capable of producing many different styles of singing: the raspy sound of a blues singer, the twang of the country balladeer, the gutsy belt of a Broadway songster, or the lyrical tones of an operatic soprano. We all try to sing, and we would like to sing well. How well we do, and what kind of sound we produce, depends on our training and our physical makeup—the lungs, vocal cords, throat, nose, and mouth are all involved in the production of vocal sound.

❋ FIGURE 3–1
In *The Fife* (1866), Édouard Manet uses, strictly in tandem, unshaded patches of color and a few simple lines to create form.

Musical Instruments

Musical instruments come in groups, or families. The symphony orchestra traditionally includes four such groups. The first is the string family, so called because these instruments produce sound by plucking or bowing a string. The second and third groups are the woodwind and brass families, both of which generate music by blowing air through a pipe or tube of one sort or another. The fourth group is the percussion family, which makes music—and sometimes just plain noise—usually by striking a suspended membrane (a drum), a block of wood, or a piece of metal with a stick of some kind. In addition, there is a fifth group of instruments, the keyboard instruments, which are not normally part of the symphony orchestra. The organ, harpsichord, and piano are the main keyboard instruments, and they make sound by means of keys and pipes (organ) or keys and strings (harpsichord and piano). The organ is usually played alone,

❋ FIGURE 3–2
Opera singer Luciano Pavarotti, now in his mid-sixties, was in his prime arguably the greatest tenor of the twentieth century.

while the piano is most often heard either by itself or as an accompaniment to another solo instrument.

Why does a composer choose a particular instrument to present a melody and not some other? In general, one instrument is chosen over another because of its capacity to express what the composer feels about the music that he or she intends to create. Invariably, the instrument with the tone color best able to portray the composer's feeling about a given musical line—and what the composer wishes to express to the listener—is the one selected. To be able to hear these subtle emotional shadings in music, it is important that we sharpen our awareness of the separate tone colors of the various instruments.

STRINGS Generally speaking, when we speak of string instruments we broadly include all instruments that produce sound by means of vibrating strings: the guitar, banjo, ukulele, and the harp, as well as the violin and its close relatives, the viola, cello, and double bass. But the guitar, banjo, ukulele, and harp usually produce their sound when plucked, whereas the violin and its relatives are normally played with a bow, not just plucked. Indeed, it is their use of a bow, along with their distinctive shape, that identifies the four members of the violin group. We traditionally associate these instruments with classical music. The guitar, banjo, ukulele, and harp, on the other hand, have their origins in folk music.

Violin Group. The violin group constituted the original core of the symphony orchestra when it was first formed during the Baroque era (1600–1750). In numbers of players, the violins, violas, cellos, and double basses still make up the largest part of any orchestra. A large symphony orchestra can easily include as many as a hundred members, at least sixty of whom play one of these four instruments.

The **violin** is chief among the string instruments. It is also the smallest—it has the shortest strings and therefore the highest pitch. Because of its high range and singing tone, it often is assigned the melody in orchestral and chamber music. The violins are usually divided into groups known as firsts and seconds. The seconds play a part slightly lower in pitch and subordinate in function to the firsts.

The sound of the violin is produced when a bow is pulled across one of four strings held tightly in place by tuning pegs at one end of the instrument and by a tailpiece at the other (Figs. 3–3 and 6–17). The strings are slightly elevated above the wooden body by means of a supporting bridge. Different sounds or pitches are produced when a finger of the left hand shortens, or "stops," a string by pressing it against the fingerboard—again, the shorter the string, the higher the pitch. Because each of the four strings can be stopped quickly in many different places, the violin possesses both great range and agility. The strings themselves are made either of animal gut or of metal wire. The singing tone of the violin, however, comes not so much from the strings as from the wooden body, known as the sound box, which amplifies and enriches the sound. The better the design, wood, glue, and varnish of the sound box, the better the tone. (For the sound of the violin, turn to Intro CD, track 11 at 1:24.)

The **viola** (Fig. 3–4) is about six inches longer than the violin and it produces a somewhat lower sound. If the violin is the string counterpart of the soprano voice, then the viola has its parallel in the alto voice. Its tone is darker,

FIGURE 3–3
Violinist Sarah Chang.

richer, and more somber than the brilliant violin. (For the sound of the viola, turn to Intro CD, track 11 at 4:27.)

You can easily spot the **cello** (violoncello) in the orchestra because the player sits with the instrument placed between the legs (Fig. 3–5). The pitch of the cello is well below that of the viola. It can provide a low bass sound as well as a singing melody. When played in its middle range by a skilled performer, the cello is capable of producing an indescribably rich, expressive tone. (For the sound of the cello, turn to Intro CD, track 11 at 3:10.)

The **double bass** (Fig. 3–6) gives weight and power to the bass line in the orchestra. Since at first it merely doubled the notes of the cello an octave* below, it was called the double bass. As you can see, the double bass is the largest, and hence lowest sounding, of the string instruments. Its job in the orchestra, and even in jazz bands, is to help set a firm base for the musical harmony. (For the sound of the double bass, turn to Intro CD, track 11, at 3:48.)

FIGURES 3–4, 3–5, AND 3–6
(top) Violist Yuri Bashmet. (above) Cellist Yo-Yo Ma. (right) Double bass player Gary Karr.

String Techniques. The members of the violin group all generate pitches in the same way: A bow is drawn across a tight string. This produces the traditional, penetrating string sound. In addition, a number of other effects can be created by using different playing techniques.

pizzicato: Instead of bowing the strings, the performer plucks them. With this technique, the resulting sound has a sharp attack, but it dies away quickly. (For an example of pizzicato, turn to Intro CD, track 11 at 2:36.)

vibrato: By shaking the left hand as it stops the string, the performer can produce a sort of controlled wobble in the pitch. This adds richness to the tone of the string because, in effect, it creates a blend of two or more pitches. (For an example of vibrato, turn to Intro CD, track 11 at 1:24.)

tremolo: The performer creates a musical "tremor" by rapidly repeating the same pitch with quick up and down strokes of the bow. Tremolo creates a feeling of heightened tension and excitement when played loudly, and a velvety, shimmering backdrop when performed quietly. (For an example of tremolo, turn to Intro CD, track 11 at 2:03.)

mute: If a composer wants to dampen the penetrating tone of a string instrument, he or she can instruct the player to place a mute (a metal or rubber clamp) on the strings of the instrument.

Harp. Although originally a folk instrument, one found in virtually every musical culture, the **harp** (Fig. 3–7) is sometimes added to the modern symphony orchestra. Its role is to add color to the orchestral sound and sometimes to create special effects, the most striking of which is a rapid run up or down the strings called a **glissando.**

WOODWINDS The name "woodwind" was originally given to this family of instruments because they emit sound when air is blown through a wooden tube or pipe. The pipe has holes along its length, and the player covers or uncovers these to change the pitch. Nowadays, however, some of these woodwind instruments are made entirely of metal. Flutes, for example, are constructed of silver, and sometimes of gold or even platinum. As with the violin group, there are four principal woodwind instruments in every modern symphony orchestra: flute, oboe, clarinet, and bassoon. In addition, each of these has a close relative that is larger or smaller in size and that possesses a somewhat different timbre and range. The larger the instrument or length of pipe, the lower the sound.

The lovely, silvery tone of the **flute** is probably familiar to you. The instrument can be rich in the lower register and then light and airy on top. It is especially agile, capable of playing tones rapidly and moving quickly from one range to another. (For the sound of the flute, turn to Intro CD, track 9 at 1:20.)

The smaller cousin of the flute is the **piccolo.** ("Piccolo" comes from the Italian *flauto piccolo,* meaning "little flute".) It can produce higher notes than any other orchestral instrument. And though very small, its sound is so shrill that it can always be heard, even when the full orchestra is playing loudly. (For the sound of the piccolo, turn to Intro CD, track 11 at 1:55.)

The **clarinet** produces sound when the player blows against a single reed fitted to the mouthpiece. The tone of the clarinet is more mellow than that of the other woodwinds, especially in the lower register of the instrument. It also has the capacity to slide or glide smoothly between pitches, and this allows for a highly expressive style of playing. The flexibility and expressiveness of the instrument have made it a favorite with jazz musicians. (For the sound of the clarinet, turn to Intro CD, track 9 at 3:35.) A lower, larger version of the clarinet is the **bass clarinet.**

The **oboe** is equipped with a double reed—two reeds tied together with an air space in between. When the player blows into the instrument through the double reed, a nasal, slightly exotic sound is created. It is invariably the oboe that gives the pitch at the beginning of every symphony concert. Not only was the oboe the first nonstring instrument to be added to the orchestra, but it is a difficult instrument to tune. Better have the other instruments tune to it than to try to have it adjust to them. (For the sound of the oboe, turn to Intro CD, track 9 at 0:48.)

✿ FIGURE 3–7

The harp's unique contribution is its glissandos, rapid runs up and down the strings that seem to color the airwaves with sound.

✿ FIGURE 3–8

(from left to right) A flute, two clarinets, an oboe, and a bassoon. The flute, clarinet, and oboe are about the same length. The bassoon is nearly twice their size.

Related to the oboe is the **English horn.** Unfortunately, it is wrongly named, for the English horn is neither English nor a horn. It is simply a larger (hence lower-sounding) version of the oboe that originated on the continent of Europe. The English horn produces a dark, haunting sound, one that was especially favored by composers of the Romantic period (1820–1900).

The **bassoon** functions among the woodwinds much as the cello does among the strings. It can serve as a bass instrument, adding weight to the lowest sound, or it can act as a soloist in its own right. When playing moderately fast or rapid passages as a solo instrument, it has a dry, almost comic tone. (For the sound of the bassoon, turn to Intro CD, track 9 at 2:30.)

There is also a double bassoon, usually called the **contrabassoon.** Its sound is deep and sluggish. Indeed, the contrabassoon can play notes lower than any other orchestral instrument.

The bassoon, contrabassoon, and English horn are all double-reed instruments, just like the oboe. Their tones, therefore, may sound more vibrant, even exotic, than those of the single-reed instruments like the clarinet and saxophone.

✺ FIGURE 3–9
Members of the Canadian Brass, with the French horn player at the left and the tuba player at the right.

Strictly speaking, the single-reed **saxophone** is not a member of the symphony orchestra, though it can be added on occasion. Its sound can be mellow and expressive but also, if the player wishes, shrill and raucous. The expressiveness of the saxophone makes it a welcome member of most jazz ensembles, while the shrill, penetrating tone of the instrument is prized by rock musicians.

BRASSES. Like the woodwind and string groups of the orchestra, the brass family consists of four primary instruments: French horn, trumpet, trombone, and tuba. Brass players use no reeds but instead blow into their instruments through a cup-shaped **mouthpiece** (Fig. 3–10). By adjusting valves or moving a slide, the performer can make the length of pipe on the instrument longer or shorter, and hence the pitch lower or higher.

✺ FIGURE 3–10
Mouthpieces for brass instruments.

The **French horn** was the first brass instrument to join the orchestra. Its sound is rich and mellow, yet somewhat veiled or covered. Because of this, composers have traditionally used the horn to add warmth and fullness to the orchestral texture. During the Romantic period (1820–1900), the horn not only provided a sonorous glue to bind the tones of the other instruments but also began to emerge as a solo instrument in its own right. (For the sound of the French horn, turn to Intro CD, track 10 at 0:00.)

Everyone has heard the high, bright, cutting sound of the **trumpet.** Whether on a parade ground or in an orchestral hall, the trumpet is an excellent solo instrument because of its agility and penetrating tone. The trumpet sounds forth with special brilliance at the beginning of Musorgsky's *Pictures at an Exhibition* (Intro CD, track 1). When provided with a mute, (a hollow plug placed in the bell of the instrument to dampen the sound), the trumpet can produce a softer tone that blends well with other instruments. Witness the effective combination of muted trumpet with woodwinds in Picture 6 of *Pictures at an Exhibition* (Intro CD, track 3 at 0:45).

Although distantly related to the trumpet, the **trombone** (Italian for "large trumpet") plays in the middle range of the brass family. It is easy to confuse the sound of the trombone with that of the French horn, because both are middle-range brass instruments and have a full, majestic sound. But the tone of the trombone is somewhat clearer and more focused, and its attack more direct than that of the French horn. (An immediate comparison of the trombone with the French horn is given on your Intro CD, track 10 at 0:20 and 0:00.)

The **tuba** is the largest and lowest-sounding of the brass instruments. It produces a full, though sometimes muffled, tone in its lowest notes. Like the double bass of the violin group, the tuba is most often used for setting a base, or foundation, of sound. On occasion, however, it can play a tuneful melodic line, as in Picture 4 of Musorgsky's *Pictures at an Exhibition* (Intro CD, track 2 at 0:00). Here, the tuba demonstrates the melodious upper range of the instrument in a lengthy solo.

PERCUSSION. Percussion instruments are those that are struck in some way, either by hitting the head of a drum with a stick or by banging or scraping a piece of metal or wood in one fashion or another. Some percussion instruments, like the timpani (kettledrums), produce a specific pitch, while others just generate noise without a recognizable musical tone. It is the job of the percussion instruments to sharpen the rhythmic contour of the music. They can also add color to the sounds of other instruments and, when they play loudly, can heighten the sense of climax in a piece. For example, much of the majesty to be heard in the climactic final tableau of Musorgsky's *Pictures at an Exhibition* (Intro CD, track 4 at 4:49) is created by the timpani, bass drum, and cymbals.

The **timpani** (Fig. 3–11) is the percussion instrument most often heard in classical music. Whether struck in single, detached strokes or hit rapidly to produce a thunderlike roll, the function of the timpani is to add depth, tension, and drama to the music. Timpani usually come in pairs, one instrument to play the tonic* note and the other to play the dominant*.

The crashing ring of the **cymbals,** the dull thud of the **bass drum,** and the rat-ta-tat-tat of the **snare drum** are sounds well known from marching bands and jazz ensembles, as well as the classical orchestra. None of these instruments produces a specific musical tone.

On the other hand, a wide spectrum of musical pitches are created by a trio of instruments that generate sound in a rather similar way: the xylophone, glockenspiel, and celesta (Fig. 3–12). The **xylophone** is a set of wooden bars that, when struck by two hard mallets, produce a dry, wooden sound. The **glockenspiel** works the same way, but the bars are made of metal so that the tone is brighter and more ringing. The **celesta,** too, produces sound when hammers strike metal bars, but the hammers are activated by keys, as in a piano; the tone of the celesta is bright and tinkling—a delightful, "celestial" sound, as the name of the instrument suggests.

FIGURES 3–11 AND 3–12
(top) Timpanist Marvin Dahlgren of the Minnesota Orchestra. (bottom) A xylophone, a celesta, and a glockenspiel.

KEYBOARD INSTRUMENTS The pipe organ, harpsichord, and piano are our most familiar keyboard instruments. The **pipe organ** (Fig. 3–13), which traces its ancestry back to ancient Greece, is by far the oldest. It works according to a simple principle: The player depresses a key that allows air to rush into a pipe, thereby producing sound. The pipes are arranged in separate groups according to their shape and material. Each group produces a full range of musical tones with one special tone quality or color. When the organist wants to bring a particular group of pipes into play, he or she simply pulls a switch, called a **stop.** The most colorful, forceful sound occurs when all the stops have been activated (thus the expression "pulling out all the stops"). The several keyboards of the organ make it possible to play several musical lines at once, each with its own timbre. There is even a keyboard for the feet!

The **harpsichord** (Fig. 3–14) was known in northern Italy as early as 1400, but it reached its heyday during the Baroque era (1600–1750). It produces sound not by means of pipes but by strings. When a key is depressed, it drives a lever upward that, in turn, forces a pick to pluck a string. The plucking creates a bright, jangling sound. Some harpsichords are equipped with two keyboards so that the player can change from one group of strings to another, each with its particular tone color and volume of sound. The harpsichord has one important shortcoming, however: The lever mechanism does not allow the performer to control the force with which the string is plucked, so each string always sounds at the same volume. (For more on the harpsichord, see page 99.)

The **piano** (Fig. 3–15) was invented in Italy in 1709, in part to remove the dynamic limitations of the harpsichord. In a piano, strings are not plucked but hit by soft hammers. A lever mechanism makes it possible for the player to regulate how hard each string is struck, thus producing softs and louds (the original piano was called the *pianoforte*, the "soft-loud"). During the lifetime of Mozart (1756–1791), the piano replaced the harpsichord as the favorite domestic musical instrument. By the nineteenth century every aspiring household had to have a piano, whether as an instrument for real musical enjoyment or as a symbol of affluence.

If the organ's familiar home is the church, where it is heard in association with religious services, the versatile piano is found almost everywhere. With equal success it can accompany a school chorus or an opera singer; it can harmonize with a rock band when in the hands of an Elton John or a Billy

❀ FIGURE 3–13
A pipe organ in the Chapel of St. Thomas Aquinas at the University of St. Thomas, Minnesota.

❀ FIGURES 3–14 AND 3–15
(left) A two-manual harpsichord built by Pascal Taskin (Paris, 1770), preserved in the Yale University Collection of Musical Instruments. (right) Pianist André Watts.

Joel; or it can become a powerful, yet expressive, solo instrument when played by a master such as Vladimir Horowitz or André Watts. The harpsichord, on the other hand, is used mainly to recreate the music of the time of Johann Sebastian Bach (1685–1750).

ELECTRONIC INSTRUMENTS. In addition to these natural musical instruments—acoustical instruments, as they are called—machines that produce musical sounds by electronic means have been invented in the twentieth century. The electric keyboard synthesizer has recently gained great favor among rock and jazz musicians because of the variety of sounds it can create and the ease with which it can be moved from job to job. Electronic instruments such as the keyboard synthesizer and electric organ and electric guitar, as well as the sound-processing computer, are discussed in Chapter 17.

Building a Symphony

The modern symphony orchestra is one of the largest and certainly the most colorful of all musical ensembles. It originated in the seventeenth century and has continually grown in size since then. When at full strength, the symphony orchestra can include upward of one hundred performers and nearly thirty different instruments, from the high piping of the piccolo down to the rumble of the contrabassoon. A typical seating plan for an orchestra is given in Fig. 3–16.

ORCHESTRAL SEATING PLAN

FIGURE 3–16
Seating plan of an orchestra.

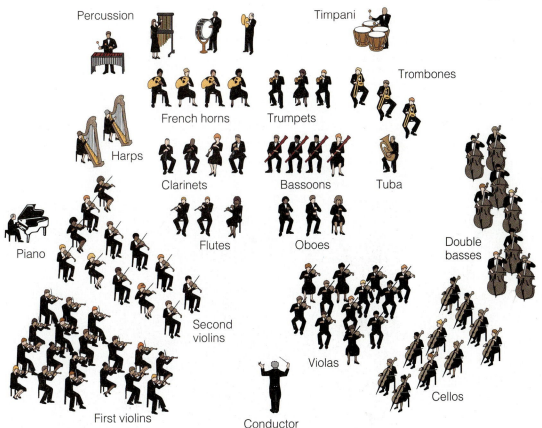

Percussion

Timpani

Trombones

French horns

Trumpets

Harps

Clarinets

Bassoons

Tuba

Piano

Flutes

Oboes

Double basses

Second violins

Violas

First violins

Conductor

Cellos

Strings are placed toward the front, and the more powerful brasses at the back. Other seating arrangements are also used, according to the special requirements of the composition to be performed.

To see how a symphony orchestra works, let's take one apart and put it back together. We will "deconstruct" the orchestra in a passage at the end of Beethoven's "Eroica" ("Heroic") Symphony, a work he composed in Vienna in 1803. Figure 3–17 shows a portion of the **orchestral score** that Beethoven created. It contains all the parts for all the instruments Beethoven selected for this work. Moving from top to bottom, the notes for the woodwinds appear first, then those of the brasses and percussion, and finally, at the bottom of the page, the music for the strings. Our passage begins with the sounds of the full orchestra as it works to a climax. All parts are playing together. Soon, however, the strings, percussion, and brasses drop out, leaving the woodwinds to present a lovely section that sounds very much like a hymn. (Beethoven did not include the flute or piccolo here, but the melody played by the oboe is repeated by these instruments on your CD to show you how they sound.) As you listen to these excerpts from Beethoven's "Eroica" Symphony, notice how each instrument has its own distinct color, and how a composer can create a variety of musical hues by combining the instruments in different ways.

FIGURE 3–17
The orchestral score of an excerpt from Beethoven's Symphony No. 3 (1803), the "Eroica," with instruments listed.

LISTENING GUIDE

Ludwig van Beethoven
Symphony No. 3 (1803), the "Eroica"
Excerpt from the 4th movement

Intro CD/9–12

The Woodwinds

Intro CD/9
0:00	Full orchestra works up to a climax and pause (Fig. 3–17)
0:14	Woodwinds play a beautiful, hymn-like passage
0:48	Oboe plays the melody
1:20	The sound of same melody, had Beethoven assigned it to a flute
1:55	The sound of same melody, had Beethoven assigned it to a piccolo
2:30	Bassoon plays the supporting bass
3:02	Oboe plays melody with the supporting bass of bassoon
3:35	Two clarinets play accompaniment in the middle of the texture
4:09	Oboe, clarinets, and bassoons together play passage as Beethoven orchestrated it

Toward the end of this passage for woodwinds alone, the French horns join in, passing the music on to the string section of the orchestra. To demonstrate how the sound of the French horn differs from that of the trombone and trumpet, the same music is then played in turn by these two instruments.

The Brasses

Intro CD/10
0:00	French horns play transition into next section
0:26	Sound of same transition, had Beethoven assigned it to the trombones
0:56	Sound of same transition, had Beethoven assigned it to the trumpets

The transition played by the French horns leads to a presentation of the hymn-like passage by the string family, to which the clarinet and oboe soon add counterpoint.

The Strings

Intro CD/11
0:00	Strings now play hymn-like passage
0:48	Violins play melody without vibrato
1:24	Violins play melody with vibrato
2:03	Violins play melody as if Beethoven had written it tremolo
2:36	Violins play melody as if Beethoven had written it pizzicato
3:10	Cellos play the supporting bass
3:48	Double basses play almost the same supporting bass an octave lower
4:27	Violas play accompaniment in middle of the texture
5:07	Clarinet and then oboe add a rising scale as counterpoint to the melody in the violins
5:46	The same passage with all the instruments, just as Beethoven orchestrated it: strings supported by the French horns with counterpoint added by the clarinet and oboe

Having taken Beethoven's symphony apart, now let's put it back together. Listen to the entire passage played by the full orchestra including a percussion instrument, the timpani. As you listen, try to follow the orchestral score, the beginning of which appears in Figure 3–17.

Full Orchestra

Intro CD/12
0:00	Full orchestra works to a climax
0:11	Woodwinds play hymn-like passage
0:33	French horns join in and pass the music to the strings
0:42	Strings supported by French horns with counterpoint added by clarinet and oboe

Even if you don't read music, a glance at the orchestral score of the "Eroica" Sympony (Fig. 3–17) will show that Beethoven had to put many, many notes on the page to achieve just a few seconds of the colorful orchestral timbres he desired. Consequently, because of Beethoven's attention to detail, during a per-

FIGURE 3–18
Conductor Seiji Ozawa of the Boston Symphony Orchestra and Vienna State Opera. By watching the gestures of the conductor, the listener is often able to follow the principal themes as they are passed from player to player or section to section.

formance the conductor has the task of attending to a dozen or more instrumental lines at once.

Surprisingly, a separate conductor was not originally part of the orchestra. For the first 200 years of its existence (1600–1800), the symphony was led by one of the performers, either a keyboard player or the principal first violinist. By the time of Beethoven (1770–1827), however, the group had so grown in size that it was thought necessary to have someone stand before it and lead, not only to keep all the players together but also to help draw out and elucidate the important musical lines. Conductors need to have very keen ears so as to be able to pick out and correct wrong pitches and rhythms in this complicated web of instrumental sounds. That's one reason the good ones, like Seiji Ozawa (Fig. 3–18), are among the highly paid superstars of the musical world.

Dynamics

Dynamics in music are the various levels of volume, loud and soft, at which sounds are produced. Dynamics work together with tone colors to affect the way we hear and react to musical sound. A high note in the clarinet has one quality—shrill and harsh—when played *fortissimo* (very loud) and quite another—vague and otherworldly—when played *pianissimo* (very soft). Following are the names of the most common musical dynamics. Since they were first used by composers working in Italy, these terms are traditionally written in Italian.

Term	Musical Symbol	Definition
fortissimo	*ff*	very loud
forte	*f*	loud
mezzo forte	*mf*	moderately loud
mezzo piano	*mp*	moderately soft
piano	*p*	soft
pianissimo	*pp*	very soft

Dynamics sometimes change abruptly, for special effects. Most common among these quick changes is the **sforzando,** a sudden, loud attack on one note or chord. A famous *sforzando* occurs in the second movement of Joseph Haydn's "Surprise" Symphony (1792), for example, in which the composer interrupts a soft melody with a thunderous crash on a single chord (6CD 2/5 at 0:30)—his intent was apparently to awaken those listeners who might have dozed off!

But changes in dynamics need not be sudden and abrupt. They can be gradual and extend over a long period of time. A gradual increase in the intensity of sound is called a crescendo, while a gradual decrease is called either a decrescendo or diminuendo.

Term	Musical symbol	Definition
crescendo	<	growing louder
decrescendo or *diminuendo*	>	growing softer

Ludwig van Beethoven was a master at writing long crescendos. The transition to the last movement of his Symphony No. 5 comes upon the listener like a great tidal wave of sound (6CD 3/5 at 5:00). An equally impressive crescendo, and then diminuendo, can be heard in Musorgsky's *Pictures at an Exhibition* (Intro CD/2 at 1:33), where the Polish ox-cart rumbles forward loudly and then disappears quietly in the distance.

Now that you have been introduced to all of the colorful sounds and dynamic possibilities of the symphony orchestra, go on to do Listening Exercise 7. Here Benjamin Britten's *The Young Person's Guide to the Orchestra* will test your ability to recognize the instruments.

✸ TEXTURE

Texture in music is the density and disposition of the musical lines that make up a musical composition. To understand this better, picture in your mind a tapestry or some other type of woven material. The individual strands, or lines, can be dense or thin; colors can be bunched toward the center or spread out more or less evenly; the lines may have either a strong vertical or a horizontal thrust. Just as a weaver or painter can fabricate a particular texture—dense, heavy, light, or thin, with independent or interdependent strands—so, too, can the composer create similar effects with musical lines. Musorgsky's *Polish Ox-Cart* (Intro CD/2), from his *Pictures at an Exhibition*, begins with a thin texture of low sounds (tuba and double basses only). As the piece progresses, the strings and then the full orchestra join in, giving the music an impressive, dense texture. Finally, toward the end, the music returns to the thin, low sounds heard at the beginning.

Monophonic, Polyphonic, and Homophonic Textures

There are three primary textures in music—monophonic, polyphonic, and homophonic—depending on the number of musical lines and the way they relate to one another. Often we call these lines, or parts, "voices" even though they may not actually be sung.

Monophony is the easiest to hear. As the name "one sounding" indicates, there is only a single line of music, with no accompaniment. When you sing by yourself, you are creating monophonic music. When a group of men (or women) sing the same pitches together—singing in unison*, as it is called—they produce monophonic texture. Even when men and women sing together at the octave*, the texture is still monophonic. Singing in unison and at the octave adds richness to the otherwise sparse sound of monophonic music.

As you may suppose from the name "many sounding," **polyphony** requires two or more lines in the musical fabric. In addition, the term "polyphonic" also implies that each of the lines will be autonomous and independent. They compete equally for the listener's attention. Usually, they move against one another, and when this happens they create what is called counterpoint. **Counterpoint** is simply the harmonious opposition of two or more independent musical lines. Because counterpoint presupposes polyphony, the terms "contrapuntal texture" and "polyphonic texture" are often used interchangeably.

What is more, there are two types of counterpoint: imitative and free. In imitative counterpoint the individual voices enter separately and the followers duplicate at least a part of what the first, or lead, voice had presented. If they copy exactly, note for note, what the first part plays or sings, then a **canon** re-

counterpoint

❋ FIGURE 3–19
Piet Mondrian's *Composition with Red, Yellow and Blue* (1939–1942) has a rather thin texture with uneven linear spacing and occasional zones of dense color.

sults. Think of *Three Blind Mice, Are You Sleeping?*, or *Row, Row, Row Your Boat*, and remember how each voice enters in turn and then exactly imitates the first voice from beginning to end. These are all short canons, or rounds, a type of strict counterpoint popular since the Middle Ages. Among the more famous *canon* longer canons in music is the well-known canon of Johann Pachelbel (1653–1706) that goes on for several minutes. Example 3–1 shows the beginning of a brief canon for three voices:

EXAMPLE 3–1

Are you sleep-ing, are you sleep-ing, broth-er John, *etc.*

Are you sleep-ing, are you sleep-ing, broth-er John, *etc.*

Are you sleep-ing, are you sleep-ing,

free counterpoint   Free counterpoint is counterpoint without any sort of imitation among the voices. The voices, or lines, may begin all together or begin separately, but they go their separate ways. Much jazz improvisation is done in free counterpoint.

Homophony means "same sounding." In this texture the voices, or lines, move to new pitches at roughly the same time. Homophony, then, differs from polyphony in that the strands are not independent but interdependent; they proceed in a tight, interlocking fashion. Usually, the lines form harmonious blocks of sound, called chords*, which support and draw attention to a higher voice that carries the melody. Hymns, Christmas carols, popular songs, and folk

FIGURE 3–20

Simultaneous Counter Composition (1929–1930), by Theo van Doesburg, comes very close to a musical definition of counterpoint: "the harmonious opposition of two or more independent [entities]."

songs almost always have a homophonic texture because they consist of a simple melody with blocks of accompanying chords below. Melody plus accompaniment then—perhaps the most common musical arrangement—produces homophonic texture. As the arrows in Exs. 3–1 and 3–2 show, in polyphonic texture the musical fabric has lines with a strong linear (horizontal) thrust, whereas in homophonic texture the fabric is marked by lines that are more vertically conceived, as blocks of accompanying chords.

EXAMPLE 3–2

changing textures

Of course, composers are not limited to just one of these three musical textures within any given work. They can change from one to another at will. By adding one or two independent lines, for example, a composer can slip easily from homophonic to polyphonic texture. In the preceding excerpt from Beethoven's "Eroica" Symphony (see page 47), a passage in homophonic texture is first played by the woodwinds (Intro CD/11 at 0:47). When it is repeated by the strings, the clarinet and oboe insert short lines of free counterpoint (Intro CD/11 at 0:49), thereby adding polyphonic density to the texture.

As a rule, the longer the piece, the greater the number of changes in texture. But such changes can come in rapid succession in short pieces as well. George Frideric Handel (1685–1759) is perhaps best known as the composer of *Messiah*, a large work for chorus and orchestra usually performed just before Christmas. By far the most familiar number within *Messiah* is the "Hallelujah" chorus, for which the audience traditionally rises to its feet.[†] To get the sound of the various textures securely in your ear, listen to this famous chorus. Notice how rapidly and how smoothly the composer moves back and forth among homophonic, polyphonic, and monophonic textures. The following Listening Guide makes it clear where the changes come.

[†]It seems that King George II (ruled 1727–1760) stood up at this point during a performance of *Messiah* in London. If the King stood, so did everyone else; hence the tradition of the audience standing.

LISTENING GUIDE   George Frideric Handel   Intro CD/14
"Hallelujah" chorus from *Messiah* (1741)

0:01	"Hallelujah! Hallelujah!"—homophony
0:25	"For the Lord God Omnipotent reigneth"—monophony
0:32	"Hallelujah! Hallelujah"—homophony
0:37	"For the Lord God Omnipotent reigneth"—monophony
0:44	"Hallelujah! Hallelujah!"—homophony
0:49	"For the Lord God Omnipotent reigneth" together with "Hallelujah"—polyphony
1:16	"The Kingdom of this world is become"—homophony

(Continued on next page)

1:35   "And He shall reign for ever and ever"—polyphony
1:58   "King of Kings and Lord of Lords" together with "Hallelujah"—homophony
2:39   "And He shall reign for ever and ever"—polyphony
2:51   "King of Kings and Lord of Lords" together with "Hallelujah"—homophony
3:01   "And He shall reign for ever and ever"—polyphony
3:07   "King of Kings and Lord of Lords" together with "Hallelujah"—homophony

When you have finished, turn to Listening Exercise 8, which
provides additional practice in hearing musical textures.

 ## FORM

Form in art is the purposeful organization of the artist's materials. It is present in every medium of creative expression. In architecture, sculpture, and painting, for example, the formal design imposes a shape and a definition on physical space. In poetry the meter, the rhyme, and the stanza give a sense of logic and coherence to the sounds, ideas, and images. And in music the melody, harmony, rhythm, tone color, and texture can be arranged to create a sequence of events that the composer and listener find pleasing and convincing.

the composer needs a plan

A composer needs formal principles to help in the process of selecting and arranging materials. Nothing is more frightening to an artist, as the composer Igor Stravinsky (1882–1971) remarked, than absolute freedom. How to begin? What to write now? What next? When and how to end? The selection of a musical form can help with these decisions by suggesting an overall shape as well as a set of operating procedures. Sometimes a composer will create a novel design because the subject matter at hand seems to demand it. Thus in his *Pictures at an Exhibition*, Modest Musorgsky fashions a long chain of musical pictures linked by a short refrain (the Promenade music). But more often a composer will fall back on a time-honored form. Using a traditional form does not tell the composer what to do at every step, but it does suggest plausible paths that might be taken—paths that other composers at other times have used and with which the listener is likely to be familiar.

the listener needs to know the plan

From the listener's standpoint, an awareness of form is perhaps the most important tool he or she can employ while listening to music. If the composer needs help in setting a broad musical plan, the listener needs formal guideposts as a means of following what the composer is trying to communicate. The music rushes by quickly: What has happened? Where am I? What is about to come? These questions are invariably asked, consciously or unconsciously, when hearing a piece for the first time. By working through the discussion and diagrams that follow, you will acquire a mental picture of the most commonly used musical forms. You will more easily comprehend the material that you hear, and be comfortable with it, because you will have met these forms before and now know what to expect. You may also gain satisfaction from hearing the composer deviate from your expectations by treating the traditional time-honored form in some new and surprising fashion.

Creating Formal Designs: Repetition, Contrast, and Variation

repetition

How are formal designs created in music? By means of repetition, contrast, and variation. **Repetition** establishes the most obvious formal units. When a distinctive melody returns, for example, it strikes the ear as an important event. Such repeating events set forth the outlines of a musical design in the same way that a steel framework outlines and holds together the materials of a building. Repetition is essential to music, perhaps because music is the most abstract of all the arts. Instead of creating tedium or boredom, each return helps to establish weight, balance, and symmetry. Because the musical material is familiar, repetition conveys to the listener a feeling of comfort and security.

Contrast, on the other hand, takes us away from the familiar and into the unknown. A quiet melody in the strings can suddenly be followed by an insistent theme blasting from the French horns, as happens, for example, in the third movement of Beethoven's well-known Symphony No. 5 (6CD 3/5). Contrasting melodies, rhythms, textures, and moods can be used as a foil to familiar material, to provide variety, even conflict. In many aspects of our lives we have a need to balance comfort and security with novelty and excitement. In music this human need is given expression through the juxtaposition of the familiar and the unknown—through the interplay of repeating and contrasting musical units.

contrast

Variation stands midway between repetition and contrast. The original melody returns, but it is altered in some way. For example, the tune may now be more complex, or new instruments may be added against it to create counterpoint. The listener has the satisfaction of hearing the familiar melody, yet is challenged to recognize in what way it has been changed.

variation

Needless to say, memory plays an important role in hearing musical form. In architecture, painting, and sculpture, form is taken in all at once by a single glance. But in music, as to some extent in poetry and literature, formal relationships only become obvious over the course of time. Here our memory must put the pieces together and show us the relationships. For this to happen, we must be able to recognize an exact repetition, a varied repetition, and a contrasting musical event. To help in this process, musicians have developed a simple system to visualize forms by labeling musical units with letters. The first prominent musical idea is designated **A.** Subsequent contrasting sections are each labeled **B, C, D,** and so on. If the first or any other musical unit returns in varied form, then that variation is indicated by a superscript number: A^1, B^2, for example. Subdivisions of each large musical unit are shown by lowercase letters (**a, b,** etc.). How this works will become clear in the following examples.

the role of memory

Musical Forms

Most musical forms transcend musical epochs—they are not unique to any one period in the history of music. The following musical forms are universal as well as timeless.

STROPHIC FORM. This is the most familiar of all musical forms because our hymns, carols, folk tunes, and patriotic songs invariably make use of it. In **strophic form** the composer sets the words of the first stanza and then uses the same entire melody for all subsequent stanzas. A good example is the Welsh holiday carol *Deck the Halls*. Notice how the first phrase (**a**) of the musical unit (**A**), or stanza, is repeated.

	a	Deck the halls with boughs of holly, fa, la, la, la, etc.
A	a	'Tis the season to be jolly, fa, la, la, la, la, etc.
	b	Don we now our gay apparel, fa, la, la, la, la, etc.
	a^1	Troll the ancient Yule-tide carol, fa, la, la, la, etc.

The basic musical unit, **A,** with the subdivisions **a, a, b, a¹,** is then heard four more times for each of the remaining stanzas, or strophes, of text. The overall form is thus:

$$
\begin{array}{ccccc}
\textbf{A} & \textbf{A} & \textbf{A} & \textbf{A} & \textbf{A} \\
\text{a a b a}^1 & \text{a a b a}^1 & \text{a a b a}^1 & \text{a a b a}^1 & \text{a a b a}^1
\end{array}
$$

A famous example of strophic form can be heard in the well-known *Wiegenlied (Lullaby)* of Johannes Brahms. Here the same music is used for each of two strophes of text (for more on this piece, see page 303).

LISTENING GUIDE

Johannes Brahms
Lullaby (1868)

Intro CD/16

0:00	Piano introduction to first strophe
0:05	Strophe one
0:50	Piano introduction to second strophe
0:56	Strophe two

THEME AND VARIATIONS If, in the preceding example, the music of the first stanza (**A**) is altered in some way each time it returns, then **theme and variations** form is present. Additions to the melody, new chords in the supporting accompaniment, and more density in the texture are the sort of changes that might occur. The return of the basic musical unit (**A**) provides a unifying element, while the changes add variety. Theme-and-variations form can be visualized in the following scheme:

$$
\begin{array}{ccccc}
\text{Statement} \\
\text{of theme} & \text{Variation 1} & \text{Variation 2} & \text{Variation 3} & \text{Variation 4} \\
\textbf{A} & \textbf{A}^1 & \textbf{A}^2 & \textbf{A}^3 & \textbf{A}^4
\end{array}
$$

When Mozart was a young man he lived briefly in Paris, where he heard the French folk song, *Ah, vous dirai-je Maman.* We know it today as *Twinkle, Twinkle, Little Star.* Upon this charming tune (**A**) he composed a set of variations for piano, the first three of which are described in the following Listening Guide (for more on this piece, see pages 165 and 175).

LISTENING GUIDE

Wolfgang Amadeus Mozart
Variations on *Twinkle, Twinkle, Little Star* (1778)

Intro CD/17

0:00	**A**	Tune played without ornamentation; melody above, harmony below
0:51	**A¹**	Variation 1: tune above decorated with florid, fast-moving figurations
1:45	**A²**	Variation 2: tune above undecorated; florid, fast-moving figurations now in bass
2:36	**A³**	Variation 3: tune above decorated with graceful arpeggios*

BINARY FORM As the name indicates, **binary form** consists of two contrasting units, **A** and **B.** In length and general shape, **A** and **B** are constructed so as to balance and complement each other. Variety is usually introduced in **B** by means of a dissimilar mood, key*, or melody. Sometimes in binary form, both **A** and **B** are immediately repeated, note for note. Musicians indicate exact repeats by means of the following sign: ‖: :‖. Thus, when binary form appears as ‖:A:‖ ‖:B:‖ it is performed **AABB.**

George Frideric Handel's Hornpipe from his *Water Music* (1717) is a jaunty country dance in binary form. There are no repeats, and hence the form is simply **AB.** The beginning of **B** is easy to hear because the melody jumps to a high range and the texture is suddenly thinner so the music sounds quieter. Because Handel's Hornpipe is very short—it lasts only forty seconds—he required that it be performed three times: On our recording it is played first by strings alone, then by woodwinds and percussion, and finally by all these instruments together. Therefore, in this example you will hear the same dance in binary form (**AB**) played three times, each with a different orchestration.

LISTENING GUIDE	George Frideric Handel Hornpipe from *Water Music* (1717)	Intro CD/18

First playing (strings alone)
0:00   **A** section
0:18   Sudden *piano* signals beginning of the **B** section

Second playing (woodwinds and percussion)
0:41   **A** section
0:58   Sudden *piano* signals beginning of the **B** section

Third playing (strings, woodwinds, and percussion together)
1:19   **A** section
1:37   Sudden *piano* signals beginning of the **B** section

TERNARY FORM **Ternary form** in music is even more common than binary. It consists of three sections. The second is a contrasting unit, and the third is a repeat of the first—hence the formal pattern is **ABA.** As we will see later (page 165), ternary form has appeared at many different times in the history of music. It is an especially satisfying arrangement because it is simple yet rounded and complete. It, too, sometimes uses musical repeats, first of the **A** section, then of both **B** and **A** together (‖:A:‖ ‖:B A:‖).

🌼 FIGURES 3–21 AND 3–22 (left) Barbara Hepworth, *Two Figures (Menhirs)* 1964. Here the two units of sculpture are distinctly different, yet mutually harmonious. This is the essence of binary form. (right) The cathedral of Salzburg, Austria, where Mozart and his father frequently performed during the 1760s and 1770s. It clearly reflects a ternary, or **ABA,** form.

LISTENING GUIDE

George Frideric Handel
Minuet and Trio from *Water Music* (1717)

Intro CD/19

0:00	French horns play phrase 1	
0:13	Trumpets play phrase 2	
0:29	Phrase 1 heard twice more	**A**
0:55	Phrase 2 heard twice more	
1:28	Shift to minor key and soft dynamics; only strings play	**B**
2:19	Full orchestra returns with phrases 1 and 2	**A**

Listen now to the opening Minuet and Trio from Handel's *Water Music*. The Minuet (**A**) is in a major key and has a sprightly melody consisting of two phrases, here introduced in turn by the French horns and the trumpets. The Trio (**B**) is in a contrasting minor key and is played softly by the strings alone. The return of the Minuet completes the ternary form: **ABA.**

RONDO FORM **Rondo form** is almost as old as music itself. It uses a simple principle: A refrain alternates with contrasting music. Perhaps because of this simplicity, rondo form has been favored by musicians of every age—Medieval songsters, Classical symphonists like Mozart and Haydn, and even contemporary rock stars like Elton John and Sting. Although the principle of a recurring refrain is a constant, composers have written rondos in several different formal patterns, including the following ones:

ABABA   ABACA   ABACABA

You may already be familiar with a rondo composed by Jean-Joseph Mouret (1682–1738), for it is used as the theme music for "Masterpiece Theater" on PBS-TV. Mouret was a composer at the French court during the reign of Louis XV (1715–1774), and his well-known *Rondeau* typifies the ceremonial splendor of the royal household during the Baroque era (1600–1750). Here the refrain (**A**), played by full orchestra with brilliant trumpets and drums, alternates with two contrasting ideas (**B** and **C**) to form a neatly symmetrical pattern. The divisions between sections are clearly audible because each unit is played by a distinctive group of instruments. As you listen to Mouret's rondo, perhaps you will agree that a simple, effective formal principle is at work here.

LISTENING GUIDE

Jean-Joseph Mouret
Rondeau from *Suite de symphonies* (1729)

Intro CD/20

0:00	**A**	Refrain played by full orchestra, including trumpets and drums, and then repeated (at 0:12)
0:24	**B**	Quieter contrasting section played by organ
0:37	**A**	Refrain returns but without repeat
0:50	**C**	New contrasting section played by organ
1:21	**A**	Refrain returns and is repeated (at 1:33)

Although these examples of musical form are all short, they clearly show that an internal logic and cohesiveness is at work in each piece. More complex musical forms, of course, do exist, and these give rise to longer, more complex compositions. Sonata–allegro form and fugal form are the principal ones. These we will discuss when we come to the music of the Baroque and Classical periods. In addition, there are also free musical forms, such as the fantasy and the prelude, which give free reign to the composer's imagination without tight formal restraints. These, too, we will meet in good time.

LISTENING EXERCISES

Instruments of the Orchestra
Benjamin Britten, *The Young Person's Guide to the Orchestra* (1946)

On your Introduction to Listening CD (track 13), you will find a performance of Benjamin Britten's *The Young Person's Guide to the Orchestra*. Britten (1913–1976) composed this piece in 1946, though he used as his main theme a melody written in 1695 by another English composer, Henry Purcell (1659–1695). *The Young Person's Guide* was originally written to provide musical examples for a film entitled *The Instruments of the Orchestra*. Britten's intent was to demonstrate first the sounds of the four instrumental families of the orchestra and then the distinctive colors of the individual instruments.

The work begins with the full orchestra playing the theme. This is followed by a presentation of the same theme, in turn, by the woodwind family alone, by the brasses, by the strings (including harp), and finally by the percussion (1–4). After the percussion holds forth, the full orchestra returns with a sweeping statement of the theme (5).

Next comes a series of thirteen variations of the theme (6–18), each of which exposes the special tone colors of one or two instruments. We begin with the flutes (6) and work our way to the percussion (18).

Finally, *The Young Person's Guide* ends with all of the instruments of the orchestra engaged in a fugue. We discuss the fugue at length in Chapter 7. For now, notice simply that the texture of the fugue is polyphonic, meaning that there are several quickly moving lines and they proceed independently of one another.

Your task is to fill in the blanks by indicating the time at which each musical event occurs, specifically, the minute and second at which the various families of instruments or individual instruments enter.
Introduction to the theme:

0:00	Full orchestra	
1. _____	Woodwinds	
2. _____	Brass	

3. _____   Strings (with harp)
4. _____   Percussion
5. _____   Full orchestra

Short transition (string tremolo and harp)

Variations on the theme:

6. 1:56   Flutes and piccolo (with harp accompaniment)
7. _____   Oboes (with string accompaniment)
8. _____   Clarinets (with tuba accompaniment)
9. _____   Bassoons (with string accompaniment)
10. 5:00   Violins sweep forward
11. _____   Violas play more quietly (with brass and woodwind accompaniment)
12. _____   Cellos offer lovely melody (with clarinet/string accompaniment)
13. _____   Double basses play comical melody (with light woodwind and percussion accompaniment)
14. _____   Harp solo (with string tremolo accompaniment)
15. _____   French horns (with string and harp accompaniment)
16. _____   Trumpets play a light gallop
17. _____   Trombones blast forth with tuba down below (with woodwind accompaniment)
18. _____   Percussion, beginning with the timpani, and then cymbals, snare drum, xylophone, and so on; ends with xylophone solo

Fugue based on the theme:

13:43   (very fast) Fugue begins with piccolo and flutes, followed by clarinets, bassoons, violins, violas, cellos, double basses, harp, horns, trumpets, trombones, and tuba

 Hearing Musical Textures

This exercise asks you to become familiar with the three basic textures of music: monophonic, polyphonic, and homophonic. On your Introduction to Listening CD (track 15), you have ten excerpts that represent these various textures. Monophonic texture, you will find, is easy to hear because it has only one line of music. More difficult is to differentiate between polyphonic texture and homophonic texture. Polyphonic texture embodies many active, independent lines. Homophonic texture, on the other hand, usually uses blocks of chords that accompany and support a single melody. Identify the texture of each of the excerpts by writing an M, P, or H in the appropriate blank.

Track 15
1. (0:00) _____ Musorgsky, *Promenade* from *Pictures at an Exhibition*
2. (0:10) _____ Britten, *The Young Person's Guide to the Orchestra*
3. (0:55) _____ Musorgsky, *Promenade* from *Pictures at an Exhibition*

4. (1:06) ____ Musorgsky, *Goldenberg and Schmuyle* from *Pictures at an Exhibition*
5. (1:32) ____ Dvořák, Symphony No. 9, "From the New World," *Largo*
6. (2:04) ____ Bach, Organ Fugue in G minor
7. (2:57) ____ Lillian Hardin and Louis Armstrong, *Droppin' Shucks*
8. (3:25) ____ Bernstein, *West Side Story*, Symphonic dance "Mambo"
9. (3:43) ____ Josquin Desprez, *Ave Maria*
10. (4:09) ____ Debussy, *Prelude to The Afternoon of a Faun*

 KEY WORDS

binary form	monophony	texture
canon	orchestral score	theme and variations
color	*piano*	timbre
counterpoint	pizzicato	tremolo
dynamics	polyphony	vibrato
forte	rondo form	‖: :‖ (indication to
"Eroica" Symphony	*sforzando*	performer to repeat
glissando	strophic form	the music)
homophony	ternary form	

HEARING MUSICAL STYLES

WHAT IS MUSICAL STYLE?

One of the challenges of listening to music is to evaluate what we hear. Consciously or not, we do this every day. When we turn on the radio, for example, we often meet an unknown work for the first time. Intuitively we try to make an educated guess as to the genre and period of the music, and perhaps the composer. Is it rap or reggae, Romantic or Baroque, Bach or Beethoven? Identifying the type and period of a composition, and even the composer, is the first step toward true musical enjoyment. This recognition is mainly an exercise in hearing musical style. But what is musical style?

Style in music is the surface sound produced by the interaction of the elements of music: melody, rhythm, harmony, color, texture, and form. The distinctive manner of presentation of all of these elements creates a style. All composers, like all creative people (Figure 1), have a personal style, one that makes their art different from all the rest. Take a work by Mozart (1756–1791), for example. A trained listener will recognize it as a piece from the Classical period (1750–1820) because of its generally symmetrical melodies, light texture, and dynamic ebb and flow. A truly experienced ear will identify Mozart as the composer, perhaps by recognizing the sudden shifts to minor keys, the intensely chromatic melodies, or the colorful writing for bassoon or clarinet—all hallmarks of Mozart's musical style.

Each period in the history of music has a musical style, too. That is to say, the music of one epoch will possess qualities common to much other music of that same time. A common set of musical practices and procedures is at work. Many motets* from the Renaissance (1475–1600) exhibit short bursts of imitative counterpoint sung by voices alone without instrumental accompaniment. A symphony* from the Romantic period (1820–1900), on the other hand, will typically exhibit long, non-imitative melodies, chromatic* harmonies, languid rhythms, and uniformly dense orchestral textures.

Historical periods, in some ways, mirror the ages of humankind. We cannot identify the precise moment in which an infant becomes a child or the child the adult. Similarly, musical styles do not change overnight; they evolve and over-

FIGURE 1

I.M. Pei's pyramid in the courtyard of the Louvre in Paris. Here two distinctive styles, one old, one new, engage in a stimulating dialogue. Against the backdrop of a heavy imperial palace, with strong elements of a classical style, stands a modern pyramid made of tempered glass and steel.

lap. Composers can stand midway between periods. For example, Guillaume Dufay (ca. 1400–1474) is a composer of the Middle Ages in his use of texture, but of the Renaissance in regard to his harmonies. Ludwig van Beethoven (1770–1827) straddles the Classical and Romantic periods, being somewhat conservative in his choice of harmonies but radically progressive in his use of form and rhythm. Despite such contradictions, historians of music, like historians of art, find it useful to discuss style in terms of historical periods. This makes it possible to conceptualize and speak about these arts in a more convenient way. Here are the stylistic periods that are discussed in the following chapters:

Middle Ages: 400–1475   Classical: 1750–1820
Renaissance: 1475–1600   Romantic: 1820–1900
Early Baroque: 1600–1710   Impressionist: 1880–1920
Late Baroque: 1710–1750   Twentieth Century: 1900–present

CHECKLIST OF MUSICAL STYLE BY PERIODS

Middle Ages: 400–1475

Melody: Moves mostly by step within a narrow range; uses diatonic and not chromatic notes of the scale

Harmony: Most surviving medieval music is monophonic Gregorian chant or monophonic *troubadour* and *trouvère* songs—hence there is no harmony

Medieval polyphony (Mass, motet, and chanson) has dissonant phrases ending with open, hollow-sounding chords

Rhythm: Gregorian chant as well as *troubadour* and *trouvère* songs sung mainly in notes of equal value without clearly marked rhythms; medieval polyphony is composed mostly in triple meter and uses repeating rhythmic patterns

Color: Mainly vocal sounds (choir or soloists); little instrumental music survives

Texture: Mostly monophonic—Gregorian chant as well as *troubadour* and *trouvère* songs are monophonic melodies

Medieval polyphony (two, three, or four independent lines) is mainly contrapuntal

Form: Strophic form of *troubadour* and *trouvère* songs; ternary form of the Kyrie; rondo form of the French *rondeau*

Representative composers: Hildegard of Bingen, Leoninus, Perotinus, Machaut, Countess of Dia, Dufay, Binchois

Principal genres: Gregorian chant, polyphonic Mass, troubadour and trouvère songs, secular polyphonic chanson, instrumental dance

Renaissance: 1475–1600

Melody: Mainly stepwise motion within a moderately narrow range; still mainly diatonic, but some intense chromaticism found in madrigals from end of period

Harmony: More careful use of dissonance than in the Middle Ages as the triad, a consonant chord, becomes the basic building block of harmony

Rhythm: Duple meter is now as common as triple meter; rhythm in sacred vocal music (Mass and motet) is relaxed and without strong down-

Representative composers: Desprez, Palestrina, Byrd, Lasso, Weelkes, Dowland

Principal genres: sacred Mass and motet, secular chanson and madrigal, instrumental dance

<table>
<tr><td></td><td>beats; rhythm in secular vocal music (chanson and madrigal) and in instrumental dances is usually lively and catchy, with frequent use of syncopation</td></tr>
</table>

	beats; rhythm in secular vocal music (chanson and madrigal) and in instrumental dances is usually lively and catchy, with frequent use of syncopation
Color:	Although more music for instruments alone has survived, the predominant sound remains that of unaccompanied vocal music, whether for soloists or for choir
Texture:	Contrapuntal, polyphonic texture for four or five vocal lines is heard throughout Mass, motet, and madrigal, though occasional passages of chordal homophonic texture are inserted for variety
Form:	Strict musical forms are not often used; most Masses, motets, madrigals, chansons, and instrumental dances are through-composed—have no musical repetitions and hence no standard formal plan

Early Baroque: 1600–1710

Representative composers: Gabrieli, Monteverdi, Purcell, Corelli, Vivaldi

Principal genres: polychoral motet, cantata, opera, sonata, concerto grosso, solo concerto, orchestral suite

Melody:	Less stepwise movement, larger leaps, wider range, and more chromaticism reflect influence of virtuosic solo singing; melodic patterns idiomatic to particular musical instruments emerge; introduction of melodic sequence
Harmony:	Stable, diatonic chords played by *basso continuo* support melody; clearly defined chord progressions begin to develop; tonality reduced to major and minor keys
Rhythm:	Relaxed, flexible rhythms of the Renaissance transformed into regularly repeating, driving rhythms
Color:	Musical timbre becomes enormously varied as traditional instruments are perfected (e.g., harpsichord, violin, and oboe) and new combinations of voices and instruments are explored; symphony orchestra begins to take shape; sudden shifts in dynamics (terraced dynamics) reflect dramatic quality of Baroque music
Texture:	Chordal, homophonic texture predominates; top and bottom lines are the strongest as *basso continuo* creates a powerful bass to support the melody above
Form:	Arias and instrumental works often make use of *basso ostinato* procedure; ritornello form emerges in the concerto grosso; binary form regulates most movements of the sonata and orchestral suite

Late Baroque: 1710–1750

Representative composers: Bach, Handel, Telemann, Vivaldi

Principal genres: cantata, opera, oratorio, sonata, orchestral suite, concerto grosso, prelude and fugue

Melody:	Grows longer, more expansive, and more asymmetrical; idiomatic instrumental style influences vocal melodies
Harmony:	Functional chord progressions govern harmonic movement—harmony moves purposefully from one chord to the next; *basso continuo* continues to provide strong bass
Rhythm:	Exciting, driving, energized rhythms propel music forward with vigor; "walking" bass creates feeling of rhythmic regularity
Color:	Instruments reign supreme; instrumental sounds, especially of violin, harpsichord, and organ, set musical tone for the era; one tone color used throughout a movement or large section of movement

Texture: Homophonic texture remains important, but polyphonic texture reemerges because of growing importance of the contrapuntal fugue

Form: Binary form in sonatas and orchestral suites; *da capo* aria (ternary) form in arias; fugal procedure used in fugue

Classical: 1750–1820

Melody: Short, balanced phrases create tuneful melodies; melody more influenced by vocal than instrumental style; frequent cadences produce light, airy feeling

Harmony: The rate at which chords change (harmonic rhythm) varies dramatically, creating a dynamic flux and flow; simple chordal harmonies made more active by "Alberti" bass

Rhythm: Departs from regular, driving patterns of Baroque era to become more stop-and-go; greater rhythmic variety within a single movement

Color: Orchestra grows larger; woodwind section of two flutes, oboes, clarinets, and bassoons becomes typical; piano replaces harpsichord as principal keyboard instrument

Texture: Mostly homophonic; thin bass and middle range, hence light and transparent; passages in contrapuntal style appear sparingly and mainly for contrast

Form: A few standard forms regulate much of Classical music: sonata–allegro, theme and variations, rondo, ternary (for minuets and trios), and double exposition (for solo concerto)

Representative composers: Mozart, Haydn, Beethoven, Schubert

Principal genres: symphony, sonata, string quartet, solo concerto, opera

Romantic: 1820–1900

Melody: Long, singable lines with powerful climaxes and chromatic inflections for expressiveness

Harmony: Greater use of chromaticism makes the harmony richer and more colorful; sudden shifts to remote chords for expressive purposes; more dissonance to convey feeling of anxiety and longing

Rhythm: Rhythms are flexible, often languid, and therefore meter is sometimes not clearly articulated. Tempos can fluctuate greatly (tempo *rubato*); tempo can slow to a crawl to allow for "the grand gesture"

Color: The orchestra becomes enormous, reaching upward of one hundred performers: trombone, tuba, contrabassoon, piccolo, and English horn added to the ensemble; experiments with new playing techniques for special effects; dynamics vary widely to create different levels of expression; piano becomes larger and more powerful

Texture: Predominantly homophonic but dense and rich because of larger orchestra; sustaining pedal on the piano also adds to density

Form: No new forms created, rather traditional forms (strophic, sonata–allegro, and theme and variations, for example) used and extended in length; traditional forms also applied to new genres such as *Lied*, symphonic poem, and orchestral song

Representative composers: Beethoven, Schubert, Berlioz, Mendelssohn, Robert Schumann, Clara Schumann, Chopin, Liszt, Verdi, Wagner, Brahms, Dvořák, Tchaikovsky, Musorgsky, Mahler, Puccini

Principal genres: symphony, program symphony, symphonic poem, concert overture, opera, Lied, orchestral song, solo concerto, character piece for piano, ballet music

Impressionist: 1880–1920

Principal genres: symphonic poem, string quartet, orchestral song, opera, character piece for piano

Representative composers: Debussy, Ravel, Fauré

Melody:	Varies from short dabs of sound to long, free-flowing lines. Melodies are rarely tuneful or singable; they often twist and turn rapidly in undulating patterns. Chromatic scale, whole-tone scale, and pentatonic scale often replace usual major and minor scales
Harmony:	Primarily homophonic; triad is extended to form seventh chords and ninth chords, and these frequently move in parallel motion
Rhythm:	Usually free and flexible with irregular accents, making it sometimes difficult to determine the meter; rhythmic ostinatos used to give feeling of stasis rather than movement
Color:	More emphasis on woodwinds and brasses and less on the violins as primary carriers of melody; more soloistic writing to show that the color of the instrument is as important as the melody line it plays
Texture:	Can vary from thin and airy to heavy and dense; sustaining pedal of the piano often used to create a wash of sound. Glissandos run quickly from low to high or high to low
Form:	Traditional forms involving clear-cut repetitions rarely used; composers try to develop a form unique and particular to each new musical work

Twentieth Century: 1900–present

Representative composers: Stravinsky, Schoenberg, Berg, Webern, Bartók, Varèse, Ives, Cage, Prokofiev, Copland, Zwilich, Adams, Tavener, Bernstein, Gershwin

Principal genres: symphony, solo concerto, string quartet, opera, ballet music, electronic music, chance music, Broadway musical

Melody:	Wide-ranging disjunct lines, often chromatic and dissonant, angularity accentuated by use of octave displacement
Harmony:	Highly dissonant; dissonance no longer must move to consonance but may move to another dissonance. Sometimes two conflicting, but equal, tonal centers sound simultaneously (polytonality); sometimes there is no audible tonal center (atonality)
Rhythm:	Vigorous, energetic rhythms; conflicting simultaneous meters (polymeters) and rhythms (polyrhythms) make for temporal complexity
Color:	Color becomes an agent of form and beauty in and by itself; composers seek new sounds from traditional, acoustical instruments, from electronic instruments and computers, and from noises in the environment
Texture:	As varied and individual as the men and women composing music
Form:	A range of extremes: sonata–allegro, rondo, theme and variations benefit from a Neo-classical revival; twelve-tone procedure allows for an almost mathematical formal control; yet chance music permits random happenings and noises from the environment to shape a musical work

MEDIEVAL MUSIC

4

Historians use the term "Middle Ages" as a catchall phrase to refer to the thousand years of history between the fall of the Roman Empire (late 400s) and the age of reawakening and discovery, exemplified by the voyages of Christopher Columbus (late 1400s). It was a period of triumphs and tragedies, of soaring cathedrals and murderous plagues, of sublime spirituality and abject poverty, of knightly chivalry and barbarous warfare. Seen from our modern perspective, the medieval period appears as a vast chronological expanse dotted by occasional outposts of dazzling architecture, stunning stained glass, and equally compelling poetry, painting, and music.

MUSIC IN THE MONASTERY

There were many kinds of music in the Middle Ages: songs for the knights as they rode into battle, songs for the men in the fields and the women around the hearth, songs and dances for the nobles in their castles, and chants for the priests as they celebrated the Christian service in the monasteries and cathedrals. Unfortunately, most of this music, and virtually all of it emanating from the common folk, is now lost because it was never written down. Only the music of the Church is preserved in any significant amount, because at that time only the men of the Church, and to a lesser degree the nuns, were educated. Even the nobility was more or less illiterate. The reading and copying of texts was the private preserve of the rural monasteries and, somewhat later, the urban cathedrals. The monks were encouraged to read and write as a means of becoming more familiar with the scriptures, and it was they who devised a system to notate and copy music. In this way, the music of the Church could be spread to other monastic communities and taught to succeeding generations of novices.

Life was rigorous in a medieval monastery. The founder of the principal monastic order, St. Benedict (died ca. 547), prescribed a code of conduct, or rule, for his followers. The Benedictines rose at about four o'clock in the morning for the night office (matins), at which they sang psalms and read scripture. After a break "for the necessities of nature" the brethren returned at daybreak to sing another service in praise of the Lord. Thereafter, the monks dispersed to farm and otherwise attend to their lands, reuniting again at seven other times during the day to sing and to pray, and to eat two communal meals. The high point of these religious services was the Mass, celebrated about nine o'clock in the morning, which, through the ritual act of communion (see page 71), commemorated Christ's sacrifice.

🌸 GREGORIAN CHANT

The music sung daily at the eight monastic hours of prayer and at Mass was what we today call Gregorian chant, named in honor of Pope Gregory the Great (540?–604). Ironically, Gregory wrote little, if any, of this music. Being more a church administrator than a musician, he merely decreed that certain chants should be sung on certain days of the liturgical year. Melodies for the Christian service had, of course, existed since the time of the Apostles, some taken over directly from the Jewish Temple. What we now call **Gregorian chant** (also called **plainsong**) is really a large body of unaccompanied vocal music, setting Latin texts, composed for the Western Church over the course of fifteen centuries—from the time of the earliest Fathers to the Council of Trent (1545–1563), which brought sweeping reforms to the Church.

chant composed for fifteen centuries

Gregorian chant is like no other music. It has a timeless, otherworldly quality that arises, no doubt, because Gregorian chant has neither meter nor regular rhythms. True, some notes are longer or shorter than others, but they do not recur in obvious patterns that would allow us to clap our hands or tap our feet. This is music intended to encourage pious reflection, not cavorting. It is free of tension and drama. All voices sing together in unison*. Thus all Gregorian chant is considered monophony*, or music for one line. There is no instrumental accompaniment, nor, as a rule, are men's and women's voices mixed when performing chant. Finally, Gregorian chant does not use time as a dimension in which to set up contrasts. Any contrast that does occur is of the mildest sort. Sometimes a soloist will alternate with a full choir. Occasionally, a passage of **syllabic singing** (only one or two notes for each syllable of text) will give way to **melismatic singing** (many notes sung to just one syllable), as in Ex. 4–1, from Hildegard of Bingen's *O Greenest Branch*.

all chant is monophonic music

EXAMPLE 4–1

The overall effect of Gregorian chant is thus one of endless peace and serenity. Through chant, the receptive listener can gradually disengage from the anxieties and tensions of the present world.

THE GREGORIAN CHANT OF HILDEGARD OF BINGEN (1098–1171)
We know the names of only a few of the composers of Gregorian chant. And what we know of their lives suggests that they thought of themselves not so much as creators or composers, but as conduits for the voice of God—vessels through which the divine message might be brought to those here on earth. One of the most remarkable contributors to the repertoire of Gregorian chant was Abbess Hildegard of Bingen (1098–1171), from whose pen we have received seventy-seven chants (Fig. 4–1). Hildegard was the tenth child of noble parents who gave her to the Church as a tithe (a donation of a tenth of one's worldly income). She was educated by Benedictine nuns and then, at the age of fifty-two, founded her own convent near the small town of Bingen, in Germany, on the west bank of the Rhine River. In the course of time, Hildegard mani-

🌸 FIGURE 4–1
A twelfth-century illumination depicting Hildegard of Bingen receiving divine inspiration, perhaps a vision or a chant, directly from the heavens. To the right a monk peeks in on her in amazement.

fested her extraordinary intellect and imagination as a playwright, poet, musician, naturalist, pharmacologist, and visionary. Popes and kings sought her advice. Though never officially canonized by the Roman Church, Hildegard is nonetheless generally regarded as a saint.

From an early age, Hildegard possessed unusual spiritual gifts. During moments that we might recognize as severe migraine attacks, she heard a voice and saw visions accompanied by great flashes of light: a serpent-like Satan devouring the petals of a scarlet rose, or the blood of Christ streaming in the heavens, for example. These images she transformed into poetry and set to music as liturgical chant—Gregorian chant. Her song to the Virgin Mary, *O viridissima virga* (*O Greenest Branch*, Ex. 4–2), vividly depicts Mary as the most verdant branch of the tree of Jesse, through whom the heat of the sun radiates like the aroma of balm. The joyful Mary brings new life to all flora and fauna of the earth.

Hildegard's *O Greenest Branch* possesses many qualities typical of Gregorian chant. It gravitates around a tonal center—here, the pitch G. Notice in the first stanza (Ex. 4–2) how the music starts on G, works up a fifth to the pitch D and then down an octave to the D below, finally returning to the initial G. Notice also how *O Greenest Branch* is a predominantly stepwise melody, one without large leaps. It also avoids chromatic* twists—added sharps and flats—that might make the chant more difficult to perform. This was, after all, choral music to be sung by the full community of musically unsophisticated monks or nuns, so it had to be simple and direct. In the case of *O Greenest Branch*, we have a chant intended to be sung at Mass. (It is a Sequentia, the sixth musical portion of the Mass—see page 71.) Finally, *O Greenest Branch* was conceived without rhythm or meter. The notes are generally of one basic value, something close to our eighth note in length. The unaccompanied, monophonic line and the absence of rhythmic drive allow a restful, contemplative mood to develop. The music is meant to float unfettered as it bears the transcendent spirit aloft.

EXAMPLE 4–2: Hildegard of Bingen, *O Greenest Branch*

🌸 FIGURE 4–2
(upper frame) A vision of Hildegard revealing how a fantastic winged figure of God the Father, the Son, and the Mystical Lamb killed the serpent Satan with a blazing sword. (lower frame) Hildegard (right) receives the vision and reports it to her secretary (left). This manuscript dates from the twelfth century.

LISTENING GUIDE

Hildegard of Bingen
Gregorian chant, *O Greenest Branch* (ca. 1150)

6CD 1/1;
2CD 1/1

Form: strophic
Texture: polyphonic and monophonic

Stanza 1

0:00   O viridissima virga, ave
     quae in ventoso flabro sciscitationis
     sanctorum prodisti.

Hail, o greenest branch
who sprang forth in the airy breeze
of the prayers of the saints.

(Continued on next page)

Chant at the Top of the Charts

In recent years, Gregorian chant has become all the rage. The excitement began in 1994 with the release, appropriately enough by Angel Records, of the CD *Chant*, which sold one million copies within the first two months of its appearance. That success spawned sequels, leading to the present *Chant IV* (Angel 56373). Much of the popularity of Gregorian chant can be attributed to the fact that it has stylistic traits in common with New Age Music. Both project smooth, uniform, rhythmically fluid sounds that are decidedly non-assertive and nonconfrontational.

Hildegard, too, has been popularized as something of a New Age mystic. She is a fixture on the World Wide Web, where you can study her chants in the original notation, find translations of her poetry, view spectacular medieval depictions of her visions, and order the latest CD. The year 1998 marked the nine-hundredth anniversary of Hildegard's birth and, right on cue, a half-dozen new Hildegard CDs appeared, as well as a lengthy video and a shorter video clip for MTV. On one recent CD entitled *Vision* (Angel 55246), Hildegard's chants are accompanied by synthesizer and bass guitar. Could the visionary nun have foreseen all this, she would doubtless have experienced yet one more of her famous migraines!

Stanza 2

0:27   Cum venit tempus,
quod tu floruisti,
in ramis tuis,
ave, ave sit tibi,
quia calor solis in te sudavit
sicut odor balsami.

So the time has come that
you flourished
in your boughs,
hail, hail to you,
because the heat of the sun radiated
in you like the aroma of balm.

Stanza 3

1:01   Nam in te floruit pulcher flos
qui odorem dedit omnibus aromatibus
quae arida erant.

For in you bloomed the beautiful
flower which scented all parched
perfumes.

Stanza 4

1:28   Et illa apparuerunt omnia
in viriditate plena.

And all things have been manifested
in their full verdure.

Stanza 5

1:46   Unde celi dederunt rorem super gramen
et omnis terra leta facta est,
quoniam viscera ipsius frumentum protulerunt
et quoniam volucres celi nidos in ipsa habuerunt.

Whence the skies set down dew on the
pasture, and all the earth was made
more joyful because her womb produced
grain, and because the birds of Heaven
built their nests in her.

Stanza 6

2:27   Deinde facta est esca hominibus
et gaudium magnum epulantium;
inde, o suavis virgo,
in te non deficit ullum gaudium.

Then the harvest was made ready for
Man, and a great rejoicing of
banqueters, because in you,
o sweet Virgin, no joy is lacking.

Stanza 7

2:59   Hec omnia Eva contempsit.
Nunc autem laus sit altissimo.

All these things Eve rejected.
Now let there be praise to you in the Highest.

(Listening Exercise 9)

✿ MUSIC IN THE CATHEDRAL

If the monastery was primarily a rural establishment, one of solitude and spiritual contemplation, the cathedral was an urban institution. Every cathedral served as the "home church" of a bishop, the spiritual leader of the people, and only in a city could a bishop minister effectively to a flock of any size. During the twelfth and thirteenth centuries, the population of the urban centers of Europe—Milan, Paris, and London, among others—grew significantly, owing to a healthy revival of trade and commerce. Much of the commercial wealth that flowed to the cities was channeled toward the construction of splendid new churches that served not only as houses of worship but also as civic auditoriums. So substantial was this building campaign that the period 1150–1350 is often called "the Age of the Cathedrals." In these years, the great urban cathedrals of England, Spain, France, Italy, and Germany rose above the city skyline; many of them are still visible today. Most were constructed in what we call the Gothic style, with pointed arches, high ceiling vaults, supporting buttresses, and richly colored stained glass.

the age of the cathedrals

Gothic architecture began in France and radiated in all directions to foreign lands, even to the Christian-held territories of the Near East. In a similar way, France was the wellspring of other intellectual and artistic developments at this time. Paris, which by the end of the thirteenth century counted eighty thousand inhabitants, had become the leading university town in Europe for the study of the arts and theology. Young clerical scholars from distant countries flocked to the Parisian schools, and when they returned to their native lands they took with them the teachings of philosophers like Peter Abelard (1079–1142) and Thomas Aquinas (1225?–1274) and also the music they had heard at the cathedral of Notre Dame (Our Lady) of Paris (Fig. 4–3).

Paris, an intellectual center

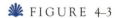 FIGURE 4–3
The cathedral of Notre Dame of Paris, begun ca. 1160, was one of the first to be built in the new Gothic style of architecture.

Notre Dame of Paris

Notre Dame of Paris was begun in the 1160s, yet was not completed until more than a hundred years later. Throughout this period the cathedral was blessed with a succession of churchmen who were not only theologians and philosophers but poets and musicians as well. Foremost among these were Master Leoninus (fl. 1169–1201) and Master Perotinus, called the Great (fl. 1198–1236). Leoninus wrote a great book of religious music (*Magnus liber organi*) to adorn the Gregorian chant sung at Notre Dame on high feasts. Perotinus revised the book of Leoninus and also composed many additional pieces of his own.

What is new about this Gothic church music is that it is written in polyphony* (two or more voices, or lines, sounding simultaneously) and not merely monophonic (one-voice) Gregorian chant. In truth, earlier church musicians had attempted to enhance the sound of the plainsong of the Church by adding another voice to it, but these efforts often required the new voice to move in exact parallel motion, usually at the interval of a fourth, a fifth, or an octave, with the preexisting chant. Leoninus, however, seized the opportunity to create an autonomous second voice, one that did not merely duplicate and amplify the plainsong but that complemented and graced it. Indeed, the added voice became the center of attention. In this musical development, we see an early instance of an artistic spirit breaking free of the constraints of the ancient authority of the Church.

LEONINUS: ORGANUM *VIDERUNT OMNES*

The expressive freedom Leoninus imparted to the new voice can be seen in his setting of the Gregorian chant *Viderunt omnes* for Mass on Christmas Day. By adding his own musical line above the chant, Leoninus created a two-voice **organum,** the name given to early church polyphony. The old chant is strung out in the lower voice and Leoninus's newly created line is on top. Soloists were assigned to the organum. Yet they sang in this new polyphonic style only for the first two words of the chant, "Viderunt omnes," which are greatly extended because of the addition of the new voice. Thereafter, the full clerical choir entered to continue and complete the remaining music in monophonic Gregorian chant. Try listening to this piece twice, first as it is given in the nearby Listening Guide, which shows the Gregorian chant in full below and a graphic indication of Leoninus's added part above. Then listen again, now trying to follow both lines of the organum as they appear in an original thirteenth-century manuscript from Paris (Fig. 4–4). As you can see in the manuscript, Leoninus's newly created upper voice undulates and even cascades in a virtuosic way as the lower voice holds the chant in long notes. Only at the beginning of the word "omnes" is any sort of rhythmic precision introduced. At this time medieval musical notation could indicate pitches accurately, but was only beginning to deal with matters of rhythm. What Leoninus has fashioned here is a rather free, rhapsodic hymn in praise of the Christ child. Imagine how these new sounds struck the ear of the medieval citizen of Paris as they rebounded around the bare stone walls of the vast, newly constructed cathedral of Notre Dame.

❀ FIGURE 4-4

A thirteenth-century manuscript preserving Leoninus's organum for Christmas, *Viderunt omnes*. Leoninus's newly created voice is on each of the upper four-line staffs, while the slower-moving Gregorian chant, with the text below, is on each of the lower staffs.

LISTENING GUIDE

Master Leoninus
Organum with Gregorian chant, *Viderunt omnes*
(ca. 1180)

6CD 1/2

Texture: polyphonic, then monophonic

0:00 Leonin's added line   1:21

Chant

Vi- de- runt   o -   - mnes fi - nes   ter -   rae

sa- lu- ta - re   De -   i   no - stri: ju- bi- la- te   De -

- o   o -   - mnis   ter - ra.

All the ends of the earth have seen the salvation of our God: Sing joyfully to God, all the earth.

0:00   Polyphonic organum sung by soloists
1:21   Monophonic chant sung by choir

Musical Portions of the Mass

PROPER OF THE MASS	ORDINARY OF THE MASS
1. Introit (an introductory chant for the entry of the celebrating clergy)	
	2. Kyrie (a petition for mercy)
	3. Gloria (a hymn of praise to the Lord)
4. Gradual (a reflective chant)	
5. Alleluia or Tract (a chant of thanksgiving or penance)	
6. Sequentia (a chant commenting on the text of the Alleluia)	
	7. Credo (a profession of faith)
8. Offertory (a chant for the offering)	
	9. Sanctus (an acclamation to the Lord)
	10. Agnus Dei (a petition for mercy and eternal peace)
11. Communion (a chant accompanying communion)	

Notre Dame of Rheims

Notre Dame of Paris was not the only important cathedral devoted to Our Lady in northern Europe. The city of Rheims, one hundred miles east of Paris in the Champagne region, was graced with a monument equally large and impressive (Fig. 4–5). In the fourteenth century it, too, benefited from the service of a poetically and musically talented churchman, Guillaume de Machaut (1300?–1377). Judging by his nearly 150 surviving works, Machaut was the most important composer of the fourteenth century. And he was equally esteemed as a narrative and lyric poet. Today, historians of literature place him on a pedestal with his slightly younger English counterpart, Geoffrey Chaucer (1340?–1400), author of the *Canterbury Tales*. Indeed, Chaucer knew and borrowed heavily from the poetic works of Machaut.

MACHAUT: *MASS OF OUR LADY*

Machaut's *Messe de Nostre Dame (Mass of Our Lady)* is deservedly the best-known work in the entire repertoire of medieval music. It is impressive for its length and novel way music is applied to the texts of the **Mass**—the central and most important service of the Roman Catholic Church. Before Machaut's time, composers writing polyphony for the Mass had set only one or two sections of what is called the **Proper of the Mass** (chants whose texts changed to suit the feast day in question). Leoninus's *Viderunt omnes*, for example, is a setting of the Gradual (see box) of the Proper of the Mass for Christmas Day. Machaut, on the other hand, chose to set all of the chants of the **Ordinary of the Mass** (chants with unvarying texts that were sung virtually every day), and he united, or linked, these together by placing a distinctive musical motive, a descending scale, in each of the five movements. Setting the Ordinary of the Mass had the obvious practical advantage that the composition could be heard more than on just one feast day of the church year. Machaut's *Mass of Our Lady*, for example, could be sung any time a Mass in honor of the Virgin Mary was celebrated. The box at the top of this page lists the musical portions of the Mass and the order in which they are sung.

Although Machaut's innovation—creating a unified setting of the Ordinary of the Mass—was not embraced immediately by all composers in all regions, by

❉ FIGURE 4–5

Interior of the cathedral of Rheims looking from floor to ceiling. The pillars carry the eye up to the ribbed vaults of the roof, creating a feeling of great upward movement, just as the Mass of Machaut, with four superimposed voices, has a new sense of verticality.

Music at the Forefront of Science

During the Middle Ages—indeed since the time of Plato—music was viewed not as an art but as a science. It was studied in the schools and universities along with geometry, astronomy, and arithmetic in a curriculum called the *quadrivium*—four core sciences the subject matter of which could be precisely measured. The musical interval of the octave, for example, could be demonstrated by means of two strings the lengths of which were in a 2:1 proportion; a fifth could be produced by strings with a ratio of 3:2, and so on. A separate curriculum, called the *trivium* (grammar, logic, and rhetoric), was devoted to the study of language and philosophy. These subjects together constituted the seven liberal arts. Such English phrases as Bachelor of Arts and Master of Arts recall this ancient formulation.

The Middle Ages gave to Western society a gift that accounts for the near total domination of the West today in matters of science and technology: rigorous quantification.

During the late Middle Ages most important modes of human experience—the measurement of time, the calculation of the value of goods and services, the mapping of the surface of the earth, even the visual layout of a painting—came to be measured in proportional units. Measurement was applied to music by means of a system of notation that regulated the two primary components of this art: sound and time (Fig. 4–6). Pitch was determined by setting symbols along a grid of horizontal lines that indicated highs and lows. Time was controlled by giving different shapes (note shapes) to those symbols so as to indicate precise durations. The larger notes were exact multiples of smaller ones. Thus by 1350, the heyday of Machaut, all the elements of modern musical notation were essentially in place. The components of this art could be precisely measured and recorded, far earlier than those in other areas of human activity. The musical staff was the West's first graph.

❋ FIGURE 4–6

A poem by Machaut, a miniature portrait of the composer at work, and a poem by him set to music. The position of the notes on the vertical axis gives the pitch, the shape of the notes on the horizontal axis indicates their duration.

the early fifteenth century his idea had come to be adopted universally in the West. Henceforth, to write a polyphonic Mass for the Church meant that a composer would set the five texts of the Ordinary (Kyrie, Gloria, Credo, Sanctus, and Agnus Dei) and find some way to bind or shape them musically into an integrated unit. This is true not only for later masters like Bach, Mozart, Beethoven, and Schubert, but also for more modern composers like Igor Stravinsky, whose Mass of 1948, by his own admission, owes much to the model of Machaut.

The *Kyrie* of Machaut's *Mass of Our Lady* is a threefold petition for mercy (*Kyrie eleison* means "Lord have mercy upon us"). As in the previous example by Leoninus, it is built on a preexisting Gregorian chant that is held in longer notes than the surrounding material. Because the men who sang the chant sustained it, they came to be called the "tenors" (from the Latin *tenere,* "to hold"). Around them Machaut added not one new line but three, thereby creating four-voice polyphony. The two voices added above the tenor came to be called the *superius* and the *contratenor altus*, whence we get our terms "soprano" and "alto." The voice added below the tenor was called the *contratenor bassus*, whence our term "bass" (for more on the four standard voice parts, see page 84). By writing for four voices and spreading these over a range of two and a half octaves, Machaut was able to create truly sonorous choral polyphony. In the *Kyrie* of his Mass, Machaut intended his four-voice polyphony to alternate with the sections of monophonic Gregorian chant.

When you listen to Machaut's *Kyrie* for the first time, you will be struck by its dark, dissonant sound. The dark quality is present because only male voices are employed here, and hence the range is rather low. Only men and boys were allowed to sing in medieval cathedrals. Sacred singing by women was confined to nunneries (for more on this point, see pages 90 and 91). As to the dissonant, biting sound, it is caused by the fact that Machaut makes use of many unusual dissonances, ones later forbidden in Western polypohonic music by music theorists. In stark contrast to these dissonances, each section of polyphony ends with an open, somewhat hollow-sounding consonant chord. These chords use only the intervals of a fifth and an octave. Such open, hollow final chords sound especially rich in buildings with very resonant, or "lively," acoustics of the sort universally found in medieval cathedrals.

LISTENING GUIDE

Guillaume de Machaut
Kyrie of the *Mass of Our Lady* (ca. 1360)

6CD 1/3

Form: ternary
Texture: polyphonic and monophonic

0:00	Kyrie eleison (polyphony)	Lord have mercy upon us
1:00	Kyrie eleison (Gregorian chant)	Lord have mercy upon us
1:23	Kyrie eleison (polyphony)	Lord have mercy upon us
2:22	Christe eleison (Gregorian chant)	Christ have mercy upon us
2:42	Christe eleison (polyphony)	Christ have mercy upon us
3:36	Christe eleison (Gregorian chant)	Christ have mercy upon us
3:57	Kyrie eleison (polyphony)	Lord have mercy upon us
4:41	Kyrie eleison (Gregorian chant)	Lord have mercy upon us
5:00	Kyrie eleison (polyphony)	Lord have mercy upon us

✿ MUSIC AT THE COURT

Outside the walls of cathedral there was yet another musical world, one of popular song and dance centered at the court. Indeed, the court embraced forms of public entertainment not permitted by church authorities. Itinerant actors, jugglers, jesters, and animal acts all provided welcome diversions. Minstrels wandered from castle to castle, bringing the latest tunes, along with bits of news and gossip. Churchmen, too, sojourned at court. Guillaume de Machaut, for example, enjoyed a double career as cleric and courtier. He composed liturgical music for the cathedral of Rheims, yet at various times in his life was employed by the king of Bohemia, the king of Navarre, and the duke of Berry. While it may seem strange that a clergyman like Machaut was active in worldly affairs at court, during the Middle Ages learned churchmen were much in demand for their ability to read and write. And because of their skill with letters and their knowledge of musical notation gained in the church, clerics were inevitably drawn to the poetry and music of the courtly song. Indeed, most of the polyphonic love songs emanating from the court in the late Middle Ages were written by ordained priests.

churchmen active at the court

The court first emerged as a center for the patronage of the arts during the years 1150–1400. The fourteenth century in particular witnessed a general decline in the authority of the Church, epitomized by the "Babylonian captivity" (1309–1377), during which the popes, driven from Rome, lived as exiles in France. Kings, dukes, counts, and lesser nobles now assumed responsibility for the defense of the land as well as for affairs of commerce and justice. The aristocratic court became a small, independent city-state. To enhance the ruler's prestige and show that he or she was a person of refinement and sensibility, the noble often engaged bands of trumpeters to herald an arrival, instrumentalists to provide dance music for the festivals of the court, and singers and poets to create lyric verse.

The first composer-poets to appear at court in any number in the West were the musicians who graced the castles of southern France and northern Spain and Italy in the late twelfth and thirteenth centuries. These musicians were very different from itinerant minstrels. They were creators, called **troubadours** because they were "finders" or "inventors" of words and melodies (*trobar* means "to find" in the medieval French of southern France). Their art was devoted mainly to the creation of songs of love that extolled the courtly ideals of faith

❋ FIGURES 4–7 AND 4–8 (above) A thirteenth-century Spanish miniature showing a medieval fiddle (the rebec) on the left and a lute on the right. (right) The Countess of Dia as depicted in a manuscript of *troubadour* and *trouvère* poetry.

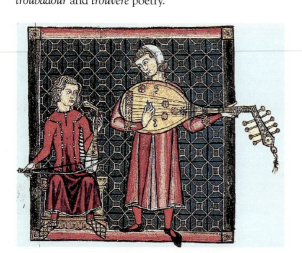

and devotion, whether to the ideal lady, to the just seigneur, or to the knight crusading in the Holy Land. Their songs were not in the Latin of the Church, but in the vernacular tongue: medieval Italian, Catalan, and Provençal (medieval French of the South). The origins of the *troubadours* were equally varied. Some were sons of bakers and drapers, others were members of the nobility, many were clerics living outside the church, and not a few were women.

In the Middle Ages, and later during the Renaissance (1475–1600), women were not allowed to sing in church, except in convents, owing to the early injunction of the Apostle Paul ("A woman must be silent in the church"). But at court, women often appeared as reciters of poetry, singers, and performers on the so-called *bas* (soft) instruments like the harp, lute, rebec (medieval fiddle), and flute (Fig. 4–7). Women *troubadours* were not merely performers, but creators in their own right. One such composer was the Countess of Dia (Fig. 4–8), who lived in southern France during the middle of the twelfth century. She was married to Count William of Poitiers but fell in love with a fellow *troubadour*, Raimbaut d'Orange (1146–1173). Her song *A chantar m'er (I Must Sing)* laments her failure in love, despite her self-proclaimed charms. It is composed of five strophes, or stanzas, each with seven lines of text and seven musical phrases. The seven-phrase melody, which owes much to the music of the Church in its stepwise movement and strong tonal feeling, displays a clear musical form, **ABABCDB** (the use of letters to indicate musical form is explained on page 53). Also in common with the chant of the Church, this *troubadour* song, as true of most, has no clearly articulated meter and rhythm, but is sung in notes of more or less equal length.

LISTENING GUIDE

Countess of Dia
Troubadour song, *I Must Sing* (ca. 1175)

6CD 1/4

0:00 Improvised introduction played on a medieval fiddle
0:26 Solo voice enters and sings first of five strophes

A chan - tar m'er de so qu'eu no vol - ri - a **A**

Tant me ran - cur de lui cui sui a - mi - a **B**

Car eu l'am mais que nul - ha ren que si - a **A**

Vas lui no'm val mer - ces ni cor - te - zi - a **B**

Ni ma bel - tatz ni mos pretz ni mos sens **C**

Qu'a - tres - si'm sui en - ga - nad' e tra - hi - a **D**

Com de-gr'es - ser s'eu fos de - sa - vi - nens. **B**

(I must sing of that which I'd rather not,
So vexed am I by him to whom I am a friend,
Because I love him more than anything that be,
But with him kindness and courtliness get me nowhere:
Neither my beauty, nor my worth, nor my wits.
In this way am I thwarted and betrayed,
Just as I would be if I were ugly.)

The Polyphonic Chanson

Gradually, the musical traditions created by the *troubadours* were carried to the north of France, where such composer-performers came to be called **trouvères,** and even to Germany, where they were called **Minnesingers.** Around 1300, some of the *trouvères* began to mix the traditions of the *troubadours* with the learned vocal polyphony coming from the Church. Soon churchmen like Guillaume de Machaut (see page 71) adopted the musical forms and poetic style of the *trouvères* to fashion a new genre of music, the polyphonic **chanson** (French for "song"). The chanson is simply a love song, normally in French, for two, three, or four voices, which usually follows a set poetic and musical form. At its best, the chanson is a small jewel of poignant lyricism.

During the fifteenth century, Gilles Binchois (1400?–1460) and Guillaume Dufay (1400?–1474) excelled at writing chansons. Both men were ordained priests, yet both moved easily between ecclesiastical and courtly circles in northern France. Dufay's *Craindre vous vueil (I Wish to Honor You)* is a lovely three-voice chanson with the structure of a **rondeau**—a musical and textual form with a recurring refrain like the rondo* (see page 56). All three voices may be sung, or the lower two may be played on accompanying instruments like the lute or rebec (see Fig. 4–7). Notice that the composer, who undoubtedly was the author of the text, has linked himself amorously to a certain woman named "Cateline" by means of an acrostic: The first letters of each line spell out "Cateline-Dufay" (*i, j,* and *y* being interchangeable in the Middle Ages, as well as *u* and *v*). A rather daring act for a priest!

EXAMPLE 4–3: Guillaume Dufay: Chanson, *I Wish to Honor You*† (ca. 1430)

†Recorded by the Medieval Ensemble of London on *Guillaume Dufay: Complete Secular Music*, L'Oiseau-lyre 237D 3.

Craindre vous vueil, douce dame de pris,
Amer, doubter, louer en fais, en dis,
Tout mon vivant, en quelque lieu que soye.
Et vous donner, m'amour, ma seule joye,
Le cuer de moy tant que je seray vis.

refrain

(I wish to honor you, sweet worthy lady,
To love, esteem, and praise you in word and deed,
All my life, no matter where I may be.
And to give you, my love, my only joy,
My heart as long as I shall live.

Iamais ne suy annuieux ne pensis
Ne douleureux, quant je voy vo clair vis
Et vo maintieng en alant par la voie.

I am never anxious or melancholy,
Or sad when I see your bright face,
And I will stand by you through life.

Craindre . . .

(repeat **refrain**)

I wish to honor . . .

De vous amer cel m'est un paradis,
Vëu les biens qui sont en vous compris;
Faire le doy quoy qu'avenir en doye.
A vous me rens, lÿes meiux que de soye,
Ioieusement, en bon espoir toudis.

To love you is paradise for me
Such are your charms.
I must do so, no matter what the future brings.
To render myself to you, in a bond tighter than silk
Joyfully, in bliss forever.

Craindre . . .

(repeat **refrain**)

I wish to honor . . .)

the court of Burgundy

At various times, both Guillaume Dufay and his colleague Gilles Binchois were employed at the court of a French nobleman, Philip the Good, duke of Burgundy (ruled 1419–1467). Owing to a succession of marriages and territorial conquests in France, Germany, and the Low Countries, the dukes of Burgundy

FIGURES 4–9 AND 4–10
(left) Dance scene at a wedding at a French court in the mid-fifteenth century. The musicians, who play shawms and a sackbut, are placed on high in a balcony. (below) A later scene, ca. 1600, showing musicians in a procession as painted by Denis van Alsloot. The instruments are, from left to right, a cornetto, two shawms, and a sackbut.

had become the most powerful rulers in Europe and their ostentatious court the envy of all the West. Here fashions, including conical headdress for women and long, pointy-toed shoes for men, attained bizarre proportions (Fig. 4–9). Equally fanciful were the evening entertainments of the court. At one banquet in Lille, in 1454, trumpets heralded, bagpipes blared, and "twenty-eight living persons playing on diverse instruments" sounded forth from within a mock castle.

Medieval Musical Instruments

In the late Middle Ages the principal musical instrument in the monastery and cathedral, indeed the only instrument admitted by church authorities, was the pipe organ. At court, however, a variety of instrumental sounds could be heard. Instruments were divided into two groups according to the amount of volume they produced: first, the loud *(hauts)* instruments, which included the trumpet, **sackbut** (forerunner of the trombone), and **shawm** (ancestor of the oboe), as well as drum; and, second, the soft *(bas)* instruments such as the flute, recorder, fiddle, harp, and lute. Dancing was an inevitable part of courtly recreation, and for this a standard "dance band" of loud instruments was required: two or three shawms, a sackbut, and perhaps a drum (see Figs. 4–9 and 4–10). The sackbut played the dance tune in long notes while the shawms or other instruments wove ornamental lines, much like a contemporary jazz quartet in which a piano and saxophone improvise above the fundamental bass notes provided by the double bass or the guitar. The late fifteenth-century tune entitled *La Spagna* (*The Spanish Tune*) is typical of the dance melodies played at the court of Burgundy during the waning years of the Middle Ages.

hauts and bas *instruments*

LISTENING GUIDE

Anonymous dance tune
The Spanish Tune (ca. 1470)
Two versions

Texture: polyphonic
0:00   Version 1: tune played by sackbut; alto shawm adds counterpoint against it
1:36   Version 2: tune played quickly and in changing rhythms by sackbut; soprano and tenor shawms add counterpoint against it, somewhat obscuring the tune

(Listening Exercise 10 asks you to focus in greater detail on the individual instruments.)

LISTENING EXERCISES

9   Hildegard of Bingen   6CD 1/1; 2CD 1/1
       Gregorian chant, *O Greenest Branch* (ca. 1150)

O Greenest Branch was intended to be sung as part of the Mass by male or female clerics, alternating a soloist with a full choir. First listen to this chant to determine which stanzas are sung by a soloist and which by a choir. Next to each stanza, write "soloist" or "choir," as appropriate.

Stanza 1 _____   Stanza 5 _____
Stanza 2 _____   Stanza 6 _____
Stanza 3 _____   Stanza 7 _____
Stanza 4 _____

Now go on to answer the following, more general, questions:

1. Does an organ accompany the female voices on this recording? _____
2. How would you describe the musical texture of this chant?
   a. monophonic   b. homophonic   c. polyphonic
3. Melismatic singing occurs in this chant
   a. more at the beginning of each stanza than at the end.
   b. more at the end of each stanza than at the beginning.

10   Anonymous dance tune   6CD 1/5
        The Spanish Tune (ca. 1470)

The Spanish Tune was a popular dance melody that first appears during the late Middle Ages and survives in more than forty different arrangements. Sometimes it is set for two instruments, sometimes for three, and occasionally for just a solo instrument like the lute. The two versions heard here make use of the shawm (predecessor of the oboe) and sackbut (ancestor of our modern trombone). Most of the following questions require you to distinguish the distinctly different sounds of these two medieval instruments.

Version 1 (0:00–1:33)

1. Which instrument is playing in a higher range, the shawm or the sackbut? _____

2. Which instrument is playing more rapidly moving pitches, the shawm or the sackbut? _____

3. Are the pitches played by the sackbut always of the same duration? _____

4. At 1:13–1:26 what does the sackbut play?
    a. an ascending scale
    b. a descending scale
    c. an ascending arpeggio

5. In the very last chord of the dance, which statement correctly describes the disposition of the instruments?
    a. The shawm is an octave higher than the sackbut.
    b. The sackbut is an octave higher than the shawm.

Version 2 (1:36–2:29)

6. How many instruments are playing? _____

7. Which instrument is playing the highest part, a shawm or a sackbut? _____

8. Are the pitches played by the sackbut always of the same duration? _____

9. Is there a drum playing in version 2 of this dance? _____

10. What is the meter of this dance, duple or triple? _____

 KEY WORDS

bas instruments	Ordinary of the Mass	shawm
chanson	organum	syllabic singing
Gregorian chant	plainsong	*trivium*
hauts instruments	Proper of the Mass	troubadour
Mass	*quadrivium*	trouvère
melismatic singing	*rondeau*	
Minnesinger	sackbut	

For a checklist of musical styles of the medieval period, see page 61.

5

RENAISSANCE

"Renaissance" means rebirth or reawakening. As a historical designation, the term was first used in the nineteenth century to characterize a great flowering of intellectual and artistic activity that occurred first in Italy and then in France, Germany, England, and the Low Countries during the years 1350–1600. In music the term is more narrowly applied to musical developments in those countries between the years 1475 and 1600. Although the Renaissance did not represent a radical split with an earlier period of darkness and ignorance, as has sometimes been assumed, it was, nonetheless, a time in which new ideas and new attitudes sprang forth and flourished in a hospitable Italian climate. As the Florentine philosopher Marsilio Ficino said in the eventful year 1492:

> If then we are to call any age golden, it is beyond doubt that age which brings forth golden talents in different places. That such is true of this our age he who wishes to consider the illustrious discoveries of this century will hardly doubt. For this century, like a golden age, has restored to light the liberal arts, which were almost extinct: grammar, poetry, rhetoric, painting, sculpture, architecture, and music, the ancient singing of songs to the Orphic lyre.

The thinkers of the Renaissance wished to renovate philosophy, literature, and education generally, not by looking to an uncertain future, but by turning backward to a glorious past. They were convinced that the best models for personal conduct could be found in the accumulated wisdom of the ancient Greeks and Romans. The cradle of the Renaissance was, of course, Italy, because so many classical texts still survived there and because the ruins of the mighty Roman colonnades and arches were everywhere to be seen. But for musicians in Italy and elsewhere, the process of reviving things classical—singing songs to the Orphic lyre—was less obvious and immediate, for almost no music from classical antiquity survived for them to imitate, and what little there was could not be deciphered. Hence, for musicians, rebirth meant not copying earlier musical styles but adopting the attitudes about music that the ancients had possessed. This was done, in part, by writing books about music—on melody, harmony, counterpoint, and rhythm—in which the author adopted the format and vocabulary of the ancient authors.

The ancient Greek writers, especially Homer and Plato, had spoken of the great emotional power of music. Their stories told how music had calmed the agitated spirit, made brave the warrior, and even induced the wanton wife to chastity. The musicians of the Renaissance eagerly embraced this notion that music could sway the emotions, even the behavior, of the listener. To heighten

FIGURES 5–1 AND 5–2
(left) *Virgin and Child with St. Anne* painted by Leonardo da Vinci in 1509–1510. Notice the human expression and near-complete absence of traditional religious symbolism, as well as the highly formalistic composition of the painting—the figures form successively larger triangles. (right) The expressive grief of the Virgin, St. John, and Mary Magdalene mark this portion of an altarpiece painted by Mathias Grünewald in 1510–1515.

the emotional intensity of music, they selected a mode (major, minor, or one of several others then in use) and a musical style that would amply suit the meaning of the text they wished to set. A hymn would be set in one style, a lament in another, a love song in yet a third. The belief in the persuasive power of music and the capacity of music to reinforce the meaning of the text were two primary articles of faith held by musicians of the Renaissance. When transformed into real compositions, these beliefs produced pieces in a great variety of musical styles and a wide range of moods. In this way music mirrored the visual arts of the Renaissance, which now likewise allowed for a great range of emotional expression. Compare, for example, the serene glow of the figures in Leonardo da Vinci's Mary, St. Anne, and the Christ child (Fig. 5–1) with the intense expressiveness of those in Mathias Grünewald's altarpiece for the parish church at Issenheim (Fig. 5–2).

the persuasive power of music

Attending the rebirth of the arts and letters of classical antiquity was a renewed interest in humankind itself. We have come to call this enthusiastic self-interest humanism. Simply said, **humanism** is the belief that people have the capacity to shape their world, to create many things good and beautiful; that they are something more than a mere conduit for gifts descending from heaven. Even the human form, in all its physical fullness, has aesthetic value (Fig. 5–3). This attitude, with its emphasis on self-esteem and human worth, differs markedly from the prevailing view in the Middle Ages, when the individual was seen as a covered, almost faceless object in a great, divine pageant. The culture of the Middle Ages was fostered by the Church; it emphasized the group and contemplation of the almighty within a cloistered setting. The culture of the Renaissance, on the other hand, with its focus on personal achievement, looked outward and indulged its passion for travel, adventure, and discovery.

new emphasis on the individual rather than God

New meaning and value were given to what artists produced in the Renaissance, as well as to the artists themselves. By the end of the fifteenth century, the system of the medieval guilds, which regulated the type of work an artist might

---

Music Becomes a Fine Art

Music enjoyed a new, higher estimation in public consciousness during the Renaissance because it was now less a science, more an art. Recall that during the Middle Ages music had been grouped with three other mathematical disciplines (arithmetic, geometry, and astronomy) to form a core curriculum called the *quadrivium* (see page 72). These subjects, along with the *trivium* of grammar, logic, and rhetoric, constituted the seven liberal arts. But now a new appreciation of the so-called mechanical arts led to a wholesale reshuffling of categories. Leonardo da Vinci himself argued that painting should be added to these seven disciplines, indeed placed at their head. So, too, poetry should join her sisters, though sculpture, because it was wrought by hard manual labor, should not. By the end of the sixteenth century, academies of painting and of music had replaced the medieval craft guilds. The expressive disciplines of poetry, painting, music, and architecture were now separated into a category of "fine arts," a worthy complement to the liberal arts and the sciences.

❈ FIGURE 5–3

Michelangelo's giant statue of David (1501–1504) expresses the heroic nobility of man in a near perfect form. Like da Vinci, Michelangelo made a careful study of human anatomy.

accept, began to break down. Now an artist might take any commission he wished. He became the intimate friend of leading citizens, and his idiosyncrasies were tolerated. No longer was he merely a craftsman who manipulated materials; he was a discoverer, an inventor, a thinker, a visionary. Consequently, the work of art itself came to be viewed as a visible record of the artist's creative mind.

This new attitude about art and about the artist affected the way in which society viewed the composer and the way in which the listener appreciated the composer's work. In the Middle Ages most compositions were preserved anonymously in manuscripts, but, from the fifteenth century on, the name of the creator was usually placed at the head of each piece. One composer even went so far as to insert his own name in a setting of a liturgical text in honor of the Virgin, a novel act of self-aggrandizement. (In a similar way the artists Raphael, Botticelli, and Michelangelo painted their own faces into various religious frescoes they created.) Composers also gained an increased awareness of the monetary value of their art. This can be seen not only in the high salaries they commanded at court but also in the astute way in which they played one patron off against another to gain additional economic benefits. Painters, too, found that money primed the pump of creativity. As one contemporary said of Michelangelo: "He would have created even greater works of art had he been paid more."

The reassessment of the arts during the Renaissance reflected the fact that society's view about music had changed. No longer was music merely the subject of scholastic theorizing; it could be a source of enjoyment and recreation. No longer was it created by humble craftsmen working only for the greater glory of God. Music in the Renaissance was composed by proud artists whose aim was to give listening pleasure. Their music was judged good or bad only to the degree that it pleased fellow human beings. Music, like the other arts, could now be freely evaluated in the secular world for its quality, and the composers ranked according to their greatness. Artistic judgment, appreciation, and criticism enters Western thought for the first time in the humanistic Renaissance.

FIGURE 5–4

The School of Athens (1505) by Raphael reflects the Renaissance attitude toward the arts in three ways: The Roman arches, antique dress, and classical sculptures reintegrate into the art of the Renaissance motifs from ancient Greece and Rome. The subject matter, which places the seven liberal arts in the context of Plato's school, likewise is drawn from classical antiquity. Finally, by depicting key figures in the likeness of himself, of Leonardo, and of Michelangelo (front left center, wearing the boots of a sculptor), Raphael suggests that the fine arts of painting and sculpture are worthy companions of the traditional liberal arts.

JOSQUIN DESPREZ (CA. 1455–1521) AND THE RENAISSANCE MOTET

FIGURE 5–5

The only surviving portrait of Josquin Desprez.

Josquin Desprez was one of the greatest composers of the Renaissance or, indeed, of any age (Fig. 5–5). He was born somewhere near the present border between France and Belgium about 1455, and died in the same region in 1521. Yet, like so many musicians of northern France, he was attracted to Italy for reasons of professional and monetary gain. Between ca. 1484 and 1504 he worked successively as a singer at the chapel of the duke of Milan, in the chapel of a cardinal in Rome, in the Sistine Chapel of the pope, and finally in the chapel of the duke of Ferrara. Several contemporary accounts, as well as his frequent movement from one employer to another, suggest that he possessed a temperamental, egotistical spirit typical of many artists of the Renaissance: He composed only when he, not his patron, wished; he demanded a salary twice that of composers only slightly less gifted; and he would break into a rage when singers tried to tamper with the notes he had written. Yet Josquin's contemporaries and immediate successors recognized his genius. Castiglione (*The Book of the Courtier,* 1528) and Rabelais (*Pantagruel,* 1535) praised him. He was the favorite of Martin Luther, who said, "Josquin is master of the notes, which must express what he desires; other composers can do only what the notes dictate." Florentine humanist Cosimo Bartoli compared him to the great Michelangelo (1475–1564), who decorated the ceiling of the chapel where Josquin had once sung (see Fig. 5–9):

Josquin, the Michelangelo of music

> Josquin may be said to have been a prodigy of nature, as our Michelangelo Buonarroti has been in architecture, painting, and sculpture; for, as there has not thus far been anybody who in his compositions approaches Josquin, so Michelangelo, among all those who have been active in these his arts, is still alone and without a peer; both one and the other have opened the eyes of all those who delight in these arts or are to delight in them in the future.

Josquin wrote more than twenty settings of the Ordinary of the Mass and a large number of French chansons (see pages 75–76). But he especially excelled in the genre of the motet. Composers had written motets in different forms and musical styles since the thirteenth century and continued to do so into the nineteenth. The **motet** in the Renaissance can be defined as a composition for a choir, setting a Latin text on a sacred subject, and intended to be sung in a church or chapel or at home in private devotion. Most motets in the Renaissance, as well as most Masses for the church, were sung **a cappella** (literally, "in the chapel"), meaning that they were performed by voices alone, without any instrumental accompaniment. (Instruments other than the organ were generally not allowed in churches during the Middle Ages and the Renaissance.) This, in part, accounts for the often serene quality of the sound of Renaissance sacred music. Indeed, the Renaissance has been called "the golden age of *a cappella* singing."

a cappella singing

Josquin's motet *Ave Maria* was written about 1485 when the composer was in Milan in the service of the duke of Milan. It was composed in honor of the Virgin Mary, and employs the standard four voice parts: soprano, alto, tenor, and bass. As the motet unfolds, the listener hears the voices enter in succession with the same musical motive. This process is called **imitation,** a procedure whereby one or more voices duplicate in turn the notes of a melody:

imitation

EXAMPLE 5–1

Josquin will also sometimes have one pair of voices imitate another, the tenor and bass, for example, imitating what the alto and soprano have just sung:

EXAMPLE 5–2

In imitative writing the voices all have a chance to present equally the melodic material and thus are all of equal importance. Moreover, because the voices all enter independently, imitative writing invariably produces counterpoint*—independent voices working with and against one another in a harmonious fashion. In Josquin's *Ave Maria*, sections in imitative counterpoint (polyphony*) alternate with passages of chordal writing (homophony*) in order to achieve musical variety. Josquin and his contemporaries favored imitative writing because the quality of balance and proportion that could be achieved by four equal voices was harmonious with the notion of balance and symmetry much prized in the visual arts during the Renaissance.

varying textures

As to the overall structure of Josquin's *Ave Maria*, it is organized in something akin to the way a humanistic orator would construct a persuasive speech or address. It begins with an introductory salutation to the Virgin sung in imitation. Thereafter, a key word, "Ave" ("Hail"), sparks a series of salutes to the Virgin, each making reference to one of her principal feast days during the church year (Conception, Nativity, Annunciation, Purification, and Assumption). At the end of this series of hails comes a final exclamation, "O mother of God, be mindful of me. Amen." These last words are set in a striking succession of imposing chords, with each syllable of text getting its own chord. The chordal, homophonic treatment allows this final sentence to stand out with absolute clarity. In this way is fulfilled the humanistic ideal that text and music work together to persuade and move the listener and, in this case, the Virgin Mary as well: that she may be mindful of the needy soul at the hour of death.

	LISTENING GUIDE	Josquin Desprez Motet, *Ave Maria* (ca. 1485)		6CD 1/6; 2CD 1/2

0:00	All four voices present each two-word phrase in turn	Ave Maria, gratia plena, Dominus tecum, virgo serena.	Hail Mary, full of grace. The Lord be with you, serene Virgin.
0:46	Soprano and alto are imitated by tenor and bass; then all four voices work to a peak on "laetitia" ("joy")	Ave cujus conceptio, Solemni plena gaudio, Coelestia, terrestria, Nova replet laetitia.	Hail to you whose conception, With solemn rejoicing, Fills heaven and earth With new joy.

(Continued on next page)

Male Choirs

Notice on our recording of Palestrina's *Sanctus* that the soprano part is performed by men singing in head voice, or what is called **falsetto voice**. This is a historically authentic manner of performance. Following an early decree of the Apostle Paul, women in the Middle Ages and Renaissance were not allowed to sing in the Roman Church, except in convents. Similarly, women were not allowed to appear in public in theatrical productions, tragic or comic, in territories under strict church control. Thus, most polyphonic church choirs in the Renaissance were exclusively male, the soprano part being performed by either choirboys or by adult men singing in *falsetto*. Beginning in 1565, however, **castratos** (castrated males) were introduced into the papal chapel, mainly as a money-saving measure. A single castrato could produce as much volume as two falsettists or three or four boys. Castrati were renowned for their power and their great lung capacity, which allowed them to execute unusually long phrases in a single breath. Surprisingly, castrati sopranos remained a hallmark of the papal chapel until 1903, when they were officially banned by Pope Pius X.

All-male choir with choirboys for the soprano part as depicted in a sixteenth-century Italian fresco.

🌸 FIGURE 5–8

A portrait of Giovanni Palestrina. Palestrina was the first important composer of the Church to have been a layman rather than a member of the clergy.

"Sabaoth," still another says "Gloria tua," with howling, bellowing, and stammering, so that they more nearly resemble cats in January than flowers in May.

Initially, the assembled prelates considered banning music altogether from the service or limiting it to just the old, monophonic Gregorian chant. But the timely appearance of a few sacred compositions by Giovanni Pierluigi da Palestrina (1525–1594), among them his *Mass for Pope Marcellus* (1562), demonstrated to the council representatives that sacred polyphony for four, five, or six voices could still be written in a clear, dignified manner. For his role in maintaining a place for composed polyphony within the established Church, Palestrina came to be called "the savior of church music."

Palestrina was born in the small town of that name outside Rome, and spent almost his entire professional life as a singer and composer at various churches in and around the Vatican: St. Peter's Basilica, St. John Lateran, St. Mary Major, and the **Sistine Chapel** (Fig. 5–9), the pope's private chapel within his Vatican apartments. Although Paul IV, one of the more zealous of the reforming popes, dismissed him from the Sistine Chapel in 1555 because he was a married layman not conforming to the rule of celibacy, Palestrina returned to papal employment at St. Peter's in 1571, holding the titles *maestro di cappella* (master of the chapel) and ultimately *maestro compositore* (master composer).

The *Sanctus* of Palestrina's *Missa Aeterna Christi munera* (*Mass: Eternal Gifts of Christ*) epitomizes the musical spirit of the Counter-Reformation that then radiated from Rome. (Remember, a *Sanctus* is the fourth of five parts of the Ordinary of the Mass* that composers traditionally set to music; see page 71.) Palestrina's *Sanctus* unfolds slowly and deliberately with long notes gradually

❀ FIGURE 5–9
Interior of the Sistine Chapel. The high altar and Michelangelo's *Last Judgment* are at the far end, the balcony for the singers at the lower right. The congregants could stand and listen from the near side of the screen.

Female Choirs in Convents

Although public church choirs in the Middle Ages and Renaissance were all-male ensembles, there was still much opportunity for women to make music. They did so as singers and performers in secular genres, such as the chanson* and madrigal*, at court and in the home. In convents, too, women formed female performing forces, yet always under the watchful eye of an outside father superior. Behind cloistered walls, the sisters sang not only Gregorian chant but also the latest polyphonic Masses and motets of Palestrina and Orlando di Lasso (ca. 1530–1594). They, too, had old manuscripts of plainsong*, and this monophonic chant they transposed into their own, higher vocal range. When it came to singing polyphony, the normally male parts of tenor and bass were played on an organ while the sisters sang alto and soprano. Thus organs and organists were of primary importance in convents. Yet, because the best organ teachers were male, the walls of the convent were a barrier to good instruction. When a nun tried to circumvent the rules of strict segregation by gender, painful consequences might result, as Sister Angela Serafina, nun and principal musician at the monastery of San Appolinare in Milan, learned in 1571:

> Suor Angela Serafina is to be without her veil [i.e. with a bare shaven head] for three months. She is relieved of the organist's duties, nor may she return to this position for six years. The large harpsichord is not to be kept in her room, but somewhere else in the house; nor can she play it or any other keyboard, nor sing polyphony for three years. And every Wednesday for six months she is to eat on the floor of the refectory, and ask forgiveness for the disturbance she caused, for the scandal of having fed the [male] organist inside the convent. (from Robert L. Kendrick, *Celestial Sirens*)

So extreme a punishment for such a seemingly minor offence! Yet here we see the tension inherent in the very thought that women might make music in the church during the austere Counter-Reformation.

Nuns in the choir stalls of their convent singing a religious service, from a fifteenth-century English manuscript.

giving way to shorter, faster-moving ones, but without catchy rhythms or a strong beat. As is true for Gregorian chant*, the melodic lines move mainly in stepwise fashion, avoiding large leaps and chromatic turns. The sober mood is created in part by the careful use of imitative counterpoint. Each phrase of text is assigned its own motive*, which appears, in turn, in each voice. A motive used in this fashion is called a **point of imitation.** Palestrina's *Sanctus* has four points of imitation (see examples in the following Listening Guide). The first enters in the order soprano, alto, tenor, bass, and the music works to a cadence*. While the soprano and bass conclude the cadence, the alto and tenor begin the second point of imitation. Soon this section cadences in the soprano and alto as the bass and tenor enter with the third point. Palestrina was a master at sewing a cadence to the beginning of a new point of imitation. The listener experiences not only a sense of satisfaction on arrival at the cadence, but also a feeling of ongoing progress as the new point pushes forward. As you listen to the *Sanctus,* follow the diagram in the Listening Guide and see if you can hear when the voices are cadencing and when a new point of imitation begins.

LISTENING GUIDE

Giovanni Pierluigi da Palestrina
Sanctus of the Mass: *Eternal Gifts of Christ* (1590)

6CD 1/8

Texture: Polyphonic

Point 1 — San - ctus, San - - - ctus — Holy, holy, holy

Point 2 — Do - mi - nus De - us Sa - ba - oth — Lord, God almighty

Point 3 — Ple - ni sunt coe - li et ter - ra glo - ri - a — The heavens and earth are filled with your glory

Point 4 — Ho - san - na in ex - cel - - sis. — Hosanna in the highest

Palestrina's serene music best captures the restrained, sober spirit of the Counter-Reformation, embodying all that Roman authority thought proper church music should be. After his death in 1594, the legend of Palestrina, "savior of church music," continued to grow. Later composers, such as Bach (*Mass in B minor*, 1733) and Mozart (*Requiem Mass*, 1791) incorporated elements of Palestrina's style into their sacred compositions. Even in our universities today, courses in counterpoint for advanced music students usually include some practice in composing in the pure, contrapuntally correct style of Palestrina. Thus the spirit of the Counter-Reformation, distilled into a set of contrapuntal rules, continued to influence musicians long after the Renaissance had come to an end.

LISTENING EXERCISES

Josquin Desprez	6CD 1/6;
Motet	2CD1/2
Ave Maria (ca. 1485)	

Ave Maria by Josquin Desprez is a fine example of a motet using imitative counterpoint, a texture that dominated the musical style of sacred motets and Masses during the Renaissance. As you work through this exercise, you will become more familiar with how the voices unfold in this imitative, polyphonic texture.

1. (0:00) What is the order in which the voices enter?
    a. bass, tenor, alto, soprano
    b. soprano, bass, tenor, alto
    c. soprano, alto, tenor, bass
2. (1:05–1:14) What is the general direction of the music during the phrase "Coelestia, terrestria" ("heaven and earth")?
    a. rises from "heaven" to "earth"
    b. falls from "heaven" to "earth"
3. (1:18) Which voice sings the final "laetitia"?
    a. soprano   b. male alto   c. bass
4. (2:26) The meter has changed here. Which is correct?
    a. It has changed from duple to triple.
    b. It has changed from triple to duple.
5. (2:57) Which voice ends this section (on the word "purgatio")?
    a. bass   b. male alto   c. soprano
6. (3:58) Is this final, chordal section written in homophony or polyphony (counterpoint)? _____
7. (4:23) On the last word ("Amen"), do the voices change pitches on the two syllables ("A" and "men"), or do they repeat their pitches?

_____

8. Which is true throughout this motet?
    a. In the imitative sections the soprano and alto always enter before the tenor and bass.
    b. In the imitative sections the tenor and bass always enter before the soprano and alto.
9. Are there any instruments accompanying the voices in this performance?

_____

10. What do we call the style of performance referred to in Question 9?

_____

Thomas Weelkes   6CD 1/7;
Madrigal   2CD 1/3
As Vesta Was from Latmos Hill Descending (1601)

So striking is the depiction of the text through music in the madrigal of the Renaissance that these instances of musical word painting are called "madrigalisms." To be sure that you are hearing this close correlation between text and music, this exercise begins by asking you to indicate the moment at which five very clear instances of word painting start.

	Text	Time	Word painting in music
Example	"descending"	0:06	musical line descends
1.	"ascending"	_____	musical line ascends
2.	"running"	_____	rapid entries, fast notes
3.	"two by two"	_____	only two voices are heard
4.	"three by three"	_____	three voices heard
5.	"all alone"	_____	solo voice

6. What is the texture of the music at the words "all alone"?
   a. imitative polyphony   b. homophony   c. monophony

7. What is the texture of the music at the words "Then sang the shepherds" (2:03–2:10)?
   a. imitative polyphony   b. homophony   c. monophony

8. What is the texture of the music at the words "Long live fair Oriana" (2:15–3:09)?
   a. imitative polyphony   b. homophony   c. monophony

9. When the bass finally enters with a presentation of "Long live fair Oriana" (2:20–2:45) are his notes moving faster or slower than the previous entries?

   _____

10. Which statement correctly describes the forces used in the performance of this madrigal?
    a. There is only one voice on each part.
    b. There are two voices singing each part.
    c. There is one voice and one instrument on each part.

 ## KEY WORDS

a cappella	humanism	point of imitation
castrato	imitation	Sistine Chapel
Council of Trent	madrigal	word painting
Counter-Reformation	madrigalism	
falsetto voice	motet	

For a checklist of musical style in the Renaissance, see page 61.

EARLY BAROQUE MUSIC

6

It is a fact of historical evolution that the fruits of any cultural period have grown from seeds sown in the preceding epoch. So it is with the Baroque era that certain qualities in the music of the late Renaissance were cultivated to the exclusion of all others. These aspects of musical style developed to the point that the art they embodied was fundamentally different from that of the preceding epoch, and soon this new art was given a new name.

"Baroque" is the term used to describe the art, architecture, dance, and music of the period 1600–1750. It is taken from the Portuguese word *barroco*, meaning a pearl of irregular shape then used in jewelry and fine decoration. During the eighteenth century the term "Baroque" was applied by various observers to indicate a rough, bold instrumental sound in music and excessive ornamentation in the visual arts. To the philosopher Jean-Jacques Rousseau (1712–1778), "A baroque music is that in which the harmony is confused, charged with modulations and dissonances, the melody is harsh and little natural, the intonation difficult, and the movement constrained." Thus, originally, "Baroque" had a pejorative meaning. It signified distortion, excess, and extravagance. Only during the twentieth century, with a new-found appreciation of the painting of Peter Paul Rubens (1577–1640), the sculpture of Gian Lorenzo Bernini (1598–1680), and the music of Antonio Vivaldi (1678–1741), among others, has the term "Baroque" come to assume a positive meaning in Western cultural history.

Baroque art and architecture have several distinctive characteristics. These qualities are observable in the music of the period as well. What strikes us most when we encounter a monument of Baroque planning, such as the basilica of St. Peter in Rome or the palace of Versailles outside of Paris, is that everything is constructed on a massive scale. The plazas, gardens, fountains, colonnades, and buildings are all of the grandest design. Similarly, human forms, as presented in the painting and sculpture of the time, are larger than life. Look at the ninety-foot-high baldachin inside St. Peter's and imagine how it dwarfs the priest at the altar below (Fig. 6–1). The nearby statue of St. Helena with Cross is almost twenty feet tall. Outside the basilica a circle of colonnades forms a courtyard large enough to encompass several football fields (Fig. 6–2). Or consider the French king's palace of Versailles, constructed during the reign of Louis XIV (1643–1715), so monumental in scope that it formed a small independent city, home to several thousand court functionaries (Fig. 6–3).

The music composed for performance in such vast expanses was also grandiose. Instrumental groups approaching the size of the modern orchestra came

🌺 FIGURE 6–1 AND 6–2

(left) Bernini's baldachin in St. Peter's, Rome. Standing more than ninety feet high, this canopy above the high altar is marked by twisted columns and curving shapes, color, and movement, all typical of Baroque art. (right) St. Peter's Square, designed by Bernini in the mid-seventeenth century. The size is so colossal it seems to swallow cars, buses, and people.

🌺 FIGURE 6–3

The chapel of the palace of Versailles (1699–1710) exalts the power of the French monarch as much as it does the Lord. Note the organ at the far end.

into being, and choral works for twenty-four, forty-eight, and even fifty-three separate vocal parts were written. Mostly intended for spacious churches, these compositions for multiple choruses with instrumental accompaniment have come to epitomize the grand or colossal Baroque.

Once the exteriors of these large Baroque palaces and churches were built, the artists of the time went to the opposite extreme, filling the long lines with an overabundance of small, decorative details. It is as if monumental space had created a vacuum into which the artist rushed with a certain nervous energy. The large painting entitled *Rape of the Sabine Women* by Nicolas Poussin (1594–1665), for example, has the spatial proportions of colossal Baroque art, anchored by the towering figure of Romulus on the left and massive Roman columns in the center; yet it has energy, power, and movement, mainly because of the great number of participants in the drama, the positioning of the figures, and the detail with which they are drawn (Fig. 6–4). The painting is at once spacious and cluttered. When filling the interior of a church the sculptor or carver employed decorative scrolls, floral capitals, and multiple layers of adornment to complete and add warmth to a large expanse (Fig. 6–5).

Similarly, when expressed in the music of the Baroque era, this love of busy detail within large-scale compositions took the form of vigorous, pulsating rhythms with strong, regular beats and many smaller subdivisions. It also was expressed by the use of musical ornaments, whether for instruments such as the violin or harpsichord (see page 99) or for voice. Notice, in Fig. 6–6, the abundance of ornaments and figural patterns in just a few bars of music for violin by Arcangelo Corelli (1653–1713). Such ornaments were equally popular with the singers of the early Baroque era, when the cult of the vocal virtuoso first began to emerge.

We observed in the music of the Renaissance (1475–1600) a growing awareness of the capacity of this art to sway, or affect, the emotions. This belief in the powers of music to move the listener intensified in the Baroque period. Musical moods now came to be called the "affections," and it was the task of the composer to fashion a musical language that could vividly express many and

🌸 **FIGURE 6–4 AND 6–5**
(left) Nicolas Poussin, *Rape of the Sabine Women* (1647). Note the larger-than-life figures and the extreme, almost melodramatic gestures. The painter said of this work that "it is violent and furious, very severe and calculated to produce amazement." (right) Church of the monastery of St. Florian, Austria (1686–1708). The powerful pillars and arches provide a strong structural framework, while the painted ceiling and heavily foliated capitals provide decoration and warmth.

varied emotions. Composers of early Baroque opera, in particular, aimed to convey impassioned speech through music.

Painters and sculptors, too, sought to increase emotional expression, which they did by means of exaggeration and distortion. The new emotionalism in Baroque art can easily be seen by comparing the *David* of Gian Lorenzo Bernini (1598–1680), with its fierce visage and twisted body (Fig. 6–7), with Michelangelo's serenely balanced treatment of the same subject done about a hundred years earlier (see page 82). Moreover, the spirit of the Baroque age required of both artist and composer that the emotional "units" they created be large, or long-lasting, and clearly defined. Baroque music does not change hurriedly from one mood to another, as was the practice, for example, in the Renaissance madrigal, where the musical feeling changed to reflect the meaning of each new phrase or word (see page 87). Instead, in the newer Baroque style each piece or each large section of a piece carried a single mood or affection throughout—

🌸 **FIGURE 6–6**
Corelli's sonata for violin and *basso continuo*, Opus 5, No. 1. The continuo provides the structural support, while the violin adds elaborate decoration above.

✻ FIGURE 6–7
Gian Lorenzo Bernini's *David* (1623) displays a vitality and restless energy of the sort that can be heard in the music of the Baroque era. Compare Michelangelo's serenely balanced treatment of the same subject (Fig. 5.3).

joy, jealousy, resignation, agony, triumph, and others. What is perhaps unique about Baroque music and Baroque art in general is not only its intense expression but also the clear-cut way in which one emotion, color, or spatial unit is kept separate and distinct from the next.

✻ CHARACTERISTICS OF BAROQUE MUSIC

The hundred and fifty years encompassed by the Baroque era (1600–1750) witnessed significant changes in musical style, from the straightforward homophony of Giovanni Gabrieli (ca. 1557–1612) to the complex polyphony of Johann Sebastian Bach (1685–1750). It also saw the introduction of many new musical forms and genres, which we discuss later in this chapter and the next: the sonata, suite, concerto, cantata, opera, oratorio, and fugue. Yet despite such stylistic evolution and formal innovation, there was one musical element that remained constant throughout the Baroque—the *basso continuo*, or "thorough bass," as it was called in seventeenth-century England.

The Basso Continuo

The **basso continuo** was a small ensemble of at least two instrumentalists who provided a foundation for the melody or melodies above. One performer played an instrument that could produce chords, usually the organ or harpsichord, but sometimes even a large lute. The other played a low-sounding instrument, like the cello, the cellolike *viola da gamba* (Fig. 6–8) or the bassoon, which played the bass line. By having the harpsichord, for example, generate the basic chords of the piece, a composition acquired a solid harmonic foundation. At the same time, the bass instrument always doubled the lowest note played by the left hand of the harpsichordist, thereby giving the bass line new and greater power.

The additional weight that the *basso continuo* lent to the bass reflected the fact that the music of the early Baroque period had assumed a new structure. In

✻ FIGURE 6–8
Basso continuo and violin. This continuo consists of a harpsichord and a large string instrument, the **viola da gamba,** or **bass viol.** The viol had six strings and produced a slightly darker, less brilliant sound than members of the violin family. The gambist playing here is Eva Linfield.

The Harpsichord

The **harpsichord** has been called the workhorse of the Baroque era because it served both as the main instrument for accompaniment and as a solo instrument in its own right (see Figs. 3–14 and 6–8). In this sense the harpsichord functioned much like the piano would later in the Classical and Romantic periods, as an accompanying and a solo instrument. The sound of the harpsichord is produced by depressing a key that pushes up a quill or (nowadays) a plastic "pick" to pluck a taut wire string. This abrupt plucking of wire is what creates the tinkling sound of the instrument. Unlike the piano, in which a complicated mechanism permits different levels of finger pressure to achieve a wide range of dynamics, the harpsichord cannot produce a louder or softer sound, because the plucking mechanism transmits a constant level of force to the string. There are, therefore, no subtle gradations of sound on the harpsichord. When greater volume is needed, an additional full set of strings is brought into play to double the sound, and all the music thereafter will be loud until this set of strings is disengaged. Thus, the harpsichord typifies the way in which sound was produced in the Baroque period. There are no gradual swells and decreases, but only abrupt changes in the amount or volume of sound. The harpsichord was invented in the late Middle Ages, reached the peak of its popularity in the Baroque era, and went out of fashion in the time of Mozart (1756–1791), replaced by the more flexible, responsive, and potentially powerful piano.

the Mass and motet of the Renaissance, the voices spin out a web of imitative counterpoint, and the character and importance of each of the lines is equal:

In early Baroque music, however, the voices are no longer equal. Rather, there is a polarity of force directed toward the top and bottom:

The soprano carries the melody; the bass provides a strong harmonic support. In between, the middle voices often do little more than fill out the texture. If Renaissance music is conceived polyphonically and horizontally, line by line, that of the early Baroque period is organized homophonically and vertically, chord by chord. The *basso continuo* helps establish a strong bass and ensures that the fundamentally chordal structure of the music holds tight.

The sound of the *basso continuo* (or simply continuo in English) pervaded almost all Baroque music. When a solo violinist or flutist played a sonata, or when a singer performed a recitative or aria (see page 106), the continuo was there; thus, three performers were involved, a principal and an accompanying cast of two (Fig. 6–8). As we shall see, the continuo also held together soloists and orchestra in the Baroque concerto, just as it unified multiple choirs in polychoral motets for the church. For church music it was the organ—the traditional instrument of the church—that played the keyboard continuo, while in virtually all other music that chord-supplying function was provided by the harpsichord. Indeed, it is the continual tinkling of the harpsichord, in step with the bass sounds of a cello, *viola da gamba*, or bassoon, that signals to the listener that the music being played comes from the Baroque era.

universal use of the basso continuo

The Rise of Instrumental Music

Composers of the early Baroque period were the first to think of instrumental music as different from vocal music. Earlier, during the Renaissance, a musical line could either be sung by the voice or played on an instrument, according to the wishes of the performer. Baroque composers not only started to differentiate between a vocal style of writing and an instrumental one, but they also began to assign specific musical lines to specific instruments, according to their natural strengths and weaknesses. The brasses, for example, were often given short figures with dotted rhythms, which maximized their capacity for sharp attacks. They would not, however, be asked to run up and down a full-octave scale, because of the difficulties in pitch they would encounter. Fast scales were most often given over to the more agile violins. Thus here, in the early Baroque era, the practice of writing music idiomatic (well-suited) for the instruments first appears.

idiomatic writing for instruments

Treatment of Musical Elements

Baroque music, as we have seen, is marked by spaciousness and grandeur, by the desire to create a powerful, unified mood within each work or large section of a work, and by its chordal framework and strong bass line, both generated by the *basso continuo*. These are qualities to be heard in all Baroque music. But there are others as well that appear as distinctive treatments of familiar musical elements. (In the next chapter we see how the stylistic traits of early Baroque music were modified and extended by Bach and Handel in the late Baroque period.)

MELODY. In the Renaissance, melody was more or less all of one type. It was a direct, uncomplicated line that could be assigned indiscriminately to either a voice or an instrument. Now, in early Baroque music, beginning about 1600, two different melodic styles begin to develop: a dramatic, virtuosic style in singing and, by contrast, a more mechanical, repetitious style in instrumental music. Despite the increasing virtuosity of vocal music, attention is no longer focused exclusively on the voice. Throughout the Baroque era there is a new emphasis on writing melodies specifically for instruments such as the harpsichord and violin. These new melodies are idiomatic in that they are well suited to the technical demands of these instruments.

melodic sequence

Early in the Baroque period a new melodic technique called sequence was applied to melody. A **melodic sequence** is the repetition of a musical motive at successively higher or lower degrees of the scale. Example 6–1 shows a sequence, indeed an exceptionally long sequence, from the music of the early Baroque composer Claudio Monteverdi (1567–1643). Notice how the initial motive is repeated seven times, each time one step lower than before.

EXAMPLE 6–1

The melodic sequence first appears extensively in the music of the Baroque era and continues to be a standard melodic device into the twentieth century.

HARMONY. Baroque harmonies are chordally conceived and tightly bound to the *basso continuo*. As the seventeenth century progresses, harmonies unfold more and more in familiar patterns as standard harmonic progressions—chord progressions*—begin to emerge. The shortest and most frequent of these is the V–I (dominant–tonic) cadence (see page 31). The advent of standard harmonic progressions like the V–I cadence gives added direction and cohesion to the music.

 chord progressions

Attending this development is the growing importance—and eventual total domination—of the major and minor system of keys. These two scale patterns, major and minor, replaced the dozen or so scales (or "modes," as they were called) used during the Renaissance and before. Moreover, as music was reduced to just two qualities of sound, the listener could more easily focus on the distinct properties of each. Composers could play minor off against major, or vice versa, to create the emotional effects so important in Baroque music.

major and minor keys

RHYTHM. Rhythm in Baroque music is characterized by uniformity. Just as a single mood, or affect, is carried from the beginning to the end of a piece, so the rhythmic patterns heard at the beginning will surface again and again, right to the end. This tendency toward rhythmic uniformity and rhythmic drive becomes more and more pronounced as the Baroque era proceeds.

DYNAMICS. Baroque music, like Baroque art, is organized in units of distinctly different, yet independent, moods and colors. Dynamics do not change gradually from one section or piece to the next. Rather, a single dynamic range, whether loud or soft, will hold fast until abruptly replaced by another. This phenomenon of shifting the volume of sound suddenly and dramatically from one level to another is called **terraced dynamics.** Changing dynamics in this fashion, especially when combined with equally abrupt changes in orchestration and shifts to major or minor tonality, helps create the clearly sectionalized sound of Baroque music. The first composer in the history of music to place dynamic marks, such as *piano* and *forte,* in the score was Giovanni Gabrieli (ca. 1557–1611), who spent his entire career in Venice.

terraced dynamics

THE VENETIAN POLYCHORAL MOTET

Venice, the Queen of the Seas, was—and remains—a city of canals, arching bridges, and colorful palaces. Reaching its zenith of commercial and economic importance in the fifteenth century, it owed its success partly to its truly republican form of government and partly to its strategic location at the head of the Adriatic Sea, which made it a natural center of trade (Fig. 6–9). By 1581 its population had reached ninety thousand. The focus of civic and spiritual life in Venice was the palace of the doge (or mayor) and the adjoining basilica of St. Mark, with its spacious piazza in front (Fig. 6–10). St. Mark's, which preserves the remains of the Apostle Mark beneath the high altar, has an architectural plan unique among the major churches of the West. It is built in the form of an equal-sided Greek cross, probably because for centuries Venice was under the political and artistic domination of the Byzantine Empire.

Beginning in the mid-sixteenth century, musicians exploited the unusual architectural plan of St. Mark's by composing motets for it for two or more choirs. At first these separate ensembles were placed in the two singers' galleries on opposite sides of the main aisle (Fig. 6–11). Later they were also stationed in the

❋ FIGURE 6–9

A map of present-day Italy showing Mantua, Venice, Florence, and Rome, each an important city for the cultivation of music during the early Baroque period.

🌸 **FIGURE 6–10**
Piazza San Marco painted by Gentile
Bellini (ca. 1429–1507). St. Mark's
was the focal point of all religious and
civic activities in Venice.

🌸 **FIGURE 6–11**
Interior of the basilica of St. Mark,
with a view of the upper galleries,
where musicians sometimes performed
polychoral motets.

other elevated galleries that adjoined the central dome. By situating groups of
musicians in these separate, elevated lofts—or loggias, as they are called—composers were able to create new sonic effects that astonished the listeners seated
or standing below. To a visitor to St. Mark's in the early seventeenth century, the
novelty of the musical environment must have been as striking as the twentieth-
century change from monophonic to multiphonic surround sound.

Giovanni Gabrieli (ca. 1557–1612)

The composer who made the most of the opportunities afforded by the architecture of St. Mark's was Giovanni Gabrieli, a native of Venice. Gabrieli wrote
little secular music and few Masses for the church. Most of his creative energy
was devoted to the composition of ceremonial motets for the semireli-
gious occasions of state that took place beneath the domes of St.
Mark's. One such piece is his polychoral motet *In ecclesiis* (*In the
Churches*), written for three choirs. Gabrieli's first musical group consists of a quartet of vocal soloists; the second is a vocal chorus; and the
third is an ensemble of six instruments: a violin, two trombones, and
three cornettos (see page 77, Fig. 4–10). Accompanying all three
groups is the *basso continuo*, here supplied by an organ.

Not only was Gabrieli the first composer to indicate in the score a
dynamic level at which the music was to be played (either *piano* or
forte), but he was also the first to prescribe specific instruments—here
violin, trombone, and cornetto. The instruments (choir 3) have their
own timbre, one distinct from the voices. They also tend to play short
bursts of music with strong attacks. The solo voices (choir 1), on the
other hand, often sing long notes or lengthy, difficult melismas*. Notice that the role of the chorus (choir 2) is simple: It regularly inserts a
chordal refrain on the word "Alleluja." Thus from beginning to end,
blocks of sound are suddenly added or subtracted to create high drama

and opulent variety. If Palestrina's music of the late Renaissance is uniformly serene from start to finish (see page 92), Gabrieli's Baroque music is full of ever-varying textures, colors, and dynamic levels. The three choirs can be contrasted with one another for dramatic effect, or they can be combined, as occurs at the end of *In ecclesiis,* to produce the impressive volume of the colossal Baroque.

LISTENING GUIDE

Giovanni Gabrieli
Motet, *In the Churches* (1612)

CD 1/9

0:00	Soprano soloist of Choir 1 plus organ *basso continuo*	In ecclesiis, benedicite Domino	In the churches, bless the Lord
0:16	Choir 2 and soprano echo, rising rapid notes on third and final time	Alleluja	
0:31	Bass soloist of Choir 1 plus continuo; peaks on "anima mea" ("my soul")	In omni loco dominationis, benedic anima mea Dominum	In every holy place, may my soul bless the Lord
1:09	Choir 2 and bass echo	Alleluja	
1:21	An instrumental interlude; begins solemnly but changes to lively dotted rhythms, ends with descending melodic sequence	Choir 3	
1:53	Tenor and alto of Choir 1 sing duet accompanied by the instrumental ensemble and continuo	In Deo salutari meo, et gloria mea	In God is my salvation and my glory
2:35	Duet continues; notes become more rapid and rise in a melodic sequence	Deus, auxilium meum et spes mea in Deo est	Lord, my help and my hope is in God
3:20	Choir 2 with alto and tenor echos	Alleluja	
3:35	Soprano and bass duet with imitation and echos	Deus noster, te invocamus, te laudamus, te adoramus	Our Lord, we call to you, we praise you, we adore you
4:17	Duet continues; change to lively triple meter on "vivifica nos" ("revivify us")	Libera nos, salva nos, vivifica nos	Deliver us, save us, revivify us
4:46	Choir 2 with soprano and bass echo	Alleluja	
5:03	Rich-sounding chords for all three choirs on "Deus," followed by long notes in the bass	Deus, adjutor noster in aeternum (repeated)	Lord, our judge forever
6:25	Choirs 2 and 3 with echoes by Choir 1 (soloists); third statement of "Alleluja" repeated; strong final cadence added	Alleluja	

(Listening Exercise 13)

✿ EARLY BAROQUE OPERA

Given the popularity of opera today—and the fact that there had been opera in China and Japan since the thirteenth century—it is surprising that this genre of music emerged comparatively late in the history of Western European culture. Not until around 1600 did opera appear, and its native soil was Italy.

Opera literally means "work": The word was first employed in the Italian phrase *opera drammatica in musica* (a dramatic work set to music). In opera, then, the lines of the actors and actresses are not merely spoken, but sung. In this way music is used to heighten the emotional intensity of the action that unfolds on the stage. Rejecting the notion that the emotions of an individual could be best

new emphasis on solo singing

expressed by a group of singers, opera stressed solo singing at the expense of the polyphonic choir. Choral singing might be a useful way to convey abstract religious thought in a Mass or motet, but to communicate raw human emotion, solo singing allowed the individual more freedom to express his or her feelings in a direct, personal way. Tying together a succession of solo songs and recitations so as to create a large-scale musical drama satisfied the Baroque desire for grandiose form as well as the Baroque need for intense, even exaggerated, personal expression.

humanists urged new attention to the word

The northern Italian city-states of Florence, Mantua, and Venice (see Fig. 6–9) possessed the most progressive musical thinkers in the early Baroque era. Their effort to create a new dramatic style was simply a continuation of the work of the humanists of the late Renaissance. The collective aim was to recapture the expressive power of ancient Greek music, as reported by Plato and others. Florence, in particular, was home to several musically gifted intellectuals, including Vincenzo Galilei (1533–1591), the father of the famous astronomer Galileo Galilei (1564–1642). These music lovers formed an aristocratic society called the Florentine *camerata* (academy) to promote their new ideals. They recognized that the power of classical drama owed much to the fact that the actors not merely spoke, but sang, their roles. The musically accompanied drama of the Greeks could be recreated, they theorized, if composers would create simple recitations sung only to the plainest of accompaniments. From these developments emerged the first full-fledged opera, Claudio Monteverdi's *Orfeo*.

✿ FIGURE 6–12 AND 6–13 (left) Portrait of Claudio Monteverdi by Bernardo Strozzi (1581–1628). (right) Adriana Basile (ca. 1580–ca. 1640), one of the first "stars" of the operatic stage. Monteverdi may have had her contralto (low alto) voice in mind when he composed the part of Orfeo, but at the first performance in 1607 the role was sung by a tenor.

Claudio Monteverdi (1567–1643)

Claudio Monteverdi was a musical genius who could manifest his enormous talents equally well in a madrigal, a motet, or an opera. He was born in the northern Italian town of Cremona in 1567 and moved to the larger city of Mantua (see Fig. 6–9) about 1590 to serve Duke Vincenzo Gonzaga as a singer and as a player of string instruments. In 1601 he was appointed director of music, and in this capacity composed two operas for the court, *Orfeo* (1607) and *Arianna* (1608). But the duke failed to pay Monteverdi what he had promised. "I have

never in my life suffered greater humiliation of the spirit than when I had to go and beg the treasurer for what was mine," said the composer some years later. Thus disenchanted with Mantua, Monteverdi accepted the much-coveted position of *maestro di cappella* at St. Mark's in Venice, which fell vacant on the death of Giovanni Gabrieli in 1612. Although called to Venice ostensibly to write church music, Monteverdi nevertheless continued to compose opera as well. Among his important later works in this genre are *The Return of Ulysses* (1640) and *The Coronation of Poppea* (1642). He died in Venice in 1643 after thirty years of faithful service.

✿ FIGURE 6–14
(left) The beginning of the third act of Monteverdi's *Orfeo* (1607), from the original print of the opera. The vocal part of Orfeo is on the staff above, the bass line of the *basso continuo* is below. (below) Orfeo charms the guardians of Hades with his lyre. A detail from a painting by Nicolas Poussin (1594–1665).

Monteverdi's first operatic masterpiece—indeed the first important opera in the history of Western music—is his *Orfeo*. Every composer of opera must begin by setting to music a dramatic text, called the **libretto.** Because the aim of early opera was to reproduce the style of ancient Greek drama, it was only natural that Monteverdi's libretto was drawn from a tale found in classical Greek mythology. Our hero is Orfeo (Orpheus), the son of Apollo, the Greek god of the sun and of music. (Indeed, the very word "music" comes from the muses that attend Apollo.) Orfeo, himself a demi-god, finds love in the form of the beautiful earthling Euridice. No sooner are they married but she is fatally bitten by a serpent and carried off to Hades (the realm of the dead). Orfeo mourns her death and vows to descend into the Underworld to rescue her and restore his love to earthly life. This he nearly accomplishes by exploiting his divine musical powers, for Orfeo can make trees sway, calm savage beasts, and even overcome the demonic forces of Hades with the beauty of his song. The theme of *Orfeo*, then, is the divine power of music.

Monteverdi's Orfeo

To convey a feeling of heightened passions, Monteverdi and other composers of early opera developed a new, more expressive and flexible style of solo singing for the stage called **stile rappresentativo** ("the representational style"). Sometimes requiring rapid declamation on a single pitch, and at other times wide-ranging vocal flourishes, *stile rappresentativo* permitted the singer to move almost imperceptibly from one mood to another. Monteverdi himself said: "I am aware that contrasts are what stir our souls, and that such stirring is the aim of all good music." In the hands of Monteverdi and later composers, *stile rappresentativo* would soon be transformed into two different and contrasting types of vocal writing, recitative and aria.

stile rappresentativo

Recitative, from the Italian word *recitativo* ("something recited"), is musically heightened speech. In opera recitative is usually used to tell the audience what has happened. Because recitative attempts to mirror the natural stresses of oral delivery, it is often made up of rapidly repeating notes followed by one or two long notes at the ends of phrases, as in the following recitative from Act II of *Orfeo*.

recitative

EXAMPLE 6–2

Al'a-ma - ra no-vel-la Ras-sem-bra l'in-fe-li - ceun mu-to sas-so
(At the bitter news the unhappy one resembled a mute stone)

Recitative in Baroque opera is accompanied only by the *basso continuo* playing simple chords. Such a sparsely accompanied recitative is called **secco recitative,** from the Italian for "dry." (By the nineteenth century, recitative will be accompanied by the full orchestra and will be called *accompagnato*.) A good example of *secco* recitative can be heard at the beginning of the vocal excerpt from Act II of *Orfeo* discussed later in the Listening Guide.

aria   If a recitative relates action, an aria expresses feeling. An **aria,** Italian for "song" or "ayre," is more passionate, more expansive, and more tuneful than a recitative. It also tends to have a clear meter and more regular rhythms. Finally, arias are usually sung with a less rapid-fire delivery and more in the way of vocal melisma* (one vowel luxuriously spread out over many notes) as can be seen, for example, in Orfeo's aria "Powerful spirit."

EXAMPLE 6–3

Pos - sen - te   Spir   -   to

e for-mi- da   -   bil   Nu   -   me
(Powerful spirit and formidable god)

Similarly, while the text of a recitative is normally written in blank verse, that of an aria is usually composed in rhyming lines organized in stanzas (strophes). The text of Orfeo's aria "Powerful spirit" consists of five three-line stanzas, each with a rhyme scheme "a-b-a." Moreover, the music for each stanza starts and ends in the same key (G minor). Tonally and textually, then, an aria constitutes a self-contained, independent musical unit. Operatic arias are nearly always accompanied not merely by the *basso continuo*, but also by part or all of the orchestra. Monteverdi gives special prominence to the violins and the cornettos in "Powerful spirit" to show how music can charm and delight even the guardians of Hades.

Recitative and aria are the two main structural units and styles of singing in Baroque opera and in opera in general. In addition, there is a third structural unit called the arioso. An **arioso** is a passage of vocal music sung in a manner halfway between aria and recitative. Its style is actually more faithful to the original concept of *stile rappresentativo* than either aria or recitative. An arioso *arioso*   is more declamatory than an aria but has fewer quickly repeating notes than a recitative. The lament that Orfeo sings on learning of the death of Euridice, "Thou art dead," is a classic example of an arioso and *stile rappresentativo* singing as well.

Like all operas, *Orfeo* begins with an introductory piece for instruments alone, here called a toccata. The term **toccata** (literally "a touched thing") refers to an instrumental piece, for keyboard or other instruments, requiring great technical dexterity of the performers. It is, in other words, an instrumental showpiece. Here the trumpet races up and down the scale while many of the lower parts rapidly articulate repeating pitches. Monteverdi instructs that the toccata be sounded three times. Brief though it may be, this toccata is sufficiently long to suggest the richness and variety of instrumental sounds available to a composer in the early Baroque period. Its theatrical function, of course, is to call the audience to attention, to signal that the action is about to begin.

| LISTENING GUIDE | Claudio Monteverdi
Orfeo (1607)
Toccata | CD 1/10 |

0:00	Trumpet highlights highest part
0:28	Repeat of toccata
0:54	Repeat of toccata

Although Monteverdi divided his *Orfeo* into five short acts, this two-hour opera was originally performed at Mantua without intermission. The first dramatic high point occurs midway through Act II, when the hero learns that his new bride, Euridice, has been claimed by the Underworld. In a heartfelt arioso, "Thou art dead," Orfeo laments his loss and vows to enter Hades to reclaim his treasure. Listen especially to the poignant conclusion in which Orfeo, by means of an ascending chromatic vocal line, bids farewell to earth, sky, and sun, and thus begins his journey to the land of the dead.

| LISTENING GUIDE | Claudio Monteverdi
Orfeo (1607)
Act II, Recitative, "At the bitter news," and Arioso, "Thou art dead" | CD 1/11 |

Characters: Orfeo and two shepherds
Situation: The shepherds relate that, on the news of the death of Euridice, Orfeo fell into a stunned silence. He soon regains his powers of expression, laments her loss, and vows to reclaim her.

Recitative

Shepherd I

0:00	Secco recitative (accompanied by *basso continuo* of bass lute)	A l'amara novella Rassembra l'infelice un muto sasso Che per troppo dolor no può dolersi.	At the bitter news the unhappy one resembles a mute stone who is too sad to express sadness.

Recitative

Shepherd II

0:16	*Secco* recitative (accompanied by *basso continuo* of harpsichord, bass viol, and bass lute)	Ahi, ben avrebbe un cor di tigre o d'orsa Chi non sentisse del tuo mal pietade, Privo d'ogni tuo ben, misero amante.	Ah, he must surely have a heart of a tiger or a bear, who did not pity thy misfortune, having lost all, unfortunate lover.

Arioso

Orfeo

0:44	*Basso continuo* of organ and a bass lute	Tu se' morta, mia vita, ed io respiro? Tu se' da me partita Per mai più non tornare, ed io rimango? No, che se i versi alcuna cosa ponno, N'andrò sicuro a'più, profundi abissi E, intenerito il cor del re de l'ombre,	Thou art dead, my life, but I still breathe? Thou hast left me, never to return and yet I remain? No, if my verses possess my power, I will go undaunted into the deep abyss. And, having softened the heart of the king of Hades,
1:44	Mention of descent into hell accompanied by fall in vocal line		

(Continued on next page)

| 2:03 | Vision of Euridice climbing to heaven causes flourish in high register | Meco trarrotti a reveder le stelle; O, se ciò negherammi empio destino, Rimarrò teco in compagnia di morte. | will transport thee to again see the stars. And, if cruel destiny works against me, I will remain with thee in the company of death. |
| 2:32 | Growing conviction portrayed by chromatic ascent in vocal line | Addio terra, addio, cielo e sole, addio. | Farewell earth, farewell heaven and sun, farewell! |

Having descended to the shores of Hades, Orfeo now invokes all his musical powers to gain entry. In the aria "Powerful spirit," he addresses Charon, the spirit who controls access to the kingdom of the dead. Orfeo's elaborate, florid vocal style and the exotic instrumental sounds he creates soon disarm the frightful guard.

LISTENING GUIDE

Claudio Monteverdi
Orfeo (1607)
Act III, Aria, "Powerful spirit" (strophes 1 and 2 only)

6CD 1/12

Characters: Orfeo and Charon
Situation: Orfeo pleads through his music that Charon grant passage into Hades

Aria (strophe 1)   Orfeo

| 0:00 | Florid singing, joined by violin flourishes, above a *basso continuo* | Possente spirto e formidabil nume, Senza cui far passaggio a l'altra riva Alma da corpo sciolta in van presume | Powerful spirit and formidable god, without whom no soul, deprived of body, may presume to pass to Hades's shore. |
| 1:35 | Instrumental postlude played by *basso continuo* and two solo violins | | |

Aria (strophe 2)   Orfeo

| 1:57 | Florid singing continues, joined now by cornettos, above a *basso continuo* | Non viv'io, no, che poi di vita è priva Mia cara sposa, il cor non è più meco, E senza cor com'esser può ch'io viva? | I live no longer, since now my dear spouse is deprived of life, I have no heart within me, and without a heart how can I still be alive? |
| 3:07 | Instrumental postlude played by *basso continuo* and two solo cornettos | | |

In the original Greek myth, the lord of Hades, Pluto, releases Euridice to Orfeo with one condition: He is to have faith in her devotion and not to look back to see if she follows him back to earth. When Orfeo yields to the temptation to embrace his beloved, she is reclaimed by Pluto forevermore. In his opera *Orfeo*, Monteverdi altered this tragic conclusion: Apollo now transforms Orfeo into a constellation, which radiates eternal spiritual harmony with the beloved Euridice. In so doing, Monteverdi established what was to become a convention for seventeenth- and eighteenth-century opera, the happy ending.

✼ FIGURE 6–15
Henry Purcell by an anonymous painter.

Henry Purcell (1659–1695)

An equally famous example of Baroque opera is *Dido and Aeneas*, by Henry Purcell. Purcell, arguably the finest of all English composers, was appointed organist at London's great Westminster Abbey in 1679 and was elevated to organist of the king's Chapel Royal in 1682. His *Dido and Aeneas*, believed by most authorities to have been composed in 1689, was among the first operas written in the English language. Yet it was apparently created not for the king's court, but for a private girls' boarding school in the London suburb of Chelsea. The students evidently served as the singers of the chorus, while professionals from

London sang the principal roles. The libretto* of the opera, one appropriate for a school curriculum steeped in classical Latin, is drawn from Virgil's *Aeneid*. The Trojan hero Aeneas, fleeing his conquered homeland, sails west to found the city of Rome, but is blown off course and onto the shores of Carthage, where the widowed Dido rules as queen. No sooner does the proud queen surrender herself to the soldier of fortune than the gods command him to depart for Italy and fulfill his divine destiny—to found the city of Rome. Betrayed and alone, Dido vents her feelings in an exceptionally beautiful aria, "When I am laid in earth," and then expires of a broken heart.

Purcell's Dido and Aeneas

Dido's aria is introduced by a brief bit of recitative, "Thy hand, Belinda." As recitative goes, this is one of the more expressive examples of what is at heart a declamatory, businesslike style. In the stepwise scale that descends an octave, one can feel the resignation of the abandoned Dido as she slumps into the arms of her servant Belinda:

EXAMPLE 6–4

Thy hand, Be - lin - da! Dark - ness shades me; on thy bo - som let me rest. More I would, but Death in - vades me: Death is now a wel - come guest.

The aria that follows is constructed of two beautifully shaped musical phrases that carry the following two lines of text:

"When I am laid in earth, may my wrongs create
   no trouble in thy breast.
Remember me, but ah! forget my fate."

Each of the lines is repeated, as are many individual words and pairs of words within them. Repetition of text is typical of an aria but not a recitative. It is one means by which the composer depicts emotion—the heroine can vocalize but cannot clearly articulate her feelings in complete sentences. The listener cares less about the syntax and more that the text and music together are emotionally charged. No fewer than six times does Dido plead with Belinda, and with us, to remember her. And, indeed, we do remember, for this plaintive aria is one of the most moving in all of opera.

Purcell constructs his aria "When I am laid in earth" on a *basso ostinato*. The term **basso ostinato** is an extension of the Italian word *ostinato* (meaning "obstinate," "stubborn," or "pig-headed") and refers to the fact that a phrase in the bass, whether just a few notes or several measures, repeats over and over. English composers of the seventeenth century called the *basso ostinato* the **ground bass** because the repeating bass provided a solid foundation on which an entire composition could be built, or grounded. The repeated bass pattern may be only a few notes or several measures in length. *Basso ostinato* is a common feature of Baroque music, often used to symbolize grief.

basso ostinato (*ground bass*)

The ostinato, or ground bass, Purcell composed for Dido's lament is five measures long and is heard eleven times. It consists of two sections (see the Listening Guide): a chromatic descent over the interval of a fourth (G, F♯, F, E, E♭, D)

Elton John and *Basso Ostinato*

For an up-to-date example of ostinato bass, we can look at a modern aria-lament by a more recent English composer, Elton John. Although not built exclusively on an ostinato figure, John's song *Sorry Seems to Be the Hardest Word* (*Live in Australia*, MCA2-8022) nonetheless has one striking affinity to the aria by Purcell—it, too, makes use of a *basso ostinato*, incorporating a chromatically descending fourth as a way of setting a very, very sad text. The ostinato pattern begins on G, with a chromatically descending fourth followed by a one-measure cadence.

It's sad (so sad), it' a sad, sad situation
Bass
G   F♯   F   E

      And it's getting more and more absurd
   E♭   D   F♯GAD
         (cadence)

This *basso ostinato*, and a slightly varied form of it, is then repeated several times for this and other lines of text. Compare Elton John's bass line with Purcell's *basso ostinato* (see page 111) and note that both laments are set in the key of G minor. Was the pop artist, who studied at the Royal College of Music in London, inspired by the famous aria of his well-coiffed countryman (see Fig. 6–15)?

Elton John (Sir Reginald Dwight)

and a two-measure cadence returning to the tonic G (B♭, C, D, G). The aria begins with one statement of this ostinato pattern played by low string instruments alone. When Dido enters she sings her phrase "When I am laid in earth, may my wrongs create no trouble in thy breast" above two statements of the ostinato. This music and text together are then repeated. The second and last phrase, "Remember me, but ah! forget my fate," is also stated and then repeated.

✳ FIGURE 6–16

Rehearsal of an Opera (ca. 1709) by Marco Ricci. A female lead rehearses for an opera in London. The small orchestra (left) includes a *basso continuo* of harpsichord and cello.

At the end of the repeat of this final line, the singer breaks off, as if unable to articulate her grief further. But the strings press on, carrying Dido's highly charged emotion across two final statements of the ostinato.

LISTENING GUIDE

Henry Purcell
Dido and Aeneas (1689)
Aria, "When I am laid in earth"

6CD 1/13;
2CD 1/4

Characters: Dido, queen of Carthage; Belinda, her servant
Situation: Having been deserted by her lover, Aeneas, Dido sings
 farewell to Belinda (and to all) before dying of a broken heart.

BRIEF RECITATIVE

0:00 Continuo played by harpsichord and cello

Thy hand, Belinda! Darkness shades me; on thy bosom let me rest. More I would—but Death invades me: Death is now a welcome guest.

ARIA

0:55	*basso ostinato* alone in cellos and double basses
1:13	*basso ostinato* with voice and strings
1:35	*basso ostinato* repeats beneath voice
1:59	*basso ostinato* repeats beneath voice
2:20	*basso ostinato* repeats beneath voice
2:45	*basso ostinato* repeats beneath voice
3:07	*basso ostinato* repeats beneath voice
3:30	*basso ostinato* repeats beneath voice
3:52	*basso ostinato* repeats beneath voice
4:19	*basso ostinato* alone with strings
4:40	*basso ostinato* alone with strings

When I am laid in earth, may my wrongs create no trouble in thy breast. Remember me, but ah! forget my fate.

(Listening Exercise 14)

❋ FIGURE 6–17

Front of a Stradivari violin photographed in ultraviolet light. During the seventeenth century the violin, along with its larger cousins, the viola and cello, came to form the core of the orchestra. By 1650 there were a number of important violin makers working in northern Italy. The most gifted was Antonio Stradiveri (1644–1737), whose better violins sell today for about $2 million each in commercial auction houses in London or New York.

❋ THE RISE OF INSTRUMENTAL MUSIC: SONATA AND CONCERTO GROSSO

The Baroque period, as we have seen, was one in which instrumental music—music without text—rose to new prominence. Indeed, during the seventeenth century, instrumental music came to rival and ultimately surpass vocal music in importance. Idiomatic instrumental music—music written specifically to exploit the technical strengths of a particular instrument—came to be cultivated by most composers. These creators likewise demanded virtuosity—the ability to play technically demanding passages rapidly and surely—of the performer. Many of the most renowned composers of the Baroque era, including Corelli (1653–1713), Vivaldi (1678–1741), and Bach (1685–1750), were themselves virtuosos on a particular instrument. Naturally, their passion for instrumental music led to the creation of new musical forms, like the fugue (see page 134), and new musical genres, such as the sonata and concerto.

The Baroque Sonata

A **sonata** is a type of chamber music to be played on an instrument. The term was first used in Venice around 1600 to indicate a composition intended specifically to be played or sounded, as opposed to one that was to be sung. Hence, a sonata is "something sounded" in distinction to a cantata (see page 126), which is "something sung."

Usually, a sonata consisted of a collection of short pieces, each of which is called a **movement.** In the Baroque era these collections of movements were of two types. One, called the **sonata da camera** (chamber sonata), was made up of a series of dancelike movements that had the name and character of a particular dance. A typical chamber sonata might consist of an allemand, sarabande, gavotte, and gigue—all dances. The second type of sonata was called the **sonata da chiesa** (church sonata), and its movements were designated only by a tempo marking such as *grave, vivace, adagio,* or *allegro* (grave, fast and lively, slow, fast)—it was thought inappropriate to have the movements of a piece destined for the church associated with secular dances. Indeed, as the names *sonata da camera* and *sonata da chiesa* indicate, the church sonata was intended to provide background music for religious services, while the chamber sonata, with its links to the dance, was usually heard at court or in the private homes of the well-to-do.

A sonata might be written for a solo keyboard instrument like the harpsichord. Or it might be composed for a solo melody instrument like the violin, in which case three performers would be involved—the violinist and two persons playing the continuo (Fig. 6–8). But whether for solo keyboard or solo melody instrument plus continuo, the work was called a **solo sonata.** Similarly, many Baroque sonatas were written for two melody instruments, two violins or violin and oboe, for example, plus continuo. Such a force was called a **trio sonata** because the composer wrote only three musical lines, even though four performers were involved—two soloists and two players on the *basso continuo.*

Arcangelo Corelli (1653–1713)

The composer-virtuoso who made the Baroque solo and trio sonata internationally popular was Arcangelo Corelli. Corelli was born in 1653 near Bologna, Italy, then an important center for violin instruction and performance. By 1675 he had moved to Rome, where he remained for the duration of his life as a teacher, composer, and performer on the violin. Although Corelli's musical output was small, consisting only of five sets of sonatas and one of concertos, his works were widely admired. Such diverse composers as Johann Sebastian Bach in Leipzig, François Couperin (1668–1733) in Paris, and Henry Purcell in London either borrowed his melodies directly or more generally studied and absorbed his style.

The most remarkable aspect of Corelli's music is its harmony. It sounds modern to our ears. That is to say, we have heard so much classical and popular music that we have come to possess an almost subconscious sense of how a succession of chords, or harmonic progression, should sound. Corelli was the first in a long line of composers to establish that harmonic norm. He was the first to write fully functional harmony; in other words, in his sonatas each chord has a specific function or role in the succession of chords. Not only does the individual chord constitute an important sound in itself, but it also prepares or leads toward the next, thereby helping to form a tightly linked chain of chords. They sound purposeful, well directed. The most basic link in the chain is the V–I (dominant–tonic) cadence (see page 31). In addition, Corelli will often construct a bass line that moves upward chromatically by half step. This chromatic, stepwise motion pulls up and into the next higher note, increasing the sense of direction and cohesiveness we feel in Corelli's music. This strong feeling of functional harmony can be heard equally well in the music of Corelli's younger contemporary, Antonio Vivaldi.

FIGURE 6–18
Arcangelo Corelli looks placid enough in this late seventeenth-century portrait. But when playing the violin, according to a contemporary, "his eyes turn red as fire, his face becomes distorted, and his eyeballs roll as if in agony."

The Baroque Concerto

The concerto was to the Baroque era what the symphony would later become to the Classical period: the most popular and important genre of instrumental music. A Baroque concerto emphasized abrupt contrasts within a unity of mood, just as striking change between the zones of light and darkness often characterizes a Baroque painting (see, for example, Fig. 6–21).

A **concerto** (from the Latin *concertare*, "to strive together") is a musical composition marked by a friendly contest or competition between a soloist and an orchestra. When only one soloist confronts the orchestra, the work is a **solo concerto.** When more than one is present and they function as a unit, the piece is a **concerto grosso.** The soloists in a concerto grosso constitute a subgroup called the **concertino** ("little concert"), and the full orchestra is called the **tutti** ("all" or "everybody"). A typical concerto grosso had a concertino of two or four violins and continuo. The soloists were not highly paid masters imported from afar, but rather the regular first-chair players who, when they were not serving as soloists, joined with the tutti to play the orchestral string parts. The contrast in sound between the heavy tutti and the lighter, more virtuosic concertino is the most distinctive feature of the concerto grosso.

concerto grosso

As written by Vivaldi, Bach, and Handel, the solo concerto and the concerto grosso usually had three movements: fast, slow, fast. The serious first movement is composed in a carefully worked-out structure called ritornello form (see page 115); the second movement is invariably more lyrical and tender; while the third movement, though usually using ritornello form, tends to be lighter, more dancelike, sometimes even rustic in mood. Both the solo concerto and the concerto grosso originated in Italy toward the end of the seventeenth century. Solo concertos for violin, flute, recorder, oboe, trumpet, and harpsichord were especially popular. The vogue of the concerto grosso peaked about 1730 and then all but came to an end about the time of the death of Bach (1750). But the solo concerto continued to be cultivated during the Classical and Romantic periods, becoming increasingly a showcase in which a single soloist could display his or her technical mastery of an instrument.

Antonio Vivaldi (1678–1741)

No composer was more influential, and certainly none more prolific, in the creation of the Baroque concerto than Antonio Vivaldi. Vivaldi, like Gabrieli, a native of Venice, was the son of a barber and part-time musician at the church of St. Mark (Figs. 6–10 and 6–11). Surprisingly, it was not unusual in the seventeenth and eighteenth centuries for barbers to be semiprofessional musicians, since their shops were frequently supplied with musical instruments with which waiting customers could amuse themselves. Young Vivaldi's proximity to St. Mark's naturally brought him into contact with the clergy. Although he became a skilled performer on the violin, he also entered Holy Orders, ultimately becoming a priest. Vivaldi's life, however, was by no means confined to the realm of the spirit: He concertized on the violin throughout Europe; he wrote and produced nearly fifty operas, which brought him a great deal of money; and for fifteen years he lived with a French soprano. The worldly pursuits of *il prete rosso* (the red-haired priest) eventually got him into trouble with the authorities of the Roman Church, and in 1737 Vivaldi was forbidden to practice his musical artistry in papally controlled lands. This ban affected his income as well as his creativity: He died poor and obscure in 1741 in Vienna, where he had gone in search of a post at the imperial court.

From 1703 until 1740 Vivaldi worked in Venice at the *Ospedale della Pietà* (Hospice of Mercy), first as a violinist and music teacher and then as its musical director. The Hospice of Mercy was an orphanage for the care and education of young women. It was one of four such charitable institutions in Venice that accepted abandoned, mostly illegitimate girls, who, as several reports state, "otherwise would have been thrown in the canals." By 1700, music had been made to serve an important role in the religious and social life of the orphanage. Each Sunday afternoon its orchestra of young women offered public performances for the well-to-do of Venice (see boxed essay). Also attending these concerts were foreign visitors—Venice was already a tourist city—among them a French diplomat, who wrote in 1739:

> These girls are educated at the expense of the state, and they are trained solely with the purpose of excelling in music. That is why they sing like angels and play violin, flute, organ, oboe, cello, and bassoon; in short, no instrument is so big as to frighten them. They are kept like nuns in a convent. All they do is perform concerts, always in groups of about forty girls. I swear to you that there is nothing as pleasant as seeing a young and pretty nun, dressed in white, with a little pomegranate bouquet over her ears, conducting the orchestra with all the gracefulness and incredible precision one can imagine.

VIOLIN CONCERTO IN E MAJOR, OPUS 8, NO. 1, "THE SPRING" (EARLY 1700s)

During the early 1700s Vivaldi composed literally hundreds of solo concertos for the all-female orchestras of the Hospice of Mercy in Venice. In 1725 he

🌀 FIGURE 6–19
Portrait of a violinist and composer believed by some to be the musician Antonio Vivaldi.

music in Venetian orphanages

Anna Maria della Pietà: Violin Virtuoso

In the early eighteenth century there were approximately four hundred girls and young women residents at the Hospice of Mercy in Venice. All received not only religious instruction but also training, both in academic disciplines and technical crafts (cooking, embroidery, lace-making, sewing, cotton-spinning, textile manufacture, health care, and music). Those who showed a special talent for music were placed within a core of forty young musicians, a prestigious group given special privileges and a distinctive red habit. Each day these talented young women studied or practiced for as many as four hours, and their musical education included tutelage in singing, ear-training, and counterpoint as well as instruction on at least two musical instruments. For these girls, the orphanage was half convent, half music conservatory.

Women musicians perform behind a grill at an eighteenth-century Venetian orphanage.

Given encouragement to their talents, it is not surprising that some of these young women developed into instrumental virtuosos. One such performer was Anna Maria della Pietà, who served, under Vivaldi's supervision, as concert-mistress of the orchestra at the Hospice of Mercy from 1712 to 1736. By 1734 she had become "the best violinist in Europe," as one contemporary observed. Vivaldi wrote approximately thirty solo violin concertos for her, many of which are still used today for teaching fledgling violinists. When performing publicly at the orphanage, Anna Maria and the other members of the musical core stood in a special gallery, a musicians' loft, and played to the outside world through a grill. Like disembodied voices, their sounds could be heard, but their faces not fully seen.

gathered twelve of the more colorful of these together and published them under the title "Opus 8." (Composers frequently use **opus,** the Latin noun meaning "work," to enumerate and identify their compositions at the time of publication; this set of concertos was thus Vivaldi's eighth published work.) In addition, he called the first four of these solo concertos **The Seasons.** What Vivaldi meant by this was that each of the four concertos in turn represents the feelings, sounds, and sights of one of the four seasons of the year, beginning with spring. So that there be no ambiguity as to what sensations and events the music represents at any given moment, Vivaldi wrote precise verbal descriptions above the notes of the players, specifying at one point that the violins are to sound "like barking dogs."

"The Spring" Concerto for solo violin and small orchestra is Vivaldi's most popular work. As is usually the case in the three-movement solo concerto, the fast first movement is composed in **ritornello** form. The Italian word *ritornello* means "return" or "refrain." In ritornello form, all or part of one main theme—the ritornello—returns again and again, invariably played by the tutti, or full orchestra. Between the tutti's statements of the ritornello, the soloist inserts fragments and extensions of this ritornello theme in virtuosic fashion.

ritornello form

The jaunty ritornello theme of the first movement of "The Spring" Concerto has two complementary parts, the second of which returns more often than the first. Between appearances of the ritornello, Vivaldi inserts the music that represents his feelings about spring. He creates the songbirds of May by asking the violins to play rapidly and staccato* in a high register. Similarly, he depicts the

FIGURE 6–20 AND 6–21
(left) A public concert by young women at the Venetian Hospice of Mercy, where Vivaldi served as a teacher and then director. Note how the performers are placed in special galleries to the left. (right) Musicians of Prince Ferdinando de Medici. The prince was a fine amateur keyboard player himself and an important patron of Vivaldi.

sudden arrival of thunder and lightning by means of a tremolo* and shooting scales, then returns to the cheerful song of the birds. Thereafter, in the slow second movement, a vision of a flower-strewn meadow is conveyed by an expansive, tender melody in the violin. Finally, during the fast finale, a sustained droning in the lower strings invokes "the festive sounds of country bagpipes." "The Spring" Concerto is thus an early example of program music, a type of descriptive instrumental writing that would flourish during the later Romantic period (see page 308). The full text of Vivaldi's "program" for the first movement of "The Spring" Concerto is given in the Listening Guide.

LISTENING GUIDE	Antonio Vivaldi Violin Concerto in E major, Opus 8, No. 1 ("The Spring"; early 1700s) First movement, *Allegro* (fast)	6CD 1/14; 2CD 1/5

Meter: duple
Texture: mainly homophonic

0:00	Ritornello part 1 played by tutti	
0:07	Ritornello part 1 repeated by tutti *pianissimo*	
0:14	Ritornello part 2 played by tutti	
0:22	Ritornello part 2 repeated by tutti *pianissimo*	

(Continued on next page)

0:30	Solo violin (aided by two violins from tutti) chirp on high	"Spring with all its festiveness has arrived And the birds salute it with happy song"
1:05	Ritornello part 2 played by tutti	
1:13	Tutti softly plays running sixteenth notes	"And the brooks, kissed by the breezes, Meanwhile flow with sweet murmurings"
1:36	Ritornello part 2 played by tutti	
1:45	Tutti plays tremolo and violins shoot up the scale	"Dark clouds cover the sky Announced by bolts of lightning and thunder"
1:51	Solo violin plays agitated, broken triads while tutti continues with tremolos below	
2:11	Ritornello part 2 played by tutti	
2:19	Solo violin chirps on high, adding an ascending chromatic scale and trill	"But when all has returned to quiet The birds commence to sing once again their enchanted song"
2:37	Ritornello part 1, slightly varied, played by tutti	
2:48	Solo violin plays rising sixteenth notes	
3:03	Ritornello part 2 played by tutti	

(Listening Exercise 15)

Vivaldi's more than 450 concertos were widely admired in the early eighteenth century, but within a few years of his death he was largely forgotten, a victim of rapidly changing musical tastes. Not until the revival of Baroque music in the 1950s were his scores resurrected from obscure libraries and dusty archives. Now his music is loved for its freshness and vigor, its exuberance and daring. Today it can be heard as background music at shopping malls, in television commercials, and in film scores. More than 150 professional recordings have been made of *The Seasons* alone. If nothing else, Vivaldi's life and posthumous reputation suggest the fickleness of fame, fortune, and public favor!

Vivaldi's posthumous reputation

LISTENING EXERCISES

13 Giovanni Gabrieli
Motet, *In the Churches* (1612)

6CD 1/9

The text of this motet is given below. First listen to the motet following the text, then answer the questions that follow:

In ecclesiis, benedicite Domino Alleluja	In the churches, bless the Lord
In omni loco dominationis, benedic anima mea Dominum Alleluja	In every holy place, may my soul bless the Lord
In Deo salutari meo, et gloria mea Deus, auxilium meum et spes mea in Deo est Alleluja	In God is my salvation and my glory Lord, my help and my hope is in God

Deus noster, te invocamus, te laudamus, te adoramus	Our Lord, we call to you, we praise you, we adore you
Libera nos, salva nos, vivifica nos Alleluja	Deliver us, save us, revivify us
Deus, adjutor noster in aeternum Alleluja	Lord, our judge forever

1. (0:08 and 0:13) At the repeat of the words "benedicite Domino," the soprano repeats the music:

   a. on a higher pitch   b. on the same pitch   c. at a lower pitch

2. (0:16–0:30) In this "Alleluja" which is true?

   a. A soloist echoes a homophonic chorus, and then they sing together.

   b. A homophonic chorus echoes a soloist, and then they sing together.

3. (0:31–0:59) In this bass solo the words "In omni loco," "dominationis," and "benedic" are each *repeated:*

   a. once   b. twice   c. three times

4. (1:43–1:52) What melodic device is used at the end of this instrumental passage?

   a. sequence   b. pizzicato   c. pedal point

5. (1:53–3:20) Do you ever hear more than two voices singing in this section? _____

6. (3:35) What happens at the beginning of this section ("Deus, te invocamus")?

   a. soprano sings first and bass answers

   b. bass sings first and soprano answers

7. (5:03–5:14 and 5:33–5:46) Do the instruments accompany the singers on the important word "Deus"? _____

8. (5:03–5:14 and 5:33–5:46) What kind of musical texture does Gabrieli choose to emphasize the word "Deus"?

   a. monophonic   b. polyphonic   c. homophonic

9. (6:58) Is the final chord major or minor (does it sound bright or dark and gloomy)? _____

10. Finally, is *In the Churches* an example of an *a cappella* motet? _____

. . . .

14 Henry Purcell   6CD 1/13; 2CD 1/4
Recitative, "Thy hand, Belinda" and aria,
"When I am laid in earth" from *Dido and Aeneas* (1689)

Your selection begins with about a minute of recitative (see page 109). Notice how Dido's deflated spirits are reflected in the music: She gradually sinks down from the C above middle C to middle C itself, touching the chromatic notes of the scale along the way. Begin, however, with the aria that follows, "When I am laid in earth." The opening is easy to recognize because it starts with a chromatically descending ostinato bass.

First draw a line beneath the text to show where each statement of the *basso ostinato* begins and ends. Then number all the lines (1–11). The lines and numbers for the opening continuo statement and the final two statements are provided for you, as is the first statement beneath the text. The repetitions in the text are included to facilitate your efforts.

1 _____   2 <u>When I am laid (am laid) in earth, may my wrongs create</u> no trouble (no trouble) in thy breast. (When I am laid, am laid in earth, may my wrongs create no trouble, no trouble in thy breast.)
Remember me (remember me), but ah! forget my fate. (Remember me, but ah! forget my fate. Remember me, remember me, but ah! forget my fate. Remember me, but ah! forget my fate.) 10 _____
11 _____

Now answer the following questions:

1. Is the recitative "Thy hand, Belinda" an example of *secco* recitative (accompanied only by *basso continuo*) or *accompagnato* recitative (accompanied by full orchestra)? _____

2. In the aria "When I am laid in earth," is the mode major or minor? _____

3. Is the meter of the aria duple or triple? _____

4. Listen once again to the end of the aria, to the last two statements of the ground bass after Dido has fallen silent. The strings play with the continuo but without the voice. Compare this to the first statement of the ostinato at the very beginning of the aria. In what way is the texture thicker now than at the beginning? _____

5. In the final two statements of the ground bass (10–11), what is the general direction of the melody?
   a. up by step
   b. up by leaps
   c. down by step
   d. down by leaps

Antonio Vivaldi   6CD 1/14; 2CD 1/5
Violin Concerto in E major, Opus 8, No. 1
("The Spring"; early 1700s)

Listen once again to the opening movement of Vivaldi's "The Spring" Concerto, and answer the following questions regarding instrumentation, rhythm, tonality, and structure.

1. Do you hear any woodwinds, brasses, or percussion playing in Vivaldi's orchestra in this concerto? _____

2. Is the harpsichord or the organ used as the keyboard instrument in the *basso continuo*? _____

3. How would you describe the rhythms of this movement?
   a. energetic with regularly repeating patterns
   b. languid with no clear sense of a downbeat

4. How would you describe the activity of the bass during the opening presentation of the ritornello theme (0:00–0:29)?
   a. moves slowly and continually up the scale
   b. moves up the scale and then repeats one pitch
   c. repeats one pitch and moves only at the end of each phrase

5. (0:30–1:05) Does the *basso continuo* play during the first solo section? _____

6. (1:05–1:12) Does the *basso continuo* play during the return of the ritornello theme? _____

7. (2:11–2:18) Is this reappearance of the ritornello theme in major or minor? _____

8. (2:19–2:29) How many statements of a chromatically rising scale do you hear the violins play in this solo section? _____

9. During this same passage and beyond (2:19–2:37), what does the cello of the *basso continuo* do?
   a. plays a pedal point* (holds one note)   b. rises by step   c. falls by step.

10. (3:11–3:23) At the very end of the movement one of the two parts of the ritornello theme is repeated quietly (*piano*). Is it part 1 or part 2 that is heard *piano*? _____

  KEY WORDS

Anna Maria della Pietà	melodic sequence	*sonata da camera*
aria	movement	*sonata da chiesa*
arioso	opera	*stile rappresentativo*
basso continuo	opus	terraced dynamics
basso ostinato (ground bass)	recitative	toccata
concertino	ritornello	trio sonata
concerto grosso	*The Seasons*	tutti
harpsichord	*secco* recitative	*viola da gamba* (bass viol)
libretto	solo concerto	
	solo sonata	

For a checklist of musical style in the early Baroque period, see page 62.

LATE BAROQUE MUSIC: BACH AND HANDEL

 The music of the late Baroque era (1710–1750), represented by the two great figures Johann Sebastian Bach and George Frideric Handel, stands as a high-water mark in Western musical culture. In this period were created such masterpieces as Bach's cantata *Awake, a Voice Is Calling* and Handel's *Messiah*. These are large, grandiose works distinguished, at various moments, by great dramatic power, broad gestures, complex counterpoint, and opulent instrumental color. At the same time they convey to the listener a sense of technical mastery—that Bach and Handel could compose with grace and skill in a variety of musical forms, techniques, and styles—building on the innovations of previous Baroque composers.

Earlier in the Baroque era, in the early 1600s, the desire for passionate expression had led to far-reaching stylistic innovations, such as the *basso continuo** and the *recitative**. Claudio Monteverdi (1567–1643) helped create an entirely new category of music, namely, opera*. Other new genres—the sonata*, the solo concerto*, and the concerto grosso*—emerged during the second half of the seventeenth century. But the opera, the sonata, and the concerto of the early Baroque era show all the signs of an art in its adolescence. They possess a certain awkwardness and instability, no matter how exciting, vital, and brash they may sound.

The late Baroque, by contrast, is not a period of musical innovation, but one of refinement. Bach and his contemporaries did not, in the main, invent new forms, styles, techniques, or genres, but rather gave greater weight, length, and polish to those established by their musical forebears. Arcangelo Corelli (1653–1713), for example, had introduced functional harmony in his sonatas, but Bach and Handel smoothed away the occasional jarring chord and made the harmony work so as to expand small musical units into larger, more compelling works of art. Bach and Handel approached the craft of composition with unbounded self-confidence. Their music has a sense of rightness, solidity, and maturity about it. Each time we choose to listen to one of their compositions, we offer further witness to their success in bringing a hundred years of musical development to a glorious culmination.

THE THEATRICAL QUALITY OF BAROQUE ART

A striking feature of much Baroque art is its theatrical quality. Drama in the arts is created by conflict, by forces that move in opposition, and yet, at the

same time, are so positioned as to project a satisfying wholeness. In late Baroque music the competing musical units are generally lengthy and unchanging in mood. Large, clearly defined blocks of sound are placed in opposition.

By the early 1700s, Bach and Handel could make music theatrical by drawing on many opposing styles, textures, colors, and performing groups. For example, a chorus could be set against instruments, a soloist against a full orchestra, an aria against a recitative, and a homophonic passage against a polyphonic one. Nonetheless, these large-scale forces compete within boundaries carefully defined by musical form. In Handel's *Messiah*, for example, ternary form* controls the flow of several arias, whereas strict fugal procedure regulates parts of the "Hallelujah" chorus. This same theatrical equilibrium is apparent in the visual arts of the late Baroque, as can be seen, for example, in Giambattista Tiepolo's *The Triumph of Nobility and Virtue over Ignorance* (Fig. 7–1). Here, two large-scale units contrast in position (high and low) and color (white and black). Yet the artist creates a grand spatial harmony because the two units have approximately the same mass and because intersecting diagonal lines within each unit pull with equal force. There is energy, movement, spectacle, and grandeur—theatricality—yet there is formal control. These are important qualities of late Baroque art, widely expressed in music as well as painting.

Baroque art: energy, movement, spectacle, and grandeur

✿ ASPECTS OF LATE BAROQUE MUSICAL STYLE

Treatment of Musical Elements

During the years 1710–1750, Bach, Handel, and their contemporaries continued to develop the distinctive elements of musical style that appeared in the early Baroque era (see pages 98–101), now amplifying and extending them. In brief, melodies became longer, rhythms more driving, harmonies more purposeful, and textures more contrapuntal.

MELODY. Melody in late Baroque music is governed by the principle of continuing development. An initial motive or theme is set forth and then continually expanded, or spun out, over an ever-lengthening line. Such a melody tends to be long and ornate. Often the notes are propelled forward by melodic sequence*, the repetition of a motive or phrase on successively higher or lower degrees of the scale. Sequence helps the melody fly higher and farther and postpones the time when it must arrive at a cadence, as is the case in this example from Handel's *Messiah*:

EXAMPLE 7–1

ex - alt - ed,

The exuberant quality of late Baroque melody, however, makes it more impressive than memorable; that is, it is hard to sing or hum, even after repeated hearings. This is due, in part, to the fact that the phrases are frequently not short, narrow, and symmetrical, but rather long, expansive, and irregular. They are also often instrumental in nature, meaning that melodic patterns that can eas-

FIGURE 7–1

The Triumph of Nobility and Virtue over Ignorance (ca. 1740) by Giambattista Tiepolo (1692–1770) offers a splendid example of late Baroque theatricality, with its grand gestures, vivid colors, and distinctly separate, yet balanced, zones of action.

ily be played on instruments are frequently transferred to the voice, where they can be difficult to sing. Bach, for example, often wrote difficult vocal lines that are instrumental in character.

RHYTHM. Rhythm is the most distinctive and exciting element of late Baroque music. If a concerto by Bach or Handel seems to chug along with an irrepressible optimism and vitality, it is because of the almost unstoppable quality of the rhythm. A piece will begin with one prominent rhythmic idea, and it or a complementary one will continue energetically to the very end of the movement. In this context, meter is firmly established by regular accents and a steady beat. Indeed, meter is more easily recognized in late Baroque music than in the music of any other period. Usually, one or two prominent instruments, often those assigned the bass line, play a regular rhythmic pattern that sets a strong beat. This clear, regular beat, in turn, makes the meter immediately audible. The strong beat and powerful bass are elements of late Baroque music that make it appealing to modern listeners. In these it has a certain affinity to contemporary rock and jazz.

driving rhythms

HARMONY. The pull of forceful chord progressions and the use of only major and minor keys were qualities of harmony found earlier, in the music of Corelli (see page 113). They continue to be embodied in the music of the late Baroque era. So, too, does the *basso continuo* (see page 98), that small ensemble of usually keyboard and a bass instrument that gives added weight to the bass and generates chords, thereby providing the harmonic support for the melody above. What chords the keyboard player is to construct are suggested to him or her by means of a **figured bass**—a numerical shorthand placed in the music that tells the player which unwritten notes to fill in above the written bass note. (Figured

bass is similar in intent to the numerical code found in "fake books" used by modern jazz pianists that indicates which chords to play beneath the written melody.)

EXAMPLES 7–2A AND 7–2B

figured bass

What is new in the harmony of the late Baroque is the regularity with which it moves. Specifically, chords appear at regular intervals and produce a constant rate of harmonic change. Chord changes may occur every beat, every other beat, or just once in each measure, but usually the rate of change is stable. Regular harmonic change and repetitious rhythms are what give the music of this period its sense of relentless, unstoppable movement.

regular chord changes

TEXTURE: THE RETURN OF COUNTERPOINT. We have seen that imitative counterpoint with independent polyphonic lines dominated the church music of the Renaissance and that, partly as a reaction to this, composers of the early Baroque era began to avoid counterpoint. In the late Baroque period, however, they returned to contrapuntal writing, in part to add richness to the middle range of what was otherwise a top–bottom (soprano–bass) dominated texture. German composers were particularly fond of counterpoint, perhaps because of their traditional love of the organ, an instrument with several keyboards and thus well suited to playing many musical lines at once. The gradual reintegration of counterpoint into the fabric of Baroque music culminates in the rigorously contrapuntal vocal and instrumental music of Bach.

more counterpoint

The Late Baroque Orchestra

During the seventeenth century, changes occurred in the makeup of the orchestra. The trumpet, which had formerly been used alone (or with drums) as a purely ceremonial or military instrument, was now welcomed into the ensemble for its bright sound, while the older, duller wooden cornetto (see Fig. 4–10) quickly disappeared. At the same time the horn left the hunting field and watchtower and took a place in the orchestra. Similarly, the oboe, usually appearing in pairs, was admitted as the principal woodwind instrument because of its penetrating sound, though it might be replaced by one or two flutes, especially if no trumpets or horns were present. Members of the violin family replaced those of the viol (see page 98), whose "still music," as Shakespeare called it, was thought too delicate; and other soft, plucked instruments from the Renaissance, like the lute, were sent packing. The core of the orchestra was now provided by the violins, violas, cellos, and double basses (which doubled the cello line an octave below). They were supported, still, by a continuo group of harpsichord (or organ in church) and cello, perhaps with a double bass playing as well. The bassoon joined the continuo group in this period to give even more strength to the bass line (see Fig. 7–2).

Many concerti grossi*, opera overtures (see page 137), and dance suites (see pages 137–38) of the late Baroque period were written for an orchestra of just string instruments and continuo. Pieces for especially festive occasions, however, would normally include a greater number of instruments for greater brilliancy. Yet never were all available instruments heard at once, even in the largest orchestral scores. If there were trumpets, there were usually no horns; if there were oboes, there were no flutes, and vice versa. Hence, by modern standards the late Baroque orchestra was at best a mid-size group. Rarely did it include more than thirty-five players, about twenty of whom belonged to the nucleus of strings.

✿ FIGURE 7–2

Detail of an orchestra playing for a Baroque opera. From left to right are a bassoon, two French horns, a cello, a double bass, a harpsichord, and then violins, violas, and oboes.

✿ JOHANN SEBASTIAN BACH (1685–1750)

In the creations of Johann Sebastian Bach, the music of the Baroque reaches its greatest glory. Bach was born to a musical dynasty, though one originally of common standing. For nearly two hundred years members of the Bach family served as musicians in small towns in Thuringia, a province in central Germany. Johann Sebastian was merely the most talented of the ubiquitous musical Bachs, though he himself had four sons who achieved international fame. Although he received an excellent formal education in the humanities, as a musician Bach was largely self-taught. To learn his craft he studied, copied, and arranged the compositions of Corelli, Vivaldi, Pachelbel, and even Palestrina. He also learned to play the organ, in part by emulating others, once traveling two hundred miles on foot to hear a great performer. By the time of his maturity he had become the most renowned virtuoso of the organ in Germany, and his improvisations on that instrument became legendary.

Bach's first position of importance was in the town of Weimar, Germany, where he served as organist to the court begin-

✿ FIGURE 7–3

Portrait of Johann Sebastian Bach painted by Elias Gottlob Haussmann in 1748.

Leipzig, St. Thomas's Church (center) and choir school (left) from an engraving of 1723, the year in which Bach moved to the city. Bach's large family occupied several floors of the choir school.

the German church cantata

cantata expands on theme of the day

ning in 1708. It was here that he wrote many of his finest works for organ, including the G minor fugue discussed later (see page 134). In 1717 Bach accepted a better position at a court in Cöthen, Germany. However, his employer in Weimar, Duke Wilhelm Ernst of Saxe-Weimar, was displeased that his organist had "jumped ship," and summarily had Bach arrested and jailed. (Composers before the era of Beethoven were little more than indentured servants who needed to obtain a release from one employer before they could enter the service of another.) After languishing in prison for some months, Bach was released to take up his duties in Cöthen, where he served as conductor of a small court orchestra. In 1723 Bach moved yet again, this time to assume the coveted position of cantor of St. Thomas's Church and choir school in Leipzig, Germany (Fig. 7–4), a post he retained until his death in 1750. He seems to have been attracted to Leipzig, then a city of about thirty thousand inhabitants, because of its excellent university where his sons might enroll at no cost.

Although prestigious, the post of cantor of the Lutheran church of St. Thomas was not an easy one. As an employee of the town council of Leipzig, Bach was charged with superintending the liturgical music of the four principal churches of that city. He also played organ for all funerals, composed any music needed for ceremonies at the university, and taught Latin grammar to the boys at the choir school of St. Thomas. But by far the most burdensome part of his job as cantor was to provide new music for the church each Sunday and religious holiday, a total of about sixty days a year. In so doing, Bach brought an important genre of religious music, the cantata, to the highest point of its development.

The Cantata

Like the opera, the sonata, and the concerto, the **cantata** was a genre of music that arose in Italy in the seventeenth century. Originally, a cantata ("something sung") was simply a sung aria, as opposed to the sonata, which was a piece played or sounded on instruments. Gradually, the cantata was expanded to several movements, including one or more arias, ariosos, and recitatives, all with instrumental accompaniment. As was true of the sonata, the cantata was heard by audiences in both the aristocratic salon and the church. Secular chamber cantatas on themes of love, morality, and politics were favored by the Italians, while the Germans preferred religious subjects. Composers like Bach and Georg Philipp Telemann (1681–1767) made the German church cantata the musical centerpiece of the German Protestant service, and their works include music for chorus as well as solo arias and recitatives.

In Bach's time St. Thomas's Church celebrated a Sunday Mass, as prescribed by Martin Luther (1483–1546) nearly two centuries earlier. The service began at seven o'clock in the morning and lasted nearly four hours. The musical high point was the cantata. It came after the reading of the Gospel and provided a commentary on the Gospel text, allowing the congregation to meditate on the word of the Lord. The preacher then delivered an hour-long sermon, which also expounded on the scriptural theme of the day. Bach wrote almost three hundred cantatas for the citizens of Leipzig (five annual cycles), though only about two-thirds of these survive. His musical forces consisted of singers from the St. Thomas choir school and instrumentalists from the university and town. The ensemble was placed in a choir loft above the west door (see Fig. 7–8), and Bach himself conducted the group, beating time with a roll of paper.

AWAKE, A VOICE IS CALLING (1731)

Bach was a devoted husband, a loving father to twenty children, and a respected burgher of Leipzig. Yet above all he was a religious man who composed not for self-expression, but for the greater glory of God. His cantata *Awake, a Voice Is Calling* reveals his abiding faith in the religious traditions of his German Lutheran community. It was written in 1731 for a service on a Sunday immediately before the beginning of Advent (four Sundays before Christmas). The text of the cantata announces the coming of a bridegroom toward his hopeful bride. Christ is the groom. A group of Wise Virgins, whose story is recounted in the Gospel of St. Matthew (25:1–13), symbolizes the bride and the entire community. Here is the Gospel of Matthew as it was read to the congregation at St. Thomas's Church immediately before Bach's cantata was performed.

> Then shall the kingdom of heaven be likened unto ten virgins, which took their lamps, and went forth to meet the bridegroom. And five of them were wise, and five were foolish. They that were foolish took their lamps, but took no oil with them. . . . And at midnight there was a cry made, Behold, the bridegroom cometh; go ye out to meet him. Then all those virgins arose, and trimmed their lamps. And the foolish said unto the wise. Give us of your oil; for our lamps are gone out. But the wise answered, saying, Not so; lest there be not enough for us and you: but go ye rather to them that sell, and buy for yourselves. And while they went to buy, the bridegroom came; and they that were ready went in with him to the marriage: and the door was shut . . . . Watch therefore, for ye know neither the day nor the hour wherein the Son of man cometh.

The message of both Matthew's Gospel and Bach's cantata was for all good Lutherans of Leipzig to awake and purify their hearts to receive the spirit of the coming Christ.

The cantata *Awake, a Voice Is Calling* is made up of a succession of seven independent movements. Those for chorus provide a structural framework, coming at the beginning, the middle, and the end. They make use of the three stanzas of text of a sixteenth-century Lutheran hymn, *Awake, a Voice Is Calling*, from which this cantata derives its name. The text of the recitatives and arias, on the other hand, is a patchwork of biblical quotations cobbled together by a contemporary of Bach's. Thus the chorus sings the verses of the traditional hymn while the soloists present the biblical excerpts in the recitatives and arias. Notice how the structure of the cantata creates a formal symmetry: recitative–aria pairs surround the central choral movement, and are preceded and followed in turn by a chorus.

FIGURE 7–5

Looking toward the altar in the interior of St. Thomas's Church, Leipzig, as it was in the mid-nineteenth century. The pulpit for the sermon is at the right.

			Movement:			
1	2	3	4	5	6	7
Chorus	Recitative	Aria (duet)	Chorus	Recitative	Aria (duet)	Chorus
1st stanza			2nd stanza			3rd stanza

Awake, a Voice Is Calling is a chorale cantata, meaning that the work is built around a chorale. A **chorale** is a well-known spiritual melody or religious folksong of the German Protestant (Lutheran) church, what other denominations would simply call a hymn. In this case the chorale had been written in 1597 and had been widely used in the Lutheran church before Bach took it up. The structure of *Awake, a Voice Is Calling* is typical of chorale melodies (see upcom-

the chorale cantata

🌸 FIGURE 7–6
Tiepolo's *Vision of St. Clement* projects three distinct levels of activity: the Trinity on high, two angels in the middle, and Pope Clement I, Christ's vicar on earth, at the bottom.

ing Listening Guide). It begins with three phrases that emphasize, in turn, the tonic, the dominant, and again the tonic of the key E♭ major. These are stated and repeated. Thereafter come four shorter phrases (4–7) that allow for tonal contrast. Finally, a concluding phrase, which is nothing other than a repeat of phrase three, rounds off the melody. The form of this chorale is thus **A(1,2,3) A(1,2,3) B(4–7,3).** And the chorale is just the starting point for Bach's complex structure!

Of the seven movements of the cantata *Awake, a Voice Is Calling*, the most remarkable is the first, a gigantic choral fantasy that displays a polyphonic mastery exceptional even for Bach. Here Bach creates a multidimensional spectacle surrounding the coming of Christ. First the orchestra announces Christ's arrival by means of a three-part ritornello* that conveys a sense of growing anticipation. Part **a** of the ritornello, with its dotted rhythm, suggests a steady march; part **b,** with its strong downbeat and then syncopations, imparts a tugging urgency; part **c,** with its rapid sixteenth notes, implies an unrestrained race toward the object of desire. Now the chorale melody enters, high in the sopranos, the voice of tradition, perhaps the voice of God. In long, steady notes placed squarely on downbeats it calls the people to prepare themselves to receive God's Son. Beneath this the voices of the people—the altos, tenors, and basses—scurry in rapid counterpoint, excited by the call to meet their savior. Lowest of all is the bass of the *basso continuo.* It plods along, sometimes in a dotted pattern, sometimes in rapid eighth notes, but mostly in regularly recurring quarter notes falling on the beat. In sum, the opening movement of *Awake, a Voice Is Calling* is the musical equivalent of a great religious painting in which the canvas is energized by several superimposed levels of activity (see Fig. 7–6). The enormous complexity of a movement such as this shows why musicians, then and now, view Bach as the greatest contrapuntalist who ever lived.

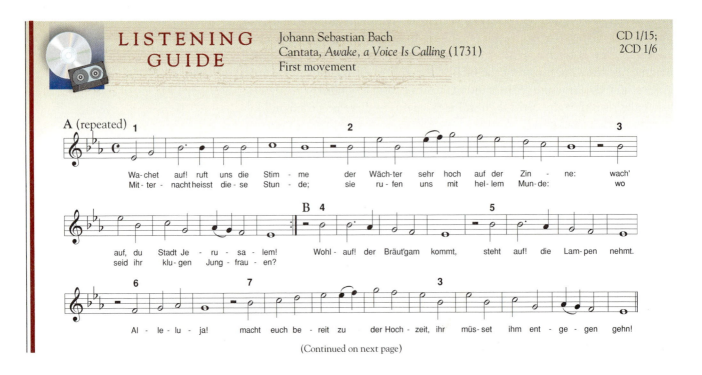

LISTENING GUIDE

Johann Sebastian Bach
Cantata, *Awake, a Voice Is Calling* (1731)
First movement

CD 1/15;
2CD 1/6

(Continued on next page)

A section of chorale tune

0:00   Ritornello parts   **a**

0:08   **b**

0:16   **c**

(Chorale phrases sung by sopranos accompanied by a horn, the instrument of the watchmen)

0:33	Chorale phrase 1	Wachet auf, ruft uns die Stimme	Awake, a voice is calling
0:52	Ritornello part **a**		
0:58	Chorale phrase 2	Der Wächter sehr hoch auf der Zinne	From the watchmen from high in the tower
1:17	Ritornello part **b**		
1:28	Chorale phrase 3	Wach auf, du Stadt Jerusalem!	Awake, Jerusalem!

* *

Repeat of **A** section of chorale tune (0:00–1:49) with new text as required by repeat in chorale tune

1:50	Ritornello parts **a, b,** and **c**		
2:22	Chorale phrase 1	Mitternacht heisst diese Stunde	Midnight is the hour
2:41	Ritornello part **a**		
2:48	Chorale phrase 2	Sie rufen uns mit hellem Munde	They call us with a clarion voice
3:07	Ritornello part **b**		
3:18	Chorale phrase 3	Wo seid ihr klugen Jungfrauen?	Where are the Wise Virgins?

* *

B section of chorale tune

3:40	Variation of ritornello parts **a, b,** and **c** leads to new keys		
4:05	Chorale phrase 4	Wohl auf, der Bräutgam kommt	Get up, the Bridegroom comes
4:19	Ritornello part **a**		
4:27	Chorale phrase 5	Steht auf, die Lampen nehmt	Stand up and take your lamps
4:44	Altos, tenors, and basses enjoy extended imitative fantasy on "Alleluja"		
5:18	Chorale phrase 6	Alleluja	Alleluia
5:30	Ritornello part **a**		
5:40	Chorale phrase 7 begins	Macht euch bereit	Prepare yourselves
5:50	Ritornello part **a**		
5:57	Chorale phrase 7 ends	Zu der Hochzeit	For the wedding
6:11	Ritornello part **b**		
6:17	Chorale phrase 3	Ihr müsset ihm entgegen gehn!	You must go forth to meet him!
6:38	Ritornello parts **a, b,** and **c**		

(Listening Exercise 16)

Movement 2. Recitative in which the Evangelist (the narrator) invites the daughters of Zion to the wedding feast; no use of chorale tune. In Bach's religious vocal music the Evangelist is invariably sung by a tenor.

Movement 3. Aria (duet) between the Soul (soprano) and Jesus (bass); no use of chorale tune. It is traditional in German sacred music of the Baroque era to assign the role of Christ to a bass.

Christ is a bass

Movement 4. For this meeting of Christ and the daughters of Zion (true believers), Bach fashioned one of his loveliest creations. Again the chorale tune serves as a unifying force, now carrying stanza two of the text. Once more Bach constructs a musical tapestry for chorus and orchestra, but a less complex one than the first movement. Here we hear only two central motifs: the chorale melody sung by all the tenors—they are the watchmen calling Jerusalem (Leipzig) to awake; and the exquisitely beautiful, lilting melody played by all violins and violas in unison—their togetherness symbolizes the unifying love of Christ for His people. This unison line is a perfect example of a lengthy, ever-expanding Baroque melody and one of the most memorable of the entire era. Beneath it we hear the measured tread of the ever-present *basso continuo*, here again playing regularly recurring quarter notes on the beat. A bass that moves at a moderate, steady pace, mostly in equal note values and often stepwise up or down the scale, is called a **walking bass.** The walking bass in this movement enhances the meaning of the text, underscoring the steady approach of the Lord.

walking bass

LISTENING GUIDE

Johann Sebastian Bach
Awake, a Voice Is Calling
Fourth movement

6CD 1/16

0:00   Violins and violas play flowing melody above walking bass
(Chorale phrases sung by the tenors)

0:43	Chorale phrases 1, 2, and 3	Zion hört die Wächter singen,	Zion hears the watchmen singing
		Das Herz tut ihr vor Freuden springen,	Her heart fills with joy
		Sie wachet und steht eilend auf.	She awakes and quickly rises.
1:12	Flowing string melody repeated		
1:55	Chorale phrases 1, 2, and 3 repeated	Ihr Freund kommt vom Himmel prächtig,	Her splendid friend arrives from Heaven
		Von Gnaden stark, von Wahrheit mächtig,	Mighty in grace, strong in truth
2:24	Flowing string melody repeated	Ihr Licht wird hell, ihr Stern geht auf.	Her light grows bright, her star arises.
2:51	Chorale phrases 4, 5, and 6	Nun komm, du werte Kron,	Now come, you worthy crown
		Herr Jesu, Gottes Sohn!	Lord, Jesus, Son of God
		Hosanna!	Hosanna!
3:09	String melody continues in minor		
3:33	Chorale phrases 7 and 3	Wir folgen all	We will follow all
		Zum Freudensaal	to the banquet hall
		Und halten mit das Abendmahl.	And share in the Lord's supper.
4:00	String melody concludes movement		

Movement 5. Recitative for Christ (bass); no use of chorale tune. Christ invites the anguished Soul to find comfort in Him.

Movement 6. Aria (duet) for bass and soprano; no use of chorale tune. This is a strict *da capo* aria (see page 142) in which Christ and the Soul sing of their mutual love.

Movement 7. Bach's cantatas usually end with a simple four-voice homophonic setting of the last stanza of the chorale. He always places the chorale tune in the soprano part, harmonizing and supporting it with the other three voices below. The instruments of the orchestra have no line of their own and merely double the four vocal parts. But more important, the members of the congregation join in the singing of the chorale melody. At that moment all of the spiritual energy of Leipzig was concentrated into this one emphatic declaration of belief. The coming Christ reveals to all believers a vision of life in the celestial kingdom.

LISTENING GUIDE

Johann Sebastian Bach
Awake, a Voice Is Calling
Seventh and last movement

CD 1/17

Time	German	English
0:00	Gloria sei dir gesungen (phrase 1) Mit Menschen und englischen Zungen (phrase 2) Mit Harfen und mit Zimbeln schon. (phrase 3)	May Glory be sung to you With the tongues of man and the angels And harps and cymbals too.
0:38	Von zwölf Perlen sind die Pforten, (phrase 1) An deiner Stadt, wir sind Konsorten (phrase 2) Der Engel hoch um deiner Thron. (phrase 3)	The gates are of twelve pearls, In your city we are consorts Of the angels high above your throne.
1:16	Kein Aug hat je gespürt, (phrase 4) Kein Ohr hat je gehört (phrase 5) Solche Freude. (phrase 6) Des sind wir froh, (phrase 7) Io, io! Ewig in dulci jubilo. (phrase 3)	No eye has ever seen, No ear has ever heard Such joy. Let us therefore rejoice, Io, io! Eternally in sweet jubilation.

Bach's Orchestral Music

In 1729 Bach became director of the Collegium Musicum of Leipzig, in addition to being cantor of St. Thomas's Church. The Collegium was an organization of university students and town musicians who voluntarily came together to give weekly concerts in a local coffeehouse (one run by a certain Gottfried Zimmerman), where the patrons sipped beer and puffed long pipes (Fig. 7–7). By means of such societies, middle-class musical culture flourished in the eighteenth century. (The Collegium has persisted in European and American universities down to the present day, though now it exists mainly to promote "early music"—the music of Bach's time and before.) Bach's association with the Collegium of Leipzig gave him the opportunity to perform secular music, most of it instrumental. Over a period of twenty-five years, from about 1705 until 1730, Bach had written an impressive array of instrumental music that the Collegium might now perform: four suites (see page 137), more than a dozen solo concertos (some of which were arrangements of works by other composers), and six concertos of the concerto grosso type. This latter set has come to be called the Brandenburg Concertos.

❀ FIGURE 7–7

An orchestra and a small chorus perform in a German coffeehouse in the mid-eighteenth century. The *basso continuo* (foreground) is comprised of harpsichord, cello, and bassoon.

THE BRANDENBURG CONCERTOS (1715–1721)

Early in his career, in 1721, Bach gathered together a half dozen of his best concertos and sent them to Margrave Christian Ludwig of Brandenburg, whose court was in the Prussian capital of Berlin. Undoubtedly, Bach was angling (unsuccessfully) for a job in the politically more important city of Berlin, and hoped that this display of skillful writing in the genre of concerto grosso would impress *the concerto grosso* his prospective employer. The concerto grosso, as we have seen (page 113), is a three-movement work involving a musical give-and-take between a full orchestra (tutti) and a much smaller group of soloists (concertino), consisting usually of just two or three violins and continuo. In the first movement, the tutti normally plays a recurring musical theme, called the ritornello. The soloists in the concertino play along with the tutti; but when the ritornello stops, they go on to present their own musical material in a flashy, sometimes dazzling show of technical skill. Each of the six Brandenburg Concertos calls for a different group of soloists in the concertino. Taken in sum, these works constitute an anthology of nearly all instrumental combinations known to the Baroque era.

Bach's aim in the Brandenburg Concertos was to show his ability to write challenging music for any and all instruments. A listener cannot fail to be impressed by the brilliant writing for the harpsichord in Concerto No. 5, for example. Here the full orchestra (tutti) is pitted against a concertino consisting of solo violin, flute, and, most important, harpsichord. In principle, the tutti plays the ritornello, and the soloists play motives derived from it. In practice, how-*ritornello form* ever, the separation between ritornello and concertino is not as distinct with Bach as it had been in the earlier concertos of Vivaldi (see page 115). In Bach's more refined treatment of ritornello form, the line between the large (loud) ensemble and the small (soft) group of soloists is less obvious. Notice here that Bach's ritornello (see Listening Guide) possesses many characteristics of Baroque melody: It is idiomatic to the violin (having many repeated notes); it is lengthy and somewhat asymmetrical (spinning out over many measures); and it possesses a driving rhythm that propels the music forward. While the sound of the violins dominates the ritornello, soon the solo harpsichord takes center stage. In fact, this work might fairly be called the first harpsichord concerto: In earlier concertos the harpsichord had appeared only as part of the *basso continuo**, not as a solo instrument. Toward the end of the movement all other instruments fall silent, leaving the harpsichord to sound alone in a lengthy section full of brilliant scales and arpeggios. Such a showy passage for soloist alone toward the end of a movement in a concerto is called a **cadenza.** One can easily imagine the great virtuoso Bach, seated at the harpsichord, dazzling patron and fellow performer alike with this bravura music.

cadenza

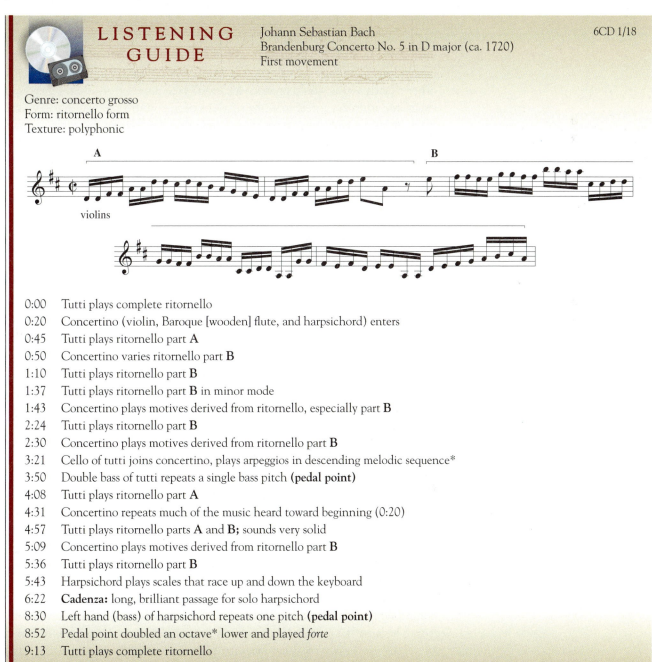

LISTENING GUIDE

Johann Sebastian Bach
Brandenburg Concerto No. 5 in D major (ca. 1720)
First movement

6CD 1/18

Genre: concerto grosso
Form: ritornello form
Texture: polyphonic

violins

0:00	Tutti plays complete ritornello
0:20	Concertino (violin, Baroque [wooden] flute, and harpsichord) enters
0:45	Tutti plays ritornello part **A**
0:50	Concertino varies ritornello part **B**
1:10	Tutti plays ritornello part **B**
1:37	Tutti plays ritornello part **B** in minor mode
1:43	Concertino plays motives derived from ritornello, especially part **B**
2:24	Tutti plays ritornello part **B**
2:30	Concertino plays motives derived from ritornello part **B**
3:21	Cello of tutti joins concertino, plays arpeggios in descending melodic sequence*
3:50	Double bass of tutti repeats a single bass pitch (**pedal point**)
4:08	Tutti plays ritornello part **A**
4:31	Concertino repeats much of the music heard toward beginning (0:20)
4:57	Tutti plays ritornello parts **A** and **B;** sounds very solid
5:09	Concertino plays motives derived from ritornello part **B**
5:36	Tutti plays ritornello part **B**
5:43	Harpsichord plays scales that race up and down the keyboard
6:22	**Cadenza:** long, brilliant passage for solo harpsichord
8:30	Left hand (bass) of harpsichord repeats one pitch (**pedal point**)
8:52	Pedal point doubled an octave* lower and played *forte*
9:13	Tutti plays complete ritornello

The fingers of the harpsichordist get a much-deserved rest in the slow-moving second movement of Brandenburg Concerto No. 5. Now an elegiac mood envelops the music as the violin and flute engage in a quiet dialogue. The fast finale is dominated by fugal writing, a style in which Bach excelled above all other composers.

Fugue

Bach was the master of counterpoint, and it is his love of contrapuntal writing that gives his music unparalleled substance and complexity. A fugue is a contrapuntal form and procedure that flourished during the late Baroque era. The word "fugue" itself comes from the Latin *fuga*, meaning "flight." Within a fugue one voice presents a theme and then "flies away" as another voice enters with the same theme. The theme in a fugue is called the **subject.** At the outset each voice presents the subject in turn, and this successive presentation is called the **exposition** of the fugue. As the voices enter, they do not imitate or pursue each other exactly—this would produce a canon* (see page 49). Rather, passages of exact imitation are interrupted by sections of free writing in which the voices more or less go their own ways. These freer sections, where the subject is not heard in its entirety, are called **episodes.** Episodes and further presentations of the subject alternate throughout the remainder of the fugue.

subject, exposition, episode

Fugues have been written for two to as many as thirty-two voices, but usually the norm is three, four, or five. These may be actual voices in a chorus or choir, or they may be simply lines or parts played by a group of instruments, or even by a solo instrument like the piano, organ, or guitar, which has the capacity to play several "voices" simultaneously. Thus, a formal definition of a **fugue** might be as follows: a composition for three, four, or five parts played or sung by voices or instruments, which begins with a presentation of a subject in imitation in each part (exposition), continues with modulating passages of free counterpoint (episodes) and further appearances of the subject, and ends with a strong affirmation of the tonic key. Fortunately, the fugue is easier to hear than to describe: The unfolding and recurrence of one subject makes it easy to follow.

ORGAN FUGUE IN G MINOR (CA. 1710)

Bach has left us nearly one hundred keyboard fugues, about a third of these for organ. The organ was Bach's favorite instrument, and in his day he was known more as a performer and improviser on it than as a composer. Bach's G minor organ fugue was composed rather early in his career, sometime between 1708 and 1717. It is written for four voices, which we will refer to as soprano, alto, tenor, and bass, and it begins with the subject appearing first in the soprano:

EXAMPLE 7–3

As fugue subjects go, this is a rather long one, but it is typical of the way Baroque composers liked to "spin out" their melodies. It sounds very solid in tonality. That's because the subject is built clearly around the notes of the G minor triad (G, B♭, D), not only in the first measure but on the strong beats of the final measures as well. The subject also conveys a sense of gathering momentum. It starts moderately with quarter notes, and then seems to gain speed as eighth notes and finally sixteenth notes are introduced. This, too, is typical of fugue subjects. After the soprano gives forth the subject, it is then presented, in turn, by the alto, the tenor, and the bass. The voices need not appear in any particular order; here Bach just decided to have them enter in succession from top to bottom.

Once Bach has each voice present the subject and join the polyphonic complex, his exposition is at an end. Now a short passage of free counterpoint follows—the first episode—which makes use of just bits and pieces of the subject. Then the subject returns, but in a highly unusual way: It begins in the tenor, but continues and ends in the soprano (see [†] in the following Listening Guide). Thereafter, Bach's G minor fugue unfolds in the usual alternation of episodes and statements of the subject. The episodes sound unsettled and convey a sense of movement. They modulate from one key to another. The subject, on the other hand, doesn't modulate. It is *in* a key, here the tonic, G minor, or the dominant, D minor, or some other closely related key. This tension between unsettled music (the episode) and stationary music (the subject) is what creates the exciting, dynamic quality of the fugue. Ultimately, Bach modulates back to the tonic key, G minor, for one final statement of the subject in the bass, and the fugue is ended. Note that, although this fugue is in a minor key, Bach puts the final chord in major. This is common in Baroque music, composers preferring the brighter, perhaps more conclusive, sound of major in the final chord.

To hear this and other fugues, then, the listener is encouraged to proceed in the following manner: Follow the unfolding of the subject as it appears in rapid succession in each voice in the exposition; identify the episodic material as distinct from the subject (sense that the subject is no longer present and that the music is changing key); listen for the subsequent alternation between episodes and further appearances of the subject, and, finally, recognize that the home key has been reached when the subject enters in strong fashion for the last time.

FIGURE 7–8
The organ presently in the choir loft of St. Thomas's Church, Leipzig. It was from this loft that Bach played and conducted.

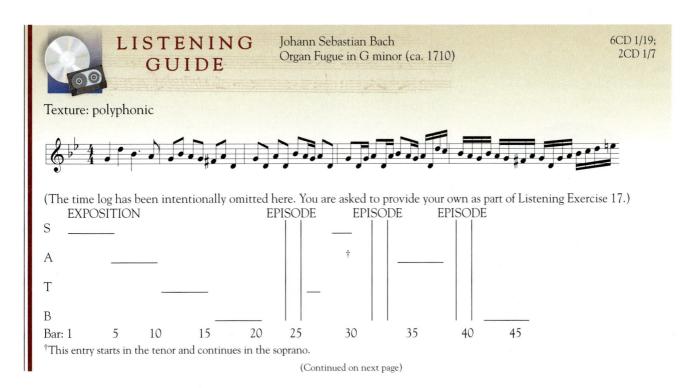

LISTENING GUIDE

Johann Sebastian Bach
Organ Fugue in G minor (ca. 1710)

6CD 1/19;
2CD 1/7

Texture: polyphonic

(The time log has been intentionally omitted here. You are asked to provide your own as part of Listening Exercise 17.)

†This entry starts in the tenor and continues in the soprano.

(Continued on next page)

Bar: 50   55   60   65
(Listening Exercise 17)

The Well-Tempered Clavier

Bach thought in fugue and fugal counterpoint. Perhaps the best-known of all collections is his *The Well-Tempered Clavier* (1720–1742), "clavier" simply being Bach's word for keyboard. It consists of two sets of twenty-four preludes and fugues. The **prelude** is a short preparatory piece that sets a mood and serves as a technical warm-up for the player before the fugue. In both sets of twenty-four there is one prelude and fugue in each of the major and minor keys: the first pair in C major, the next in C minor, the next in C♯ major, then C♯ minor, and so on. Through this arrangement Bach showed that it was possible to write a piece—in this case a prelude and fugue—in every key, something that had not been done in a systematic fashion up to that time.

Toward the end of his life Bach composed the *Art of Fugue* (1742–1750), an encyclopedic treatment of all known contrapuntal procedures set forth in nineteen canons and fugues. The final fugue, one in which Bach combines four related subjects, was broken off by his death in 1750. The *Art of Fugue* was thus Bach's valedictory statement of a musical form he brought to supreme mastery. It remains a fitting testimony to this composer's stylistic integrity, grand design, and superhuman craftsmanship.

❀ FIGURE 7–9
Portrait of George Frideric Handel painted by Balthasar Denner ca. 1727.

✿ GEORGE FRIDERIC HANDEL (1685–1759)

The careers of Bach and Handel could hardly have been more different. While Bach spent his life confined to towns in central Germany, his cosmopolitan countryman Handel traveled the world—from Rome, to Venice, to Hamburg, to Amsterdam, to London, to Dublin. If Bach was most at home conducting chorale cantatas and playing organ fugues from the church choir loft, Handel was a man of the public theater, a denizen of the orchestra pit, by training and temperament a composer of opera. And if Bach fell into virtual obscurity at the end of his life, retreating into a world of esoteric counterpoint, Handel's stature only grew larger on the international stage. He became the most famous composer in Europe and a treasured national institution in England.

George Frideric Handel (as he styled himself after becoming a naturalized English citizen) was born in the town of Halle, Germany, in 1685, and died in London in 1759. Although his father had decreed a program of study in law, the young Handel managed to cultivate his intense interest in music, sometimes secretly by candlelight. At the age of eighteen he got his first taste of opera in the city of Hamburg, where he had gone to take a job as violinist in the public opera theater. But since the musical world around 1700 was dominated by things Italian, he, too, set off for Italy to learn his trade and broaden his horizons. He

moved between Florence and Venice, for which cities he wrote operas, and Rome, where he composed mainly secular cantatas. In 1710 Handel returned to North Germany to accept the post of chapel master to the elector of Hanover, but on the condition that he be given an immediate leave of absence to visit London. Although he made one additional voyage back to his employer in Hanover in 1711 and many subsequent visits to the Continent, Handel conveniently forgot about his obligation to the Hanoverian court. London became the site of his musical activity and the place where he won fame and fortune.

After four years in Italy, London must have seemed a cultural backwater to Handel. Many of the streets were unpaved, the buildings were black with the soot of coal fires, and there was none of the art and architecture that graced Venice, Florence, or Rome. But there was opportunity. Handel soon found employment in the homes of the aristocracy and became the music tutor to the English royal family. As fate would have it, his continental employer, the elector of Hanover, became King George I of England in 1714, when the Hanoverians acceded to the throne on the extinction of the Stuart line. Fortunately for Handel, the new king bore his truant musician no grudge, and he was called on frequently to compose festival music to entertain the court or mark its progress. For these events Handel produced such works as *Water Music* (1717), *Music for the Royal Fireworks* (1749), and *Coronation Service* (1727), parts of which have been used at the coronation of every English monarch since its first hearing.

FIGURE 7–10
The Prince of Wales (the future King George III) and his sisters, painted in 1733 by Philip Mercier. The Prince plays the cello and Princess Anne the harpsichord. Handel was the music tutor to the English royal family.

Handel and the Orchestral Dance Suite

WATER MUSIC (1717)

Aside from *Messiah*, Handel's most beloved composition is his *Water Music*. Handel's *Water Music* belongs to a genre of composition called a dance suite, a term derived from the French word *suite* (a succession of pieces). The **dance suite** is a collection of dances, usually varying from four to seven, all in one key and for one group of instruments, be it full orchestra, trio, or solo. *Water Music*, in fact, is a collection of three suites for orchestra that were performed one after the other. The listeners did not dance the music of Handel's suites. These were stylized, abstract dances. But it was the job of the composer to bring each one to life, to make it recognizable to the audience by incorporating the salient elements of rhythm and style of each particular dance.

the dance suite

Most Baroque dance suites begin with an overture, usually a **French overture,** so called because this style of overture was first created at the French royal court by Jean Baptiste Lully (1632–1687), the favored composer of King Louis XIV. (The French overture consists of two sections, the first slow, in duple meter, with dotted rhythms, and the second fast and light with imitative counterpoint.) After the overture comes the succession of dances. Among the dances that Handel popularized in his orchestral suites are the following.

Allemande: A stately dance in $\frac{4}{4}$ meter with gracefully interweaving lines.

Courante: A lively dance in $\frac{6}{4}$ with a pickup* and frequent changes of metrical accent.

Saraband: A slow, elegant dance in $\frac{3}{4}$ with a strong accent on the second beat.

Minuet: A moderate dance in $\frac{3}{4}$ usually followed by another, shorter dance in the same style called the trio (see page 165).

FIGURE 7–11

This view of London and the Thames River by Canaletto (1697–1768) captures vividly the setting for Handel's *Water Music*.

Hornpipe: An energetic dance, derived from the country jig, in either $\frac{3}{2}$ or $\frac{2}{4}$ time.

Gigue: A fast dance in $\frac{6}{8}$ or $\frac{12}{8}$ with a constant eighth-note pulse that produces a galloplike effect.

But no matter what the rhythm or style of the dance, the form of each dance movement in the Baroque era was invariably the same: binary form* (see page 54). Binary form, of course, is a musical form with only two sections, **A** and **B,** each of which may be repeated. Normally **A** takes the movement from tonic to dominant, while **B** brings it back home to the tonic. Some dance movements are followed by a second, complementary dance, as the minuet is followed by a trio. In such cases the first dance should be repeated after the second.

Water Music

Handel composed his *Water Music* during the summer of 1717 to please his patron, King George I, who was trying, in turn, to please his subjects. The German-born George I, the first of those stalwart Hanoverian monarchs who have sat on the throne of Great Britain up to the present day, was not universally loved. He refused to speak a word of English, preferring his native German. He fought with his son, the Prince of Wales, and banned him from court. His subjects thought the king dimwitted, "an honest blockhead," as one contemporary said.

To counter the growing unpopularity of the royal family, the king's ministers urged a program of public entertainments, including an evening of diversion on the River Thames for the lords of Parliament and the lesser people of London. Thus on July 17, 1717, the King and his court left London, accompanied by a small navy of boats, and progressed up the Thames to the strains of Handel's orchestral music. An eyewitness describes this nautical parade in detail:

About eight in the evening the King repaired to his barge, into which were ad-mitted the Duchess of Bolton, Countess Godolphin, Madam de Kilmansech, Mrs. Were and the Earl of Orkney, the Gentleman of the Bedchamber in Waiting. Next to the King's barge was that of the musicians, about 50 in number, who played on all kinds of instruments, to wit trumpets, horns, hautboys [oboes], bassoons, German flutes, French flutes [recorders], violins and basses; but there were no singers. The music had been composed specially by the famous Handel, a native of Halle [Germany], and His Majesty's principal Court Composer. His Majesty so greatly approved of the music that he caused it to be repeated three times in all, although each performance lasted an hour—namely twice before and once after supper. The evening weather was all that could be desired for the festivity, the number of barges and above all of boats filled with people desirous of hearing the music was beyond counting.

Water Music heard on the River Thames

So broad are Handel's musical gestures and so brilliant his orchestral effects that even the "blockhead" king was enchanted by the fifty musicians playing *Water Music* on the neighboring barge. What makes the dance movements of *Water Music* so easy to comprehend is their formal clarity. Notice in the Minuet how Handel asks the French horns and trumpets first to announce both the **A** and **B** sections before passing this material on to the woodwinds and then to the full orchestra.

LISTENING GUIDE

George Frideric Handel
Water Music (1717)
Minuet and Trio

Intro CD/19

Genre: dance suite
Form: ternary

Minuet (triple meter, major key)
0:00   French horns introduce part **A**

0:12   Trumpets introduct part **B**

0:29   Winds and continuo play **A**
0:42   Full orchestra repeats **A**
0:55   Winds and continuo play **B**
1:08   Full orchestra repeats **B**

Trio (triple meter, minor key)
1:28   Strings and continuo play part **C**
1:43   Strings and continuo play part **D**

Minuet
2:19   Full orchestra plays **A**
2:31   Full orchestra plays **B**

The jaunty triple-meter Hornpipe is very brief, the complete dance requiring only forty seconds. For such a short piece to have an effect, Handel directed that it be played three times, first by strings and continuo, then by woodwinds

and continuo, and finally by both strings and woodwinds together, along with continuo. The Minuet and the Hornpipe are just two of the twenty dances that make up Handel's *Water Music*.

LISTENING GUIDE

George Frideric Handel
Water Music
Hornpipe

Intro CD/18

Genre: dance suite
Form: binary
(triple meter, major key)

0:00   Strings and continuo play part **A**

0:18   Sudden *piano* signals beginning of part **B**

(Hornpipe is repeated with new orchestration)
0:41   Woodwinds, drum, and continuo play part **A**
0:58   Woodwinds, drum, and continuo play part **B**

(Hornpipe is repeated with new orchestration)
1:19   Strings, woodwinds, drum, and continuo play part **A**
1:37   Sudden *piano* signals beginning of part **B**

Handel and the Oratorio

Handel moved to London in 1710, not for the chance to entertain the royal family, and certainly not for the climate or cuisine, but for the potentially lucrative opportunity to compose opera. With the rare exception of a work such as Purcell's *Dido and Aeneas* (see page 108), there was no English opera at this time. Instead, spoken plays with occasional musical interludes dominated the London stage. Handel intended to fill this void by importing Italian opera, which was then enormously popular on the Continent. Guaranteed a healthy share of the profits from the operas he produced, Handel rented the theater, composed the music, engaged high-paid soloists from Italy, led the rehearsals, and conducted the finished product from the harpsichord in the orchestral pit. From 1710 until 1728 he had great artistic and some financial success, produc-

Handel as composer of opera seria

ing two dozen examples of Italian **opera seria** (literally, serious, as opposed to comic, opera). Foremost among these was *Giulio Cesare* (*Julius Caesar*; 1724), a recasting of the story of Caesar's conquest of the army of Egypt and its queen, Cleopatra. But opera is seldom a profitable business, and in 1728 the company Handel had founded went bankrupt, a victim of the exorbitant fees paid the star singers and competition from other, upstart operatic companies. Handel continued to write opera into the 1730s, but he increasingly turned his attention to a musical genre similar in construction to opera, oratorio.

An **oratorio** is literally "something sung in an oratory," an oratory being a hall or chapel used specifically for religious devotion as expressed in prayer and music. Thus, the oratorio as it first appeared in seventeenth-century Italy was

an extended musical setting of a sacred text intended for the spiritual edification of the faithful and performed in a special hall or chapel. By the time it reached Handel's hands, however, the oratorio had become in most ways nothing but an opera with a religious subject.

Both Baroque oratorio and opera begin with an overture, are divided into acts, and are composed primarily of recitatives and arias. But there are a few important differences, aside from the obvious fact that oratorio treats a religious subject. Oratorio, being a quasi-religious genre, is performed in a church, a theater, or a concert hall, but makes no use of staging and costumes. Because the subject matter is almost always sacred, there is more of an opportunity for moralizing, a dramatic function best performed by a chorus. Thus the chorus assumes greater importance in an oratorio. It sometimes serves as a narrator, but more often functions, like the chorus in ancient Greek drama, as the voice of the people commenting on the action that has transpired. Add to these the fact that oratorio in England is sung in English (not Italian), and its potential impact on a large segment of English society becomes obvious.

oratorio and opera compared

By the 1730s oratorio appeared to Handel as an attractive alternative to the increasingly unprofitable opera in London. He could do away with the irascible and expensive castrati and prima donnas. He no longer had to pay for elaborate sets and costumes. He could draw on the ancient English love of choral music, a tradition that extended well back into the Middle Ages. And he could exploit a new, untapped market—the faithful of the Puritan, Methodist, and growing evangelical sects in England who had viewed the pleasures of foreign opera with distrust and even contempt.

advantage of oratorio

MESSIAH (1741)

Beginning in 1732 and continuing over a twenty-year period, Handel wrote upward of twenty oratorios. The most famous of these is his *Messiah*, composed in the astonishingly short period of three and a half weeks during the summer of 1741. It was first performed in Dublin, Ireland, the following April as part of a charity benefit, with Handel conducting. Having heard the dress rehearsal, the local press waxed enthusiastic about the new oratorio, saying that it "far surpasses anything of that Nature, which has been performed in this or any other Kingdom." Such a large crowd was expected for the work of the famous Handel that ladies were urged not to wear hoopskirts, and gentlemen admonished to leave their swords at home. In this way could an audience of 700 be squeezed into a hall possessing only 600 seats.

Messiah premiere in Dublin

Buoyed by his artistic and financial success in Dublin, Handel took *Messiah* back to London, made minor alterations, and performed it in Covent Garden Theater. In 1750 he again offered *Messiah*, this time in the chapel of the Foundling Hospital for orphans in London (Fig. 7–12), and again there was much popular acclaim for Handel as well as profit for charity. This was the first time one of his oratorios was sung in a religious setting rather than a theater or a concert hall. The annual repetition of *Messiah* in the Foundling Hospital chapel during Handel's lifetime and long after did much to convince the public that his oratorios were essentially religious music to be performed in church.

early performances of Messiah

In a general way, *Messiah* tells the story of the life of Christ. It is divided into three parts (instead of three acts): (I) the prophecy of His coming and His Incarnation; (II) His Passion and Resurrection, and the triumph of the Gospel; and (III) reflections on the Christian victory over death. In *Messiah* dramatic

🌀 FIGURE 7–12
The chapel of the Foundling Hospital, London, where *Messiah* was performed annually for the benefit of the orphans.

confrontation is replaced by a mood of lyrical meditation and, ultimately, exaltation. The music consists of fifty-three numbers: Nineteen are for chorus, sixteen are solo arias, sixteen are recitatives, and two are purely instrumental pieces.

There are many beautiful and stirring arias in *Messiah*, including "Every valley shall be exalted," "O thou that tellest good tidings to Zion," and "Rejoice greatly, O daughter of Zion." Significantly, "Rejoice greatly, O daughter of Zion" is on the same topic as Bach's cantata, *Awake, a Voice Is Calling* (see page 127): It tells of the joy felt by all true believers, here personified by the daughter of Zion, at the coming of the Messiah.

da capo *aria*

Handel composed "Rejoice greatly, O daughter of Zion" in the form of a modified *da capo* aria. A **da capo aria** has two musical sections, **A** and **B,** with the second usually having a different key and mood. When the singer reaches the end of part **B,** he or she is instructed by the words "da capo" to "take it from the top" and thus repeat **A,** note for note. What results is **ABA,** another example of ternary form* in music. Composers such as Handel and Bach sometimes change **A** when it returns so as to achieve variety. A modified *da capo* aria (**ABA′**) is thus created. When such a modification is effected, it usually allows the soloist to build to a final climax of vocal virtuosity. At the end of "Rejoice greatly, O daughter of Zion," for example, what was a relatively easy passage of simple stepwise motion at the end of **A** is transformed into a more difficult, and dramatic, series of leaps of octaves and sevenths in **A′.**

EXAMPLE 7–4

be- hold, thy   King   cometh   un - to   thee   be- hold, thy King cometh un - to thee, be- hold, thy King

Examples of *da capo* form and modified *da capo* form abound in arias in both oratorio and opera of the late Baroque era. Indeed, the line of distinction between these two Baroque musical genres, between the sacred oratorio and the

profane opera, was a thin one. Although the text of "Rejoice greatly, O daughter of Zion" comes from scripture (Zechariah 9:9–10), the flamboyant style of singing has its origins in the more worldly opera house.

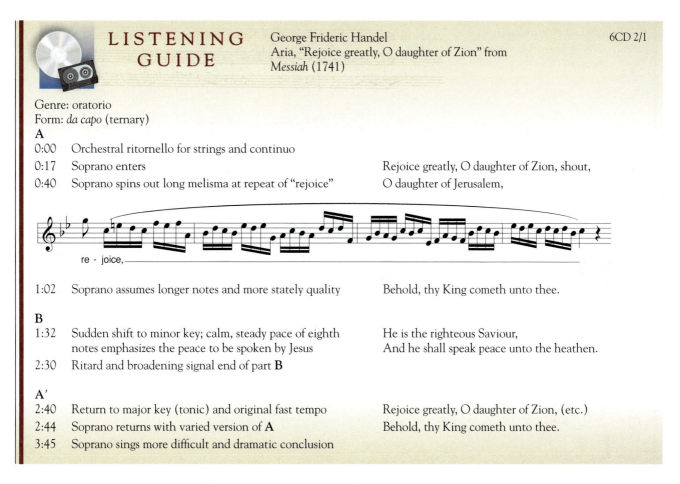

LISTENING GUIDE

George Frideric Handel
Aria, "Rejoice greatly, O daughter of Zion" from
Messiah (1741)

6CD 2/1

Genre: oratorio
Form: *da capo* (ternary)

A

0:00	Orchestral ritornello for strings and continuo	
0:17	Soprano enters	Rejoice greatly, O daughter of Zion, shout,
0:40	Soprano spins out long melisma at repeat of "rejoice"	O daughter of Jerusalem,

re - joice,

1:02	Soprano assumes longer notes and more stately quality	Behold, thy King cometh unto thee.

B

1:32	Sudden shift to minor key; calm, steady pace of eighth notes emphasizes the peace to be spoken by Jesus	He is the righteous Saviour, And he shall speak peace unto the heathen.
2:30	Ritard and broadening signal end of part **B**	

A′

2:40	Return to major key (tonic) and original fast tempo	Rejoice greatly, O daughter of Zion, (etc.)
2:44	Soprano returns with varied version of **A**	Behold, thy King cometh unto thee.
3:45	Soprano sings more difficult and dramatic conclusion	

Despite the bravura quality of the arias, the true glory of *Messiah* is to be found in its choruses. Handel was arguably the finest composer for chorus who ever lived. As a world traveler with an unsurpassed ear, he had absorbed the German tradition of the fugue and the Lutheran chorale; he knew the Venetian polychoral style of Gabrieli (see page 101) and the powerful English church anthems* (extended motets) of Henry Purcell; and, of course, he had a flair for the dramatic, gained from a lifetime in the theater.

Handel's choruses

Nowhere is Handel's choral mastery more evident than in the justly famous "Hallelujah" chorus that concludes Part II of *Messiah*. Here a variety of choral styles are displayed in quick succession: chordal, unison, chorale, fugal, and fugal and chordal together. The opening word "Hallelujah" recurs throughout as a powerful refrain, yet each new phrase of text generates its own distinct musical idea. The vivid phrases speak directly to the listener, making the audience feel like a participant in the drama. So moved was King George II when he first heard the great opening chords, as the story goes, that he rose to his feet in admiration, thereby establishing the tradition of the audience standing for the "Hallelujah" chorus—for no one sat while the king stood. Indeed, this movement would serve well as a royal coronation march, though in *Messiah*, of course, it is Christ the King who is being crowned.

"Hallelujah" chorus

LISTENING GUIDE

George Frideric Handel
"Hallelujah" chorus from *Messiah* (1741)

Intro CD/14

0:00   Brief string introduction

0:06   Chorus enters with two salient motives:

0:16   Five more chordal exclamations of the "Hallelujah" motive, but at a higher pitch level

0:25   Chorus sings new theme in unison answered by chordal cries of "Hallelujah"

0:35   Music repeated but at a lower pitch

0:47   Fuguelike imitation begins with subject   "For the Lord God omnipotent reigneth"

1:13   Quiet and then loud; set in chorale style   "The kingdom of this world is become the Kingdom of our Lord . . ."

1:31   New fuguelike section begins with entry in bass

1:53   Altos and then sopranos begin long ascent in long notes   "King of Kings and Lord of Lords"

2:33   Basses and sopranos reenter with   "And he shall reign for ever and ever"

2:44   Tenors and basses sing in long notes   "King of Kings and Lord of Lords"

3:00   Incessant major tonic chord   "King of Kings"

3:26   Broad final cadence   "Hallelujah"

(Listening Exercise 18)

The "Hallelujah" chorus is a strikingly effective work mainly because the large choral force creates a sense of heavenly power and strength. In fact, however, Handel's chorus for the original Dublin *Messiah* was much smaller than those used today. It included no more than five singers on the alto, tenor, and bass parts and eight choirboys singing the soprano. The orchestra was equally slight. For the Foundling Hospital performances of the 1750s, however, the orchestra grew to thirty-five players. Then, in the course of the next hundred years, the chorus progressively swelled to as many as four thousand with a balancing orchestra of five hundred in what were billed as "Festivals of the People" in honor of Handel (Fig. 7–13).

Handel's fame grows   And just as there was a continual increase in the performing forces for his *Messiah*, so too Handel's fortune and reputation grew. Toward the end of his life he owned a squire's house in the center of London, bought paintings, including a large and "indeed excellent" Rembrandt, and, on his death, left an enormous estate of nearly twenty thousand pounds, as the newspapers of the day were quick to report. More than three thousand persons attended his funeral in Westminster Abbey on April 20, 1759, and a sculpture of the composer holding an aria from *Messiah* was erected above his grave and is still visible today (Fig. 7–14). As a memento of Handel's music, *Messiah* was an apt choice, for it is still performed each year at Christmas by countless amateur and professional groups throughout the world.

LISTENING EXERCISES

16   Johann Sebastian Bach   6CD 1/15; 2CD 1/6
        Cantata, *Awake, a Voice Is Calling* (1731)
        First movement

The purpose of this listening exercise is to have you learn to recognize a chorale tune and to differentiate it from the surrounding musical texture. First, read through the questions. Then listen to the entire first movement, following the Listening Guide on page 129. This will give you an overall sense of the relationship of the chorale to the other voices and to the instruments. If some of these questions seem complex, so is Bach's writing in this impressive choral fantasy!

1. Throughout the course of this movement, does the soprano part do anything other than sing the chorale tune in long note values? _____ If so, what? _____

2. Which part is moving the fastest in this complex musical texture?
   a. the bass line played by cellos and double basses
   b. the soprano part with the chorale tune
   c. violins

3. Which part is moving the slowest in this texture?

🌿 FIGURE 7–13 AND 7–14
(left) An enormous orchestra, and even larger chorus, performing an oratorio of Handel's at the Great Handel Festival, London, 1859. (right) Handel's funeral monument at Westminster Abbey. The composer holds the aria "I know that my Redeemer liveth" from *Messiah*.

a. the bass line played by cellos and double basses

b. the soprano part with the chorale tune

c. violins

4. (0:33–0:51) The sopranos enter with the first phrase of the chorale melody. Do the other voices (altos, tenors, and basses) enter before or after them? _____

5. (0:33–0:51) While the sopranos sing on high, what are the cellos and double basses playing?
   a. slow equal notes
   b. fast running notes
   c. notes of varying durations

6. (0:58–1:16) The second phrase of the chorale tune now is heard in the soprano part while the lower voices enter in ascending lines of counterpoint against it. What do the cellos and double basses do at 1:08 in response to this rising counterpoint?
   a. They continue with the dotted note pattern.
   b. They continue with the slow equal notes.
   c. They join in the counterpoint, rising rapidly, as had the voices.

7. (1:28–1:49) Here the sopranos sing the third phrase of the chorale. Do the other voices, which have been singing counterpoint against the sopranos, disappear in this section? _____

8. (1:50–3:39) Now the previous music (0:00–1:49) is repeated with new text. Are the roles of the various parts still the same in the repeat? (Do sopranos still carry the chorale; altos, tenors, and basses provide a counterpoint; violins play a ritornello; and cellos and basses set a harmonic foundation?) _____

9. (4:44–5:27) Here on the word "Allelujah" the altos, tenors, and then basses enter joyfully and in succession. What musical texture do they create?
   a. imitative polyphony
   b. nonimitative polyphony
   c. chordal homophony

10. Now go on to listen to the opening (0:00–0:47) of the famous "Hallelujah" chorus of Handel's *Messiah* (Intro CD/14). In what ways is Handel's writing for chorus different from Bach's as exhibited in this first movement of his cantata? Specifically, circle each of the following statements that is correct.
    a. Handel has the voices, not the instruments, begin his piece.
    b. Handel makes no use of a chorale tune in long notes in the soprano.
    c. Handel has no instrumental ritornello that is different in mood and style from the choral parts.
    d. Handel has his chorus sing the first word, "Hallelujah," in clear, chordal homophony.

 Johann Sebastian Bach   6CD 2/19; 2CD 1/7
Organ Fugue in G minor (ca. 1710)

The following diagram is essentially the same as that found on page 135. It charts the flow of the music as Bach's Organ Fugue in G minor unfolds from the straightforward exposition, through the increasingly lengthy episodes, to the final statement of the subject in the bass. For this exercise, you are asked to make your own time log, or listening guide, for the nine entries of the subject. Above the blank line that shows each subject entry (_____), write in the time at which the subject appears. The first, of course, will be "S0:00." You don't have to indicate times during the episodes, but see if you can sense that modulations are occurring.

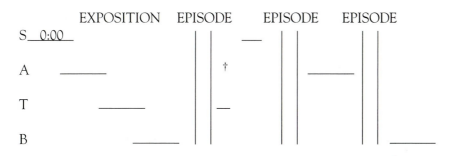

†This entry starts in the tenor and continues in the soprano.

9. How many musical instruments are performing this fugue? _____
10. Does Bach's Fugue in G Minor end on a major chord or a minor one? _____

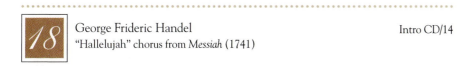

18   George Frideric Handel   Intro CD/14
      "Hallelujah" chorus from *Messiah* (1741)

1. How many musical lines are prominent during the instrumental introduction?
    a. one: basses (cellos and double basses)
    b. two: violins and basses (cellos and double basses)
    c. three: oboes, violins, and basses (cellos and double basses)
2. In what kind of musical texture do the voices sing when they enter with "Hallelujah"?
    a. homophony   b. polyphony   c. monophony
3. (0:25–0:31; "For the Lord God omnipotent reigneth") As the chorus sings in unison, do the violins double (play the same line as) the voices?

    _____
4. Unison singing and playing creates what kind of texture?

    _____
5. (0:47–1:12; "For the Lord God omnipotent reigneth") Now we have a passage of imitative, fuguelike writing in which a subject is presented in succession in the voices. In what order do the voices enter with this subject?
    a. soprano, male voices, alto

    b. soprano, alto, male voices

    c. alto, male voices, soprano

6. (1:32–1:52; "And he shall reign for ever and ever") Again, Handel offers another passage of fugal writing, with a new subject. In what order do the voices enter?

    a. bass, tenor, soprano, alto

    b. bass, tenor, alto, soprano

    c. bass, soprano, alto, tenor

    d. bass, alto, tenor, soprano

7. (2:06–2:30) What are the sopranos doing here?

    a. rising by leap

    b. rising by step

    c. rising in an arpeggio

8. (beginning at 2:52) Which brass instrument reinforces and ornaments the soprano line from here to the end? _____

9. (3:22–3:24) In a brilliant stroke Handel sets off and highlights the final statement of "Hallelujah" (and the final cadence) in which of the following ways?

    a. precedes it by a "pregnant pause," a long rest

    b. anticipates the "Hallelujah" with an entry in the bass

10. What is it that creates the drama and grandeur in this choral movement?

    a. the skillful use of a variety of textures and styles

    b. a very clear setting of the English text (music reflecting the natural stresses in the words)

    c. the concentration of all voices and instruments on a few, simple musical gestures

    d. all of the above

KEY WORDS

Art of Fugue	exposition	prelude
cadenza	figured bass	subject
cantata	French overture	*The Well-Tempered*
chorale	fugue	*Clavier*
da capo aria	*opera seria*	walking bass
dance suite	oratorio	
episode	pedal point	

For a checklist of musical style of the late Baroque period, see page 62.

CLASSICAL IDEALS: THE WORLD OF HAYDN AND MOZART

8

"Classical" as a musical term has two separate, though related, meanings. We use the word "classical" to signify the "serious" or "art" music of the West as distinguished from folk music, popular music, jazz, and the traditional music of various ethnic cultures. We call this music "classical" because there is something about the excellence of its form and style that makes it enduring, just as a finely crafted watch or a vintage automobile may be said to be a "classic" because it has a timeless beauty. Yet in the same breath we may refer to "Classical" music (now with a capital C), and by this we mean the music of a specific historical period, 1750–1820, a period of the great works of Haydn and Mozart and the early masterpieces of Beethoven. The creations of these artists have become so identified in the public mind with musical proportion, balance, and formal correctness—with standards of musical excellence—that this comparatively brief period has given its name to all music of lasting aesthetic worth.

"Classical" derives from the Latin *classicus*, meaning "something of the first rank or highest quality." To the men and women of the eighteenth century, no art, architecture, philosophy, or political institutions were more admirable, virtuous, and worthy of emulation than those of ancient Greece and Rome. Other periods in Western history also have been inspired by classical antiquity—the Renaissance heavily, the early Baroque less so, and our own century to some degree—but no period more than the eighteenth century. This was the time of the discovery of the ruins of Pompeii (1748), of the publication of Winkelmann's *History of Ancient Art* (1764) and Gibbon's *Decline and Fall of the Roman Empire* (1788).

It was also the period in which young English aristocrats made the "grand tour" of Italy and carted back to their country estates Roman statues, columns, and parts of entire villas. Classical architecture, with its formal control of space, geometric shapes, balance, and symmetrical design, became the only style thought worthy for domestic and state buildings of consequence. European palaces, opera houses, episcopal residences, and country homes all made use of it. Thomas Jefferson also traveled to Italy in these years while American ambassador to France, and later was instrumental in establishing Classical design in this country. Our nation's capitol, many state capitols, and countless other governmental and university buildings abound with the well-proportioned columns, porticos, and rotundas of the Classical style.

❋ FIGURE 8–1 AND 8–2
(left) The fourth-century Pantheon in Rome. (right) The Library of the University of Virginia, designed by Thomas Jefferson in the late eighteenth century. Jefferson had visited Rome and studied the ancient ruins while ambassador to France (1784–1789). The portico, with columns and triangular pediment, and the central rotunda are all elements of Classical style in architecture.

❀ THE ENLIGHTENMENT

The Classical era in music, art, and architecture coincides with the period in philosophy and letters called the Enlightenment. During the Enlightenment, also referred to as the Age of Reason, thinkers gave free rein to the pursuit of truth and the discovery of natural laws. This is the era that saw the rise of a natural religion called Deism, the belief that a Creator made the world, set it in motion, and has left it alone ever since. This is also the age of such scientific advances as the discovery of electricity and the invention of the steam engine. The first *Encyclopedia Britannica* appeared in 1771 and the French *Encyclopédie* between 1751 and 1772, a twenty-four volume set whose authors discarded traditional religious convictions and superstitions in favor of more rational scientific, philosophical, and political beliefs. In France the encyclopedists Voltaire (1694–1778), Rousseau (1712–1778), and Diderot (1713–1784) espoused the principles of social justice, equality, religious tolerance, and freedom of speech. These Enlightenment ideals subsequently became fundamental to all democratic governments and were enshrined in our American constitution.

Needless to say, the notion that all persons are created equal and should enjoy full political freedom put the thinkers of the Enlightenment on a collision course with the defenders of the existing social order. The old political structure had been built on the mysteries of the church, the privileges of the nobility, and the divine right of kings. Voltaire attacked the habits and prerogatives of both clergy and aristocracy, and championed middle-class virtues: honesty, common sense, and hard work. The extravagant gestures, sword, and wig of the frivolous courtier were an easy target for his pen. A more natural appearance, one appropriate to a tradesman, merchant, or manufacturer, now became the paradigm. Spurred on by economic self-interest and the principles of the philosophers, an increasingly

❋ FIGURE 8–3
Thomas Jefferson, by the French sculptor Houdon, 1789.

🌀 FIGURE 8–4

"Cherubino is discovered by the Count," an illustration of a scene in Pierre Beaumarchais's play *The Marriage of Figaro* (1784).

numerous and self-confident middle class in France and America rebelled against the monarchy and its supporters. The Age of Reason gave way to a newer Age of Revolution.

✿ MUSIC AND SOCIAL CHANGE: COMIC OPERA

Music was affected by these profound social changes, and in some ways it helped to precipitate them. A new form of opera, comic opera, proved to be a powerful vehicle for social reform. Opera in the Baroque period had been dominated by *opera seria** (see page 140). It was beautiful, grandiose, somewhat stiff, and expensive to mount. Portraying the deeds of mythological heros, gods and goddesses, and historical emperors and kings, it was the quintessential opera of the aristocracy. By contrast, the new **comic opera,** called **opera buffa** in Italy, was the opera of the middle class. It made use of everyday characters and situations; it employed spoken dialogues and simple songs in place of recitatives and *da capo** arias; and it was liberally spiced with sight gags, slapstick comedy, and bawdy humor. The librettos, such as they were, either poked fun at the nobility for its pomposity and incompetence or criticized it for being heartless.

opera buffa

Like seditious pamphlets, comic operas appeared in every country; among them were John Gay's *The Beggar's Opera* (1728) in England, Giovanni Pergolesi's *La serva padrona* (*The Maid Made Master,* 1733) in Italy, and Jean-Jacques Rousseau's *Le devin du village* (*The Village Soothsayer,* 1752) in France. And composers of greater stature were seduced by the charms of this middle-class entertainment. Mozart, who was treated poorly by the nobility throughout his short life, set one libretto in which a barber outsmarts a count and holds him up to public ridicule, *Le nozze di Figaro* (*The Marriage of Figaro,* 1786) (Fig. 8–4), and another, *Don Giovanni* (1787), in which the villain is a leading nobleman of the town. The play that served as the basis for Mozart's *Figaro* was banned by the authorities when it first appeared in Paris. By the time of the French Revo-

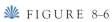 FIGURE 8–5

A public concert in the Vauxhall Gardens, London. A singer (right) performs from the balcony, with an accompanying orchestra (left) behind her.

lution (1789), comic opera, a rebellious upstart, had nearly driven the established *opera seria* off the eighteenth-century stage.

PUBLIC CONCERTS

The social changes of the eighteenth century, in turn, affected who it was that listened to music. In an earlier day a citizen might only hear sacred vocal music in a church or a bit of instrumental music at court, if he or she happened to be lucky enough to be an invited guest. But by mid-century the bookkeeper, physician, cloth merchant, and customs agent collectively had enough disposable income to organize and patronize their own concerts. In Leipzig, for example, the merchants got together to form the *Gewandhaus* ("Clothiers' House") concerts, which were held in the great hall of that guild; this *Gewandhaus* orchestra is still active today. Entrepreneurs in London offered concerts in the Vauxhall Gardens, where music could be heard inside in the orchestra room and outside as well (Fig. 8–5).

In Paris, then a city of 500,000, one could attend, as a citizen of the day said, "the best concerts every day with complete freedom." The most successful Parisian concert series was the *Concert spirituel*, which was advertised to the public by means of flyers or handbills distributed in the streets. To make its offerings accessible to a broad stratum of society, it also instituted a two-tiered system of prices (four livres for boxes and two livres for the pit). Thus we can trace to the middle of the eighteenth century the tradition of middle-class citizens attending public performances in return for an admission fee. Music was becoming public entertainment. The institution of "concerts" as we know them and the development of a broadly based listening audience date from this time.

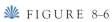 FIGURE 8–6

Mozart's piano, preserved in the house of his birth in Salzburg. The keyboard spans only five octaves, typical for the late eighteenth-century piano.

THE ADVENT OF THE PIANO

The newly affluent middle class wished not only to listen to music but also to play it. Most of this music making was centered in the home and around an instrument that first entered public consciousness in the Classical period: the piano. Invented in Italy about 1700, the piano gradually replaced the harpsichord as the keyboard instrument of preference (Fig. 8–6)—and with good reason, for the piano could play at more than one dynamic level (hence the original name **pianoforte,** "soft-loud"). Compared with the harpsichord, the piano could produce gradual dynamic changes, more subtle contrasts, and—ultimately—more power.

Those who played this new domestic instrument were mostly amateurs, and the great majority of these were women. Young ladies were encouraged to show skill on the piano as a means of demonstrating their refinement. This social requirement, in turn, encouraged a simpler, more homophonic keyboard style, one that would presumably not tax the technical limitations of the female performer. The spirit of democracy may have been in the air, but this was still very much a sexist age. It was assumed that ladies would not wish, as one publication said, "to bother their pretty little heads with counterpoint and harmony," but would be content with a tuneful melody and a few rudimentary chords to flesh it out. Collections such as *Keyboard Pieces for Ladies* (1768) were directed at these new musical consumers.

✿ FIGURE 8–7

Jean Baptiste Wicar's *Virgil Reading the Aeneid to Augustus* (1790–1793). In addition to its subject matter, this painting is marked by classical columns, classical costumes and gestures, and classical motifs (the laurel wreath to symbolize the poet Virgil, for example).

✿ CLASSICAL SIMPLICITY AND BALANCE

Painting of the late eighteenth century is often called Neoclassical, because it draws heavily on the themes and styles of classical antiquity. Many of the major artists of the day—among them American Benjamin West (1738–1820), Frenchman Jean Baptiste Wicar (1762–1834) (Fig. 8–7), and Englishwoman Angelica Kauffman (1741–1807)—traveled to Rome between 1760 and 1790 to study the architecture, mosaics, and sculpture that remained in the Roman forum and elsewhere around the city. They incorporated in their works not only the style and ornament of Roman dress but also the clarity, simplicity, and formal balance inherent in ancient classical design.

Angelica Kauffman's painting *The Artist [Angelica Kauffman] in the Character of Design Listening to the Inspiration of Poetry* (Fig. 8–8) shows a pair of balanced figures in Roman costume, Design on the left and Poetry on the right. Poetry is crowned with the laurel wreath of the Roman poet laureate. In addition, each figure holds a symbol of her art, Design a drawing board and Poetry a lyre. To their left are a pair of Greek columns, which similarly invoke a feeling of antiquity and at the same time balance the female pair. Nowhere to be seen are secondary figures who might clamor for the viewer's attention. Our eyes focus solely on Design and Poetry. The simplicity, balance, and static quality of the painting creates a feeling of calm, serenity, and repose.

These same features are to be found in the aria "Voi che sapete" ("You ladies who know") from Mozart's comic opera *The Marriage of Figaro* (1786). Here our ears concentrate exclusively on the melody. It consists of a succession of short phrases, almost all of them four measures in length. The opening provides a very clear example of a couplet of four-bar phrases arranged as an antecedent–consequent* pair. Subsequent phrases are also usually grouped in pairs. The simple chordal harmony (spaced out beneath as arpeggios*) supports, but in no way competes with, the lyrical top line. Toward the end, the opening phrase returns to round off the whole. The text is a succession of couplets, one pair for

✿ FIGURE 8–8

Angelica Kauffman's *The Artist in the Character of Design Listening to the Inspiration of Poetry* (1782).

each stanza. All is clarity, balance, and simplicity. Yet somehow, from the simplest of materials, the genius of Mozart creates a musical object of sublime beauty. The aria "You ladies who know" embodies classical perfection.

LISTENING GUIDE

Wolfgang Amadeus Mozart
Aria, "You ladies who know"
from the comic opera *The Marriage of Figaro* (1786)

6CD 2/2

Characters: Cherubino, an infatuated youth, and Suzanna, the older, wiser betrothed of Figaro. [Because Cherubino is a young adolescent, Mozart wrote the part for a high (soprano) voice. It is traditionally sung by a woman dressed as a boy.]
Situation: Cherubino (a soprano), sings to Suzanna of the pains and pleasures of love.

0:00	Orchestral introduction with antecedent–consequent phrases		
0:17	Voice enters with the antecedent phrase, inserts a new four-bar phrase, and then moves on to the consequent phrase	Voi che sapete che cosa è amor, donne, vedete s'io l'ho nel cor.	You ladies who know the nature of love, see if I have it within my heart.
0:42	A succession of paired phrases	Quello ch'io provo vi ridirò; è per me nuovo, capir non so. Sento un affetto pien di desir,	What I experience I will explain; it's so new to me I don't understand it. I have a feeling full of desire,
1:08	Charming major on "delightful" turns to anguished minor on "tormenting"	ch'ora è diletto, ch'ora è martir. Gelo, e poi sento l'alma avvampar, e in un momento torno a gelar. Ricero un bene fuori di me, non so chi'l tiene, non so cos'è.	sometimes delightful, sometimes tormenting. At first I freeze, and then my spirit burns, and then in a moment I turn to ice. I seek a treasure outside myself, I don't know who holds it, I don't even know what it is.
1:50	Rising repetitions insistently suggest "sighing and groaning"	Sospiro e gemo senza voler, palpito e tremo senza saper. Non trovo pace notte, nè dì ma pur mi piace languir così.	I sigh and groan without wanting to, I shake and tremble and know not why. I find no peace night or day, yet it only pleases me to languish so.
2:10	Peace is restored with return of opening phrase	Voi che sapete che cosa è amor, donne, vedete s'io l'ho nel cor.	You ladies who know the nature of love, see if I have it within my heart.

VIENNA: A CITY OF MUSIC

During the second half of the eighteenth century, Vienna rose to prominence as a place hospitable to the growth of music in the new Classical style. Indeed, Vienna became so important as a center of musical composition that the late eighteenth century is often called the age of the Viennese Classical style. The city owed its importance to a fortuitous location. As the capital city of the old Holy Roman Empire, Vienna was the administrative center for portions of modern-day Germany, Croatia, Bosnia, Serbia, Slovakia, The Czech Republic, Hungary, and Italy, in addition to all of Austria, and thus was a cultural crossroads for Central Europe (see Fig. 8–9). Musicians such as Christoph Gluck (1714–1787) from Bohemia (The Czech Republic), Antonio Salieri (1750–1825) from northern Italy, Franz Joseph Haydn (1732–1809) from Rohrau in lower Austria, Wolfgang Amadeus Mozart (1756–1791) from Salzburg in upper Austria, and Ludwig van Beethoven (1770–1827) from the German Rhineland gravitated toward Vienna for its rich musical life. There were theaters for German and Italian opera, concerts in the streets on fine summer nights, and ballroom dances where as many as four thousand persons might sway to a minuet, a contradance, or even a waltz by Mozart or Beethoven. In a city of nearly 200,000 inhabitants (the fourth largest in Europe behind London, Paris, and Naples), there were estimated to be 300 piano teachers. "There cannot be many cities in which musical amateurism is as widespread as it is here. Everybody plays, everybody takes music lessons," reported a journal of the day. And the musical allure of Vienna continued into the nineteenth century. In addition to native-born Franz Schubert (1797–1828), outsiders such as Anton Bruckner (1824–1896), Johannes Brahms (1833–1897), and Gustav Mahler (1860–1911) spent many of their most productive years there. Even today Vienna remains the capital of a nation (Austria) that spends nearly as much money on its state opera as it does on national defense.

❀ FIGURE 8-9

A map of eighteenth-century Europe showing the Holy Roman Empire and the principal musical cities.

❀ FRANZ JOSEPH HAYDN (1732–1809)

Thus, it was only natural that Franz Joseph Haydn, the son of a wheelwright from Rohrau in lower (eastern) Austria, should be sent to the capital to nurture his obvious musical talent. Haydn was born in 1732, and by the age of eight his pleasing voice had caught the attention of local church authorities. Soon he was singing among the choirboys at the cathedral of St. Stephen in Vienna. After nearly ten years of service his voice broke and he was abruptly dismissed. For most of the 1750s Haydn eked out a meager living as a free-lance musician—"miserable breadwinning" he called it: He gave keyboard lessons, accompanied singers, and sang or played violin or organ at three churches each Sunday, moving quickly from one to the next. All the while he studied musical composition. By 1761 he had progressed to the point where he was able to obtain a position as composer and leader of the orchestra at the court of Prince Esterházy.

✲ FIGURE 8–10

A portrait of Franz Joseph Haydn painted in 1791, when the composer was in London.

composing before the time of copyright

Haydn in London

The Esterházy were a noble Hungarian family with extensive landholdings southeast of Vienna and a passionate interest in music. As did many wealthy aristocrats of the time, Prince Nikolaus Esterházy (1714–1790) maintained an orchestra, a chapel for singing religious music, and a theater for opera. When Haydn was first engaged he was required to sign a contract of employment, one that suggests the subservient place of the composer in eighteenth-century society:

> [He] and all the musicians shall appear in uniform, and the said Joseph Haydn shall take care that he and all the members of the orchestra follow the instructions given, and appear in white stocking, white linen, powdered, and with either a pigtail or a tiewig. . . .
>
> The said [Haydn] shall be under obligation to compose such music as his Serene Highness may command, and neither to communicate such compositions to any other person, nor to allow them to be copied, but he shall retain them for the absolute use of his Highness, and not compose for any other person without the knowledge and permission of his Highness.

Thus, not only did Haydn lead the life of a liveried servant at court, dressing like the other domestics, but he also was prohibited from circulating his music without the express permission of his patron. But Nikolaus Esterházy was a benign ruler, and Haydn's symphonies, quartets, and sonatas came to be known not only in Vienna but also in foreign capitals. In the 1770s they surfaced in Amsterdam, London, and Paris in "pirated" editions. Since there was no international copyright in those years, a publisher might simply print a work from a copyist's score without the composer's knowledge or consent. When Haydn signed another contract with Prince Nikolaus in 1779, there was no such "exclusive use" provision, and he began to sell his works to various publishers, sometimes consigning the same piece to two or three at the same time!

For a period of nearly thirty years Haydn served Nikolaus Esterházy, writing symphonies and divertimentos* for evening entertainment, operas for the court theater (see Fig. 10–3), and string trios in which the prince himself might participate. When Nikolaus died in 1790, the Esterházy orchestra was dismissed in favor of a smaller, military band. Haydn retained his title as court composer as well as his full salary, but he was now free to travel as he wished. After settling briefly in Vienna, he journeyed to London where he had been engaged at a substantial fee to compose and conduct. From this commission resulted the twelve **London symphonies,** which were first performed in the Hanover Square Rooms (see Fig. 9–7), a large public concert hall built in part with capital supplied by Johann Christian Bach, old Bach's youngest son. Haydn stayed in London during 1791–1792 and returned again for the concert season 1794–1795. He was presented to the king and queen, received the honorary degree of doctor of music at Oxford, and was generally accorded the status of a visiting celebrity, as a letter written within a fortnight of his arrival attests:

> Everyone wants to know me. I had to dine out six times up to now, and if I wanted, I could have an invitation every day; but first I must consider my health and second my work. Except for the nobility, I admit no callers 'til 2 o'clock in the afternoon.

After Haydn returned home to Vienna for good in the summer of 1795, he wrote mainly Masses for chorus and orchestra and two oratorios, *The Creation* (1798) and *The Seasons* (1801)—it seems that he had been deeply impressed by the performances of Handel's oratorios he had heard while in England. His last public appearance was in 1808 for a performance of *The Creation* given in his

A public performance of Haydn's oratorio *The Creation* given at the university in Vienna in 1808 to mark the composer's seventy-sixth birthday. Haydn is seated at the lower center. The orchestra, which can be seen on the podium at the rear, is being conducted by Antonio Salieri.

honor in the festival hall of the university and conducted by court chapel master Antonio Salieri (Fig. 8–11). He died the following spring, on May 31, 1809, just two weeks after the besieging armies of Napoleon had conquered Vienna.

Haydn's long life, commitment to duty, and unflagging industry resulted in an impressive number of musical compositions: 104 symphonies, about 70 string quartets, nearly a dozen operas, 52 piano sonatas, 15 Masses, and 2 oratorios. He began composing before the death of Bach (1750) and did not put down his pen until about the time Beethoven set to work on his Fifth Symphony (1808). Thus, Haydn not only witnessed but, more than any other composer, helped to create the mature Classical style.

Haydn's works

Despite his accomplishments, he did not rebel against the modest station assigned to him in traditional eighteenth-century society: "I have associated with emperors, kings, and many great people," he said, "and I have heard many flattering things from them, but I would not live in familiar relations with such persons; I prefer to be close to people of my own standing." And though keenly aware of his own musical gifts, he was quick to recognize talent in others, especially Mozart: "Friends often flatter me that I have some genius, but he [Mozart] stood far above me."

❖ WOLFGANG AMADEUS MOZART (1756–1791)

Indeed, Wolfgang Amadeus Mozart may be the greatest musical genius the world has ever known. Mendelssohn (1809–1847) and Schubert (1797–1828) were perhaps his equals as youthful composers. But who, except possibly Bach, can match the diversity, breadth of expression, and perfect formal control present in the best works of Mozart?

The stories of Mozart's prodigious musical talent are many. As a child he could identify the notes played in any chord, judge the pitch of an instrument within an eighth of a tone, or pick out a wrong note in a musical score while crawling on his back across a table. As a youth he heard a motet sung in the Sistine Chapel in Rome, went to his room, and wrote it down by memory, note for note. He frequently copied one of his finished compositions onto a score while working out a new piece in his head. Little wonder that the great German poet Goethe (1749–1832), who had heard Mozart play as a child, referred to him as "the human incarnation of a divine force of creation."

An unfinished portrait of Mozart executed by his brother-in-law Joseph Lange during 1789–1790.

❊ FIGURE 8–13 AND 8–14
(left) Young Mozart at the keyboard, with his sister, Nannerl, and his father, Leopold, painted in Paris, 1763–1764, during their three-year tour of Europe. (right) Archbishop Colloredo, the unsympathetic patron of both Wolfgang Mozart and his father Leopold.

Mozart was born in Salzburg, Austria, in 1756. His father, Leopold, was a violinist in the orchestra of the archbishop of Salzburg, and his older sister, Nannerl, was also a talented performer (Fig. 8–13). Leopold was quick to recognize the musical gifts of his son, who by the age of six was playing the piano, violin, and organ as well as composing. The Mozart family coached off to Vienna, where the children displayed their musical wares before Empress Maria Theresa (1717–1780). They then embarked on a three-year tour of Northern Europe that included extended stops in Munich, Brussels, Paris, London, Amsterdam, and Geneva. In London, Wolfgang sat on the knee of Johann Christian Bach (1735–1782) and improvised a fugue. And here, at the age of eight, he heard his first two symphonies performed. Eventually, the Mozarts made their way back to Salzburg. But in 1768 they were off again to Vienna, where the now twelve-year-old Wolfgang staged a production of his first opera, *Bastien und Bastienne,* in the home of the famous Dr. Franz Anton Mesmer (1733–1815), the inventor of the theory of animal magnetism (hence, "to mesmerize"). The next year father and son visited the major cities of Italy, including Rome, where the pope dubbed Wolfgang a Knight of the Golden Spur. Although the aim of this globe-trotting was to acquire fame and fortune, the result was that Mozart, unlike Haydn, was exposed at an early age to a wealth of musical styles—French Baroque, English choral, German polyphonic, and Italian vocal. His extraordinarily keen ear absorbed them all, and ultimately they increased the breadth and substance of his music.

Mozart and *Amadeus*

Perhaps you have seen the extraordinary film *Amadeus* (1985) by Milos Forman, based on a play by Peter Schaffer, and wondered if the Mozart portrayed there bore any relation to the real Mozart. The answer is, in a few ways, yes; in most ways, no. To be sure, Mozart's lifestyle was somewhat chaotic, he had expensive tastes, and he was often downright silly in his behavior. Yet there is no hint of drunkenness in the contemporary documents; he had an excellent, if erratic income; and his childish behavior, according to his brother-in-law Joseph Lange, was the way in which he released excess tension built up during concentrated periods of creative activity. Mozart did not die poor. Indeed, his income from two major operas in 1791 and the famous Requiem Mass made his last year one of his most lucrative. Nor was he abandoned to suffer a pauper's funeral. He received the same sort of burial (placed in a common grave) as eighty-five percent of the upper-middle-class in Vienna at that time. Nor, finally, was Mozart poisoned by his principal rival in Vienna, the composer Antonio Salieri (1750–1825). Salieri, court composer to Emperor Joseph II and his two successors, was a universally respected, if not supremely gifted, musician who later went on to become, at various times, the teacher of Beethoven, Schubert, Liszt, and even one of Mozart's two sons. Salieri may have been a mediocre composer, but he was no murderer.

A scene from Amadeus.

A period of relative stability followed: For much of the 1770s Mozart resided in Salzburg, where, like his father, he had been taken on as a violinist and composer to the archbishop. Unfortunately, the reigning archbishop, Colloredo (Fig. 8–14), was a stern, somewhat miserly man who had little sympathy for Mozart, genius or not. As was the custom since medieval times, this prince of the Church, whom Mozart refers to in his letters as "the Archboobie," was as much a political figure as a spiritual leader. Mozart was given a place in the orchestra, a small salary, and his board. Like the musicians at the court of Esterházy, those at Salzburg ate with the cooks and valets. For a Knight of the Golden Spur who had played for kings and queens across Europe, this was humble fare indeed, and Mozart chafed under this system of aristocratic patronage. After several unpleasant scenes in the spring of 1781, the twenty-five-year-old composer cut himself free of the archbishop and determined to make a living as a freelance musician in Vienna.

Mozart chose Vienna partly because of the city's rich musical life and partly because it was a comfortable distance from his overbearing father. In a letter to his sister written in the spring of 1782, Wolfgang spells out his daily regimen in the Austrian capital.

> My hair is always done by six o'clock in the morning and by seven I am fully dressed. I then compose until nine. From nine to one I give lessons. Then I lunch, unless I am invited to some house where they lunch at two or even three o'clock. . . . I can never work before five or six o'clock in the evening, and even then I am often prevented by a concert. If I am not prevented, I compose until nine. Then I go to my dear Constanze.

※ FIGURE 8–15
Antonio Salieri (1750–1825). History has unfairly portrayed him as Mozart's nemesis.

🌸 FIGURE 8-16

St. Stephen's Cathedral, Vienna, where Mozart was married in 1782 and where his funeral was held in 1791.

Against the advice of his father, Wolfgang married his "dear Constanze" (Weber) in the summer of 1782. But, alas, she was as romantic and impractical as he, though less given to streaks of hard work. In addition to his composing, teaching, and performing, Mozart now found time to study the music of Bach and Handel, play chamber music with his friend Joseph Haydn, and join the Freemasons. Although still very much a practicing Catholic, he was attracted to this fraternity of the Enlightenment because of its belief in tolerance and universal brotherhood. His opera *Die Zauberflöte* (*The Magic Flute*, 1791) is viewed by many as a hymn in praise of masonic ideals.

The years 1785–1787 witnessed the peak of Mozart's success and the creation of many of his greatest works. He had a full complement of pupils, played several concerts a week, and enjoyed lucrative commissions as a composer. Piano concertos, string quartets, and symphonies flowed from his pen, as well as his two greatest Italian operas, *The Marriage of Figaro* and *Don Giovanni*. But *Don Giovanni*, a huge success when first performed in Prague in 1787, was little appreciated when mounted in Vienna in the spring of 1788. "The opera is divine, perhaps even more beautiful than *Figaro*," declared Emperor Joseph II, "but no food for the teeth of my Viennese." Mozart's music was no longer in vogue. His pupils began to dwindle and the elite failed to subscribe to his concerts. His style was thought to be too dense, too intense, too dissonant. One publisher warned him: "Write in a more popular style or else I cannot print or pay for more of your music."

Mozart's last year

Although now in declining health, Mozart was still capable of creating the greatest sort of masterpieces. In his last year (1791) he composed a superb clarinet concerto and the German comic opera *The Magic Flute*, and began work on a Requiem Mass, one he was never to finish. Mozart died on December 5, 1791, at the age of thirty-five. The precise reason for his death has never been determined, though kidney failure made worse by needless bloodletting was the most likely cause. No single event in the history of music was more tragic than the premature loss of Mozart. What he would have given to the world had he enjoyed the long life of a Bach or a Haydn!

🌸 CLASSICAL STYLE IN MUSIC

Even for a music lover of many years' experience, it is sometimes difficult to distinguish the sound of Haydn from that of Mozart or, similarly, to differentiate late Haydn or Mozart from early Beethoven. This easy confusion points up the fact that music in the Classical period is more homogeneous in style than in any other period in the history of music—pieces in the same genre but by different composers tend to sound like one another. Clearly, there was then a consensus among creative musicians as to what music was supposed to sound like, an ideal tacitly agreed upon, not only by Haydn, Mozart, and Beethoven in Vienna but also by lesser composers working in Milan, Paris, London, and elsewhere. The Viennese Classical style embodied universal principles in an age that greatly valued universal ideals.

classical balance and symmetry

Much has been written about the Classical style in music: its quiet grace, noble simplicity, purity, and serenity. It is certainly "classical" in the sense that extreme emphasis is placed on formal clarity, order, and balance. Compared with the relentless, grandiose, sometimes pompous sound of the Baroque, Classical music is lighter in tone, more natural, yet less predictable. It is even capable of humor and surprise, as when Mozart again and again leads up to, but carefully avoids, a cadence, or when Haydn explodes with a thunderous chord in the midst of a sea of quiet. But what is it in precise musical terms that creates this feeling of levity and grace, of clarity and balance, in Classical music?

MELODY. Perhaps the first thing that strikes the listener about the music of Haydn or Mozart is that the theme is often tuneful, catchy, even singable. Not only are melodies simple and short but also the phrases tend to be organized in antecedent–consequent*, or question–answer, pairs. Indeed, antecedent-consequent phrases in significant number appear for the first time in the history of music in the Classical period. The melody usually progresses by playing out these short phrases in symmetrical groups of two, three, four, eight, twelve, or sixteen bars. The brevity of the phrase and frequent cadences allow for ample light and air to penetrate the melodic line.

antecedent and consequent phrases

Below is the theme from the second movement of Mozart's Piano Concerto in C major (1785). It is composed of two three-bar phrases—an antecedent and a consequent phrase. The melody is light and airy, yet perfectly balanced. It is also singable and quite memorable—indeed, it has been turned into a popular movie theme (the "love song" from *Elvira Madigan*). Compare this with the long, asymmetrical melodies of the Baroque that were often instrumental in character (see page 122).

EXAMPLE 8–1

HARMONY. After about 1750 all music assumed a more homophonic, less polyphonic character. The new tuneful melody was supported by a simple harmony. In the preceding example only two chords, tonic and dominant, support Mozart's lovely melody. The bass still generates the harmony, but it does not always move in the regular, constant fashion typified by the Baroque walking bass*. Rather, the bass might sit on the bottom of one chord for several beats, even several measures, then move rapidly, and then stop again. Thus, the rate at which chords change—the harmonic rhythm as it is called—is much more fluid and flexible with Classical composers.

flexible harmonic rhythm

To avoid a feeling of inactivity when the harmony is static, Classical composers invented new accompanying patterns. Sometimes, as in Ex. 8–1, they simply repeat the accompanying chord in a uniform triplet rhythm. More common is the pattern called the **Alberti bass,** named after the minor Italian keyboard composer Domenico Alberti (1710–1740) who popularized this figure. Instead of playing the pitches of a chord all together, the performer spreads them out to provide a continual stream of sound. Mozart used an Alberti bass at the beginning of his famous C major piano sonata (1788):

EXAMPLE 8–2

Alberti bass

The Alberti pattern serves essentially the same function as the modern "boogie-woogie" bass. It provides a feeling of harmonic activity for those moments when, in fact, the harmony is stationary.

RHYTHM. Rhythm, too, is more flexible in the hands of Haydn and Mozart. It animates the stop-and-go character of their melodies and harmonies. Rapid motion may be followed by repose and then further quick movement, but there is little of the driving, perpetual motion of Baroque musical rhythm.

TEXTURE. Musical texture was also transformed in the latter half of the eighteenth century, mainly because composers began to concentrate less on writing dense counterpoint than on creating charming melodies. No longer are inde-*light harmonic texture* pendent polyphonic lines superimposed, layer upon layer, as in a fugue of Bach or a polyphonic chorus of Handel. The lessening of counterpoint, then, made for a lighter, more transparent sound, especially in the middle range of the texture. Mozart, after a study of Bach and Handel in the early 1780s, infused his symphonies, quartets, and concertos with greater polyphonic content, but this seems to have caused the pleasure-loving Viennese to think his music too dense!

The Classical Orchestra

The development of the orchestra during the Classical period is discussed in connection with the creation of the Classical symphony in Chapter 10 (page 185). For the moment, suffice it to say that during the late eighteenth century the orchestra grows in size as a direct response to the larger audience that crowded into the new public concert halls. The strings still constitute the core of the orchestra, but the woodwinds—oboes, flutes, bassoons, and the new clarinets—gain increased autonomy. They no longer merely double or echo the violins and the bass line as they had during the Baroque era. Henceforth, they enter and depart, seemingly at will, now to play a theme as a solo, now to thicken momentarily the musical texture or to add a dash of instrumental color.

The Dramatic Quality of Classical Music

What is perhaps most revolutionary in the music of Haydn, Mozart, and their younger contemporary, Beethoven, is its capacity for rapid change and endless fluctuation. Recall that in earlier times a work by Purcell, Corelli, Vivaldi, or Bach would establish one "affect," or mood, to be rigidly maintained from beginning to end—the rhythm, melody, and harmony all progressing in a continuous, uninterrupted flow. Such a uniform approach to expression is part of the "single-mindedness" of Baroque art. Now, with Haydn, Mozart, and the young

Beethoven, the mood or character of a piece may change radically within a few short phrases. An energetic theme in rapid notes may be followed by a second one that is slow, lyrical, and tender. Similarly, textures may change quickly from light and airy to dense and more contrapuntal so as to create tension and excitement. For the first time composers began to call for crescendos and diminuendos, a gradual increase or lessening of the dynamic level, so that the volume of sound might continually fluctuate. When skilled orchestras made use of this technique, audiences were fascinated and rose to their feet. Keyboard players, too, now took up the crescendo and diminuendo, assuming that the new multi-dynamic piano was at hand in place of the old, less flexible harpsichord. These rapid changes in mood, texture, color, and dynamics give to Classical music a new sense of urgency and drama. The listener feels a constant flux and flow, not unlike the continual swings of mood we all experience.

frequent changes in mood

crescendos and diminuendos

Classical Forms

How did composers of the Classical period reconcile their desire to express changing moods, colors, and textures with the Classical principles of grace, order, and balance? They did so, in a word, by means of form. All of the elements of expression—themes, harmonic relationships, colors, textures, dynamics—are precisely positioned within the boundaries of strict musical form. Limits are set as to where the changing or conflicting elements may be placed, how intense they may be, and how long they may last. By placing the musical events, or sections, in a carefully regulated order, grace, balance, and proportion are achieved. As one critic observed in 1777: "A knowledge of the proper ordering of sections is essential to any friend of music who wishes to be a conoisseur and who desires to derive pleasure from the workings of this art." Indeed, so important is form in Classical music that the subject requires a chapter unto itself.

form controls the unfolding of musical events

KEY WORDS

Alberti bass	Nikolaus Esterházy	*The Magic Flute*
Antonio Salieri	*opera buffa*	*The Marriage of Figaro*
comic opera	*pianoforte*	
London symphonies	Salzburg	

A checklist of musical style in the Classical era is given on page 63.

9

CLASSICAL FORMS

To understand and appreciate Classical music, it is especially important to understand musical form. For in the Classical period, more so than any other, a small number of forms—ternary, sonata–allegro, rondo, and theme and variations—regulated nearly all music. Indeed, there are few compositions written during the years 1750–1820 that are not shaped according to one of these. At the same time, it is important to realize that none of these forms was unique to the Classical period. Ternary form can be found in the earliest examples of Gregorian chant* as well as in all *da capo** arias of the Baroque era (1600–1750). The rondo had its origins in the popular dances and songs of the Middle Ages, though its repetitive structure has made it attractive to such diverse musicians as Mozart, Beethoven, Elton John, and Sting. And theme and variations, as both a musical and a literary process, is at once ancient and eternal. Only sonata–allegro form actually came into being in the Classical period. It dominated musical structure during the time of Mozart and Haydn, but it also remained a potent force in the works of most composers of the Romantic era (1820–1900) and in the creations of some twentieth-century musicians as well. Thus, the forms discussed in this chapter

❀ FIGURE 9–1 A ball at the Redoutensaal in the emperor's palace in Vienna ca. 1800. Mozart, Haydn, and, later, Beethoven composed minuets and "German dances" for officially sponsored events there. The orchestra can be seen in the gallery at the left.

should be thought of not as belonging to the Classical period alone, but in the broader meaning of the term "classical." With the single exception of the more recent sonata–allegro form, they are all timeless and universal.

TERNARY FORM

Ternary structure (**ABA**) is a form often encountered in the history of music. Yet the simple principle of presentation, contrast, and return was especially favored by Classical composers for its simplicity and directness. Everyone is familiar with the tune *Twinkle, Twinkle, Little Star* (also the tune of *Bah, Bah, Black Sheep*, and *A, B, C, D, E, F, G*). Less well known is the fact that it began life as a French folk song, *Ah, vous dirai-je, Maman* (*Ah, Let Me Tell You, Mama*). Wolfgang Amadeus Mozart (1756–1791) came to know the melody when he toured France as a youth, and he wrote it down in a keyboard version. Here is his setting of it:

EXAMPLE 9-1

Notice that both units (**A** and **BA**) are repeated. Observe also that **A** is in the tonic, **B** emphasizes a contrasting key (here the dominant), and the returning **A** is again in the tonic. If a piece in ternary form is in a minor key, the contrasting **B** section will usually be in what is called the **relative major.**[†] Needless to say, most pieces in ternary form are more complex than *Twinkle, Twinkle*. Most have more contrast of melody, key, and/or mood between the **B** section and the surrounding units of **A.**[††]

Minuet and Trio

The most common use of ternary form in the Classical period is found in the minuet and trio. Strictly speaking, the **minuet** is not a form, but rather a genre of dance implying an elegant musical style, stately tempo, and constant triple

---

[†]Relative keys are keys that share the same key signature, E♭ major and C minor (both with three flats), for example.

[††]Note for instructors: on the designation "ternary form" for this piece, see the Preface.

meter. It first appeared at the French royal court early in the reign of King Louis XIV (1643–1715). Most minuets in the Baroque era were in binary form*. But by 1770 the minuet was usually composed in ternary form and grouped with a second minuet possessing a much lighter texture. Because this second minuet had originally been played by only three instruments, it was called the **trio,** a name that persisted into the nineteenth century, no matter how many instrumental lines were required in this second minuet. Once the trio was finished, convention dictated that there be a return to the first minuet, now performed without repeats. Since the trio also was composed in ternary form, an **ABA** pattern was heard three times in succession. (In the following, the **ABA** structure of the trio is represented by **CDC,** to distinguish it from the minuet.) And, since the trio

✿ FIGURE 9–2

Couples in the late eighteenth century dancing the stately minuet.

was different from the surrounding minuet, the entire movement minuet–trio–minuet formed an **ABA** arrangement.

A (minuet)	B (trio)	A (minuet)
‖: A :‖: BA :‖	‖: C :‖: DC :‖	ABA

Mozart's *Eine kleine Nachtmusik (A Little Night Music)*, written in the summer of 1787, is among his most popular works. It is a **serenade,** a light, multi-movement piece for strings alone or small orchestra, one intended for public entertainment and often performed outdoors. Although we do not know the precise occasion for which Mozart composed it, we might well imagine *A Little Night Music* providing the musical backdrop for a torch-lit party in a formal Viennese garden. The *Menuetto* appears as the third of four movements in this serenade, and is a model of grace and concision.

Mozart's A Little Night Music

EXAMPLE 9-2

As you can see, the **B** section is only four measures long, and the return to **A** does not reproduce the full eight bars of the original but only the last four—thus, this pattern might be viewed as **ABA′**. In the trio that follows, a lighter texture is created as the first violin plays a solo melody quietly above a soft accompaniment in the lower strings. The **D** section of the trio is distinguished by a *forte* stepwise run up and down the scale, and then the quiet melody of **C** returns to complete the ternary form. Finally, the minuet appears once again, but now without repeats.

<table>
<tr><td colspan="2">LISTENING GUIDE</td><td>Wolfgang Amadeus Mozart
Serenade, A Little Night Music (1787)
Third movement, Minuet and Trio</td><td>6CD 2/4;
2CD 1/9</td></tr>
</table>

Form: ternary

MINUET		Form	Number of bars
0:00	Strong violin melody with active bass	A	8
0:10	Repeat of **A**		
0:20	Softer violin scales	B	4
0:26	Return of violin melody	A′	4
0:30	Repeat of **B** and **A′**		
TRIO			
0:41	Soft, stepwise melody in violins	C	8
0:52	Repeat of **C**		
1:03	Louder violins	D	4
1:09	Return of soft stepwise melody	C	8
1:20	Repeat of **D** and **C**		
MINUET			
1:37	Return of **A**	A	8
1:48	Return of **B**	B	4
1:54	Return of violin melody **A′**	A′	4

We have said that Classical music is symmetrical and proportional. Note here how both minuet and trio are balanced by a return of the opening music (**A** and **C**) and how all the sections are either four or eight bars in length.

a more extended minuet

If Mozart's *Menuetto* represents the minuet in its most succinct form, the minuet of Haydn's Symphony No. 94 (The "Surprise" Symphony) offers a more typically symphonic presentation of this ternary design. The form is considerably extended, in part because Haydn was writing for a full orchestra rather than a small string ensemble as in Mozart's serenade. (It is axiomatic in music that the larger the performing force, the more extended the musical form.) But keeping the model of Mozart's simple ternary minuet in our ears, we can easily follow Haydn's more expansive formal plan.

LISTENING GUIDE

Franz Joseph Haydn
Symphony No. 94, The "Surprise" Symphony (1791)
Third movement, Minuet and Trio

6CD 2/6

Form: ternary

MINUET [ ] = repeats

			Form
0:00		Rollicking dance in triple meter begins	**A**
0:19		Repeat of **A**	
0:40	[1:33]	Imitation and lighter texture	**B**
0:50	[1:43]	Strong harmonic movement	
0:58	[1:51]	Bass sits on dominant note	
1:05	[1:59]	Return of **A**	**A'**
1:13	[2:07]	Pause on dominant chord	
1:23	[2:17]	Gentle rocking over tonic pedal point*	

TRIO

2:27		Light descending scales for violins and bassoon	**C**
2:37		Repeat of **C**	
2:46	[3:08]	Two-voice counterpoint for 1st and 2nd violins	**D**
2:58	[3:21]	Bassoon reentry signals return of **C**	**C**

MINUET

3:30		Return to minuet	**A**
3:51		Return of **B**	**B**
4:16		Return of **A**	**A'**

SONATA–ALLEGRO FORM

Sonata–allegro form is at once the most complex and most satisfying of musical forms. It is also the only form to originate during the Classical period (1750–1820). We must keep in mind, however, the distinction between the general term "sonata" and the more specific term "sonata–allegro form"—that is, between the multimovement composition called the sonata and the single-movement form called sonata–allegro.

Recall that in the Baroque period a multimovement work was often called a sonata, either a solo sonata or a trio sonata. These consisted of a succession of binary-form movements that often proceeded slow–fast–slow–fast (see page 112). By the early Classical period, however, the usual arrangement of movements for a sonata had become fast–slow–minuet–fast, or occasionally just fast–slow–fast. When played by a solo instrument like the piano, this group of movements is called a solo sonata. When this same sort of three- or four-movement composition is written for string quartet or quintet, it is called simply a string quartet or quintet. And when intended for a full symphonic orchestra, it is called a symphony.

Yet no matter what the performing force, the form of each of these movements can be one of several different types. As we have seen, if there are four movements the third is usually a minuet with trio. The second and fourth movements might be, for example, in rondo form or theme and variations form (both discussed later in the chapter). The fast first movement, however, is almost invariably written in what is called **sonata–allegro form.** Thus, the term "sonata–allegro" derives from the fact that sonata–allegro form was usually applied to the fast (allegro) first movement. Slow second movements and fast finales sometimes make use of sonata–allegro form as well. To show at least two typical arrangements, here are the movements and forms of Mozart's *A Little Night Music* and Haydn's Symphony No. 94:

FIGURE 9–3
In this painting, the six-year-old Mozart is dressed in the court costume given him by Empress Maria Theresa in 1762.

Mozart, *A Little Night Music* (1787)			
Fast	Slow	Minuet and Trio	Fast
(sonato–allegro)	(rondo)	(ternary)	(rondo)

Haydn, Symphony No. 94 (1791)			
Fast	Slow	Minuet and Trio	Fast
(sonata–allegro)	(theme and variations)	(ternary)	(sonata–allegro)

Sonata–allegro form came into being around 1750 as a means of incorporating more drama and conflict into a single movement of music. Like a great play, sonato–allegro form has the potential for dramatic presentation, conflict, and resolution. That sonata–allegro form would continue to serve composers into the Romantic period and beyond attests to its compelling logic and great flexibility. It gave composers a formal backdrop on which a musical drama could play out in any number of individual ways.

The Shape of Sonata–Allegro Form

To get a sense of what might happen in a typical first movement of a sonata, string quartet, symphony, or serenade, look at the diagram at the top of page 170. As with all models of this sort, this one is an ideal, an abstraction of what commonly occurs in sonata–allegro form. It is not a blueprint for any composition. Composers have exhibited countless individual solutions to the task of writing in this and every other form. Yet such a model can be of great use to the listener because it gives a clear picture of what we might expect to hear. Ultimately, once we have embraced the form and are familiar with its workings, we will take as much delight in having our musical expectations foiled or delayed as in having them fulfilled.

SONATA-ALLEGRO FORM

In its broad outline, sonata–allegro form looks much like ternary form. It consists of an **ABA** plan, with the **B** section providing contrast in mood, key, and thematic treatment. The initial **A** in sonata–allegro form is called the exposition, the **B** the development, and the return to **A** the recapitulation. In the early Classical period the exposition **(A)** and the development and recapitulation **(BA)** were each repeated, as in ternary form. But Haydn and Mozart eventually dropped the repeat of the development and recapitulation, and composers of the Romantic period gradually dispensed with the repeat of the exposition. Let's take each of these sections in turn and see what we are likely to hear.

EXPOSITION. The purpose of the **exposition** is to present, or expose, the main thematic material of the movement, just as the exposition of a fugue exposes the subject.

presentation

First theme. The exposition begins with a first theme, or group of themes, and can be anywhere from four to forty measures or more in length. If not easily singable, the first theme is at least distinctive, memorable enough so that later returns and references to it will be recognized and enjoyed by the listener. The first theme is always in the tonic key (I).

Transition. The aim of the **transition,** or **bridge** as it is sometimes called, is to carry the music from the tonic to the dominant (from tonic to relative major if the movement is in a minor key) and prepare for the arrival of the second theme. The transition is usually made up of rapidly moving figural patterns— running scales, arpeggios*, and the like—which are frequently put forth as melodic sequences*. In order to effect the tonic-dominant (I–V) modulation, the bass becomes active and generates quick chord changes. This lively harmonic movement may subside if the transition ends with a solid cadence.

Second theme. Not only does a new melody usually appear at this point, but it enters in the fresh context of a new key, the dominant or, less frequently, the relative major. The second theme often contrasts in mood with the first: If the first is rapid and assertive, the second may be more languid and lyrical. Because a clear-cut theme holds center stage here, the accompanying harmonic material is stable, not modulatory. The listener's attention is focused on melody, not on harmonic movement.

Closing theme. The second theme usually gives way to a closing theme, one that is normally light and carefree in style. It often ends in a harmonically simple way, merely rocking back and forth between dominant and tonic chords. The

FIGURE 9–4

The autograph manuscript of *A Little Night Music* (1787). Mozart was composing here with a score of four staffs: First and second violins are on the top two staffs, violas on staff three, and cellos and double basses on four. One can sense with what extraordinary speed, yet accuracy, Mozart could set music on paper.

static harmony and repeated full cadences* signal the conclusion of the exposition. The piece has stopped moving forward, and therefore the exposition is at an end. Tradition requires that the exposition now be repeated note for note.

DEVELOPMENT. As the name indicates, the **development** is a section in which there is a further working out, or developing, of the thematic material presented in the exposition. Both the first and the second theme may be manipulated, and occasionally even the closing theme is exploited as well. A theme may be elaborated on and expanded, or, just as often, it may be taken apart, reduced to just a few notes to be tossed around from instrument to instrument. One typical technique is for the composer to show the contrapuntal possibilities lurking within a theme by using it as the subject of a brief fugue*. (A fugue within a movement of a sonata is called a **fugato.**) Like the transition, the development tends to have unstable harmonies. The use of both melodic and harmonic sequence is plentiful, and this encourages rapid modulation from one key, or tonal center, to another. Only toward the end of the development, in the area called the **retransition,** does tonal stability return, often in the form of a pedal point* on the dominant note. The retransition helps prepare the ear for the return of the tonic key and the restatement of the first theme.

confrontation

RECAPITULATION. After the dramatic disruptions of the development, the listener greets the return of the first theme and the tonic key of the exposition with welcome relief. Though the **recapitulation** is not an exact, note-for-note repetition of the exposition, it nonetheless presents the same musical events in the same order, reaffirming the logic and integrity of the original. The only change that regularly occurs in this restatement is the rewriting of the transition, or bridge. Because the movement must end in the tonic, the bridge must not modulate to the dominant (or relative major) as before but stay at home in the tonic key. Thus, the recapitulation imparts to the listener not only a feeling

resolution

of return to familiar surroundings but also an increased sense of harmonic stability, as all themes are now heard in the tonic key.

The following two elements are optional to sonata–allegro form.

optional elements

INTRODUCTION. About half the mature symphonies of Haydn and Mozart have brief introductions before the exposition begins. These are, without exception, slow and stately and usually filled with ominous or puzzling chords designed to set the listener wondering what sort of musical excursion he or she is about to undertake. That the introduction is not part of the exposition is shown by the fact that it is never repeated.

CODA. As the name **coda** (Italian for "tail") indicates, this is a section added to the end of the sonata–allegro movement. It may be just a few bars long, as is most often the case with Mozart, or it may, in the hands of Beethoven, for example, expand into an independent section, one equal in size to the development. The melodic material is usually no more than a short motive extracted from the first theme or sometimes from the closing theme, or it may be a newly created motive. But whatever the source, normally this motive is sounded again and again in conjunction with repeating dominant–tonic chords, or merely the tonic chord alone played over and over, all intended to create a grand effect and announce to the listener that the movement is at an end. Again, thematic repetition at the same pitch level and static harmony are two ways a composer can signal the end of a section or the end of a piece. The more of this that goes on, the greater the feeling of conclusion.

Hearing Sonata–Allegro Form

Given its central place in the music of Mozart and Haydn, and later in Beethoven, Schubert, Brahms, and Mahler, among others, sonata–allegro is perhaps the most important of all musical forms. But it is also the most complex and the most difficult for the listener to follow. A sonata–allegro movement tends to be long, lasting anywhere from a minimum of four minutes in a simple piece of the Classical period to twenty minutes or more in a full-blown movement of the Romantic era. Moreover, it embodies many kinds of musical events and many styles of writing—thematic and transitional, for example. And finally, sonata–allegro form does not merely involve one theme but incorporates several, and all of these have to be remembered and their development followed.

the challenge of sonata–allegro form

How does one get the better of this musical beast? First of all, be sure you have the model of sonata–allegro form clearly in mind. This will help you know what to expect, what you are likely to hear. Next, sharpen your ability to grasp and remember melodies, or at least the beginnings of melodies. If necessary, return to Chapter 2 and practice some melodic graphing (see page 20). And finally, think carefully about the four principal styles of writing found in sonata–allegro form. Each has its own distinct character. A thematic section has clearly recognizable themes or melodies, sometimes even singable tunes. The transition is full of melodic movement, sequences, and rapid chord changes. The development is also disjunct, agitated, contrapuntal, and harmonically active, but it makes use of a recognizable theme, albeit extended or cut up into small pieces. And a concluding passage, whether at the end of the exposition, in the retransition at the end of the development, or in the coda at the end of the movement, tends to repeat motives or cadential phrases over and over above a static harmony. Each of these four styles has a specific function within sonata–allegro form: to state, to move, to develop, or to conclude. The composer employs a rhetoric of music, just as the orator practices a rhetoric of speech. Much of your success in hearing sonata–allegro form will come from your ability to recognize each of these four functional types of music. With this by way of preparation, let's listen to a movement in sonata–allegro form.

For this we once again turn to the familiar sound of Mozart's *A Little Night Music*. The first movement *(Allegro)* of this four-movement serenade offers a concise, graceful example of sonata–allegro principle. Yet even a straightforward sonata–allegro-form movement such as this requires the listener's full attention. The following Listening Guide is not typical of this book. It is unusually lengthy so as to lead you through the difficult process of hearing sonata–allegro form. First read the description in the center column, then listen to the music, stopping where indicated to rehear each of the principal sections of the form.

LISTENING GUIDE

Wolfgang Amadeus Mozart
A Little Night Music (1787)
First movement, *Allegro* (fast)

6CD 2/3;
2CD 1/8

Form: sonata–allegro

FIRST THEME GROUP [ ] = repeats

0:00 [1:37] The movement opens aggressively with a leaping, fanfarelike motive. It then moves on to a more confined, pressing melody with sixteenth notes agitating beneath, and ends with a relaxed, stepwise descent down the G major scale, which is repeated with light ornamentation.

STOP: LISTEN TO THE FIRST THEME GROUP AGAIN

TRANSITION

0:30 [2:08] This starts with two quick turns and then races up the scale in repeating sixteenth notes. The bass is at first static, but when it finally moves it does so with great urgency, pushing the modulation along until a cadence. The stage is then cleared by a brief pause, allowing the listener an "unobstructed view" of the new theme that is about to enter.

0:30 Rapid scales
0:40 Bass moves
0:45 Cadence and pause

STOP: LISTEN TO THE TRANSITION AGAIN

SECOND THEME

0:48 [2:26] With its *piano* dynamic level and separating rests, the second theme sounds soft and delicate. It is soon overtaken by a light, somewhat humorous closing theme.

STOP: LISTEN TO THE SECOND THEME AGAIN

(Continued on next page)

CLOSING THEME

1:01   [2:39]   The light quality of this melody is produced by its repeating note and the simple rocking of dominant-to-tonic harmony below. Toward the end of it more substance is added when the music turns *forte*, and good counterpoint is inserted in the bass. The bass closing theme is then repeated, and a few cadential chords are tacked on to bring the exposition to an end.

1:09   Loud; counterpoint in bass
1:14   Closing theme repeated
1:33   Cadential chords

STOP: LISTEN TO THE CLOSING SECTION AGAIN

1:37–3:14   The exposition is now repeated.

DEVELOPMENT

3:15   Just about anything can happen in a development, so the listener had best be on guard. Mozart begins with the fanfarelike first theme again in unison, as if this were yet another statement of the exposition! But abruptly the theme is altered and the tonal center slides up to a new key. Now the closing theme is heard, but soon it, too, begins to slide tonally, down through several keys that sound increasingly remote and bizarre. From this arises a unison scale (all parts move up stepwise together) in a dark-sounding minor key. The dominant note is held, first on top in the violins and then in the bass. This is the retransition. The mode changes from dark minor to bright major, and the first theme returns with force in the tonic key, signaling the beginning of the recapitulation.

3:15   First theme developed
3:20   Quick modulation
3:25   Closing theme developed
3:32   More modulations
3:41   Rising scale in unison
3:48   Held note (dominant) in violins and then bass

STOP: LISTEN TO THE DEVELOPMENT AGAIN

RECAPITULATION

3:52   It is this "double return" of both the tonic key and the first theme that makes the arrival of this and all recapitulations so satisfying. We expect the recapitulation to more or less duplicate the exposition, and this one holds true to form. The only change comes, as usual, in the transition, or bridge, where the modulation to the dominant is simply omitted—there's no need to modulate to the dominant since tradition demands that the second theme and the closing theme appear in the tonic.

3:52   Loud return of first theme
4:23   Transition much abbreviated
4:38   Second theme
4:51   Closing theme
5:05   Closing theme repeated
5:23   Cadential chords

CODA

5:26   After the cadential chords that ended the exposition are heard again, a brief coda begins. It makes use of a fanfare motive that strongly resembles that of the opening theme, but this one is supported below by a pounding tonic chord that drives home the feeling that the movement has come to an appropriate end.

What we have just heard is an example of sonata–allegro form in miniature. Rarely has this design been produced in less time, or space, and almost never as artfully. But sonata–allegro is a dynamic, flexible form, one that can serve equally well as an appropriate vessel for a large symphonic movement, a dramatic overture to an opera, or a Romantic tone poem*. We will meet it again in several later compositions. Listening Exercise 19 presents another, even more dramatic, unfolding of sonata–allegro form: the overture to Mozart's tragic-comic opera *Don Giovanni*.

✿ THEME AND VARIATIONS

After the complexity of sonata–allegro form, a movement in theme and variations form seems relatively simple and straightforward. This is partly because just one theme is used and that theme is subjected to only one sort of compositional treatment: variation. For theme and variations to be effective, the theme itself must be easy to grasp and clearly stated at the outset. As the Enlightenment philosopher Jean-Jacques Rousseau said in his *Dictionnaire de musique* (1768): "Through all the embroidery, one must always be able to recognize the essence of the melody."

To that end composers of the Classical period and beyond often chose themes that were already well-known to the listener: folk songs, popular tunes, and favorite arias and marches from successful operas, for example. Patriotic songs have always seemed especially apt for musical variation. Those so treated include *God Preserve Franz the Emperor* (Haydn), *God Save the King* (Beethoven), *Rule Britannia* (Beethoven), and later *Yankee Doodle* (Vieuxtemps) and *America* (Ives). Such tunes are popular, in part, because they are simple, and this, too, is an advantage for the composer. Melodies that are spare and uncluttered can more easily be dressed in new musical clothing. The essence of theme and variations, then, is to present a simple, direct melody and restate it again and again, each time musically varying or disguising the theme in some novel fashion.

How is variation of a theme brought about? It is done one of two ways: either by merely ornamenting the theme, overlaying it with figural patterns, or, what produces a more radical transformation, by altering its shape—changing its rhythmic, harmonic, or melodic profile in some way. In the two examples that follow, one by Mozart and one by Haydn, the specific techniques of ornamentation and alteration of a melody will become apparent. You will be challenged to retain a familiar tune in your ear as the composer embellishes or transforms it.

In the Classical period it was common for a composer-pianist to improvise in concert a set of variations on a well-known tune, perhaps one called out from the audience. Contemporary reports tell us that Mozart was especially skilled in this art of spontaneous variation. In 1778 he published, as was mentioned earlier, a set of such improvised variations built on the French folk song *Ah, vous dirai-je, Maman,* which we know as *Twinkle, Twinkle, Little Star.* With a tune as well known as this, it is easy to follow the melody as it is subjected increasingly to ornamentation and transformation in the course of twelve variations. (Only the first eight bars of the theme are given here; for the complete melody, see page 165; the music can be heard on Intro CD/17.)

EXAMPLE 9–3a: *Twinkle, Twinkle, Little Star,* Basic Theme (0:00)

Variation 1 ornaments the theme and almost buries it beneath an avalanche of sixteenth notes. Would you know that *Twinkle, Twinkle* lurks herein (see the asterisks) if you did not have the tune securely in your ear?

🔹 F I G U R E 9–5

A portrait of the young Mozart at the keyboard painted during his first trip to Italy, in 1770.

Mozart's variation on Twinkle, Twinkle

EXAMPLE 9–3b: Variation 1 (0:51)

FIGURE 9–6
Emperor Joseph II with two of his sisters. Mozart made a point of meeting the musically knowledgeable emperor in 1781. The score on the piano is by Mozart's rival at court, Antonio Salieri.

In variation 2 the rushing sixteenth notes are transferred to the bass, so that the theme surfaces again rather clearly in the upper voice.

EXAMPLE 9–3c: Variation 2 (1:45)

In variation 3, triplets* appear in the right hand, and only the general contour of the melody is audible. Thus, the melody here is transformed.

EXAMPLE 9–3d: Variation 3 (2:36)

After the same technique has been applied to the bass (variation 4), a thematic alteration again occurs in variation 5. Here the rhythm of the melody is "jazzed up" by placing part of it off the beat, in syncopated fashion.

EXAMPLE 9–3e: Variation 5

Of the remaining seven variations, some change the tune to minor, others add Bach-like counterpoint against it, while the final variation presents this duple-meter folk tune reworked into a triple-meter waltz! Yet throughout all of Mozart's magical embroidery, the theme remains clearly audible, so well ingrained is *Twinkle, Twinkle* in our musical memory.

*   *   *   *   *

Joseph Haydn (1732–1809) was the first composer to take theme and variations form and use it for a movement inside a symphony. His Symphony No. 94 (The "Surprise" Symphony) has been his most celebrated composition ever since it was first performed in London early in 1792.

We have already discussed the third movement, the minuet (see page 168). But the work owes its popularity, and its nickname, to the slow second movement *(Andante)*, written in theme and variations form. The famous opening theme possesses both simplicity and immediate appeal. Notice how the beginning is shaped by laying out in succession the notes of a tonic triad (I) and a dominant chord (V) in C major. The chordal implications of the tune account for its folk-song–like quality and make it easy to remember during the variations that follow (see the first example in the Listening Guide). These first eight bars (**A**) are stated and then repeated quietly. And just when all is ending peacefully, the full orchestra comes crashing in with a *fortissimo* chord, as if to shock the drowsy listener back to attention. What better way to show off the latent dynamic power of the larger Classical orchestra? The surprise *fortissimo* chord is a dominant chord that leads into the **B** section of the theme (second example in the Listening Guide), another eight-bar phrase, which is also repeated but with added flute and oboe accompaniment. With the simple yet highly attractive binary theme now in place, Haydn proceeds to compose four variations on it, adding a superb coda at the end.

LISTENING GUIDE

Joseph Haydn
Symphony No. 94, The "Surprise" Symphony (1791)
Second movement, *Andante* (moving)

6CD 2/5

Form: theme and variations

THEME

0:00   First part (**A**) of the theme
0:16   **A** repeated softly, then *fortissimo* chord

0:33   Second part (**B**) of the theme
0:49   **B** repeated with flute and oboe added

VARIATION 1

1:06   **A** played by second violins while first violins and flute add counterpoint above
1:22   **A** repeated
1:39   **B** with counterpoint continuing above in first violins and flutes
1:55   **B** repeated

VARIATION 2

2:11   **A** played loud and in minor key, shift (2:19) to rich major chord
2:27   **A** repeated
       (Variation of **B** omitted)
2:43   Full orchestra develops **A** in minor key
3:11   First violins alone, playing in unison

VARIATION 3

3:20   **A** ornamented rapidly by oboe
3:34   **A** repeated; melody in strings with oboe and flute ornamenting above
3:50   **B** now in strings with oboe and flute ornamenting above
4:05   **B** repeated

VARIATION 4

4:23   **A** loud, in full orchestra, with violins playing running scales
4:38   **A** repeated with theme rhythmically varied
4:55   **B** varied further by the violins
5:11   **B** repeated loudly by full orchestra
5:27   Transition to coda, pause (5:35)

CODA

5:40   Reminiscences of theme in its original form

After listening to this movement by Haydn, you can now understand that hearing theme and variations form requires listening to discrete units of music. Each block (variation) is marked by some new treatment of the theme. In the

A Rondo By Sting

While the rondo may have enjoyed its greatest favor in the sphere of art music during the Baroque and Classical periods, it has continued to live on in the realm of folk and popular song, undoubtedly because the refrain–digression pattern has such universal appeal. Traditional ballads such as *Tom Dooley* make use of it, and so do more recent pop songs by artists such as Arlo Guthrie in *City of New Orleans*. Sting's *Every Breath You Take* produces a rondo pattern (**ABACABA**) that in its symmetrical, indeed palindromic, shape would do any Classical composer proud:

Sting (Gordon Sumner)

Every breath you take	Every single day	
Every move you make	Every word you say	
Every bond you break	Every game you play	**A**
Every step you take	Every night you stay	
I'll be watching you.	I'll be watching you.	

O can't you see, you belong to me
How my poor heart aches, with every step you take.   **B**

Every move you make
Every vow you break
Every smile you fake   **A**
Every claim you stake
I'll be watching you.

Since you've gone I've been lost without a trace
I dream at night I can only see your face
I look around but it's you I can't replace   **C**
I feel so cold and I long for your embrace
I keep crying baby please.

Instrumental interlude (no text) to **A** music,   **A**

O can't you see, you belong to me . . . (etc.)   **B**

Every move you make . . . (etc.)   **A**

Coda (fade out)

(Available on A & M Records CD 75021 3902 2)

Classical period all the units are usually the same size, that is, the same number of measures. The variations become progressively more complicated as more ornamentation and transformation are applied. The addition of a coda after the last variation gives extra weight to the end, so that the listener feels the set of variations has reached an appropriate conclusion. If such extra bars were not appended, the audience would be left hanging, expecting yet another variation to begin.

RONDO FORM

Rondo form is an ancient musical structure in which a refrain continually alternates with contrasting material. We have previously seen this formal plan at work in the music of the Middle Ages (see page 76) and of the Baroque era (see pages 56 and 115). During the Classical period composers like Haydn and Mozart took the principle of rondo form and expanded and enlivened it. Not only were simple designs like **ABABA** and **ABACA** used, but sometimes more complex arrangements as well, such as **ABACABA** and **ABACADA.** What is more, they borrowed a style of writing found in sonata–allegro form. The more expansive and dramatic musical treatment of the transitions and development

ancient form expanded and enlivened

sections of sonata–allegro form was brought into the rondo. The rondo of the Classical period, therefore, is not merely a collection of short sections linked back to back, as is usually true of the Baroque rondo (see page 56), but an elastic, flexible form in which the recurring theme and the subordinate ideas develop and expand to new proportions. The subordinate ideas may be themes in their own right (lettered **B, C,** and **D**), or they may simply be digressions (**X**) away from the periodic refrain. Haydn uses the latter approach—refrain–digression—in the last movement of his Symphony No. 88 (1789). Here the theme (refrain) is a carefree tune in bright G major, and, though lengthy, it has a clear **aba'** shape to it.

LISTENING GUIDE

Joseph Haydn
Symphony No. 88 (1789)
Fourth movement, *Allegro con spirito* (fast with spirit)

6CD 2/7;
2CD 1/10

Form: rondo

Rondo form

0:00	Statement of **a**	
0:07	Repeat of **a**	
0:14	Beginning of **b**	**aba'** form
0:26	Statement of **a'**	with repeats
0:34	Repeat of **b** and **a'**	

A (refrain)

0:54	Scales and rapid movement
1:11	Hint of **a** and turn to minor
1:23	More scales and active bass

X (digression)

1:39	**a** and **b** but without concluding **a'** and without repeats

A

2:00	Development of turn motive
2:36	Texture thins out to just two repeating notes

X

2:43	Return of **aba'** but without repeats

A

3:09	Chords signal beginning of coda; then running scales and final cadential chords

Coda

(Listening Exercise 20)

The general mood of this movement by Haydn is typical of the lively rondo, which tends to be lighter and more jovial in spirit than does a movement in sonata–allegro form. Classical composers most often used rondo form as the final movement (finale) of a sonata, quartet, or symphony. The tuneful refrain and easily grasped digressions produce a light-hearted ending intended to leave the audience, if not euphoric, at least in a pleasant state of mind.

FORM, MOOD, AND THE LISTENER'S EXPECTATIONS

The audience of the late eighteenth century brought to the concert hall certain expectations, not only about the structure but also about the mood of the music that was to be performed. Listeners had a notion of what the form, tempo, and general character would be of each movement of a sonata, quartet, or symphony. For the Classical period we might summarize these as follows:

Movement:	1	2	3	4
Tempo:	Fast	Slow	Lively	Fast
Form:	Sonata–allegro	Large ternary, theme and variations, or rondo	Minuet and trio in ternary form	Sonata–allegro, theme and variations, or rondo
Mood:	Serious and substantive despite fast tempo	Lyrical and tender	usually light and elegant, sometimes spirited	Bright, light-hearted, sometimes humorous

Ludwig van Beethoven (1770–1827) and later composers of the Romantic period (1820–1900) modified somewhat this conventional format—the third movement, for example, was often treated as a boisterous scherzo (see page 191) rather than as an elegant minuet, and the finale became a more serious, weighty conclusion, with the result that the lighthearted rondo fell out of fashion. Yet the Classical model was well established in the mind of the listener. For, unlike previous periods in the history of music, succeeding generations did not forget the music of Haydn, Mozart, and their contemporaries. Their sonatas, quartets, and symphonies enjoyed undiminished favor with the listening public, and the formal designs they created or popularized have remained, with a few exceptions, the norm for the concert hall down to the present day.

lasting influence of the Classical model

  LISTENING EXERCISES

 Wolfgang Amadeus Mozart   6CD 2/11
Overture to the opera *Don Giovanni* (1787)

As is typical of overtures in the Classical period, the one Mozart wrote to precede his opera *Don Giovanni* (1787) is composed in sonata–allegro form. (The opera itself is discussed at length in the following chapter.) Mozart begins his overture with a slow introduction that incorporates many of the musical motives he will later use within the opera. This ominous beginning is written in D minor, which brightens to D major at the start of the exposition. Since this is an overture and not a symphony, there is no repetition of the exposition.

In the exercise that follows, the sections of the exposition are identified for you so that you become familiar with the main thematic material of this piece. Then, beginning with the development and continuing through the recapitulation and brief coda, you are asked a series of questions that follow the unfolding of sonata form.

0:00   Introduction commences with slow, sinister chords that give way to twisting chromaticism, and, finally, writhing scales.

1:56   Exposition begins fast but quietly in major key with first theme in the strings.

2:15   Cadential pattern brings first theme group to a close.

2:20   Transition starts with scalar theme presented in sequence.

2:30   Continues with unstable chords that build tension.

2:35   Transition ends with strong cadence.

2:41   Second theme marked by scalar descent and then "birdlike fluttering" in woodwinds.

3:00   Light closing theme.

3:10   Static, cadential harmony signals end of exposition.

Questions:

1. 3:20   Which theme is used here at the beginning of the development? _____

2. 3:31   This same theme is now heard in the woodwinds in which guise?
   a. in overlapping imitation
   b. as a chorale
   c. as a cadence

3. 3:40   Which theme enters? _____

4. 3:54   Which theme now returns? _____

5. 4:20–4:26 Retransition: In this section is the harmony active or static? _____ [Listen to the double basses and tim-pani. Are they moving to different pitches (active harmony) or just repeating one note (static harmony)?]

6. 4:27   Now the recapitulation begins. Does it commence as expected, with the first theme? _____

7. 4:49   Does the transition return again at this point?

_____

8. 5:08   Do both the descending scale and the "flutter" motive appear as the second theme returns? _____

9. 5:29   Does the closing theme return? _____

10. 5:45   A brief coda begins here. A reminiscence of which theme is heard as the main melodic material? _____

N.B. There are no *forte* cadential chords to produce a "big bang" ending for this overture. Rather, Mozart writes an orchestral fadeout designed to coincide with the raising of the curtain and to lead into the music of the first scene of the opera.

· ·

Joseph Haydn   6CD 2/7; 2CD 1/10
Symphony No. 88 (1789)
Fourth movement, *Allegro con spirito* (fast with spirit)

The first four questions of this exercise pertain to issues of orchestration; the final six address the form and general feeling of a rondo. Be sure you are famil-iar with the Listening Guide on page 180.

1. (0:00–0:13) Which woodwind instrument plays along with the strings dur-ing the first part (**a**) of the refrain?
   a. flute   b. bassoon   c. clarinet

2. (0:27–0:34 and 0:48–0:54; for both passages the answer is the same) Which two woodwind instruments play the return of the first part (**a'**) of the refrain?
   a. flute and clarinet   b. flute and bassoon   c. clarinet and bassoon

3. (1:39–1:46) Which woodwind instrument plays the refrain here at its first return?
   a. flute   b. bassoon   c. clarinet

4. (2:43–2:50) Which woodwind instruments play the refrain here at its sec-ond return?
   a. flute and clarinet   b. flute and bassoon   c. clarinet and bassoon

5. The refrain, or theme **A,** of this rondo has an **aba'** structure, which is simi-lar to which form from the Baroque era?
   a. *da capo* aria form   b. rondo form   c. fugal form

6. Is there a second theme in this movement, one that contrasts with the re-frain (**A**)? _____

7. (0:54–1:12 and 2:00–2:23) In this rondo the sections that begin to digress from the refrain are *least* like which functional type of music found in sonata–allegro form?
   a. transitional   b. developmental   c. cadential

8. What is the overall mood of this rondo?
    a. lyrical and hymnlike
    b. serious, even anguished
    c. light and carefree
9. What helps create this mood?
    a. There is much staccato playing throughout.
    b. The movement is mostly in a major key.
    c. The tempo is fast.
    d. There are many short notes that repeat quickly.
    e. all of the above
10. What is the function of the coda in this rondo?
    a. adds cadential material to give feeling of conclusion
    b. allows for one final statement of the refrain

KEY WORDS

coda	minuet	serenade
development	recapitulation	sonata–allegro form
exposition	relative major	transition (bridge)
fugato	retransition	trio

A checklist of musical style in the Classical period is given on page 63.

CLASSICAL GENRES

 In music the general term "genre" refers to that special quality of musical style, form, performing medium, and even place of performance that we associate with one class or type of music. The string quartet is a genre of music just as is the country music ballad, the cabaret song, the military march, and even the straight-ahead rock 'n' roll tune. When we choose to hear pieces of one genre or another, we listen with certain expectations as to how these works will sound, how they will progress, and how long they will last. We may even go to a special place, an opera house or a bar, and dress a certain way—in tuxedo or black leather jacket, for example—depending upon the genre of music we will hear. In simplest terms, then, a musical genre is a general type of music.

In the Classical period there were five main genres of secular art music: the symphony, string quartet, sonata, concerto, and opera. Though performed by different forces and usually in different environments, the same sort of audience might attend each. One of these genres, the opera, was taken over from the Baroque era and, though modified by Classical composers, retained its fundamental structure. Two others, the sonata and concerto, had also existed during the Baroque period, but were so changed by Haydn, Mozart, and their contemporaries that they were now tantamount to new genres. And still two others, the symphony and the string quartet, had no immediate ancestors in the Baroque era but were created wholly new during the Classical period.

THE SYMPHONY

It was during the Classical era that the symphony sprang forth to become the preeminent musical genre. That Haydn composed so many (104) and Mozart an even more astonishing number (41), given his short life, shows that the symphony had become, and would remain, the genre through which an aspiring composer might test his mettle and start on the road to international fame.

The symphony traces its origins to the late seventeenth-century Italian opera overture called the **sinfonia** ("a harmonious sounding together"). Around 1700 the typical Italian *sinfonia* was a one-movement instrumental work in three sections, fast–slow–fast. Soon Italian musicians and foreigners alike took the *sinfonia* out of the opera house and expanded it into three separate and distinct movements. A fourth movement, the minuet, was inserted by composers north of the Alps beginning in the 1740s. Thus, by mid-century the symphony had emerged as an independent genre and assumed its familiar four-movement format, fast–slow–minuet–fast.

The public favor the symphony came to enjoy was tied directly to certain revolutionary social changes that swept Europe during the Enlightenment. Not the least of these, as we have seen, was the impressive growth of public concerts (see page 152). The center of musical life in such cities as London, Paris, and, to a lesser degree, Vienna gradually shifted from the aristocratic court to the newly constructed or refurbished public concert hall. Larger audiences and greater financial gain for the composer could be had at public concerts like those mounted in the Hanover Square Rooms in London (see page 156) or the Burgtheater in Vienna (Figs. 10–1 and 10–2), where commoner and aristocrat met on more-or-less equal footing. Although some members of the nobility, notably the elector at Mannheim and the Esterházy princes, were important patrons of the early symphony, the genre ultimately flourished in an upper-middle-class environment. All but a few of Haydn's last twenty symphonies were composed for public performance in Paris and London, and Mozart apparently wrote no symphonies for a court patron during the last ten years of his life. His G minor symphony was apparently first performed in a casino (see Fig. 10–4)—that's where the people were and that's where the money was to be found. Henceforth, the listening public, and not the aristocratic prince, provided the principal support for the symphony and for the instrumental ensemble that performed it, the symphony orchestra.

Naturally, as the place of performance of the symphony moved from the aristocratic salon to the public auditorium, the size of the audience and the size of the concert hall increased. The orchestra of Haydn's patron, Prince Nikolaus Esterházy, was never larger than twenty-five, and the audience at court was often only the prince and his staff (Fig. 10–3). But when Haydn went to London to appear before the public in 1791, his "London Symphonies" were performed in the Hanover Square Rooms (see Fig. 9–7), which accommodated between eight hundred and nine hundred persons. Indeed, for one of his public

❧ FIGURE 10–1

At the right, the Burgtheater, Vienna, where many symphonies, concertos, and operas by Mozart were first heard. The building to the left now serves as the famous Spanish Riding School.

❧ FIGURE 10–2

The interior of the Burgtheater, which could accommodate an audience of about seven hundred. Mozart directed four of his operas and performed several of his piano concertos there. Beethoven made his Viennese debut in this theater on March 29, 1795.

concerts in the spring of 1792, nearly 1,500 eager patrons crowded in. To fill these larger halls with sound, a larger orchestra was needed. Mozart mentions an orchestra of at least eighty players, including forty violins, ten violas, eight cellos, and ten double basses, for a public concert in the Burgtheater in Vienna in 1781 (Fig. 10–2). And although this ensemble was unusually large, orchestras of fifty or sixty players for public performance were not uncommon in Paris and London by the end of the century.

The heart of the Classical orchestra, as had been true of the earlier Baroque orchestra, was the string section: the ensemble of violins, violas, cellos, and double basses. But not only were there now more instruments in the group, the violin was modestly different as well. To produce a larger, more penetrating tone, metal strings, which could be strung to greater tension, began to replace those of animal gut. The winds were also increased in number so as to be heard in the midst of the large string sound. Now, instead of just one flute or one bassoon, there were usually pairs. And a new woodwind was introduced, the clarinet. Mozart was particularly delighted when he first heard the clarinet used as an orchestral instrument during a visit to the Mannheim court in 1778. "Ah, if only we had clarinets too! You cannot imagine the glorious effect of a symphony with flutes, oboes, and clarinets," he wrote to his father back in provincial Salzburg. Later Beethoven and Schubert would share his love for the rich color of this instrument. By the 1780s, then, the full Classical orchestra consisted of strings, two oboes, two flutes, two clarinets, two bassoons, two horns, and, for especially festive symphonies, two trumpets and timpani.

🌿 FIGURE 10–3
Haydn leading the orchestra at the court of the Esterházy princes during a performance of a comic opera. The composer is seated at the keyboard, surrounded by the cellos. The higher strings and woodwinds are seated at the desk.

Mozart: Symphony No. 40 in G minor (1788)

Mozart's celebrated symphony in G minor requires all of the full instrumental sound and disciplined playing the late eighteenth-century orchestra could muster. This is not a festive composition (hence no trumpets and drums), but rather an intensely brooding work that suggests tragedy and feverish despair. While we might be tempted to associate the minor key and despondent mood with a specific event in Mozart's life, apparently no such causal relationship exists. This was one of three symphonies, his last three, that Mozart produced in the incredibly short span of six weeks during the summer of 1788, and the other two are sunny, optimistic works. Rather than responding to a particular disappointment, it is more likely that Mozart invoked the tragic muse in this G minor symphony by drawing on a lifetime of disappointments and a premonition—as his letters attest—of an early death.

a composer's mood; a composer's music

FIRST MOVEMENT (*MOLTO ALLEGRO*)
Exposition: Although Mozart begins his G minor symphony with a textbook example of Classical phrase structure (four-bar antecedent, four-bar consequent

phrases), an unusual sense of urgency is created by the repeating, insistent eighth-note figure at the beginning. This urgent motive is immediately grasped by the listener and, indeed, is the most memorable theme of the work.

EXAMPLE 10–1

What is not so quickly seized, but yet contributes equally to the sense of urgency, is the accelerating rate of harmonic change. At the outset chords are set beneath the melody at an interval of one chord every four measures, then one every two bars, then one every measure, then two chords per measure, and finally four. Thus, the harmony, or harmonic rhythm, is moving sixteen times faster at the end of this section than at the start. This is how Mozart creates the drive and urgency we all feel yet may be unable to explain. After this quickening start, the first theme begins once again, but soon veers off its previous course and into the transition. Transitions are filled with motion, especially running scales, and this one is no exception. What is unusual is that a motive is inserted, one so distinctive we might call it a transition theme (see the example in the following Listening Guide). As if to reciprocate for an extra theme here, Mozart dispenses with one toward the end of the exposition, at the point where we would expect a closing theme to appear. Instead, as closing material he makes use of the persistent motive and rhythm from the beginning of the first theme, and this rather nicely rounds off the exposition. Finally, a single, isolated chord is heard, one that leads back to a repeat of the exposition, or, second time through, launches into the development.

accelerating harmonic rhythms

Development. In the development Mozart employs only the first theme (and then only the first four bars), but subjects it to a variety of musical treatments. First he carries it through several distantly related keys, next shapes it into a fugue subject for use in a fugato*, then sets it as a descending melodic sequence, and finally inverts the direction of the motive.

manipulation of the motive

The retransition* is suddenly interrupted by *sforzandi* (loud attacks). But soon a dominant pedal point* is heard in the bassoons, and above it the flute and clarinets begin to cascade down to the tonic pitch. This use of soloistic woodwinds in the retransition is a hallmark of Mozart's symphonic style.

Recapitulation. As expected, the recapitulation offers the themes in the same order in which they appeared in the exposition. But now the transition theme, which Mozart has left untouched since its initial appearance, receives extended treatment, creating something akin to a second development section as it is pulled through one new key after another, only to end up back in the original tonic minor. When the lyrical second theme finally reappears, it has a more somber, plaintive mood now that it is in minor. Because the repeating figure of the first theme rounds off the recapitulation by way of a closing theme, only the briefest coda is needed to end this passionate, haunting movement.

LISTENING GUIDE

Wolfgang Amadeus Mozart
Symphony No. 40 in G minor (1788)
First movement, *Molto allegro* (very fast)

6CD 2/8;
2CD 1/11

Form: sonata–allegro

EXPOSITION   [ ] = repeat

0:00	[1:53]	Urgent, insistent first theme
0:21	[2:15]	First theme begins to repeat but is cut short
0:30	[2:23]	Transition
0:36	[2:28]	Rapid, ascending scales
0:44	[2:38]	Strong cadence ending transition, pause to clear the air
0:47	[2:41]	Lyrical second theme, major key contributes to brighter mood
0:56	[2:50]	Second theme repeated with new orchestration
1:09	[3:02]	Crescendo leading to closing material (taken from first theme)

DEVELOPMENT

3:49	Opening motive of first theme taken through several distant keys
4:01	First theme used as fugue subject in basses and then violins
4:23	First theme reduced to just opening motive
4:43	*Sforzandi* (loud attacks) give way to retransition
4:52	Dominant pedal point* in bassoons with cascading flute and clarinets above

RECAPITULATION

4:59	First theme returns
5:19	First theme begins to repeat but cut off by transition
5:27	Transition theme returns but is greatly extended
5:55	Rapid, ascending scales
6:04	Cadence and pause
6:07	Second theme now in (tonic) minor
6:17	Second theme repeated with new orchestration
6:30	Return of crescendo leading to closing material (taken from first theme)

CODA

7:11	Begins with rising chromatic scale
7:18	Opening motive returns, then three final chords

(Listening Exercise 21)

🌸 FIGURE 10-4
The New Market in Vienna as painted in 1759. The building on the right housed the city casino, and it was here that Mozart's G minor symphony was first performed in 1788. Even today famous musicians, such as Luciano Pavarotti, still perform in casinos—that's where the money is!

chamber music: one player per part

SECOND MOVEMENT (*ANDANTE*)

After the feverish excitement of the opening movement, the slow, lyrical *Andante* comes as a welcome change of pace. What makes this movement exceptionally beautiful is the extraordinary interplay between the light and dark colors of the woodwinds against the constant tone of the strings. If there is no thematic contrast and confrontation here, there is, nonetheless, heartfelt expression brought about by Mozart's masterful use of orchestral color.

THIRD MOVEMENT (*MINUETTO: ALLEGRETTO*)

We expect the aristocratic minuet to provide elegant, graceful dance music. But much to our surprise, Mozart returns to the intense, somber mood of the opening movement. This he does, in part, by choosing to write in the tonic minor key—a rare minuet in minor.

FOURTH MOVEMENT (*ALLEGRO ASSAI*)

The finale starts with an ascending rocket that explodes in a rapid, *forte* flourish—and only carefully rehearsed string playing can bring off the brilliant effect of this opening gesture. The contrasting second theme of this sonata–allegro form movement is typically Mozartean in its grace and charm, a proper foil to the explosive opening melody. Midway through the development musical compression takes hold: There is no retransition, only a pregnant pause before the recapitulation; the return dispenses with the repeats built into the first theme; and a coda is omitted. This musical foreshortening at the end produces the same psychological effect experienced at the very beginning of the symphony—a feeling of urgency and acceleration.

🌸 THE STRING QUARTET

If the symphony is the ideal genre for the public concert hall and aims to please a large listening public, the string quartet is intended for the private chamber and sometimes for an audience of just the performers themselves. Unlike the symphony, which even in the Classical era might have a dozen violinists joining on the first violin line, the **string quartet** has only one player per part: one first violinist, one second violinist, one violist, and one cellist (Fig. 10–5). Moreover, there is no conductor. All performers function equally and communicate directly among themselves. No wonder the German poet Johann Wolfgang von Goethe (1749–1832) compared the string quartet to a conversation among four intelligent people. Although chamber music can include many modes of performance, ranging from a solo piano or violin to a piano trio, wind quintet, or even a string octet, all employ just one player on a part. Of these chamber media, the string quartet is historically the most important.

In the Baroque era the favored ensemble for chamber music was the trio sonata*, a group of two melody instruments, usually violins, and a *basso continuo** (including keyboard), which set the harmonies from below. With the emphasis shifting from the bottom-heavy Baroque to the lighter, simpler melodies of the early Classical period, the trio sonata ceded pride of place in the 1750s to the string quartet. The *basso continuo* gradually disappears and a new type of bass line emerges, one played by an agile cello alone. Moreover, the middle of the texture is given greater substance by assigning an active role to the viola, the instrument playing immediately above the cello.

❀ FIGURE 10–5

A representation of a string quartet at the end of the eighteenth century. The string quartet was at first an ensemble for playing chamber music in the home. Not until 1804 did a string quartet appear in a public concert in Vienna, and not until 1814 in Paris.

Joseph Haydn created this new style of chamber music. In his mature quartets the spectrum of sound from top to bottom is covered evenly by four instruments that participate more or less equally in a give and take of theme and motive. As with most Classical quartets, Haydn's have the usual succession of four movements, fast–slow–minuet–fast. But in a set he wrote in 1772 Haydn dubbed each minuet a **scherzo** (Italian for "joke"), suggesting the high-spirited style of playing intended for this movement and the string quartet in general.

It was the chance to play string quartets together that gave rise to a lasting friendship between Haydn and Mozart. During the summer of 1784 and winter of 1785, the two men met in Vienna, sometimes at the home of an aristocrat, sometimes in Mozart's own apartments. Haydn played first violin, Mozart viola in their quartet. As a result of this experience, Mozart was inspired to dedicate a set of his best works in this genre to the older master, which he published in 1785 (Fig. 10–6). Yet in this convivial, domestic music-making, Haydn and Mozart merely joined in the fashion of the day. For whether in Vienna, Paris, or London, aristocrats and members of the well-to-do middle class were encouraged to play quartets with friends as well as to engage professional musicians to entertain their guests. Haydn, Mozart, Beethoven, and young Schubert wrote some of their finest works for these amateur and professional ensembles. Their trios, quartets, and quintets have come to occupy such an important place in the repertoire that Classical chamber music has become almost synonymous with chamber music itself.

Haydn: Opus 76, No. 3, The "Emperor" Quartet (1797)

Haydn's "Emperor" Quartet, written in Vienna during the summer of 1797, is counted among the best works of the string quartet genre. It is known as the "Emperor" because it makes liberal use of *The Emperor's Hymn*, a melody Haydn himself composed the previous January in honor of Emperor Franz II. The invasion of imperial lands by the armies of Napoleon in that year had started a patriotic firestorm in Vienna, and Haydn's tune, set to the text "Gott erhalte Franz

❀ FIGURE 10–6

Title page of six string quartets by Mozart dedicated to Haydn (1785). Mozart offers them to Haydn as "six children," asking Haydn to be their "father, guide, and friend."

den Kaiser" ("God preserve Franz the Emperor"), was all the rage. (With altered texts it subsequently became, in addition to a Protestant hymn, the national anthem of Austria [1853] and Germany [1950].) Although the charming minuet makes no use of the emperor's tune, and the opening and closing movements of this quartet only allude to it, the slow second movement uses the majestic melody as the basis of a theme and variations set. The theme (see the example in the following Listening Guide) is first presented by the first violin, and harmonized in simple chords. Four variations follow. In these all four instruments are given equal opportunity to hold forth with the tune. Example 10–2 shows how in the Classical string quartet the melodic profile of each of the lines is pretty much the same, a far cry from the melody–walking-bass* polarity that typified the earlier Baroque trio sonata.

equality of instruments

EXAMPLE 10–2

Had Haydn been writing for a symphony orchestra, he could not have composed his bass line in this fashion. For the lowest string instrument in the symphony is the low double bass, which plays an octave below the cello and in that range produces a resonant, yet slightly muddled sound. But the more flexible fingering and singing tone of the cello make it possible for even the lowest in-

❉ FIGURE 10–7

A performance of a sonata for piano and cello as depicted in 1775 by Joseph Zophany. This is one of the earliest paintings to show a piano rather than a harpsichord. Here the piano is a square piano of the type then manufactured in London.

strument of the string quartet to participate as an equal partner. What the quartet gives up by way of depth and richness of sound, it gains in increased motivic interaction and in a more transparent texture.

LISTENING
GUIDE

Joseph Haydn
String Quartet, Opus 76, No. 3, The "Emperor" Quartet (1797)
Second movement, *Poco adagio cantabile* (rather slow, songlike)

6CD 2/9;
2CD 1/12

Form: theme and variations

THEME

(repeat)

(repeat)

0:00   Theme played slowly in first violin; lower three parts provide chordal accompaniment

VARIATION 1

1:19   Theme in second violin while first violin ornaments above it

VARIATION 2

2:35   Theme in cello while other three instruments provide counterpoint against it

VARIATION 3

4:04   Theme in viola; other three instruments only gradually enter

VARIATION 4

5:31   Theme returns to first violin, but now the accompaniment is more contrapuntal than chordal

(Listening Exercise 22)

THE SONATA

The **sonata** was another important genre of chamber music that flourished during the Classical period. No longer was it a succession of four or five dance movements, as was usually the case during the Baroque era (see page 112). Now the sonata was a work in three movements (fast–slow–fast), each of which might make use of one or another of the forms favored by Classical composers: sonata–allegro, ternary, rondo, or theme and variations.

The sonata came to enjoy great popularity during the Classical period. According to publishers' inventories from the end of the eighteenth century, more sonatas were printed than any other type of music. The explanation for this sudden vogue is tied to the equally sudden favor experienced by the piano. Indeed, the word "sonata" has become so closely associated with the piano that

the piano sonata

unless otherwise qualified as "violin sonata," "cello sonata," or the like, we usually assume that "sonata" refers to a three-movement work for piano.

Who played this flood of new sonatas for the piano? Amateur musicians, mostly women, who practiced and performed for polite society in the comfort of their own homes. As we have seen (page 152), in Mozart's time the ability to play the piano, to do fancy needlework, and to utter a few selected words of French were thought by male-dominated society all that was necessary to be a cultured young lady. To teach the musical handicraft, instructors were needed. Mozart, Haydn, and Beethoven all served as piano teachers in fashionable circles early in their careers. The piano sonatas they composed for their numerous pupils were not intended to be played in the public concert halls. Sonatas were to provide students with material that they might practice to develop technique and that they might play as musical entertainment in the home. Even among the splendid thirty-two piano sonatas that Beethoven composed, only one was ever performed at a public concert in Vienna during his lifetime.

piano sonatas for women

(An example of a Classical piano sonata by Beethoven, his *Pathétique* Sonata, is found on 6CD 3/1 and 2CD 1/13. It is discussed in detail on page 211.)

✿ THE CONCERTO

With the genre of the concerto we leave the salon or private chamber and return once again to the public concert hall. For the Classical concerto is a large-scale, three-movement work for instrumental soloist and orchestra, and thus of the same magnitude as the symphony itself. And while the symphony might provide the greatest musical substance at a concert, more often than not the audience was lured to the hall by the prospect of hearing a virtuoso performer play a concerto. Audiences then as now had a special fascination with personal virtuosity and all the daring and excitement that a stunning technical display might bring. The soloist in such concertos was a single performer whose place in the musical firmament was that of a star. Gone was the Baroque tradition of the concerto grosso*, which pitted an orchestra (tutti*) against a *group* of soloists (the concertino*). From now on the concerto was a **solo concerto,** usually for piano, but sometimes for violin, cello, or wind instrument.

solo concerto offers technical display

Development of the solo concerto for piano had begun with the two sons of Johann Sebastian Bach, one living in Berlin, the other in London. The Berlin Bach, Carl Philip Emanuel Bach (1714–1788), was the keyboard player for the flute-playing King Frederick the Great (1712–1786) of Prussia, who drilled his troops during the day and played concertos in the evening. Johann Christian Bach (1735–1782), the London Bach as he was called, experimented with the piano concerto in connection with a series of public concerts he gave both in London and Paris during the 1760s and 1770s. But no one did more to bring the form and style of the piano concerto to maturity than Wolfgang Amadeus Mozart.

Mozart's concertos

Mozart wrote twenty-three piano concertos, more than any other important composer. He did so mainly because his economic livelihood depended on it, especially after he took up residence in Vienna as a freelance musician in 1781. Most of his masterpieces in this genre were composed so that Mozart himself might showcase his talents at public concerts that he alone had organized, for to attract attention in this period a composer not only had to write the music

FIGURE 10–8

A young woman performs a keyboard concerto supported by a small orchestra (from an engraving of 1777). Notice that the lid of the instrument has been removed to allow the sound to project farther.

but also had to serve as performer, concert manager, and ticket seller all in one (see Fig. 10–9). It was up to Mozart to rent the hall (see Figs. 10–1 and 10–2), hire the orchestra, solicit an audience, and offer his paying public a collection of his newest creations. A musical journal for March 22, 1783, reports one of Mozart's more successful ventures of this sort:

> Today the celebrated Chevalier Mozart gave a musical concert for his own benefit at the Burgtheater in which pieces of his own music, which was already very popular, were performed. The concert was honored by the presence of an extraordinarily large audience and the two new concertos and other fantasies which Mr. Mozart played on the Forte Piano were received with the loudest approval. Our Monarch [Emperor Joseph II], who contrary to his custom honored the entire concert with his presence, joined in the applause of the public so heartily that one can think of no similar example. The proceeds of the concert are estimated at sixteen hundred gulden.

With a take such as this, Mozart could, at least for a time, indulge his expensive tastes.

FIGURE 10–9

One of the few surviving tickets to a concert mounted by Mozart in Vienna.

Mozart: Piano Concerto No. 17 in G Major (1784)

Mozart composed this concerto, not for himself, but for one of his more talented pupils, the nineteen-year-old Barbara Ployer. In it the Classical love of balance is immediately evident, for the piano and orchestra appear in equal measure. Of all the solo instruments, the piano, with its capacity for melody, for speed of execution, and for full sound, is perhaps most up to the task of competing with an orchestra in a spirited give-and-take of musical material. When the orchestra comes forward with a rich, full sound or varied instrumental color, the piano can counter with a line of tender expression, a virtuosic run, or a passage of *fortissimo* chords. Although Mozart's piano was small by standards of

a contest between piano and orchestra

Barbara Ployer: Concert Pianist

In 1781 Mozart broke from his patron, the Archbishop of Salzburg, to establish himself as a freelance musician in Vienna. To earn a living, he took on a small number of piano students whom he visited daily for their lessons. Most of these were young women, and for the more talented of them he composed piano sonatas and concertos. Among the best was Barbara Ployer (1765–1811), the daughter of an old and wealthy acquaintance from Salzburg. It was for Fraulein Ployer "who paid me handsomely" that Mozart composed his Concerto No. 17 in G. When it came time to perform the work publicly in June 1784, Ployer did so at a concert organized in the town of Döbling outside of Vienna. For this premier, Mozart brought along the well-known composer Giovanni Paisiello (1740–1816) to show off both his pupil and concerto. The next year Ployer was described as "a marvelous pianist." She also studied musical composition with Mozart, and some alternative cadenzas* for his concertos are thought to be from her hand.

FIGURE 10–10

Another view of Mozart's piano. Mozart purchased this instrument in Vienna in 1784, the year he wrote his Concerto No. 17 in G.

a virtuoso cadenza

today (Fig. 10–10), during the performance of a concerto the lid was often removed (Fig. 10–8) to permit the sound to project more freely.

FIRST MOVEMENT (ALLEGRO)

As with all of Mozart's concertos, this one is in three movements (there is never a minuet or scherzo in a concerto). And, as is invariably the case, the first movement is written in sonata–allegro form. However, here it is modified to meet the special demands and opportunities of the concerto. What results is **double exposition form,** an extension of sonata–allegro form in which the orchestra plays one exposition and the soloist then plays another. First, the orchestra presents the first, second, and closing themes, all in the tonic key. Next, the soloist enters and, with orchestral assistance, offers the piano's version of the same material, but modulating to the dominant in the transition. Then a surprise in the middle of the transition: A new lyrical theme sounds forth in the piano alone. This is another feature of the Classical concerto—a melody held back, or saved, for presentation by the soloist. Toward the end of this second exposition a part of the first theme returns, a throwback to the ritornello* principle of the old Baroque concerto grosso.

The development focuses more on harmonies than themes, as the piano leads the orchestra through a succession of striking chord changes. The recapitulation compresses the two expositions into one, presenting the themes in the same order as before but now all in the tonic key. Finally, toward the end of the movement the orchestra suddenly stops its forward motion and comes to rest on a single chord. Using this chord as a springboard, the pianist plunges headlong into a flight of virtuosic fancy, the cadenza*. Now playing alone, the performer mixes rapid runs, arpeggios, and snippets of previously heard themes into a fantasy-like improvisation. Although Mozart wrote down these cadenzas, when he performed them the notated score was merely a stimulus to his imagination, just as in our own century a talented jazz musician might depart from a musical sketch to improvise an extended solo. After a minute or so of this razzle-dazzle, the pianist plays a trill* in the right hand to signal the orchestra that it is time for it to reenter the competition. From here to the end the orchestra holds forth, making use of the closing theme. There is much to follow in the Listening Guide for this movement in double exposition form, but the glorious music of Mozart will amply reward the attentive listener.

LISTENING GUIDE

Wolfgang Amadeus Mozart
Piano Concerto No. 17 in G major (1784)
First movement, *Allegro* (fast)

6CD 2/10

Form: double exposition sonata–allegro

EXPOSITION 1 (orchestra)

0:00   Strings present elegant first theme, part **a**

0:29   *Forte:* Full orchestra presents first theme part **b**

0:39   Transition: running scales, agitation, then calm cadence

1:02   Strings and then woodwinds play quiet, plaintive second theme

1:27   Bold harmonic shift momentarily sends music off course

1:43   Strings quietly present closing theme part **a**

2:03   Full orchestra loudly plays closing theme part **b**

EXPOSITION 2 (piano and orchestra)

2:15   Piano ornaments first theme part **a**
        with Alberti bass* accompaniment

2:48   Woodwinds and then full orchestra play first theme part **b**
2:59   Transition begins with piano playing runs and then arpeggios

3:16   Piano, solo, injects a graceful new theme

3:44   Transition continues as piano plays falling arpeggios
4:07   Piano plays second theme, then woodwinds take it over
4:32   Piano plays passage of rapid figuration, scales, and arpeggios
5:03   Full orchestra brings back first theme part **b**
5:15   Full orchestra plays closing theme part **b**

DEVELOPMENT

5:26   Bold harmonic shift, then piano plays arpeggios in midst of continually shifting harmonies
6:14   Piano develops turning motive from "new" theme in minor key
6:28   French horns play pedal point* signalling retransition back to recapitulation

(Continued on next page)

RECAPITULATION

6:43 Strings play first theme part **a**

7:09 Full orchestra plays first theme part **b**

7:20 Transition begins with runs in the violins

7:35 Piano gradually leads up to "new" theme

8:10 Transition continues through minor keys

8:32 Piano plays second theme, then woodwinds take it over

8:58 Piano plays scales, then arpeggios, and then a trill

9:23 Bold harmonic shift

9:33 Full orchestra plays loud, syncopated chords, then holds a chord

9:42 **Cadenza** for piano alone: references to first theme, second theme, and "new" theme; ends with trill signalling orchestra to recommence playing

11:00 Full orchestra plays closing theme parts **a** and **b**

11:27 Final cadential chords

SECOND MOVEMENT (*ANDANTE*)

Mozart saved some of his most heart-wrenching music for the slow, middle movements of his piano concertos. In this typical *andante* (gently moving movement) in **aba′** form, the expressive dialogue is mainly between the piano and the woodwinds.

THIRD MOVEMENT (*ALLEGRETTO*)

Mozart's bird

The finale is a straightforward set of variations on a simple theme. The theme, however, may have an unusual origin. It was apparently given to Mozart by a bird, a pet starling the composer purchased in the spring 1784. When he bought the bird, Mozart entered into his expense book its cost as well as a seventeen-note, four-measure tune it could mimic—the first seventeen notes of the theme of this finale.

EXAMPLE 10–3

In truth, it is not certain whether Mozart had taught this tune to the bird, or if the bird already knew it. At the least, it suggests that in the Classical period, even birds could be made to think in balanced, four-bar phrases!

✿ OPERA

Opera in the Classical period maintained the broad features passed on to it from the Baroque era. It still began with an overture, was divided into two or three acts, and made use of a succession of arias and recitatives along with an occasional choral number. Also, needless to say, it still was performed in a theater, one large enough to accommodate both an orchestra and elaborate stage sets.

Yet while the genre of opera retained its overall shape, it nonetheless underwent important internal changes during the second half of the eighteenth century. Italian comic opera (*opera buffa*), a powerful voice for social change in the Enlightenment (see page 151), came to dominate the stage and gradually replace the serious opera (*opera seria*) of the Baroque period. The statuelike gods and goddesses, emperors and queens, of the older style have departed, replaced by more natural, realistic characters drawn from everyday life. Gone, too, are the rigid sectional divisions between aria, recitative, and chorus set in place to segregate one emotion from another. Baroque opera posed magnificently; Classical opera moves gracefully. Although aria and recitative were still differentiated, in Classical opera they now flow more easily one to another. The mood of the music changes rapidly to reflect the up-and-down emotions of the characters. The more fluid Classical style is better suited to comic situations that invariably involve a quick give-and-take between characters.

easy flow of comic opera

Comic opera also brought a new element into the opera house, the **vocal ensemble.** While recitatives are still used to narrate action and arias to express emotion, now a variety of emotions can be expressed simultaneously by means of a vocal trio, quartet, or even sextet of soloists. One character might sing of her love, another of his fear, another of her outrage, while a fourth pokes fun at the other three. Vocal ensembles are especially favored at the ends of acts. No longer does the curtain fall after a solo "exit aria" from a famous **prima donna** (leading lady), but after a vocal ensemble including the principals—another manifestation of the collective spirit, and better dramatic sense, of the late eighteenth century.

the vocal ensemble

The master of Classical opera, and of the vocal ensemble in particular, is Wolfgang Amadeus Mozart. While Haydn wrote more than a dozen operas and conducted others (see Fig. 10–3, page 187), he lacked Mozart's instinct for what would work in the theater and what would not. Nor did he have Mozart's uncanny ability to depict and differentiate characters through music. With its lightning-quick changes in mood and color, and juxtaposition of themes of different character, Mozart's music is inherently theatrical and perfectly suited to the genre of opera.

Mozart wrote Italian *opera seria* of the old Baroque sort as well as German comic opera, which was called *Singspiel*. Like a Broadway musical, a **Singspiel** is made up of spoken dialogue (instead of recitative) and songs. Mozart's best work of this type is *Die Zauberflöte* (*The Magic Flute*, 1791), more recently popularized in a film version (1975) by the Swedish director Ingmar Bergman. But Mozart also wrote operas more in the tradition of Italian comic opera. These include his masterpieces *Le nozze di Figaro* (*The Marriage of Figaro*, 1786), *Don Giovanni* (1787), and *Così fan tutte* (*Thus Do They All*, 1790), all three with text (libretto) by Lorenzo da Ponte.

Mozart: *Don Giovanni* (1787)

Don Giovanni has been called not only Mozart's greatest opera but also the greatest opera ever written. The story tells the tale of a wicked philanderer, a Don Juan, who seduces and murders his way across Europe before being pursued and finally dragged down to hell by the ghost of a man whom he has killed. Since the seducer and mocker of public law and morality is a nobleman, *Don Giovanni* is implicitly critical of the aristocracy, and Mozart and da Ponte danced quickly to stay one step ahead of the imperial censor before production. Mozart's opera was first performed on October 29, 1787, at the Nostitz Theater (Fig. 10–11) in Prague, a city in which his music was especially popular. As fate would have it, the most notorious Don Juan of the eighteenth century, Giovanni

❀ FIGURE 10–11
A view of the Nostitz, or National Theater, Prague, where *Don Giovanni* was first performed on October 29, 1787. The theater still stands today and has been used for the filming of *Amadeus* (1985) and *Immortal Beloved* (1994).

overture

character depiction through music

Casanova (1725–1798), was in the audience that first night in Prague. It turns out that he had had a small hand in helping his friend da Ponte shape the libretto.

The overture to *Don Giovanni,* as we have seen (6CD 2/11; Listening Exercise 19), is written in sonata–allegro form. It begins with a slow introduction that incorporates several themes or motives important later in the opera. Just as an author postpones writing a preface until after a book is finished, so a composer saves the overture for the end of the creative process. In this way the overture can not only prefigure important themes in the opera but also characterize the overall tone of the work. Mozart, as was his custom, postponed much of the writing of *Don Giovanni* to the last minute, and the overture was not completed until the night before the premiere, the copyist's ink still wet on the pages as the music was handed to the orchestra.

As the last strains of the overture die away, the curtain rises on the comic figure Leporello, Don Giovanni's faithful, though somewhat reluctant, servant. He has been keeping a nocturnal vigil outside the house of Donna Anna while his master is at work inside. Grumbling as he paces back and forth, Leporello sings about how he would gladly trade places with the fortunate aristocrat ("I would like to play the gentleman"; 6CD 2/12). Immediately, we see Mozart working to establish the musical character of Leporello: He sets this opening aria in F major, a traditional key for the pastoral in music, showing that Leporello is a rustic fellow; he gives him a narrow vocal range, yet no fancy chromaticism; and he has him sing quick repeated notes, almost as if he were stuttering. This last technique, called "patter song," is a stock device used to depict low-caste, inarticulate characters in comic opera.

As Leporello concludes his complaint, the masked Don Giovanni rushes on stage, chased by the virtuous Donna Anna. Here the strings rush up the scale and the music modulates up a fourth (at 1:32) to signify that we are now dealing with the highborn. It seems that the Don has been checked in his advances toward Donna Anna, and the affronted lady wants him captured and unmasked. While the gentleman and lady carry on a musical tug-of-war in long notes above, the cowering Leporello patters away fearfully below. The vocal ensemble makes clear the conflicting emotions of each party.

Now the cast of characters in the ensemble changes as Donna Anna runs to get help and her father enters to challenge Don Giovanni. The listener senses that this bodes ill—there is an ominous tremolo* in the strings, and the music shifts from major to minor (2:50). Our fear is immediately confirmed as the Don, first refusing to duel, draws his sword and attacks the aging Commandant. In the brief exchange of steel, Mozart depicts the rising anxiety by means of ascending chromatic scales and tight, tense chords (3:32). At the very moment Don Giovanni's sword pierces the Commandant, the action stops and the orchestra holds on a painful **diminished chord** (3:44)—a chord made up of all minor thirds. Mozart then clears the air of discord with a simple texture and accompaniment as Don Giovanni and Leporello gaze in horror on the dying Commandant. The listener can feel the Commandant expire, his life sinking away through the slow descent of a chromatic scale (4:52). In its intensity and compression, the opening scene of *Don Giovanni* has no equal outside of Shakespeare's *King Lear*.

a duel set to music

Lorenzo da Ponte: Librettist to Mozart

Mozart's principal librettist during the 1780s was Lorenzo da Ponte, whose own life was more unbelievable than the theatrical characters he created. Born in northern Italy of Jewish parents, he received his only formal education in a Catholic seminary. He became a teacher of Italian and Latin literature and then an ordained priest, but was banned from his native Venice for his unreligious thinking and adulterous liaisons. Having made his way to Vienna in 1781, he was introduced to Emperor Joseph II by the imperial court composer Antonio Salieri (see page 159). Da Ponte became the official court librettist ("Poet to the Imperial Theaters"), and both Salieri and Mozart made use of his talents. But when Joseph died in 1790 and Mozart the following year, da Ponte's fortunes in Vienna declined.

After passing time with another famous Venetian adventurer, Giovanni Casanova (1725–1798), da Ponte made his way to London, where he opened a bookstore. But he was soon charged with shady financial dealings, so in 1805 da Ponte stole away from London for America, one step ahead of his creditors. After a brief stop in New York, he established himself in Sunbury, Pennsylvania, as a trader, distiller, and occasional gunrunner during the War of 1812. Eventually, he gave this up and returned to New York, becoming the first professor of Italian literature at Columbia University in 1825. The high point of his final years came in May 1826, when he helped bring *Don Giovanni* to the stage in New York, the first opera by Mozart to be performed in America.

Lorenzo da Ponte (1749–1838).

LISTENING GUIDE

Wolfgang Amadeus Mozart
Opera, *Don Giovanni* (1787)
Act I, Scene 1

6CD 2/12

Characters: Don Giovanni, a rakish lord; Leporello, his servant; Donna Anna, a virtuous noblewoman; the Commandant, her father, a retired military man

ARIA

Leporello

0:00   The watchful Leporello grumbles as he awaits his master Don Giovanni

Notte e giorno faticar,   On the go from morn 'til night
per chi nulla sa gradi,   for one who shows no appreciation,
piova e il vento sopportar,   sustaining wind and rain,
mangiar male e mal dormir.   without proper food or sleep.

Voglio far il gentilumo   I would like to play the gentleman
e non volgio più servir . . .   and no more a servant be . . .

(Leporello continues in this vein)

1:32   Violins rush up the scale and music modulates upward as Don Giovanni and Donna Anna rush in

ENSEMBLE (TRIO)

Donna Anna

1:38   Donna Anna trys to hold and unmask Don Giovanni while Leporello cowers on the side

Non sperar, se non m'uccidi,   Do not hope you can escape
ch'io ti lasci fuggir mai'.   unless you kill me.

Don Giovanni

Donna folle, indarno gridi,   Crazy lady, you scream in vain,
chi son io tu non saprai.   you will never know who I am.

Leporello

Che tumulto, oh ciel, che gridi   What a racket, heavens, what screams,

il padron in nuovi guai.   my master in a new scrape.

Donna Anna

Gente! Servi! Al traditore!   Everyone! Help! Catch the traitor!
Scellerato!   Scoundrel!

Don Giovanni

Taci et trema al mio furore!   Shut up and get out of my way!
Sconsigliata!   Fool!

Leporello

Sta a veder che il malandrino   We will see if this malefactor
mi fara recipitar. . . .   will be the ruin of me. . . .

(The trio continues in this manner with liberal repeats of text and music.)

2:50   String tremolo and shift from major to minor as the Commandant enters

ENSEMBLE (TRIO)

Commandant

     The Commandant comes forward to fight; Don Giovanni first refuses, then duels; Leporello tries to flee

Lasciala, indegno!   Let her go, villain!
Battiti meco!   Fight with me!

Don Giovanni

Va! non mi degno   Away, I wouldn't deign
di pugnar teco!   to fight with you!

Commandant

Così pretendi   So you think
da me fuggir!   you can get away thus?

Leporello (aside)

Potessi almeno   If I could only
di qua partir!   get out of here.

(Continued on next page)

			Don Giovanni	
		Misero! attendi		You old fool! Get ready then,
		se vuoi morir!		if you wish to die!
3:32	Musical duel (running scales and tense diminished chords)			
3:44	Climax on intense chord (the Commandant falls mortally wounded), then a pause			

ENSEMBLE (TRIO)

			Commandant	
3:50	Don Giovanni and Leporello look on the dying Commandant; the "ticking" sound in the strings freezes time	Ah, soccorso! son tradito. L'assassino m'ha ferito, e dal seno palpitante sento l'anima partir.		Ah, I'm wounded, betrayed The assassin has run me through, and from my heaving breast I feel my soul depart.

	Don Giovanni	
Ah, gia cade il sciagurato, affannoso e agonizzante, gia del seno palpitante Veggo l'anima partir.		Ah, already the old fool falls, gasping and writhing in pain, and from his heaving breast I can see his soul depart.

	Leporello	
Qual misfatto! qual eccesso! Entro il sen dallo spavento palpitar il cor mi sento. Io non so che far, che dir.		What a horrible thing, how stupid! I can feel within my breast my heart pounding from fear. I don't know what to say or do.

4:52	A slow, chromatic descent as the last breath seeps out of the Commandant

When we next meet the unrepentant Don Giovanni, he is in pursuit of the country girl Zerlina. She is the betrothed of another peasant, Masetto, and the two are to be married the next day. Don Giovanni quickly dismisses Masetto and turns his charm on the naive Zerlina. First he tries verbal persuasion carried off in *secco* recitative* (the harpsichord is still used to accompany *secco* recitatives in Classical opera, a vestige of the older Baroque practice). Zerlina, he says, is too lovely for a common swain like Masetto. Her beauty demands a higher state: She will become his wife.

This preliminary discussion in *secco* recitative now gives way to more passionate expression in the form of a charming duet, "Là ci darem la mano" ("Give me your hand, oh fairest"). Don Giovanni begins with a seductive melody (**A**) cast squarely in the Classical mold of two four-bar phrases. Zerlina repeats and extends this, but is still singing alone and untouched. The Don becomes more insistent in a new phrase (**B**), and Zerlina, in turn, becomes flustered, as her quick sixteenth notes reveal. The initial melody (**A**) returns but is now sung together by the two principals, their voices intertwining—musical union accompanies the act of physical touching that occurs on stage. Finally, as if to further affirm this coupling through music, a concluding section (**C**) is added in which the two characters skip off, arm in arm ("Let's go, my treasure"), their voices linked together, mainly in parallel-moving thirds to show unity of feeling and purpose. These are the means by which a skilled composer like Mozart can underscore, through music, the drama unfolding on the stage.

❀ FIGURE 10–12
Don Giovanni (Thomas Hampson) and Zerlina (Marie McLaughlin) sing the duet "Là ci darem la mano" from *Don Giovanni*.

LISTENING GUIDE

Wolfgang Amadeus Mozart
Opera, *Don Giovanni* (1787)
Act I, Scene 7

6CD 2/13

Characters: Don Giovanni and the peasant girl Zerlina

Situation: Don Giovanni tries, and apparently succeeds, in the seduction of Zerlina.

RECITATIVE

Don Giovanni

0:00   Alfin siam liberati, Zerlinetta gentil,
da quel sioccone.
Che ne dite, mio ben,
sò far pulito?

At last, gentle Zerlina,
we are free of that clown.
And say, my love, didn't
I handle it well?

Zerlina

Signore, è mio marito . . .

Sir, he is my fiance.

Don Giovanni

Chi? Colui?

Who? Him?

Vi par che un onest'uomo,
un nobil cavalier, qual io mi vanto,
possa soffrir che quel visetto d'oro,
quel viso inzuccherato
da un bifolcaccio vil sia strapazzato?

Do you think that an honorable
man, a noble cavalier as I
believe I am, could let such a
golden face, such a sweet
beauty, be profaned by that
clumsy oaf?

Zerlina

Ma, signor, io gli diedi
parola di sposarlo.

But sir, I have already given
my word to marry him.

Don Giovanni

Tal parola non vale un zero.
Voi non siete fatta per esser paesana;
un altra sorte vi procuran quegli
occhi bricconcelli, quei labretti si
belli, quelle dituccia candide e
odorose, par me toccar giuncata e
fiutar rose.

Such a promise counts for
nothing. You were not made
to be a peasant girl, a higher
fate is in store for those
roguish eyes, those beautiful
lips, those milky, perfumed
hands, so soft to touch,
scented with roses.

Zerlina

Ah! . . . Non vorrei . . .

Ah! . . . I do not wish . . .

Don Giovanni

Che non vorreste?

What don't you wish?

Zerlina

Alfine ingannata restar.
Io sò che raro colle donne voi
altri cavalieri siete onesti e sinceri.

In the end to be decieved.
I know that rarely with
women are you noblemen
honest and sincere.

Don Giovanni

Eh, un'impostura della gente plebea!
La nobiltà ha dipinta negli occhi
l'onestà. Orsù, non perdiam tempo;
in questo istante io ti voglio sponsar.

A vile slander of the low
classes. Nobility can be
seen in honest eyes. Now
let's not waste time. I
will marry you immediately.

Zerlina

Voi?

You?

(Continued on next page)

Don Giovanni

Certo, io. Quell casinetto è mio.	Certainly I. That villa
Soli saremo, e là, gioiello mio,	over there is mine. We
ci sposeremo.	will be alone, and there, my
	little jewel, we will be married.

ARIA (DUET)

A

1:45
              Don Giovanni

Là ci da-rem la ma-no, là mi di-rai di sì.

Là ci darem la mano,	Give me your hand, oh fairest,
là mi dirai di sì.	whisper a gentle "yes."
Vedi, non è lontano:	See, it's not far,
partiam, ben mio, da qui.	let's go, my love.

              Zerlina

2:03	Vorrei, e non vorrei,	I'd like to but yet I would not.
	mi trema un poco il cor;	My heart will not be still.
	felice, è ver, sarei,	Tis true I would be happy,
	ma può burlarmi ancor.	yet he may deceive me still.

B
              Don Giovanni

Vie-ni, mio bel di-let-to!

2:26	Vieni, mio bel diletto!	Come with me, my pretty!

              Zerlina

Mi fa pietà Masetto!	May Masetto take pity!

              Don Giovanni

Io cangierò tua sorte!	I will change your fate!

              Zerlina

Presto, non son più forte.	Quick then, I can no longer resist.

A′

2:51   Repeat of first eight lines, but with Don Giovanni's and Zerlina's parts moving closer together

B′

3:14   Repeat of next four lines

C

3:42   Change of meter to dancelike 6/8 as the principals skip off together

              Together

(Zerlina)
An-diam, an-diam, mio be-ne, a ri-sto-rar le pe-ne d'un' in-no-cen-te a-mor!

(Don Giovanni)
An-diam, an-diam, mio be-ne, a ri-sto-rar le pe-ne d'un' in-no-cen-te a-mor!

Andiam, andiam mio bene,	Let's go, let's go, my treasure,
a ristorar le pene	to soothe the pangs
d'un innocente amor!	of innocent love.

Ultimately, in the duet "Give me your hand, oh fairest," Don Giovanni persuades Zerlina to extend her hand and the prospect of a good deal more. The tune, perhaps the most memorable of the opera, became a popular favorite in the nineteenth century. No less so *Don Giovanni*. From the moment of its first performance in Prague, Mozart's tragic-comic opera has enjoyed enormous favor with all who are moved by alluring melodies and passionate drama. *Don Giovanni* is one of those rare instances in the fine arts of a work that has immediate popular appeal, yet is universally judged to be a masterpiece of the highest order.

LISTENING EXERCISES

Wolfgang Amadeus Mozart   6CD 2/8; 2CD 1/11
Symphony No. 40 in G minor (1788)
First movement, *Molto allegro* (very fast)

Mozart's Symphony No. 40 in G minor has been discussed in detail (page 187), as has the development of the symphony orchestra in the Classical period. The following questions focus on the various instruments and instrumental families of the orchestra as they work within the framework of sonata–allegro form. This is not a festive symphony, so there are no trumpets and drums. Mozart is writing for French horns, woodwinds, and strings. How does he use these instrumental forces to achieve his musical aims?

0:00–0:20   Beginning of first theme
   1. Which instruments are playing the melody here?
       a. violins   b. violas   c. cellos
   2. At what time do the woodwinds finally enter? _____

0:30–0:45   Transition
   3. (0:37–0:45) Which statement is true regarding the function of the French horns in this, and most, Classical symphonies?
       a. They stand out by playing independent solo melodies.
       b. They add to the "background" resonance of the orchestra by repeating one or two pitches.

0:47–1:04   Second theme
   4. Which is true?
       a. The strings dominate this second theme area.
       b. The strings and woodwinds participate equally.

1:22–1:32   Echoes of the first theme provide a closing
   5. Which woodwind instrument plays the main motive of the first theme?
       a. French horn   b. bassoon   c. flute

1:53–3:45   Repeat of exposition

3:49–4:28   Development section, first of two parts
   6. Which family of instruments dominates this contrapuntal working out of the first theme?
       a. strings   b. woodwinds   c. brasses

4:52–4:58   Retransition at the end of the development
 7. Which family of instruments dominates this retransition?
    a. strings   b. woodwinds   c. brasses

4:59–5:26   Beginning of recapitulation
 8. Which of the following is true?
    a. The orchestration here at the beginning of the recapitulation is mostly
        the same as that at the beginning of the movement (strings followed by
        later woodwind entry).
    b. Mozart has radically changed the orchestration. The woodwinds come
        in first with the theme, and the strings come in later.

5:27–6:05   Transition
 9. Which family of instruments dominates this extended transition?
    a. strings   b. woodwinds   c. brasses

6:07–6:25   Second theme

6:48   Echoes of first theme provide a closing
10. Which of the following is true generally about this movement?
    a. The woodwinds introduce all themes, the violins add color and counter-
        point, and the brasses play melodies in the foreground.
    b. The violins introduce all themes, the woodwinds add color and counter-
        point, and the brasses play sustaining pitches in the background.

Joseph Haydn   6CD 2/9; 2CD 1/12
Opus 76, No. 3, The "Emperor" Quartet (1797)
Second movement, *Poco adagio cantabile* (rather slow, songlike)

The string quartet is a type of chamber music, and its musical style is different
from that of the symphony. Here we have a quartet by the aging Haydn in
which the slow movement is composed in the form of theme and variations.
Go back and have another look at the melody that constitutes the theme (page
193) and then answer the following questions.

0:00–1:17   Theme
 1. Listen to the theme as it is played by the first violin. Is it in a major or a
     minor key? _____
 2. Why does this melody sound so secure and firm?
    a. because all the notes are the same length
    b. because each phrase ends on a dominant or a tonic note
    c. because there are many modulations

1:19–2:33   Variation 1
 3. The second violin has the theme while the first violin rapidly ornaments
     above. Do the viola and cello (the lowest two instruments) play at all dur-
     ing this variation? _____

2:35–4:02   Variation 2
 4. The cello has the theme in this variation. Would you say the instrument is
     playing in the higher or the lower part of its range? (Listen especially to the
     last section of the melody.) _____

4:04–5:29   Variation 3

5. The viola has the melody but is gradually joined by the other instruments. Which instrument is the *last* to enter in this variation?

a. first violin   b. second violin   c. cello

6. Is the style of writing in this variation homophonic (chordal) or polyphonic (contrapuntal)? _____

5:31–6:55   Variation 4

7. The theme now returns to the first violin. When the violin repeats the first phrase of the melody, it does so

a. an octave higher.   b. an octave lower.   c. at the same pitch level.

6:56–end   A brief coda

8. What does the cello do for much of the coda (6:56–7:06)?

a. sustains a pedal point*

b. plays an arpeggio

c. repeats a melodic sequence

9. In what way does Haydn conclude the movement?

a. has the players accelerate for a *fortissimo* climax

b. has the players execute a "fadeout" by means of a ritard* and *diminuendo*

10. A general question about this movement: Which of the following is true?

a. In this set of theme and variations Haydn keeps the theme pretty much intact and changes, or varies, the context in which it appears.

b. In this set of theme and variations Haydn radically transforms the theme while keeping its context pretty much intact.

KEY WORDS

cadenza	scherzo	string quartet
diminished chord	*sinfonia*	*The Emperor's Hymn*
double exposition form	*Singspiel*	vocal ensemble
Lorenzo da Ponte	solo concerto	
prima donna	sonata	

A checklist of musical style in the Classical period is given on page 63.

THE BRIDGE TO ROMANTICISM: LUDWIG VAN BEETHOVEN

 No composer is more revered than Ludwig van Beethoven (1770–1827), no music more loved than his. Indeed, when one conjures up the image of a composer of music, most likely it is the figure of Beethoven that comes to mind—the angry, defiant, disheveled Beethoven. Is it not the bust of Beethoven, rather than the elegant Mozart or the stalwart Bach, that sits atop the piano in the comic strip *Peanuts*? Is it not Beethoven who is the namesake of popular canine movies (*Beethoven* and *Beethoven 2nd*) and whose love-life is likewise chronicled on film (*Immortal Beloved*)? Is it not Beethoven who is the butt of all "decomposing" jokes? Such observations are not mere trivialities. The image of Beethoven is deeply ingrained in our popular culture. For many, Beethoven personifies the ideal of "the musician as artist"; for some he is the consummate "artist as hero."

His music, too, enjoys great public favor. Statistics show that Beethoven's symphonies, sonatas, and quartets are performed in concert halls and heard on radio more than those of any other classical composer. His works are tender but powerful, perfectly balanced yet bursting with energy. And just as Beethoven the composer struggled to overcome personal adversity—his growing deafness—so his music imparts a feeling of struggle and ultimate victory. It has a sense of rightness, even morality, about it. It elevates and inspires the listener, and for that reason it has an immediate and universal appeal.

Beethoven's life spanned the last quarter of the eighteenth century and the first quarter of the nineteenth. For the most part his music belongs to the tradition of the Viennese Classical masters. He composed predominantly in the Classical genres of symphony, piano sonata, concerto, string quartet, and opera; and he wrote within the Classical forms of sonata–allegro, rondo, and theme and variations. Yet even in the compositions of his youth, there is unmistakably a new spirit at work in his music, one that foreshadows the musical style of the Romantic period (1820–1900). An intense, lyrical expression is heard in his slow movements, while his allegros abound with striking themes, pounding rhythms, and startling dynamic contrasts. He stays within the bounds of Classical forms, yet he pushes their confines to the breaking point, so great is his urge for personal expression. Though a pupil of Haydn and a lifelong admirer of Mozart, he nonetheless elevated music to new heights of eloquence and dramatic power. For this reason he can rightly be called the prophet of Romantic music.

A somewhat glamorized portrait of 1819 showing Ludwig van Beethoven at work on his *Missa solemnis*. In reality Beethoven had a pock-marked face and was usually unshaven.

Beethoven and the aristocracy

 ## THE EARLY YEARS (1770–1802)

Like Bach and Mozart before him, Beethoven came from a family of musicians. His father and grandfather were performers at the court of the Elector at Bonn, Germany, a small town on the Rhine River where Beethoven was born on December 17, 1770. Seeing great musical talent in his young son, Beethoven's father, a violent, alcoholic man, forcibly made him practice at the keyboard all hours, day and night. Soon he tried to exploit his son as a child prodigy, a second Mozart, telling the world the diminutive boy was two years younger than he actually was. At the age of seventeen Beethoven was packed off to faraway Vienna to study with Mozart himself. But no sooner had he arrived and played for the master than his mother became seriously ill, and he was forced to return to Bonn. Five years later, in 1792, Beethoven finally went to Vienna for good. As one of his benefactors said, "You are going to Vienna in fulfillment of your long-frustrated wishes . . . you will receive the spirit of Mozart from the hands of Haydn."

Mozart had died since Beethoven's last visit, so he now took up the study of musical composition with Haydn. But alas the aging Haydn and the youthful, impetuous Beethoven were not compatible. So when Haydn set off for his second sojourn in London in 1794 (see page 156), Beethoven began to work with other teachers, including a certain Johann Albrechtsberger (1736–1809), with whom he studied fugue, and the ever-present Antonio Salieri (1750–1825; see page 159), who taught him the Italian vocal style. At the same time Beethoven tried to make himself acceptable to polite society in Vienna: He bought new clothes, located a wigmaker, and found someone who could give him dancing lessons.

Beethoven's aim was to gain an entrée into the homes of the wealthy of the Austrian capital. And this he soon did, not because of his skill as a composer, and less because of his social graces, but because of his phenomenal talent as a pianist. His playing was louder, more violent, more forceful, yet more expressive than the aristocrats of the salons had ever heard. He possessed an extraordinary technique—even if he did hit occasional wrong notes—and this he put to good use, especially in his fanciful improvisations. As a contemporary witness observed: "He knew how to produce such an impression on every listener that frequently there was not a single dry eye, while many broke out into loud sobs, for there was a certain magic in his expression."

The aristocracy was captivated. One patron put a string quartet at his disposal, another made it possible for Beethoven to experiment with a small orchestra, and all showered him with gifts. He acquired well-to-do pupils; he sold his compositions ("I state my price and they pay," he said with pride in 1801); and he requested and eventually received an annuity from three noblemen so that he could work undisturbed. The text of this arrangement includes the following lines:

> It is recognized that only a person who is as free as possible from all cares can consecrate himself to his craft. He can only produce these great and sublime works which ennoble Art if they form his sole pursuit, to the exclusion of all unnecessary obligations. The undersigned have therefore taken the decision to ensure that Herr Ludwig van Beethoven's situation shall not be embarrassed by his most necessary requirements, nor shall his powerful genius be hampered.

What a contrast between Beethoven's contract and the one signed by Haydn four decades earlier! Music is no longer merely a craft and the composer a servant. It is now an exalted Art, and the great creator a Genius who must be pro-

tected and nurtured—this is a new notion of the value of music, one of the Romantic age. And Beethoven did his best to encourage a belief in the exalted mission of the composer as artist. He would not stand at the beck and call of a master. When one patron demanded that he play for a visiting French general, Beethoven stormed out of the salon and responded by letter: "Prince, what you are, you are through the accident of birth. What I am, I am through my own efforts. There have been many princes and there will be thousands more. But there is only one Beethoven!"

Piano Sonata, Opus 13, The *Pathétique* Sonata (1799)

The bold originality in Beethoven's music can be heard in one of his most celebrated compositions, the *Pathétique* Sonata. A sonata*, as we have seen, is a multimovement work for solo instrument or an instrument with keyboard accompaniment. That Beethoven himself supplied the title *Pathétique* for this solo piano sonata suggests the passion and pathos he felt within this work. It has more drama and intensity, and requires more technical skill of the pianist, than any piano sonata of Mozart or Haydn. Beethoven himself frequently performed the *Pathétique* in the homes and palaces of the Viennese aristocracy.

FIRST MOVEMENT. Contemporaries recount how Beethoven the pianist played with "superhuman" speed and force, and how he banged so hard on one occasion that he broke six strings. The crashing C minor chord that opens the *Pathétique* Sonata suggests Beethoven's sometimes violent approach to the instrument. After this startling opening gesture, Beethoven the dramatist continues by juxtaposing music of wildly differing moods: the *sforzando* chord is immediately followed by quiet lyricism, only to be interrupted by another chordal thunderbolt. This slow introduction probably is a written-out version of the sort of improvisation at the piano that gained Beethoven great fame in Vienna. The introduction leads to a racing first theme that rises impetuously in the right hand. The sense of anxiety the listener feels is amplified by the bass, where the left hand of the pianist plays broken octaves (the alternation of two tones an octave apart) reminiscent of the rumble of distant thunder.

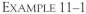 FIGURE 11–2

A fanciful, yet in some ways accurate, depiction of Beethoven in the midst of creative chaos. The illustrator has assembled many objects from Beethoven's daily life: his ear-trumpet, used in a vain attempt to counteract his growing deafness; the bowl of porridge about to spill into the keyboard; and the broken strings protruding from the back of his Graf piano. When composing, Beethoven was famously given to cursing, howling, and pounding on the piano.

EXAMPLE 11–1

Thereafter the movement plays out as a struggle of the impetuous, racing themes pitted against the sound of the stormy introduction, which is reintroduced at regular intervals. There is much passion and intensity here, yet there is also Classical formal control: The crashing chords come back at the beginning of both the development and the coda in this sonata–allegro form movement. Thus the chords simultaneously set the formal boundaries and prevent the racing themes from flying out of control.

LISTENING GUIDE

Ludwig van Beethoven
Piano Sonata, Opus 13, The *Pathétique* Sonata (1799)
First movement, *Grave; Allegro di molto e con brio*
(grave; very fast and with gusto)

6CD 3/1;
2CD 1/13

Form: sonata–allegro

INTRODUCTION

0:00	Crashing chords alternate with softer, more lyrical chords
0:46	Softer chords continually cut off by crashing chords below
1:10	Melody builds to a climax and then rapid descent

EXPOSITION [ ] = repeats

1:41 [3:14]   Rising agitated melody in right hand against broken octaves in left (first theme)

1:59 [3:34]   Transition with modulation to new key, thinner texture
2:11 [3:44]   Bass, followed by treble, initiates a "call and response" (second theme)

2:39 [4:12]   Right and left hands race in opposite directions (closing theme, part 1)
2:58 [4:31]   Rapid scales in right hand above simple chords in left (closing theme, part 2)
3:04 [4:37]   Reminiscence of first theme
[3:14–4:47]   Repeat of exposition

DEVELOPMENT

4:48	Crashing chords and softer chords from introduction
5:32	First theme extended and varied
6:09	Rapid twisting descent played by right hand leads to

RECAPITULATION

6:15	Rising agitated melody in right hand (first theme)
6:25	Transition
6:35	Call and response between bass and treble (second theme)
6:59	Hands move rapidly in opposite directions (closing theme, part 1)
7:18	Scale runs in right hand (closing theme, part 2)
7:24	Reminiscence of first theme

CODA

7:35	Recall of chords from the introduction
8:14	Reminiscence of first theme leads to a drive to the final cadence

(Listening Exercise 23)

Beethoven's Confession: The Heiligenstadt Testament

Beethoven was a physically powerful, proud, egotistical man who suffered no fools and had few doubts about his own worth as a musician. The loss of his hearing, which began in 1798, was a near fatal blow. It not only jeopardized his profession but also caused him to withdraw increasingly from society, creating the image of Beethoven the loner, the outcast, the misanthrope. The Heiligenstadt Testament is a lengthy, public letter that Beethoven, having finally decided against suicide, wrote in the fall of 1802. It is a remarkable document—part plea for understanding, part artistic manifesto. The name "Heiligenstadt" derives from the fact that Beethoven penned it in the village of that name, just to the north of Vienna, where he had gone in 1802 for a "cure" for his deafness. Here are a few lines of Beethoven's public declaration:

Oh my fellow men who consider me an unfriendly, hostile, peevish man or even misanthropic, how greatly you wrong me. For you do not know the secret reason why I appear to be so to you. . . . Though endowed with a passionate and lively temperament and even fond of the distractions offered by society, I was soon obliged to withdraw and live in solitude. . . . I could not bring myself to say to people: "Speak up, shout, for I am deaf." Alas, how could I possibly mention the loss *of a sense* which in me should be more perfectly developed than in other people, a sense which at one time I possessed in the greatest perfection, even to a degree few in my profession possess or have ever possessed. . . . But how humiliated I have felt if somebody standing beside me heard the sound of a flute in the distance and *I heard nothing!* Such experiences made me despair. I would have ended my life—it was only *my art* that held me back.

SECOND MOVEMENT. Eyewitnesses who heard Beethoven at the piano remarked on the "legato" quality of his playing, and contrasted it with Mozart's lighter, more staccato style. Beethoven himself said in 1796 that "one can sing on the piano, so long as one has feeling." We can hear Beethoven sing through the legato melodic line that dominates the slow second movement of the *Pathétique* Sonata. Indeed, the expression mark he gave to the movement is *cantabile* ("songful"). The singing quality of the melody seems to have appealed to pop star Billy Joel, who borrowed this theme for the refrain of his song "This Night" on the album *Innocent Man* (Columbia/CBS CK 38837).

THIRD MOVEMENT. A comparison of the second and third movements of the *Pathétique* Sonata will show that musical form does not determine musical mood. Although both the *Adagio* and the fast finale are in rondo form, the first is a lyrical hymn and the latter a passionate, but slightly comical, chase. The finale has hints of the crashing chords and stark contrasts of the first movement, but the earlier violence and impetuosity have been softened into a mood of impassioned playfulness.

Beethoven cut a strange, eccentric figure as he wandered the streets of Vienna, sometimes humming, sometimes mumbling, and sometimes jotting on music paper. Adding to the difficulties from his somewhat unstable personality was the fact that he was gradually going deaf—a serious handicap for any person, but a tragic condition for a musician. The symptoms first manifested themselves in the late 1790s, and, quite understandably, the victim suffered considerable anguish and depression. His deafness perhaps least affected his work as a composer—good musicians can hear with an "inner ear" and do not need actual sound. But it caused him to retreat from society even more, and it all but ended his career as a performer, since he could no longer gauge how hard to press the piano keys. By late 1802 Beethoven recognized that he would suffer a gradual, though ultimately total, loss of hearing. Yet he emerged from his period of depression with a renewed conviction to do great things. His music had

growing deafness

sustained him: "I would have ended my life—it was only *my art* that held me back," he said. He would now "seize Fate by the throat."

✿ THE "HEROIC" PERIOD (1803–1813)

It was in this resurgent, defiant mood that Beethoven entered what we call his "heroic" period of composition (1803–1813). His works became longer, more assertive, and full of grand gestures. Simple, often triadic, themes predominate, and these are repeated, sometime incessantly, as the music swells to majestic proportions. When these themes are played *forte* and given over to the brass instruments, a heroic, triumphant sound results.

Symphony No. 3 in E♭ Major ("Eroica," 1803)

As its title suggests, Beethoven's "Eroica" Symphony epitomizes the grandiose, heroic style. More than any single orchestral work, it changed the historical direction of the symphony. Its length, some forty-five minutes, is nearly twice that of a symphony of Haydn or Mozart. It assaults the ear with startling rhythmic effects and chord changes that were shocking to early-nineteenth-century listeners. The slow movement is a funeral march, while the finale not merely ends the symphony but provides a culmination of all that has preceded. Most novel for Beethoven, the work has biographical content, for the hero of the "Eroica" Symphony, at least originally, was Napoleon Bonaparte.

Beethoven and Napoleon

Austria and the German states were at war with France during the early years of the nineteenth century. Yet German-speaking Beethoven was much taken with the enemy's revolutionary call for liberty, equality, and fraternity. Napoleon Bonaparte became his hero, and the composer dedicated his third symphony to him, writing on the title page "intitolata Bonaparte." But when news that Napoleon had declared himself emperor reached Beethoven, he flew into a rage saying "Now he, too, will trample on all the rights of man and indulge his ambition." Taking up a knife, he scratched so violently to erase the name Bonaparte from the title page that he left a hole in the paper (Fig. 11–3). When the

🌸 FIGURE 11–3

The title page of the autograph of Beethoven's "Eroica" Symphony: "Sinfonia grande/intitolata Bonaparte." Note the hole where Beethoven scratched out Napoleon's name with a knife.

work was published, Napoleon's name had been removed in favor of the more general title, "Heroic Symphony: To Celebrate the Memory of a Fallen Hero." In musical terms, the fallen hero Beethoven buries in "Eroica" Symphony is the style of the older Classical symphony, so radical is this new work. It is music that is the real hero of the "Eroica."

FIRST MOVEMENT (ALLEGRO CON BRIO)

To an audience accustomed to the elegance and formal balance of Mozart, Beethoven's "Eroica" Symphony must have sounded bizarre indeed: The development is half again as long as the exposition; a French horn begins the recapitulation four bars too soon; and the coda is almost as long as the gigantic development—truly a case of the *coda* (Italian for "tail") wagging the dog! But it all works. Long passages of tonic harmony, a solid triadic principal theme, and incessant repetition provide a rock-solid base, an appropriate counterweight to Beethoven's radical experiments with musical form.

sonata–allegro form expanded

MARCIA FUNEBRE (ADAGIO ASSAI)

Having heard legions of military bands during the Napoleonic Wars, both in Bonn and Vienna, Beethoven had in his ear a set of musical stereotypes required of all funeral marches: a slow tempo, duple meter, steady dotted rhythms (imitating a drum beat), and a mournful minor key. These elements he transforms and extends, changing the traditional funeral march into a symphonic slow movement full of pathos and nostalgia for a fallen hero.

SCHERZO (ALLEGRO VIVACE)

Following the example set by his teacher, Haydn, Beethoven abandoned the stately minuet* and replaced it with a rollicking scherzo* (this change will be discussed at length on page 222). The scherzo of the "Eroica" Symphony is less a dance than a frenzied whirl.

FINALE (ALLEGRO MOLTO)

Before Beethoven, the finale of a symphony had traditionally been a light send-off, a pleasing "curtain closer" without much weight or substance. With his "Eroica" Symphony, however, Beethoven showed that the finale could equal the opening movement in length and emotional content. This represented an important change in the structure and psychology of symphonic design, and subsequent composers of the Romantic era followed Beethoven's example. If the center of gravity has not entirely shifted from the first movement to the last, henceforth these two antipodes were at least of equal weight and density. The finale is no longer merely an ending, it is a summation.

Beethoven wished to achieve something new in this finale, and to do so he returned to something old: a theme that he had used in three previous compositions in theme-and-variations form. In fact, it is a double theme, one with a treble (melody) and a bass component (see Listening Guide). Part of the increased gravity of the finale of the "Eroica" Symphony derives from the fact that Beethoven is varying not one, but two themes. Granted, the themes are constructed as a pair of eight-bar antecedent-consequent phrases typical of the Classical period. But Beethoven treats his themes in a new way, reaching out beyond the confines of traditional theme-and-variations form. In Variation 3, for example, he transforms the bass theme into

FIGURE 11–4

As a young officer, Napoleon Bonaparte seized control of the government of France in 1799 and established a new form of Republic. When Napoleon elevated himself to emperor in 1804, Beethoven changed the title of his Symphony No. 3 from "Bonaparte" to "Eroica." The portrait by Jacques-Louis David shows the newly crowned Napoleon in full imperial regalia. Liberator had become oppressor.

theme-and-variations form expanded

the subject of a lengthy fugato*, while in Variation 6 he exploits motives from both themes to create a development section, much like one would find in a movement in sonata–allegro form. As a result, the basic sixteen-bar unit is greatly expanded. Variation 6, for example, extends over eighty-two measures. By contrast, Mozart and Haydn had composed variations of approximately the same length—a chain of equal-size links. Beethoven's expanded treatment of Classical form allows him to work toward higher and higher peaks. Here the apex is reached in Variation 8 when the French horns blare forth in heroic fashion, a climax of towering force.

LISTENING GUIDE

Ludwig van Beethoven
Symphony No. 3, The "Eroica" (1803)
Fourth movement, *Allegro molto* (very fast)

CD3/2

Form: theme and variations

0:00	Brief, energetic introduction
0:13	Strings play **bass theme** softly and pizzicato
0:50	**Variation 1:** Second violins play bass theme while first violins and cellos add contrapuntal embellishment
1:26	**Variation 2:** First violins play bass theme while other strings add rapidly moving counterpart
2:01	Oboe and then first violins present **treble theme**
2:38	Brief modulation to relative minor*
2:46	**Variation 3:** Bass theme in minor mode used as a subject in a fugato*
3:37	**Variation 4:** Flute with violin support plays and varies treble theme
4:09	**Variation 5:** Treble theme (varied) and bass theme are transformed into a gypsy dance in minor mode
4:53	**Variation 6:** Process of development applied to motives from both themes; all instruments hold a dominant chord
6:22	**Variation 7:** Woodwinds and then strings present treble theme in luxuriant homophonic texture[†]
8:15	**Variation 8:** Brilliant French horns, *fortissimo* dynamics, and slow, majestic tempo lend heroic quality to treble theme
9:23	Brief modulation
9:28	**Variation 9:** Violins quietly vary melodic contour, mode, and rhythm of treble theme; then all parts participate in a grand crescendo (9:45)
10:51	Coda: recalls energetic introduction and interjects noisy filler that emphasizes the tonic triad; final fireworks by French horns

[†]To hear all the instruments individually play their parts in Variation 7, return to the section "Building a Symphony" (page 47).

Beethoven wrote nine symphonies in all, six of them in his "heroic" period. Although few in number compared with earlier Classical composers, Beethoven's symphonies nonetheless set the standard for the genre of the symphony for the remainder of the nineteenth century. Noteworthy, in addition to the "Eroica" (Third), are the famous Fifth Symphony, the Sixth (called the "Pastoral" because it tries to evoke the ambiance of the Austrian countryside), the Seventh, and the monumental Ninth. In these Beethoven introduces new orchestral colors by bringing new instruments into the symphony orchestra: the trombone (Symphony Nos. 5, 6, and 9), the contrabassoon (Symphony Nos. 5 and 9), the piccolo (Symphony Nos. 5, 6, and 9), and even the human voice (Symphony No. 9).

Symphony No. 5 in C Minor (1808)

At the center of Beethoven's symphonic output stands his remarkable Symphony No. 5. Its novelty rests in the way the composer conveys a sense of psychological progression over the course of four movements. An imaginative listener might feel the following sequence of events: (1) a fateful encounter with elemental forces, (2) a period of quiet soul-searching, followed by (3) a further wrestling with the elements, and, finally, (4) a triumphant victory over the forces of Fate. Beethoven himself is said to have remarked with regard to the famous opening motive of the symphony: "There Fate knocks at the door!"

a symphony with a psychological progression

The rhythm of the opening—perhaps the best-known moment in all of classical music—animates the entire symphony. Not only does it dominate the opening *Allegro* but it reappears in varied form in the three later movements as well, binding the symphony into a unified whole.

EXAMPLE 11–2

FIRST MOVEMENT. At the very outset the listener is jolted to attention, forced to sit up and take notice by a sudden explosion of sound. And what an odd beginning to a symphony—a blast of three short notes and a long one, followed by the same three shorts and a long, all now a step lower. The movement can't quite get going. It starts and stops, then seems to lurch forward and gather momentum. And where is the theme or melody? This three-shorts-and-a-long pattern is more a motive or musical cell than a melody. Yet it is striking by virtue of its power and compactness. As the movement unfolds, the actual pitches of the motive prove to be of secondary importance. Beethoven is obsessed here with rhythm. He wants to demonstrate the enormous latent force that lurks within even the simplest rhythmic cell just waiting to be unleashed by a composer who understands the secrets of rhythmic energy.

a famous musical motive

To control the sometimes violent forces that will emerge, the musical processes unfold within the traditional confines of sonata–allegro form. The basic four-note motive provides all the musical material for the first theme area:

EXAMPLE 11–3

There is a brief transition played by a solo French horn. It is only six notes long and is formed simply by adding two notes to the end of the basic four-note motive. As expected, the transition moves the tonality from the tonic (C minor) to the relative major* (E♭ major):

EXAMPLE 11–4

The second theme seems to offer a moment of escape from the rush of the motive, but even here the pattern of three shorts and a long is heard underneath in the low strings:

EXAMPLE 11–5

The closing theme, too, is none other than the motive once again, now presented in a somewhat different guise:

EXAMPLE 11–6

With the development, the opening motive returns and assumes all, if not more than all, of the force it had at the beginning. It soon takes on different melodic forms, as it is tossed back and forth between instruments, though the rhythmic shape remains constant:

EXAMPLE 11–7

Following a rhythmic climax and a brief imitative passage, Beethoven reduces the six-note motive of the transition down to merely two notes, and then just one, and he passes these around *pianissimo* between the strings and the winds:

EXAMPLE 11–8

❧ FIGURE 11–5

Interior of the Theater an der Wien, Vienna, where Beethoven's Symphony No. 5 received its premiere on December 22, 1808. During this first performance the orchestra frequently halted because of the difficulties in playing Beethoven's radically new music.

Beethoven was a master of the process of musical fragmentation—stripping away all extraneous material to get to the core of a musical idea. Here in this mysterious *pianissimo* passage he holds up the irreducible minimum of his motive: a single note. In the midst of this quiet, the original four-note motive tries to reassert itself *fortissimo*, yet at first cannot do so. Its explosive force, however, cannot be held back. A thunderous return of the opening chords signals the beginning of the recapitulation.

Although the recapitulation offers a repeat of the events of the exposition, Beethoven has one surprise in store. No sooner has the motive regained its momentum than an oboe interjects a tender, languid, and wholly unexpected solo. Though a deviation from the usual path of sonata–allegro form, this brief oboe cadenza* allows for a momentary release of excess energy. The recapitulation then resumes its expected course.

What is not expected is the enormous coda that follows. It is even longer than the exposition! A new form of the motive appears and it, too, is subjected to development. In fact, what Beethoven does here is write a second development section, so great is his urge to exploit the latent power of this one simple musical idea.

a coda longer than the exposition

LISTENING GUIDE

Ludwig van Beethoven
Symphony No. 5 in C minor (1808)
First movement, *Allegro con brio* (fast with gusto)

6CD 3/3;
2CD 1/14

Form: sonata–allegro

EXPOSITION [   ] = repeats

0:00	[1:23]	Two statements of the motive
0:06	[1:29]	Motive builds momentum in a crescendo working up to climax and three chords, the last of which is held
0:23	[1:46]	Another crescendo begins as motive is piled upon itself in imitative counterpoint
0:40	[2:06]	Loud climax on two chords
0:43	[2:08]	Short transition played by solo French horn
0:45	[2:09]	Quiet second theme in new major key (relative major)
0:58	[2:22]	Crescendo
1:04	[2:27]	Loud string passage prepares arrival of closing theme
1:13	[2:36]	Closing theme

| [1:23–2:44] | Repeat of exposition |

DEVELOPMENT

2:46	Motive played *fortissimo* by horn and strings and then passed back and forth between woodwinds and strings
3:07	Another crescendo or "Beethovenian swell"
3:13	Rhythmic climax in which motive is pounded incessantly
3:20	Short passage of imitative counterpoint using transition motive
3:30	Two notes of transition motive passed back and forth
3:40	One note passed back and forth between winds and strings; gets quiet
3:50	Basic four-note motive tries to reassert itself loudly
3:54	More *pianissimo* one-note alternation between winds and strings
3:58	Motive reenters insistently

RECAPITULATION

4:04	Return of motive
4:10	Motive gathers momentum and cadences with three chords
4:20	Unexpected oboe solo

4:36	Motive returns and moves hurriedly to a climax
4:56	Transition now played by bassoon instead of horn
4:59	Quiet second theme with timpani now playing rhythm of motive
5:15	Crescendo leading to closing theme
5:23	Closing theme

(Continued on next page)

CODA

5:40   Motive pounded *fortissimo* on one note, then again a step higher

5:53   Imitative counterpoint

6:07   Rising quarter notes form new four-note pattern

6:19   New four-note pattern alternates between strings and woodwinds

6:39   Pounding on a single note, then motive as at beginning

6:53   Succession of I–V–I chords brings movement to abrupt end

(Listening Exercise 24)

SECOND MOVEMENT. After the pounding we have been subjected to in the explosive first movement, the calm, noble *Andante* comes as a welcome change of pace. The key is now major (A♭), the mood serene, and the melody expansive—instead of beginning with a four-note motive, the opening theme here runs on for twenty-two measures. The musical form is also a familiar one: theme and variations (see pages 175–179). But this is not the simple, easily audible theme and variations of Haydn. There are, as in the finale of the "Eroica" Symphony, two themes, and the first one has three parts. Not only do the variations become more complex as the movement progresses, but also, beginning with variation 2, Beethoven shuffles the order in which the themes and parts of themes appear.

a more complex theme and variations

LISTENING GUIDE

Ludwig van Beethoven
Symphony No. 5 in C minor (1808)
Second movement, *Andante con moto* (progressing with movement)

6CD 3/4

Form: theme and variations

THEMES

0:00   Violas and cellos play beginning of theme 1

0:24   Woodwinds play middle of theme 1

0:38   Violins play end of theme 1

0:54   Clarinets, bassoons, and violins play theme 2

(Continued on next page)

1:16   Brasses play theme 2 in fanfare style

1:34   Mysterious *pianissimo*

VARIATION 1

2:01   Violas and cellos vary beginning of theme 1 by adding sixteenth notes

2:24   Woodwinds play middle of theme 1

2:34   Strings play end of theme 1

2:53   Clarinets, bassoons, and violins play theme 2

3:14   Brasses return with fanfare (theme 2)

3:32   More of the mysterious *pianissimo*

VARIATION 2

4:00   Violas and cellos overlay beginning of theme 1
      with rapidly moving ornamentation

4:36   Pounding repeated chords with theme below in cellos and basses

4:53   Rising scales lead to a fermata (hold)

5:12   Woodwinds play fragments of beginning of theme 1

5:54   Fanfare (theme 2) now returns in full orchestra

6:43   Woodwinds play beginning of theme 1 detached and in a minor key

VARIATION 3

7:23   Violins play beginning of theme 1 *fortissimo*

7:48   Woodwinds play middle of theme 1

7:58   Strings play end of theme 1

CODA

8:12   Tempo quickens as bassoons play reminiscence of beginning of theme 1

8:28   Violins play reminiscence of theme 2

8:37   Woodwinds play middle of theme 1

8:48   Strings play end of theme 1

9:09   Ends with repetitions of the rhythm of the very first measure of the movement

THIRD MOVEMENT. In the Classical period the third movement of a symphony or quartet was usually a graceful minuet and trio (see page 165). Haydn and his pupil Beethoven wanted to infuse this third movement generally with more life and energy, so they often wrote a faster, more rollicking piece and

the scherzo called it a scherzo, meaning "joke." There is nothing really humorous about the mysterious and sometimes threatening sound of the scherzo of Beethoven's Symphony No. 5, yet it is certainly far removed from the elegant world of the courtly minuet.

The formal plan of Beethoven's scherzo, **ABA′**, is taken over from the ternary form of the minuet, as is the triple meter heard here. The scherzo, **A,** is in the tonic key of C minor, while the trio, **B,** is in C major. This conflict, or juxtapo-

the trio sition, of major and minor, of dark and light, is just one of several confrontations that is resolved in the course of the four-movement symphony.

Now, a stroke of genius on Beethoven's part: He links the third and fourth movements by means of a musical bridge. Holding a single pitch as quietly as possible, the violins create an eerie sound, while the timpani beats menacingly in the backbround. A three-note motive grows from the violins and is repeated over and over as a wave of sound begins to swell from the orchestra. With enormous force the wave finally crashes down, and from it emerges the triumphant beginning of the fourth movement—one of the most thrilling moments in all of music.

a bridge to the finale

LISTENING GUIDE

Ludwig van Beethoven
Symphony No. 5 in C minor (1808)
Third movement, *Allegro* (fast)

6CD 3/5

Form: ternary

SCHERZO

0:00	Cellos and basses creep in with theme 1 and pass it on to higher strings	
0:08	Repeat	
0:21	French horns enter with theme 2	
0:38	Cellos and basses come back with theme 1	
0:52	Crescendo	
0:59	Full orchestra again plays theme 2 *fortissimo*	
1:18	Development of theme 1	
1:41	Ends with theme 2 *fortissimo*, then *piano*	

TRIO

1:47	Cellos and basses present subject of fugato
	Violas and bassoons enter with the subject
	Second violins enter with the subject
	First violins enter with the subject
2:01 – 2:22	Repeat of these imitative entries
2:23 – 2:49	Subject enters imitatively again: cellos and basses, violas and bassoons, second violins, first violins, and then flutes are added
2:50 – 3:17	Subject enters imitatively again in the same instruments and the flutes extend it

SCHERZO

3:15	Quiet return of theme 1 in cellos and basses
3:24	Pizzicato (plucked) presentation of theme 1 in cellos accompanied by bassoons
3:36	Ghostlike return of theme 2 in short notes in winds and pizzicato in strings

BRIDGE TO FOURTH MOVEMENT

4:26	Long note held *pianissimo* in strings with timpani beating softly below
4:40	Repeating three-note pattern emerges in the first violins
5:00	Great crescendo leads to fourth movement

FOURTH MOVEMENT. When Beethoven arrived at the finale, he was faced with a nearly impossible task: how to write a conclusion that would lift the tension of the preceding musical events yet provide an appropriate, substantive balance to the weighty first movement. He did so by fashioning a monumental work in sonata–allegro form, the longest movement of the symphony, and by bringing some unusual forces into play. To his orchestra he added three trombones, a contrabassoon (low bassoon), and a piccolo (high flute), the first time any of these instruments had been used in a symphony. He also wrote big, bold, and in most cases, triadic themes, assigning these, often as not, to the powerful brasses. It is these instruments and these themes, along with the final turn from C minor to C major, that cause the finale to project a strong feeling of optimism, a sense that a superhuman will has triumphed over adversity.

new instruments give added force

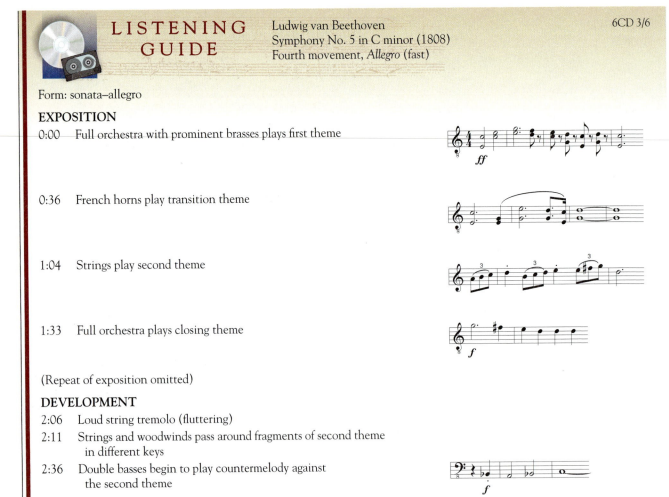

LISTENING GUIDE

Ludwig van Beethoven
Symphony No. 5 in C minor (1808)
Fourth movement, *Allegro* (fast)

6CD 3/6

Form: sonata–allegro

EXPOSITION

0:00   Full orchestra with prominent brasses plays first theme

0:36   French horns play transition theme

1:04   Strings play second theme

1:33   Full orchestra plays closing theme

(Repeat of exposition omitted)

DEVELOPMENT

2:06   Loud string tremolo (fluttering)

2:11   Strings and woodwinds pass around fragments of second theme
           in different keys

2:36   Double basses begin to play countermelody against
           the second theme

2:46   Trombones play countermelody

3:13   Woodwinds and brasses play countermelody above
           dominant pedal point in cellos and basses

3:30   Climax and pause on dominant triad

3:48   Ghostlike theme from the scherzo with four-note rhythm

(Continued on next page)

RECAPITULATION

4:17   Full orchestra plays first theme *fortissimo*

4:54   French horns bring in transition theme

5:26   Strings play second theme

5:54   Woodwinds play closing theme

CODA

6:26   Violins play second theme

6:37   Brasses and woodwinds play countermelody

6:50   V–I, V–I chords sound like final cadence

6:59   Bassoons, French horns, flutes, clarinets, and then piccolo continue
         with transition theme

7:27   Trill high in piccolo

7:50   Tempo changes to *presto* (very fast)

8:14   Brasses recall first theme but now twice as fast

8:21   V–I, V–I cadence followed by pounding tonic chord

Beethoven's Symphony No. 5 reveals his genius in a paradox: From minimal material (the basic cell) he derives maximum sonority. Climaxes are achieved by incessantly repeating the cell-like motive. Long crescendos swell like tidal waves of sound. Wildly different moods are accommodated within a single movement. In the quiet string music of the *Andante* (second movement), for example, we are never far from a heroic brass fanfare. Everywhere there is a feeling of raw, elemental power pushed forward by the newly enlarged orchestra. Beethoven was the first to recognize that massive sound could be a potent psychological weapon. No wonder that during World War II (1939–1945) both sides used the music of this symphony to symbolize "Victory."[†]

Beethoven's symphonic style

[†]In Morse code, short–short–short–long is the letter "V," as in "Victory."

❀ FIGURE 11–6
Beethoven at work on the second movement of his Symphony No. 5. The many corrections in different-colored inks and red pencil suggest the turmoil and constant evolution involved in Beethoven's creative process.

✻ FIGURE 11–7
A drawing of the deceased Beethoven sketched on the morning of March 28, 1827, the day after the composer's death. It was made by Josef Danhauser, the same artist who painted the group portrait that serves as the cover of this book.

Ode to Joy

✻ FIGURE 11–8
Beethoven's tombstone in the Central Cemetery in Vienna. Schubert and Brahms are buried only a few feet away.

❊ THE FINAL YEARS (1814–1827)

By 1814 Beethoven had become totally deaf and had withdrawn almost completely from society. His music, too, took on a more remote, inaccessible quality, placing heavy demands on both performer and audience. In these late works Beethoven requires the listener to connect musical ideas over long spans of time, to follow the variation of a theme when that variation has become quite remote from the original theme itself. Most of these late works are piano sonatas and string quartets—intimate, introspective chamber music. But two pieces, the Mass in D (*Missa solemnis*, 1823) and the Symphony No. 9 (1824), are large-scale compositions for full orchestra and chorus. In these works for larger forces, Beethoven seems again to wish to communicate directly to a broad spectrum of humanity.

Beethoven's Symphony No. 9, his last, was the first work in the history of this genre to include a chorus. It is as if the composer's need for expression in his final symphonic work was so great that the instruments of the orchestra alone were no longer sufficient. Something more was necessary: text and voices. And so they enter in the finale of this four-movement work. The text, *An die Freude (Ode to Joy)*, was written by the German poet Friedrich von Schiller in 1786. It is a hymn, in the spirit of the French Revolution, in honor of universal brotherhood, a theme that had been important to Beethoven since his earliest years. Beethoven set Schiller's text to a melody that has become well known to all of us as his *Ode to Joy*. (In recent times the tune has been popularized in a TV commercial, a movie score, as a Christmas song, and, more appropriately, as an anthem for the United Nations.) Beethoven intentionally constructed a melody that is folk song-like, even commonplace in shape, a fitting musical companion to a text extolling the commonality of humankind. (For the melody and a discussion of its structure, see page 27 and Listening Exercise 5.)

The *Ode to Joy* serves as a theme for a magnificent set of variations, twenty-five minutes in length, that marches toward a grandiose climax. Beethoven pushes the voices to sing louder and louder, higher and higher, faster than they can enunciate the text. The instrumentalists, too, are driven by the *presto* tempo to go so quickly they can scarcely play the notes. All performers strain to exceed the limits of their physical abilities, to accomplish the impossible. The sound is not so much beautiful as it is overwhelming, for the chorus and orchestra speak as all humanity. Their message is Beethoven's message: With divine guidance and superhuman effort humankind will triumph.

The figure of Beethoven towered over all the arts during the nineteenth century. He had shown how personal expression might expand the confines of Classical form with astonishingly powerful results. He had given music "the grand gesture," stunning effects like the crashing introduction of the *Pathétique* Sonata or the gigantic crescendo leading to the finale of the Fifth Symphony. He had shown that pure sound—sound divorced from musical idea—could be glorious in and of itself. At once he had made music both grandiose and intensely lyrical. His works became the standard against which later composers of the Romantic era measured their worth. The cover of this book shows poet, novelist, playwright, performer, and composer all turning in reverence toward the bust of Beethoven. Beethoven, larger than life, gazes down from Olympian heights, a monument to all that is noble and sublime in art.

LISTENING EXERCISES

 Ludwig van Beethoven   6CD 3/1; 2CD 1/13
Piano Sonata, Opus 13, The *Pathétique* Sonata (1799)
First movement, *Grave; Allegro di molto e con brio*
(grave; very fast and with gusto)

This exercise is designed to suggest how drama can be created in music by the use of contrast, pitting loud against soft, high against low, fast against slow, and, in the case of textures, thin against thick.

0:00–1:40 Introduction

1. The introduction creates an unsettled, uncertain feeling in the mind of the listener. What specifically does Beethoven do to create this feeling? (Circle the one answer that is *not* correct.)
    a. contrasts high and low ranges of the piano
    b. puts very loud and very soft sounds in close proximity
    c. starts with major chords and moves to minor ones
    d. contrasts slow chords with racing scales
2. (1:36–1:39) The end of the introduction is marked by a long descent. Which hand of the pianist plays this descent? _____

1:41–3:13 Exposition

3. (1:33–1:53) The descent gives way to the first theme (1:42) and the tempo changes. Which statement is true?
    a. A fast tempo gives way to an even faster one.
    b. A fast tempo gives way to a slower one.
    c. *Grave* (grave) gives way to *allegro con brio* (fast with gusto).
4. (1:59–2:09) A rumbling broken-octave bass had accompanied the agitated first theme (1:41–1:58). Now here in this section of modulation, can these broken octaves still be heard in the bass? _____
5. (2:11–2:38) What about now during the second theme. Are the broken octaves still present? _____
6. (2:39–2:56) Here, in the first part of the closing theme, the right hand drives rapidly to the top range of the piano while the left hand dives deep into the bass. Is this one long, twenty-second passage of music, or two presentations (statement and repeat) of a shorter, ten-second passage? _____
7. (3:07–3:13) The final cadence at the very end of the exposition is marked by a thick texture. How is this created?
    a. The left hand alternates chords in the top and middle ranges while the right plays ascending broken chords.
    b. The right hand alternates chords in the top and middle ranges while the left plays descending broken octaves.

3:14–4:47 Now comes the repeat of the exposition. As you listen, check your answers to questions 4–7.

4:48–6:14 Development

8. (5:15–5:40) The development begins with a return to the chords of the introduction and then proceeds with the first theme. Which statement is true about the tempo in this passage?
   a. The music gets progressively slower, almost stopping, and then suddenly becomes fast.
   b. The music proceeds at a moderate pace and then suddenly becomes fast.
   c. The music accelerates and then becomes progressively slower.

9. (6:09–6:14) Does the left hand (bass) rest during the rapid twisting descent at the end of the development? In other words, is this a solo for the right hand? _____

6:15–7:34 Recapitulation

7:35–8:24 Coda

10. (8:18–8:24) How does this movement end?
    a. with the crashing chord of the introduction
    b. with the closing theme
    c. with a soft fadeout

Ludwig van Beethoven   6CD 3/3; 2CD 1/4
Symphony No. 5 (1808)
First movement, *Allegro con brio* (fast with gusto)

There is perhaps no more famous single movement in classical music than the first movement of Beethoven's Symphony No. 5. The following questions refer to places that correspond to the major formal divisions of the movement. They are designed to show how Beethoven honored, and sometimes broke with, the usual Classical treatment of sonata–allegro form.

1. (0:00–0:30) Which instruments carry the motive and its immediate repetitions?
   a. strings   b. woodwinds   c. brasses   d. percussion

(0:41 French horn plays short transition

2. (0:45–0:51) When the quiet, brief second theme enters it is played three times in succession by three different instruments. In what order do these instruments present the theme?
   a. flute, clarinet, violins
   b. clarinet, violins, flute
   c. violins, clarinet, flute

3. (0:45–0:51) Is this second theme in the major or the minor mode?
   _____

4. (1:13–1:28) In this passage we have the closing theme and final chords of the exposition, and then the return to the beginning, which commences the repeat of the exposition. What happens to the mode in this passage from the end of the exposition back to the beginning?
   a. The minor mode shifts back to major.
   b. The major mode shifts back to minor.

1:23–2:44 Repeat of the exposition. Check your answers to questions 1–3.

5. (2:46–2:49) When the solo horn announces the beginning of the development, does it do so with the four-note version of the motive or the six-note version used in the transition (see page 218)? _____

6. (3:58–4:08) Here at the end of the development the orchestra insistently repeats the motive, and then the recapitulation begins. What is the dynamic level?

   a. *forte*   b. *fortissimo*   c. *piano*   d. *pianissimo*

7. (4:20–4:36) An oboe suddenly interrupts the recapitulation. Was this lyrical solo heard in the exposition? _____

8. (4:56–5:08) Beethoven reorchestrates and rewrites the transition and second theme in the recapitulation. The brief transition, which was played by a solo French horn in the exposition, is now given over to a solo bassoon. Then the short second theme is played four times and this passage, too, is reorchestrated. Circle the choice that correctly represents the orchestration applied to the four statements of the second theme.

   a. violins, flutes, violins, flutes
   b. clarinet, violins, flute, clarinet
   c. flutes, clarinet, violins, clarinet

9. (4:59–5:08) What is the mode of the second theme here in the recapitulation, major or minor? _____

10. Identify at least one way in which Beethoven breaks out of the usual confines of sonata–allegro form in this movement. What does he do that is unusual?

_____

 KEY WORDS

"Eroica" Symphony   *Ode to Joy*   *Pathétique* Sonata
Heiligenstadt Testament

12

THE ROMANTIC SPIRIT (1820–1900)

The mature music of Beethoven, with its powerful crescendos, pounding rhythms, imitations of nature, and larger, more colorful orchestra, announces the arrival of an important change in music in the first decades of the nineteenth century. This is the change from Classicism to Romanticism. It coincides with similar changes in style in the poetry, literature, and painting of the period. In all the arts revolutionary sentiments were in the air: a new desire for liberty, self-expression, bold action, passionate feeling, and a love of nature. And just as the impatient Beethoven finally cast off the wig and powdered hair of the eighteenth century, so now the formal constraints of the old Classical art were thrown aside.

REVOLUTIONARY SENTIMENT AND ROMANTIC CREATIVITY

Romanticism is often defined as a revolt against the Classical adherence to reason, rules, forms, and traditions. Whereas artists of the eighteenth century sought to achieve unity, order, proportion, and a balance of form and content, those of the nineteenth century strove for self-expression, to communicate with passion no matter what sort of imbalance, contradiction, or formal inconsistency might result. If Classical architecture, painting, and music drew its inspiration from the monuments of ancient Greece and Rome, Romantic literature, poetry, painting, and music found creative encouragement in the newly proclaimed liberty of man and in the wonders of nature. The Romantic artist exalted instinctive feelings, human and natural, above all else. These were not the feelings of the masses that Beethoven addressed in his Ninth Symphony, however, but individual, personal, private feelings. Music and her sister arts now withdrew from Beethoven's vision of humanity. They became more intensely expressive yet highly personal and introspective.

If there was a single feeling or sentiment that pervaded the Romantic era it was love. Indeed, love, or "romance," is at the very heart of the word "Romantic." The loves of Romeo and Juliet and of Tristan and Isolde, for example, captured the imagination of the Romantic century. These were ardent tales in which desire, anguish, longing, and despair were felt far more powerfully than any enjoyment or happiness in love. The endless pursuit of love, the search for the unattainable, became an obsession that, when expressed as music, produced the sounds of longing and of yearning heard in so much of Romantic music. Berlioz, Liszt, and Wagner not only wrote about the pursuit of ideal love through their music, but also lived this quest in their personal lives. As art imitates life, so the Romantic composer could not write love-music without being in love.

Yet love was only one of many emotions felt strongly by the Romantics. Despair, revenge, pride, frenzy, and heavenly exaltation were a few of the others they communicated effectively in their music and poetry. Classical music had, in general, exhibited only a narrow range of emotional expression. Romantic music, on the other hand, was marked by wide swings of mood, just as the composers themselves sometimes indulged in wild extremes of behavior. Just how the range of expression was broadened in Romantic music can be seen in the "expression marks" that came into being at this time: *espressivo* (expressively), *dolente* (sadly), *presto furioso* (fast and furiously), *con forza e passione* (with force and passion), *misterioso* (mysteriously), and *maestoso* (majestically). Although these are directives to the performer explaining how a passage is to be played, they also reveal what the composer felt about the music.

Feelings about nature also received unprecedented attention with the Romantics. Nature came to be seen as the source of ultimate truth, of certainty and perfection, a reflection of God and His Eternal Mind. Romantic painters, like J. M. W. Turner (1775–1851) and Caspar David Friedrich (1774–1840), stood in awe of nature's powerful, mysterious forces (see Fig. 12–1). The English Romantic poets John Keats (1795–1821), William Wordsworth (1770–1850), and Lord Byron (1778–1824) communed with her verdant woods, dissolving mists, and tender twilights. Musicians, too, paid homage to nature through sounds that sought to capture her lyrical song, spacious majesty, and destructive fury. Beethoven's "Pastoral" Symphony (Symphony No. 6), with its bird calls and summer storm, was the first of these evocative pieces. Schubert's "Trout" Quintet, Liszt's *Lake of Wallenstadt*, Schumann's *Forest Scenes*, and Strauss's "Alpine" Symphony are just a few of the musical works that continue the tradition.

Associated with this desire to be at one with nature was a passion for travel, what the Germans call a *Wanderlust*. Far-off places and people stirred the imagination of the Romantics. The German composer Felix Mendelssohn (1809–1847) journeyed to Italy, to Scotland, and to the Hebrides Islands to find inspiration for his symphonies and overtures. The English poet Byron sailed to Greece and Turkey and infused his art with a sense of the exotic.

FIGURE 12–1

A Traveler Looking over a Sea of Fog (ca. 1818). The themes of isolation, solitude, oblivion, and endless time are explored in this early Romantic painting by Caspar David Friedrich. Friedrich's credo was: "The artist's feeling is his law."

MUSIC AND NATIONALISM

Byron had gone to Greece to foment a revolution—to help the Greeks break free from the empire of the Ottoman Turks. The struggle of the Greeks was symptomatic of the desire of many of Europe's people to throw off the rule of foreign powers or oppressive monarchs. In the 1830s, Poland fought (unsuccessfully) for freedom from Russia, Belgium broke free from the Dutch, and Italy, long controlled by the Austrian Empire and by Spain, began its long march toward liberation and national unity. In 1830, and again in 1848, Paris rebelled against a repressive king. The uprising of 1848 sparked similar revolts

wars of independence

in many cities throughout German- and Italian-speaking lands. The composer Hector Berlioz took to the streets of Paris, revolver in hand, during the insurgence of 1830. Richard Wagner led, and then fled, the unsuccessful revolt in Dresden in 1849. Verdi's name was an acronym for the Italian liberation movement (see page 281). In 1861, Italy finally achieved full unification, with Rome as its capital. Ten years later a German Empire, under the political leadership of Chancellor Otto von Bismarck (1815–1898), was formally recognized. Pride in a national culture and character was likewise felt by smaller groups, such as the Czechs, Hungarians, Poles, and Finns, each of which was trying to free itself from more powerful countries such as Germany, Austria, and Russia.

revolution in Europe

Not surprisingly, patriotism was accompanied by musical **nationalism.** A flood of national anthems, native dances, military marches, protest songs, rescue operas, and victory symphonies gave musical voice to the rising tide of nationalism. At the same time, national identity was fostered by incorporating folk art into more "serious" forms of music, literature, poetry, and painting. National color in music was communicated by means of indigenous folk elements—folk songs, native scales and dance rhythms, and local instrumental sounds.

Earlier we met a staunch proponent of musical nationalism, the composer Modest Musorgsky (see page 6). Musorgsky was one of "The Russian Five," a group of composers dedicated to creating purely Russian art. In 1859 he declared: "I have been a [European] cosmopolitan, but now there's been some sort of regeneration. Everything Russian is becoming dear to me." Musorgsky's musical nationalism sounds forth in the opening *Promenade* (Intro CD/1) of his *Pictures at an Exhibition* (1874). The tempo is marked "Fast but resolute, in the Russian manner"; the meter is irregular, as in a folk dance, mixing groups of five

✹ FIGURE 12–2

Eugène Delacroix's *Liberty Leading the People* was inspired by the Parisian Revolution of 1830. The allegorical figure Liberty leads an urban worker, a middle-class merchant, and a pistol-toting street urchin. The composer Berlioz participated in and wrote music to commemorate those killed in this revolt.

Lord Byron's *Know You the Land*

George Gordon, Lord Byron, was the epitome of the Romantic hero: dashing, passionate, self-absorbed, idealistic, and guilt ridden (he had had an affair with his half sister). "He is mad, bad, and dangerous to know," said one of his lovers. Byron climbed the Swiss Alps, swam the Hellespont (separating Europe from Asia Minor), and died, at age thirty-six, fighting for Greek independence from Turkish rule. His poem *Know You the Land* (from *The Bride of Abydos: A Turkish Tale*) possesses several of the sensibilities dear to the hearts of the Romantics: the colors and sounds of nature, the sights and perfumes of the exotic East, and a hint of forbidden love.

Know you the land of the cedar and vine,
Where the flowers ever blossom, the beams ever shine;
Where the light wings of Zephyr, oppress'd with perfume,
Wax faint o'er the gardens of Gul in her bloom;
Where the citron and olive are fairest of fruit,
And the voice of the nightingale never is mute:
Where the tints of the earth, and the hues of the sky,
In colour though varied, in beauty may vie,
And the purple of Ocean is deepest in dye;

A portrait of the English poet Lord Byron in the dress of an Albanian adventurer.

Where the virgins are soft as the roses they twine,
And all, save the spirit of man, is divine?

from Lord Byron's *Know You the Land* (1813)

beats with those of six; and the melody is built on a folk-influenced scale, called a **pentatonic scale,** which uses only five notes instead of the usual Western scale of seven, here B♭, C, D, F, and G:

EXAMPLE 12–1

(For another example of musical nationalism, turn to the Polish mazurka of Frédéric Chopin, which is discussed on page 269).

✿ MUSIC AND THE LITERARY IMAGINATION

If nationalism offered hope for the future, imagination brought escape from the oppressive present. Fantasy, dreams, even nightmares were the stuff of creative inspiration for the Romantics. Composers gave free reign to their musical imaginations in countless pieces called "fantasies" and "romances." Writers like the brothers (Jacob and Wilhelm) Grimm wrote fairy tales that expressed the dark side of human nature. Other authors were swept away by the bizarre, the macabre, and the demonic. Johann von Goethe's *Faust* (1808 and 1831), perhaps the most influential work of the nineteenth century, tells the tale of a scholar who sells his soul to the devil, finding beauty and honor in pain. The gothic novel, with its haunted castles, ghosts, and terrified heroines, had arrived. In

Romantic fantasy

1818 Mary Shelly (1797–1851) published her *Frankenstein,* and in 1831 Victor Hugo (1802–1885) gave to his readers *The Hunchback of Notre Dame,* both showing empathy for the deformed and the grotesque. In music, as we shall see, magic bullets cast by the devil (in Weber's *Die Freischütz,* 1821), an evil elfking (in Schubert's *Erlkönig,* 1815), and a witches' black Mass (in Berlioz's *Symphonie fantastique,* 1830) reflect the attraction of the supernatural for the Romantic temperament. To understand all that was good, the artist must know evil as well.

literature and music

As parallel developments in music and literature attest, word and tone were never more closely allied than during the nineteenth century. The poets viewed music as the womb from which sprang all true art; sounds were capable of expressing emotions and feelings more powerfully, more subtly, more perfectly than could mere words. For their part, composers were as much enraptured by literature as they were by music—Berlioz, Schumann, Liszt, and Wagner were writers of poetry as well as music. They sought to bring external stimuli—poetic and literary themes—into their musical creations as if thereby to double the emotional impact of pure sound. Byron, Goethe, and, above all, Shakespeare struck resonant chords with Romantic composers, who turned the poetry and plays of these writers into overtures, symphonic poems, and operas. Now for the first time Shakespeare became widely read on the Continent, in part because of the publication of an authoritative German translation of his works in 1801. Rare was the Romantic composer who failed to capture in music the spirit of one of the Bard's great plays.

✿ THE MUSICIAN AS ARTIST, MUSIC AS ART

Besides fostering a tight bond between sound and word, the spirit of Romanticism encouraged a new attitude about music as an art. The forceful pens of musician-writers like Berlioz, Schumann, and Wagner persuaded the public that the composer was no longer a mere craftsman but an artist, someone above an ordinary mortal. Bach had been a municipal civil servant, devoted and dutiful, to the town government in Leipzig. Haydn and Mozart served, and were treated, as domestics in the homes of the great lords of Europe. But Beethoven began to break the chains of submission. He was the first to demand, and receive, the respect and admiration due a great creative spirit. Ultimately, Franz Liszt and Richard Wagner, as much through their literary works as through their musical compositions, caused the public to view the artist as a sort of demigod, a prophet able to inspire the audience through the creation of music that was morally uplifting as well as beautiful. They fostered the idea that the artist was a superior being, endowed with exceptional powers of expression. Never was the position of the creative musician loftier than in the mid-nineteenth century.

the artist as prophet to the world

Just as the musician changed from craftsman to artist in the public mind at this time, so the music he or she produced changed from handicraft to work of art. Classical music had been created for the immediate gratification of patron and audience, with little thought given to its lasting value. With the mature Beethoven and the early Romantics, this attitude began to change. Symphonies, quartets, and piano sonatas sprang to life, not to give immediate pleasure to a listener, but to gratify a deep-seated creative urge within the composer. They became extensions of the artist's personality. These works might not be understood by the creator's contemporaries, as was true of the late piano sonatas of Beethoven and the orchestral works of Hector Berlioz, for example, but they would be understood by posterity, by future generations of listeners. The idea of "art for art's sake"—art free of all functional concerns—was born of the Romantic spirit.

art for art's sake

The new exalted position of the composer and his work of art soon brought a more serious tone to the concert hall. Before 1800 people gathered to listen to music more for the opportunity for social interchange than for the chance to enjoy an aesthetic experience. They talked, smoked, drank, ate, played cards, flirted, and wandered about. The audience was loud and demonstrative; if the music went well, people applauded not only at the end of pieces, but also between movements. Sometimes they demanded an immediate encore, sometimes they hissed their disapproval. By the 1830s, however, this had changed. With the revered figure of the Romantic composer-performer now before them, the members of the audience sat in respectful silence. The work of art was surrounded by a sacred aura of devotion and absolute attention (see cover). More was expected of the listener, partly because symphonies and sonatas were longer and more complex. But the listener, in turn, expected more from the music: not mere entertainment but an emotionally satisfying encounter that would leave the attentive person exhausted yet somehow purified and uplifted by the artistic experience.

the concert hall becomes silent

Romantic Ideals and Today's Concert Hall

Romanticism has kept its grip on the Western imagination. Belief in the artist as hero, reverence toward the work of art as an object of moral inspiration, and the expectations of silence and even formal dress at a concert—these are all attitudes that developed in the early Romantic period. What is more, the notion that a particular group of pieces should get a repeated hearing gains currency at this time. Prior to 1800 almost all music was disposable music: It was written for the enjoyment of the moment and then was no longer in vogue. But the generation following Beethoven began to see his best symphonies, concertos, and quartets, as well as those of Mozart and Haydn, as worthy of continued performance and preservation. These and the best works of succeeding generations came to constitute a "canon" of music—a body of music possessing attributes of unity, expression, and form that should be continually revisited. Such masterpieces, as they were correctly viewed, came to form the core of today's concert repertoire. Thus what we think about the composer, how we view the work of art, what we can expect to hear at a concert, and even how we behave during the performance are not ideals, with us since time immemorial, but are paradigms created during a special period in history. In many respects, the attitudes about art and music that arose in the early nineteenth century still govern our thinking today.

a core repertoire for the concert hall

✿ THE STYLE OF ROMANTIC MUSIC

The Romantic spirit rebelled against Classical ideals in ways that allow us to generalize these two artistic movements as pairs of opposites: rational against irrational, intellect opposed to heart, conformity versus originality, and the masses in contradistinction to the individual. Yet in purely musical terms, the works of the Romantic composers represent not so much a revolution against Classical ideals as an evolution that goes beyond them. Romantic music is an expansion and amplification of the style created by the Classical masters. The Romantics introduced no new musical forms and only one or two new genres. Instead, Romantic composers took the musical materials received from the hands of Haydn, Mozart, and young Beethoven and made them more intensely expressive, more original, more personal, and, in some cases, more bizarre.

Romantic Melody

The Romantic period witnessed the apotheosis of melody. Melodies become broad, powerful streams of sound intended to sweep the listener away. They go beyond the neat symmetrical units of two plus two, four plus four, inherent in the Classical style. They become longer, rhythmically more flexible, and more irregular in shape. At the same time, Romantic melodies continue a trend that developed in the late eighteenth century in which themes became vocal in conception, more singable. Melodies of Chopin, Tchaikovsky, and Rachmaninoff have been turned into popular songs in our own day. Similarly, today's popular collections of "40 All-Time Favorite Classical Melodies" draw primarily from the symphonies, sonatas, and operas of the Romantic period, simply because these themes are so profoundly expressive. They sigh and lament. They grow and become ecstatic. They start haltingly and then build to a grandiose climax, sublime and triumphant. Example 12–2 is a melody by Hector Berlioz, the principal theme of his *Symphonie fantastique* (1830). Notice that it is long and rhythmically rather free, with many syncopations* that cross the bar lines and obscure the downbeats*. Observe, too, that by means of an ascending melodic sequence (see brackets) the melody climbs inexorably upward to a lofty climax, from where it relaxes back down to the tonic note.

the popular quality of Romantic melodies

EXAMPLE 12–2

Colorful Harmony

Part of the emotional intensity of Romantic music is generated by a new, more colorful harmony. Classical music had, in the main, made use of chords built only on the seven notes of the major or minor scale—the so-called diatonic* notes of the scale (see page 24). Romantic composers went farther by constructing chords on the five additional notes within the full twelve-note chromatic scale—the so-called chromatic* notes. This gave more colors to their harmonic palette. It also gave fluency to the sound, as chords and inner voices glide smoothly to notes only a half step away. Using chromatic chords similarly made

chromatic harmony

it easier for the composer to modulate to distant keys, to carry the music tonally away to some far-off, exotic land of six flats or seven sharps.

The rich, lush sounds of the Romantics are also created by setting up novel relationships between chords. In the Baroque and Classical periods, harmony often moved along in chord progressions in which the roots of the chords were an interval of a fifth apart. Now chords only a third apart are frequently set in close proximity, and these can require radically different key signatures*—a harmony with four sharps might be followed immediately by one with four flats, for example. The striking sound that results from these unusual relationships is appropriate for music that seeks to express a wider range of feeling.

bold choral progressions

Finally, much of the sound of pain and anguish that we hear in Romantic music comes about because of a greater use of dissonance. Dissonant notes are not only more numerous, but they are held for longer periods of time as well. Since dissonance always wants to move, or resolve, to consonance, the delay of the resolution produces a feeling of anxiety, longing, and searching, all sentiments appropriate for music that often deals with the subject of love.

dissonance longs for consonance

All three of these qualities of Romantic harmony—chromaticism, bold chordal relationships, and dissonance–consonance movement—come in quick succession at the end of Franz Liszt's *Liebestraum* (*Love-Dream*, 1850). Neither you nor the author can hear all the music given in Ex. 12–3 simply by looking at it. (To hear it, turn to 6CD 4/5 at 3:57.) We can, however, visualize here some of the music's inner workings—first the chromaticism, then the shift from a chord with three sharps to one with four flats, and finally dissonance resolving to consonance. In this way we may begin to understand, when hearing the rich, sensuous sound of Romantic music, how it is created.

EXAMPLE 12–3

Romantic Tempo: *Rubato*

In keeping with an age that glorified personal freedom and tolerated eccentric behavior, tempo in music was cut loose from the restraints of a regular beat. The watchword here was *rubato* (literally "robbed"), an expression mark for the performer written into the score by the composer. A performer playing tempo **rubato** stole some time here and gave it back there, moving faster or slower so as to effect an intensely personal performance. The free approach to tempo was often reinforced by fluctuating dynamic levels—ritards were done with diminuendos* and accelerations with crescendos*—as a way of explaining, even exaggerating, the flow of the music. Whatever excesses might result, could be excused under license of artistic freedom.

🌿 FIGURE 12–3

A natural French horn of the late eighteenth century, the sort of horn contemporary with the symphonies of Mozart, Haydn, and Beethoven.

🌼 EXPRESSIVE TONE COLORS, GREATER SIZE, GREATER VOLUME

From the listener's perspective, perhaps the most striking aspect of Romantic music is the color and sheer volume of the sound. Sometimes all thematic and harmonic movement stops and nothing but pure sound carries the moment. During the nineteenth century the orchestra became larger and more varied, the piano bigger and more powerful. Composers demanded, and received, musical forces equal to the task of expressing the extremes of emotion, changing moods, and extravagant gestures of the Romantic spirit.

The Romantic Orchestra

The Industrial Revolution brought with it mechanical innovations that made the instruments of the symphony orchestra essentially what they are today. The wood of the flute was replaced by silver, and the instrument was supplied with a new fingering mechanism that added to its agility and made it easier to play in tune. Similarly, the trumpet and French horn were provided with valves that improved technical facility and accuracy of pitch in all keys. These brass instruments were now capable of playing intricate, chromatic melodies as well as providing the traditional backdrop of sonic support for the rest of the orchestra. The horn, in particular, became an object of special affection during the Romantic period. Its rich, dark tone and its traditional association with the hunt—and by extension nature—made it the Romantic instrument par excellence. Composers often called on a solo horn when they wished to express something mysterious or distant.

Besides improvements to existing instruments, several new instruments were added to the symphony orchestra during the nineteenth century. We have seen how Beethoven brought the piccolo (a high flute), the trombone, and the con-

🌿 FIGURE 12–4

A modern French horn with valves, an invention of the 1820s. The valves allowed the performer to engage different lengths of tubing instantly, and thereby play a fully chromatic scale.

The Growth of the Symphony Orchestra

Mozart (1788) Symphony in G minor	Berlioz (1830) *Symphonie fantastique*	Mahler (1889) Symphony No. 1
1 flute	1 piccolo	3 piccolos
2 oboes	2 flutes	4 flutes
2 clarinets	2 oboes	4 oboes
2 bassoons	1 English horn	1 English horn
2 French horns	2 B♭ clarinets	4 B♭ clarinets
1st violins (8)[†]	1 E♭ clarinet	2 E♭ clarinets
2nd violins (8)	4 bassoons	1 bass clarinet
violas (4)	4 French horns	3 bassoons
cellos (4)	2 trumpets	1 contrabassoon
double basses (3)	2 cornets	7 French horns
	3 trombones	5 trumpets
	2 ophicleides (tubas)	4 trombones
	1st violins (15)[†]	1 tuba
	2nd violins (14)	1st violins (20)[†]
	violas (8)	2nd violins (18)
	cellos (12)	violas (14)
	double basses (8)	cellos (12)
	2 harps	double basses (8)
	timpani	1 harp
Total: 36	bass drum	timpani (2 players)
	snare drum	bass drum
	cymbals and bells	triangle, cymbals
		tam-tam
	Total: 89	
		Total: 115

[†]Number of string players estimated according to standards of the period.

trabassoon (a bass bassoon) into the orchestra in his famous Symphony No. 5 (1808). In 1830 Hector Berlioz went even farther, requiring an ophicleide* (an early form of the tuba), an English horn* (a low-pitched oboe), a cornet*, and two harps in his *Symphonie fantastique*. Berlioz, the embodiment of the Romantic spirit, had a typically grandiose notion of what the ideal symphony orchestra should contain. He wanted no fewer than 467 instrumentalists including 120 violins, 40 violas, 45 cellos, 35 double basses, and 30 harps. Needless to say, such a gigantic instrumental force was never assembled, but Berlioz's utopian vision indicates the direction in which Romantic composers were headed. By the second half of the nineteenth century, orchestras with nearly a hundred players were not uncommon. Compare the instruments and their number required for a typical eighteenth-century performance of Mozart's G minor symphony with the symphony orchestra called on to play Berlioz's *Symphonie fantastique* and that required for Gustav Mahler's Symphony No. 1 (see box above). Our ears today have been desensitized by an over-exposure to electronically amplified sound to the point that we can hardly imagine the overwhelming impact that a large symphony orchestra had on concertgoers in the nineteenth century.

larger orchestras

The Conductor

Naturally, someone was needed to coordinate the efforts of the enlarged orchestra. Previously, in the days of Bach and Mozart, the orchestra had been led from within, either by the keyboard player of the *basso continuo** gesturing with his head and hands or by the chief violinist directing with his bow. When Beethoven played and conducted his piano concertos, he did so seated at his instrument. When he led one of his symphonies, especially toward the end of his life, he stood before the orchestra, back to the audience, waving his hands. In 1820 the composer Louis Spohr became the first to use a wooden baton to lead the orchestra and to rehearse the musicians carefully through the problematic spots of his compositions. In the course of the nineteenth century the leader of the orchestra became increasingly a privileged interpreter, sometimes dictator, of the musical score. The modern conductor had arrived.

The Piano

During the nineteenth century the piano became what the computer is today, something of a home entertainment center. Every aspiring household had to have one, as well as the software to make it work. The software then was the **piano transcription**—a reduction for piano solo of some larger orchestral or operatic work. Thus the symphonies of Beethoven and Berlioz were transcribed for piano, as were the opera overtures of Rossini and entire operas by Bellini and many others. Music lovers in Brussels, Baltimore, or Birmingham might never have the chance to hear a "live" performance of a Beethoven symphony, but they might come to know it at home by means of a piano transcription by Liszt, for example. Before the age of electronically produced sound, the piano transcription was the medium by which the general listening public became familiar with the major works composed for the symphony hall or opera house.

That the piano provided a good two-handed approximation of the symphony orchestra suggests that it, too, grew considerably in size during the early 1800s. Here also the new technology of the Industrial Revolution was decisive. Although still surrounded by a wooden shell, the internal wooden frame was replaced by a cast-iron one that allowed for greater tension on the strings. This necessitated thicker strings which, in turn, greatly increased the volume of sound. The pianist could bang away and no strings would break. To soften the blow, hammers were covered with felt, which made the instrument "sing" with a mellow tone, in contrast to the "ping" of the pianos of Mozart's day. The range of the instrument was extended both high and low, expanding from the five-octave piano of the 1790s to a seven-octave instrument by the 1840s. By mid-century, all pianos were equipped with at least two pedals: a **sustaining pedal** (right), which enabled some strings to continue to sound while others were being struck; and a **soft pedal** (left), which allowed the instrument to play at a softer dynamic by shifting the position of the keyboard. Finally, in the 1850s, the Steinway Company of New York began **cross-stringing** the piano, a practice whereby the strings of the lowest keys ride up over those of the middle register, thereby producing a richer, more homogenous sound. By the mid-nineteenth century, all the essential features of the modern piano were in place: The basic design of the piano has not changed in 150 years.

❧ FIGURE 12–5
Silhouette of Karl Maria von Weber conducting with a rolled sheet of music so as to highlight the movement of his hand.

❧ FIGURE 12–6
The grand piano made by C. Bechstein (Berlin, 1864) at which Richard Wagner finished the opera *Tristan und Isolde* (1865), now preserved in the Yale University Collection of Musical Instruments. It is a vastly larger and more powerful instrument than Mozart had at his disposal (see page 196).

The Virtuoso

Appropriate for an era that glorified the individual, the nineteenth century was the age of the solo virtuoso. Of course, there had been instrumental virtuosos before—Bach on the organ, Mozart on the piano, to name just two—but now enormous energy was expended by many musicians to raise their performing skills to an unprecedented height. Pianists and violinists in particular practiced long hours just on technical exercises—arpeggios, tremolos, trills, and scales played in thirds, sixths, and octaves—to develop wizardlike hand speed on their instrument. Naturally, some of what they played for the public was lacking in musical substance, tasteless show pieces designed to appeal immediately to the large audiences that packed the ever-larger concert halls. Pianists developed tricks of playing to make it appear they had more hands than two (see Fig. 13–20). Franz Liszt (1811–1886) sometimes played at the keyboard with a lighted cigar between his fingers. The Italian Niccolò Paganini (1782–1840) secretly tuned the four strings of his violin in ways that would allow him to negotiate with ease extraordinarily difficult passages (see Ex. 12–4). If one of his strings broke, he could play with just three; if three broke, he could continue apace with just one. As the composer Debussy later remarked, "The attraction of the virtuoso is like that of the circus performer, there's always the hope that something disastrous will happen." The musical showman had taken center stage. Fortunately, as we shall see, some of these showmen were also gifted composers.

EXAMPLE 12–4: Paganini, Caprice, Opus 1, No. 5

FIGURE 12–7 AND 12–8 (right) Niccolò Paganini. (left) *Paganini and the Witches,* a lithograph by an unknown artist. Paganini's extraordinary powers on the violin led some to believe he was in league with the devil. The fourth string of his violin was said to be made of the intestine of his mistress, whom he had murdered with his own hands. None of this was true, and Paganini undertook several libel suits to disprove it.

Forms: Monumental and Miniature

The musical forms that had earlier served Haydn and Mozart continued to satisfy the needs of the nineteenth-century composer. Sonata–allegro form, in particular, remained useful because its flexible format could accommodate any number of individual solutions. What developed, then, was not a rush to invent new forms but a trend to extend the existing ones. As composers laid out *colossal symphonies*

broad, sweeping melodies, indulged in gigantic crescendos, and reveled in the luxurious sound of the enlarged orchestra, the length of individual movements increased dramatically. Mozart's G minor symphony (1788) lasts about twenty minutes, depending on the tempo of the performance. But Berlioz's *Symphonie fantastique* (1830) takes nearly fifty-five minutes, and Mahler's Symphony No. 2 (1894) nearly an hour and a half. Perhaps the longest of all musical works is Richard Wagner's four-opera *Ring* cycle (1853–1876), which continues some seventeen hours during the course of four evenings. In these extended visions the Romantic composer seems to be saying along with the poet: "Romanticism is beauty without bounds—the beautiful infinite."

character pieces

Yet, paradoxically, Romantic composers were fascinated by miniature forms as well. In brief works of a scant minute or two, they tried to capture the essence of one single mood, sentiment, or emotion. Such a miniature was called a **character piece.** It was usually written for the piano and often made use of simple binary (**AB**) or ternary (**ABA**) form. Because the character piece passes by in a twinkling of an eye, it was sometimes given a whimsical title, such as bagatelle (a trifle), humoresque, arabesque, musical moment, caprice, romance, intermezzo, or impromptu. Schubert, Schumann, Chopin, Liszt, Brahms, and Tchaikovsky all enjoyed creating these musical miniatures, perhaps as antidotes to their lengthy symphonies and concertos.

✿ NEW GENRES: THE SYMPHONIC POEM AND THE ART SONG

The Classical genres of the symphony, concerto, string quartet, piano sonata, and opera remained fashionable, though somewhat altered in appearance, throughout the nineteenth century. The symphony, as we have seen, now grows in length, embodying the widest possible range of expression, while the concerto becomes increasingly virtuosic, as a heroic soloist does battle against an orchestral mass. In addition, two new genres of music are created during the Romantic century, specifically, the symphonic poem and the art song.

program music: inspired by another source

The advent of the symphonic poem (discussed shortly) is tied to the broad development of program music generally in the nineteenth century. **Program music** is a piece of instrumental music, usually for symphony orchestra, that seeks to recreate in sound the events and emotions portrayed in some extramusical source: a story, a play, a historical event, or even a painting. The theory of program music rests on the obvious fact that specific kinds of music can evoke particular feelings and associations. A lyrical melody may recall memories of love, harshly dissonant chords may create a sense of conflict, rapidly flowing notes may produce a vision of a mountain stream, distant trumpet calls may suggest the imminent arrival of a hero. By stringing these together in a convincing sequence, music might be made to tell a story. Program music is fully harmonious with the strongly literary spirit of the nineteenth century.

absolute music: music without an external source

Some Romantic composers, notably Johannes Brahms (1833–1897) and Anton Bruckner (1824–1896), resisted the allure of program music and continued to write what came to be called **absolute music**—symphonies, sonatas, quartets, and other instrumental music without extramusical or programmatic references. But most composers succumbed to the temptation to make their instrumental works take on an overtly narrative character. The programmatic influence crept into established genres like the overture and symphony. It also gave rise to an entirely new genre, the symphonic poem. The principal kinds of nineteenth-century program music can be defined as follows:

Symphonic poem (also called the **tone poem**): A one-movement work for orchestra that gives musical expression to the emotions and events associated with a story, play, political occurrence, personal experience, or encounter with nature. It is usually a lengthy piece composed in any one of several forms including sonata–allegro, theme and variations, and rondo. Examples include Liszt's *Les Préludes* (1854), Modest Musorgsky's *Night on Bald Mountain* (1867), Tchaikovsky's *Romeo and Juliet* (1869), and Richard Strauss's *Don Juan* (1888).

Program symphony: A symphony with the usual three, four, or five movements, but now the individual movements together tell or depict a succession of specific events or scenes drawn from some extramusical work or story. Examples include Berlioz's *Symphonie fantastique* (1830) and Liszt's "Faust" Symphony (1857).

Overture (to an opera or a play): A one-movement work, usually in sonata–allegro form, which foretells in music the essential dramatic events that will follow in an opera or a play. Many overtures, because of unusual color or special effects, became popular with the listening public and came to be performed by themselves. Examples include Rossini's Overture to his opera *William Tell* (1829) and Mendelssohn's Overture to Shakespeare's play *A Midsummer Night's Dream* (1826).

Concert overture: Similar to the overture but *not* designed to precede an opera or play; thus, an independent one-movement work of programmatic content originally intended for the concert hall. Examples include Mendelssohn's *Hebrides Overture* (1830) and Tchaikovsky's *1812 Overture* (1880). In fact, there is little difference between the symphonic poem and the concert overture. Both are one-movement programmatic works intended for the concert hall.

Incidental music: Music to be inserted between the acts or during important scenes of a play to add an extra dimension to the drama. Examples include Mendelssohn's incidental music to Shakespeare's *A Midsummer Night's Dream* (1843) and Edvard Grieg's music to Henrik Ibsen's play *Peer Gynt* (1875).

About 1850 Franz Liszt, a leading advocate of program music, said that an explicit program gave the composer "a means by which to protect the listener against a wrong poetical interpretation and to direct his attention to the poetical idea of the whole." Soon we will hear and discuss three imaginative examples of program music: Berlioz's *Symphonie fantastique* (a program symphony), Mendelssohn's Overture to *A Midsummer Night's Dream* (an overture to a play), and Tchaikovsky's *Romeo and Juliet* (a symphonic poem). You will be able to decide whether the presence of a program is useful, allowing you to make sense of the music more easily, or harmful, restricting your creative imagination as you listen.

The other new musical genre that flourished in the nineteenth century was the art song. An **art song** is simply a piece for solo voice and piano accompaniment with high artistic aspirations. Of course, there had been songs of artistic merit for voice and accompanying instrument since the Middle Ages. But one of the hallmarks of the Romantic movement, as we have seen, was a quickening interest in literature and especially in poetry. The Romantic poets like

❁ FIGURE 12–9

The Balcony Scene of Romeo and Juliet (1845) by Eugène Delacroix typifies the nineteenth-century fascination with Shakespeare. Berlioz sought to capture the spirit of the play in a five-movement program symphony (*Roméo et Juliette*, 1839); Tchaikovsky tried to do so in a one-movement symphonic poem (*Romeo and Juliet*, 1869).

does a program increase the enjoyment of listening?

the art song

Wordsworth, Keats, Shelley, and Byron burst on the English scene in the early 1800s, and they had their counterparts in Germany in the person of the great Goethe and the gifted Heinrich Heine (1797–1856). Literally thousands of odes, sonnets, stanzas, ballads, and romances poured from their pens and those of lesser talent. Swept up in this new-found enthusiasm for poetry, composers set many of these texts for voice and piano, believing that music could intensify poetic sentiments by expressing things words alone could not. Because the art song was cultivated mainly in German-speaking lands, the genre is also called the **Lied** (plural, **Lieder**), German for "song." The first important composer of the *Lied* was Franz Schubert (1797–1828), and it is to his music and that of the other early Romantics that we now turn.

the Lied

LISTENING EXERCISE

25   Comparing Orchestral Works of the Classical and Romantic Periods

Listen again to the first movement of Mozart's Symphony No. 40 in G minor (1788) (6CD 2/8; 2CD 1/11) and compare it with the finale of Hector Berlioz's *Symphonie fantastique* (1830) (6CD 3/10; 2CD 2/1).

1. Which work uses a larger, more colorful orchestra? _____
2. Which work has a consistently uniform tempo to it? _____
3. Which work employs the orchestra to create "special effects," much as in a score for a modern-day motion picture? _____
4. Which has greater "mood swings," in which the music oscillates between louds and softs, high pitches and low pitches? _____
5. In which work are all themes presented first by the violins? _____
6. Which uses a brass instrument to play a solo melody? _____
7. Which uses a percussion instrument to play a solo melody? _____
8. Which work is more progressive, in that it moves purposefully and without delay from one section to another? _____
9. In what ways does Berlioz use the orchestra to express sentiments and feelings typical of the Romantic period (passion, isolation, terror, the bizarre)?

    _____
    _____
    _____

10. Now sit back and listen again to both pieces, giving free reign to your creative imagination. Try to construct in your mind's eye a scenario or a series of visual images that correspond to the music you hear. Which composition lends itself more readily to this sort of creative flight of fancy, and why?

    _____
    _____
    _____
    _____

KEY WORDS

absolute music	nationalism	*rubato*
art song	overture	soft pedal
character piece	pentatonic scale	sustaining pedal
concert overture	piano transcription	symphonic poem
incidental music	program music	tone poem
Lied	program symphony	

THE EARLY ROMANTICS

 The decade 1803–1813 was perhaps the most auspicious in the history of music. In this short span of time were born the composers Hector Berlioz (1803), Felix Mendelssohn (1809), Frédéric Chopin (1810), Robert Schumann (1810), Franz Liszt (1811), Giuseppe Verdi (1813), and Richard Wagner (1813). Add to this the shining figure of Franz Schubert (born 1797) and this brilliant galaxy of musical geniuses is complete. We call them Romantics because they were part of, indeed they created, the Romantic movement in music. But with the possible exception of Mendelssohn, they were very unconventional people. Their lives typify all that we have come to associate with the Romantic spirit: self-expression, passion, excess, the love of nature and literature, as well as a certain selfishness, irresponsibility, and even a bit of lunacy. Not only did they create great art, but life, and how they lived it, also became an art.

THE ART SONG†

The genre of the art song, or *Lied**, for solo voice and piano became a popular type of musical expression during the early 1800s. The enormous outpouring of the Romantic poets was matched by the creative enthusiasm of the Romantic composers, who set hundreds of ballads, odes, and romances to music. Franz Schubert was the greatest of these composers. His special talent was to fashion music that captures both the spirit and the detail of the text, creating a sensitive mood painting in which the voice and, especially, the piano accompaniment express every nuance of the poem. Schubert said, "When one has a good poem the music comes easily, melodies just flow, so that composing is a real joy."

Franz Schubert (1797–1828)

Franz Schubert was born in Vienna in 1797. Among the great Viennese masters—Haydn, Mozart, Beethoven, Schubert, Brahms, and Mahler—only he was native-born to the city. Schubert's father was a schoolteacher, and the son, too, was groomed for that profession. Yet the boy's obvious musical talent made it imperative that he also have music lessons, so his father taught him to play the violin and his older brother, the piano. At the age of eleven Schubert was ad-

†The art song is discussed more fully on page 243.

mitted as a choirboy in the emperor's chapel (the group today is called the Vienna Choirboys). Proximity to the royal palace brought young Schubert into contact with Antonio Salieri, erstwhile rival of Mozart and still imperial court composer (see page 159). He began to study composition with Salieri in 1810. Soon Schubert was composing his own musical works at an astonishing rate.

After his voice changed in 1812, young Franz left the court chapel and enrolled in a teacher's college. He had been spared compulsory military service because he was below the minimum height of five feet and his sight was so poor he was compelled to wear the spectacles now familiar from his portraits (Fig. 13-1). By 1815 he had become a teacher at his father's primary school. But he found teaching demanding and tedious and so, after three unpleasant years, Schubert abandoned this profession to give himself over wholly to music.

"You lucky fellow; I really envy you! You live a life of sweet, precious freedom, can give free rein to your musical genius, can express your thoughts in any way you like." This was Schubert's brother's view of the composer's newfound freedom. But as many Romantics would find, the reality was harsher than the ideal. Aside from some small income he earned from the sale of a few songs, he lacked a means of support. Schubert, unlike Beethoven, kept no company with aristocrats and thus received no patronage from them. Instead, he lived a Bohemian life, helped along by the generosity of his friends, with whom he often lodged when he was broke. His mornings were consumed passionately composing music; his afternoons were passed in cafes discussing literature and politics; and his evenings were often spent playing his songs and dances before friends and admirers.

While Schubert was coming to his artistic maturity, the era of the great aristocratic salon was drawing to an end. Its place, as a focus for artistic expression, was taken by the middle-class parlor or living room. Here in less pretentious surroundings, groups of men and women with a common interest in music, the novel, drama, or poetry would meet to read and hear all that was new in these arts. The gatherings at which Schubert appeared, and at which only his compositions were played, were called **Schubertiades** by his friends. It was in small, purely private assemblies such as these (Fig. 13-2), not in large public concerts, that most of his best songs were first performed.

In 1822 misfortune befell the composer: He contracted syphilis. His lyrical Symphony in B minor of that fateful year was left incomplete (hence the title, the Unfinished Symphony). Yet during the years that remained before his premature death in 1828 he created some of his greatest works: the song cycles *Die schöne Müllerin* (*The Pretty Maid of the Mill*, 1823) and *Winterreise* (*Winter Journey*, 1827), the "Wanderer" Fantasy for piano (1822), and the great C major Symphony (1828). When Beethoven died in 1827, Schubert served as one of the torchbearers at the funeral. The next year, he too was dead, the youngest of the great composers.

In his brief life of thirty-one years, Franz Schubert wrote eight symphonies, fifteen string quartets, twenty-one piano sonatas, seven Masses for chorus and orchestra, and four operas—a sizable *oeuvre* by any standards. Yet in his day Schubert was known almost exclusively as a writer of art songs. Indeed, he composed more than six hundred works of this genre, many of them minor masterpieces. In a few cases, Schubert chose to set several texts together in a series. In so doing he created what is called a **song cycle**—a tightly structured group of individual songs that tell a story or treat a single theme. *The Pretty Maid of the*

※ FIGURE 13–1
Franz Schubert.

※ FIGURE 13–2
A Schubertiade as depicted in water colors in 1821. The composer, seated at the piano, entertains his friends.

ERLKING (1815)

To gain an idea of Schubert's extraordinary musical talent, we need only listen to his song *Erlkönig (Erlking)*, written when he was just seventeen. The text itself is a ballad—a dramatic story told in alternating narrative verse and dialogue—from the pen of the famous poet Goethe. It relates the tale of the evil King of the Elves and his quest for the soul of a young boy, for legend had it that whosoever was touched by the King of the Elves would die. According to the account of one of Schubert's friends, the composer was reading a book of Goethe's poetry, pacing back and forth in his room. Suddenly, he sprang to the piano and, as fast as he could write, set the entire ballad to music. From there Schubert and his friend hastened to the composer's college to play it for a few kindred spirits. In his lifetime *Erlking* became Schubert's best-known song, one of the few that brought him any money.

FIGURE 13–3

A contemporary painting of the story of the Erlking, showing the evil king, the father and son, and the king's comely daughters.

The opening line of the poem sets the frightful nocturnal scene: "Who rides so late through night and wind?" With his feverish son cradled in his arms, a father rides at breakneck speed to an inn to save the child. Schubert captures both the general sense of terror in the scene and the detail of the galloping horse; he creates an accompanying figure in the piano that pounds on relentlessly just as fast as the pianist can make it go:

EXAMPLE 13–1

The specter of death, the Erlking, beckons gently to the boy. He does so in seductively sweet tones, in a melody with the gentle lilt and folksy accompaniment of a popular tune:

EXAMPLE 13–2

(Thou dearest boy, come go with me!)

The frightened boy cries out to his father in an agitated, then chromatic, line:

EXAMPLE 13–3

(Dear father, my father, say, did'st thou not hear the Erlking whisper promises in my ear?)

This cry is heard again and again in the course of the song, each time at a successively higher pitch and with increasingly dissonant harmonies. In this way the music mirrors the growing terror of the boy. The father tries to calm him and does so in low tones that are steady, stable, and repetitive. Thus, each of the three characters of the story is portrayed with a specific musical quality. This is musical characterization at its finest: The melody and accompaniment not only support the text but also intensify and enrich it. Suddenly, the end is reached. The hand of the Erlking has touched his victim. The accompaniment figure is abruptly choked off as the narrator announces in increasingly somber (minor) tones: "But in his arms, his child was dead!"

characterization through music

LISTENING GUIDE

Franz Schubert
Art song, *Erlking* (1815)

6CD 3/7;
2CD 1/15

Form: through composed

0:00   Introduction by piano accompaniment; pounding triplets in the right hand and an ominous minor motive in the left

Narrator

0:23

Wer reitet so spät
durch Nacht und Wind?
Es ist der Vater
mit seinem Kind.
Er hat den Knaben
wohl in dem Arm,
er fasst ihn sicher,
er hält ihn warm.

Who rides so late
through night so wild?
A loving father
with his child.
He clasps his boy close
with his arm,
He holds him tightly
and keeps him warm.

Father

0:56

"Mein Sohn, was birgst
du so bang dein Gesicht?"

"My son, what makes you hide
your face in fear?"

Son

1:05   With agitated leaps

"Siehst, Vater, du
den Erlkönig nicht?
Den Erlenkönig
mit Kron' und Schweif?"

"Father don't you see
the Erlking—
the Erlking
with crown and shroud?"

Father

1:20   In low, calming tones

"Mein Sohn, es ist ein
Nebelstreif."

"My son, it's only some streak
of mist."

(Continued on next page)

1:30	With a seductive melody in major key	"Du liebes Kind, komm, geh' mit mir! gar schöne Spiele spiel' ich mit dir; manch' bunte Blumen sing an dem Strand, meine Mutter hat manch' gülden Gewand."	**Erlking** "You dear child, come along with me! I'll play some very fine games with you; where varied blossoms sing on meadows fair and my mother has golden garments to wear."
1:55	Tension depicted by tight chromatic movement in voice	"Mein Vater, mein Vater und hörest du nicht, was Erlenkönig mir leise verspricht?"	**Son** "My father, my father, do you not hear how the Erlking whispers promises in my ear?"
2:07	In low, steady pitches	"Sei ruhig, bleibe ruhig, mein Kind, in düren Blättern säuselt der Wind."	**Father** "Be calm, stay calm, my child, Through wither'd leaves the wind blows wild."
2:18	With a happy, lilting tune in major key	"Willst, feiner Knabe, du mit mir geh'n? Meine Töchter sollen dich warten schön, meine Töchter führen den nächtlichen Reih'n, und wiegen und tanzen und singen dich ein."	**Erlking** "My handsome young lad, will you come with me? My beauteous daughters wait for you, With them you would join in the dance every night, and they will rock and dance and sing you to sleep."
2:36	Same intense chromatic notes as before, but now a step higher; minor key	"Mein Vater, mein Vater und siehst du nicht dort Erlkönigs Töchter am düstern Ort?"	**Son** "My Father, my father, don't you see at all the Erlking's daughters over there in the dusk?"
2:48	Low register, but more leaps (agitation) than before	"Mein Sohn, mein Sohn, ich seh' es genau, es scheinen die alten Weiden so grau."	**Father** "My son, my son, the form you there see, is only the aging gray willow tree."
3:06	His music is no longer seductive but now threatening and in minor key	"Ich liebe dich, mich reizt deine schöne Gestalt; und bist du nicht willig, so brauch' ich Gewalt."	**Erlking** "I love you, I'm charmed by your fine appearance; And if you're not willing, I'll seize you by force!"
3:18	Piercing cries in highest range	"Mein Vater, mein Vater jetzt fasst er mich an! Erlkönig hat mir ein Leids gethan!"	**Son** "My father, my father, now he's got me, the Erlking has seized me by his trick."
3:32	With a rising and then falling line	Dem Vater grausets; er reitet geschwind, er hält in den Armen das ächzende Kind. Erreicht den Hof mit Müh und Noth: in seinen Armen das Kind war todt!	**Narrator** The father shudders, he rides headlong, holding the groaning child in his arms. He reaches the inn with toil and dread, but in his arms, his child was dead!
3:47	Piano slows and then stops, recitative		

(Listening Exercise 26)

Tension in Schubert's *Erlking* rises continually from the beginning to the very end. As the story is told, the music, too, unfolds continually without repetition of material, though the cries of the son provide something of a constant refrain. Compositions made up of ever-changing music are called **through composed.** *Erlking* is thus a through-composed *Lied*. For texts that do not tell a story or project a series of changing moods, however, **strophic form** is often preferred. Here a single poetic mood is maintained from one stanza, or strophe, of the text to the next. Accordingly, the same music is repeated, again and again, for each strophe, as in a hymn or a folk song. Schubert used strophic form, for example, when setting a prayer found in Sir Walter Scott's *The Lady of the Lake*. The result was his immortal *Ave Maria* (1825), a song in which the music for each of three strophes is identical, note for note.

through composed and strophic forms

THE TROUT (1817)

Schubert's *Die Forelle (The Trout)* shows how both the Romantic poet and the musician were attracted to the charms of nature. Picture a fresh mountain stream where a trout darts happily about. Schubert captures this vision with a lively tune and a bubbling accompaniment figure in the piano—whether a spinning wheel, a rippling stream, or a galloping horse, Schubert knew better than anyone how to create the musical equivalent of such graphic details. The poem is composed of three eight-line stanzas, each with the rhyme scheme ABABCDCD. The first sets the scene of the crystal-clear stream, the second introduces a fisherman on the opposite bank, and the third tells how the invader tricks and catches the trout. Each strophe is set to the same music, with one exception. At the beginning of the third stanza, where the fisherman tricks the trout by muddying the stream, the bubbling accompaniment figure is replaced momentarily by a swirling effect using minor chords. Such a change within the basic strophic form produces **modified strophic form.** It allows the composer to highlight a particular detail without disturbing the overall structure of strophic form.

modified strophic form

Unlike the dramatic *Erlking* of Goethe, the lyrical text of *The Trout* (by one Daniel Schubart) is in no way exceptional as a poem. What is remarkable is the

LISTENING GUIDE

Franz Schubert
Art song, *The Trout* (1817)

6CD 3/8

Form: modified strophic

0:00   Piano introduces the rippling
        accompaniment figure in bright
        major key

(Continued on next page)

0:07	First strophe	In einem Bächlein helle,	A streamlet clear and sunny
		Da schoss in froher Eil'	With ripples all about,
		Die launische Forelle	Was once the bath for pretty
		Vorüber wie ein Pfeil.	For gentle little trout.
		Ich stand an dem Gestade	On shore I stood observing
		Und sah in süsser Ruh'	With exquisite delight,
		Des muntern Fischleins Bade	The happy little creature
		Im klaren Bächlein zu.	It was a lovely sight.
0:39	Second strophe: exact repeat of music of first strophe	Ein Fischer mit der Rute Wohl an dem Ufer stand Und sah's mit kaltem Blute, Wie sich das Fischlein wand. Solang dem Wasser Helle, So dacht ich, nicht gebricht, So fängt er die Forelle Mit seiner Angel nicht.	A fisher with his angle Stood on yonder shore Trying to entangle The fish from water's floor. I thought if clear the water Still races all about, He'd never, never capture My lovely, little trout.
1:13	Third strophe: minor replaces major; chords replace rippling figure; return to major tonality and rippling figure	Doch endlich ward dem Diebe Die Zeit zu lang. Er macht Das Bächlein tückisch trübe, Und eh' ich es gedacht. So zuckte seine Rute, Das Fischlein zappelt dran, Und ich mit regem Blute Sah die Betrog'ne an.	Yet the robber had no patience To while away the time He made the brook all muddy Ere I sensed the crime. His line went inward reeling My little fish so sweet, Then saw I with raging feeling The cheated and the cheat.

way that Schubert can make even the most ordinary verse into a song of extraordinary beauty.

THE "TROUT" QUINTET (1819)

In the summer of 1819, two years after he wrote his song *The Trout*, Schubert decided to vacation in the hills west of Vienna, to enjoy the stunning beauty of the Austrian countryside. There an amateur cellist asked the composer to arrange for string quartet his charming song about a fish. Schubert accepted the challenge but changed the medium of performance. He decided to add a fifth instrument, a piano, to the ensemble (making it a piano quintet) and to replace the usual second violin of the quartet with a double bass. This would give added weight to the bass line and allow the piano to roam with little competition in the upper register. Having selected his instrumental forces, he then composed a five-movement piano quintet, the "Trout" Quintet, perhaps the most lyrical of all works of chamber music.

The fourth movement of Schubert's "Trout" Quintet makes prominent use of the lovely tune of the *Lied* and does so in the form of a theme and six variations. The two phrases of the melody (**A** and **B**) are stated and immediately repeated within each variation, though the repeat of **B** extends only to the last four bars (**B′**). Each instrument has its turn to present the melody—the piano does so in variation 1, the viola in variation 2, and the double bass, cello, and violin in variations 3, 5, and 6, respectively. Variations 4 and 5 take us away from the bright tonic key of D major, to D minor and B♭ major, but variation 6 returns us to the tonic major.

a theme and six variations

Schubert was fond of making use of the melodies of his songs in his instrumental chamber music. The "Trout" Quintet shows that he was not merely a songsmith but could also compose instrumental music with the sort of lyricism, fluidity, and grace that even Mozart might have envied.

LISTENING GUIDE

Franz Schubert
Piano Quintet in A major, the "Trout" Quintet (1819)
Fourth movement, *Andantino* (gently moving)

6CD 3/9

Form: theme and variations

0:00	**THEME** (in D major)	Strings play the theme quietly; both phrases of the melody (**A** and **B**) are repeated (**A** exactly, **B** as **B′**)
0:57	**VARIATION 1**	Piano finally enters and decorates theme with trills; violin flutters against the theme adding trills in high range
1:53	**VARIATION 2**	Viola has the theme; violin plays countermelody of stepwise scales above; piano echoes phrases of the theme
2:53	**VARIATION 3**	Double bass has the theme; piano plays virtuosic passagework against the melody
3:46	**VARIATION 4**	Sudden shift to minor; *fortissimo* then *piano* chords followed by quiet dialogue between piano and violin; growing lyricism in cello, viola, and violin
4:47	**VARIATION 5**	Cello plays theme with only thin accompaniment; the repeat of phrase B is rewritten and extended by a dialogue between cello and violin
6:16	**VARIATION 6**	Violin has theme as piano plays accompaniment figure from song; cello has theme as violin plays this accompaniment figure; music fades out as figure is passed around to other instruments

🌼 FIGURE 13-4

Hector Berlioz at the age of twenty-nine.

🌼 FIGURE 13-5

A satirical engraving suggesting the public's impression of Berlioz conducting his vastly enlarged symphony orchestra. The large instrument on the upper right is an ophicleide (early tuba).

🌸 PROGRAM MUSIC†

More than any other period, the nineteenth century was a time in which composers sought and received inspiration from sources outside music. An encounter with nature, the impressions of a voyage, a disappointment in love, a popular legend, or an entire play might provide a story, a scene, or an idea that could be described in music. Of course, music could not actually tell a tale. But it could, by using different colors, moods, and sound effects, suggest a particular sequence of events to a sensitive listener. To this end composers wrote overtures*, concert overtures*, incidental music*, symphonic poems*, and program symphonies*, which taken together constitute a sizable part of the repertoire of Romantic music. Two of the best composers of this sort of descriptive music were Hector Berlioz and Felix Mendelssohn.

Hector Berlioz (1803–1869)

Hector Berlioz was one of the most original figures in the history of music. He was born in 1803 near the mountain city of Grenoble, France, the son of a local doctor. What he learned of music in the home and at school was scanty: no thorough training in music theory or composition and little exposure to the music of the great masters. Local tutors taught him to play the flute and guitar. Among the major composers of the nineteenth century, he was the only one without fluency at the keyboard. He never studied piano, and could do no more than bang out a few chords; yet he would become one of the greatest orchestrators of all time.

At the age of seventeen Berlioz was sent off to Paris to study medicine, his father's profession. For two years he pursued a program in the physical sciences, earning a degree in 1821. But Berlioz found the dissecting table repulsive and the allure of the opera house and concert halls irresistible. After a period of soul searching, and the inevitable falling out with his parents over the choice of a career, he vowed to become "no doctor or apothecary but a great composer."

His dismayed father immediately cut off his living stipend, leaving young Berlioz to ponder how he might support himself while studying composition at the Paris Conservatory (the French national school of music). Other composers had relied on teaching as a means to earn a regular income: Mozart, Haydn, Beethoven, Chopin, and Liszt, for example, all gave piano lessons as young men. But what could Berlioz teach? He had no particular skill on any instrument. So he turned to music criticism, writing reviews and articles for literary journals. Berlioz was the first composer to earn a livelihood as a music critic, and criticism, not the sale of his music, remained his primary source of income for the rest of his life.

Perhaps it was inevitable that Berlioz turned to writing about music, for literature was, and would remain, a powerful force in his life and art. As a boy his father had taught him to read Virgil's *Aeneid* in the original Latin; later he would use episodes from this classical epic to form the libretto of an opera called *Les Troyens* (*The Trojans*, 1858). As a young man he read Lord Byron's *Childe Harold's Pilgrimage* and Goethe's *Faust*, works that inspired his concerto for viola called *Harold in Italy* (1834) and his dramatic symphony *The Damna-*

†Nineteenth-century program music is discussed more fully on pages 242–243.

tion of Faust (1846). But of all literary influences, none was greater than that of Shakespeare. As we have seen (page 233), Shakespeare burst upon the consciousness of continental Europe for the first time early in the nineteenth century. For Berlioz the experience was shattering: "Shakespeare, coming upon me unawares, struck me like a thunderbolt. The lightning flash of that discovery revealed to me at a stroke the whole heaven of art." Berlioz devoured the English poet's plays and gave musical expression to four: for *The Tempest* and *King Lear* he wrote concert overtures*—one-movement pieces that sum up the spirit of the drama; for *Hamlet* he composed a funeral march for the death of this prince; and for *Romeo and Juliet* he created a five-movement program symphony*, *Roméo et Juliette* (1839), in which a chorus and solo voices intermittently sing Shakespeare's own words.

Berlioz and Shakespeare

In these works inspired by literature, as well as in his religious music, Berlioz called for enormous orchestral and choral forces—hundreds and hundreds of performers. He also experimented with new instruments: the **ophicleide** (an early form of the tuba), the **English horn** (a low oboe), the harp (an ancient instrument now brought into the symphony orchestra for the first time), the **cornet** (a brass instrument with valves, borrowed from the military band), and even the newly invented saxophone. His approach to musical form was also iconoclastic; he rarely wrote in strict sonata–allegro form or theme and variations, for example. His French compatriots found his compositions "bizarre" and "monstrous" and thought him something of a madman. Increasingly, he crisscrossed Europe to conduct his works before foreigners, who more readily appreciated his unique new sounds. To London, Bonn, Vienna, Prague, Leipzig, and even Moscow he went to introduce such works as *Symphonie fantastique*, *Damnation of Faust*, *Roméo et Juliette*, and *The Trojans*. He died in Paris in 1869, isolated and embittered. The little recognition he received in his native France came "too late," as he said, to help his career or self-esteem.

new instruments in the orchestra

SYMPHONIE FANTASTIQUE (1830)

Berlioz's most celebrated work, then and now, is his *Symphonie fantastique*, perhaps the single most influential composition of the entire nineteenth century. Its form and orchestration are revolutionary. But what is more, it tells in music a vivid story and, as such, is the first complete program symphony. The story surrounding the creation of the descriptive program of the work is as fascinating as the program itself.

In 1827 a troupe of English actors came to Paris to present Shakespeare's *Hamlet* and *Romeo and Juliet*. Berlioz, of course, had read some of Shakespeare's plays in a French translation, but was eager to see these works performed on stage. Though he understood little English, he was overwhelmed by what he saw. The human insights, touching beauty, and onstage action in Shakespeare's work far surpassed the virtues found in traditional French theater. Not only was Berlioz smitten by Shakespeare, but he also fell in love with the leading lady who played Ophelia to Hamlet and Juliet to Romeo, one Harriet Smithson (Fig. 13–6). Like a lovesick adolescent Berlioz swooned at her sight and wrote such violently passionate letters that the frightened starlet refused to meet the student composer. Eventually, his ardor cooled—for a time he even became engaged to someone else. But the experience of an all-consuming love, the despair of rejection, and the vision of darkness and possible death furnished the stimulus—and story line—for an unusually imaginative symphony.

🌸 FIGURE 13–6
The actress Harriet Smithson became an obsession for Berlioz and the source of inspiration for his *Symphonie fantastique*. At the time Berlioz wrote this symphony (1830), she was a good deal more famous than he.

Berlioz wrote the *Symphonie fantastique*, not in the usual four movements of a symphony, but in five, an arrangement that may have been inspired by Shakespeare's use of a five-act format. Movements 1 and 5 balance each other in length and substance, as do 2 and 4, leaving the leisurely third movement as the center of the work. But symmetry is not the only element holding the symphony together. Berlioz creates a single melody that reappears as a unifying force, movement after movement, a total of eight times during the symphony. Earlier, Beethoven had experimented with thematic recall and transformation in his fifth and ninth symphonies. But Berlioz takes this technique one step farther by recalling the melody constantly and by associating it with an object, his beloved. The vision of his loved one, and her attending melody, become an obsession. Berlioz called this musical fixation his **idée fixe** ("fixed idea"). As his feelings about the beloved change from movement to movement, so the *idée fixe* is transformed to reflect these various moods. To make sure that the listener has no doubt as to what these moods are, Berlioz prepared a written program to be read as the music is performed.

idée fixe: a recurring melody

First Movement: Reveries, Passions

> Program: A young musician . . . sees for the first time a woman who embodies all the charms of the ideal being he has imagined in his dreams. . . . The subject of the first movement is the passage from this state of melancholy reverie, interrupted by a few moments of joy, to that of delirious passion, with movements of fury, jealousy, and its return to tenderness, tears, and religious consolation.

A slow introduction ("this state of melancholy reverie") prepares the way for the first vision of the beloved, carried forward by the first appearance of the main theme, the *idée fixe*. (The entire melody is given earlier in Ex. 12–2.)

EXAMPLE 13–4

idée fixe transformed

The movement unfolds in sonata–allegro form. The "recapitulation," however, does not so much repeat the *idée fixe* as it does transform the melody to reflect the artist's feelings of sorrow and tenderness.

Second Movement: A Ball

> The artist finds himself . . . in the midst of the tumult of a party.

A lilting waltz now begins, but it is interrupted by the unexpected appearance of the *idée fixe*, the rhythm changed to accommodate the triple meter of the waltz. Four harps add a graceful accompaniment when the waltz returns, and, toward the end, there is even a lovely solo for cornet. The sequence of waltz–*idée fixe*–waltz creates, once again, ternary form.

Third Movement: Scene in the Country

> Finding himself one evening in the country, the artist hears in the distance two shepherds piping. . . . He reflects upon his isolation and hopes that soon he will no longer be alone.

The dialogue between the shepherds is presented by an English horn and an oboe, the latter played offstage to give the effect of a distant response. The unexpected appearance of the *idée fixe* in the woodwinds suggests that the artist has hopes of winning his beloved. But has she falsely encouraged him? The shepherd's tune recurs, but the oboe doesn't answer. There is only the lonely call of the English horn and the empty rumble of distant thunder in the timpani.

Fourth Movement: March to the Scaffold

> Having realized that his love goes unrecognized, the artist poisons himself with opium. The dose of the narcotic, too weak to kill him, plunges him into a sleep accompanied by the most horrible visions. He dreams that he has killed the one he loved, that he is condemned, led to the scaffold, and now witnesses his own execution.

This drug-induced nightmare centers on the march to the scaffold where the artist is to be executed. The steady beat of the low strings and the muffled bass drum sound the steps of the procession. Near the end the image of the beloved returns in the clarinet, only to be suddenly cut off by a *fortissimo* crash by the full orchestra. The guillotine has fallen.

Fifth Movement: Dream of the Witches' Sabbath

> He sees himself at the witches' sabbath surrounded by a troop of frightful shadows, sorcerers, and monsters of all sorts, gathered for his funeral. Strange noises, groans, bursts of laughter, distant cries echoed by others. The beloved melody returns again, but it has lost its noble, modest character and is now only base, trivial, and grotesque. An outburst of joy at her arrival; she joins in the devilish orgy.

In this monstrous finale Berlioz creates his personal vision of hell. A crowd of witches and other ghouls is summoned to dance around the corpse of the artist on its way to the inferno. Weird sounds are produced by the strings, using mutes, and by the high woodwinds and French horn, playing glissandos*. A piercing clarinet enters with a burlesque parody of the *idée fixe* as Harriet Smithson, now in the frightful garb of a wicked old hag, comes on stage.

EXAMPLE 13–5

She is greeted by a joyous *fortissimo* outburst by the full assembly as all proceed to dance to the now perverted *idée fixe*. Suddenly, the music becomes ominously quiet and, in one of the most strikingly original moments in all of music, great Gothic church bells are heard. Against this solemn backdrop sounds the burial hymn of the medieval Church, the **Dies irae,** played by ophicleides (tubas) and bassoons. (Recently, the *Dies irae* has been used to signal doom and gloom in three "horror" films: *Nightmare before Christmas*, *Sleeping with the Enemy*, and *The Shining*.)

🌸 FIGURE 13–7
Witches' Sabbath by Francisco de Goya (1746–1828) bears the same title as the finale of Berlioz's *Symphonie fantastique*. Both create images of the bizarre and the macabre so dear to the hearts of Romantic artists (see page 233).

Dies irae: *a chant from the medieval Church*

EXAMPLE 13–6

[Di - es i - rae di - es il - la sol - vet   sae - clum   in fa - vil - la]
[Day of anger, day of wrath, on which the ages will be changed to ash]

a mockery of the Church

Not only is the orchestration sensational, the musical symbolism is sacrilegious. Just as the painter Goya parodies the Catholic Mass in his *Witches' Sabbath*—making babies serve as communion wafers (Fig. 13–7), so Berlioz creates a mockery of one of the most venerable Gregorian chants of the Catholic Church. First the *Dies irae* is played by the horns twice as fast (a process called rhythmic **diminution**). Then the sacred tune is transformed into a jazzed-up dance tune played by a shrill, high clarinet, the entire scene now becoming a blasphemous black Mass.

EXAMPLE 13–7

a parody of the fugue

As the ceremony proceeds, the witches begin to dance. But they do so in a strange way: They enter one by one and create a fugato*, a fugal passage within a symphonic movement. What is a learned fugue doing here in the middle of hell? Presumably because, having just mocked the ancient music of the Catholic Church, Berlioz now decides to ridicule the musical establishment and its strictest form, the academic fugue. But beyond this, the regular entry of more and more voices, or dancing witches, creates the effect of a growing tumult around the corpse of the artist.

EXAMPLE 13–8

col legno technique

A climax is reached as the theme, or subject, of the witches, played by the strings, as well as the *Dies irae* melody, played by the brasses and woodwinds, sound together, though in different keys, a bizarre example of **double counterpoint.** Stranger still is the sound that follows, for Berlioz instructs the violins to play **col legno** ("with the wood")—to strike the strings, not with the usual front of the bow, but with the wooden back, creating a noise something akin to the crackling or burning of hellfire.

   To the audience that first heard the *Symphonie fantastique* on December 5, 1830, all of this must have seemed incomprehensible: new instruments, novel playing effects, simultaneous melodies in different keys, and a form that is not traditional, like sonata–allegro or rondo, but grows out of the events in a soap-opera–like program. But it all works. Here is a rare example in the history of art in which a creator has not only undertaken to experiment radically but has done so in a way that produces a wholly integrated, unified, and ultimately satisfying work. The separate effects may be revolutionary and momentarily shocking, but they are consistent and logical among themselves when subsumed in the total artistic concept. Had Berlioz never written another note of music, he would be justly famous for this single masterpiece of Romantic invention.

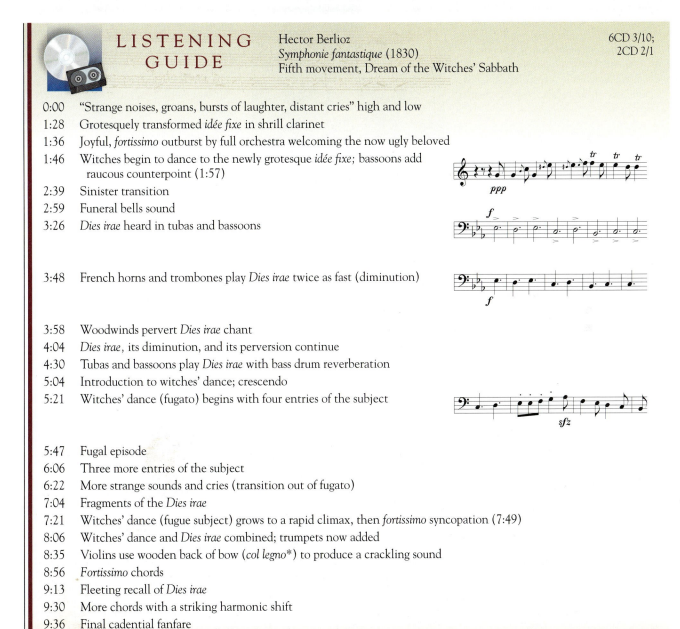

LISTENING GUIDE

Hector Berlioz
Symphonie fantastique (1830)
Fifth movement, Dream of the Witches' Sabbath

6CD 3/10;
2CD 2/1

0:00	"Strange noises, groans, bursts of laughter, distant cries" high and low
1:28	Grotesquely transformed *idée fixe* in shrill clarinet
1:36	Joyful, *fortissimo* outburst by full orchestra welcoming the now ugly beloved
1:46	Witches begin to dance to the newly grotesque *idée fixe*; bassoons add raucous counterpoint (1:57)
2:39	Sinister transition
2:59	Funeral bells sound
3:26	*Dies irae* heard in tubas and bassoons
3:48	French horns and trombones play *Dies irae* twice as fast (diminution)
3:58	Woodwinds pervert *Dies irae* chant
4:04	*Dies irae*, its diminution, and its perversion continue
4:30	Tubas and bassoons play *Dies irae* with bass drum reverberation
5:04	Introduction to witches' dance; crescendo
5:21	Witches' dance (fugato) begins with four entries of the subject
5:47	Fugal episode
6:06	Three more entries of the subject
6:22	More strange sounds and cries (transition out of fugato)
7:04	Fragments of the *Dies irae*
7:21	Witches' dance (fugue subject) grows to a rapid climax, then *fortissimo* syncopation (7:49)
8:06	Witches' dance and *Dies irae* combined; trumpets now added
8:35	Violins use wooden back of bow (*col legno**) to produce a crackling sound
8:56	*Fortissimo* chords
9:13	Fleeting recall of *Dies irae*
9:30	More chords with a striking harmonic shift
9:36	Final cadential fanfare

(Listening Exercise 27)

The Real End of the Program

In Berlioz's programmatic *Symphonie fantastique*, art imitates life—he constructs a musical narrative to mirror events (real and imagined) in his young life. But how did the story of Berlioz and his beloved Harriet Smithson really end? In truth, Berlioz did meet and marry Harriet, but the two lived miserably together ever after. Harriet died in 1854 and was buried in a small graveyard in Paris. In 1864, that cemetery was to be closed and the remains of all the deceased transferred to a new, larger burial ground. It fell to widower Berlioz to remove Harriet's corpse to the new cemetery, as he recounts in his memoirs:

> One dark, gloomy morning I set forth alone for the sad spot. A municipal officer was waiting, to be present at the disinterment. The grave had already been opened, and on my arrival the gravedigger jumped in. The coffin was still en-

The Parisian painter Eugène Delacroix's depiction of the graveyard scene in Hamlet (1829).

tire, thought it had been ten years underground; the lid alone was injured by the damp. The man, instead of lifting it out, tore away the rotten lid, which cracked with a hideous noise, and brought the contents of the coffin to light. He then bent down, took up the crowned, decayed head of the *poor Ophelia*—and laid it in a new coffin awaiting it at the edge of the grave. Then, bending down a second time, he lifted with difficulty the headless trunk and limbs—a blackish mass to which the shroud still adhered, resembling a heap of pitch in a damp sack. I remember the dull sound . . . and the odor. (Hector Berlioz, *Memoirs*)

Berlioz had begun by playing Romeo to Harriet's Juliet, and ended by playing Hamlet to her Ophelia. He cast his music, and his life, in terms of Shakespearean drama.

Felix Mendelssohn (1809–1847)

Berlioz was a child of the Romantic age: He tried suicide at least twice, ran around Italy with a gang of bandits in imitation of Lord Byron, and married an image, an ideal of a woman, with disastrous consequences. Felix Mendelssohn was an altogether different personality, anything but the stereotype of the rebellious, self-absorbed, struggling artist.

Mendelssohn was born in 1809 into a prosperous, indeed wealthy, Jewish family. His father was a banker, and his grandfather, Moses Mendelssohn (1726–1786), was a noted philosopher. At the family home in Berlin young Felix had every advantage: He studied languages, literature, and philosophy with private tutors, as well as painting, dancing, riding, and even gymnastics. In 1816 Mendelssohn's parents had their four children baptized Christians, partly so they might enjoy full legal equality and move freely in all social circles. Indeed, their home became a gathering place for artists and intellectuals of all sorts: the poet Heine, the philosopher Hegel, and the geographer Humboldt (discoverer of the Humboldt current) were all frequent guests. Because Felix had shown extraordinary musical talent, he was not only given piano lessons but also provided with a small orchestra on Sunday afternoons to try out his youthful compositions. At the age of sixteen he composed a masterpiece, his octet for strings. The next year (1826) witnessed an equally astonishing work, the Overture to *A Midsummer Night's Dream*. As a composer Mendelssohn was even more precocious than either Mozart or Schubert.

Taking advantage of his privileged station in life, Mendelssohn spent the years 1829–1835 traveling across Europe to discover its natural beauty and to meet the great artists of the day. He walked across most of Switzerland, sketching and painting as he went. He met Goethe in Weimar, Berlioz in Rome, Liszt, Chopin, and the painter Delacroix (see Fig. 13–14) in Paris, and the novelist Sir Walter Scott outside Edinburgh. The itinerant years ended in the spring of 1835 when he was appointed musical director of the Gewandhaus Orchestra in Leipzig, Germany.

Founded in 1781 by the merchants of Leipzig, the **Gewandhaus Orchestra** ("Clothiers' House" Orchestra) played in the guild hall of that trade association (Figs. 13–9 and 13–10). Mendelssohn recruited better players, increased their salaries, established a pension fund for the orchestra, and conducted as a musical interpreter, not just as a mere time-beater. By so doing he soon made the Gewandhaus Orchestra one of the finest in Europe, a position it has continued to hold to the present day. Mendelssohn was director of this ensemble for a dozen years, from 1835 until 1847, when he died prematurely by stroke at the age of thirty-eight.

During his tenure in Leipzig, Felix Mendelssohn changed the very purpose of the symphony orchestra. He established the modern notion that a symphony exists not only to promote contemporary music but also to preserve a past repertoire of musical masterpieces. In 1829 he mounted the first performance in almost a hundred years of Bach's great *St. Matthew Passion,* thereby bringing the long-forgotten Bach to the public's attention. ("And to think that it should be a Jew who gives back to the world the greatest of Christian works," he said at the time.) So, too, he programmed the works of other composers of historical interest: Handel, Haydn, and Mozart. The idea spread. From this time forward a concert by a symphony orchestra served not only as a forum for new or recent works but also as a museum for the old.

Given the fact that Mendelssohn revived the music of the eighteenth-century masters, it is not surprising that his own compositions are the most conservative, the most "classical," of the great Romantic composers. His harmonies are colorful but not revolutionary; his orchestration distinctive but not shocking—a light, dancing string sound is his hallmark; and his use of form is traditional, as seen in his heavy reliance on sonata–allegro form. Never does he indulge in startling outbursts of sound. The classical ideals of unity, grace, and formal balance predominate.

What then makes Mendelssohn a musical Romantic? Program music. Nature, travel, and literature provided stimuli for many of his creations. A trip to Italy in 1830–31 gave rise to his "Italian" Symphony, just as a lengthy sojourn in Scotland a year earlier had planted the seeds for the "Scottish" Symphony. On this same northern voyage he visited the windswept Hebrides Islands and soon captured the spirit of the churning sea

FIGURE 13–9

Exterior of the Gewandhaus in Leipzig, Germany, as depicted by Felix Mendelssohn. In addition to being a musician and composer and speaking four languages fluently, Mendelssohn was a gifted painter, his preferred medium being water color.

FIGURE 13–10

A concert in progress, ca. 1840, in the Gewandhaus, the hall where Mendelssohn, Liszt, Berlioz, and Clara and Robert Schumann frequently performed.

influence of nature, travel, and literature

and rocky coast in his *Hebrides Overture* (1830). Mendelssohn commented on the difficulty he faced when trying to harness a raging ocean within the confines of sonata–allegro form: "The whole development section smells more of counterpoint than of blubber, gulls, and salted cod."

As to literary influences, he heard the voices of Goethe and Shakespeare most clearly. To Goethe's *Faust* the composer owed the inspiration for the *Scherzo* of his early Octet (1825) and several later orchestral works. And to Shakespeare, of course, can be traced the genesis of the music for *A Midsummer Night's Dream*.

OVERTURE TO *A MIDSUMMER NIGHT'S DREAM* (1826)

Mendelssohn began to compose, or "to dream *A Midsummer Night's Dream*," as he says, during July 1826, when he was an impressionable youth of seventeen. His aim was to transform the romantic fantasy of Shakespeare's play into an independent concert overture (a piece for the concert hall, not the theater). Some years later, in 1843, he was commissioned by the king of Prussia to create incidental music (music to be heard during an actual performance) for a production of the play planned for Berlin. Among these incidental pieces is his famous *Wedding March*—originally written to accompany the marriage of the characters Theseus and Hippolyta, but now traditionally played at weddings as the recessional march.

a concert overture

To enter fully into the enchanted world of Mendelssohn's Overture to *A Midsummer Night's Dream*, we must know something of the play—the program—that inspired it. The drama begins in an imaginary city called Athens, where the ruler, Duke Theseus, is about to marry Hippolyta, queen of the Amazons. Nearby is an enchanted forest ruled by Oberon, king of the elves, and his estranged queen, Titania. Into this magical grove come Lysander and Hermia, another pair of would-be lovers. Then enters a group of common craftsmen, led by the blockheaded Bottom, who have come to prepare for the royal wedding. Finally, the hunting party of Theseus and Hippolyta joins the woodland scene. Confusion reigns as an agent of fairy king Oberon, the spirit Puck, administers a love potion to the wrong parties; fairy queen Titania falls in love with the clownish Bottom, who is made to wear the head of an ass. Eventually, all is set right and the nobles and gentry return to the court of Athens. The events in the enchanted forest had been no more real than a midsummer night's dream.

Shakespeare's play

Mendelssohn's Overture closely follows the play. Separate and distinctly different musical colors and styles make the various characters clearly identifiable

※ FIGURE 13–11
Oberon, Titania and Puck with Fairies Dancing by the English artist and poet William Blake (1757–1827).

and the events easy to follow. At the same time, the music unfolds in sonata–allegro form. There is a slow four-chord introduction, a first theme (the dancing fairy music), a transition (royal music of the court of Athens), a second theme (the lovers' music), and a closing theme group (the craftsmen's music and the hunting calls). The fairies dominate the development section, and in the coda (or epilogue) they have the last word, just as in Shakespeare's play. Mendelssohn's own thoughts best describe the ending: "After everything has been satisfactorily settled and the principal players have joyfully left the stage, the elves follow them, bless the house, and disappear with the dawn. So ends the play, and my overture too."

LISTENING GUIDE

Felix Mendelssohn
Overture to *A Midsummer Night's Dream* (1826)

6CD 4/1

Form: sonata–allegro

| Program: | Musical Events: |

EXPOSITION

0:00 Introduction to enchantment — Four sustained chords in the winds (introduction)

0:20 Fairies' music — Rapid, light, staccato notes in violins (first theme)

1:04 Duke Theseus and his court — Full orchestra *fortissimo* (transition)

1:34 — Fairies' music mixes into transition

2:08 Lovers' music — Quiet melody in woodwinds and strings grows more passionate (second theme)

3:00 Bottom's music — Raucous motive sounds like braying of a donkey (closing theme, part 1)

3:22 Hunting calls of regal party — Fanfares in brass and woodwinds (closing theme, part 2)

DEVELOPMENT

3:46 Fairies' music developed — Music of the fairies (first theme) worked out in different keys

4:22 French horn blasts

4:52 Fairies' music extended — String pizzicato and string tremolo

5:27 Lysander and Hermia sleep — Ritard, soft string sound, music seems to come to a stop

RECAPITULATION

5:52 Return to enchantment — Four introductory chords return

6:14 Fairies' music — Dancing fairies' music returns (first theme), but transition is eliminated

6:58 Lovers' music — Lyrical melody in woodwinds and strings (second theme) as before

7:47 Bottom's music — Again raucous *fortissimo* music of the ass (closing theme, part 1)

8:52 Hunting party — Fanfares (closing theme, part 2) serve as ending to recapitulation

CODA

9:16 Epilogue by fairy Puck — Light, quick music of the fairies; toward the end Duke Theseus and the four opening chords are recalled

✿ THE PIANISTS

By the 1840s the piano had evolved into essentially the instrument we know today (see also page 240). Its thundering power, rapid action, singing tone, and wide range of expression made it the most popular instrument of the Romantic period. No self-respecting middle-class home could be without one. No education was thought complete without lessons at it. Spurred by the extraordinary *vogue of the piano* vogue of the instrument, a host of virtuoso performers set upon the concert halls of Europe with fingers blazing. What they played was often more a display of digital fireworks—rapid octaves, racing chromatic scales, thundering chords—than of musical substance. Happily, however, several of the greatest piano virtuosos of the nineteenth century were also gifted composers. While these artists sometimes wrote songs, symphonies, or concertos, the piano—and piano style—was at the heart of their creative process.

vogue of the piano

Robert Schumann (1810–1856)

In many ways Robert Schumann's life was a failure, indeed a tragedy. Sent to university at Heidelberg to study law, he attended not a single class—he had no more affinity for law than Berlioz had for medicine. With his mother's grudging consent, Schumann moved on to Leipzig to study piano, determined to become a virtuoso. But after two years of lessons with the eminent Friedrich Wieck (1785–1873), all he had to show for his labors was a permanently damaged right hand. His career as a virtuoso now frustrated, composition and music criticism became the focus of his creative energies. During the 1830s he produced a remarkable series of works for solo piano, mostly sonatas, variations, and collections of character pieces*. He also founded and served as editor for the new musical periodical, the *Neue Zeitschrift für Musik (New Journal of Music)*. Schumann became the apostle for new music within the German Romantic movement, championing the works of such "radical" composers as Berlioz, Chopin, Mendelssohn, Liszt, and the young Johannes Brahms.

✿ FIGURE 13–12
Robert Schumann.

While studying piano in the Leipzig home of Friedrich Wieck, Schumann met, and soon fell in love with, Wieck's beautiful and talented daughter, Clara. They were married in 1840, over the violent objections of her father. The year of their union was one of feverish creation for Robert; from his pen flowed more than 125 *Lieder**, mostly love songs, for voice and piano. These include several now-famous song cycles* such as *Dichterliebe (Poet's Love)* and *Frauenliebe und -leben (Women in Love and Life)*, individual songs of which are the equal in quality to the works of the great Franz Schubert in this genre. Clara now encouraged him to extend himself beyond art songs and character pieces for piano, *Lieder and character pieces for the piano* and into orchestral and chamber music. But in these larger forms he had only mixed success. His piano concerto (1845) and piano quintet (1842) are supreme accomplishments, but his four symphonies are not uniformly compelling. At heart Schumann was a miniaturist whose creativity was inextricably bound to the keyboard. And unlike his idol Beethoven, who composed on sketchbooks as he walked through forest and field, Schumann was unable to generate music except at the piano. Touch and sensation were intrinsic to his creative process.

Life between the Schumanns was marked by symbiotic artistry and personal agony. Husband and wife read poetry together, and each made suggestions on the other's musical compositions. But from his earliest years Robert Schumann had been afflicted with what psychiatrists now call bipolar disorder. His moods swung from nervous euphoria to suicidal depression. Naturally, this disease affected his creativity, both for good and for ill. In some years he produced a torrent of music, in others virtually nothing. As time progressed, Schumann's condition grew more extreme. He began to hear voices, both heavenly and hellish, and one morning, pursued by demons within, he jumped off a bridge into the Rhine river. Nearby fishermen pulled him to safety, but from that point on, by his own request, he was confined to an asylum, where he died of dementia in 1856. In his final, tragic years, his creative output dwindled to nothing.

growing insecurity

SCENES FROM CHILDHOOD (1838)

To hear Schumann in a sunny, optimistic mood, let us turn to a set of miniature keyboard pieces he wrote in 1838, *Kinderszenen (Scenes from Childhood)*. These are not pieces intended for children but musical recollections of events or sensations from childhood—"reminiscences of a grown-up for grown-ups," the composer said. Each of the thirteen works in the set has its own suggestive title, such as *By the Fireside*, *Catch-as-Catch-Can*, or *Bogeyman's Coming*. Each invites the listener to enter the very private world of the imagination, to make one's own retrospective associations with the sounds. And each is a perfect example of the Romantic character piece*—a short work conveying a single character or mood in which that feeling is distilled to its very essence. In their musical form, the scenes are quite uncomplicated, usually in simple ternary structure (**ABA**). What is remarkable is the way in which a vision or sensation is instantly created and then, just as quickly, vanishes. The first of the scenes, *Von fremden Ländern und Menschen (Of Foreign Lands and People)*, may allude to a child's bright eyes seeing far-off places. Another, *Träumerei (Dreaming)*, suggests a child engrossed in a world of dreams. *Dreaming*, incidentally, was the character piece the great pianist Vladimir Horowitz (1904–1989) traditionally played as the last of his encores.

each a Romantic character piece

LISTENING GUIDE

Robert Schumann
Scenes from Childhood (1838)

CD 3/11-12

Genre: character piece
Form: ternary

Of Foreign Lands and People

0:00	Bright melody in major key with triplet accompaniment	**A**
0:15	**A** section repeated	
0:30	Change to minor key as melody falls and then rises by step	**B**
0:43	Brief fermata (hold)	
0:45	Bright melody returns back in tonic major	**A**
1:00	**B** and final **A** repeated	

(Continued on next page)

Dreaming
0:00   Dreamlike melody in major key rises, falls, and then rises to a climax and falls again   **A**

0:44   **A** section repeated
1:25   Melody extended through several major and minor keys   **B**
2:04   Dreamlike melody returns but now set in a new harmony   **A**

Where Were the Women?

You may have noticed that female composers are poorly represented in this book. We have seen the works of some, Hildegard of Bingen (page 66) and the Countess of Dia (page 74), for example, and we will meet those of Ellen Taaffe Zwilich later (page 368). But in general, although women have been actively engaged as performers of secular music since the Middle Ages, only rarely, until the twentieth century, did they become composers. While the causes of this condition are numerous, one factor stands out above all others: People then had no faith in the capacity, or the propriety, of female creativity. Although a young lady might learn to play the piano in a show of domestic refinement, a woman's function in society was defined as nurturer of children (preferably male) and handmaiden of husband. Fanny Mendelssohn Hensel (1805–1847), the gifted sister of Felix Mendelssohn, was fifteen and considering music as a profession when she received the following directive in a letter from her father: "What you wrote to me about your musical occupations, and in comparison to those of Felix, was rightly thought and expressed. But though music will perhaps become his profession, for you it can and must only be an ornament, never the core of your existence."

Fanny Mendelssohn

With no encouragement to become a creative force outside the home, little wonder that self-doubt arose among women of talent. As Clara Schumann wrote in her diary in 1839: "I once believed that I possessed creative talent, but I have given up this idea; a woman must not desire to compose. There has never yet been one able to do it. Should I expect to be that one?"

Composing a symphony or a string quartet is a complex process requiring years of schooling in harmony, counterpoint, and instrumentation. Women did not have access to such formal training in composition. For example, the Paris Conservatory was founded in 1793 but did not admit women into the classes in advanced music theory and composition until almost a century later. (Similarly, women who wished to become painters were barred from anatomy classes, instruction crucial to the figural arts.) Only in those exceptional cases in which a daughter received an intense musical education at home, as did Fanny Mendelssohn and Clara Schumann, did a woman have a fighting chance to become a musical creator.

Clara Wieck Schumann (1819–1896)

Unlike her husband, Robert, a gifted composer but failed performer, Clara Wieck Schumann was one of the great piano virtuosos of the nineteenth century. A child prodigy, she made her debut at the age of eleven in the Gewandhaus (see Figs. 13–9 and 13–10) in Leipzig, Germany, the city of her birth. She then undertook a concert tour of Europe during which she impressed and befriended Mendelssohn, Berlioz, Chopin, and Liszt. In Austria, the Emperor named her "Royal and Imperial Chamber Virtuosa"—the first time that exalted title had been given to a Protestant, a teenager, or a woman.

When she married Robert Schumann in 1840, Clara Wieck was much better known on the international stage than he. Nevertheless, she put aside her own career to play the roles of wife and mother to the eight children she soon bore him (one died in infancy). Her compositions became few and far between, her public performances limited to an occasional tour. But when Robert Schumann was institutionalized in 1854 Clara was compelled by economic necessity again to pursue the concert circuit. There were annual tours to England and more than one to Russia. She continued to concertize until the age of seventy, having become a legend in her own time. Said the famous London music critic and playwright George Bernard Shaw (1856–1950), "She is an artist of the sort that is the Grail of the critic's quest."

Not only was Clara Schumann a piano virtuoso but she was also a gifted composer. As a child she had received the kind of exacting education in harmony and counterpoint that was exceptional for her sex. Later, when married to Robert Schumann, she studied the fugues of an earlier musician from Leipzig, J. S. Bach. The dense textures and intensely chromatic inner parts found throughout Clara's music can be attributed to this rigorous early training and thorough exposure to Bach.

❈ FIGURE 13–13
Clara Schumann.

a legendary pianist and composer

ROMANCE FOR PIANO AND VIOLIN, OPUS 22, NO. 3 (1853)

A **romance** is a brief instrumental work, usually in a slow tempo, that conveys a single, intensely lyrical mood. It, too, belongs to that genre of music called the character piece* (see page 242). Clara Schumann wrote numerous romances for piano alone. And even in this set of three for piano with violin, it is the pianist who does most of the work, creating a rich chromatic texture, providing the harmony, and sometimes supplying the melody as well. What is of interest in this romance is the composer's unflagging industry and integrity. There are two themes, **a** (heard four times) and **b** (heard twice). Where a lesser composer might have relied on simple repeats, Clara Schumann continually varies the surrounding musical context each time the themes reappear. Here beauty is created through the subtle way in which the two themes continually take on new expressive meaning in an ever-changing sea of harmonic color.

LISTENING GUIDE

Clara Wieck Schumann
Romance for Piano and Violin, Opus 22, No. 3 (1853)

6CD 4/2;
2CD 2/2

Genre: character piece
Form: ternary

0:00   Theme **a** in violin; piano plays harmony as rapid arpeggios   **A**

(Continued on next page)

0:33	Piano briefly joins in return of **a**
0:54	Extension and development of **a**
1:24	Violin plays trills in V–I cadence leading to
1:34	Theme **b** in violin; piano plays harmony as staccato chords **B**

1:53	Piano plays theme **b**; violin plays harmony as pizzicato chords
2:11	Extension and development of **b**
2:32	Piano plays **b** while violin adds counterpoint
3:00	Theme **a** in violin; piano plays arpeggios **A'**
3:19	Extension and development of **a**
3:55	Piano plays **a** while violin adds counterpoint
4:12	Fragments of **a** and rich harmonies **CODA**

(Listening Exercise 28)

Frédéric Chopin (1810–1849)

a French father, a Polish mother

In the compositions of Frédéric Chopin, the piano and its music have their most perfect union. This "poet of the piano," as he was called, was born near Warsaw, Poland, of a French father and a Polish mother. The father taught at an elite secondary school for the sons of Polish nobility, and it was there that Frédéric not only gained an excellent general education but acquired aristocratic friends and tastes as well. He then moved on to the newly founded Warsaw Conservatory, where, between 1826 and 1829, he concentrated on the study of piano and composition. It was during this period that he composed his first major work, a brilliant set of variations for piano and orchestra on Mozart's duet "Là ci darem la mano" ("Give me your hand") from *Don Giovanni* (on the duet, see page 205). Warsaw was now thought to be too small, too provincial, for a young man of his musical talents. So in 1830 he departed to seek his fortune in Vienna and Paris. The next year Poland's fight for freedom was crushed by Russian troops, and Chopin never returned to his homeland.

After an unsuccessful year in Vienna, the twenty-one-year-old Chopin arrived in Paris in September 1831. His inaugural concerts caught Parisians' fancy, and his imaginative playing soon became the stuff of legends. But Chopin was not cut out for the life of the public virtuoso. He was introverted, physically slight, and somewhat sickly. Consequently, he chose to play at private *musicales* (musical evenings) in the homes of the aristocracy and to give lessons for a fee only the very rich could afford. "I have been introduced all around the highest circles," he said within a year of his arrival. "I hobnob with ambassadors, princes, and ministers. I can't imagine what miracle is responsible for all this since I really haven't done anything to bring it about."

In October 1836 Chopin was introduced to Baroness Aurore Dudevant (1803–1876), a writer who under the pen name of George Sand poured forth a steady stream of Romantic novels roughly akin to our Silhouette Romances. Sand was an ardent individualist and bisexual who often dressed in men's clothing and smoked cigars (see cover and Fig. 13–15). Six years Chopin's senior, she became his lover and protector. Many of the composer's best works were written at Nohant, her summer residence 150 miles south of Paris. After their relationship ended in 1847, Chopin undertook a taxing concert tour of England and Scotland. While this improved his depleted finances, it weakened his delicate health. He died in Paris of tuberculosis at the age of thirty-nine.

CHOPIN AND NATIONALISM: MAZURKA IN B♭ MAJOR, OPUS 7, NO. 1 (1832)

Although Frédéric Chopin spent most of his adult life in France, he was an ardent Polish nationalist. As a youth he had vacationed with his family in the Polish countryside where he heard native dances such as the mazurka and the polonaise. The **mazurka** is a fast dance in triple meter with an accent on the second beat. Its melody draws upon native folk tunes, some of them of Jewish ancestry, and its harmony suggests the droning of a village bagpipe. Chopin's Mazurka in B♭ major begins much like a triple meter waltz, except that the strong accent often falls on beat two, not beat one. Yet midway through (in section **C**), the mode switches from major to

minor, a strange scale sounds in the melody, and a drone appears in the accompanying bass. We have been transported from the world of the Parisian salon to a Polish village, from the familiar to the exotic. Chopin was something of a national hero in Poland, and his music was embraced as a way of preserving a national heritage. In Chopin's day these mazurkas were experienced as music or as dance: the Parisians listened, the Poles danced.

❀ FIGURE 13–14
A superbly Romantic portrait of Chopin by Eugène Delacroix. It was originally painted with Chopin next to George Sand (see Fig. 13–15). But in 1870 a vandal slashed the double portrait, thereby (unintentionally) creating two canvases.

❀ FIGURE 13–15
Novelist Aurore Dudevant (George Sand) by Eugène Delacroix. Both the painter Delacroix and the composer Chopin often stayed at her summer home in Nohant in the south of France.

LISTENING GUIDE

Frédéric Chopin
Mazurka in B♭ major, Opus 7, No. 1 (1832)

6CD 4/3

Form: **ABACA** (with repeats)

0:00   Rapid dance with triple-meter accompaniment and accent on beat two (**A**)
0:16   Repeat of **A**
0:34   Lyrical interlude (**B**)
0:47   Return to **A**
1:03   Repeat of **B** and **A**
1:31   Exotic melody supported by constantly repeating (drone) bass (**C**)

1:46   Return to **A**
2:03   Repeat of **C** and **A**

Chopin applied his elegant style to several musical genres—all for piano. Besides stylized dance music, he composed three full-length sonatas for piano solo, and two concertos for piano and orchestra. His shorter works include twenty-one nocturnes* and a set of twenty-four preludes (brief character pieces, one in each of the major and minor keys). Perhaps most remarkable is his set of twenty-four etudes, an **etude** being a short, one-movement piece designed to improve one specific aspect of a performer's technique. In these Chopin's genius transforms an otherwise dreary exercise into a dazzling show piece.

❈ FIGURE 13–16

A painting done from memory by the Polish artist Siemiradski shows Chopin playing in the drawing room of Prince Anton Radziwill (seated center), himself a talented amateur musician.

CHOPIN AND REVOLUTION: THE "REVOLUTIONARY" ETUDE, OPUS 10, NO. 12 (1831)

Social unrest and wars of revolution rocked Europe between 1830 and 1848, as we have seen (page 232). Frédéric Chopin, weighing less than a hundred pounds and infected with tuberculosis, hardly cut the figure of a soldier. But he could, and did, express his patriotism through music. When news reached him in September 1831 that Russian troops had suppressed the revolt of Polish nationals, his excited mind sketched what was to become the "Revolutionary" Etude. The finished product of his nationalistic fervor, completed some months later, was a two-and-a-half-minute outburst. Here Chopin assails the misfortune of his country, family, and, especially, father, who had been a member of the Polish National Guard. Crashing chords and dissonances sound forth in the right hand. But the real action—and the exercise for the pianist—is to be found in the left hand, where a succession of twisting chromatic intervals race along at breakneck speed. What began for Chopin as an expression of anger, remains today a technical challenge for even the most accomplished pianist.

LISTENING GUIDE

Frédéric Chopin
The "Revolutionary" Etude, Opus 10, No. 12 (1831)

6CD 4/4;
2CD 2/3

Form: ternary

A

0:00   Introduction: right hand chord followed by rapid descent to the bass
0:16   Theme **a:** heroic chords in the right hand against racing figures in the left

B

0:51   Theme **b:** music less intense, but left hand must play difficult chromatic patterns

A′

1:24   Chord and descent to the bass lead to a return of theme **a**
1:33   Theme **a:** heroic chords in the right hand now appear in varied form
2:03   Music gradually becomes quiet, less threatening
2:42   Sudden *fortissimo* descent to the bass and crashing final chords

Chopin dedicated this etude to his close friend Franz Liszt, and it was he who gave it the nickname "Revolutionary." Thus was Chopin's quiet passion passed on to a more sensational virtuoso, the pianist Liszt.

Franz Liszt (1811–1886)

Franz Liszt was born in Hungary of German-speaking parents. His ambitious father moved the family to Vienna in 1822 so that his gifted son might study with the very best teachers. From Vienna it was on to Paris to establish the boy as the latest child prodigy, the newest infant virtuoso. But some years later, when his father died suddenly of typhoid fever, the sixteen-year-old youth was left in

🌿 FIGURE 13–17
Franz Liszt at the age of twenty-four.

🌿 FIGURE 13–18
Marie d'Agoult. She was a novelist in her own right, and some of the tracts on music that appeared under Liszt's name were probably penned by her. Like many female writers of the day, including George Sand and George Eliot, she wrote under a masculine *nom de plume*, Daniel Stern.

Paris more or less on his own. He gave piano lessons, became something of a religious fanatic, and tried to enter a Parisian seminary in hopes of becoming a priest.

But in 1831 Liszt heard the great violin virtuoso Niccolò Paganini (see page 241), and this changed his life. "What a man, what a violin, what an artist! O God, what pain and suffering, what torment in those four strings." Liszt vowed to bring Paganini's technical virtuosity to the piano, and he did. Practicing four to five hours a day—unusual dedication for a prodigy—he taught himself to play on the piano what had never been played before: tremolos, leaps, double trills, glissandos, simultaneous octaves in both hands, all at breathtaking speed. When he returned to the stage for his own concerts, he overwhelmed the audience. He had become the greatest pianist of that era, perhaps of all time.

Then, in 1833, Liszt's life took another unexpected turn. He met the Countess Marie d'Agoult (see cover and Fig. 13–18) and decided to give up the life of the performing artist in exchange for domestic security. Although she was already married and the mother of two children, she and Liszt eloped, first to Switzerland and then to Italy. Residing in these countries for four years, the couple had three children of their own. (Their youngest daughter would become the wife of Richard Wagner; see Fig. 14–9, page 289.)

Beginning in 1839, and continuing until 1847, Liszt once more took to the road as a touring virtuoso. He played more than a thousand concerts: from Ireland to Turkey, from Sweden to Spain, from Portugal to Russia. Everywhere he went the handsome pianist was greeted with the sort of mass hysteria today reserved for rock stars. Audiences of three thousand crowded into the larger halls. Women tried to rip off his silk scarf and white gloves. They fought for a lock of his hair. **Lisztomania** swept across Europe.

Despite their obvious sensationalism, Liszt's concerts in the 1840s established the format of our modern-day piano recital. He was the first to play entire programs from memory (not reading from music). He was the first to place the piano parallel with the line of the stage so that neither his back nor full face, but rather his extraordinary side profile, was visible to the audience. He was the first to perform on the stage alone—up to that point concerts traditionally had included numerous performers on the program. At first these solo appearances were called "soliloquies," then "recitals," suggesting they were something akin to poetic recitations.

While concertizing in Russia in 1847, Liszt met another married woman who would profoundly change the course of his life—Princess Sayn-Wittgenstein. (He and Marie d'Agoult had separated in 1844.) This new woman persuaded him to give up the life of an itinerant virtuoso and concentrate on composing. Liszt accepted a position at the court of Weimar, Germany, and took up residence with his new mistress. Because a full orchestra was now at his disposal at Weimar, he produced a steady stream of large-scale orchestral works. In 1861 the couple moved to Rome, where it was hoped that the princess would secure a divorce. When this was not forthcoming, Liszt entered the lower Holy Orders of the Roman Church, styled himself "Abbé Liszt," and for a while even lived in the Vatican! But he continued traveling and performing to the very end. He died at the age of seventy-five in Bayreuth, Germany, where he had gone to hear the latest opera of his son-in-law, Richard Wagner.

Liszt wrote a dozen symphonic poems*—one-movement works for orchestra that capture the spirit and sentiments of a preexisting story, literary theme, or

FIGURE 13–19

Lisztomania. A recital by Liszt in the mid-nineteenth century was likely to create the sort of sensation that a concert by a rock star might generate today. As Liszt modestly said, "Le concert, c'est moi!"

poetic idea—as well as two program symphonies* and three piano concertos. He also composed more than sixty religious works, including two oratorios*, almost all dating from his stay in Rome. In his instrumental music Liszt developed the idea of "thematic transformation," in which a single main theme and its offshoots dominate an entire movement or all the movements of a work. In this he was carrying forward Berlioz's use of an *idée fixe* (see page 256).

But Liszt was first and foremost a pianist, and it is for his piano music that he is known above all else. If Chopin composed in a way that made the piano sound at its best, Liszt wrote in a style that made him sound best at the piano. He had large hands and unusually long fingers (see Fig. 13–17). He could play a melody in octaves when others could play only the single notes of the line. If others could execute a passage in octaves, Liszt could dash it off in more impressive-sounding tenths (octave plus third). So he wrote daredevil music of this sort. His *Transcendental Etudes* and *Hungarian Rhapsodies* are among the most difficult pieces ever written for piano. Only the most skilled virtuosos attempt them.

LIEBESTRAUM (LOVE-DREAM) NO. 3 (1850)

During the late 1840s Franz Liszt set to music three Romantic love poems and entitled them *Liebesträume*. In 1850 he returned to these three *Lieder* and arranged them for a piano solo, now calling each one a "nocturne"—a **nocturne,** or night piece, is a slow, introspective type of piano music suggesting moonlit nights, romantic longing, and a certain painful melancholy. The melody of the third *Liebestraum* has remained a favorite

FIGURE 13–20

The aged Liszt, still dazzling audiences and destroying pianos, executes what appears to be the "eight-hand trick" (see page 274).

down to the present day, having been reworked in recent years into more than one popular song and movie theme.

Liszt was a piano virtuoso and showman, and to everything he touched—even a gentle nocturne—he brought pianistic razzle-dazzle. At the beginning of *Liebestraum* he performs the "three-hand trick." The treble and bass make up two musical lines, with the melody, a third line, couched in the middle range. Sometimes played by the thumb of the left hand and sometimes by the thumb of the right, the middle part suggests the presence of a third hand (see first example in the next Listening Guide). Soon the melody returns, and the technical display grows more complex and demanding. Finally, in a third and last statement of the theme, Liszt implies the presence of four hands by creating four very different musical lines: (1) a harmonic bass, (2) an arpeggiated inner voice, (3) a lyrical melody, and (4) a two-chord counterpoint to the melody high in the treble. To bring off this "four-hand trick," the left hand must quickly pass over the right and play in the highest register (see second example in the Listening Guide at 4). In *Liebestraum*, poetry and wizardry unite in an artistry of the highest order.

Liszt's "four-hand trick"

LISTENING GUIDE

Franz Liszt
Liebestraum No. 3 (1850)

6CD 4/5

Genre: nocturne
0:00   Theme, part 1, in middle voice

0:42   Theme, part 2, rises upward
1:24   Rapid flourish of thirds and sixths leads to
1:34   Return of theme, now in the high register
2:02   Theme, part 2, played by right hand in octaves
2:45   A whirlwind of seconds, thirds, and arpeggios
3:01   Theme returns in soprano, with left hand crossing over to play chords in the highest range

3:57   Coda: chromatic chords, bold harmonic shift, dissonance resolving to consonance

LISTENING EXERCISES

Franz Schubert   6CD 3/7; 2CD 1/15
Art song, *Erlking* (1815)

Schubert was a master at bringing to life the essential characters and sentiments of the poetry he set to music. This exercise suggests how he used two
very basic musical elements, a shift in mode and a change in the accompaniment, to intensify Goethe's dramatic ballad *Erlking*.

1. (0:00–0:22) Is this opening section, with rapidly repeating notes in the
   right hand of the accompanist and an ominous motive below in the left,
   written in a major key or a minor key? _____
2. (1:30–1:52) When the Erlking enters, is the ominous motive still heard in
   the accompaniment? _____
3. (1:30–1:52) Does the Erlking sing in a major key or a minor key?
   _____
4. (1:55–2:06) As the son returns to speak, what happens in the piano accompaniment?
   a. Rapidly repeating notes return in the accompanist's right hand and the
      mode shifts from major to minor.
   b. Rapidly repeating notes return in the accompanist's left hand and the
      mode shifts from minor to major.
5. (2:18–2:34) For the second appearance of the Erlking, which is true?
   a. Arpeggios replace the rapidly repeating notes in the right hand and the
      mode is major.
   b. The rapidly repeating notes in the right hand continue and the mode is
      minor.
6. (3:06–3:17) For the third and final appearance of the Erlking, which is true?
   a. The repeating notes in the right hand continue and the mode changes
      quickly from major to minor.
   b. The accompaniment pattern changes to arpeggios in the right hand and
      the mode remains in major throughout.
7. (3:47–3:58) How does Schubert tell us that the galloping horse has arrived
   at the inn?
   a. The piano accompaniment stops abruptly.
   b. The piano accompaniment gradually ritards and then comes to a stop.
8. (4:06–4:11) How does Schubert emphatically emphasize that the child has
   died and that there will be no happy ending?
   a. He writes an abrupt V–I cadence in a major key.
   b. He writes an abrupt V–I cadence in a minor key.
9. Excluding the narrator, how many characters are portrayed in Schubert's
   Erlking? _____
10. How many voices actually sing the *Lied**? _____

27
Hector Berlioz   6CD 3/10; 2CD 2/1
Symphonie fantastique (1830)
Fifth movement, Dream of the Witches' Sabbath

Imagine that you were among the audience in Paris on December 5, 1830, when Berlioz's *Symphonie fantastique* was first performed. If you had been a dedicated concertgoer up to that time, you might have heard one or two of the latest symphonies of Beethoven. This would have been the extent of your exposure to "radical" new music. How would you have reacted? Of course, it is now impossible to gauge the impact of Berlioz's progressive gestures—our ears have become accustomed to them in the music of other, later composers. The following set of questions asks you to focus on a few special aspects of orchestration and form in this astonishingly new work. As always, be sure that you have read the discussion of this movement in the text (page 257) and have listened to it at least once following the Listening Guide (page 259).

1. (0:00–0:09) The opening sounds eerie because the high strings are divided into many parts and are playing with a special string technique. What is this technique called?
   a. pizzicato   b. tremolo   c. ostinato

2. (0:19–0:23) Now another string technique is employed by the upper strings. Which is it?
   a. pizzicato   b. tremolo   c. ostinato

3. (1:28–1:36) The *idée fixe* returns, now transformed. The passage sounds weird because of the unusual orchestration Berlioz employs. What characterizes it?
   a. *idée fixe* in oboe against pounding timpani
   b. *idée fixe* in high clarinet against pounding bass drum

4. (2:39–2:56) The "sinister transition" leading to the introduction of the *Dies irae* chant is a gradual descent. Which family of instruments does *not* participate?
   a. string   b. woodwind   c. brass

5. (3:48–3:58) The French horns now play the *Dies irae* theme twice as fast as before. What is this sort of reduction of note values in music called?

   _____

6. (4:28–4:47) In this passage the *Dies irae* melody continues in the low brasses against a pounding sound produced by the bass drum. Which of the following is true?
   a. The low brasses are playing the melody on the downbeat while the bass drum syncopates against it.
   b. The bass drum is playing on the downbeat while the low brasses syncopate against it.

7. (5:21–5:48) Now the fugato begins. Its structure is made clear, in part, because the composer cuts off the subject each time so as to announce the next entry. He does this by means of a burst of syncopated chords in the brasses. How many times does this occur? _____

8. (7:04–7:18) Which instruments play a reminiscence of the *Dies irae* chant?
   a. bells   b. tubas   c. cellos and double basses

9. (8:06–8:27) Now the *Dies irae* and the witches' dance (fugue subject) are heard simultaneously. How are they orchestrated?

a. *Dies irae* in violins, witches' dance in trumpets

b. *Dies irae* in trumpets, witches' dance in violins

10. (8:35–8:48) As the strings produce the crackling sound by playing *col legno* (with the wood of the bow and not the horsehair), a melody is heard in the woodwinds. Which is it?

a. the *idée fixe*

b. the *Dies irae* chant

c. the witches' dance (fugue subject)

 Clara Wieck Schumann   6CD 4/2; 2CD 2/2
Romance for Piano and Violin, Opus 22, No. 3 (1853)

Clara Schumann's Romance consists of a lovely melody with two parts (**a** and **b**), played mostly by the violin, and an accompaniment, furnished mainly by the piano. The piano usually plays the accompaniment as arpeggios, but sometimes plays chords. Occasionally, moreover, the roles of the instruments are reversed, with the piano now not only providing the accompaniment but also playing the melody, while the violin either joins in the accompaniment or sets a counterpoint against the melody. Four different ways in which the musical material is allocated to the piano are identified here as A, B, C, and D. Indicate which musical arrangement governs at the important musical moments listed below.

A. piano plays accompaniment only as arpeggios (violin has melody)

B. piano plays accompaniment only as chords (violin has melody)

C. piano plays melody and its own accompaniment as arpeggios

D. piano plays melody and its own accompaniment as chords

0:00 _____   2:32 _____   3:55 _____
1:34 _____   2:47 _____   4:12 _____
1:53 _____   3:00 _____
2:11 _____   3:34 _____

 KEY WORDS

col legno	Gewandhaus Orchestra	recital
cornet	Harriet Smithson	romance
Dies irae	*idée fixe*	Schubertiade
diminution	Lisztomania	song cycle
double counterpoint	mazurka	strophic form
English horn	modified strophic form	through composed
etude	nocturne	
George Sand	ophicleide	

A checklist of musical style in the Romantic period is given on page 63.

ROMANTIC OPERA

The nineteenth century is often called "the golden age of opera." It is the century of Rossini, Bellini, Donizetti, Verdi, Wagner, Gounod, Bizet, and early Puccini. Even today, two-thirds of the operas produced by the San Francisco Opera Company, the Metropolitan Opera in New York, Covent Garden in London, and La Scala in Milan, for example, are works written during the years 1820–1900.

Italy, of course, is the home of opera. The Italian language, with its evenly spaced, open vowels, is perfectly suited for singing, and the people of Italy seem to have an innate love of melody. The first operas were created, beginning around 1600, for the cities of Florence, Rome, Venice, and Mantua (see page 103). For nearly two centuries Italian opera dominated the international stage. When Handel wrote operas for London in the 1720s, for example, he composed Italian operas, as did Mozart when he created musical theater for the courts of Germany and Austria in the 1770s and 1780s. With the onset of the nineteenth century, however, other people, driven by an emerging sense of national pride, developed idiomatic opera in their native tongues. Although Italian opera remained the dominant style, it now had to share the stage, not only with traditional French opera but also with the newer forms of Russian, Czech, and especially German opera.

ROMANTIC OPERA IN ITALY

During the early decades of the nineteenth century, the primacy of Italian opera was maintained almost single-handedly by Gioachino Rossini (1792–1868). Surprising as it may seem today, Rossini was the most popular composer in Europe during the 1820s, far exceeding in celebrity Beethoven and Schubert. He owed his public favor not only to the charm of his music but also to the fact that the genre of music within which he chose to work—opera—was then the most popular form of public musical entertainment, much more so than the symphony or string quartet, for example. Rossini continued, and indeed brought to a glorious close, the eighteenth-century tradition of comic opera, or *opera buffa* (see page 151). Catchy, oft-repeating melodies, vivacious rhythms, and rollicking crescendos were his trademarks. His best-known comic opera, *The Barber of Seville*, has never disappeared from the operatic stage since it first appeared in 1816. Even casual music lovers know a little of this enduring work in the form of the "Figaro, Figaro, Figaro" call from the opening aria for the resourceful bar-

ber, Figaro. Rossini could also write in a more serious style, as exemplified in his last opera, *William Tell* (1829). This stormy drama, too, has achieved a measure of popular immortality, the overture providing the theme music for the radio and film character of the Lone Ranger.

Italian *Bel Canto* Opera

Whereas German operatic composers would come to emphasize the dramatic power and instrumental color of the orchestra, Italians after Rossini increasingly focused all of their energies on the solo voice and on melody—on the art of beautiful singing, or **bel canto.** The two most gifted of the early creators of *bel canto* opera were Gaetano Donizetti (1797–1848) and Vincenzo Bellini (1801–1835). In their works there is little orchestral color and almost no counterpoint. The orchestra merely provides a simple harmonic support for the soaring, sometimes divinely beautiful, lines of the voice. Look at the opening of the famous aria "Casta diva" from Bellini's *Norma* (1831), in which the heroine sings a prayer to a distant moon goddess. Here the orchestra functions like a giant guitar. Simple chords are fleshed out as arpeggios by the strings while an even simpler bass line is plucked below. All of the musical interest is in the rapturous sound of the human voice. One Italian newspaper of the day declared "In the theatrical arts it is said that three things are required: action, action, action; likewise, three things are demanded for music: voice, voice, voice."

🌀 FIGURE 14–1
Gioachino Rossini.

EXAMPLE 14–1

(Chaste goddess, who does bathe in silver light these hallowed, ancient trees)

Not surprisingly, by placing such importance on the solo singer, *bel canto* opera fostered an environment in which a star system was bound to flourish among the cast. Usually, it was the lyric soprano—heroine and "prima donna"—who held the most exalted position in the musical firmament. By the 1880s, she would be called a **diva,** which, as in the aria "Casta diva," means "goddess." Indeed, the goddess of the beautiful female voice would rule Italian opera right through the nineteenth century, from the early *bel canto* operas of Donizetti and Bellini through the mature works of Giuseppe Verdi (1813–1901) and Giacomo Puccini (1858–1924).

cult of the diva

FIGURE 14–2
Giuseppe Verdi.

Giuseppe Verdi (1813–1901)

The name Giuseppe Verdi is virtually synonymous with Italian opera. For six decades, from the time of *Nabucco* in 1842 until *Falstaff* in 1893, he had almost no rival for the affections of the opera-loving public in Italy and elsewhere throughout Europe. Even today the best-loved of the twenty-six operas of Verdi are more readily available—in opera houses, in TV productions, and on videotape—than those of any other composer.

Verdi was born near Busseto in northern Italy in 1813, the son of a tavern keeper. He was apparently no musical prodigy, for at the age of eighteen he was rejected for admission to the Conservatory of Music in Milan because he was already too old and his piano technique faulty. But Verdi stayed on in Milan to study composition. He returned to Busseto in 1835 to serve as the town's bandmaster, and then four years later went back to Milan to earn his livelihood as a composer.

To be a composer in nineteenth-century Italy was to be a composer of opera. Verdi's first, *Oberto*, was produced at the famous La Scala Opera House in Milan (Fig. 14–3) in 1839, and it achieved a modicum of success. But his *Nabucco* of 1842 was a popular triumph, receiving an unprecedented fifty-seven performances at La Scala in that year alone. Through subsequent productions in other

FIGURE 14–3
La Scala Opera House about 1830. Verdi's first four and last two operas had their premieres at La Scala, then and now the foremost opera house in Italy.

theaters, Verdi's name was quickly carried throughout Italy, Europe, and both North and South America. His career was launched.

The text, or libretto*, of *Nabucco*, as well as most of the other operas Verdi composed in the 1840s, concerns the suppression of a people by a cruel foreign power—and by implication the people of Italy by Austria, which then ruled much of the peninsula. Verdi had become a spirited liberal and an Italian patriot. Normally, we do not think of music as expressing political ideas, but opera was such an important part of Italian popular culture that it had the capacity to inspire political revolution. In his libretti Verdi inserted and then set for chorus or solo voice such fiery words as "You may have the universe, so long as I keep Italy" and "Long live Italy! A sacred pact binds all her sons." Partly through such patriotic music and partly by accident, Verdi became a leader in the Risorgimento, the movement for a united Italy free of foreign domination. By handy coincidence, the letters of the composer's last name produced an acronym for **V**ittorio **E**manuele **R**e **d'I**talia (King Victor Emanuel being the people's choice for the throne of a united Kingdom of Italy). Thus, cries of "Viva, Verdi!" echoed throughout Italy in hopes of unification. In 1861, after that goal had been largely achieved, Verdi was elected to the country's first parliament, and later, in 1874, to its senate.

Verdi as political leader and symbol of Italian unification

But in the late 1840s the drive for Italian independence was far from complete. Indeed, the liberal Revolution of 1848 failed to oust the Austrians from Milan, and Verdi for a time became disillusioned with politics. He now turned his attention to domestic themes and more personal drama, producing a trio of much-admired operas: *Rigoletto* (1851), *La traviata* (1853), and *Il trovatore* (1853). For most of the early-to-mid-1850s, Verdi lived away from the area of Milan, residing in Paris or traveling throughout Europe to oversee the production of his increasingly numerous works. He called these years of toil and intense productivity "my years as a galley slave."

On his return to his homeland in 1857, the pace of Verdi's opera production slackened. He composed only when the subject was of interest or the fee so substantial he couldn't refuse. *La forza del destino* (*The Force of Destiny*, 1861) was written for St. Petersburg for the enormous commission of 60,000 francs; *Don Carlo* (1867) was composed for Paris for an equally large amount; and *Aïda* (1871), written for Cairo shortly after the opening of the Suez Canal, for the astonishing sum of 150,000 francs. Verdi had become more than a little wealthy, and he retired to his estate in northern Italy to lead the life of a country squire— or so he thought.

later operas

But like a performer who feels he owes the audience more, or has something more to prove to himself, Verdi returned to the theater for two final encores: *Otello* (1887) and *Falstaff* (1893), both exceptionally well-crafted operas based on dramas of Shakespeare. The latter work was written when the composer was on the threshold of eighty, a feat without parallel in music history or the annals of the dramatic stage. He died peacefully at his country home in 1901, a much-respected national institution.

VERDI'S DRAMATURGY AND MUSICAL STYLE

When the curtain goes up on a Verdi opera, the listener will find elements of dramaturgy—how the drama is put together—and musical style that are unique to this composer. For Giuseppe Verdi conflict was at the root of every emotion, and he expressed conflict, whether personal or national, by juxtaposing self-contained, yet clearly differentiated, units of music. A rousing march, a patriotic chorus, a passionate recitative, and a lyrical aria follow one after the other in quick succession. In each vivid number there is no mistaking which emotion is being communicated to the audience. The composer aims not at musical and dramatic subtlety but rather at immediate effect and direct appeal to the listener's sensibilities. The emotional states of the characters are so clearly drawn, sometimes overdrawn, that the drama comes perilously close to melodrama—excessively sentimental or sensational. But it is never dull. There is action, passion, and intensity. "I would be willing to set even a newspaper, or a letter, to music," he said in 1854, "but in the theater the public will stand for anything except boredom."

How does Verdi generate this feeling of intense passion and nonstop action? He does so by creating a new kind of recitative and a new style of aria. Verdi continues to use the former to narrate the action and the latter to express feeling. But now the old *secco* recitative, with mere keyboard accompaniment, gives way to orchestrally accompanied recitative (**recitativo accompagnato**). This allows the action to flow smoothly from orchestrally accompanied aria to orchestrally accompanied recitative and back without a jarring change of texture. As to the aria, Verdi brings to it a new intensity. Yes, he is a composer squarely in the tradition of Italian *bel canto* opera. He, too, focuses all attention on the solo voice, and on a lyrical, beautiful vocal line. Indeed, no composer had a greater gift for writing simple, memorable melodies that the audience could whistle on the way out of the theater. Yet Verdi also adds intensity and passion to these arias by pushing the singers to the utmost of their range. The tenor is asked to sing up to the B above middle C, the soprano two octaves and more above middle C. The thrilling moments in which the hero (the tenor) or the heroine (the soprano) go right to the top are literally the high points of any Verdi opera.

※ FIGURE 14–4
Verdi's long-time mistress and ultimately his wife, Giuseppina Strepponi (1815–1897) holding the score of his early opera *Nabucco*.

LA TRAVIATA (1853)

We may measure the high intensity and passion in Verdi's operas by listening to a portion of his *La traviata* (1853). *La traviata* literally means "The Woman Gone Astray." It tells the story of the sickly Violetta Valery, a courtesan, or "kept woman," who resists and then succumbs to the love of a new suitor, the young Alfredo Germont. For a while the couple retires from Paris to lead a quiet life in the country. But without explanation Violetta deserts Alfredo, in truth so that her former life will not bring disgrace on his respectable family. The hot-tempered Alfredo now publicly insults Violetta, fights a duel with her new "protector," and is banished from France. When the nature of Violetta's sacrifice is revealed, Alfredo rushes back to Paris. But it is too late. She is dying of tuberculosis—her fate is dictated by an operatic convention that requires the heroine to sing one last show-stopping aria and then expire.

the plot

Verdi first heard this sentimental tale, one that pits passionate love against middle-class morality, when in Paris during the winter of 1852. There he and his mistress, the singer Giuseppina Strepponi (Fig. 14–4), were captivated by a new play of Alexandre Dumas the younger entitled *The Lady of the Camellias*, now known to English audiences simply as *Camille*. The main character of the drama, Violetta Valery, was modeled after a real-life figure, Marie Duplessis (Fig. 14–5), who had been the mistress of playwright Dumas and, briefly, of composer Franz Liszt as well. Like many in this period, she, too, died young of tuberculosis, at the age of twenty-three. Verdi's compassion toward this heroine

a true story

probably was sparked by the fact that his mistress, too, was held in general disrepute at this time, having by then given birth to four illegitimate children.

We join *La traviata* toward the end of the first act. A gala party is in progress in a fashionable Parisian salon, and here the dashing Alfredo has finally managed to cut Violetta away from the crowd to profess to her his love. He does so in the aria "Un dì felice" ("One Happy Day"), which is lovely, yet somber in tone. The seriousness of his intent is underscored by the slow, square, even plodding accompaniment in the orchestra. When Violetta enters she is supported by the same accompaniment, but the mood of the aria is radically changed to one that is light and carefree. Witness how Verdi's direct musical characterization works: Alfredo's slow melody with a hint of minor is replaced by Violetta's flighty sound of high, rapidly moving notes. Eventually, the two join in a duet: he below, somberly proclaiming the mysteries of love; she above, making light of them.

After the duet has come to a cadence, a friend, Gaston, briefly interrupts, singing in accompanied recitative. But soon the voices of Alfredo and Violetta are once more joined. The tempo of the music increases and so does their growing ardor for each other, shown musically by the way the singers rush in breathlessly on successively higher notes. This rapid, final portion of the duet is called a **cabaletta**—the concluding fast section of any two- or three-section aria complex. The cabaletta was an oft-used dramatic device in Italian opera because the increased speed of the music allowed one or both of the singers to race off stage at the end of a scene or act. Here Alfredo kisses Violetta's hand and excitedly departs.

 FIGURE 14–5
Marie Duplessis. The end of her brief, scandalous life is the subject of Giuseppe Verdi's opera *La traviata*.

LISTENING GUIDE

Giuseppe Verdi
La traviata (1853)
Act I, Scene 4

6CD 4/6

Characters: Alfredo, a young man of good standing; Violetta, a kept woman leading a wanton life in Paris
Situation: A party in a Parisian salon around 1850; Alfredo professes his love to Violetta, who at first rejects him.

Aria

Alfredo (tenor)

0:00		Un dì felice, eterea,	One happy day,
		Mi balanaste innante,	you appeared to me.
		E da quel dì tremante	And from this day, trembling,
		Vissi d'ignoto amor.	I have lived in that
		Di quell'amor ch'è palpito	unspoken love, in that love
		Dell'universo intero,	which animates the world,
	Shift to minor	Misterioso, altero,	mysterious, proud, pain
		Croce e delizia al cor.	and delight to the heart.

Violetta (soprano)

1:22	Violetta changes aria to lighter mood through faster tempo and shorter notes	Ah, se ciò èver, fugitemi.	If that's true, leave me.
		Solo amistade io v'offro;	Only friendship I offer you.
		Amar non so, nè soffro	I don't know how to love
		Un cosi eroico amore.	or suffer such a heroic love.
		Io sono franca, ingenua;	I'm being honest and sincere.
		Altra cercar dovete;	You must find another.
		Non arduo troverete	It won't be difficult.
		Dimenticarmi allor.	Just leave me.

(Continued on next page)

(Duet)

1:46   Alfredo and Violetta together
in rapturous duet

		Alfredo
	Oh amore!	Oh love!
	Misterioso, altero,	mysterious, proud, pain
	Croce e delizia al cor.	and delight to the heart.
		Violetta
	Non arduo troverete	It won't be difficult.
	Dimenticarmi allor.	Just leave me.
	"Ah"	"Ah"

2:48   Exuberant vocal flourishes for both

Recitative

3:26   Gaston interrupts

		Gaston
	Ebben? che diavol fate?	Well, what the devil's going on?
		Violetta
	Si folleggiava!	Just fooling around.
		Gaston
	Ah, ah, sta ben! restate!	Well then, continue!

Strains of a waltz heard from ballroom

(Duet)

3:35   Continues as dialogue

		Violetta
	Amor dunque non più.	Well then, no more about love!
	Vi garba il patto?	Is that a promise?
		Alfredo
	Io v'obbedisco. Parto.	I'll obey you. I'm leaving.
		Violetta
	A tal giungeste	So it's come to that already?
	(Si toglie un fiore	(She takes a flower from
	dal seno.)	her bosom.)
	Predete questo fiore.	Take this flower.
		Alfredo
	Perchè?	Why?
		Violetta
	Per riportarlo.	So that you can bring it back.
		Alfredo
	Quando?	When?
		Violetta
	Quando sarà appassito.	When it's withered.
		Alfredo
	O ciel! Domani?	Good god, you mean tomorrow?
		Violetta
	Ebben, domani.	Oh well, tomorrow.

Cabaletta

4:01   Tempo increases

		Alfredo
	Io son, Io son felice!	I'm so happy.
		Violetta
	D'amarmi dite ancora?	Do you still say you love me?
		Alfredo
	Oh! quanto v'amo!	Oh, how much I love you.
	Io son felice.	I'm so happy.
		Violetta
	Partite?	Are you going?
		Alfredo
	Parto.	I'm going.
		Violetta
	Addio.	Adieu.
		Alfredo
	Di più non bramo.	I need nothing more.
	Addio. (esce)	Adieu. (exits)

The musical-dramatic design of the concluding scene of Act I of *La traviata* shows a similar tripartite structure: aria, brief recitative, cabaletta. Violetta is left alone on stage. She reveals, in a slow strophic aria, "Ah, fors'è lui" ("Ah, perhaps he's the one"), that Alfredo may be the lover she has long desired. But then, in an impassioned recitative ("Folly! Folly! What sort of crazy dream is this!"), she jumps to her feet to proclaim that she must always remain free of the entanglements of love. This aria, "Sempre libera" ("Always free") is one of the great showpieces for soprano voice. Yet it also helps define through music the character of Violetta—the extraordinary, carefree flourishes on the word "pleasure," for example, reinforce her "enjoy-ourselves-while-we-may" approach to life. This declaration of independence is momentarily broken by the voice of Alfredo, who from outside her window expresses again his feelings about the mysterious powers of love. Violetta brushes these aside and repeats her vow always to be free. Of course, she does not remain emotionally free; she falls fatally in love with Alfredo as Acts II and III reveal. Listen now to the final scene of Act I of Verdi's *La traviata*. You will have the pleasure of hearing two of the greatest voices of the twentieth century, Joan Sutherland (soprano) and Luciano Pavarotti (tenor).

❀ FIGURE 14–6
The great Australian soprano Joan Sutherland singing the role of Violetta and tenor Luciano Pavarotti as Alfredo in Verdi's *La traviata*.

LISTENING GUIDE

Giuseppe Verdi
La traviata (1853)
Act I, Scene 6

6CD 4/7
6CD 4/8;
2CD 2/4

Characters: Violetta and Alfredo (outside her window)
Situation: Violetta at first believes Alfredo to be the passionate love she has long sought, but then rejects this notion, vowing to remain free.

Aria

First strophe

0:00	Soprano sings first phrase	Ah, fors'è lui che l'anima Solinga ne' tumulti Godea sovente pingere De' suoi colori occulti.	Ah, perhaps he's the one whom my lonely heart delighted often to paint with vague, mysterious colors.
0:35	First phrase repeated		
0:58	Voice rises up in melodic sequence	Lui, che modesto e vigile All'egre sogli ascese, E nuova febbre accese Destandomi all'amor!	He who, so modest and attentive during my illness, waited and with youthful fervor aroused me again to love!
1:24	Return of Alfredo's major-key refrain from previous aria	A quell'amor ch'è palpito Dell'universo intero, Misterioso altero, Croce e delizia al cor.	To that love which animates the universe, mysterious, proud, pain and delight to the heart.

(Continued on next page)

Second strophe

2:26	Return of first phrase	A me, fanciulla, un candido E trepido desire,	To me, a girl, this was an innocent, anxious desire,
2:53	First phrase repeated	Quest'effgiò dolcissimo Signor dell'avvenire.	this sweet vision, lord of things to come.
3:17	Voice rises up in melodic sequence	Quando ne' cieli il raggio Di sua beltà vedea E tuta me pascea Di quel divino error.	When in the heavens I saw rays of his beauty I fed myself completely on that divine error.
3:44	Return of Alfredo's major-key refrain from previous aria	Sentia che amore è il palpito Dell'universo intero, Misterioso altero, Croce e delizia al cor.	I felt that love which animates the universe, mysterious, proud, pain and delight to the heart.
4:18	Highly ornamental final cadence with lengthy trill		

6CD 4/8; 2CD 2/4

Recitative   Violetta

0:00	Accompanied by orchestra	Follie! Follie! delirio vano è questo! Povera donna, sola, abbandonata, in questo populoso deserto che appellano Parigi. Che spero or più? Che far degg'io?	Folly! Folly! What sort of crazy dream is this! Poor woman, alone, adandoned in this populated desert that they call Paris. What hope have I? What can I do?
0:49	Flights of vocal fancy as she thinks of pleasure	Gioir! Di voluttà ne' vortici perir! Gioir!	Pleasure! Perish in a whirl of indulgence! Pleasure!
1:05	Introduction to cabaletta		

Cabaletta   Violetta

1:16		Sempre libera degg'io Folleggiare di gioia in gioia, Vo' che scorra il viver mio Pei sentieri del piacer. Nasca il giorno, o il giorno muoia, Sempre lieta ne' ritrovi, A diletti sempre nuovi Dee volare il mio pensier.	Always free I must remain to reel from pleasure to pleasure, running my life along the paths of joy. From dawn to dusk I'm always happy finding new delights that make my spirit soar.

    Alfredo

2:01	Echoes of his previous aria	Amor è palpito dell'universo, misterioso, altero, croce e delizia al cor.	Love that animates the world, mysterious, proud, pain and delight to the heart.

    Violetta

2:48	Extravagant flourishes	Follie! Follie! Gioir! Gioir!	Folly! Folly! Pleasure! Pleasure!

Cabaletta returns

3:17	this time even more brilliant in its showy, superficial style	Sempre libera . . .	Always free . . .

(Listening Exercise 29)

❀ ROMANTIC OPERA IN GERMANY

Before 1820 opera was mainly an Italian affair. It was first created in Italy around 1600 and then, during the next two hundred years, was exported to all parts of Europe and eventually to North and South America. But German opera, by comparison, was rather weak and provincial. Before 1820 the only German opera heard outside German-speaking lands was Mozart's *Die Zauberflöte* (*The Magic Flute*, 1791), which owed its widespread appeal to the glories of Mozart's music rather than any fondness for the somewhat primitive conventions of German opera.

What passed as native opera in German-speaking lands went by the name of *Singspiel*. A **Singspiel** ("singing play") is a musical comedy or light musical drama that has, by sheer coincidence, many elements in common with our present-day Broadway musical: plenty of topical humor, tuneful solo songs, energetic choral numbers, and spoken dialogue instead of sung recitative. Mozart, in *The Magic Flute* (1791), and Beethoven, in his only opera, *Fidelio* (1805), each wrote a *Singspiel* in which he tried to bring greater seriousness and unity to the genre. A somewhat younger contemporary of Beethoven, Karl Maria von Weber (1786–1826), likewise attempted to develop a tradition of serious German opera distinct from the Italian style. His *Der Freischütz* (1821) makes use of German folk songs, or folklike melodies, as well as a libretto that delights in magic and the supernatural. (Its most memorable moment is the "Wolf Glen" scene at the beginning of the second act during which magical silver bullets are cast in a Satanic ritual.) The German passion for horror subjects and supernatural tales in the Romantic period can be seen in other works, such as Heinrich Marschner's *The Vampire* (1828) and Richard Wagner's *The Flying Dutchman* (1843).

a Singspiel *has much in common with a Broadway musical*

horror subjects and supernatural tales

Richard Wagner (1813–1883)

The composer who realized the German dream of a truly national opera was the titanic figure Richard Wagner. Wagner's theories and his art have made him both the object of almost religious adoration and, at the same time, the most detested composer in the history of music. In fact, he was not merely a composer but also a politician, philosopher, propagandist, and bully for his particular vision of dramatic music. For Wagner, opera was the most perfect form of artistic expression and the composer a religious prophet who could reveal a musical kingdom to his congregation, namely, the listening audience. Wagner's music is, indeed, often inspiring. It contains moments of grandeur unmatched by any other composer. His influence on the musical style of other composing musicians at the end of the nineteenth century was enormous. Yet his reception by the musical public at large, then and now, has been divided. Some listeners are immediately converted to adoring Wagnerites at the first sound of the heroic themes and powerful orchestral climaxes. Others are left cold, believing the music long-winded and the operatic plots devoid of real human drama.

Who was this controversial artist who has stirred such mixed feelings within the musical public for more than a century? Richard Wagner was born into a theatrical family in Leipzig, Germany, in 1813. His first passion was not music but poetry, drama, and the theater. Only in his late teens, when he began to immerse himself in the music of Beethoven, did he begin to consider music as a profession. He made piano transcriptions* of the orchestral music of Beethoven, and took lessons in composition from the cantor of Leipzig's St. Thomas's

❀ FIGURE 14–7
Richard Wagner.

🌿 FIGURE 14-8
Bayreuth Festival Theater, an opera house built especially to produce the music dramas of Richard Wagner—and only Wagner.

Church, Bach's church (see page 126). After a succession of jobs as an opera director in several small German towns, Wagner and his young family moved to Paris in 1839 in hopes of seeing his first opera produced there. Instead of meeting success in Paris, as had Liszt and Chopin before him, Wagner was greeted by thundering indifference. No one could be persuaded to produce his work. Reduced to poverty, he spent a brief sojourn in a Parisian prison for nonpayment of debts.

When Wagner's big break came it was not in Paris but in his native Germany, in the city of Dresden. His opera *Rienzi* was given a hearing there in October 1842 and generated such an enthusiastic response that the composer was offered the post of opera director for the king of Saxony in this important city. During the next six years three additional German Romantic operas by Wagner were given there: *The Flying Dutchman* (1844), *Tannhäuser* (1845), and *Lohengrin* (1848). In the aftermath of the political revolution that swept much of Europe in 1848, Wagner was forced to flee Dresden, though in truth he took flight as much to avoid his creditors as to escape any repressive government.

Wagner found a safe haven in Switzerland, which was to be his home, on and off, for the next dozen years. Exiled now from the major opera houses in Germany, he began to imagine a complex of music dramas on a vast and unprecedented scale. What he ultimately created was *Der Ring des Nibelungen (The Ring of the Nibelung)*, a set of four operas intended to be performed during the course of four successive evenings. *Das Rheingold,* the first, lasts 2½ hours; *Die Walküre* and *Siegfried* each run nearly 4½; while the finale, *Götterdämmerung (Twilight of the Gods)*, goes on for no less than 5½ hours. The thread of a single story runs from beginning to end. But instead of drawing his theme from a play or a set of historical events, Wagner reached back into Germanic mythology for his subject matter. The scene is set in the smoky mists of primeval time, in a land of gods, river nymphs, dwarfs, giants, dragons, and sword-wielding heroes.

the Ring *cycle*

Although the plot of the *Ring* is complex in the extreme, it is best viewed as an allegory exploring the themes of power, greed, lust, honor, and bravery in contemporary nineteenth-century society. Power, for example, is symbolized by the ring belonging to the dwarfish Nibelungs, bravery by the exploits of the hero Siegfried. While these are universal themes, they were harmonious with the growing feeling of German national identity. The German philosopher Friedrich Nietzsche (1844–1900), for a time a friend and confidant of Wagner, modeled his concept of the superhero, or superman, on Wagner's heroic character. In the twentieth century, Adolph Hitler would exploit Wagnerian symbolism to foster the notion of a superior German race, building, for example, a Siegfried Line on the Western Front.

plot of the Ring

Needless to say, publishers and producers were at first reluctant to print or mount the operas of Wagner's *Ring*, given their massive scope and fantastic subject matter. They would, however, pay well for the rights to more traditional works by him. So in the midst of his labors on the *Ring* cycle, the always penurious Wagner interrupted the project for a period of years to create *Tristan und Isolde* (1865) and *Die Meistersinger von Nürnberg (The Mastersingers of Nuremberg,* 1868). But these, too, were long and not easy to produce. The bulky scores piled up on his desk.

In 1864 Wagner was rescued from his plight by King Ludwig II of Bavaria, who paid off his debts, gave him an annual allowance, encouraged him to complete the *Ring* tetralogy, and helped him to build a special theater where his giant operas could be mounted according to the composer's own specifications. This opera house, or Festival Theater as Wagner called it, was constructed at Bayreuth, a small town between Munich and Leipzig in southern Germany. The first "Bayreuth Festival" took place in August 1876 with three successive performances of the entire *Ring* cycle. Wagner's last opera, *Parsifal*, premiered there as well, in 1882. Following Wagner's death the next year, his remains were interred on the grounds of the Wagner villa in Bayreuth. To this day the theater at Bayreuth continues to stage the music dramas of Wagner—and only Wagner. Each summer thousands of opera lovers make the pilgrimage to this theatrical shrine to one of art's most determined, and ruthless, visionaries.

Bayreuth Festival Theatre

Wagner's "Music Dramas"

With a few very minor exceptions, Richard Wagner wrote only musical works intended for the theater. He did not call these operas, however, but "music dramas." A **music drama** for Wagner was a musical work for the stage in which all the arts—poetry, music, acting, mime, dance, and scenic design—function as a harmonious ensemble. Such an artistic union Wagner referred to as a **Gesamtkunstwerk** ("total art work"). Thus combined, the unified force of the arts would generate real drama. No longer would the dramatic action grind to a halt in order to spotlight the vocal flourishes of a soloist, as often happened in Italian opera.

the Gesamtkunstwerk

Indeed, Wagner's music drama differs from conventional Italian opera in several important ways. First, it is not made up of distinct and separate numbers—aria, recitative, duet, and the like—but of an almost seamless flow of undifferentiated solo singing and declamation. Second, ensemble singing is almost entirely absent—duets, trios, choruses, and full-cast finales—are rare in the extreme. Finally, the tuneful aria is banished to the wings. Wagner avoids repetition, symmetry, and regular cadences—all things that can make a melody "catchy"—in favor of long-flowing, nonrepetitive, not particularly songlike lines. As the tuneful aria decreases in importance, the role of the orchestra increases.

With Wagner the orchestra is everything. It sounds forth the main musical themes, develops and exploits them, and thereby "plays out" the drama through pure instrumental music. On stage the words and actions of the singers give the audience supplementary clues as to what the musical drama in the orchestra is all about. In the 1850s Wagner drank deeply of the philosophy of Arthur Schopenhauer (1788–1860), who wrote that "music expresses the innermost basis of the world, the essence behind appearances." In music drama what happens on the stage is the appearance; what happens in the orchestra is the reality, the drama at a deeper level.

As had Beethoven and Berlioz before him, Wagner continued to expand the size of the orchestra. He called for triple woodwinds and greatly enlarged the brass section, requiring more trombones and tubas. A bigger orchestra

✹ FIGURE 14–9
Cosima Wagner (daughter of Franz Liszt and Marie d'Agoult), Richard Wagner, and Liszt at Wagner's villa in Bayreuth in 1880. At the right is a young admirer of Wagner, Hans von Wolzogen, who first coined the term "leitmotif" (see page 290).

demanded, in turn, more forceful singers. To be heard above an orchestra of nearly a hundred players, a large, specially trained voice was needed, the so-called Wagnerian tenor or Wagnerian soprano. Yet during moments of climax even these powerful voices are scarcely audible. Imagine an opera of Verdi in which the voice of the hero or heroine cannot be heard. Impossible! But in a music drama of Wagner, the virtual disappearance of the voice does not matter. By design the singer is ultimately consumed by the greater reality of an all-powerful orchestra. Let us see how the orchestra brings this about in Wagner's music drama *Tristan und Isolde*.

Wagnerian tenor, soprano

TRISTAN UND ISOLDE (1865)

Wagner began to compose *Tristan und Isolde* during 1857 when living in Switzerland and supported in part by a wealthy patron, Otto Wesendonck. Although still married, the composer began an affair with Wesendonck's wife, Mathilde—so fully did Wagner the man live his life as Wagner the artist that it was impossible for him to create an opera dealing with passionate love without being passionately in love himself. Eventually, his own wife, Minna, caused such a scene that the composer fled to Venice. By 1864 Wagner had made his way to Munich for the first production of the now finished *Tristan*. Having long since forgotten both Mathilde and his wife, he now fell in love with Cosima von Bülow, the wife of the man scheduled to conduct *Tristan*. Cosima was the illegitimate daughter of Franz Liszt and Marie d'Agoult (see Fig. 13–18 and page 272), and she and Wagner soon produced three illegitimate children of their own. The first of these, a daughter born on the first day of rehearsals for *Tristan*, was christened Isolde.

The story of *Tristan und Isolde* comes from an old Arthurian legend. Briefly, it is the tale of the love of a captive Irish princess, Isolde, betrothed to King Mark of Cornwall (England), and of Tristan, the king's trusted knight. Tristan is sent to conduct the reluctant Isolde to her wedding with King Mark. Wishing only for revenge and then death, Isolde asks for a deadly potion, but her devoted servant instead substitutes a love potion, which the unknowing Tristan and Isolde consume. On arrival in Cornwall this passionate, soon adulterous, love is revealed to the court. Despairing of any happy union with Isolde in this world, Tristan allows himself to be mortally wounded in combat and sails off to his native Brittany to die. Isolde pursues him but arrives only in time to have him expire in her arms. Knowing that their union will only be consummated through death, Isolde sings her *Liebestod (Love-Death)*, an ecstatic vision of their love beyond the grave, and then she, too, expires next to her lover's body. This was the sort of all-consuming, sacrificial love so dear to the hearts of Romantic artists.

❋ FIGURE 14–10
Original costume designs for the premiere of Wagner's *Tristan und Isolde*, June 1865.

Wagner begins *Tristan*, not with a rousing, self-contained overture, but with a simple yet beautiful prelude that sets the general tone of the drama and leads directly to the raising of the curtain. The first sound we hear is a plaintive call of the cellos, answered by one in the woodwinds. Each is not so much a lengthy theme as it is a short, pregnant motive. Wagner's disciples called each a **leitmotif,** a brief, distinctive unit of music that is designed to represent a character, object, or idea and that returns repeatedly in order to facilitate the progress of the drama. We have encountered a representational, or programmatic, theme before in the form of Berlioz's *idée fixe* (see page 256). But Wagner's leitmotifs are much shorter than Berlioz's lengthy melody, and there are many more of them. They are usually not sung but only played in the orchestra. In this way an element of the subconscious can be brought to the drama: The orchestra can

the leitmotif

Leitmotifs in *Star Wars*

The technique of the leitmotif, as developed by Richard Wagner, has been borrowed by many composers of Hollywood film music. To name just one: John Williams, the creator of the music for George Lucas's *Star Wars* series. When Williams wrote the music for *Star Wars*, *The Empire Strikes Back*, and *The Return of the Jedi*, he composed for each main character (and theme or force) a particular musical motive. Below are two of Williams's leitmotifs, the first signifying the hero Luke Skywalker, the second (merely an insistent rhythm) symbolizing the evil Darth Vader.

Like Wagner, Williams also sets these leading motives in the orchestra and thereby tells the audience what the char-

acter is thinking or what the future may hold. When young Luke is confined to his uncle's farm, for example, we learn that greater things await him: The orchestra plays the heroic Force leitmotif in the background. In fact, *Star Wars* has more than just leitmotifs in common with Wagner's music dramas. Both Wagner and Lucas started with a core of three dramas and added a fourth as a preface or "prequel" (*Das Rheingold* was prefixed to the *Ring* and *The Phantom Menace* to *Star Wars*). Both four-drama cycles play out a succession of epic battles between larger-than-life heros and villains, mythical forces for good and evil.

Luke's Theme

Darth Vader's Theme

give a sense of what a character is thinking even when he or she is singing about something else. By developing, extending, varying, contrasting, and resolving these representational leitmotifs, Wagner is able to play out the essence of the drama almost without recourse to his singers.

Leitmotifs in *Tristan* are associated mainly with feelings rather than concrete objects or persons. Typical are the leitmotifs representing "Longing," "Desire," and "Ecstasy."

EXAMPLE 14–2

"Longing"

"Desire"

"Ecstasy"

leitmotifs *in Wagner's* Tristan

intense chromaticism

Notice how both the "Longing" and "Desire" motifs involve chromatic lines, the first descending, the second ascending (see arrows). This sort of linear chromatic motion made it easy for the composer to wind continually through many different keys, not stopping long enough to establish any one as a home base, or tonic*. Wagner's intense use of chromaticism loosened the feeling of key and eventually led to the collapse of tonality as the main organizing force in Western music, as we shall later see (page 336). Here he uses twisting chromatic lines for a specific expressive purpose, to convey a sense of the anxiety and pain to be felt by the ill-fated lovers.

a glorious conclusion

As you listen to the final scene of *Tristan* you can feel Wagner trying to draw you into his all-enveloping world of love, longing, desire, and death. Here Isolde cradles the body of the dying Tristan and prepares to share his fate. As she sings her justly famous *Liebestod (Love-Death)*, four leitmotifs sound forth, each heard previously in the opera. They frequently appear in sequences*, usually moving upward so as to convey a sense of continual longing and rising tension. Cadences are avoided, thereby increasing the restless mood. Dissonances are placed at points of climax to heighten the feeling of pain and anguish. Finally, the music reaches one last, glorious climax (4:25) and hereafter all is consonance and reduced movement—Isolde has joined Tristan in the world beyond. First listen to the *Liebestod*, concentrating on the leitmotifs as they are worked out by the voice but even more by the orchestra. Then play it once more, this time just drinking it in, like a love potion, all of Wagner's divinely inspired sound. If there is such a thing as a transcendental experience in Romantic music, you will have it here.

LISTENING GUIDE

Richard Wagner
Liebestod, from *Tristan und Isolde* (1865)

6CD 4/9;
2CD 2/5

Characters: The lovers Tristan and Isolde
Situation: Tristan's castle in Brittany; Isolde cradles Tristan in her arms as she prepares to join him in death.

0:00   Isolde, gazing at Tristan, slowly sings the "Love-Death" leitmotif, which is then taken up by the orchestra

Mild und leise wie er lächelt,
Wie das Auge hold er öffnet—
Seht ihr, Freunde? Seht ihr's nicht?
Immer lichter wie er leuchtet,
Stern-umstrahlet hoch sich hebt?

Oh how tenderly and gently he smiles,
As he opens his eyes—
Do you see, Friends, don't you see it?
Ever brighter, how he shines,
Glowing in starlight raised on high?

1:02   The orchestra continues with the "Love-Death" motif as the singer goes her own way

Seht ihr's nicht?
Wie das Herz ihm mutig schwillt,
Voll und hehr im Busen ihm quillt?

Do you not see it?
How his heart proudly swells,
Full and brave beating in his breast?

1:30   The "Ecstasy" leitmotif enters, not in the voice, but in the high woodwinds and then the violins

Wie den Lippen, wonnig mild
Süsser Atem sanft entweht—
Freunde! Seht!

How from his lips, blissfully tender,
Sweet breath gently flutters—
Do you not see, Friends?

(Continued on next page)

2:08	Reapperance of the ascending, chromatic "Desire" motif from the Prelude	Fühlt und seht ihr's nicht?	Don't you feel and see it?
2:15	"Love-Death" motif returns in voice and orchestra, followed by "Ecstasy" motif and then "Desire" motif in voice	Höre ich nur diese Weise Die so wundervoll und leise, Wonne klagend, alles sagend, Mild versöhnend aus ihm tönend, In mich dringet, auf sich schwinget, Hold erhallend um mich klinget?	Do I alone hear this melody Which, so wonderfully and gently, Moaning bliss, expressing all, Gently forgiving, coming from him Pierces me, soars upwards, Blessedly echoing all around me?
3:18	"Transcendent Bliss" leitmotif appears in violins		
3:39	Tension increases as "Desire" motif rises by chromatic steps in the orchestra	Heller schallend, mich umwallend, Sind es Wellen sanfter Lüfte? Sind es Wolken wonniger Düfte Wie sie schwellen, mich umrauschen, Soll ich atmen, soll ich lauschen? Soll ich schlürfen, untertauchen? Süss in Düften mich verhauchen? In dem wogenden Schwall, in dem tönenden Schall.	Resounding clearly all around me, Are they waves of gentle air? Are they clouds of delightful fragrance? As they swell and envelop me, Should I breathe, should I listen? Should I sip them, plunge beneath them? Breathe my last in such sweet fragrance? In the growing swell, the surging sound.
4:25	Glorious climax with the "Transcendent Bliss" motif shining forth in the orchestra	In des Welt-Atems wehendem All— Ertrinken, versinken— Unbewusst— Höchste Lust!	In the vastness of the world's spirit To drown, sink down— Unconscious— Supreme bliss!

The orchestra then fades away into silence as the curtain descends

(Listening Exercise 31)

LATE NINETEENTH-CENTURY OPERA

Verismo Opera

If Wagner's operas center on the deeds of mythical heroes, and Verdi's "domestic operas" on those of the upper middle class, the late nineteenth-century works of Giacomo Puccini (1858–1924) and his competitors focus on the actions of the lower stratum of society. They depict the grimy, everyday life of industrialized nineteenth-century Europe and are tinged with just a hint of eroticism and the threat of violence. This turn to social realism on the musical stage produced what is called *verismo* ("realism") opera. **Verismo opera** was part of a general late-Romantic movement that held that in art and literature the ugly and the vulgar have their place because truth has aesthetic value. The goal for poets like Charles Baudelaire (1821–1867), painters like J.-F. Millet (1814–1875), and novelists like Charles Dickens (1812–1870) and Emile Zola (1840–1902) was to transform the mundane and commonplace into art, to find the poetic and mystical in even the most ordinary of human experience. No more do we hear of gods and goddesses, Nordic giants, or benevolent kings and queens. A gypsy girl who works in a cigarette factory (Carmen in Bizet's *Car-*

realism in opera

men, 1875), a jealous clown who stabs his wife (Canio in Leoncavallo's *Pagli-acci*, 1892), and a distraught singer who murders the chief of police (Tosca in Puccini's *Tosca*, 1900)—these are the heros and heroines of *verismo* opera.

Giacomo Puccini (1858–1924)

Giacomo Puccini did not have to look far for a profession. He was the scion of four generations of musicians from the northern Italian town of Lucca. His fa-ther and his grandfather had both written operas, and before that his forebears had composed religious music for the local cathedral. But Puccini was no child prodigy. For a decade following his graduation from the Milan Conservatory he lived in poverty as he struggled to develop a distinctive operatic style. Not until the age of thirty-five did he score his first triumph, the *verismo* opera *Manon Lescaut* (1893). Thereafter, successes came in rapid succession: *La bohème* (1896), *Tosca* (1900), *Madama Butterfly* (1904). The heir to Verdi, the king of Italian opera, had been found. Growing famous, wealthy, and a bit complacent, Puc-cini worked less and less frequently. His last, and many believe his best, opera, *Turandot*, was left unfinished at the time of his death from throat cancer in 1924.

FIGURE 14–11
Giacomo Puccini.

LA BOHÈME (THE BOHEMIAN GIRL, 1896)
Puccini's most famous opera is *La bohème*. Indeed, statistics show that it is the most performed of all operas. *La bohème* is typical of *versimo* opera because the characters are portrayed as living a bohemian life in miserable poverty. The hero, Rodolfo (a poet), and his pals, Schaunard (a musician), Colline (a philoso-pher), and Marcello (a painter), are starving artists who inhabit an unheated attic on the Left Bank of Paris. The heroine, Mimi (the "bohemian girl"), their neighbor, is a poor, tubercular seamstress. Rodolfo and Mimi meet and fall in love. He grows obsessively jealous while she becomes progressively sickly. They separate for a time, only to return to each other's arms immediately before Mimi's death. In truth, this is not much of a plot, nor is there much character develop-

the libretto

ment. The theatrical setup on stage is merely a pretext to allow each of us to feel love, hope, and despair. The words of the singers and their particular dra-matic situation, in the last analysis, don't matter. In a singers' opera such as *La bohème* it is the glorious sound of the human voice that carries the moment. When Rodolfo, for example, sings of Mimi's frozen little hand in the aria "Che gelida manina" we escape the cold, hopeless world of a Left Bank attic. The soaring sound of Rodolfo's high tenor voice, not his words, invites us to experi-ence feelings and sensations far beyond the mundane. With the expansive arias of Puccini the golden century of Italian opera, which began with Rossini and embraced all of Verdi, comes to a fitting end.

LISTENING GUIDE

Giacomo Puccini
La bohème (1896)
Aria, "Ah, what a frozen little hand"

6CD 4/10

Characters: The poor poet Rodolfo and the equally impoverished seamstress Mimi
Situation: Mimi has knocked on Rodolfo's door to ask for a light for her candle. Charmed by the lovely stranger, he natu-rally obliges. The wind again blows out Mimi's candle, and amidst the confusion she drops her key. As the two search for it in the darkness, Rodolfo by chance touches her hand and, then holding it, seizes the moment to tell her about himself and his hopes.

(Continued on next page)

Time	Description	Italian	English
0:00	Rodolfo begins conversationally, much like in a recitative	Che gelida manina / se la lasci riscaldar. / Cercar che giova? / Al buio non si trova. / Ma per fortuna / è una notte di luna, / e qui la luna / l'abbiamo vicina.	Ah, what a frozen little hand, / let me warm it up. / What's the good of searching? / We won't find it in the dark. / But by good luck / there is moonlight tonight, / and here / we have the moon nearby.
	(Mimi tries to withdraw her hand)	Aspetti, signorina, / le dirò con due parole / chi son, e che faccio, / come vivo. Vuole? / Chi son? Sono un poeta. / Che cosa faccio? Scrivo. / E come vivo? Vivo!	Wait, young lady, / I will tell you in two words / who I am and what I do, / how I live. Would you like this? / Who am I? I'm a poet. / What do I do? I write. / How do I live? I live!
1:03	Voice increases in range, volume, and intensity		
	(Rodolfo proceeds to explain who he is and what he does)	In povertà mia lieta / scialo da gran signore / rime et inni d'amore. / Per sogni et per chimere / e per castelli in aria, / l'anima ho milionaria.	In my delightful poverty / I grandiosely scatter / rhymes and songs of love. / Through dreams and reveries / and through castles in the air, / I have the soul of a millionaire.
1:52	Return to conversational style		
2:30	Voice grows more expansive with longer notes and higher range; orchestra doubles voice in unison	Talor dal mio forziere / ruban tutti i gioielli / due ladri: gli occhi belli. / V'entrar con voi pur ora, / ed i miei sogni usati / e i bei sogni miei / tosto si dileguar! / Ma il furto non m'accora,	Sometimes from the strongbox / two thieves steal all the jewels: / two pretty eyes. / They came in with you just now / and my usual dreams, / my lovely dreams / vanish at once! / But the theft doesn't bother me
3:24	Orchestra sounds melody alone; then is joined by voice for climactic high note "hope"	poichè v'ha preso stanza / la speranza!	because their place / has been taken by hope!
	(As the music diminishes, Rodolfo asks for a response from Mimi)	Or che mi conoscete, / parlate voi, deh! parlate. / Chi siete? Vi piaccia dir!	Now that you know who I am, / Tell me about yourself, speak. / Who are you? Please speak.

LISTENING EXERCISES

29 Giuseppe Verdi, *La traviata* (1853)   6CD 4/7–8; 2CD 2/4
Act I, Scene 6: Aria "Ah, perhaps he's the one"
Recitative "Folly! Folly"
Cabaletta "Always free"

In *La traviata* Verdi has created what is very much a "singers' opera"—the listener's attention is drawn almost entirely to the voices. The orchestra plays a subordinate role, often limited to setting up a background accompaniment with simple rhythms and regular meters. The following questions illuminate the way in which Verdi makes the voice the center of attention, pausing from time to time to enjoy a moment of vocal bravura, yet still keeps the tempo of the opera moving at a rapid pace.

1. (0:00–1:00) What are the meter and the mode at the beginning of this aria?
   a. duple and major   b. duple and minor
   c. triple and major   d. triple and minor

2. (0:12–0:33) What does the orchestra do while Violetta (soprano) sings?
   a. provides simple chordal homophony
   b. provides simple imitative polyphony

3. (0:35–0:58) When the voice repeats the first phrase, does the nature of the accompaniment change? _____

4. (1:24–2:11) Here Violetta sings the expansive refrain introduced previously by Alfredo in Scene 4. The orchestral accompaniment now changes to the "big guitar" effect. How does Verdi create this big guitar in the orchestra?
   a. Strings play pizzicato chords and clarinet plays arpeggios.
   b. Strings play tremolo chords and flute plays arpeggios.
   c. Strings play vibrato chords and flute plays arpeggios.

5. (2:26–5:32) Violetta now sings the second strophe of her aria. When the expansive refrain returns (3:44–4:30), does the orchestra still produce the "big guitar" effect? _____

6CD 4/8; 2CD 2/4

6. During Violetta's accompanied recitative "Folly! Folly!" there is a passage in which she expresses her fear at being merely "a poor woman alone, abandoned in this populated desert that they call Paris" (0:13–0:23). The orchestra helps heighten this feeling of fear by playing:
   a. string tremolo and rising stepwise motion in the bass
   b. string pizzicato and falling stepwise motion in the bass
   c. string *rubato* and rising stepwise motion in the bass

7. After her recitative, and following some vocal fireworks on the word "gioir" ("pleasure"), Violetta launches into her brilliant cabaletta "Sempre libera" ("Always free"). Which number has a clear-cut, regular meter?
   a. the recitative "Folly! Folly!"   b. the aria "Always free"

8. At the end of "Always free" the voice of Alfredo enters (at 2:01) with his familiar refrain "Love that animates the world." Which of the following is true about Alfredo's music?
   a. The tempo speeds up and a guitar accompanies the voice.
   b. The tempo slows down and a harp accompanies the voice.

9. (3:00–3:15) Again Violetta vows to dedicate herself to a life of pleasure ("gioir"). What does the orchestra do during this vocal flourish?
   a. merely plays chordal homophony
   b. creates the "big guitar" effect
   c. nothing

10. Now Violetta repeats "Always free" (3:17), swearing to remain free of the snares of love. Where does the vocal high point of "Always free" occur—where does the soprano go to the top of her range?
    a. at the end of the first time Violetta sings the aria (1:55–2:01)
    b. at the end of the second time Violetta sings the aria (4:34–4:49)

Richard Wagner   6CD 4/9; 2CD 2/5
Liebestod, from *Tristan und Isolde* (1865)

Isolde's *Liebestod (Love-Death)*, which brings *Tristan und Isolde* to a glorious conclusion, is a unique musical composition. It is written for soprano voice—indeed, for a dramatic Wagnerian soprano—with orchestra, yet it is a very different sort of piece from Giuseppe Verdi's aria "Always free" from *La traviata*, which we have previously heard. The following queries begin by asking for specific responses to the music and conclude with a more general question regarding your reaction to the *Liebestod*.

1. Is there an easily perceptible duple or triple meter in the *Liebestod*?
   _____

2. When the soprano sings the "Ecstasy" leitmotif (2:35–2:57) she does so to what for Wagner is exceptionally "square" poetry—lines of 4 + 4 syllables with internal rhyme. (Try saying the German to yourself.)

   Wonne klagend, alles sagend   Moaning bliss, expressing all
   Mild versöhnend aus ihm tönend   Gently forgiving, sounding from within

   What is the course of the soprano line during this couplet?
   a. falls   b. falls in a sequence   c. rises   d. rises in a sequence

3. Immediately after (2:58–3:17), the music rises toward a climax to reflect the sentiment of the next couplet:

   In mich dringet, auf sich schwinget,   Pierces me, rises upwards,
   Hold erhallend, um mich klinget?   Blessedly echoing all around me?

   How is this rising tension brought about in the music?
   a. Tremolos are played by the strings.
   b. The voice rises up chromatically.
   c. There is a gradual crescendo.
   d. all of the above

4. (3:39–4:25) Wagner now builds to a final climax with the "Desire" leitmotif churning in the orchestra. But along the way, on the word "Lauschen" ("listen"), he suddenly changes dynamics. To which does he change?
   a. *pianissimo*   b. *fortissimo*

5. (4:45–5:18) The great climax has been reached. How does Wagner now musically depict the final words of Isolde "to drown, to sink down, in supreme bliss"?
   a. The vocal line falls, then soars up and holds a note.
   b. The vocal line soars up, then falls.
   c. The vocal line continually falls.

6. Which leitmotif is heard softly in the oboes (at 5:36) immediately before the final chord?
   a. "Ecstacy"   b. "Desire"   c. "Transcendent Bliss"

7. Who has the "last word" (who is heard at the very end of the *Liebestod*)?
   a. the voice   b. the orchestra

8. Which musical force could be omitted without serious loss to the music?
   a. the voice   b. the orchestra

9. Is the *Liebestod* through-composed (without large-scale repetition), or in *da capo* aria form? _____

10. Do you find this an exceptionally moving musical creation? Are you now a convert to the music of Wagner, a "perfect Wagnerite," to use George Bernard Shaw's phrase? _____

KEY WORDS

Bayreuth Festival Theater

bel canto

cabaletta

diva

Gesamtkunstwerk

La Scala

leitmotif

Liebestod

music drama

recitativo accompagnato

Ring cycle

Singspiel

verismo opera

LATE ROMANTICISM

When historians speak of "late Romanticism," they refer to the artistic developments that occurred in the West from about 1870 until 1900–1910, from the time of the Franco–Prussian War (1870) until shortly before the outbreak of World War I (1914). Of course, human activity, artistic or otherwise, rarely occurs within tidy chronological units. As we shall see, a strong anti–Romantic movement developed in France as early as the 1880s. Yet while some progressive artists began to turn away from Romanticism at this early date, other more conservative ones continued to compose in the late Romantic style into the 1940s. Romanticism had a strong hold on the consciousness of the listening public, one that it has not entirely relinquished even today.

During the last decades of the nineteenth century, orchestral music, especially German orchestral music, increasingly came to dominate the European musical scene. The continued growth in the size and color of the orchestra made listening to a symphony orchestra the most powerful aesthetic experience that a citizen of the late nineteenth century could enjoy. Not surprisingly, the force of the ever-larger orchestra affected the development of musical genres. We have seen that Wagner wrote operas in which the instrumental ensemble sometimes overwhelmed and absorbed the voice into its rich orchestral tapestry. Similarly, the orchestra began to infiltrate the realm of the art song, so that now the singer of a *Lied** was often accompanied not merely by a piano but by a full orchestra. So, too, the symphony orchestra expropriated the overture, taking it out of the theater and bringing it into the concert hall. And all the while the traditional four-movement symphony grew longer and more complex, a direct response to the increased number and variety of instruments. Let us review briefly the development of the symphony and concerto during the nineteenth century.

THE LATE ROMANTIC SYMPHONY AND CONCERTO

The four-movement symphony came into being during the Classical period, in the orchestral works of Haydn and Mozart (see page 185). Throughout the nineteenth century it remained a favorite with audiences everywhere, except in Italy, where opera was a national obsession. Symphonic composers in the Romantic period generally followed the four-movement format inherited from *composers write few, but long, symphonies and concertos*

their Classical forebears—fast, slow, minuet or scherzo, fast. But now the third movement might be almost any sort of light, contrasting creation, while the finale increasingly took on a more serious tone. As we have seen (page 242), the movements of a symphony grew in length in the course of the nineteenth century. Perhaps as a consequence of this greater length and seriousness, composers wrote fewer symphonies. Schumann and Brahms composed only four, Mendelssohn five, Tchaikovsky six, Dvořák, Bruckner, and Mahler each nine. No one approached the 40-odd symphonies of Mozart, to say nothing of the 104 of Haydn.

Similarly for the concerto, with expanded length came a reduction in number. A Classical concerto may last twenty minutes, a Romantic one forty; Mozart gave us twenty-three piano concertos, but Beethoven only five. Beethoven, Mendelssohn, Brahms, and Tchaikovsky penned just a single violin concerto, yet each is a substantial showpiece for the soloist. Despite its growing length, the Romantic concerto retained the three-movement plan established during the Classical period—fast, slow, fast.

the legacy of Beethoven

For a Romantic composer contemplating the creation of a symphony or concerto, no figure loomed larger than Beethoven. Wagner asked why anyone after Beethoven bothered to write symphonies at all, given the dramatic impact of Beethoven's Third, Fifth, and Ninth. Wagner himself wrote only one, Verdi none. Some composers, notably Berlioz and Liszt, turned to a completely different sort of symphony, the program symphony*, in which an external scenario determined the nature and order of the musical events. But these works sometimes lacked the force, internal unity, and compelling logic of a Beethoven symphony. It was not until the late Romantic period, nearly fifty years after the death of Beethoven, that someone came forth to claim the title of successor to Beethoven the symphonist. That figure was Johannes Brahms.

Johannes Brahms (1833–1897)

Brahms was born in the north German port city of Hamburg in 1833. He was given the Latin name Johannes to distinguish him from his father Johann, a street musician and "beer-hall" fiddler. Although Johannes's formal education never went beyond primary school, his father saw to it that he had the best training on the piano and in music theory. He was fed a heavy diet of the great masters: Bach's *The Well-Tempered Clavier* (see page 136), Beethoven's piano sonatas, and Haydn's chamber music. While he studied these by day, by night he earned money playing out-of-tune pianos in "stimulation bars" on the Hamburg waterfront. To get his hands on better instruments, he practiced daily in the showrooms of local piano stores.

Brahms first came to the public's attention in 1853, when Robert Schumann published a highly laudatory article announcing him to be something of a musical Messiah, the heir apparent of Haydn, Mozart, and Beethoven and their great legacy. Brahms, in turn, embraced both Schumanns, Robert and his wife Clara (see page 264), as his musical mentors. When Robert was confined to a mental institution in 1854, Brahms moved into the Schumann home for two years to help Clara raise her seven children. Not surprisingly, his respect and affection for Clara ripened into love, despite the fact that she was fourteen years his senior. Yet for whatever reason—they both later destroyed many of their letters to each other—their mutual affection did not culminate in marriage after

❉ F I G U R E 15–1
Johannes Brahms in his early thirties. Said an observer of the time: "The broad chest, the herculean shoulders, the powerful head, which he threw back energetically when playing—all betrayed an artistic personality replete with the spirit of true genius."

Robert's death. Brahms remained a bachelor for the duration of his life.

Disappointed first in love and then in his attempts to gain an official position in his native Hamburg, Brahms in 1862 moved to Vienna. He contracted to conduct choral groups from time to time, but for the most part was able to maintain his modest lifestyle—"very un-Wagnerian" he called it—with fees earned as a concert pianist and with royalties accruing from the publication of his ever-growing list of compositions. His fame increased dramatically in 1868 with performances of his *A German Requiem*, which was sold to amateur choruses around the world. Honorary degrees were offered from Cambridge University (1876) and Breslau University (1879). After Wagner's death in 1883, he was generally considered the greatest living German composer. His own death, from liver cancer, came in the spring of 1897. He was buried in the central cemetery of Vienna, thirty feet from the graves of Beethoven and Schubert.

FIGURE 15–2
Brahms's composing room in Vienna. On the wall, looking down on the piano, is a bust of Beethoven. The spirit of Beethoven loomed large over the entire nineteenth century (see also the cover) and over Brahms in particular.

That Brahms should choose Vienna as his home is not surprising—it was then a city of nearly a million people, the fifth largest in the world. But, more important, Vienna had been the home of Haydn, Mozart, Beethoven, and Schubert. In the music of these past masters the conservative Brahms sought inspiration. He returned again and again to the genres (symphony, concerto, quartet, and sonata) and forms (sonata–allegro, theme and variations, and rondo) that they had established or popularized. Most telling, Brahms composed no program music—what to other nineteenth-century musicians like Liszt and Berlioz was the very soul of Romantic music. Instead, he chose to write **absolute music,** chamber sonatas, symphonies, and concertos without any sort of program. In these, Brahms did not indulge in unrestrained expression as had Berlioz, Liszt, and Wagner, but maintained a sense of balance by setting Romantic themes within the tight confines of traditional music forms. Brahms could write songful Romantic melodies, but he was at heart a contrapuntalist, a "developer" in the tradition of Bach and Beethoven. Indeed, soon he would be dubbed the last of the musically famous "three B's": Bach, Beethoven, and Brahms.

Brahms the conservative

VIOLIN CONCERTO IN D MAJOR (1878)

In 1870 Johannes Brahms wrote: "I shall never compose a symphony! You have no idea how the likes of us feel when we hear the tramp of a giant like him behind us." Brahms, of course, was referring to Beethoven. He was terrified by the prospect of competing with the symphonies of that "giant." But Brahms did go on to write a symphony—indeed, four of them, each in four movements. They were first performed, in turn, in 1876, 1877, 1883, and 1885. In the midst of this symphonic activity, Brahms also wrote his only violin concerto, a worthy rival of the earlier violin concerto of Beethoven.

By training and profession, Brahms was a pianist, not a violinist. For help with regard to violin bowing and fingering he turned to his long-time friend and playing partner Johann Joachim (Fig. 15–3). When the concerto received its premiere at the Gewandhaus (see Figs. 13–9 and 13–10), it was virtuoso Joachim who played the solo part while Brahms conducted the orchestra. One technical skill that Brahms required of the soloist is the art of playing **double stops.** Usually we think of the violin as a monophonic* instrument, capable of executing only one line of music. But a good violinist can hold (stop) two and sometimes more strings simultaneously and sweep across them with the bow. This imparts a richer, more brilliant sound to the soloist's part. Example 15–1 shows how Brahms incorporates double stops into the melody of the last movement of his concerto.

EXAMPLE 15–1

🌸 FIGURE 15–3
Johann Joachim (1831–1907), the virtuoso who first performed Brahms's Violin Concerto.

When he arrived at the finale of his Violin Concerto, Brahms the conservative turned to a form traditionally used in the last movement of a concerto: the rondo. Recall that a rondo centers on a single theme that serves as a musical refrain. Here the refrain has the flavor of a gypsy tune, like the Hungarian dances Brahms often heard in the Prater Park in Vienna as he sipped beer and chatted with friends. What marks this refrain is its lively rhythm (♩♪♪♪♩ ♪♪♪♪). Above this foot-tapping motive the violin sometimes soars with difficult passage work (scales, arpeggios, and double stops). The technical demands placed on the soloist caused one musician of the day to complain that Brahms had not written a concerto "for" the violin but rather "against" it. To which a later virtuoso replied: "Brahm's concerto is not against the violin, but for violin against orchestra—and the violin wins."

LISTENING GUIDE

Johannes Brahms
Violin Concerto in D major (1878)
Third movement, *Allegro giocoso, ma non tropo vivace*
(fast and playful, but not too lively)

6CD 4/11;
2CD 2/6

Form: rondo

0:00	Refrain played by violin and then by orchestra	A	
0:56	Transition: racing scales in violin		
1:20	New theme moves up, and then down, a major scale	B	
2:09	Violin returns with refrain; orchestra repeats it	A	
2:49	Violin plays more lyrical theme built on arpeggio	C	

(Continued on next page)

Time	Description	Section
3:55	Rising scale in violin, answered by falling scale in orchestra	B
4:46	Elaboration of rhythm of refrain	
5:07	Orchestra plays refrain *fortissimo*	A
5:35	Violin plays very brief cadenza*, then rhythm of refrain developed	
6:46	Another brief cadenza*	
6:55	Rhythm of refrain becomes march-like	CODA

(Listening Exercise 31)

VOCAL MUSIC FROM CRADLE TO GRAVE. Brahms wrote very serious music. When he wanted to "lighten up," he did so in his *Lieder,* songs for solo voice and piano. Brahm's most famous *Lied,* perhaps the best-known art song ever written, is his *Wiegenlied (Lullaby).* He drew the text from a collection of folk poetry, and fashioned the melody from a tune a girlfriend had once sung to him. The piano accompaniment is a syncopated waltz. Above it the voice sings a melody that is as profoundly simple as it is beautiful.

LISTENING GUIDE

Johannes Brahms
Lullaby (1868)

Intro CD/16

Meter: triple
Genre: *Lied*
Form: strophic

0:00	Piano introduction		
0:05	Soprano sings first strophe	Guten Abend, gut Nacht,	Good evening, good night,
		Mit rosen bedacht,	Covered with roses,
		Mit Näglein besteckt	Adorned with carnations,
		Schlupf unter die Deck':	Slip under the covers.
		Morgen früh, wenn Gott will,	Tomorrow early, if God so wills,
		Wirst du wieder gewecht.	You will awake again.
0:50	Repeat of piano introduction		
0:56	Soprano sings second strophe of text to same melody	Guten Abend, gut Nacht,	Good evening, good night,
		Von Englien bewacht,	Watched over by angels,
		Die zeigen im Traum	Who in dreams show
		Dir Christkindleins Baum:	You the Christ child's tree.
		Schlaf nun selig und süss,	Now sleep blissful and sweetly,
		Schau im Traum's Paradies.	Behold Paradise in your dreams.

The serious—and conservative—Brahms can be heard again in his *A German Requiem.* The idea of composing a Mass for the Dead gradually coalesced in his mind following the death of his teacher, Robert Schumann, and then, in 1865, of his mother. What Brahms created was not a burial service for either the official Catholic church or the German Lutheran church. Nowhere can be heard the voice of the wrathful God of judgment. Rather, *A German Requiem* is

A German Requiem

a personal, nonsectarian confession of faith, full of sounds of solace for all who have suffered loss through death. For texts of consolation, Brahms drew equally from the Old and New Testament. For musical inspiration, he again turned to the music of past masters. Brahms had studied and conducted the motets* of Palestrina and the cantatas* of Bach. He wedded their old-style counterpoint to the sound of the large-scale nineteenth-century chorus.

The emotional core of this hour-long, seven-movement work is its fourth movement. "How lovely is Thy dwelling place," says the text of Psalm 84, and before us looms an image of the heavenly House of the Lord. Imitating the bliss-ful souls in heaven, a four-part chorus sings praises to the Lord in a skillful blend of homophonic and polyphonic textures. The interplay between chorus and or-chestra is evident at the very outset. The opening phrase played by the wood-winds is immediately sung in mirror image by the sopranos (see musical example in the Listening Guide). Such contrapuntal details rest at the heart of Brahm's compositional style. The challenge to the listener is to hear the counterpoint in the midst of the richly soothing sound of the Romantic chorus and orchestra.

Brahms's counterpoint

| LISTENING GUIDE | Johannes Brahms
A German Requiem (1868)
Fourth movement, "How lovely is Thy dwelling place" | 6CD 4/12 |

Text: Psalm 84, verses 1, 2 and 4

0:00   Woodwinds play peaceful melody

0:07	Sopranos respond in same mood	Wie lieblich sind deine Wohnungen, Herr Zebaoth!	How lovely is Thy dwelling place, O, Lord of Hosts!
0:44	Tenors sing same text, basses, altos and sopranos follow in imitative counterpoint		
1:23	More imitative counterpoint sung by chorus	Meine Seele verlanget und sehnet sich nach den Vorhöfen des Herrn;	My soul longs and thirsts for the courts of the Lord;
1:56	Chorus sings homophony with strong accents in orchestra	Mein Leib und Seele freuen sich in dem Lebendigen Gott.	My body and soul rejoice in the living God.
2:26	Return of opening music in orchestra and then chorus	Wie lieblich . . .	How lovely . . .
3:15	Chorus quietly sings chordal homophony	Wohl denen, die in deinem Hause wohnen,	Blessed are they who dwell in Thy House,
3:38	Chorus declaims its praise of the Lord in forceful imitative counterpoint	die loben Dich immerdar.	where they praise you ever after.
4:27	Return of opening music and text	Wie lieblich . . .	How lovely . . .

Antonín Dvořák (1841–1904)

"There is no doubt that he is very talented. He is also very poor." Thus Johannes Brahms wrote to the music publisher Simrock in 1876 describing the then-unknown thirty-five-year-old Antonín Dvořák. Dvořák, the son of a butcher, had come from Bohemia, an area of the Czech Republic south of Prague. Young Antonín, too, passed an apprenticeship to be a butcher, but a prosperous uncle saw musical talent in the teenager and sent him to study organ in Prague for a year. Thereafter, for nearly two decades, Dvořák eked out a living as a freelance violist and organist in Prague, playing in dance bands, the opera orchestra, and in church. All the while he composed tirelessly—operas, symphonies, string quartets, and songs, almost all of which went unheard.

Brahms's intervention with the publisher Simrock proved decisive in Dvořák's career. Soon the Czech composer's charming *Slavonic Dances* for piano duet were available in music stores across Europe, and they caught on like wildfire. Simrock's firm got rich from this publication, though Dvořák received only the equivalent of two months of his usual salary. (There was no such thing as artists' royalties at this time; the composer or author simply sold the work for a flat fee to the publisher, who took all risks and kept all revenues.) What Dvořák did receive from his publications was recognition. Commissions from various orchestras and conductors now came like a flood. During the 1880s his symphonies, string quartets, and choral works were heard in London, Berlin, Vienna, Dresden, Leipzig, Moscow, Budapest, and even Cincinnati, which then had a strong Bohemian component to its population.

In the spring of 1892 Dvořák received an offer he couldn't refuse. He was promised the astonishing sum of $15,000 per year (the equivalent of about $500,000 today) to became the Director of the newly founded National Conservatory of Music in New York City. So on September 17, 1892, Dvořák set sail for America and ultimately took up residence at 327 East 17th Street (see Fig. 15–5). It was here that he began work on his "American" Quartet and his Symphony "From the New World." Instead of returning to Prague that summer, Dvořák and his family traveled by train and carriage to Spillville, Iowa, spending three months among the mainly Czech-speaking people of this rural farming community. After two more winters in New York City as Director of the National Conservatory, he returned to his native Bohemia for good. He died in Prague in 1904, the Czechs' most famous and beloved composer.

🌸 FIGURE 15–4 AND 15–5
(above) Antonín Dvořák conducting: a painting now hanging in the Dvořák Museum in Prague. (left) 327 East 17th Street, Dvořák's residence in New York City during 1892–1894.

Dvořák moves to the "New World"

DR. DVORAK'S
GREAT SYMPHONY.

"From the New World" Heard for
the First Time at the Philharmonic Rehearsal.

ABOUT THE SALIENT BEAUTIES.

First Movement the Most Tragic, Second
the Most Beautiful, Third the
Most Sprightly.

INSPIRED BY INDIAN MUSIC.

The Director of the National Conservatory Adds a Masterpiece to
Musical Literature.

Dr. Antonin Dvorak, the famous Bohemian
composer and director of the National Conservatory of Music, dowered American art with a
great work yesterday, when his new symphony
in E minor, "From the New World," was played
at the second Philharmonic rehearsal in Carnegie Music Hall.
The day was an important one in the musical
history of America. It witnessed the first public
performance of a noble composition.
It saw a large audience of usually tranquil
Americans enthusiastic to the point of frenzy
over a musical work and applauding like the
most excitable "Italianissimi" in the world.
The work was one of heroic proportions. And
it was one cast in the art form which such poet
musicians as Beethoven, Schubert, Schumann,
Mendelssohn, Brahms and many another "glorious one of the earth" has enriched with the
most precious outwellings of his musical imagination.

✺ FIGURE 15-6

A review of the premiere of the Symphony "From the New World" in the *New York Herald*, December 16, 1893.

SYMPHONY "FROM THE NEW WORLD" (1893)

The Symphony "From the New World" in E minor, Dvořák's ninth and last symphony, is by far his best-known work. It received a rousing premiere in New York City, at the newly built Carnegie Hall, on December 16, 1893. As Dvořák wrote to his publisher, Simrock, the following week:

> The success of the symphony was tremendous. The papers write that no composer has ever had such a triumph (see Fig. 15–6). I was in a box. The hall was filled with the best New York audience. The people clapped so much that I had to thank them from the box like a king! You know how glad I am if I can avoid such ovations, but there was no getting out of it, and I had to show myself like-it-or-not.

The title that Dvořák gave to this symphony, "From the New World," might suggest that he placed within it musical elements that are distinctly American. Yet while Dvořák showed a keen interest in the indigenous music of African Americans and American Indians, none of the many tuneful melodies heard in this symphony can be identified as a preexisting folk song. They came from Dvořák's own head and heart. And although these melodies, especially those of the famous *Largo*, do possess a "folk style" quality, they may be as much Czech as American in inspiration.

First movement (Adagio: Allegro molto; "Slow: Very fast"). A satisfying blend of forceful energy and tuneful lyricism mark this opening movement in strict sonata–allegro form. Solo wind instruments—French horn, oboe, and flute—introduce the principal themes, and then leave it to the strings to propel the music forward.

Second movement (Largo; "Slow and broad"). The "emotional soul" of this symphony rests in this second movement, the famous Largo. The essence of musical Romanticism can be felt here in the prolonged gestures—as heard in the low brass introduction—and the wealth of beautiful melodies—such as the haunting English horn solo (see Fig. 15–7). This latter tune was soon extracted from the symphony and became a popular American song under the title "Goin' home."

✺ FIGURE 15-7

An autograph sketch of the famous English horn theme from the second movement (*Largo*) of Dvořák's Symphony "From the New World."

LISTENING GUIDE

Antonín Dvořák
Symphony No. 9, "From the New World" (1893)
Second movement, *Largo* (Slow and broad)

6CD 4/13

Form: **ABCA**

A

0:00   Solemn introductory chords by low brass choir, then timpani

0:50   English horn solo, the "Goin' home" melody

1:18   Clarinet joins English horn, then strings join as well

2:33   Introductory chords now played by high woodwinds and French horn, concluded by brasses and timpani

3:05   Strings play and extend "Goin' home" melody

3:59   Melody returns to English horn and is completed by strings and woodwinds

4:41   French horn echoes the melody

B

5:08   Faster tempo and new theme (**B1**) in flute and oboe

5:35   Second new theme (**B2**) in clarinets above bass pizzicato

6:22   Melody **B1** played more insistently by violins

7:18   Melody **B2** played more intensely by violins

C

8:22   Oboe leads chirping of high woodwinds

8:49   Brasses play *fortissimo* recall of first theme of first movement

9:02   Diminuendo and lovely transition back to

A

9:18   English horn brings back "Goin' home" melody

9:48   Pairs of violins and violas play melody but break off, as if choked by emotion

10:23   Solo cello and solo violin play melody, then full strings join

11:02   Quiet, monophonic soliloquy by violins

11:30   Final return and extension of opening chords

Third movement (Molto vivace; "Very fast and lively"). Dvořák said this scherzo was intended to depict "a feast in the woods where the Indians dance." Yet the only time Dvořák actually heard "live" American Indian music was when he saw a performance of Buffalo Bill's Wild West Show, and there the commercialized songs had little to do with authentic Indian melodies. For most listeners this scherzo is more suggestive of frolicking Bohemian peasants than dancing American Indians.

Fourth movement (Allegro con fuoco; "Fast with fire"). The stirring finale presents a succession of exciting themes in the brasses while also recalling melodies from the three previous movements, thereby binding the symphony into a satisfying whole.

✿ LATE ROMANTIC PROGRAM MUSIC

Program music, as we have seen (pages 242–243), was at the very heart of the creative works of the early Romantics, like Berlioz, Mendelssohn, and Liszt. While Brahms, later in the century, held fast to the Classical ideal of absolute music*, most late Romantic composers continued to yield to the allure of music inspired by some sort of extramusical element—a play, an experience with nature, even a painting. The late-nineteenth-century composer who achieved the greatest popular success in writing program music was Peter Tchaikovsky. Tchaikovsky was not a Russian nationalist*; rather, he composed in the then-dominant German orchestral style.

Peter Tchaikovsky (1840–1893)

Tchaikovsky was born in 1840 into an upper-middle-class family in provincial Russia. He showed a keen ear for music in his earliest years, and by the age of six could speak fluent French and German (an excellent musical ear and a capacity to learn foreign languages often go hand in hand). As to his career, his parents determined that law would provide the easiest route to fame and fortune. Thus, young Tchaikovsky spent seven years, 1852–1859, at the School of Jurisprudence in St. Petersburg and four more years as a clerk in the Ministry of Justice. Then, like Robert Schumann before him, he realized that it was music, not law, that fired his imagination. He made his way to the St. Petersburg Conservatory of Music, from which he was graduated in 1866. That same year, he went to the newly formed Moscow Conservatory, where he assumed the position of professor of harmony and musical composition.

In truth, it was not his official position in Moscow that supported Tchaikovsky during most of his mature years, but rather a private arrangement with an eccentric patroness, Madame Nadezhda von Meck (Fig. 15–9). This wealthy, music-loving widow furnished him an annual income of six thousand rubles on the condition that she and the composer never meet—a requirement not always easily fulfilled, since the two sometimes resided at the same summer estate. In addition to this annuity, in 1881 Tsar Alexander III awarded Tchaikovsky an annual pension of three thousand rubles in recognition of his importance to Russian cultural life. Being a man of independent means meant that Tchaikovsky not only was able to travel extensively in Western Europe, and even to America, but could also enjoy the freedom he found so necessary to creative activity.

Tchaikovsky's creative output touched every genre of nineteenth-century music: opera, song, string quartet, piano sonata, concerto, symphony, and symphonic poem. It is, however, his large-scale works for orchestra that have best stood the test of time. Tchaikovsky's musical strengths—sweeping melodies, colorful instrumentations, dramatic contrasts, and grand gestures—could only be fully expressed by a large symphony orchestra. Not surprisingly, he also achieved unparalleled success as a composer of orchestral music for ballet, a type of music in which short bursts of colorful sounds and evocative rhythms are necessary to

❀ FIGURE 15–8
Peter Tchaikovsky.

❀ FIGURE 15–9
Nadezhda von Meck was the widow of an engineer who made a fortune constructing the first railroads in Russia during the 1860s and 1870s. She used her money, in part, to support composers like Tchaikovsky and, later, Claude Debussy.

create distinctly different moods for each new scene. His *Swan Lake* (1876), *Sleeping Beauty* (1889), and *Nutcracker* (1892) are the most popular works in the entire repertoire of grand Romantic ballet, beloved by young and old alike.

Despite his considerable popular success, Tchaikovsky's life was not a happy one. He was a manic-depressive, a neurotic, and a hypochondriac. He was also a homosexual, and this was a time when there was little sympathy for homosexuality or awareness of its biological causes. He died suddenly in 1893, at the age of fifty-three, after drinking unboiled water during an epidemic of cholera.

SYMPHONIC POEM, *ROMEO AND JULIET* (1869)

Tchaikovsky was at his best when writing illustrative music for large orchestra, whether a program symphony, a one-movement symphonic poem*, or music for ballet. He called his most overtly programmatic works sometimes simply "overture," sometimes "overture fantasy," and sometimes "symphonic fantasy." We may broadly group these one-movement programmatic pieces in the general category of symphonic poem. As with Berlioz, Mendelssohn, and Liszt before him, it was the plays of Shakespeare that provided the strongest extramusical stimulation. Of his three symphonic poems based on works of Shakespeare—*Romeo and Juliet* (1869), *The Tempest* (1877), and *Hamlet* (1888)—the earliest is best. Indeed, it was his first masterpiece.

his program music

Just as Mendelssohn captures the spirit, not the letter, of Shakespeare's *Midsummer Night's Dream* (see page 262), so Tchaikovsky offers a free, not literal, presentation of the principal dramatic elements of *Romeo and Juliet*. In fact, he distills these into just three musical themes: the compassionate music of the kindly Friar Laurence, whose plan to unite the lovers goes fatally awry; the fighting music, which represents the feud between the Capulets and Montagues; and the love theme, which expresses the passion of Romeo and Juliet. Once again, sonata–allegro form provides the arena in which the musical drama will be played out. The introduction presents the music of Friar Laurence, then anguished dissonant sounds in the strings and French horn, and finally a succession of beautifully mysterious chords with strumming by a harp, as if Friar Laurence, like a medieval bard, were about to narrate a tragic tale. When the exposition begins, we hear angry, percussive music, racing strings, and syncopated cymbal crashes: This is the violent world of the Capulets and Montagues. Soon the fighting subsides and the love theme emerges. As appropriate for a pair of lovers, it is in two parts, each of which has the capacity to grow and become more passionate when pushed upward in ascending sequences:

themes from Shakespeare's Romeo and Juliet

EXAMPLE 15–2A

EXAMPLE 15–2B

The brief development pits the feuding families against the increasingly ada-
mant pleas of Friar Laurence. The recapitulation, true to sonata form, begins
with the feud music, but moves quickly to an expanded, more ecstatic presentation of the love theme (part 2 first, then part 1), which is eventually cut off by
a noisy return of the feuding clans. The beginning of the dramatic coda is an-
nounced by a foreboding *fortissimo* roll on the timpani. As we hear the steady
drumbeats of a funeral procession and fragments of the broken love theme, we
know that Romeo and Juliet are dead. A celestial hymnlike passage (a transformation of the love theme) suggests the lovers have been united above, a feeling
then confirmed by the return of the love theme in high violins. There only remains to bring the curtain down on the story of the star-crossed lovers, which
Tchaikovsky does with seven *fortissimo* hammer strokes for full orchestra, all on
the tonic chord.

a Romantic ending

Shakespeare wrote *Romeo and Juliet* as a tragedy: "For never was a story of
more woe/Than this of Juliet and her Romeo," say the final lines of the play. By
incorporating a "celestial conclusion" into his coda—a hymnlike choir of an-
gelic woodwinds followed by the transcendent love theme on high in the violins—Tchaikovsky has changed the final import of the play. True child of the
Romantic age, he suggests that the love-death of Romeo and Juliet was, in fact,
not a tragedy but their spiritual triumph.

| LISTENING GUIDE | Peter Tchaikovsky Symphonic poem, *Romeo and Juliet* (1869) | 6CD 5/1 |

Form: sonata–allegro

INTRODUCTION

0:00   Friar Laurence theme sounding organlike in the woodwinds

0:36   Anguished, dissonant sound in strings and French horn
1:25   Harp alternates with flute solo and woodwinds
2:07   Friar Laurence theme returns with new accompaniment
2:34   Anguished sound returns in strings and French horn
3:23   Harp strumming returns
3:56   Timpani roll and string tremolos build tension; hints of Friar Laurence theme in woodwinds
4:31   Anguished sound again returns, then yields to crescendo on repeating tonic chord

EXPOSITION

5:01   Feud theme in agitated minor; angry rhythmic motive in woodwinds,
         racing scales in strings

5:48   Crashing syncopations (with cymbal) running against scales

(Continued on next page)

6:19   Gentle transition, with release of tension, to second theme

6:57   Love theme (part 1) played quietly by English horn and viola

7:13   Love theme (part 2) played quietly by strings with mutes

7:51   Love theme (part 1) returns with growing ardor in high woodwinds while
        French horn plays counterpoint against it

8:51   Lyrical closing section in which cellos and English horn engage in dialogue against backdrop of gently plucked
        chords in harp

DEVELOPMENT

9:52   Feud theme against which French horn soon plays Friar Laurence theme (10:04)

10:11   String syncopations, again against Friar Laurence theme

10:38   Feud theme and Friar Laurence theme continue in opposition

11:23   Cymbal crashes signal climax of development as trumpet blares forth with Friar Laurence theme (11:30)

RECAPITULATION

11:58   Feud theme in woodwinds and brasses against racing strings

12:21   Love theme (part 2) softly in woodwinds

13:00   Love theme (part 1) sounds ecstatically with all its inherent force and sweep

13:41   Love theme begins again in strings, with counterpoint in brasses

14:01   Fragments of Love theme in strings, then brasses

14:28   Love theme begins again but is cut off by Feud theme; syncopated cymbal crashes (14:36)

14:43   Feud theme and Friar Laurence theme build to a climax

15:43   Timpani roll announces coda

CODA

15:52   Timpani beats a funeral march while strings play fragments of Love theme

16:38   Love theme (part 2) transformed into the sound of a heavenly chorale* played by woodwinds

17:43   Transcendent Love theme sounds from on high in violins

18:18   Timpani roll and final chords

(Listening Exercise 32)

 THE ORCHESTRAL SONG

We began our discussion of Romantic music with two art songs* of Franz Schubert (pages 246–252), and we end it with an orchestral song by Gustav Mahler (1860–1911). This is an appropriate framework in which to experience Romantic music, for the nineteenth century was marked throughout by an exceptionally strong union between music and poetry. If poetry had the power to communicate feelings of love, grief, pain, or longing, these typically Romantic sentiments could not fail to be intensified when set to music. Thus, the art song came into being in the early nineteenth century. At about the same time, Beethoven incorporated song into the finale of his Ninth ("Choral") Symphony (1824), as Berlioz and Liszt would also do in their later programmatic symphonies. Naturally, it was only a matter of time before the genres of art song and symphony began to interact and influence each other, producing something new: the orchestral song. In its simplest form the **orchestral song** was an

art song in which the full orchestra replaced the piano as the medium of accompaniment. Yet because the orchestra could supply more color and add a greater number of contrapuntal lines, the orchestral song grew to be longer, denser, and more complex than the piano-supported art song. Berlioz, Brahms, and Wagner all experimented with the orchestral song in various ways, but not until Gustav Mahler did this hybrid musical genre reach maturity.

Gustav Mahler (1860–1911)

Gustav Mahler was born in 1860 into a middle-class Jewish family in Bohemia, then part of the Austrian Empire but now encompassed by the new Czech Republic. At the age of fifteen he was admitted to the prestigious Vienna Conservatory of Music, where he studied musical composition and conducting. Mahler felt his mission in life was to conduct—to interpret—the works of the masters ("suffer for my great masters," he said). Like most young conductors, he began his career in provincial towns, gradually working his way to larger and more important musical centers. His itinerary as resident conductor took him along the following route: Bad Hall (1880), Laibach (1881–1882), Olmütz (1883), Kassel (1883–1884), Prague (1885–1886), Leipzig (1886–1888), Budapest (1888–1891), Hamburg (1891–1897), and finally back to Vienna.

In May 1897 Mahler returned triumphantly to his adopted city as director of the Vienna Court Opera, a position Mozart had once coveted. The next year he also assumed directorship of the Vienna Philharmonic, then and now one of the world's great orchestras. But Mahler was a demanding autocrat—a musical tyrant—in search of an artistic ideal. That he drove himself as hard as he pushed others was little comfort to the singers and instrumentalists who had to endure his wrath during rehearsals. After ten stormy but artistically successful seasons (1897–1907), Mahler was dismissed from the Vienna Opera. About this time he accepted a call from New York to take charge of the Metropolitan Opera and, eventually, he conducted the New York Philharmonic as well. Here, too, there was both controversy and acclaim. And here, too, at least at the Met, his contract was not renewed after two years, though he stayed on longer, until February 1911, with the Philharmonic. He died in Vienna in May 1911 of a lingering streptococcal infection that had attacked his weak heart—a sad end to an obsessive and somewhat tormented life.

Mahler is unique among composers in that as a mature artist he wrote only orchestral songs and symphonies. These he managed to create during the summers when freed of his conducting duties. His five orchestral song cycles* typically contain settings of four, five, or six poems by a single author. *Kindertotenlieder* (*Children's Death Songs*, 1901–1904), for example, is a collection of five songs for voice and orchestra to words by Friedrich Rückert (1788–1866). They express the poet's overwhelming grief on the loss of two young children to scarlet fever. By tragic coincidence, no sooner had Mahler finished setting Rückert's painfully personal memorials than his own eldest daughter died of scarlet fever at the age of four, a loss from which the intensely sensitive composer never recovered.

🌿 FIGURE 15–10
Gustav Mahler.

🌿 FIGURE 15–11
Gustav Mahler conducting in the orchestra pit of the Vienna Court Opera. Mahler earned his living as a conductor and was free to devote himself to composition only during the summer months.

What is also unique to Mahler is the extent to which he borrowed from his own orchestral songs when he sat down to compose a symphony. It is as if the songs served as a musical repository or vault to which the composer could return for inspiration while wrestling with the problems of a large, multimovement work for orchestra. Mahler's First Symphony (1889), though entirely instrumental, makes use of melodies already present in his song cycle *Lieder eines fahrenden Gesellen* (*Songs of a Wayfaring Lad*, 1885). His Second (1894), Third (1896), and Fourth (1901) symphonies incorporate various portions of the *Wonderhorn Songs* (1892–1899) as solo vocal parts within the symphony. Symphonies Five (1902) and Six (1904) are again purely instrumental, but once more incorporate preexisting melodies, in this case from *Children's Death Songs* and *Five Rückert Songs* (1901–1902). Altogether Mahler wrote nine symphonies, seven of which make use of his own orchestral songs or other preexisting vocal music.

songs and symphonies

But to Mahler a symphony was much more than just an extended orchestral song. "The symphony is the world; it must embrace everything," he once said. And so he tried to embrace every sort of music within it. There are folk dances, popular songs, military marches, off-stage bands, bugle calls, and even Gregorian chant* at various points in his symphonies. What results is a collage of sound on the grandest scale, one achieved, in part, by employing massive forces and a greatly extended sense of time. Mahler's Symphony No. 2, for example, calls for ten horns and eight trumpets, and lasts an hour and a half. The first performance of his Symphony No. 8 in Munich in 1910 involved 858 singers and 171 instrumentalists. With good reason it has been nicknamed the "Symphony of a Thousand."

"Symphony of a Thousand"

Gustav Mahler was the last in the long line of great German symphonists that extended back through Brahms, Schubert, and Beethoven to Mozart and, ultimately, to Haydn. What had begun as a modest instrumental genre with a limited emotional range had grown in the course of the nineteenth century into a monumental structure, the musical equivalent, in Mahler's view, of the entire cosmos.

Life Among the Artists

In 1901 middle-aged Gustav Mahler married the dazzling Viennese beauty Alma Schindler (1879–1964). She was the daughter of a noted Austrian landscape painter and was in her own right a talented pianist and budding composer. As a precondition to their marriage, however, Mahler insisted that Alma give up her own career in music to serve his art. Given this infringement of her liberty and the fact that she was just slightly more than half Mahler's age, it is not surprising that their marriage was not a tranquil one. At one point, in 1910, Mahler consulted the famous Sigmund Freud, father of psychoanalysis, in hopes of coming to a better understanding of himself and his union with Alma. (Freud declined to treat Mahler, apparently for fear of destroying the latter's creative process.) After the composer's death in 1911, Alma went on to have affairs with the conductor Bruno Walter and the painter Oskar Kokoschka, and later to marry the architect Walter Gropius and the novelist Franz Werfel. Obviously, Alma Schindler had a keen eye for talent. Her tongue was equally sharp, as can be seen in the following extracts from her memoirs *And the Bridge Was Love*, which describe Mahler's work habits at their lakeside summer home in southern Austria.

Alma Schindler Mahler in 1902, shortly after her marriage to Gustav Mahler

"Mahler got up at six or six-thirty every day. As soon as he was awake, he rang for the cook, who promptly prepared his breakfast and carried it up a steep, slippery trail to his forest study, two hundred feet above the house. (She was forbidden to use the regular road, lest he meet her on his way up; before work, he could not stand seeing anyone.) The study was a one-room brick hut with a door and three windows, a grand piano, a bookshelf with the collected works of Kant and Goethe. No music but Bach's. About noon he came down, changed, and went for a swim. . . . Our afternoons were spent walking. Rain or shine, we walked for three or four hours, or rowed around the gleaming, heat-spewing lake. . . . Often he stopped and stood with the sun burning down on his hatless skull, drew out a notebook, wrote, thought, wrote some more. Sometimes he beat time in the air before writing the notes down. This could go on for an hour or more, with me sitting on a tree trunk or in the grass, not daring to look at him. Mahler made sure that everything in his personal life revolved around his own genius."

ORCHESTRAL SONG, *I AM LOST TO THE WORLD*, FROM THE *FIVE RÜCKERT SONGS* (1901–1902)

It is the everyday world, not the grand cosmos, that concerns Mahler in his setting of Friedrich Rückert's *Ich bin der Welt abhanden gekommen (I Am Lost to the World)*. Rückert was a minor German Romantic poet whose verse, nonetheless, enjoyed favor with Schubert, Schumann, and Brahms because of its structural regularity. During the summers of 1901 and 1902, Mahler chose to set five among the many hundreds of poems by Rückert. The subject of these five verses was dear to the composer because it expresses in various ways his outlook on life and on art.

an artist withdraws into the world of music

I Am Lost to the World speaks of the artist's growing remoteness from the travails of everyday life and of withdrawal into a private, heavenly world of music, here signified by the final word *Lied* (song). Although the poem has three stanzas, Mahler chose not a strophic setting*, but a through-composed* one. The first strophe sets the mood of the song as a mournful English horn begins to play a halting melody, one then picked up and extended by the voice. The second stanza moves to a faster tempo and more rapid declamation in the voice, as if the mundane world should be quickly left behind. The final strophe returns to a slow tempo. It also sets the notes of the bass on the beat and on the roots of triads*, all of which help project a settled, satisfied feeling—the self-absorbed

poet-composer has withdrawn into the peaceful world of art. Toward the end Mahler shows how music has the capacity to sum up in a few brief sounds the entire progress of the poem, the movement from the dissonance of the world to the peace of the inner self. First the strings (at 6:23) play an extended dissonance (F against E♭), which resolves to a consonance (E♭ against E♭), and this is repeated at the very end (6:39) by the English horn, "dying out expressively" as the composer requests. The desire to escape from this dissonant world into the consonant realm of art has been fulfilled.

I Am Lost to the World has been called Mahler's best orchestral song. That he made use of some of this same music in the beautiful slow movement of his Symphony No. 5 suggests that these musical ideas were important to him and express, as he said at the time, "his very self." Both song and symphony have a certain world-weariness about them, as if Mahler had a premonition that both the artist's life and the Romantic era were coming to an end.

FIGURE 15–12

Mahler spent his summers at various villas in the Austrian mountains, but he made sure that each was supplied with a "forest hut" where he could go each morning to compose without distraction. The last of these composing chalets, at Alt-Schluderbach, is today one of the more accessible ones.

LISTENING GUIDE

Gustav Mahler
Orchestral song, *I Am Lost to the World,*
from the *Five Rückert Songs* (1901–1902)

6CD 5/2

Form: through composed

0:00	English horn haltingly rises with the melody		
1:00	Voice enters and extends the melody	Ich bin der Welt abhanden gekommen, mit der ich sonst viele Zeit verdorben; sie hat so lange nichts von mir vernommen,	I am lost to the world, in which I've squandered so much time; it has known nothing of me for so long,
1:56	English horn returns with the melody	sie mag wohl glauben, ich sei gestorben!	it may well think that I am dead!
2:34	Triplets in harp; faster tempo, recitative quality in the voice	Es ist mir auch gar nichts daran gelegen, ob sie mich für gestorben hält. Ich kann auch gar nichts sagen dagegen, denn wirklich bin ich gestorben der Welt.	I don't really care, if it takes me for dead. Nor can I contradict, for really I am dead to the world.
3:39	Melody returns in English horn; slow, peaceful conclusion	Ich bin gestorben dem Weltgetümmel und ruh' in einem stillen Gebiet! Ich leb' allein in meinem Himmel, in meinem Lieben, in meinem Lied.	I am dead to the world's commotion, and rest in a world of peace. I live alone in my own heaven, in my love, in my song.
5:47	English horn returns with melody		
6:23	Dissonance–consonance in violins		
6:39	Dissonance–consonance in English horn		

(Listening Exercise 33)

LISTENING EXERCISES

 Johannes Brahms   6CD 4/11; 2CD 2/6
Violin Concerto in D major (1878)
Third movement, *Allegro giocoso, ma non troppo vivace*
(fast and playful, but not too lively)

We derive our term "concerto" from the Italian word *concertare*. A concerto involves a concerted effort, and sometimes a friendly competition, between a soloist and an orchestra. In the finale of Brahm's Violin Concerto, the violin and orchestra vie for control of the theme, and sometimes there is a real tug of war between the two. At other moments, however, the orchestra merely accompanies the virtuosic flights of the soloist. The following questions focus on the nature of the musical "struggle" between violin and orchestra. Who in fact does "win"?

At the beginning of the movement the refrain is heard three times. Indicate below which is true for each of the three statements.

    a. The orchestra has the refrain and the violin accompanies.

    b. The orchestra has the refrain and the violin is silent.

    c. The violin has the refrain and the orchestra accompanies.

1. 0:00–0:11 _____

2. 0:12–0:22 _____

3. 0:38–0:49 _____

4. (1:09–1:20) At the end of the transition, what is the relationship between the forces here?

    a. The orchestra has the melody and violin plays counterpoint.

    b. The violin plays runs against pizzicato accompaniment in the orchestra.

5. (1:21–1:25) Now a new theme enters, specifically a rising scale. Which is true?

    a. There is a true dialogue here: The violin goes up with the theme, the orchestra comes down it.

    b. Only the violin has the theme, going both up and down with it.

6. (2:32–2:48) Again, there is another transition to a new theme. Which is true?

    a. The orchestra has the melody and the violin plays counterpoint.

    b. The violin plays difficult arpeggios to a background accompaniment of simple chords in the orchestra.

7. (5:07–5:23) The refrain returns. Which is true?

    a. The violin has the melody and the orchestra is silent.

    b. The orchestra has the melody and the solo violin is silent.

8. Now an unusual moment (5:35–5:55):

    a. The violin plays entirely by itself and the orchestra gradually sneaks back in.

    b. The orchestra plays alone and the violin gradually sneaks back in.

9. Following the violin cadenza (6:47–6:54), the refrain is transformed into a march-like melody (6:55). Which is true?

a. The violin plays the transformed refrain, and the orchestra provides an accompaniment.

b. The orchestra plays the transformed refrain, and the violin provides an accompaniment.

10. Finally, what, in your opinion, is the outcome of this musical contest?
    a. Violin is dominant.   b. Orchestra is dominant.   c. It's a draw.

 Peter Tchaikovsky   6CD 5/1
Symphonic poem, *Romeo and Juliet* (1869)

Peter Tchaikovsky might be called the quintessential Romantic composer, given his brilliant orchestrations and sweeping, if sometimes sentimental, melodies. Tchaikovsky was not a "developer" in the tradition of Beethoven and Brahms, but usually chose instead to repeat large sections of music. These repetitions he would often partly disguise by means of a new and different orchestration. The following questions focus your attention on various aspects of Tchaikovsky's use of repetition in the symphonic poem *Romeo and Juliet*.

Introduction

1. (0:00–0:35) The opening woodwind passage, which sounds faintly religious, is a musical depiction of the kindly Franciscan monk, Friar Laurence. How would you describe the texture?
    a. monophonic   b. polyphonic   c. homophonic

0:36–1:05 Anguished dissonances in strings and French horn

2. (1:25–2:06) We hear solo flute and harp strumming. How many times does the harp play its sequence of strumming chords?
    a. once   b. twice   c. three times

3. (2:07–2:33) The Friar Laurence theme now returns. In what way is it different?
    a. Bassoon plays in unison with the melody in woodwinds.
    b. Trumpet plays fanfare against the melody in woodwinds.
    c. Strings provide pizzicato accompaniment to the melody in woodwinds.

2:34–3:04 Repeat of anguished dissonances in strings and horn

4. (3:23–3:55) The harp strumming returns. In what way is it different?
    a. solo flute has been replaced by high violins
    b. flute now plays pizzicato
    c. Friar Laurence theme now heard as a counterpoint

5:01 *Exposition* begins with Feud theme

5. (6:19–6:40) Which sentence best describes what occurs in the transition between the Feud theme and the Love theme?
    a. Strings ascend and there is a release of tension.
    b. Strings descend and there is a release of tension.
    c. Woodwinds gradually descend and there is a release of tension.

6. (7:51–8:10 and again 8:33–8:50) As the love theme is played passionately by the woodwinds, the French horn provides a counterpoint. How would you describe it?

a. three-note phrases that gradually ascend by step
b. two-note phrases that gradually ascend by step
c. two-note phrases that gradually descend by step

8:51–9:46 Lovely closing section

11:57 *Development*

7. Is the Love theme anywhere to be heard in the development?
   a. yes   b. no

Recapitulation

8. (11:58–12:21) Has the transition music from the exposition (6:19–6:40) been eliminated here in the recapitulation?
   a. yes   b. no
9. (13:00) When the Love theme returns in its full glory, why does it this time sound so much more passionate and powerful?
   a. because the melody is now played by sweeping strings
   b. because the melody in now played by full brass section
   c. because woodwinds now play the melody louder
10. (13:00–14:00) Does the French horn return again with its counterpoint against the Love theme?
    a. yes   b. no

Gustav Mahler
Orchestral song, *I Am Lost to the World,*
from the *Five Rückert Songs* (1901–1902)

CD 5/2

Gustav Mahler's orchestral song *I Am Lost to the World* exploits both the rich-ness of the human voice and the color of the late Romantic orchestra. Listen to this lovely composition and respond to the following questions.

1. At the very beginning, which instrument provides a bass accompaniment below the melody in the English horn?
   a. viola   b. French horn   c. harp
2. Which is the voice that enters?
   a. an alto   b. a tenor   c. a baritone
3. (2:16–2:32) How is the word "gestorben" ("dead") treated?
   a. There is a vocal flourish that is answered by the French horn.
   b. There is a French horn flourish that is answered by the voice.
4. At the end of the second stanza (after "gestorben der Welt"), which musi-cal device is used?
   a. an ascending pizzicato line in the violins
   b. a descending sequence in the violins
   c. an ostinato in the bass
5. For the beginning of the third and final strophe, how would you describe the range of the voice?
   a. falls to the singer's lowest register
   b. continues up to a climax in the singer's highest register
6. The last line of the poem is a fitting epitaph for the entire Romantic era: "in meinem Lieben, in meinem Lied" ("in my love, in my song"). Which is

the more correct description of the musical treatment of these two alliterative phrases?

   a. music climaxes on "Lieben" and dies out on "Lied"

   b. starts quietly on "Lieben" and climaxes on "Lied"

7. The movement from dissonance to consonance toward the end, first in the violins (6:23) and then in the English horn (6:39), creates which feeling?

   a. longing and satisfaction   b. a march   c. a waltz

8. This is an orchestral song, and although Mahler later published a version of it with piano accompaniment instead of the orchestra, this later arrangement is not as effective a piece. Which of the following correctly explains why the orchestral version is more successful?

   a. The orchestra can create more colors.

   b. Individual lines of the counterpoint are more audible when assigned to distinctive-sounding instruments.

   c. Winds and strings are better able to sustain pitches than is a piano.

   d. all of the above

9. What role do the brasses play here in Mahler's orchestral song? _____

10. Is the vocal part of this song strophic or through composed? _____

KEY WORDS

absolute music

double stops

A German Requiem

Nadezhda von Meck

orchestral song

Alma Schindler Mahler

symphonic poem

16

FROM ROMANTIC TO MODERN: IMPRESSIONISM

 Romantic music reached its apogee during the late nineteenth century in the grandiose works of Wagner, Tchaikovsky, Brahms, and Mahler. But by 1900 this German-dominated musical empire was in danger of crumbling, shaken by forces both within and without. Some composers outside the mainstream of Romanticism were becoming downright hostile toward the German style, epitomized by the music of Wagner. Not surprisingly, the most powerful anti-German sentiment was felt in France. (France and Germany went to war in 1870 and would do so again in 1914.) After first embracing Wagner during the 1870s and 1880s, the avant-garde of French music had, by the 1890s, turned antagonistic. It began to ridicule the sentimentality of Romanticism in general and the monumental structures of the Germans in particular. German music was said to be too heavy, too pretentious, too bombastic. Wagner's system of obvious leitmotifs* was now deemed overly simplistic—just as clumsy as one of his Nordic giants. True passion, they said, might be expressed in more subtle ways, in something other than sheer volume of sound and epic length.

IMPRESSIONISM IN PAINTING AND MUSIC

The movement that arose in France in opposition to German Romantic music has been given the name **Impressionism.** We are, of course, more familiar with this term as a designation for a school of French painters living and working in Paris during the last decades of the nineteenth century. That group included Claude Monet (1840–1926), Edgar Degas (1834–1917), Camille Pissarro (1830–1903), Alfred Sisley (1839–1899), Auguste Renoir (1841–1919), and the American Mary Cassatt (1844–1926). Impressionist painters were not overtly anti-German like their musical counterparts. There was no need to be, for French painting had a long and secure tradition (Figs. 6–4, 8–7 and 13–14), one not subject to threat of foreign domination. Their rebellion was against the traditional, academic style of painting of their native land.

The Impressionist movement in painting began in the early 1870s when Monet and his colleagues were forbidden to show their canvases in the official Parisian Salon. Consequently, they launched their own exhibition. In the uproar that followed, the artists were jeeringly called "impressionists" for the sometimes-vague quality of their art. The painters accepted the name, partly as an act of defiance against the establishment, and soon the term was universally adopted.

❋ FIGURE 16–1

The painting that gave its name to an epoch, Claude Monet's *Impression: Sunrise*, was exhibited at the first group exhibition organized by Monet, Renoir, Degas, and Pissarro, in Paris in 1874. The ships, rowboats and other elements in the early morning light are more suggested than fully drawn. Said the critic Louis Leroy derisively of this painting at the time: "Wallpaper in its most embryonic state is more finished than that seascape."

❋ FIGURE 16–2

Claude Monet, *Woman with Umbrella* (1886). The Impressionist canvas is not a finished surface in the traditional sense. Rather, the painter breaks down light into separate dabs of color and juxtaposes them for the viewer's eye to reassemble. Here Monet's bold brush strokes convey an astonishing sense of movement, freshness, and sparkling light.

It is ironic that this style of French painting generated such controversy, for no school of painters is now more popular with the general public than the Impressionists. Indeed, judging by museum attendance and the number of books and reproductions sold, there is an almost limitless enthusiasm for the works of Monet, Degas, Renoir, and their associates—precisely the paintings that the artists' contemporaries mocked and jeered. But what is it about the Impressionist style that then caused such a furor?

The Impressionists were the first to turn against representational art, the idea that a painting should exactly represent an object, as in a photograph. Instead, they tried to recreate the impression that the object produced on their senses. The key here is light: The Impressionists saw all objects as awash in vibrant rays of light and sought to capture the aura that the light-bathed object created in the eye of the beholder. To accomplish this they covered their canvases with small, dablike brushstrokes in which light was broken down into spots of color. This creates a sense of constant movement and fluidity. Shapes are not clearly defined but blurred, more suggested than delineated. Minor details disappear. Sunlight is everywhere and everything shimmers (Fig. 16-2).

As impressions and sensations became paramount for these painters, it is not surprising that they showed an intensified interest in music. What art form is more elusive and suggestive? What medium allows the receiver—the listener—more freedom to interpret the sensations he or she perceives? Painters began to speak in musical terms. Paul Gauguin (1848–1903) referred to the harmonies of line and color as the "music of painting," and Vincent Van Gogh (1853–1890) suggested "using color as the music of tones." Paul Cézanne (1839–1906) painted an "overture" in homage to Wagner, while James Whistler (1834–1903), an American who worked in Paris in the 1860s and 1880s, created "nocturnes" and "symphonies." The artist envied the musician's good fortune to work in a

�' FIGURE 16–3
Claude Debussy.

medium in which flux and change could be continually expressed—rather than one that required the artist to seize the moment and fix it on canvas. At the same time Claude Debussy, the musician whose work most consistently displayed the Impressionist style in music, found inspiration for his work in the visual arts. He called various collections of his pieces *Sketches, Images,* and *Prints.* Rare are the moments in history when the aesthetic aims of painters and musicians were as closely allied.

Claude Debussy (1862–1918)

Claude Debussy, French musician and innovator par excellence, was born in 1862 into a modest family living in a small town outside Paris. Since neither of his parents was musical, it came as a surprise when their son demonstrated talent at the keyboard. At the age of ten he was sent off to the Paris Conservatory for lessons in piano, composition, and music theory. Owing to his skills as a performer he was soon engaged for summer work in the household of Nadezhda von Meck, a wealthy patroness of the arts and the principal supporter of Tchaikovsky (see Fig. 15–9). This employment took him, in turn, to Italy, Russia, and Vienna. In 1884 he won the Prix de Rome, an official prize in composition supported by the French government, one that required a three-year stay in Rome. But Debussy was not happy in the Eternal City. He preferred the Bohemian life of Paris, the atmosphere of the bistros and the cafes.

Returning to Paris more or less permanently in 1887, the young Frenchman continued to learn his craft and search for his own independent voice as a composer. He had some minor successes, and yet, as he said in 1893, "There are still things that I am not able to do—create masterpieces, for example." But the next year, in 1894, he did just that. With the completion of *Prélude à L'Après-midi d'un Faune (Prelude to The Afternoon of a Faun)*, he gave to the public what has become his most enduring orchestral work. Debussy's later compositions, including his opera *Pelléas et Mélisande* (1902), the symphonic poem *La Mer* (*The Sea*, 1905), and his two books of *Preludes* for piano, met with less popular favor. Critics complained of a certain formlessness and a lack of melody. Today, with the advantage of a century of hindsight, these works are seen as early beacons pointing straight down the road to musical modernism. *La Mer* has become a staple in the repertoire of every professional orchestra, *Pelléas* is a standing production of every major opera house, and the *Preludes* form part of the required literature for every would-be concert pianist. Illness and the outbreak of World War I (1914) brought Debussy's musical productivity to a virtual standstill. He died of cancer in the spring of 1918 while the guns of the German army were shelling Paris from the north.

prophet of modernism

PRELUDE TO THE AFTERNOON OF A FAUN (1894)
Debussy spent his time more in the company of poets and painters than with musicians. His orchestral *Prelude to The Afternoon of a Faun*, in fact, was written to precede a staged reading of the poem *The Afternoon of a Faun* by his friend and mentor Stéphane Mallarmé (Fig. 16–4).

Mallarmé was the spiritual leader of a group of versifiers in *fin-du-siècle* Paris called the **Symbolists,** poets whose aesthetic aims were in harmony with those of the Impressionist painters. They worked to create a suggestive verse in which the sound of the word, and the associations that that sound might produce,

Symbolist poetry

were more important than the literal meaning of the word. Symbolism is certainly at the heart of Mallarmé's evocative *The Afternoon of a Faun*, which applies suggestive language to an ancient Greek theme. The faun of Mallarmé's poem is not a young deer but a satyr (a mythological beast that is half man, half goat). He spends his days in pursuit of sexual gratification at the expense of the nymphs who inhabit the forest. On this afternoon we see the faun, exhausted from the morning's escapades, reclining on the forest floor in the still air of the midday heat. He contemplates future conquests while piping listlessly on his flute. A passage from the poem suggests the dreamlike mood, vague and elusive, that Debussy was challenged to recreate.

> No murmur of water in the woodland scene,
> Bathed only in the sounds of my flute.
> And the only breeze, except for my two pipes,
> Blows itself empty long before
> It can scatter the sound in an arid rain.
> On a horizon unmoved by a ripple
> This sound, visible and serene,
> Mounts to the heavens, an inspired wisp.

Debussy wisely made no effort to follow Mallarmé's poem closely—the poem is just a succession of feelings, not a narrative program. Debussy, moreover, was no composer of programmatic music like Berlioz or Tchaikovsky. As he said at the time of the first performance in December 1894: "My *Prelude* is really a sequence of mood paintings, throughout which the desire and dreams of the Faun move in the heat of the midday sun." When Mallarmé had heard the music, he, in turn, said the following about Debussy's musical response to the poem: "I never expected anything like it. The music prolongs the emotion of my poem and paints its scenery more passionately than colors could."

Significantly, both musician and poet refer to *Prelude to The Afternoon of a Faun* in terms of painting. But how does one create a painting in music? Here a tableau is depicted by using the distinctive colors of the instruments, especially the woodwinds, to evoke vibrant moods and sensations. The flute has one tim-

❀ FIGURE 16–4
The poet Stéphane Mallarmé, author of *The Afternoon of a Faun*, as painted by the great predecessor of the Impressionists, Edouard Manet (1832–1883). Mallarmé was a friend and artistic mentor of the composer Debussy.

❀ FIGURE 16–5
Mallarmé's *The Afternoon of a Faun* created something of a sensation among late nineteenth-century French artists. This painting by Ker-Xavier Roussel (1867–1944) is just one of several such representations of the Faun surrounded by woodland nymphs.

bre, the oboe another, the clarinet yet a third. Debussy has said, in effect: Let us focus on the sound-producing capacity of the instruments, let us see what new shades can be elicited from them, let us try new registers, let us try new combinations. Thus a solo flute begins in its lowest register (the pipes of the faun), followed by a harp glissando*, then dabs of color from the French horn. These tonal impressions swirl, dissolve, and reform, but seem not to progress: There is no regular rhythm or discernible meter to push them along. All is languid beauty, a music that is utterly original yet shockingly sensual.

the tone color of the instrument is paramount

LISTENING GUIDE

Claude Debussy
Prelude to The Afternoon of a Faun (1894)

6CD 5/3;
2CD 2/7

Form: ternary

A

0:00   Solo flute plays twisting chromatic line

0:25   Harp glissandos and dabs of color from French horns

0:57   Flute continues with melody, then (1:23) passes it to oboe

1:37   Crescendo that disappears before it can climax

2:03   Return of melody to flute

B

3:17   Clarinet and then flute play rapid chromatic arabesques

4:15   Crescendo that melts into clarinet solo

5:11   Sweeping Romantic theme in woodwinds

5:50   Sweeping theme repeated in violins, then solo violin (6:42)

A′

7:05   Solo flute, then oboe (7:38) return with twisting chromatic line

8:19   Solo flute plays theme again above string tremolo (shimmering effect) with solo violin high above

9:06   Solo viola in low range of instrument plays chromatic line

9:30   Oboe offers complement to the line

CODA

9:54   Ostinato* in harps

10:03   Violins and French horns move up and down in lock step (parallel motion)

10:15   Dabs of sound in various instruments

(Listening Exercise 34)

Debussy's voluptuous *Prelude* creates an entirely new world of musical aesthetics, one very different from the German Romantic school of Mendelssohn, Wagner, and Brahms. Where a composer in the German Romantic tradition asserts a strongly profiled theme, a French Impressionist like Debussy will insinuate a tiny motive. Instead of clear meters and regular rhythms, the Impressionist favors constantly shifting accents that obscure the pulse. Instead of working toward a thunderous climax and a strong cadence, the Impressionist prefers to avoid a climax by placing a diminuendo before the cadence, thereby creating an anticlimax. Instead of moving purposefully along a well-directed harmonic progression, the Impressionist chooses to sit on a single static harmony and let the colorful instruments work their magic. Most important, instead of having musical color reinforce the musical theme, the Impressionist prefers to call on the instruments to demonstrate their sonorities independent of theme. What is radically new about Debussy's music is that beautiful sonorities are allowed simply to exist without having constantly to progress, by means of themes, to some distant goal.

Indeed, with the opening notes of the faun's flute in his *Prelude*, Claude Debussy breathed new life into the art of music, introducing an element of modernism. Think back to the orchestral music of Mozart, Beethoven, Brahms, or Tchaikovsky. When a new theme enters in their works, it is almost invariably presented and carried forward by a new instrument or group of instruments. Instrumental color thus reinforces and gives profile to the theme. The exposition and development of the themes, working in tandem with harmony, in turn create the musical form. With Debussy, on the other hand, color becomes independent of melody. Instruments enter with a distinct color but no easily discernible theme. The instrumental groupings can be more dense or less dense. Thus color and texture begin to replace melody as the primary agents in the creation of musical form. The revolutionary figures of twentieth-century music who use colors and textures exclusively to generate form—among them Ives, Varèse, and Cage (see Chapter 17)—found a precedent for their modernist approach to musical form in the compositions of the Impressionist Claude Debussy.

PRELUDES FOR PIANO (1910, 1913)

Debussy's last and most far-reaching attempt at descriptive writing in music is found in the two books of *Preludes* for piano that he published in 1910 and 1913. Here the challenge to create musical impressions was all the greater, for the piano has a more limited musical palette than the multicolor orchestra. The evocative titles of some of these short pieces

❀ FIGURE 16–6

In 1912 the music of Debussy's *Prelude to The Afternoon of a Faun* was set as a ballet by the famous *Ballets russes* (see page 348). Here the dancer Vaslav Nijinsky assumes the role of the faun.

❀ FIGURE 16–7

August Renoir, *Young Ladies at the Piano* (1892). Our present-day love of Impressionist art is due at least in part to the relaxed mood created by the pastel hues and diffused light. Also, because the Impressionists usually painted scenes from everyday life, a deep knowledge of religious symbolism and pictorial conventions is not a precondition for enjoyment.

❋ FIGURE 16–8
Claude Monet's *Sailboats on the Seine* (1874). The gentle rocking of the boats is suggested by the exaggerated reflections on the water.

allude to their mysterious qualities: *Steps in the Snow*, *The Sunken Cathedral*, *What the West Wind Saw*, and *Sounds and Perfumes Swirl in the Night Air*. Timbres and textures can be produced in music, and images and events can be suggested, if not actually depicted. But can music really stimulate our sense of smell? Can it create perfume? Perhaps for some. That Debussy suggests it might shows how intent he was to create an ideal sort of music, one involving all the senses. As he says of this perfect music, "It would involve a mysterious collaboration of the air, of the movement of leaves and of the perfume of flowers along with music; music would serve to bind all these elements in a way so natural that their unity would seem to grow from all of them."

music as perfume?

Voiles (Sails) (1910)

Voiles (Sails), from the first book of Preludes, takes us to the sea. In our mind's eye is implanted the vision of a boat resting on becalmed waters. The sails flap listlessly in a fluid descent, mostly in parallel thirds. The hazy, languid atmosphere is created in part by the special scale Debussy employs, the **whole-tone scale.** All the notes of the whole-tone scale are a whole step apart:

EXAMPLE 16–1

whole-tone scale

Because in the whole-tone scale each note is the same distance from its neighbor, no one pitch is heard as the tonal center—they all seem equally important. The composer can stop on any note of the scale and it will sound no more central, or final, than any other note. The music floats without a tonal anchor. Then, as if impelled by a puff of wind, the boat seems to rock on the now-rippling waters. Debussy creates this gentle rocking by inserting a four-note ostinato* into the texture. Ostinatos are frequently employed by Impressionist composers. They help account for the often static, restful feeling in the harmony. By definition, ostinatos involve repetition rather than dramatic movement.

EXAMPLE 16–2

ostinatos

A new ostinato now appears in the upper register (right hand), while a succession of four-note chords sounds in the middle register (left hand). Notice that all the four notes of each chord consistently move in what is called parallel motion. In **parallel motion** all parts move together, locked in step, in the same direction.

parallel motion, the opposite of counterpoint

EXAMPLE 16–3

Parallel motion is the antithesis of counterpoint, the traditional musical technique in which two or more lines usually move in directions opposite to one another. Parallel motion was an innovation of Debussy, and it was one way he expressed his opposition to the German school of Wagner and Brahms, so heavily steeped in counterpoint.

Suddenly a gust of wind shakes the ship as the pianist races up the scale in a harplike glissando*. This scale, however, is different from the preceding whole-tone one. It is a pentatonic scale*. There are only five notes within each octave, here the five notes corresponding to the black keys on the piano. We have seen before that the pentatonic scale is often found in folk music (see page 232). Debussy first encountered it in the Indonesian music he heard at the Paris International Exposition of 1889 (see Fig. 16–11).

EXAMPLE 16–4

pentatonic scale

Following this energized whirl around the pentatonic scale, the seascape regains its placid demeanor as the whole-tone scale returns and, ultimately, the descending thirds with which the piece began. At the end Debussy directs the pianist to push down and hold the sustaining pedal (the right-most of the three pedals). Once the sustaining pedal is pressed and held, all notes sounded thereafter will blur into a vague haze, similar to the hazes and mists that envelop many Impressionist paintings (see Fig. 16–1).

LISTENING GUIDE

Claude Debussy
Voiles (Sails), from *Preludes*, Book I (1910)

6CD 5/4

0:00	Descending parallel thirds using whole-tone scale
0:14	Bass pedal point* enters
1:11	Ostinato enters in middle register
1:40	Ostinato moves into top register; chords move in parallel motion in middle register
2:14	Harplike glissandos using pentatonic scale
2:28	Chords moving in parallel motion above pedal point
2:51	Glissandos now employing whole-tone scale
3:38	Opening descending thirds return
3:57	Glissandos blur through use of sustaining pedal

 FIGURE 16–9

Claude Monet, *La Japonaise* (*Madame Camille Monet in Japanese Costume*, 1876). America and Europe began to show an enthusiasm for things Japanese after the opening of trade with Japan in the 1850s. Fashionable Parisian women wore kimonos and furnished their homes with oriental furniture, prints, and *objets d'art*.

 ## THE EXOTIC IN MUSIC

One of the magical qualities of music is its capacity to carry us to distant lands. Far-off places can be experienced in our minds, if only through the strange and mysterious sounds we associate with them. Composers at the turn of the twentieth century delighted in such vicarious journeys, and their music is brimming with the "exotic." Claude Debussy experienced the allure of the Orient in 1889 when he attended the International Exposition in Paris, the world's fair for which the Eiffel Tower was constructed (Fig. 16–11). There he not only saw newfangled inventions like electric lighting and electric-powered elevators but he also heard the colorful sounds of a gamelan* orchestra from Java (Indonesia). Some years later he recalled to a friend: "Do you not remember the Javanese music that was capable of expressing every nuance of meaning, even unmentionable shades, and makes our tonic and dominant sounds seem weak and empty." This Eastern influence accounts in part for the ostinatos, the static harmonies, the pentatonic and whole-tone scales, and the shimmering surfaces found in Debussy's music.

But Claude Debussy was not the only artist to feel the allure of the "other" in these years. The painter Claude Monet lined the walls of his home in Giverny, France, not with his own canvases, but with prints and water colors from Japan. Their influence can be seen in the startling portrait of his wife in traditional Japanese costume (Fig. 16–9). Modernists like Pablo Picasso (1881–1973) and Georges Braque (1882–1963) began collecting African art in Paris during the years 1905–1908. Some historians believe that the Cubist movement in painting (see page 334) was born of Picasso's interest in African sculpture and ceremonial masks. Paul Gaugin (1848–1903) followed his passion for non-Western art farthest afield. His love of oceanic colors and costumes took him to Tahiti and the nearby Marquesas Islands, where he died in 1903 (Fig. 16–10).

❀ FIGURE 16–10

The painter Paul Gauguin went farthest afield in a quest for the exotic, spending much of the last twelve years of his life in the South Seas. His painting *Musique barbare* (1892) is a rendering of an Indonesian gamelan orchestra. Three years earlier, Debussy came under the sway of Indonesian music in Paris.

What was the exotic in music? Anything outside Western European musical culture. It might be a non-Western melody, scale, rhythm, or musical instrument, like the tambourine* or gong*, that signified the exotic. It might also be an alien subject matter. Giacomo Puccini fashioned operas using stories set in Japan (*Madam Butterfly*, 1904), China (*Turandot*, 1924), and even the American West (*The Girl of the Golden West*, 1910). For French Impressionists like Claude Debussy and Maurice Ravel, nearby Spain was thought to be exotic. Debussy composed an orchestral piece (*Ibéria*, 1908) and a piano work ("Evening in Grenada," 1903) using Spanish melodies. Ravel wrote his first orchestral work (*Rapsodie espagnole*, 1907) and his last

❀ FIGURE 16–11

The Cambodian Pagoda at the International Exposition in Paris in 1889. Here Debussy heard the music of Cambodia, China, and Indonesia, and he began to formulate a musical aesthetic different from the prevailing German symphonic tradition.

ballet (*Bolero*, 1928), as well as an opera (*The Spanish Hour*, 1911) on Spanish subjects. Yet neither Debussy nor Ravel set foot in Spain. In art, the evocative powers of the imagination are often a more potent force than mundane reality.

Maurice Ravel (1875–1937)

"He was the eternal traveller who never went there," said an acquaintance of Maurice Ravel. Indeed, Ravel spent almost all of his life in Paris, a modest music teacher and composer earning a modest living. Only through his music did he journey to Spain, Arabia, ancient Greece, and the Far East—all lands he sought to evoke through exotic-sounding elements in his music. Yet there was one exception to Ravel's life of the imagination: In 1928 he embarked on a four-month concert tour of the United States. He heard jazz in Harlem with American composer George Gershwin (1898–1937), and had breakfast in Hollywood with Charlie Chaplin (1889–1977); he visited Niagara Falls and the Grand Canyon. Having performed and conducted his music in twenty-five American cities, Ravel returned to Paris with what was then the enormous sum of $27,000. He was financially secure for the remainder of his life.

RAPSODIE ESPAGNOLE (1907)

Ravel's first composition, written in 1895 at the age of twenty, was a work for piano entitled *Habanera*. A **habanera** is a slow, seductive dance named after Havana, the capital of the then Spanish colony of Cuba. The rhythms that mark its progress are, however, West African, a musical legacy of the slave trade to Cuba. In 1907 Ravel arranged his *Habanera* for orchestra and added three additional pieces to it to form his four-movement *Rapsodie espagnole*. Like the progress of a Spanish day, the musical moods move from a mysterious, flower-scented night (*Prelude to the Night*), through two dances (*Malagueña* and *Habanera*), to the blistering brilliance of the noonday sun (*Feria*). Musical elements of the exotic include the habanera rhythm, which involves alternating groups of three and two eighth-notes as well as syncopations (see Listening Guide). A **tambourine** (a small drum hung with jingles) from Basque (a region of Spain) is heard in *Habanera* as well as castanets* in *Feria*. Yet everywhere in *Rapsodie espagnole* there are glissandos*, hints of themes rather than sweeping melodies, and lines moving in parallel motion. This is exotic Spain, but Spain filtered through the musical sensibilities of a French Impressionist.

❀ FIGURE 16–12
Portrait of Maurice Ravel playing the piano (ca. 1909) by Achille Ouvré.

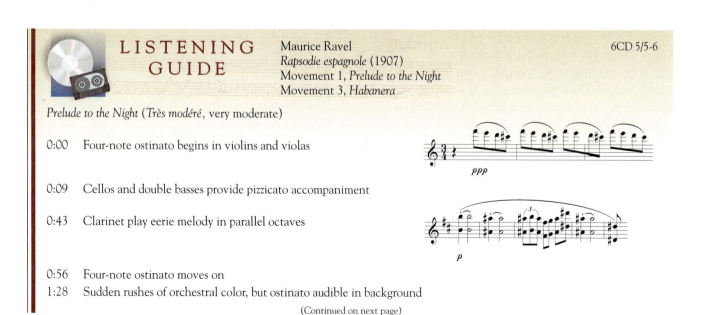

LISTENING GUIDE

Maurice Ravel
Rapsodie espagnole (1907)
Movement 1, *Prelude to the Night*
Movement 3, *Habanera*

6CD 5/5-6

Prelude to the Night (*Très modéré*, very moderate)

0:00   Four-note ostinato begins in violins and violas

0:09   Cellos and double basses provide pizzicato accompaniment

0:43   Clarinet play eerie melody in parallel octaves

0:56   Four-note ostinato moves on
1:28   Sudden rushes of orchestral color, but ostinato audible in background

(Continued on next page)

2:29   Sharp, dissonant *cadenza ad libitum* (freely played) for two clarinets
2:55   Solo violin, viola, and cello play eerie melody
3:22   Two bassoons now play cadenza
3:48   Ostinato returns and fades away

Habanera (*Assez lent et d'un rhythm las;* rather slow and with a jaded rhythm)
0:00   Introduction: syncopated rhythm and glissandos in the strings
0:21   Habanera melody in oboe and English horn

0:47   Solo violin and viola continue Habanera melody
1:01   French horns move from minor triad to major triad against Habanera rhythm

1:13   Violins play Habanera melody in parallel motion

1:40   Tambourine enters as woodwinds continue with Habanera melody
2:00   Violins continue Habanera melody with tambourine in background
2:09   French horns play Habanera melody
2:22   Trumpets slide from minor triad to major triad at the end

The love of the exotic, the foreign, and the mysterious were all part of a final expression of Romanticism in the arts. The Romantic writer, beginning with Lord Byron (see page 233), had taught that a free spirit must experience all that the world has to offer. Reality could be found in different forms and in many different lands. The Romantic spirit would go forth to embrace them all. But these distant visions, exotic fantasies, and escapist desires could not last long in the face of global warfare. Such late-Romantic sentiments were soon pushed aside by the grim events of the twentieth century.

LISTENING EXERCISE

 Claude Debussy   6CD 5/3; 2CD 2/7
Prelude to The Afternoon of a Faun (1894)

Debussy, as we have seen, was a master at extracting new sonorities and textures from the traditional Western orchestra. The following questions, therefore, deal mainly with issues of color and texture.

1. (0:00–0:23) What is the musical texture at the beginning?
   a. monophonic   b. polyphonic   c. homophonic
2. (0:57–1:20) When the flute returns with the twisting chromatic line, is the texture the same as it was at the beginning of the piece? _____

3. (1:37–2:03) Here is an instance where Debussy avoids a climax by repeating a motive as it fades away. By continually repeating a motive on the same pitches Debussy is employing
   a. an arpeggio   b. an ostinato   c. a pedal point

4. (1:37–2:03) Which dynamic markings does Debussy prescribe to create this feeling of an evasion and anticlimax?
   a. crescendo–diminuendo   b. diminuendo–crescendo

5. (2:03, 2:18, 2:40, and 7:05) When the flute returns with the twisting chromatic line, which instrument provides a colorful background?
   a. harp   b. French horn   c. English horn

6. Appropriately enough, what is this instrument playing to help create this background "wash of sound"? The playing of this passage is particularly clear at 7:05–7:20.
   a. chromatic scales   b. pedal points   c. arpeggios

7. (3:21–3:46) Which is a correct description of the music at this point?
   a. Various instruments dart in and out with tiny motives, creating colorful sonorities but a discontinuous texture.
   b. The violins sweep forward with a sensuous, rhythmically free melody based on a whole-tone scale.

8. (5:50–7:02) In this beautiful passage Debussy comes closest to recreating the lush sentimentality more typical of Romantic than Impressionist music. Which statement is *not* correct?
   a. There is a long, sweeping, rhythmically free melody.
   b. The melody is played expressively by the violins.
   c. There is a solo for French horn and then violin at the beginning.
   d. There is a solo for French horn and then violin at the end.

9. A passage with a prominent flute is stated (7:05–7:32) and then repeated at a lower pitch (7:36–8:09), now featuring an oboe. What happens to the texture and orchestration in the course of each of these two passages?
   a. Homophonic texture and unchanging orchestration give way to polyphonic texture and discontinuous orchestration.
   b. Polyphonic texture and discontinuous orchestration give way to homophonic texture and unchanging orchestration.

10. In a typical Romantic work for symphony orchestra, it is usually the strings, particularly the violins, that present and develop most themes. In Debussy's Impressionist *Prelude*, however, the instruments of which family introduce most melodic motives? _____

 KEY WORDS

Impressionism   parallel motion   whole-tone scale
habanera   Symbolists

A checklist of the musical style of Impressionist composers is given on page 64.

THE TWENTIETH CENTURY

 By the standards of any age, the twentieth century must be seen as an eventful, even calamitous, period. Two world wars, a worldwide depression, the extermination of millions of people, the atomic bomb, the cold war, biological weapons, and acts of terrorism have marked this century. At the same time, scientific advances have improved the quality and length of life: The automobile and airplane, radio and television, antibiotics, organ transplants, computers, and the Internet have had a profound impact on our daily lives. Some inventions—the radio, long-playing records, magnetic tape recorder, compact disc, and the Internet—have greatly affected our musical culture, bringing serious music to a much larger segment of the populace and stimulating the growth of popular and commercial music in an unprecedented way. Thus, the tenor of the age has been one of discovery as well as of fear and anxiety brought about by the constant threat of war, nuclear annihilation, or ethnic "cleansing." During the first half of the twentieth century in particular, scarcely a family in Europe and America went untouched by the Depression and two world wars. All of the composers whose works are discussed early in this chapter had their lives drastically altered by one or the other of the wars and the rise of Naziism in Europe. The anxiety and disjunction that you will feel in much of their music is an artistic expression of the social upheavals and underlying uncertainties of the twentieth century.

MODERNISM: DIVERSITY AND EXPERIMENTATION

Given all the good and ill that have marked the last hundred years, it is hardly surprising to find that in matters of culture the twentieth century has experienced great diversity and what appears to be a corresponding lack of cohesion. Where is its artistic core? What have been the main artistic currents? Where lies the path to the twenty-first century?

In previous periods in the history of music, each era seems to have developed a general musical style that constituted a sort of synthesis of what that age believed to be the norm, or model, for the music of that time. Not so for the twentieth century. We have seen a bewildering variety of styles come and go: atonal music, twelve-tone music, electronic music, chance music, Neo-classicism, and Minimalism have all enjoyed favor at various times. Composers themselves have often adopted one style or another as their careers evolved, just as the painter Picasso, for example, moved from Cubism (Fig. 17–1) to Neo-classicism (see Fig. 17–26). We will discuss each of these styles in this chapter, but no one of them can be said to be the mainstream of musical modernism. From a vantage point at the end of this century, the last hundred years appears as a time of alienation, fragmentation, experimentation, and diversity. It is the radically experimental quality of this music, and of our culture in general, that allows us to call it modern or avant-garde.

Radical experimentation in music began shortly before World War I (1914–1918). The new music was not a further evolution of the German-dominated symphonic style of late Romanticism but a sharp turning away from it. It renounced the notion that music should be beautiful and pleasing, expressive or elevating, that it should delight or comfort the listener. Instead, it resorted to

distortion, even violence, of sound, to shock the listening audience. Arnold Schoenberg's early experiments with dissonance were received with hoots by a hostile public in Vienna in 1913; Igor Stravinsky's dissonant chords and pounding rhythms caused a riot at the first performance of *Le Sacre du printemps* (*The Rite of Spring*) in Paris the same year. The intent of the avant-garde composer was to shake the listener out of a state of cultural complacency, just as the artist of the period offended middle-class sensibilities by means of radical visual distortions.

Indeed, there are clear parallels between the music and the art of the early twentieth century. The increasingly angular melody and discontinuous rhythm of the new music found analogous expression in an artistic style called **Cubism.** A Cubist painting is one in which the artist fractures and dislocates formal reality into geometrical blocks and planes, as in Pablo Picasso's

❀ FIGURE 17–1 AND 17–2 (above) One of the first statements of Cubist art, Picasso's *Les Demoiselles d'Avignon* (1907). The ladies of the evening are depicted by means of geometric shapes on a flat, two-dimensional plane. Like much avant-garde music of the time, Cubist paintings reject the emotionalism and decorative appeal of nineteenth-century art. (right) Wassily Kandinsky's *Impression III (Concert)* (1911). Kandinsky was one of the founders of the Expressionist movement, which was centered in Vienna and Munich. This painting of an audience at a concert does not depict the concert so much as a psychological state—the audience's reaction to the concert.

(1881–1973) famous *Les Demoiselles d'Avignon* (1907) (Fig. 17–1), where the female form has been recast into angular, interlocking shapes. During the 1910s and 1920s, Picasso and Stravinsky were friends and occasional artistic collaborators in Paris. So disjointed did the musical line become in the works of Arnold Schoenberg that melody as we know it all but disappeared. At that very time a group of painters working mainly in Germany in a style called Expressionism (see page 347), because they expressed intense internal feelings, so distorted formal reality that objects in their paintings were sometimes barely recognizable. The women are discernible in Picasso's *Les Demoiselles d'Avignon* but where is the audience in Wassily Kandinsky's *Concert* (1911) (Fig. 17–2)? Even more shocking art was produced by the Dadaists (a movement begun in Zurich in 1916) and the Surrealists (formed in Paris in 1922), the latter group glorifying the mysteries of the subconscious (Fig. 17–3). Cubism, Expressionism, Dadaism, Surrealism, and later Abstract Expressionism, Optical art, and Pop art are a few of the diverse artistic movements that have left their mark on the twentieth century. Diversity and radical experimentation are hallmarks of modern art no less than they are of modern music.

❀ FIGURE 17–3

Like the Expressionists, the Surrealists sought to probe the subconscious mind, where unexpected associations might lurk. René Magritte's *Portrait* (1935) calls into question our belief in reality and traditional classification of art by genre. Does the eye in the midst of a piece of ham make this still life a portrait?

❀ FIGURE 17–4

The angularity and disjointed quality of much early twentieth-century melody can also be seen in contemporary painting. In Picasso's *Woman in an Armchair* (1941), for example, the usually contiguous body parts are intentionally set out of alignment. Compare the disjunct melody of Arnold Schoenberg given in Example 17–1.

✿ TWENTIETH-CENTURY MUSICAL STYLE

Despite its diversity, there are, nonetheless, several constant qualities of modern music that create a consistent musical style. These are most forcefully expressed in the elements of melody, harmony, rhythm, and tone color.

Melody: More Angularity and Chromaticism

asymmetrical, angular themes

octave displacement

Music in the Romantic era focused on melody—long sweeping lines that tended to unfold in balanced phrases. The Romantic melody was generally conjunct* in its motion (moving more by steps than by leaps) and built on the notes of the diatonic* scale, though chromatic notes became increasingly frequent toward the end of the nineteenth century. By the early twentieth century, however, this sort of smooth, controlled melody was becoming out of fashion. The young avant-garde composers now favored themes that were more asymmetrical, fragmented, and angular. They bent over backward to avoid writing conjunct, stepwise lines. Rather than moving up a half-step from C to D♭, for example, they were wont to jump down a major seventh to the D♭ an octave below. Avoiding a simple interval for a more distant one an octave above or below is called **octave displacement** and it is a feature of modern music. So, too, is the heavy use of chromaticism. In the following example by Arnold Schoenberg (1874–1951), notice how the melody makes large leaps where it might more easily move by steps and also how several sharps and flats are introduced to produce a highly chromatic line:

EXAMPLE 17–1

Unlike the melodies of the Romantic period, many of which are song-like in style and therefore easily sung and remembered, there are very few themes in twentieth-century music that the listener goes away humming. In fact, melody per se is less important to the avant-garde composer than is a pulsating rhythm, an unusual texture, or a new sonority.

Harmony: More Dissonance, New Chords, New Systems

the liberation of dissonance

Throughout the Baroque, Classical, and Romantic eras, the basic building block of music was the triad*—a consonant, three-note chord. Dissonance was inserted in order to provide tension and variety, but like a hot spice it had to be used sparingly and resolved to a blander consonance. By the late Romantic period, however, composers like Richard Wagner (1813–1883) began to enrich their music with more and more chromaticism. This, in turn, created greater dissonance simply because the added chromatic notes generated more and more chords that were not consonant triads. By the first decade of the twentieth century, some composers, such as Arnold Schoenberg, were using so much chromaticism that the triad all but disappeared. Dissonance became so frequent that it was almost as common as consonance—the exception was becoming the norm. As Igor Stravinsky (1882–1971) said about this reassessment, "Dissonance is now no more an agent of disorder than consonance is a guarantee of security." Hence, the music of the early avant-garde composers took on a harsher, more strident sound, one that has been maintained in modern music, with rare exception, down to the present day. In the course of time we have simply come to accept a greater level of dissonance in the music that we hear, not only in art music but also in popular idioms like film scores and heavy metal rock.

In addition to creating dissonance by chromatically obscuring the triad, twentieth-century composers created dissonance by means of new chords. This was done mainly by superimposing more thirds on top of the consonant triad. In this way were produced not only the **seventh chord** (a seventh chord spans seven letters of the scale, from A to G, for example) but also the **ninth chord** and the **eleventh chord.** The more thirds that were added on top of the basic triad, the more dissonant the sound of the chord:

new chords

EXAMPLE 17–2

seventh chord ninth chord eleventh chord

Some composers, including Stravinsky, Béla Bartók (1881–1945), and Charles Ives (1874–1954), created new dissonant chords by stacking one triad or seventh chord upon another to create a **polychord.** A very dissonant sound is produced if the bottom notes of the two triads are at a dissonant interval from each other, say a major or a minor second away:

polychords

EXAMPLE 17–3

C major triad D major triad dissonant polychord

Polychords help create the jarring, clashing sound that is so much a part of modern music.

But perhaps the most challenging harmonic issue facing composers of the twentieth century was the question "What do we do without tonality?" As we have seen, both Richard Wagner and Claude Debussy in different ways moved away from major–minor tonality, a system that had ruled music for nearly two hundred years. Tonality, with its network of closely related keys, provided a structure for music. Without it composers had to find a new basis for structure. The long ostinatos* of Stravinsky and the twelve-tone* method of Schoenberg (both discussed later in the chapter) are modern responses to this need to impose musical structure in the absence of traditional tonality.

What to do without tonality?

Rhythm: New Asymmetrical Rhythms and Irregular Meters

Most art music before the twentieth century, and indeed all of our pop and rock music down to the present day, is built on regular patterns of duple (2/4), triple (3/4), or quadruple (4/4) meter. Romantic music of the previous generation of composers had many qualities to recommend it: direct expression, broad themes, powerful climaxes, and moments of tender lyricism, to name a few. But only

FIGURE 17-5

Lines of varying lengths can be seen as analogous to measures of different lengths caused by changing meters. Theo van Doesburg's *Rhythm's of a Russian Dance* (1918) was likely inspired by the Russian folksongs in Igor Stravinsky's *The Rite of Spring* (1913).

rarely was it carried along by an exciting, vital rhythm, staying instead within the comfortable confines of regular accents and duple or triple meter.

At the turn of the century composers of art music began to rebel against the rhythmic and metric regularity that had governed much of nineteenth-century music. In abandoning the traditional structures of rhythm and meter, they were no different from modern poets, like Gertrude Stein (1874–1946) and T. S. Eliot (1888–1965), who dispensed with traditional poetic meters and repeating accents in favor of free verse. Musicians such as Stravinsky and Bartók began to write music in which syncopations and measures with odd numbers of beats made it all but impossible for the listener to feel regular metrical patterns. Accents moved from one pulse to another, meters changed from measure to measure. The following passage from Stravinsky's *Petrushka* (1911) gives a sense of how unpredictable modern meter and rhythm can be. Notice how measures with five pulses per unit appear alongside the more traditional measures with two or three, and note how the meter changes for each bar:

EXAMPLE 17–4

In addition, **polyrhythms** (two or more rhythms at once), **polymeters** (two or more meters at once), and rhythmic ostinatos (continually repeating rhythms) now all came into vogue. Each of these is explained in greater detail on pages 342–343. For the moment, it is enough to observe that rhythm in the twentieth century assumed an energy and drive that had not been heard since the Baroque era. But unlike Baroque music, which rejoiced in rhythmic and metric regularity, much of the great force and tension in modern music, its excitement and flamboyance, comes from its irregular rhythms and meters.

Tone Color: New Sounds from New Sources

Twentieth-century composers have created a brave new world of sound. This came about mainly because many musicians were dissatisfied with the string-dominated tone of the Romantic symphony orchestra. The string sound, with its lush vibrato, was thought to be too expressive, perhaps too mushy and senti-

more percussive effects

mental, for the harsh realities of the modern world. So the strings, which had been the traditional melody carriers, relinquished this role to the sharper, crisper woodwinds. Instead of playing a sweeping melody, the violinists might now be called on to beat on the strings with the wooden part of the bow or to take their hands and strike the instrument on its sound box. This preference for percussive effects was also expressed in the new importance assigned the instruments of the percussion family. Entire pieces were written for them alone. In-

new percussion instruments

struments such as the xylophone*, glockenspiel*, and celesta* were added to the group (see Fig. 3–12), and objects that produced an unfixed pitch, like the cow bell, brake drum, and police siren, were also heard on occasion. The piano, which in the Romantic era had been favored for its lyrical "singing" tone, came to be used as an orchestral instrument prized for the decisive way in which the hammers could be made to bang into the strings. The voice, too, was often asked to abandon its traditional lyrical tone and to replace it with declamatory speech, hisses, whoops, cries, grunts, and other novel sounds. What is more, by mid-century an entirely new way of generating and processing sound had been developed, by means of the electronic synthesizer. This allowed for even more new and different tone colors, ones that could not be produced on traditional acoustical instruments.

Producing new tones in novel ways, whether by new "instruments" or by traditional instruments using new playing techniques, is only part of the story of sound in modern music. A more fundamental development is the new way of thinking about musical color, or timbre, as an independent element in music. During the Classical and Romantic periods, sounds of different colors and different volumes had been used mainly as a way to highlight the progress of the themes and thus to articulate the form of a composition. When the second theme entered in sonata–allegro form, for example, it was usually assigned to a new instrument to tell the listener that this was, in fact, a new theme; when a final climax was near, more and more instruments, including the powerful brasses, were usually added to increase the level of sound, signaling that the end was close at hand. The use of tone color and volume as mere servants of melody came to an end at the turn of the twentieth century. Claude Debussy (see page 325) was the first to use color, independent of melody, to give form to a work. But this development was carried to radical lengths in the compositions of modernists such as Edgard Varèse (1883–1965), Charles Ives (1874–1954), and John Cage (1912–1992), whose pieces sometimes do nothing except progress from bright tones spaced far apart to dark tones densely grouped together. There may be no melody or harmony as we usually think of these, but only clusters or streams of sounds with changing colors. This approach to color and line is, of course, similar to the one followed by avant-garde painters who deconstruct recognizable objects so as to emphasize the emotional power of pure color (see Fig. 17–6).

❄ FIGURE 17–6

Henri Matisse's *The Red Studio* (1911). Here color is not a subordinate element employed to delineate the various objects in the room. Color and line have been separated and color per se has gained unprecedented power.

density of texture: an independent element

❋ THE EARLY AVANT-GARDE: STRAVINSKY, SCHOENBERG, AND BARTÓK

Faced with the extraordinary diversity of modern music, today's conductors and performers have a difficult time selecting a musical repertoire for the listening public. What kinds of modern music should be performed and how much of it? Audiences are notorious for preferring the tried-and-true "chestnuts" of the

Classical and Romantic periods to any sort of new or experimental music. The masterpieces by the composers discussed next are not only compelling works of art in themselves but they also have offered answers for other composers in regard to the fundamental question of modern music—how to create cogent new music in a world marked by increasing cultural diversity and artistic fragmentation. All of these works have now become accepted into the standard repertoire of concert music, though not all of the composers have become icons of popular culture like Beethoven or Mozart.

Igor Stravinsky (1882–1971)

Igor Stravinsky is arguably the most significant composer of the twentieth century, both for the music he produced and for his influence on other composers. He created masterpieces in many different genres: opera, ballet, symphony, church Mass, and cantata. His versatility was such that he could write a ballet for baby elephants (*Circus Polka*, 1942) just as easily as he could set to music a Greek classical drama (*Oedipus Rex*, 1927). Throughout his long life he traveled with the fashionable set of high art. Although reared in St. Petersburg, he later lived in Paris, Venice, Lausanne, New York, and Hollywood. Forced to become an expatriate by the Russian Revolution (1917), he took French citizenship in 1934, and then, having moved to the United States at the outbreak of World War II, became an American citizen in 1945. He counted among his friends the painter Pablo Picasso (1881–1973), the novelist Aldous Huxley (1894–1963), and the poets Dylan Thomas (1914–1953) and T. S. Eliot (1888–1965). On his eightieth birthday, in 1962, he was honored by President John Kennedy at the White House and, later in the same year, by Premier Nikita Khrushchev in the Kremlin. He died in New York in 1971 at the age of eighty-eight.

Stravinsky rose to international fame as a composer of ballet music. In 1908 some of his early work caught the attention of the legendary impresario (producer) of Russian opera and ballet, Sergei Diaghilev (1872–1929). Diaghilev wanted to bring Russian ballet to Paris, at that time the artistic capital of the world. So he formed a company, called the **Ballets russes** (Russian ballets), and hired, over the course of time, the most progressive artists he could find: Pablo Picasso and Henri Matisse for scenic designs, George Balanchine (later the force behind the New York City Ballet) as a choreographer, and Debussy, Ravel, and Stravinsky, among others, as composers. Stravinsky soon became the principal composer of the company, and the *Ballets russes* became the focus of his musical activity for the next ten years. Accordingly, the decade 1910–1920 has become known as Stravinsky's Russian ballet period. He would have others—a Neo-classical period (1920–1951) when he returned to classical forms and a smaller orchestra, and a twelve-tone period (1951–1971) during which he adopted the so-called serial style of composing (see page 349)—but his

✳ FIGURE 17–7 AND 17–8 (left) Pablo Picasso's *Portrait of Igor Stravinsky* (1920) and (right) Sergei Diaghilev. Diaghilev was a cultural impresario who exported Russian art, opera, and ballet to the West. His greatest talent was recognizing and encouraging the genius of artists like Picasso, Matisse, Stravinsky, and Ravel.

fame was made through his early ballets. Motion, whether of dancers or of musical performers, was always foremost in his mind's eye. As Stravinsky said in his autobiography, "I have always had a horror of listening to music with my eyes shut, with nothing for them to do. The sight of the gestures and movements of the various parts of the body . . . is fundamentally necessary if music is to be grasped in its fullness."

The three most important ballets Stravinsky wrote for Diaghilev's company were *The Firebird* (1910), *Petrushka* (1911), and *The Rite of Spring* (1913). All are built around stories taken from Russian folk tales—a legacy of musical nationalism*—and all make use of the large, coloristic orchestra of the late nineteenth century. Unlike symphonic music, however, music for ballet does not explore, or develop, carefully integrated musical themes. Rather, the composer creates a succession of short, independent vignettes designed to express the action being danced and mimed on the stage. The dance of Diaghilev's *Ballets russes* is not the elegant, graceful classical ballet in the French and Russian tradition, the sort that we associate with Tchaikovsky's *Swan Lake* (1877) and *The Nutcracker* (1892). It is a new, modern style of dance influenced by "primitive" Russian folk dancing and folk art; it is heavier, more physical, more driving. Rhythm becomes the driving force of these Russian ballets and of Stravinsky's music in general.

❋ FIGURE 17–9

In 1909 Henri Matisse painted the first of two canvases entitled *Dance*. Here he achieves a raw primitive power by exaggerating a few basic lines and employing a few cool tones. Two years later he created an even more intense vision of the same scene (see Fig. 17–10).

LE SACRE DU PRINTEMPS (THE RITE OF SPRING) (1913)

"*The Rite of Spring* serves as a point of departure to all who seek to mark the beginning of what is still called 'contemporary' music," said the composer Pierre Boulez (b. 1925). Yet at the premiere, *The Rite of Spring* provoked not admiration, but a riot of hostility. This opening, the most notorious "first night" in the history of music, took place on an unusually hot evening, May 29, 1913, at the newly built Théâtre Champs-Élysées in Paris. With the very first sounds of the orchestra, many in the packed theater voiced, shouted, and hissed their displeasure. Some called for a doctor, others for two. There were arguments and flying fists as opponents and partisans warred over this Russian brand of modern art. To restore calm, the curtain was lowered momentarily and the house lights were turned on. All in vain. The musicians still could not be heard, and the dancers had difficulty following the pulse of the music. The disorder was experienced first-hand by a visiting critic of the *New York Press*, who reported as follows:

a riot at the premiere

> I was sitting in a box in which I had rented one seat. Three ladies sat in front of me and a young man occupied the place behind me. He stood up during the course of the ballet to enable himself to see more clearly. The intense excitement under which he was laboring, thanks to the potent force of the music, betrayed itself presently when he began to beat rhythmically on the top of my head with his

🌸 FIGURE 17–10

Dance (1911) by Henri Matisse uses greater angularity and more intense colors, and thereby creates a more intense reaction to this later version of a primitive dance scene (see Fig. 17–9).

fists. My emotion was so great that I did not feel the blows for some time. They were perfectly synchronized with the beat of the music!

In truth, the violent reaction to *The Rite of Spring* was in part a response to the modernist choreography of Vaslav Nijinsky (see Fig. 16–6). His mode of dance was no less "primitive" than Stravinsky's score. But what specifically is there in Stravinsky's music that so many that night found shocking?

Percussive Orchestra. First, there is a new percussive—one might say "heavy metal"—approach to the orchestra. The percussion section is enlarged to include four timpani, a triangle, a tambourine, a guiro*, cymbals, antique cymbals, a bass drum, and a tam-tam*. Even the string family, the traditional provider of warmth and richness in the symphony orchestra, is required to play percussively, attacking the strings with repeated down-bows at seemingly random moments of accent.

Irregular Accents. Stravinsky intensifies the effect of his harsh, metallic sounds by placing them where they are not expected, on unaccented beats, thereby creating explosive syncopations. Notice in the following example, the famous beginning of "Augurs of Spring," how the strings accent (>) the second, fourth, and then first pulses of each four-pulse measure. In this way Stravinsky destroys ordinary 1, 2, 3, 4 meter and forces us to hear, in succession, groups of 4, 5, 2, 6, 3, 4, and 5 pulses—a conductor's nightmare!

EXAMPLE 17–5

Polyrhythms. The rhythm of *The Rite of Spring* is complex because the composer often superimposes two or more independent rhythms simultaneously. Look at the reduced score given in Ex. 17–6. Every instrument seems to be doing its own thing! In fact, six distinctly different rhythms can be heard.

EXAMPLE 17–6

Ostinato Figures. Notice also in Ex. 17–6 how most of the instruments are play-ing the same motive over and over at the same pitch level. Such a repeating figure, as we have seen, is called an ostinato*. In this instance we hear multiple ostinatos. Stravinsky was not the first twentieth-century composer to use osti-natos extensively—Debussy had done so earlier in his Impressionist scores (see page 327). But Stravinsky employs them more often and does so for longer spans. In *The Rite of Spring*, ostinatos give the music its incessant, driving quality, es-pecially in the sections with fast tempos.

Polymeters. Not only do individual parts often play separate rhythms but they also sometimes project distinctly different meters, each with a different time signature, either written or implied. Notice in Ex. 17–7 that the oboe plays in 6/8 time, the E♭ clarinet plays in 7/8, while the B♭ clarinet is in 5/8.

EXAMPLE 17–7

Dissonant Polychords. The harsh, biting sound that is heard throughout much of *The Rite of Spring* is often created by having two triads*, or a triad and a seventh chord*, sound at once. When these chords are only a step* or a half step* apart, the resulting polychord is especially dissonant. In Ex. 17–8, the passage from the beginning of "Augurs of Spring," a seventh chord* built on E♭ is played simultaneously with a major triad* built on F♭.

EXAMPLE 17–8

♨ FIGURE 17–11

As polychords create two or more tonal centers sounding at once, so the Cubist painting *The Violin* (1916), by Juan Gris, refracts the violin and the bow into two and sometimes three simultaneous images.

The plot of the ballet *The Rite of Spring* is suggested by its subtitle: "Pictures of Pagan Russia." Part 1 is called "The Kiss of the Earth" and depicts the springtime rituals of primitive Slavic tribes; part 2 is entitled "The Sacrifice," and here a virgin dances herself to death as an offering to the god of Spring. Stravinsky's music is sometimes lyrical and sensuous, but more often percussive, dissonant, and even violent. Throughout he makes use of Russian folk songs, fragments of folk songs, and his own brief imitations of these. Yet as Stravinsky said, he had little tradition or precedent to direct him: "I had only my ears to guide me. I heard and I wrote what I heard. I am the vessel through which *The Rite of Spring* passed."

Following the *succès de scandale* that attended the premiere of *The Rite of Spring*, Stravinsky immediately removed the music from the ballet itself and had it played as an independent orchestral suite. The music alone was now recognized as an important, if controversial, statement of the musical avant-garde. Later, in 1940, the score of *The Rite of Spring* furnished the music for an important segment of Walt Disney's early full-length animated film, *Fantasia*. Musical modernism had become mainstream.

LISTENING GUIDE

Igor Stravinsky
The Rite of Spring (1913)
Introduction and Scenes 1–3

6CD 5/7–10;
2CD 2/8–9

Genre: Ballet music
Introduction (the awakening of the earth)

0:00	Bassoon writhing in high register
0:20	Other winds (bass clarinet, English horn, another bassoon, high clarinet) gradually enter
1:37	Flutes play in parallel motion
1:53	Writhing woodwinds continue
2:34	Ostinato in bass supports gradual orchestral crescendo
2:57	Bassoon melody returns, clarinet trills

Augurs of Spring: Dances of the Adolescents (youthful dancers pound onto the stage; male and female groups entice one another; attention shifts to more folklike dances of the girls)

0:00	Elemental pounding of dissonant string chords punctuated by blasts from the French horns and trumpets (see Ex. 17–5)

(Continued on next page)

0:46   Bassoons and then trombones play stepwise motive

1:15   *Fortissimo* chords and timpani blows
1:39   French horn plays folklike melody

1:59   Flute plays melody
2:13   Trumpets play new folklike melody

2:47   Gradual orchestral crescendo

(2CD stops here)

Game of Abduction (macho gestures of "kidnapping" a girl)

0:00   Wild, chaotic playing in orchestra peppered with blows on the timpani and blasts from the French horn
0:53   Quickly changing meters; syncopated percussion blows

Spring Rounds (round dances by groups of male and female adolescents)

0:00   Flutes trill while clarinets play in parallel motion
0:26   Low strings set up mournful accompaniment
1:04   Folklike melody now played by violins and flutes, then French horn

1:59   Folklike melody played dissonantly by full orchestra
2:41   Dissonant, syncopated, percussive music for male dancers
2:58   Return of opening flute trill and opening melody

(Listening Exercise 35)

Arnold Schoenberg and the Second Viennese School

If Paris was the artistic capital of Europe before the First World War, Vienna was second in importance. The city of Mozart and Beethoven was blessed with strong musical traditions and a large, if conservative, audience. But the musical expectations of the Viennese were now challenged by a trio of native composers who were to take modern music on a radically different course: Arnold Schoenberg (1874–1951), Alban Berg (1885–1935), and Anton Webern (1883–1945). The close association of these three innovative musicians has come to be called the "Second Viennese School," the first, of course, being that of Mozart, Haydn, and Beethoven.

Arnold Schoenberg, the leader of this group, almost single-handedly thrust modern music on a reluctant Viennese public. Schoenberg was from a Jewish family of modest circumstances and was largely self-taught as a musician. As a young man he worked as a bank clerk during the day, but studied literature, philosophy, and music at night, becoming a competent performer on the violin and cello. He came to know the music of Brahms, Wagner, and Mahler, mostly by playing their scores and attending concerts. Having "left the world of bank notes for musical notes" at the age of twenty-one, he earned a modest living by

from bank clerk to musician

FIGURE 17–12
Arnold Schoenberg, *Self Portrait* (1910).

conducting a men's chorus, orchestrating operettas—the Viennese counterpart of our Broadway musicals—and giving lessons in music theory and composition. Eventually, his own compositions began to be heard in Vienna, though they were usually not well received.

Schoenberg's earliest works are written in a typical late Romantic style, with rich harmonies, chromatic melodies, expansive forms, and programmatic content. But by 1908 his music had begun to evolve in unexpected directions. Having been strongly influenced by Wagner's chromatic melodies and harmonies, Schoenberg started to compose works in which there was no tonal center. If Wagner could write winding chromatic passages that temporarily obscured the tonality, why not go one step farther and create fully chromatic pieces in which there is no tonality? This Schoenberg did, and in so doing created what is called **atonal music**—music without tonality, music without a key center.

But Schoenberg not only abandoned music with a tonal center—a stable point of reference for the listener—he also dispensed with the triad as the basic building block of music. Earlier, tonal music had unfolded in chord progressions built mainly of consonant triads. Dissonance, which adds an element of tension and anxiety, was carefully controlled and required to resolve to a stable consonance, usually a triad. With Schoenberg's new atonal music, however, dissonance is freed from the necessity of resolving to consonance—it can wander off chromatically to another dissonance and then yet another. We have, in Schoenberg's words, "the emancipation of dissonance." Most listeners today are at first hostile to atonal music, in part because there is no tonal center but more so because it is so highly dissonant. Small wonder that in Schoenberg's day some Viennese musicians refused to play his atonal music, or that when they did the audience's reaction was sometimes violent. (At one concert, March 31, 1913, the police had to be called out to restore order.) Despite the hostility, Schoenberg remained true to his own artistic vision:

Whether one calls oneself conservative or revolutionary, whether one composes in a conventional or progressive manner, whether one tries to imitate old styles or is destined to express new ideas—whether one is a good composer or not—one must be convinced of the infallibility of one's own fantasy and one must believe in one's own inspiration.

FIGURE 17–13
This 1909 Viennese theater poster by Oskar Kokoschka shows the Expressionist affinity for the dramatic and grotesque. The effect is created by the use of strong, almost crude, lines and bold contrasting colors.

Expressionism and Atonality

Arnold Schoenberg and his students Alban Berg and Anton Webern were not alone in creating a radically new style of art. As we have seen, there appeared at this same time a powerful movement in the visual arts called Expressionism. Expressionism was initially a German–Austrian development that arose in Berlin, Munich, and Vienna. Its aim was not to depict objects as they are seen but to express the strong emotion that the object generated in the artist; not to paint a portrait of an individual but to create an expression of the subject's innermost feelings, anxieties, and fears. In Edvard Munch's early Expressionist painting *The Scream* (1893), the subject cries out to an unsympathetic and uncomprehending world. Schoenberg's statement in this regard can be taken as a credo for the entire Expressionist movement: "Art is the cry of despair of those who experience in themselves the fate of all Mankind" (1910). Gradually, realistic representations gave way to highly personal and increasingly abstract expression. Artists such as Oskar Kokoschka (1886–1980) and Wassily Kandinsky (1866–1944) used harsh colors, macabre images, and distorted figures to show intense psychological states, sometimes with shocking results (see Figs. 17–2 and 17–13). Schoenberg, a personal friend of both Kokoschka and Kandinsky, was himself a painter and exhibited his works with the Expressionists in 1912 (Figs. 17–12 and 17–14). In fact, the music and art of this movement can be described in rather similar terms. The clashing of strong colors, the disjointed shapes, and the jagged lines of the painters have their counterparts in the harsh dissonances, asymmetrical rhythms, and angular, chromatic melodies of Schoenberg and his followers. It is surely not an accident that Schoenberg moved from tonality to atonality in music (1908–1912) at precisely the time Kandinsky and others turned away from realistic representation to abstract expression.

The Scream, by Edvard Munch

PIERROT LUNAIRE (MOONSTRUCK PIERROT) (1912)

Moonstruck Pierrot, Schoenberg's best-known composition, is an exemplary work of Expressionist art. It is a setting for chamber ensemble and female voice of twenty-one poems by Albert Giraud. Here we meet "Moonstruck Pierrot," a white-faced clown from the world of traditional Italian pantomime and puppet shows. Yet in this Expressionist poetry the fun-loving clown suffers the endless anxiety of a sensitive artist-lover whose only confidante is the moon. Pierrot's inner feelings are projected by means of a new vocal technique invented by Schoenberg called **Sprechstimme**—"speech-voice." *Sprechstimme* requires the vocalist to declaim the text more than sing it. The voice is to execute the rhythmic values exactly; but once it hits a pitch, it is to quit the tone immediately, sliding away in either a downward or an upward direction. This creates exaggerated declamation, even a feeling of hysteria, a sentiment appropriate for this hyperexpressive text.

Sprechstimme, a new vocal technique

Poems 6 and 7 of *Moonstruck Pierrot* reveal two different aspects of the clown's feverish state of mind. In number 6 Pierrot offers a hymn of solace to the suffering Madonna; and in number 7 he projects on the face of the moon his own love pains. Each poem is cast as a *rondeau,* an old musical and poetic form characterized by the use of a refrain (see pages 56 and 76). Traditionally, composers had used the appearance of a textual refrain to repeat part or all of the melody as well. This helped create a unity of text and music and gave the work formal coherence. But Schoenberg, true to his iconoclastic ways, avoids musical repetition in his atonal works. His music unfolds in an ever-varying continuum, like a stream of consciousness. His dissonances, disjunct rhythms,

an ever-varying continuum

changing textures, and nonrepeating melodies place unprecedented demands on the listener. Your first reaction to the seemingly formless flow of dissonance in *Moonstruck Pierrot* may be decidedly negative. Yet with repeated listenings the force of the jarring elements of the atonal style begins to lessen and a bizarre, eerie sort of beauty emerges, especially if you are sensitive to the meaning of the text.

LISTENING GUIDE

Arnold Schoenberg
Moonstruck Pierrot (1912)
Number 6, *Madonna*
Number 7, *The Sick Moon*

6CD 5/11–12;
2CD 2/10

Number 6, *Madonna*, draws its inspiration from the vision of the sorrowful Mother of Christ at the Cross. The traditional association of the image of the Cross with musical chromaticism, one extending at least back to Bach, may have given rise to the ascending chromatic line, played pizzicato, in the cello. The angular movement of the voice is typical of Schoenberg's atonal melodic line:

(*Sprechstimme* — "speech-voice")

Steig,   O Mut - ter al - ler Schmer zen, auf den Al - tar mei - ner   Ver - se!

Steig, O Mutter aller Schmerzen	**Arise, O Mother of all sorrows**
Auf den Altar meiner Verse!	**On the altar of my verse!**
Blut aus deinen magern Brüsten	Blood from your thin breast
Hat des Schwertes Wut vergossen.	Has spilled the rage of the sword.
Deine ewig frischen Wunden	Your eternally fresh wounds
Gleichen Augen, rot und offen,	Like eyes, red and open,
Steig, O Mutter aller Schmerzen	**Arise, O Mother of all sorrows**
Auf den Altar meiner Verse!	**On the altar of my verse!**
In den abgezehrten Händen	In your thin and wasted hands
Hältst du deines Sohnes Leiche	You hold the body of your Son
Ihn zu zeigen aller Menschheit,	To show him to all mankind,
Doch der Blick der Menschen meidet	Yet the look of men avoids
Dich, **O Mutter aller Schmerzen.**	You, **O Mother of all sorrows.** (2CD set stops here)

Number 7, *Der kranke Mond (The Sick Moon)*, is a soliloquy for voice and accompanying flute. As do the Expressionist painters, here the poet transfers to the object (the moon) the internal feelings of the subject (the artist Pierrot). Thus, as Pierrot speaks, the moon begins to reflect his inner turmoil, becoming feverish, tormented, death-sick with love. The silvery tones of the flute help evoke an aura of moonlight, "death-sick" as it may be.

Du nächtig todeskranker Mond	**You nocturnal, death-sick moon**
Dort auf des Himmels	**There on heaven's**
schwarzem Pfühl,	**dark couch,**
Dein Blick, so fiebernd übergross	Your look, so feverishly swollen,
Bannt mich wie fremde Melodie.	Charms me like a foreign melody.
An unstillbarem Liebesleid	In unending pain of love
Stirbst du, an Sehnsucht, tief erstickt,	You die, in yearning consumed,
Du nächtig todeskranker Mond	**You nocturnal, death-sick moon**
Dort auf des Himmels	**There on heaven's**
schwarzem Pfühl.	**dark couch.**
Den Liebsten, der im Sinnenrausch,	The lover who, in sensual frenzy,
Gedankenlos zur Liebsten geht,	Steals to the beloved without a care,
Belustigt deiner Strahlen Spiel,	Rejoices in your play of light,
Dein bleiches, qualgebornes Blut,	Your pale, tormented blood,
Du nächtig todeskranker Mond.	**You nocturnal, death-sick moon.**

Needless to say, this music of the extreme avant-garde did not sit well with the anti-intellectual Nazis who took power in Germany in 1933 and Austria in 1938. Hitler and his National Socialists not only harbored a hatred of Jews, but they also made it virtually impossible for "degenerate" modern art like *Moonstruck Pierrot* to be seen or heard. So Schoenberg fled the German lands, as did thousands of other progressive spirits, including Thomas Mann (1875–1955), Kurt Weill (1900–1950), and Albert Einstein (1879–1955). He ultimately made his way to this country and to Los Angeles, where he died peacefully in 1951 at the age of seventy-six.

SCHOENBERG'S TWELVE-TONE MUSIC

When Arnold Schoenberg and his followers did away with tonal chord progressions and melodies that repeated, they found themselves facing a serious artistic problem: how to write large-scale compositions in the new atonal style. For centuries musical structures, like fugue and sonata–allegro form, had been generated by means of a clear tonal plan and the repetition of broad musical themes. Forms created by repetition were useful to the composer and most welcome to the listener seeking to make sense of a new musical composition. But Schoenberg's chromatic, atonal, nonrepeating melodies made traditional musical forms all but impossible. What other formal plan might be used? If all twelve notes of the chromatic scale are equally important, as is true in atonal music, why choose any one note at a given spot in a piece and not another?

By 1923 Schoenberg had solved the problem of formal anarchy—or absence of form—caused by total chromatic freedom. He had discovered a new way of creating music that he called "composing with twelve tones." **Twelve-tone composition** is a method of writing that employs each of the twelve notes of the chromatic scale set in a fixed, predetermined order. The composer chooses the succession of twelve notes to achieve the desired "melody" and places them in a row. Throughout the composition the twelve notes must come in the same order. Music in which elements such as pitch, timbre, or dynamics come in a fixed series is called **serial music.** In twelve-tone music the twelve-note series may unfold not only as a melody but also as a melody with accompaniment, or simply as a progression of chords, since two or more notes of the row may sound simultaneously. Moreover, in addition to appearing in its basic form, the row might go backward (retrograde*) or upside down (inversion*) or both backward and upside down at the same time (retrograde inversion). While such arrangements might seem wholly artificial and very unmusical, we should remember that composers such as J. S. Bach in the Baroque era and Josquin Desprez in the Renaissance had subjected their melodies to similar permutations. The purpose of Schoenberg's twelve-tone method was to create musical unity by basing each piece on a single, orderly arrangement of twelve tones, thereby guaranteeing the perfect equality of all pitches so that none would seem like a tonal center.

TRIO FROM *SUITE FOR PIANO* (1924)

The first steps along this radical twelve-tone path were tentative and, not surprisingly, the pieces that resulted were short, very short. Among Schoenberg's first serial compositions was his *Suite for Piano*, a collection of seven brief dance movements, including the Minuet and Trio to be discussed here. The tone row for the *Suite*, along with its three permutations, is as follows:

❊ FIGURE 17–14

As a young man Schoenberg was undecided whether his future lay in music or painting. Like many Expressionist paintings before World War I, his *Hatred* (ca. 1910) gives a sense of the subject's inner feeling.

serial music

Row														Retrograde											
E	F	G	D♭	G♭	E♭	A♭	D	B	C	A	B♭			B♭	A	C	B	D	A♭	E♭	G♭	D♭	G	F	E
1	2	3	4	5	6	7	8	9	10	11	12			12	11	10	9	8	7	6	5	4	3	2	1

Inversion														Retrograde-inversion											
E	E♭	D♭	G	D	F	C	F♯	A	G♯	B	B♭			B♭	B	G♯	A	F♯	C	F	D	G	D♭	E♭	E
1	2	3	4	5	6	7	8	9	10	11	12			12	11	10	9	8	7	6	5	4	3	2	1

Schoenberg allows the row or any of its permutations to begin on any pitch, so long as the original sequence of intervals is maintained. Notice in the Trio, for example, that the row itself begins on E but is also allowed to start on B♭ (see Listening Guide). In the second part, measures 6–9, the exact serial progression of the row breaks down slightly. The composer explained this as a "justifiable deviation," owing to the need for tonal variety at this point. Notice as well that the rhythms in which the notes appear may likewise be changed for the sake of variety. As you listen to the Trio, see if you can follow the unfolding of the row and all its permutations. Listen many times—the piece is only fifty-one seconds long! Its aesthetic effect is similar to that of a constructivist painting of an artist like Theo van Doesburg (Fig. 17–15). If you like the painting, you should like Schoenberg's twelve-tone piano piece as well.

❧ FIGURE 17–15

The same rational processes at work in Schoenberg's twelve-tone music can be seen in Theo van Doesburg's *Composition IV* (1917). Notice the retrograde motion: The pattern proceeding downward from the top left is the same as that upward from the bottom right.

LISTENING GUIDE

Arnold Schoenberg
Trio from *Suite for Piano* (1924)

6CD 5/13

(Continued on next page)

As the years progressed, Schoenberg used his twelve-tone method to construct longer compositions for larger forces. In 1932 he completed most of a full-length opera, *Moses and Aaron,* and in 1947 he finished a cantata*, *A Survivor from Warsaw,* that tells of Nazi atrocities in Poland. Both works are twelve-tone in style throughout. But the listening public never embraced Schoenberg's twelve-tone music. The style is still very much that of dissonant, atonal music. For most listeners, it sounds irrational and arbitrary, indeed completely "out of control." Schoenberg was philosophical about the public's general dislike of his music: "If it is art, it is not for all, and if it is for all, it is not art."

Béla Bartók (1881–1945)

The music of the Hungarian composer Béla Bartók is decidedly modern, yet distinctly different in sound from that of Stravinsky or Schoenberg. While it can be atonal, like the music of Schoenberg, it is often highly tuneful, making use of sweeping melodies. And while it is frequently percussive and highly rhythmic, like the motor-driven sounds of Stravinsky, Bartók's rhythmic force derives mainly from folk music. Bartók's creative imagination was fired by folk materials of his native Hungary. He saw the return to the simple, direct style of folk music as a way to counter the tendency in Romantic music toward ostentation and sentimentality.

The life of Béla Bartók was strongly affected by the turbulent events that occurred in Eastern Europe during the first half of the twentieth century. He was born in 1881 in Hungary, but in a part of that nation that was later given over to Rumania at the end of World War I. Throughout his life he was an ardent Hungarian nationalist, and chose to develop his obvious musical talents at the Academy of Music in Budapest rather than at the German-dominated Vienna Conservatory, where he had also been admitted. As a student at the Academy in Budapest he studied composition and piano, quickly acquiring a reputation as a concert pianist of the highest quality. By the 1920s he had achieved an international reputation both as a pianist and as a composer of music in the modern vein. His tours even carried him to the western part of the United States, where one newspaper alerted the public to his coming with the following headline: "Hungarian Modernist Advances upon Los Angeles." As both a Hungarian modernist and nationalist, Bartók was an outspoken critic of the supporters of Nazi Germany who gained control of the Hungarian government in the late 1930s. He called the fascists "bandits and assassins," cut off ties with the Ger-

🌸 FIGURE 17–16
Béla Bartók.

an ardent anti-Nazi

man firm that published all his music, and banned the performances of his works in Germany and Italy, thereby losing considerable performance fees. Ultimately, in 1940, he fled to the United States. Bartók died of leukemia in New York City in 1945, and not until 1988 were his remains returned, at the request of his sons, to his beloved Hungary.

Bartók and folk music

Béla Bartók is unique among composers in that he was as much interested in musical research, specifically in the study of Eastern European folk music, as he was in musical composition. He traveled from village to village in Hungary, Rumania, Bulgaria, Turkey, and even North Africa using the newly invented recording machine of Thomas Edison. In this way his ear became saturated with the driving rhythms and odd-number meters of peasant dances, as well as the unusual scales on which the folk melodies of Eastern Europe were constructed. If the cosmopolitan Stravinsky took his folk melodies from printed anthologies, Bartók found his among the people.

The musical heritage of Eastern Europe is heard continually throughout Bartók's music, from his first string quartet (1908) to his great final works for orchestra: *Music for Strings, Percussion and Celesta* (1936), *Divertimento for Strings* (1939), and *Concerto for Orchestra* (1943). This last-named work is probably Bartók's best-known composition. Certainly, it is among his most alluring creations.

CONCERTO FOR ORCHESTRA (1943)

The title of this composition, as Bartók wrote in the program notes for its first performance, "is explained by [the work's] tendency to treat the single orchestral instruments in a 'concertante' or soloistic manner." Instead of having one unchanging group function as soloists, as in a Baroque concerto grosso*, Bartók's group of soloists has a continually revolving membership, drawing at various times on different instruments of the orchestra. Now one, now another instrument or combination of instruments steps forward to display its distinctive tonal

a modern-day concerto grosso

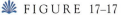
FIGURE 17–17
Béla Bartók recording folk songs among Czech-speaking peasants in 1908. The performers sang into the megaphone of a wax-cylinder recording machine invented by Thomas Edison.

color against the backdrop of the full orchestra. There are five movements: The first is "written in a more or less regular sonata form," as the composer says, and makes use of the folklike pentatonic* scale; the second is a colorful parade of pairs of instruments; the third is an atmospheric nocturne*, an example of what is called Bartók's "night music," in which the woodwinds slither around chromatically above a misty tremolo in the strings; the fourth is an unusual intermezzo; while the fifth is a vigorous peasant dance in sonata–allegro form. Let us focus our attention on the fourth movement, *Intermezzo interrotto (Broken Intermezzo)*.

An **intermezzo** (Italian for "between piece") is a light musical interlude intended to separate and thus break the mood of two more serious surrounding movements. But here, as the title *Broken Intermezzo* indicates, the light intermezzo is itself rudely interrupted by contrasting music. A sophisticated mood is first established by a charming theme in the oboe. As is usual for Bartók, this melody shows the influence of the Hungarian folk song both in its pentatonic construction (the five notes that make up the scale of the melody are B, C$\sharp$, E, F$\sharp$, and A$\sharp$) and in the way it switches back and forth between an even 2/4 and an odd 5/8:

Hungarian melodies

EXAMPLE 17–9

After the tune is passed among several wind instruments, an even more ingratiating melody emerges in the strings. It, too, is Hungarian in style. In fact, it is Bartók's idealized reworking of the song *You Are Lovely, You Are Beautiful, Hungary.*

EXAMPLE 17–10

But the nostalgic vision of the homeland is suddenly interrupted by a new, cruder theme in the clarinet, and it also tells a tale. Bartók took this clarinet melody from the Russian composer Dimitri Shostakovitch's Symphony No. 7, a programmatic work depicting the German invasion of Russia (1942). Bartók borrowed the theme Shostakovitch had written to signify the invading Germans, believing its simple quarter-note descent to be appropriately heavy and trite.

EXAMPLE 17–11

Thus, Bartók's intermezzo can be heard as an autobiographical work in which, as the composer related to a friend, "the artist declares his love for his native land in a serenade which is suddenly interrupted in a crude and violent manner; he is seized by rough, booted men who even break his instrument." Bartók

tells us what he thinks of these "rough, booted men" by surrounding them with rude, jeering noises in the trumpets and woodwinds. Ultimately, he brings back the idyllic vision of the homeland by returning to the opening two themes. The main events of the *Broken Intermezzo* are enumerated in the short Listening Guide that follows. A more detailed description of the piece will emerge as you complete Listening Exercise 36.

an anti-Nazi work

LISTENING GUIDE

Béla Bartók
Concerto for Orchestra (1943)
Fourth movement, *Broken Intermezzo*

6CD 5/14;
2CD 2/11

Genre: Concerto

0:00		Four-note introduction
0:06	**A**	Oboe introduces theme
1:07	**B**	Violas introduce theme
1:49	**A**	Oboe briefly plays theme
2:14	**C**	Clarinet introduces theme (borrowed from Shostakovich)
2:22		Rude noises in trumpets and woodwinds
2:36	**C**	Parody of theme in violins
2:44		More rude noises
2:52	**C**	Theme played in inversion by the violins
2:56		More rude noises
3:04	**B**	Theme returns in violas
3:23	**A**	Theme returns in English horn, flute, and clarinet

(Listening Exercise 36)

❋ THREE AMERICAN EXPERIMENTALISTS: IVES, VARÈSE, AND CAGE

There are times in the history of art when the rejection of a previously dominant system coincides with radical experimentation, as new ideas compete to fill a void. In music this happened at the turn of the seventeenth century, when many composers suddenly gave up on imitative polyphony, as well as at the turn of the twentieth century, when tonality and consonance no longer seemed important. Painting, too, experienced a revolution after the turn of the twentieth century, when it was confirmed that photographic realism in art was no longer desirable. Radical experimentation continued into mid-century. Painters Jasper Johns (Fig. 17–18) and Andy Warhol (Fig. 17–25), for example, explored a host of new ways that paint, and other materials, could be applied to canvas. Simultaneously, musicians sought new ways to organize pitch, density, and spacial relationships.

anything is possible

✹ FIGURE 17–18

The American Optical artist Jasper Johns has taken a venerable object and created unexpected effects of light, motion, and color in his *Three Flags* (1958).

Among the most radical of these exploratory musical thinkers were Charles Ives (1874–1954), Edgard Varèse (1883–1965), and John Cage (1912–1992). By creating a novel style of collage art, Ives gave new meaning to traditional and popular music material; Varèse worked to remove the element of pitch from music so as to concentrate on color and texture; and Cage brought noises from the everyday world into the concert hall and asked why these, too, were not music, thereby questioning our very definition of this art. That all three of these experimental composers were American suggests the probing, independent, sometimes scientific quality of American musical thought during the twentieth century.

✹ FIGURE 17–19

Young Charles Ives in the baseball uniform of Hopkins Grammar School, New Haven, Connecticut. A better baseball player than student, Ives needed a year of preparatory school before he entered Yale. At Hopkins he studied English, German, Latin, and Greek, but not music.

Charles Ives (1874–1954)

Charles Ives was the greatest, and most eccentric, of American composers. He was born in Danbury, Connecticut, the son of George Ives (1845–1894), a bandleader in the Union Army who had served with General Grant during the Civil War. The senior Ives gave his son a highly unorthodox musical education, at least by European standards. True, there was the obligatory study of the three B's—Bach, Beethoven, and Brahms—along with harmony and counterpoint, as well as lessons on the violin, piano, organ, cornet, and drums. But young Ives was also taught how to "stretch his ears," as he said. In one exercise he was made to sing *Swanee River* in E♭ while his father accompanied him on the piano in the key of C—a useful lesson in polytonality*! The sounds that stuck in his ears were those of marches, popular and patriotic songs, fiddlers' jigs, minstrel tunes, and church hymns.

Since his forebears had gone to Yale, it was decided that Charles should enroll there, too. At Yale he took courses in music with Horatio Parker (1863–1919), a composer of some capability who had been trained in Germany. But Ives's youthful, independent ideas about how music should sound clashed with Parker's traditional European notions of harmony and counterpoint. The stu-

🌿 FIGURE 17–20
William Harnett's *Music and Good Luck* (1888) creates a satisfying collage by melding various objects from a horse barn and the world of music.

dent learned to leave his more radical musical experimentations, such as a fugue with a subject entering in four different keys, outside Parker's classroom. Ives became heavily involved in extracurricular activities, including fraternity musicals, and maintained a D+ average (a "gentleman's" mark before the days of grade inflation).

When he graduated with the class of 1898, Charles Ives decided not to pursue music as a profession. He realized that the sort of music he had in his head was not the kind the public would pay to hear. So he headed for New York City, and in 1907 he and a friend formed the company of Ives and Myrick, an agency that sold insurance as a subsidiary of Mutual of New York (MONY). Ives and Myrick grew to become the largest insurance agency in the United States, and in the year in which Ives retired, 1929, had sales of $49 million.

But Charles Ives led two lives: insurance executive by day, frantic composer by night. During the twenty years between his departure from Yale (1898) and the American entry into World War I (1917), Ives wrote the bulk of his 43 works for symphony or band, 41 choral pieces, approximately 75 works for piano solo or various chamber ensembles, and more than 150 songs. Almost without exception they went unheard. Ives made little effort to get his music performed— composition was for him a very private matter. Gradually, however, word of his unusual creations spread among a few influential performers and critics. In 1947 he was awarded the Pulitzer Prize in music for his Third Symphony, one he had written forty years earlier! In his usual gruff, eccentric way, Ives told the members of the Pulitzer committee, "Prizes are for boys. I'm grown up."

THE FOURTH OF JULY (1911–1913)

No piece could be more representative of Ives's distinctly American brand of musical experimentalism than *The Fourth of July*. Ives's own words best capture the panoramic vision of a small-town Fourth of July that inspired this one-movement orchestral work.

> Cannon on the Green, Village Band on Main St., fire crackers, shanks mixed on cornets, strings around big toes, torpedoes, Church-bells, lost finger, fifes, clam-chowder, a prize-fight, drum-corps, burnt shins, parades (in and out of step), saloons all closed (more drunks than usual), baseball game (Danbury All-Stars vs. Beaver Brook Boys), pistols, mobbed umpire, Red, White and Blue, runaway horse,—and the day ends with the sky-rocket over the Church-steeple, just after the annual explosion sets the Town-Hall on fire.

a giant collage of sound

The Fourth of July is a piece of program music*, but not one in which a succession of musically described events unfold in logical order. Instead, Ives superimposes many musical references to create a giant collage of sound. Marching bands playing in different keys, army buglers, sailors, country fiddlers, and church choirs can all be heard more or less simultaneously. They are depicted musically by the more than fifteen patriotic songs, popular tunes, hymns, and marches that Ives borrowed, reaching back into the musical memory of his youth. All of these he brings together to produce a jumble of melody, an ear-splitting dissonance, and rhythms of such complexity that they are almost impossible to play. The most oft-quoted tune is *Columbia, the Gem of the Ocean* (see Listening Guide), our unofficial "national anthem" before *The Star-Spangled Banner* was adopted as such in 1931. Snippets of the *Battle Hymn of the Republic, The Battle Cry of Freedom,* and *Reveille* can also be heard. Most of the borrowed melodies, however, including *Yankee Doodle* and *Dixie,* are inaudible in

the midst of the incredible din of twisted tunes and dissonant harmonies. The cacophony comes to a climax with the burst of a skyrocket toward the end. All of this sounds very wrong, but as Ives instructed his copyist about *The Fourth of July:* "Dear Mr. Price: Please don't try to make things nice! All the wrong notes are right."

What is Ives trying to do in this wild, seemingly chaotic ride through America's past? Above all, he is playing with our musical memories, our nostalgia for the familiar tunes of our youth. He evokes these treasured songs, but then refuses to set them in the traditional tonal, consonant background we remember and expect. Instead, he places the familiar objects in an alien, hyperdissonant environment. In a manner akin to that of an avant-garde artist who reinterprets fragments of reality in surprising ways (see Fig. 17–20), Ives defamiliarizes the familiar. He challenges us to look at the ordinary in a new light, suggesting that truth may lurk therein. We might prefer the musically familiar and comfortable—the old world of tonality and consonance—but Ives is saying, in effect: What is past is past and will be no more; let us not mourn the loss, but exalt in the possibilities unleashed by a new world of vibrant sound.

a new view of the familiar

LISTENING GUIDE

Charles Ives
The Fourth of July (1911–1913)

6CD 5/15

O Co - lum - bia, the gem of the o - cean, The home of the brave and the free, ___

0:00	Violins play slow variation of *Columbia*
0:36	Basses do the same
0:55	Tuba joins the basses
1:30	Piccolo plays variation of *Columbia*
1:42	Strings play dissonant variation of *Columbia*
2:01	Piccolo plays variation of *Columbia*
3:05	Strings and winds play *Battle Hymn of the Republic*
3:17	Horns play *The Battle Cry of Freedom*
3:27	Horns and then trumpet play *Reveille*

ff

3:39	Trombone plays *Columbia*
3:49	A march begins with the entry of the drums
3:59	Piccolo sneaks in phrase of *The Girl I Left Behind Me*
4:09	Orchestral explosion: the fireworks have begun
4:35	March begins again with *Columbia* in the French horns
4:44	Fragments of many tunes are played in various instruments, including *Columbia* (trombones), *Battle Hymn of the Republic* (cornet), *Dixie* (piccolo), and *Yankee Doodle* (piano and xylophone), but most can't be heard
5:43	Pause before the strings carry the skyrocket over the church steeple
6:05	Remnants of the rocket quietly fizzle back to earth

Edgard Varèse (1883–1965)

Passage to a land of new aesthetic frontiers was also the goal of Edgard Varèse. Thus in 1915 this French musician left old-world Europe and sailed for the United States. An accidental fire caused the loss of some of the scores he had brought with him from Paris. He then destroyed the rest, obliterating in this symbolic act all traces of his European musical past. Significantly, Varèse entitled his first work written in this country *Amériques* (1921), suggesting not only a new geography but also a new world of musical sound. Besides the usual complement of strings, brasses, and woodwinds, *Amériques* also requires a battery of new percussion instruments, including sirens and sleigh bells, most of which had never before been heard in a symphony orchestra. Later compositions, such as *Hyperprism* (1923) and *Intégrales* (1925), likewise experiment with percussion instruments, to the virtual exclusion of the traditional strings. Eventually, Varèse did away entirely with conventional acoustical instruments, creating something called **musique concrète** (see boxed essay on page 360).

Varèse not only uses more percussion instruments than any other composer, but he employs them in a most untraditional way. In earlier centuries, orchestral composers customarily called on the percussion for purposes of accent. By means of taps, thuds, and bangs these instruments helped delineate the main features, and especially climaxes, of the musical structure. Like a spice, they added character, but did not change—and did not constitute—the essence of the music.

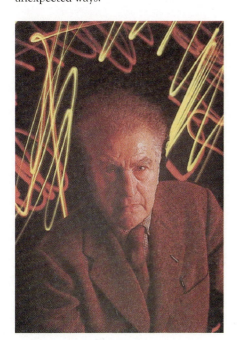

❀ FIGURE 17–21 AND 17–22 (left) Composer Edgard Varèse surrounded by a light sculpture. (right) Just as the composer Edgard Varèse creates interacting "sound masses" of varying color and density, so the American sculptor Alexander Calder, in his mobiles such as *Lobster Trap and Fish Tail* (1939), creates "spatial zones" of different color and density that, on the slightest breath of air, interact in unexpected ways.

IONIZATION (1931)

In *Ionization*, however, Varèse completely turns the musical tables. Now there are no instruments other than percussive ones. Thirteen performers play thirty-seven different instruments, including two sirens, two tam-tams, a gong, cymbals, anvils, three different sizes of bass drum, bongos, snare drums, various Cuban rattles and gourds, slap-sticks, Chinese blocks in three registers, sleigh bells, chimes, a piano, and more. There are no strings,

brasses, or woodwinds. Percussive sounds do not reinforce the music—they are the music.

Most important, nearly all the instruments required in *Ionization* generate sounds of indefinite pitch—they produce no one continuous frequency or musical tone. They cannot play melody and harmony. They can, however, set rhythms, show colors, and fill in sonic space. Consequently, what Varèse creates is a succession of blocks of sound, each with a distinctive color, texture, and density. He called these blocks "zones of intensity." Varèse's zones collide, repel, interact, and reform, not unlike the changing modules of color with a mobile (see Fig. 17–22). As does the avant-garde sculptor, so too this modern composer shows that compelling works of art can be created by focusing on color, texture, density, and registral distribution (ups and downs, highs and lows). The message of *Ionization*: Music need not always be a linear narrative (unfolding melody supported by harmony) but can be a "sound sculpture" made up of ever-changing sonic zones.

color, texture, and density, but no melody or harmony

LISTENING GUIDE

Edgard Varèse
Ionization (1931)

6CD 6/1

0:00	Sound zone 1: shimmer of cymbals, drums, gongs, and sirens
0:27	Sound zone 2: snare drum and tam-tam create sharply defined rhythms, thin texture
0:42	Sound zone 1 returns briefly
0:52	Sound zone 2 expanded, becomes denser as more instruments added
1:47	Siren from sound zone 1 penetrates into sound zone 2
1:58	Sound zone 3: pounding intensity (*fortissimo*), denser texture in low register (bass drums)
2:33	Sound zone 4 (high-sounding anvils) interacts with sound zone 1
2:47	Sound zones 1–4 interact at various levels of intensity (louds and softs)
3:57	Sound zone 5 (piano and chimes) added to the mix
4:40	Fadeout: intensity diminishes, texture thins as accumulated sonority of five sound zones fades away

John Cage (1912–1992)

John Cage was born in Los Angeles, the son of an inventor. He was graduated valedictorian of Los Angeles High School and spent two years at nearby Pomona College before going to Europe to learn more about art, architecture, and music. Arriving in New York in 1942, he worked variously as a wall washer at the YWCA, teacher of music and mycology (the science of mushrooms) at the New School for Social Research, and as music director of a modern dance company.

From his earliest days as a musician, Cage had a special affection for percussion instruments and the unusual sounds they can create. His *First Construction (in Metal)* (1939) has six percussionists play piano, metal thunder-sheets, oxen bells, cowbells, sleigh bells, water gongs, and brake drums, among other things. By 1941 he had collected three hundred percussion objects of this kind—anything that might make an unusual noise when struck or shaken. Cage's tinkering with percussive sounds led him to invent the **prepared piano:** a grand piano outfitted with screws, bolts, washers, erasers, and bits of felt and plastic all in-

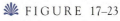 FIGURE 17–23

"I have nothing to say and I am saying it." John Cage.

Electronic Music

Most classical music is **acoustical music**—music produced by instruments that make sound "naturally" by means of vibrating strings, pipes, or drums, for example. Since World War II, however, scientific developments have made possible **electronic music**—music produced by machines that generate sound using electronic circuitry.

The earliest experiments with the creation of electronic sound gave rise to *musique concrète*. **Musique concrète** is so-called because the composer works directly, or concretely, with sounds recorded from the natural world, not with intermediary symbols (musical notation) and the middlemen (performers). A car horn, a jackhammer, or a dog's bark may be recorded and doctored in some way, and then reassembled (mixed) to form an unexpected montage of sound. Pierre Schaeffer working in Paris and Edgard Varèse in New York were among the first practitioners of *musique concrète*, Varèse's *Poème electronique* (1958) being a landmark in the history of this sort of synthetic music. More recently, the principle of *musique concrète* has been employed by George Lucas at his Skywalker Sound Studio (see below) in the *Star Wars* films. The sound of the Imperial Walkers, for example, was created by modifying and layering the noise of a bicycle chain being dropped on a concrete floor—a literal example of the principle of *musique concrète!*

The most important device for electronic music today is the **synthesizer,** a machine that creates, transforms, and combines (or synthesizes) electronic sounds. If *musique concrète* involves recorded sounds from the everyday world, a synthesizer creates its own sounds electronically by means of an os-cillator. An **oscillator** is a device that, when activated by an electronic current, pulses back and forth, producing an electronic signal that can be modified in various ways: It can be made higher or lower, not just by a tone or semitone, but by every small fraction of an interval in between; its color (timbre) can be changed—a clarinet sound turned into that of a trombone, a violin tone into that of an organ—by modifying the waveform and the relative prominence of the overtones*. When hooked up to a keyboard, the synthesizer places at the fingertips of the user a new range of hitherto-unknown and unimaginable sounds. More important, a single electronic instrument can now approximate the sounds of many different acoustical instruments. Keyboard synthesizers such as the Yamaha SY-22 have become indispensable for both "serious" composers and rock performers alike.

Most synthesizers today are driven by computers, and the union of the two has created a new genre of "serious" music called computer music. The principle of **computer music** is this: all aspects of musical sound—pitch, duration, color, volume, attack and decay—can be measured and expressed quantitatively in binary numbers. Such numbers can be stored and manipulated by the computer and, on command, turned into electrical voltages that can then be pushed through speakers to produce audible sound. Avant-garde compositions can be created in this fashion. (This same technology—the capacity to store and retrieve digital sound—allows music to be sent over the Internet.) Today the computer-driven synthesizer can produce sounds that are almost indistinguishable from those of a ninety-piece orchestra. Needless to say, this has revolutionized the world of commercial music. The computer-equipped recording studio now generates much of the music we hear on radio and television and at the movies.

At Skywalker Sound, the sound studio of George Lucas in Marin County, California, there are no walls between art music and popular music. This state-of-the-art facility has created the sound tracks for the recent *Star Wars* films by exploiting the latest electronic sound systems as well as more traditional acoustical music, recorded in London. At the heart of the studio is the Skywalker Scoring Stage. Here a full symphony orchestra can record on as many as forty-eight tracks, as the film shows on screen. The sound of the acoustical instruments can then be enhanced by computers for special effects. The hall also has acoustical panels on all surfaces to alter dramatically the reverberation characteristics of the room. Besides serving as a center for the creation of film music, the facility is also in high demand for pop, jazz, and classical recording sessions.

The television composer W. G. (Snuffy) Walden at a keyboard synthesizer in his electronic studio near Los Angeles.

Scoring stage at the Skywalker Ranch, Marin County, California.

FIGURE 17–24
John Cage's "prepared piano." By putting spoons, forks, screws, paper clips, and other sundry objects into the strings of the piano, the composer changes the instrument from one producing melodic tones to one generating percussive impacts.

serted between the strings (Fig. 17–24). This transformed the piano into a one-man percussion band that could produce a great variety of sounds and noises—twangs, zaps, rattles, thuds, and the like—no two of which were exactly the same in pitch or color. In creating the prepared piano, Cage was merely going farther along the experimental trail first blazed by his spiritual mentor, Edgard Varèse: "Years ago, after I decided to devote my life to music, I noticed that people distinguished between noises and sounds. I decided to follow Varèse and fight for noises, to be on the side of the underdog."

Cage's glorification of everyday noise began in earnest during the 1950s. Rather than engage in a titanic struggle to shape the elements of music, as did Beethoven, he decided to sit back, relax, and just let noises occur around him. In creating this sort of purposeless, undirected music, Cage invented what has come to be called chance music, the ultimate in musical experimentation. In **chance music,** musical events are not carefully predetermined by the composer but come in an unpredictable sequence as the result of traditionally unmusical activities such as using astrological charts, tossing coins, throwing dice, or shuffling the pages of music any which way. In *Music Walk* (1958), for example, one or more pianists connect lines and dots in any fashion to create a musical "score" from which to play. Such "scores" only suggest in the most vague way what the musician is to do. The musical "happening" that results is the sort of spontaneous group experience that was to flower during the 1960s. More radical still is Cage's work *0'00"* (1962), which allows the performer total artistic freedom. When performed by Cage himself in 1962, he sliced and prepared vegetables at a table on a stage, put them through a food processor, and then drank the juice, all the while amplifying and broadcasting the sound of these activities around the hall. In a funny way, Cage's attempts to elevate the random, ordinary noise of food processing to the level of art is rather like Andy Warhol's glorification of the Campbell's soup can (Fig. 17–25).

FIGURE 17–25
The *Campbell's Soup Can* (1965) painted by Andy Warhol (1930–1987) asks the fundamental question: What is art?

Must music, too, be "goal oriented"?

Naturally, music critics called Cage a joker and a charlatan. Most would agree that his "compositions" in and of themselves are not of great musical value. But he did have a philosophy about music that he articulated by means of questions implied in his music. By focusing on the chance appearance of ordinary noise, Cage aggressively asks us to ponder the fundamental principles that underlie most Western music. Why must sounds of similar range and color come one after the other, why must music have form and unity, why must it have "meaning," why must it express something, why must it develop and climax, why must it be goal oriented, as is so much of human activity in the West?

4′33″ (1952)

The "composition" of Cage that causes us to focus on these questions most intently is his *4′33″*. Here one or more performers carrying any sort of instrument come out on the stage, seat themselves, open the music, and play nothing. For each of the three carefully timed movements there is no notated music but only the indication *tacet* ("it is silent"). With no organized sound to be heard during the four minutes and thirty-three seconds of silence that follows, the listener gradually becomes aware of the background noise in the hall—a creaking floor, a passing car, a dropped paper clip, an electrical hum. It turns out there is no such thing as absolute silence. Cage asks us to embrace these random, everyday noises—to tune our ears in innocent sonic wonder. Are these sounds not of artistic value too? What is music? What is noise? What is art?

Can random noise be music?

Needless to say, we have not filled your tapes and CDs with four minutes and thirty-three seconds of background noise. You can create your own, and John Cage would have liked that. Listen to *4′33″* with the following guide and note what you hear. Perhaps this experiment will make you more aware of how important conscious organization is to the art we call music. If nothing else, Cage makes us realize that music, above all, is a form of communication from one person to the next and that random background noise can do nothing to express or communicate ideas and feelings.

LISTENING GUIDE

John Cage
4′33″ (1952)

0:00–0:30	First movement—silence (?)
0:31–2:53	Second movement—silence (?)
2:54–4:33	Third movement—silence (?)

 ## THREE TRADITIONALISTS: SERGEY PROKOFIEV, AARON COPLAND, AND ELLEN TAAFFE ZWILICH

While experimental composers in this century, such as Varèse and Cage, have sought to break with the traditions of Western music, other musicians have tried to extend and invigorate the past by imposing on it modern idioms and styles. In this sense composers like Aaron Copland and Ellen Taaffe Zwilich, to name only two among the traditionalists, are more evolutionary than revolutionary. Their aim is to show that traditional values of form, balance, melodiousness, warmth, emotion, and meaning in music have validity in the modern sonic world. Modernity, of course, could never fully eradicate tradition. The two aesthetics continue to exist side by side. Each offers an ongoing critique of the other, and thereby further identifies and defines itself.

Toward the end of the first World War (1914–1918), a new artistic movement called **Neo-classicism** sought to revive the balanced forms and conjunct melodies of earlier music, specifically of the Baroque and Classical periods. The resourceful Igor Stravinsky turned away from his large-scale, colorful Russian ballets like *The Rite of Spring* to write for a much smaller, leaner orchestra of strings and woodwinds. "I attempted to build a new music on eighteenth-century classicism," he said. Neo-classicism rejected not only the large orchestra and the emotionalism of the Romantics but also the extreme sort of dissonance and atonality being advanced by modernists such as Arnold Schoenberg and his Second Viennese School (see page 345). Needless to say, the listening public, which had never taken kindly to the experimental works of the radical avant-garde, welcomed the greater simplicity, clarity, and even humor in the Neo-classical style. The earliest and perhaps most enjoyable example of musical Neo-classicism is Sergey Prokofiev's *Classical Symphony* (1917).

Sergey Prokofiev (1891–1953)

The career of Sergey Prokofiev is full of contradictions and ironies, caused in part by the place he occupied in Russian history. The son of a well-to-do farm administrator, he fled the Communist Revolution in 1917, only later to celebrate in music the most murderous of the revolutionaries, Joseph Stalin (1879–1953). He was known as the dissonant, atonal "bad boy" of the St. Petersburg Conservatory, where he received his musical education, but later wrote such pleasantly benign works as *Peter and the Wolf* (1936). He thought of himself above all as a serious composer—the author of seven symphonies, six operas and six ballets, five piano concertos, and nine piano sonatas—but today is remembered mainly for his lighter works: the *Classical Symphony*, *Peter and the Wolf*, and the film scores *Lieutenant Kijé* and *Alexander Nevsky*. He and Joseph Stalin died within minutes of each other on the night of March 5, 1953, but news of Prokofiev's death was withheld for days so as not to deflect attention away from the deceased dictator. No flowers could be bought for the great composer's coffin: The funeral of the supreme murderer, without exaggeration, had claimed them all.

CLASSICAL SYMPHONY (1917)

There is a sense of historical irony present as well in Prokofiev's *Classical Symphony*. It is the irony created by a clash of musical systems and values: those of the eighteenth century against those of the modern world. Prokofiev creates a model of Neo-classicism by invoking the orchestra and the musical forms of Joseph Haydn. He hypothesized: "It seemed to me that had Haydn lived in our day, he would have retained his own style while accepting something new at the same time." The "something new" in this four-movement Neo-classical symphony is the following: a melody that is more disjunct and extended than Haydn would have written, a harmony that slides suddenly to unexpected chords, and a dissonance so biting and so frequent as to be unknown to classical composers. What is more, Prokofiev distorts our traditional sense of timing and balance; in this very short symphony every musical idea seems to end be-

FIGURE 17–26
Just as Stravinsky, after the example of Prokofiev, entered a Neo-classical period during the 1920s, so the artist Pablo Picasso painted in a lighter, more transparent Neo-classical style in that decade. Although the figures in his *Mother and Child* (1921–1922) are somewhat extended and abstract, the formal composition of this painting, which harks back to a Madonna and Child of the Renaissance, is classical.

FIGURE 17–27
Sergey Prokofiev.

fore it has begun. By juxtaposing the classical and the modern in a single work, the composer focuses attention on the question: "What makes musical style?" Thus, as we listen to the *Classical Symphony* we enjoy the music in and of itself, but we also think about the interaction of contrasting musical styles. Prokofiev's work is simultaneously art and a critique of art.

LISTENING GUIDE

Sergey Prokofiev
Classical Symphony (Symphony No. 1; 1917)
First movement, *Allegro* (fast)

6CD 6/2

Genre: Symphony
Form: Sonata–allegro

EXPOSITION

0:00   Violins play racing first theme

0:23   Woodwinds lead lively transition
0:55   Violins softly play second theme above bassoon counterpoint

1:28   *Forte* closing theme

DEVELOPMENT

1:44   First theme returns briefly
1:54   Transition material developed and extended to different keys
2:13   *Fortissimo* expansion of second theme
2:40   Closing theme used as retransition*

RECAPITULATION

2:54   First theme returns
3:04   Woodwinds lead transition
3:30   Soft violins bring back second theme above bassoon counterpoint
3:58   *Forte* closing theme

Aaron Copland (1900–1990)

The tradition embodied in the music of Aaron Copland is, simply said, our American musical heritage. He does not reuse materials taken from eighteenth-century Europe but instead employs American hymn tunes, cowboy songs, and jazz idioms. These he sets not in a collage of dissonant atonality, as did his older contemporary, Charles Ives, but in a conservative backdrop of generally consonant harmony.

an American in Paris

Copland was born in Brooklyn of Jewish immigrant parents. After a rudimentary musical education in New York City, he set sail for Paris to broaden his artistic horizons. In this he was not alone, for the City of Light at this time attracted young writers, painters, and musicians from across the world, including Stravinsky, Picasso, James Joyce (1882–1941), Gertrude Stein (1874–1946), Ernest Hemingway (1898–1961), and F. Scott Fitzgerald (1896–1940). After three years of study Copland returned to the United States, determined to compose a kind of music that was distinctly American. Like other young expatriate artists during the Twenties, Copland had to leave his homeland to learn what was distinctive about it: "In greater or lesser degree, all of us discovered America in Europe."

At first Copland sought to forge an American style by incorporating into his music elements of jazz, recognized the world over as a uniquely American creation. His debt to the Jazz Age is especially apparent in his *Piano Concerto* (1926), written two years after George Gershwin's *Rhapsody in Blue for Jazz Band and Piano* (see page 389). Then, beginning in the late 1930s, Copland turned his attention to a series of projects that had rural and western America as their subjects. The ballet scores *Billy the Kid* (1938) and *Rodeo* (1942) are set in the West and make use of classic cowboy songs like *Goodbye, Old Paint* and *The Old Chisholm Trail*. Another ballet, *Appalachian Spring* (1944), recreates the ambience of the farm country of Pennsylvania, and his single opera, *The Tender Land* (1954), is set in the cornbelt of the Midwest.

In these distinctly American works, Copland's musical voice is unique and consistently conservative. He uses folk and popular elements to soften the dissonant harmonies and disjunct melodies of European modernism. Copland's melodies tend to be more stepwise and diatonic than those of other twentieth-century composers, perhaps because Western folk and popular tunes are fundamentally conjunct and without chromaticism. His harmonies are almost always tonal and often slow-moving in a way that can evoke the vastness and grandeur of the American landscape. The triad, too, is still important with Copland, perhaps for its stability and simplicity, but he frequently uses it in a modern way, as we shall see, by having two triads sound simultaneously, creating mildly dissonant polychords. But perhaps the most important component in the distinctive "Copland sound" is his clear, luminous orchestration. He does not mix colors to produce rich Romantic blends, but keeps the four families of instruments (strings, woodwinds, brasses, and percussion) more or less to their own group. And he distributes the instruments of the orchestra so as to construct a solid bass, a very thin middle, and a top of one or two high, clear tones. It is this separation and careful spacing of the instruments that creates the fresh, wide-open sound so pleasing in Copland's music.

The clarity and simplicity of Aaron Copland's music is not accidental. During the Great Depression of the 1930s, he became convinced that the gulf between modern music and the ordinary citizen had become too great—that dissonance and atonality had little to say to most music lovers. "It made no sense to ignore them and to continue writing as if they did not exist. I felt that it was worth the effort to see if I couldn't say what I had to say in the simplest possible terms." Thus, he not only wrote appealing new tonal works like *Fanfare for the Common Man* (1942) but also was attracted to traditional tunes such as *The Gift to Be Simple*, which he uses in *Appalachian Spring*.

APPALACHIAN SPRING (1944)

Appalachian Spring is a one-act ballet that tells the story of "a pioneer celebration of spring in a newly built farmhouse in Pennsylvania in the early 1800s." A new bride and her farmer-husband express through dance the anxieties and joys of life in pioneer America. The work was composed in 1944 for the great lady of American choreography, Martha Graham (1893–1991), and it won Copland a Pulitzer Prize the following year. It is divided into eight connected

FIGURE 17–28
Aaron Copland conducting one of his scores at a recording session at CBS.

his musical style

a clear, wide-open sound

an American ballet

sections that differ in tempo and mood. Copland has provided a brief description of each of these orchestral scenes.

Section 1. "Introduction of the characters one by one, in a suffused light." The quiet beauty of the land at daybreak is revealed as the orchestra slowly spaces out the notes of the tonic and then dominant triad.

EXAMPLE 17–12

While this simultaneous presentation of two triads should be heard as a polychord, the effect is only mildly dissonant because of the slow, quiet way in which the notes of the two chords are introduced. The serene simplicity of the introduction sets the tone for the entire work.

Section 2. "A sentiment both elated and religious gives the keynote of this scene." The early calm is suddenly broken by a lively dance with a salient rhythm played aggressively in the strings. As the dance proceeds, a more restrained, hymnlike melody emerges in the trumpet.

Section 3 is a dance for the two principals, in ballet parlance a pas de deux, accompanied by lyrical writing for strings and winds. Sections 4 and 5 are musical depictions of the livelier aspects of country life, with 4 including a toe-tappin' hoedown, while Section 6 recalls the quiet calm of the opening of the ballet.

Section 7. "Calm and flowing. Scenes of daily activity for the Bride and her Farmer-husband." For this section Copland chose to make use of a traditional tune of the Shakers, an extreme religious sect that prospered in the Appalachian region in the early nineteenth century and whose members showed their spiritual intensity in frenzied singing, dancing, and shaking. The tune, as Copland first presents it in the clarinet, is given in example 17–13. Since the action of the ballet at this point concerns "scenes of daily activity," the original text of the Shaker song is harmonious with what is occurring on stage:

EXAMPLE 17–13

a Shaker tune

'Tis the gift to be simple,
'Tis the gift to be free,
'Tis the gift to come down where we ought to be,
And when we find ourselves in the place just right,
'Twill be in the valley of love and delight.

❀ FIGURE 17–29
A scene from Martha Graham's ballet *Appalachian Spring*, with music by Aaron Copland.

Thereafter come five variations in which *The Gift to Be Simple* is not so much varied as it is clothed in different instrumental attire.

Section 8. "The Bride takes her place among her neighbors." Serenity returns to the scene as the strings, then the woodwinds, and then the strings and woodwinds together play a slow, mainly stepwise descent "like a prayer." The hymnlike melody from section 2 is heard again in the flute, followed by the quiet landscape music from the beginning of the ballet. Darkness has again descended on the valley, leaving the young pioneer couple "strong in their new house" and secure in their community.

LISTENING GUIDE

Aaron Copland
Appalachian Spring (1944)
Sections 1, 2, 7, and 8

6CD 6/3–6;
2CD 2/12–15

Genre: Ballet music

SECTION 1 (6CD 6/3; 2CD 2/12)

0:00	Quiet unfolding of triads by clarinet and other instruments
0:45	Soft violin melody descends
1:11	More triads in woodwinds and trumpet
1:36	Oboe and then bassoon solos
2:19	Clarinet plays concluding triad

SECTION 2 (6CD 6/4; 2CD 2/13)

0:00	Percussive rhythm (♫ ♩ ♫ ♩) in strings and rising woodwinds
0:19	Rhythm gels into sprightly dance
0:44	Trumpet plays hymnlike melody above dance

(Continued on next page)

1:13   Rhythmic motive scattered but then played more forcefully
2:09   Hymn heard in strings, with flute counterpoint above
2:36   Rhythmic motive skips away in woodwinds

SECTION 7 (6CD 6/5; 2CD 2/14)
0:00   Clarinet presents Shaker tune

0:36   Variation 1: Oboe and bassoon play tune
1:06   Variation 2: Violas and trombones play tune at half its previous speed
1:51   Variation 3: Trumpets and trombones play tune
2:16   Variation 4: Woodwinds play tune more slowly
2:31   Variation 5: Final majestic statement of tune by full orchestra

SECTION 8 (6CD 6/6; 2CD 2/15)
0:00   Serene, stepwise string music
0:44   Woodwinds continue placid mood
0:58   Strings and winds together play more loudly
1:20   Flute enters with hymnlike tune from section 2
2:14   Clarinet plays triad from the beginning of ballet
2:29   Soft, mild polychords in strings

(Listening Exercise 37)

🌸 FIGURE 17–30
"I never have to work for themes; they can hit me at any time, and usually do." Ellen Taaffe Zwilich.

Ellen Taaffe Zwilich (b. 1939)

Like the late Aaron Copland, Ellen Taaffe Zwilich works to integrate musical modernism with earlier musical traditions. She draws not so much upon American folk music but more upon the traditions of the European concert hall. Her string quartet, four symphonies, and twelve concertos, among other works, reflect her desire to honor the traditional genres of classical music. Yet her aim is always the same: to communicate directly with the audience and thereby show that modern music can be enjoyed by the average listener. As she has said, "Most people have the mistaken impression that classical music is written by dead people."

The daughter of an airline pilot, Zwilich was born in Miami and educated at Florida State University. She then moved to New York City, where she played violin in the American Symphony Orchestra, studied composition at the Juilliard School, and worked for a time as an usher at Carnegie Hall. Zwilich's big "break" came in 1983, when she became the first woman to win the Pulitzer Prize in music. During 1995–1998 she was the first person of either sex to occupy the newly created Composer's Chair at Carnegie Hall—usher had become director. Today Zwilich enjoys a status to which all modern composers aspire: She is free to devote herself exclusively to writing music, sustained by her royalties and commissions. Recently, the New York Philharmonic and the Chicago Symphony Orchestra each paid five-figure sums for a single new piece from her pen.

The tradition of the Baroque concerto grosso* lies at the heart of Zwilich's five-movement *Concerto Grosso 1985*. Commissioned by the Washington Friends of Handel, this work honors the composer George Frideric Handel (see page 136), a leading exponent of the concerto grosso. Zwilich borrows a melody directly from Handel (the opening theme of his Violin Sonata in D major). She also embraces several elements of Baroque musical style: a regular rhythmic pulse, a repeating bass pedal point*, a walking bass*, and a harpsichord*. Yet Zwilich adds twisting chromaticism to Handel's melody (see Listening Guide) and sets it in a biting, dissonant harmony. Most important, she demands an insistent, pounding style of playing that would have shocked Handel. The composer says that the emotional core of this concerto grosso is its slow third movement, marked *Largo*. When Handel composed a largo, he invariably made it noble and serene. In Zwilich's *Largo*, everywhere lurks a brooding, menacing sound suggestive of the modern age.

Handel made modern

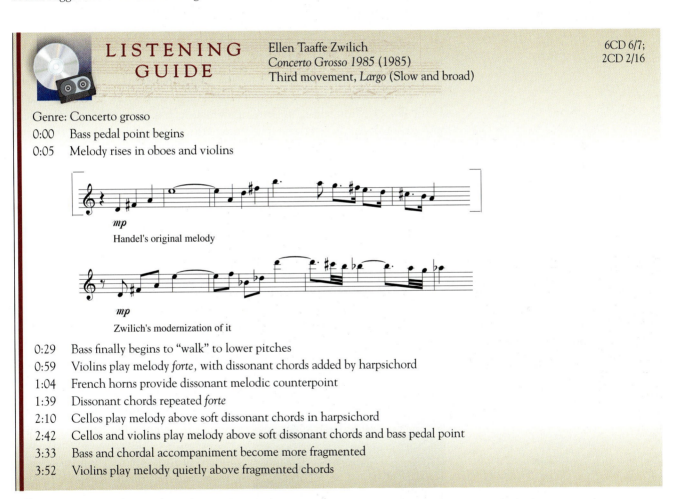

LISTENING GUIDE

Ellen Taaffe Zwilich
Concerto Grosso 1985 (1985)
Third movement, *Largo* (Slow and broad)

6CD 6/7;
2CD 2/16

Genre: Concerto grosso

0:00   Bass pedal point begins
0:05   Melody rises in oboes and violins

mp

Handel's original melody

mp

Zwilich's modernization of it

0:29   Bass finally begins to "walk" to lower pitches
0:59   Violins play melody *forte*, with dissonant chords added by harpsichord
1:04   French horns provide dissonant melodic counterpoint
1:39   Dissonant chords repeated *forte*
2:10   Cellos play melody above soft dissonant chords in harpsichord
2:42   Cellos and violins play melody above soft dissonant chords and bass pedal point
3:33   Bass and chordal accompaniment become more fragmented
3:52   Violins play melody quietly above fragmented chords

❋ NEW TRENDS: MINIMALISM AND POSTMINIMALISM

Composers at the end of the twentieth century have faced a perplexing question: Where is the mainstream of musical modernism? Should they follow Arnold Schoenberg's dissonant twelve-tone* method and create works in which all aspects of melody and harmony are strictly predetermined? Or should they head in the opposite direction and travel the freely experimental route of John Cage, even though this more chancy path can sometimes lead to musical happenings that border on the silly? Should they recreate the warmth and sentiment of nineteenth-century music, a Neo-romantic sound produced by tradi-

Where's the path to the future?

tional acoustic instruments? Or should they try to create wholly new sonorities generated electronically by means of synthesizers and computers? One recent trend, which rejects all of these solutions, is a movement in composition called Minimalism. Minimalist composers, like their counterparts the Minimalist artists (see Fig. 17–31), strive to do away with both time-honored processes and modern technical complexities.

Minimalism is a style of modern music, begun in the early 1960s, that takes a very small amount of musical material and repeats it over and over to form a composition. A three-note melodic cell, a single arpeggio, or two alternating chords is the sort of small, "minimal" element a composer will introduce, reiterate again and again, modify or add to, and then begin to repeat once more. The basic material is usually simple, tonal, and consonant. By repeating these minimal figures incessantly at a steady pulse, the composer creates a hypnotic effect—"trance music" is the name sometimes given this music. The trancelike quality of Minimalist music has influenced rock musicians (Talking Heads and Pink Floyd), as well as cinema composers (*The Truman Show* with music by Philip Glass). Minimalism, in both art and music, has been mainly an American movement. Its most successful musical practitioners are Steve Reich (b. 1936), Philip Glass (b. 1937), and John Adams (b. 1947).

John Adams (b. 1947)

John Adams, educated at Harvard and presently living in Berkeley, California, was not the first Minimalist composer. Indeed, he is not even a strict Minimalist, in that from time to time a warm, traditional-sounding melody will creep into his constantly repeating, minimal patterns. For that reason he might best be termed a "post-Minimalist"—a Minimalist who blends other materials into the minimal sonorities. Moreover, the two works for which Adams is best known, *Nixon in China* (1987) and *The Death of Klinghoffer* (1991), are anything but minimal in size—both are lengthy, three-act operas.

SHORT RIDE IN A FAST MACHINE (1986)

Let's take a brief excursion through a Minimalist work by Adams, one commissioned in 1986 by the Pittsburgh Symphony. *Short Ride in a Fast Machine* is scored for full orchestra and two electronic keyboard synthesizers*. Example 17–14 shows how the music is composed of short (mostly four-note) motives that continually repeat. There are five sections to this work (we'll call them laps). In each lap the machine seems to accelerate, not because the tempo gets faster but because more and more repeating motives are added. The effect created is that of a powerful, twentieth-century engine firing on all cylinders. As Adams has said about his Minimalist work: "You know how it is when someone asks you to ride in a terrific sports car, and then you wish you hadn't?"

🌿 F I G U R E 17–31
Frank Stella, *Los Alamitos*, from his Race Track series of 1972. Here the minimal material—repeating concentric ovals—takes its point of departure from a racetrack in Los Angeles.

🌿 F I G U R E 17–32
John Adams.

EXAMPLE 17–14

LISTENING GUIDE

John Adams
Short Ride in a Fast Machine (1986)
Delirando (with exhilaration)

6CD 6/8

Time	Description
0:00	Lap 1: woodblock, woodwinds, and keyboard synthesizers begin; brasses, snare drum, and glockenspiel* gradually added
1:06	Lap 2: bass drum "backfires"; motives rise in pitch and become more dissonant
1:47	Lap 3: starts quietly with sinister repeating motive in bass; syncopation and dissonance increase
2:40	Lap 4: two-note falling motive in bass
2:55	Lap 5: trumpets play fanfarelike motives (this is the "victory lap")
4:03	Coda: return to sounds of the start

BACK TO THE FUTURE

Among the very newest styles of contemporary music is one that, ironically, makes use of the oldest of musical materials. "Time travelers" such as Peter Maxwell Davies (b. 1934), Arvo Pärt (b. 1935), and John Tavener (b. 1944) have composed in ways that suggest that the path to the future may circle back to the music of the most distant past: to early Celtic hymns, the chants of the medieval Church, and the *a cappella** singing of the Middle Ages and Renaissance. They borrow from ancient Eastern and Western religious rituals so as to create spiritual music for a new age.

influences from the distant past

John Tavener (b. 1944)

John Tavener was born in London and received a conservative musical education at The Royal Academy of Music. During the swinging 1960s, however, he hung out with Beatles leader John Lennon. More recently, Tavener's music was featured, along with that of Elton John, at the funeral of Diana, Princess of Wales. Tavener is a visionary who looks both forward and backward. His music creates dramatic force by means of contrasting textures and sonorities; a feeling of religious ritual grows from a constant repetition of simple blocks of sound.

Among the ancient sources from which Tavener draws inspiration are the venerable rites of the Greek Orthodox Church, to which faith he belongs.

"MYSTICAL PRAYER TO THE HOLY SPIRIT" FROM *IKON OF LIGHT* (1984)

In this work for four-voice choir, Tavener has set a prayer coming from the Greek Orthodox Church. The text was fashioned by St. Simeon the New Theologian (942–1022), and thus is a thousand years old. The music, on the other hand, sounds like a mix of medieval polyphony and New Age Music. There are open fifths typical of the Middle Ages (see page 73); the singing proceeds, like Gregorian chant, without clear meter and rhythm; and the music is performed in the old *a cappella** style (without instruments). But the sounds are also repetitious, consonant, and non-confrontational, like "mystical" New Age Music. Tavener's choral sonorities seem to hang in midair, as might rays of light. The light begins on high (very high sopranos) and gradually descends (through tenors and then baritones) to earth (very low basses). When all the voices sound together in the stunning conclusion, the entire cosmos seems filled with the radiance of God as Light.

❀ FIGURE 17–33
John Tavener.

LISTENING GUIDE

John Tavener
"Mystical Prayer to the Holy Spirit" from *Ikon of Light* (1984)

6CD 6/9

Genre: *a cappella* motet

Text: Greek

0:00	Two soprano lines, one stationary, the other moving down and up by step	
	Elthe to phos to alithinon.	Come, true light.
0:15	Two tenor lines (singing in falsetto* voice), one stationary, the other moving down and up by step	
	Elthe i eonios zoi.	Come, eternal life.
0:32	Two baritone lines, one stationary, the other moving down and up by step	
	Elthe to apokekrimenon mistirion.	Come, hidden mystery.
0:53	Two bass lines, one stationary, the other moving down and up by step	
	Elthe to akatonomastos thisavros.	Come, nameless treasure.
1:13	Sopranos	
	Elthe to anekphoniton pragma.	Come, reality beyond all words.
1:34	Tenors	
	Elthe to akatanoiton prosopon.	Come, person beyond all understanding.
1:55	Baritones	
	Elthe i aidhios agalliasis.	Come, rejoicing without end.
2:16	Basses	
	Elthe to anesperon phos.	Come, light that knows no evening.
2:36	Sopranos (minor-key intervals toward the end)	
	Elthe pandon ton mellondon sothine alithini prozdokia.	Come, unfailing expectation of the saved.
3:02	Tenors overlap sopranos (minor-key intervals toward the end)	
	Elthe ton kimenon i egersis.	Come, the raising of the fallen.

(Continued on next page)

3:23	Baritones	
	Elthe ton nekron i anastasis.	Come, the resurrection of the dead.
3:42	Basses	
	Elthe o dhinatos o panda ai pion ke	Come, all powerful, for endlessly you create,
	metapion ke allion mono to voulesthe.	refashion and change all things by your will alone.
4:23	Sopranos (two moving lines against two stationary ones)	
	Elthe o aoratos ke aphanis pandi ke apsilaphitos.	Come, invisible, whom none may touch and handle.
4:49	Tenors (two moving lines against two stationary ones) overlap sopranos	
	Elthe o ai menon ametakinitos ke kathoran	Come, for you continue always unmoved, yet
	olos metakinoumenos ke erkhomenos pros imas	at every instant you are wholly in movement; you draw
	tous en to adhi kimenous, o iperano pandon	near to us who lie in the inferno, yet you remain higher
	ton ouranon.	than the heavens.
5:53	Baritones overlap sopranos and tenors, singing a line much like Gregorian chant	
	Elthe to peripothiton onama ke thriloumenon,	Come, for your name fills our hearts with longing and
	lalithine dhe parimonoper is i gnosthine,	is ever on our lips; yet who you are and what your nature,
	ipios i potapos olos imin anepidhekton.	we cannot say or know.
6:55	Basses overlap sopranos, tenors, and baritones in glorious burst of sound	
	Elthe i. eonios khara.	Come, eternal joy.

LISTENING EXERCISES

35   Igor Stravinsky   6CD 5/7–8; 2CD 8–9
The Rite of Spring (1913)
Introduction and Scene 1

Stravinksy, more than any other modern composer before the recent Minimalists (see page 370), made use of the musical ostinato—the repetition of a motive, over and over at the same pitch. The ostinato imparts to his music a feeling of kinetic energy continually being recycled and renewed. At the same time, the static quality of a repeating motive allows Stravinsky to work against the functional chord progression* and "goal-oriented" melodic expansion of Romantic music. A stationary musical moment can be maintained and enjoyed in and of itself. The following exercise asks you to focus on the ostinatos heard in the Introduction and Scene 1 of *The Rite of Spring*. Listen to the listed passages, and state if an ostinato is or is not present. Sometimes this will require listening carefully to the inner parts.

Ostinato present? (yes or no)

1. 0:35–0:56 _____   6CD 5/8; 2CD 2/9
2. 2:08–2:20 _____   6. 0:24–0:36 _____
3. 2:34–2:55 _____   7. 1:14–1:22 _____
4. 2:57–3:10 _____   8. 1:23–1:36 _____
5. 3:28–3:34 _____   9. 1:59–2:29 _____
10. Judging from your responses, are there more moments in *The Rite of Spring* making use of an ostinato than those that do not? _____

Béla Bartók
Concerto for Orchestra (1943)
Fourth movement, *Broken Intermezzo*

6CD 5/15; 2CD 2/11

The fourth movement of Bartók's *Concerto for Orchestra* is entitled *Intermezzo interrotto (Broken Intermezzo)*, and this title may be seen as a metaphor for Bartók's life in his native Hungary, broken or interrupted by the arrival of Nazi troops. The movement incorporates three themes: the first (**A**) is rather light and playful and marked by three staccato notes; the second (**B**) is a lush, lilting Hungarian melody played by the strings; while the third (**C**), representing the German soldiers, is a straight quarter-note descent, spiced with triplets, introduced by the clarinet. The themes are given here. Study them and become familiar with the general outline of each. Then listen to the movement and complete the time log for it. Remember that the movement unfolds **ABACBA,** with the second appearance of **A** being very brief.

Theme **A**

Theme **B**

Theme **C**

0:00	Brief introduction
0:06	**A** in oboe
_____	**A** flute plays inversion* of **A** with harp accompaniment
_____	**A** (varied) in French horn
_____	**A** in oboe, with counterpoint in flute
1:07	**B** enters in violas
_____	**B** heard again more forcefully in violins, with counterpoint in lower strings
_____	**A** returns briefly in oboe
2:14	**C** enters in clarinet (rude noises)
_____	**C** in strings varied by means of rapid repeating notes (rude noises)
_____	**C** now ascends in violins (rather than descends) (rude noises)
3:05	**B** returns in strings
_____	**A** returns in English horn, flute and clarinet
_____	Cadenza by flute supported by sustaining chord in strings
_____	Reminiscences of **A** played by various woodwinds lead to quiet end

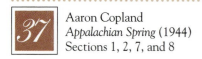

Aaron Copland   6CD 6/3–6; 2CD 2/12–15
Appalachian Spring (1944)
Sections 1, 2, 7, and 8

The following questions focus on musical themes, textures, and colors. They also ask you to consider the ways in which Copland the conservative softens the sometimes biting sound of twentieth-century music.

Section 1 (6CD 6/3; 2CD 2/12): Introduction

1. (0:00–2:31) Which family of instruments provides the bulk of the **soloists** for this opening section?
   a. percussion   b. brass   c. strings   d. woodwinds

2. (0:45–1:09) Why does this passage sound more like Romantic music than modern music?
   a. lovely French horn call suggests nature
   b. warm, primarily stepwise melody played by violin
   c. exotic English horn plays stepwise melody

3. (2:19) As the clarinet rises to end the opening section, what do the strings do?
   a. continue with the melody
   b. play a dissonant chord above the clarinet
   c. hold a single note below

Section 2 (6CD 6/4; 2CD 2/13): Joys and anxieties of pioneer life

This section is composed of two musical ideas: an energetic dance theme and a more restrained hymnlike tune (see examples on page 367).

4. The dance theme begins in the strings (at 0:19) and then the hymnlike tune enters in the trumpet (0:43). Which is more percussive and dissonant—hence more modern sounding?
   a. dance theme   b. hymnlike theme

5. (1:20–2:07) Now the lively dance theme dominates. Identify three qualities of the music you hear in this passage that are reminiscent of the music of Igor Stravinsky, a composer whom Copland greatly admired.
   a. violent, percussive strokes in the timpani, piano, and xylophone
   b. a rhythmic ostinato in the flutes and harp
   c. a sweeping melody in the cellos
   d. tone clusters in the brasses
   e. strong, irregular accents

Section 7 (6CD 6/5; 2CD 2/14): Variations on a Shaker tune *The Gift to Be Simple* (see Example 17–13 on page 366)

    0:00 Tune in the clarinet
    0:36 Oboe and bassoon present variation 1
    1:06 Violas and then violins present variation 2

6. During variation 2 (1:06–1:41), what do the woodwinds and percussion (piano, harp, and glockenspiel) do?
   a. play a flowing countermelody
   b. establish an ostinato as a sonorous backdrop

7. At the end of variation 2 is a brief transition (1:46) to variation 3 (1:51). Which of the following occurs in this transition?
   a. a rising scale in trombone and trumpet that produces a modulation to a new, higher key
   b. a descending scale in dotted notes in the strings but no modulation

   1:51 Trumpets and trombones present variation 3, against which the violins and violas interject running scales as counterpoint

8. In variation 3 (1:51–2:13) the Shaker tune appears in note values that are played in what speed?
   a. twice as fast as the previous variation
   b. the same as the previous variation
   c. twice as slow as the previous variation

   2:16 Woodwinds quietly carry the tune in variation 4

9. (2:31) The full orchestra offers the fifth and final variation. How would you describe what the strong bass line is doing in this statement?
   a. descending slowly, mainly by step
   b. descending quickly in large intervals
   c. rising slowly, mainly in large intervals

Section 8 (6CD 6/6; 2CD 2/15): "Like a prayer"

This begins with a quiet interlude in which all the strings play a slow, mainly stepwise descent. This is repeated by all the woodwinds (at 0:44) and then by strings and woodwinds together (at 0:58).

10. (2:24–2:50) At the very end the music is warm and glowing, and although polychords are present there is no feeling of harsh dissonance. Why not?
    a. because the polychords are played percussively
    b. because the notes of the polychords enter slowly and quietly, one by one
    c. because the Shaker hymn is heard in the flute

KEY WORDS

atonal music	minimalism	prepared piano
Ballets russes	*musique concrète*	serial music
chance music	Neo-classicism	seventh chord
computer music	ninth chord	*Sprechstimme*
Cubism	octave displacement	synthesizer
electronic music	oscillator	twelve-tone
eleventh chord	polychord	composition
Expressionism	polymeter	
intermezzo	polyrhythm	

A checklist of musical styles of the twentieth century is given on page 64.

AMERICAN POPULAR MUSIC: BLUES, JAZZ, BROADWAY, AND ROCK

American popular music, specifically jazz and rock, along with Hollywood films, now dominate popular culture around the world. But what is popular music? Is it music for all the people? Is it a commodity that can be mass produced and sold everywhere? Is it music more loved or favored than some other types of music and hence "popular," like a movie star or sports hero? Although lovers of classical music can be just as passionate about Mozart as goth rock fans are about Marilyn Manson, for example, the truth is that popular music is enjoyed by a much larger segment of society than is "serious" music. Popular music is heard everywhere. It is "broadcast" in the literal sense of the word. Popular CDs outsell classical discs by about nine to one. For the most part, popular music is simple and direct. It requires little or no formal training in music. It is made to be enjoyed for the moment without concern for lasting artistic value.

Popular music is similar, but not identical to, folk music. Folk music, too, is enjoyed by all societies. But, unlike popular music, different folk songs are known to different groups. Moreover, true folk music is not created by an identifiable individual; it springs from the entire community and is part of that group's unique heritage. Popular music, on the other hand, is not only created by an "artist" but also is intended to be reproduced and sold as a commodity to a mass audience, whether in written form as sheet music or in digital audio format as CDs. The homespun folk singer who wails a centuries-old ballad—like *The Streets of Laredo* (see page 29)—is a far cry from the professional pop singer who performs his or her latest hit in Madison Square Garden. Yet from the folk music of both white and black America have sprung our most distinctive genres of popular music: blues, jazz, and rock.

BLUES

Why, where, and how the blues originated is a story that will probably never be fully told. We cannot even hazard a guess as to who gave this style of singing the name "blues," though the expression "the blue devils" had been used to describe a melancholy mood since Shakespeare's time. All that can be said with certainty is that the **blues** are a form of black folk song that originated in the South sometime during the 1880s and 1890s. Like all true folk music, the blues were passed along by oral tradition, one performer learning directly from another without benefit of written music. Comparisons with other forms of folk

origins

music suggest that the blues had two immediate ancestors. First and most important was the work song and field holler (or cry) of the black laborers, which bequeathed to the blues a wailing vocal style, a particular scale (see later), and a body of subjects or topics for singing the blues. The second was the Anglo-American folk ballad, which imparted the regular, predictable pattern of chord changes that characterize the blues. Blues were first printed as sheet music in 1912 (*The Memphis Blues* and *The Dallas Blues*), and the first blues recordings, all made by black artists, were cut in 1920.

a succession of three-line stanzas

A singer sings the blues to relieve a melancholy soul, to give vent to feelings of pain and anger. Poverty, loneliness, oppression, family troubles, infidelity, and separation are typical subjects of the blues. The lyrics are arranged in a succession of stanzas, usually three to six to a song, and each stanza is made up of three lines. The second line normally repeats the first, and the third rounds off the idea and concludes with a rhyme. At the end of each line an instrument inserts a short response, called an **instrumental break,** as a way of replying to the cry of the voice. Thus, the blues perpetuates the age-old African performing style of "call and response," the form of which is shown in the following blues stanza:

Call	*Response*
The moon looks lonesome when	
it's shining through the trees.	(instrumental break)
Yes, the moon looks lonesome,	
shining through the trees.	(instrumental break)
And a man looks lonesome when	
his woman packs up to leave.	(instrumental break)

guitar accompaniment

By the turn of the twentieth century the guitar had become the accompanying instrument favored by blues singers. It could not only supply a solid harmonic support but also provide an expressive "second voice" to answer in the instrumental break after the previous call in the vocal line. "Bending" the guitar strings at the frets produced a whining, mournful sound in keeping with the general feeling of the blues.

blues scale

The object of the blues is not so much to tell a story, as in the white folk ballad, but to express emotion. The voice sometimes moans and sometimes shouts, it is often raspy or frayed, and it always twists and bends the pitch. Instead of hitting a tone directly, the singer usually approaches it by slide from above or below. In addition, a particular scale, called **blues scale,** is used in place of a major or minor scale. The blues scale has seven notes, but the third, fifth, and seventh are sometimes flat, sometimes natural, and sometimes in between. The three "in between" tones are called **blue notes.** The blues scale is an integral part of virtually all African-American folk music, including the work song and spiritual as well as the blues.

EXAMPLE 18–1

        � = blue note

Good blues singers indulge in much spontaneous expression, adding and subtracting text and improvising around the basic melody as the spirit moves them. Such liberties are possible because these mournful songs are built above the bedrock of a twelve-bar harmonic pattern that repeats, over and over, one statement for each stanza of text. Singing the blues means singing in a slow 4/4 above this simple I–IV–I–V–I chord progression in the following manner:[†]

Vocal lines:	Line 1		break		Line 2		break		Line 3		break	
Chord:	I ——————————————				IV —————		I —————		V —————		I ———	
Measure:	1	2	3	4	5	6	7	8	9	10	11	12

the twelve-bar blues

Sometimes additional chords are inserted between the basic ones for greater harmonic interest. Yet the simplicity of the pattern is its greatest resource. Thousands of tunes have been constructed over this basic harmonic progression, by solo singers, by solo pianists, by Dixieland jazz combos, and by rock 'n' roll bands.

Bessie Smith (1894–1937)

Although there have been and are many great blues singers—Blind Lemon Jefferson, Leadbelly, Muddy Waters, and B. B. King, to name just a few—perhaps the greatest of them all was Bessie Smith, called the "Empress of the Blues." A native of Tennessee, Bessie Smith was "discovered" singing in a bar in Selma, Alabama, and brought to New York to record for Columbia Records. The blues recordings she made between 1924 and 1927 catapulted her to the top of the world of popular music. In her first full year as a recording artist, her disks sold more than two million copies, and she became the highest-paid black artist, male or female, of the day. In fact, all of the great blues singers who achieved recording success during the 1920s were women, perhaps because so many of the texts of the blues have to do with male–female relations and are written from the woman's perspective. Tragically, Bessie Smith's career was cut short by a fatal automobile accident in 1937.

Lost Your Head Blues, recorded in 1926, reveals the huge, sweeping voice of Bessie Smith. She was capable of great power, even harshness, one moment, and then in the next breath could deliver a phrase of tender beauty. She could hit a note right on the head if she wanted to, or bend, dip, and glide into the pitch, as she does, for example, on the words "days," "long," and "nights" in the last stanza of *Lost Your Head Blues*. In this recording Bessie is backed by Fletcher Henderson (piano) and Joe Smith (trumpet), and they begin with a four-bar introduction. Then the voice enters and the twelve-bar blues harmony starts up, one full statement of the pattern for each of the five stanzas of text. Each time Bessie Smith sings her melody above the repeating bass, she varies it slightly by means of vocal inflections and off-key shadings. Her expressive vocal line, the soulful, improvised responses played by the trumpet, and the repeating twelve-bar harmony carried by the piano are the essence of the blues.

🌸 FIGURE 18–1
Bessie Smith, the "Empress of the Blues," was a physically powerful woman with an exceptionally flexible, expressive voice.

[†]Chord progressions of this sort are discussed on page 31.

LISTENING GUIDE

Lost Your Head Blues
sung by Bessie Smith (recorded in New York, 1926)

6CD 6/10

0:00   Four bar introduction
0:11   Line 1: I was with you baby when you did not have a dime. (trumpet)
       Chords: I ——————————————————————————————
0:22   Line 2: I was with you baby when you did not have a dime. (trumpet)
       Chords: IV ———————————————— I ————————————
0:32   Line 3: Now since you got plenty money you have throw'd your good gal down. (trumpet)
       Chords: V ———————————————— I ————————————

(For the next three stanzas the chord changes and instrumental breaks continue as above;
in the last stanza the breaks come in the middle of the lines as well as at the end.)

0:44   Once ain't for always, two ain't for twice.
       Once ain't for always, two ain't for twice.
       When you get a good gal, you better treat her nice.

1:16   When you were lonesome, I tried to treat you kind.
       When you were lonesome, I tried to treat you kind.
       But since you've got money, it's done changed your mind.

1:49   I'm gonna leave baby, ain't gonna say goodbye.
       I'm gonna leave baby, ain't gonna say goodbye.
       But I'll write you and tell you the reason why.

2:20   Days† are lonesome, nights are long†.
       Days are lonesome, nights† are so long.
       I'm a good gal, but I've just been treated wrong.

†Note the vocal "slides" here.

(Listening Exercise 38)

The impact of the blues on the popular music of the twentieth century has been enormous. In addition to being in itself a genre of music of great feeling and power, the blues gave to jazz a much-used harmonic pattern and an expressive style of playing. Many jazz and rock greats—from Louis Armstrong (*Gut Bucket Blues*) to Wynton Marsalis (*The Majesty of the Blues*) to Tracy Chapman (*Give Me One Reason*) to Cream (*Strange Brew*)—have improvised around the blues. Equally important, it was from the blues and its offspring, rhythm and blues, that rock 'n' roll was born.

enduring influence of the blues

 JAZZ

Jazz has been called America's classical music. To be sure, it manifests many different musical currents from the New World, including the marches of John Philip Sousa (1854–1932), the fiddle tunes and jigs of white Appalachia, and, most important, the spirituals and blues of American blacks in the South. The four-square sense of phrasing and strong, regular harmonies of the Anglo-American styles merged with the complex rhythms, percussive sounds, and flexible vocal production of African-American music to produce a dynamic new sound. Jazz originated about 1910 almost simultaneously in many southern and midwestern cities: New Orleans, St. Louis, Kansas City, and Chicago, to name a few. Because its style was different from city to city and because various other styles of jazz would later evolve—swing*, bebop*, cool*, and third-stream* among others—jazz must be defined in rather general terms.

roots

Jazz is lively, energetic music with pulsating rhythms and scintillating syncopations, usually played by a small instrumental ensemble (a combo) or a somewhat larger group (a big band). Jazz tends to be polyphonic, since several instruments play independent lines. And it also includes a strong element of improvisation that gives individual performers the freedom to follow their own flights of musical fancy. Tension and excitement are created as virtuosic soloists play off against a regularly changing harmony and a steady beat provided by the rhythm section (usually drums, piano, and a string bass). Playing jazz is like playing a competitive team sport: It requires teamwork, imagination, skill and endurance, and the outcome is never certain!

jazz style

Ragtime: A Precursor of Jazz

Ragtime music was an immediate precursor of jazz and shares with it many of the same rhythmic features. To black musicians, "to rag" meant to play or sing music in a heavily syncopated, jazzy style—with "ragged time." Ragtime music originated in brothels, saloons, and dancehalls during the 1890s—the Gay Nineties—and the jaunty, upbeat sound of ragtime captured the spirit of that age. Most rags were written by black pianists who played in houses of ill repute because it was difficult in those years for black musicians to find employment elsewhere. Piano rags, which first began to be published in 1897, took America by storm, more than two thousand titles appearing in print by the end of World War I. Sold as sheet music of a thin page or two, piano rags quickly moved from the saloon into middle-class homes, where musically literate amateurs played them on the parlor piano.

from saloons to parlors

✳ FIGURE 18–2

One of the few surviving images of ragtime composer Scott Joplin.

The undisputed "King of Ragtime" was Scott Joplin (1868–1917). The son of a slave, Joplin managed to acquire for himself a solid grounding in classical music while he earned a living playing in honky-tonk bars in and around St. Louis. In 1899 he published *Maple Leaf Rag*, which sold an astonishing one million copies. Though he went on to write other immensely popular rags, such as *The Entertainer* and *Peacherine Rag*, Joplin gradually shed the image of barroom pianist and moved to New York to compose rag-oriented opera.

The *Maple Leaf Rag*, which was all the rage at the turn of the century, is typical of the style of Joplin and his fellow ragtime composers. Its form is similar to that of a traditional military march, consisting of a succession of sixteen-bar units, each of which is repeated. And its harmonies are also European in origin, moving purposefully from chord to chord with slight chromatic inflections—Joplin knew his Schubert and Chopin! But what makes ragtime so infectious is its bouncy, syncopated rhythm. Syncopation, of course, is the momentary displacement of an accent from on the beat to off the beat. In piano ragtime the left hand keeps a regular "um-pah, um-pah" beat, usually in 2/4 meter, while the right hand lays on syncopations against it. In the following example from the *Maple Leaf Rag*, syncopation (S) occurs when long notes (either an eighth note or two sixteenth notes tied together) sound off (between) the steady eighth-note beats of the bass:

FIGURE 18–3
FIGURE 18–3

A New Orleans street band in the 1990s. The tradition of playing jazz in the streets of New Orleans, at parades, funerals, and functions of fraternal orders, extends back to the late 1800s and continues today.

EXAMPLE 18–2

New Orleans (Dixieland) Jazz

Although jazz sprang up almost simultaneously in towns up and down the Mississippi River, its focal point and probable place of origin was New Orleans. Not only was New Orleans the home of many of the early jazz greats—King Oliver (1885–1938), Jelly Roll Morton (1890–1941), and Louis Armstrong (1898–1971)—but it enjoyed an exceptionally lively and varied musical life that encouraged the development of new musical styles. Culturally, New Orleans looked more toward France and the Caribbean than it did to the Anglo-American north. The city air was filled not only with opera tunes, marches, and ballroom dances from imperial France but also African-American blues and ragtime and Cuban dance rhythms. The end of the Spanish-American War (1898) brought a flood of used military band instruments into second-hand shops in New Orleans at prices that were affordable even to impoverished blacks. Musicians, black and white alike, found ready employment in ballrooms of the well-to-do, in the bars and brothels of Storyville (a thirty-eight-square-block red-light district in the center of the city), at parades, picnics, weddings, and funerals associated with the many New Orleans societies and fraternal orders. Music was everywhere. Even today in New Orleans bands of various sorts, some good, some bad, can be heard on the streets of the city's French Quarter at almost any hour, day or night.

New Orleans, a musical and cultural melting pot

What marks the sound of New Orleans jazz? Syncopation combined with a free treatment of melody. A given march, rag, blues or popular tune is played with off-beat accents and a spontaneous sliding into and around the pitches of the tune. The rag had phrases (strains) of sixteen bars, many popular songs of the period had four four-bar phrases, and the traditional blues, as we have seen, consisted of a steady stream of twelve-bar units. Within the square formal confines of these four-, eight-, twelve- and sixteen-bar patterns, the New Orleans jazz combo found a security that allowed the solo instruments the greatest sort of freedom of expression. The melody was usually played in some jazzed-up way by a cornet or trumpet; a clarinet supported this lead instrument and further embellished the tune; a trombone added counterpoint against the melody in a lower range; down below, a tuba set the harmonies if the group was marching, but if it did not, that job was handed over to a string bass, piano, banjo, and/or guitar. These same instruments (tuba, string bass, piano, banjo, and guitar), along with the drums, formed the **rhythm section** because they not only set the harmony but also helped the drums give out the beat in a steady fashion. Finally, New Orleans–style bands, then and now, never play from written music. They count, or feel, when the chords must change and they improvise and re-fashion the tune so as to fit those changes.

Dixieland style

playing without written music

Louis Armstrong (1898–1971)

When the brothels and gambling houses of the red-light district of New Orleans were closed by the U.S. government in 1917, many places of employment for jazz musicians disappeared. Performers began to look elsewhere for work—in New York, Chicago, and even Los Angeles. One of those who eventually made his way to Chicago was Louis "Satchmo" ("Satchelmouth") Armstrong. Armstrong was born in New Orleans in 1898, and in 1923 followed his mentor, King

❋ FIGURE 18–4
Louis Armstrong (seated) with his band The Hot Fives at a recording session sometime during 1925–1926. The songwriter and pianist Lillian Hardin, who became Armstrong's wife, is at the right.

Oliver, to Chicago to join the latter's Creole Jazz Band. By this time Armstrong was already recognized by his peers as the best jazz trumpeter alive. He soon formed his own band in Chicago, The Hot Fives, to make what was to become a series of landmark recordings. When the vogue of classic New Orleans–style jazz gave way to the sound of the swing band around 1930, Armstrong moved to New York, where he "fronted"—played as featured soloist—in a number of large bands. He invented the practice of "scat singing"—singing nonsense syllables in jazz style–and eventually became known as much for the gravelly sound of his voice, in songs such as *Hello Dolly* and *Mack the Knife*, as for his trumpet playing. His last years were spent in almost continual travel, sent around the world by the U.S. State Department as "Ambassador Satchmo." He died at his home in Queens, New York, in 1971.

"Ambassador Satchmo"

Although cut in Chicago, Armstrong's early recordings are classics of New Orleans–style jazz. The tune *Droppin' Shucks*, by pianist Lillian Hardin, is only sixteen bars long, but it appears seven times, each time varied in some way in the Dixieland style. In a jazz piece of this sort each presentation of the tune is called a **chorus,** whether played by a soloist or the entire ensemble. Although there are three melody instruments here—trumpet, trombone, and clarinet—it is Armstrong's strong, clean trumpet sound that dominates the group. He is also heard as a vocalist in choruses 3 and 4, a jilted lover who has had "shucks" dropped on him by an unfaithful woman, but who is about to drop some of his own.

LISTENING GUIDE

Droppin' Shucks, a song by Lillian Hardin, played by Louis Armstrong's The Hot Fives (recorded in Chicago, 1925)

6CD 6/11

0:00	Introduction (minor-key sound)
0:24	Chorus 1—full ensemble
0:48	Chorus 2—piano (Lillian Hardin) and banjo (Johnny St. Cyr)
1:11	Chorus 3—vocal (Louis Armstrong)
1:34	Chorus 4—vocal
1:51	Chorus 5—clarinet (Johnny Dobbs)
2:16	Chorus 6—trombone (Kid Ory)
2:39	Chorus 7—full ensemble

The liberties Armstrong takes with the text and melody of *Droppin' Shucks* points out a general principle of jazz: Musicians are superior to the songs they perform. To many this is a radical notion, given that in classical music the performer must adhere faithfully to the written text. But in jazz the performer is the text. As the saying goes: "Tain't what you do, 'tis the way you do it."

Big Bands and Swing

The recordings of Louis Armstrong and The Hot Fives sold as fast as they could be pressed. Jazz became the rage of the 1920s, just as ragtime had been the craze at the turn of the century. It was, in the words of novelist F. Scott Fitzgerald, the "Jazz Age." So popular did jazz become that it was now performed in ballrooms, large dancehalls, and movie theaters, in addition to the smaller bars and

the Big Band era

supper clubs where New Orleans–style jazz had its home. And just as the small supper club gradually gave way to the ballroom, so too did the small jazz combo cede pride of place to the big band—for to be heard above the stomping and swaying of many hundreds of pairs of feet, an ensemble larger than the traditional Dixieland combo of five or seven players was needed. Thus was born the big-band era, the glory days of the bands of Benny Goodman (1909–1986), Duke Ellington (1889–1974), Count Basie (1904–1984), and Glenn Miller (1904–1944).

Though not "big" by the standard of today's marching band, the **big band** of the 1930s and 1940s was at least double the size of the New Orleans–style jazz combo. In 1943, for example, Duke Ellington's orchestra consisted of four trumpets, three trombones, five reed players (men who played both clarinet and saxophone), plus a rhythm section of piano, string bass, guitar, and drums—a total of sixteen players (Fig. 18–6). Most big-band compositions were worked out ahead of time and set down in written arrangements called "charts." The fact that jazz musicians now for the first time had to play from written notation suggests that a more disciplined, polished, orchestral sound was desired. The addition of a quintet of saxophones gave the ensemble a more mellow, blended quality. The new sound has little of the sharp bite and wild syncopation of the earlier New Orleans–style jazz. Rather, the music is mellow, bouncy, and flowing. In a word, it "swings." **Swing,** then, can be said to be a popular style of jazz played by a big band in the 1930s and 1940s. The present revival of "swing dancing" suggests that an elegant dance style that is distinctly jazzy can enjoy enduring popularity.

FIGURE 18–5 AND 18–6
(left) Benny Goodman, the "King of Swing," during a radio broadcast in the early 1940s. (right) Duke Ellington (seated at the piano) and his big band in 1943. Unlike other band leaders of this time, Ellington was as much a composer and arranger as he was a performer.

swing and swing dancing

Bebop

The craze for big-band swing jazz reached its peak immediately before and during World War II. It had become, in effect, the popular music of America. Swing jazz was heard at home on the radio, on jukeboxes, at college proms, in hotel ballrooms, in theaters, and even in New York's Carnegie Hall, the hallowed home of classical music. Then, for reasons that are not fully known, it fell out of favor. One cause was that many of the best young performers found that playing from written big-band charts limited their freedom and creativity.

return of the jazz combo

FIGURE 18-7
Charlie "Bird" Parker about 1950.
Parker developed a fast, snapping,
syncopated style of playing that often
sounds like the word "bebop" said
quickly.

They wanted to return to a style of playing in which improvisation was more important than composition and where the soloist, not the ensemble, was king. Choosing their playing partners carefully, they worked or "jammed" in small, elite groups in clubs in midtown Manhattan and in Harlem, and in so doing created a new virtuosic style of jazz called bebop.

Bebop is an angular, hard-driving style of jazz played by a small combo without written music. It derives its name from the fact that the fast, snappy melody sounds like the word "bebop, bebop" said quickly. Typically, bebop requires a quintet of trumpet, saxophone, piano, double bass, and drums. The best players, among them saxophonist Charlie Parker (1920–1955) and trumpeter Dizzy Gillespie (1917–1993), had astonishing technique and played at breakneck speed. Their love was improvisation, and the solos they created were more complex than those heard in either swing or New Orleans–style jazz. They overlaid the melody with so much rapid, jarring embroidery that the tune soon became unrecognizable. They also changed chords more rapidly than earlier jazz players and went to more remote keys. Only the most gifted performers could keep up and "make the changes." Bebop was for an elite few.

Charlie "Bird" Parker (1920–1955)

Perhaps the most gifted of the bebop artists was Charlie "Yardbird" or "Bird" Parker, the subject of Clint Eastwood's movie *Bird* (1988). Parker was a tragic figure, a drug-addicted, alcoholic, antisocial man whose skills as an improviser and performer, nonetheless, were greater than all other jazz musicians, save Louis Armstrong. Indeed, the lives of Armstrong and Parker make an interesting comparison. Both were born into the extreme poverty of the ghetto, Armstrong in New Orleans and Parker in Kansas City, and both rose to the top of their profession through extraordinary talent and hard work. But Armstrong was an extroverted person who viewed himself as a public entertainer as much as an artist. Parker didn't care whether people liked his music or not, and he managed to alienate everyone around him including, finally, his friend and longtime playing partner Dizzy Gillespie. He died of the effects of his many excesses, alone and broke, at the age of thirty-four. Parker's life may have been a mess, but his rapid, inventive style of playing changed irrevocably the history of jazz.

In 1950 Parker and Gillespie recorded a bebop version of a sentimental love song called *My Melancholy Baby* (1911). Like many popular tunes from the early part of this century, *My Melancholy Baby* is sixteen bars long and divided into four four-measure phrases (here **ABAC**). After a four-bar introduction by pianist Thelonious Monk, Parker plays the tune more or less "straight," with only moderately complex elaborations. But when Dizzy Gillespie enters for the second chorus, the ornamentation becomes more complex by means of racing thirty-second notes and continues to do so through the third and final chorus, which Monk and Parker divide. Try to follow the original tune of *My Melancholy Baby* as each soloist embroiders it. As you listen, notice that there is no group ensemble playing at the end and no strong beat. Instead, in bebop we find frenetic solos for a single instrument set against a quiet, relaxed rhythm section. What results is a music more for listening than for dancing. Bebop is the "chamber music" of jazz, a style designed to appeal to only a small number of aficionados.

"far-out" improvisations above
obscure harmonies

LISTENING GUIDE

My Melancholy Baby
Charlie Parker, saxophone; Dizzy Gillespie, trumpet;
Thelonious Monk, piano; Curly Russell, bass; Buddy
Rich, drums (recorded in New York, 1950)

6CD 6/12

A
Come to me, my mel - an - chol - y   ba - by, Cud - dle up and don't   be   blue;

B
All your fears are fool - ish fan - cy,   may - be, You know, dear, that I   am strong for   you.

A
Ev - 'ry cloud must have a   sil - ver   lin - - ing,   Wait, un - til   the sun   shines   through,

C
Smile, my hon - ey dear, while I   kiss a - way each tear, Or   else I shall be mel - an - chol - y   too.

0:00   Four-bar introduction
0:13   Chorus I—**ABAC,** saxophone
1:12   Chorus II—**ABAC,** trumpet (with mute)
2:13   Chorus III—**AB,** piano
2:40   . . . . **AC,** saxophone
3:05   ritard and tag (short coda) by saxophone and trumpet

(Listening Exercise 39)

Jazz Styles Since 1950

The heyday of bebop (1945–1955) marked the beginning of a decline in the popularity of jazz. If you couldn't dance to it, why listen? The decade also saw the beginning of a fragmentation and proliferation of jazz styles—no one type of jazz was able to capture the public's imagination. **Cool jazz,** sometimes called "soft bebop" because of its more relaxed, less-frenzied solos, grew out of bebop and gained a modest following in the 1950s. Its main practitioners were trumpeter Miles Davis (1926–1991) and saxophonists Gerry Mulligan (b. 1927) and Stan Getz (1927–1991). Their delivery was soft, gradual, and nonaggressive, a welcome change of pace to the dramatic, hard-driving sound of bebop. By the 1960s the fragmentation and abstraction begun by Parker and Davis had led to the playing of saxophonist John Coltrane (1926–1967) and **free jazz,** a style in which a musician could improvise without the constraints of rhythm, melody, or harmony. Many listeners wondered if jazz would ever return to earth.

beyond bebop

Return it did, and to rock-solid ground. In the 1970s jazz began to assimilate some of the traits of rock. The cause of this stylistic change was simple: money.

a fusion of jazz and rock

Jazz recordings—whether bebop, cool, or free jazz—were not selling. What was selling was rock. So jazz musicians, driven by economic reality, began to adopt the rhythms of the rock drummer and the simple, repetitious harmonies outlined by the Fender bass guitar. **Jazz-fusion** is the name given this mixture of jazz and rock. Young trumpeters, such as Lew Soloff (b. 1943) and Chuck Mangione (b. 1941), stopped playing like Miles Davis and went off to form jazz-rock bands, such as Blood, Sweat and Tears, Chicago, and the Chuck Mangione Ensemble. They have made great music—and gotten rich—by blending the driving rhythms and harmonies of rock with the big-band brass sounds and the virtuosity of the jazz improviser. The moral of the story, as it pertains to the history of jazz and its listening public, is that any popular music without a catchy tune or a foot-stomping beat won't be popular for long.

Wynton Marsalis (b. 1961)

At present, jazz is enjoying something of a renaissance, simply by returning to its roots—to blues, Dixieland jazz, and the classically elegant sound of Duke Ellington. Appropriately enough, the leader of this revival, Wynton Marsalis, is a native of New Orleans, the birthplace of traditional jazz. Marsalis is the son of pianist Ellis Marsalis and the younger brother of saxophonist Branford Marsalis (leader of the *Tonight Show* band during the early 1990s). He received his first trumpet at the age of six from New Orleans jazz great Al Hirt. To build a virtuosic technique and to "know what makes music great," Marsalis studied the classical repertoire, enrolling at the Juilliard School in New York City in 1980. In 1984 he became the only person to win a Grammy simultaneously as a classical performer (for a recording of the Haydn trumpet concerto) and as a jazz performer (for his album *Think of One*). His oratorio *Blood on the Fields,* which treats the subject of slavery in America, won the Pulitzer Prize for Music in 1997, the first time this award has been given to a composer writing in a jazz idiom. To reinvigorate jazz, Marsalis has returned to New Orleans rag, stomp*, Dixieland jazz, and blues. He also made himself familiar with the popular ballads that had earlier served Duke Ellington and Charlie Parker so well. *In the Afterglow* is Marsalis's arrangement of a ballad fashionable in the 1920s. In it we hear traditional elements such as eight-plus-eight-bar phrasing and ternary form. Yet we also experience more sophisticated harmonies, including ninth and eleventh chords*, and a smoother style of playing typical of Ellington. The rhythm, too, has a certain freedom that approaches the flexibility of Parker—the beat is sometimes difficult to locate at the ends of phrases, for example. All of this is attributable to Marsalis's obsession with jazz's past. As he says, "Study is the only protection against folly."

✳ FIGURE 18–8

According to jazz revivalist Wynton Marsalis, "Jazz musicians are making the same mistakes that the classical musicians made. Like modern European classical music, their jazz has become abstract and pessimistic."

LISTENING GUIDE	*In the Afterglow* Wynton Marsalis, trumpet; Marcus Roberts, piano; Robert Hurst, bass; Jeff Watts, drums	From album *Marsalis Standard Time* Columbia Records, CD CK 40461, track 10

Form: ternary
(meter: triple; tempo: slow)

0:00	Phrase **a**	A
0:32	Phrase **b**	
1:00	Phrase **c**	B
1:31	Phrase **d**	
1:47	Transition	
1:59	Phrase **a**	A
2:30	Phrase **b**	
3:01	Transition	
3:14	Coda	**CODA**

GEORGE GERSHWIN: FROM SYMPHONIC JAZZ TO BROADWAY

George Gershwin (1898–1937) brought jazz into the Broadway musical, just as he sometimes brought jazz into the classical symphony and concerto. Born to Rose and Morris Gershovitz in New York on September 26, 1898, his mother soon did as many upwardly mobile middle-class matrons in America: She bought her family an upright piano on the installment plan. Only young George could play it, however, picking out every sort of rag, march, and show tune by ear. Soon he was taking formal lessons in classical music, studying Mozart, Chopin, and Debussy. By the age of fifteen music had become Gershwin's life, so he quit high school and took a job as a piano "plugger," a pianist who played new songs for prospective buyers all day in a music publisher's showroom—there were no radios or CD stores at this time where a customer might try out the latest tunes. In 1919 Gershwin stopped plugging the music of others and began to promote his own. In that year he published his song "Swanee," which soon sold two and a half million copies around the world. Other hits, like "I Got Rhythm" (from his Broadway show *Girl Crazy*) and "Summertime" (from his folk opera *Porgy and Bess*), would follow. By the age of twenty Gershwin was already rich and famous.

But George Gershwin did not forget his strongly classical upbringing. Throughout his life he continued to study the works of Bach and Mozart, and especially those of Impressionists Debussy and Ravel. In three large-scale orchestral compositions (*Rhapsody in Blue*, 1924; *Concerto in F*, 1925; and *An American in Paris*, 1928) Gershwin created something called **symphonic jazz,** a fusion of jazz styles with the genres and forms of classical music. Of these the most famous is *Rhapsody in Blue*, which critics dubbed "a jazz concerto." Here the framework is traditional: a classical medium (symphony orchestra),

FIGURE 18–9
George Gershwin.

genre (piano concerto), and form (theme and variations). But everywhere elements of jazz abound. The opening glissando for clarinet comes straight from the jazz band, as does the later "wah-wah" effect on the trumpet played with a mute (0:57). Gershwin even includes a reference to the Charleston (3:53), a popular, syncopated dance of the Roaring Twenties. *Rhapsody in Blue* is a synthesis of styles that once outraged some classical and jazz purists, but has eternally delighted the general listening public.

LISTENING GUIDE

George Gershwin
Rhapsody in Blue (Part 1)

6CD 6/13

Genre: Jazz concerto

Time	Description
0:00	Introduction: clarinet glissando*
0:16	Clarinet plays first theme

with freedom

| 0:44 | Saxophones play second theme |

mf   *poco rit.*

0:57	Trumpet with mute plays first theme
1:07	Piano enters and begins to vary first theme
1:42	Piano solo (improvisations on first theme)
2:04	Piano and orchestra vary first theme
2:27	Piano solo (improvisations on first theme)
3:01	Impressionist sounds borrowed from Debussy: whole-tone scale* and parallel motion*
3:24	Full orchestra plays and then varies first theme
3:53	Orchestra plays dance tune recalling the Charleston
4:29	Full orchestra varies second theme in the style of a march
4:54	Clarinet slides and trumpet "wa-wa's" recall opening

BROADWAY

"Broadway" is the name given to a district in New York City, centered at the junction of Broadway and 42nd Street, where more than thirty theaters provide a stage for plays and musicals alike. The Broadway musical has its roots in many diverse forms of popular drama—the Viennese operetta of Johann Strauss, the English operetta of Gilbert and Sullivan, French *opéra comique,* and even traditional Yiddish (Jewish) theater from Eastern Europe. An **operetta** is simply a "light" opera, one involving romance and comedy in equal measure. It differs from opera most fundamentally in that the dialogue is spoken, not sung as recitative. **Musical comedy** is a genre similar to the operetta but even more popular in style. It too uses spoken dialogue, yet its subject matter concerns the proverbial man-in-the-street, his "gal," and their everyday problems. In musical comedy, interest is concentrated in a few carefully placed songs—appealing

the American musical comedy, or musical

tunes that make no demands for vocal virtuosity on the leads. The earliest Broadway musicals were written by native-born Americans, most notably George M. Cohan (*Little Johnny Jones*, 1906, which included "Give my regards to Broadway") and Jerome Kern (*Showboat*, 1927). The often-revived *Showboat*, with its signal song "Ol' Man River," is especially noteworthy in that it includes strains of uniquely American music, specifically blues, jazz, and the Negro spiritual. The treatment of the African-American experience in Kern's *Showboat* and Gershwin's *Porgy and Bess* paved the way for other ethnic subjects in later works, like *Fiddler on the Roof* (Yiddish stories) and *West Side Story* (Puerto Rican immigrants).

The collaboration of composer Richard Rodgers (1902–1979) with lyricist Oscar Hammerstein (1895–1960) marked the beginning of a golden era for the American musical theater. In a span of less than two decades this gifted team produced a succession of blockbuster musicals, beginning with *Oklahoma!* (1943), continuing with *Carousel* (1945), *South Pacific* (1949), and *The King and I* (1951), and concluding with *The Sound of Music* (1959). *Oklahoma!* ran originally for 2,248 performances, *The King and I* for 4,625. Moreover, these were the first musicals in which sales of records, movie rights, and touring companies brought in more money than the box office receipts of the original Broadway production. Rodgers and Hammerstein struck gold by blending tasteful, if sentimental, lyrics with uplifting, if square-cut, melodies. The "Broadway songbooks" performed at home today are filled with such standards as "Oh, what a beautiful mornin'" (*Oklahoma!*), "You'll never walk alone" (*Carousel*), "Some enchanted evening" (*South Pacific*), "Getting to know you" and "Shall we dance?" (*The King and I*), and "Climb ev'ry mountain" (*The Sound of Music*)—all Rodgers and Hammerstein creations.

Rodgers and Hammerstein

Today the Broadway scene is dominated by the megahits of Englishman Andrew Lloyd Webber (*Evita, Cats, Starlight Express, Phantom of the Opera*, and *Sunset Boulevard*), which rely more on dazzling scenic effects and heavily amplified sound than they do on inspired musical invention. These and the equally successful French import *Les Misérables* (1987) have put American musical comedy into a state of temporary eclipse. At the moment Broadway offers more revivals of American musicals (*Annie Get Your Gun, The Sound of Music*, and *Fascinating Rhythm*) and musical versions of movies (*Beauty and the Beast, The Lion King*, and *Saturday Night Fever*) than new productions.

❋ FIGURE 18–10

Leonard Bernstein. His podium style was sometimes majestic, more often wild and frenetic, leading to the nickname "Leaping Lenny."

Leonard Bernstein (1918–1990)

One of the most original shows ever mounted on Broadway was Leonard Bernstein's *West Side Story*, a musical as brash and energetic as Bernstein himself. Bernstein was educated at Harvard and at the Curtis Institute in Philadelphia, where he studied conducting. He went on to become one of the great conductor-interpreters of this century. But Bernstein was a protean figure of frenetic energy and diverse talents. As a writer of "serious" music he created symphonies and ballet scores; as a composer in more popular styles he produced a film score (*On the Waterfront* starring Marlon Brando) and four musicals (*Wonderful Town, On the Town, Candide*, and *West Side Story*); as a virtuoso pianist he appeared often as a soloist with his own orchestra; as an educator he introduced a generation of youthful Americans to the joys of classical music through his "Young People's Concerts" broadcast nationally on CBS-TV; and as an advocate for the

❋ FIGURE 18–11
Still of a dance scene from the 1961 movie version of *West Side Story*. Members of the Jets and the Sharks tauntingly strut their stuff.

cate for the arts he exercised influence on presidents, especially John F. Kennedy. America has never enjoyed a more dynamic musical leader than the lionlike Bernstein.

WEST SIDE STORY (1957)

In *West Side Story* Bernstein takes the age-old story of Romeo and Juliet and gives it modern significance. The feuding Capulets and Montagues are replaced by New York street gangs, one "American" (the "Jets") and one Puerto Rican (the "Sharks"). The scenario crystallized for Bernstein one day during a ride through New York's Spanish Harlem:

> All around, Puerto Rican kids were playing—with a huge causeway as a background in a classic key, pillars, and Roman arches. The contrast between the setting and the kids was striking, fascinating. Right then and there we had our theme for *West Side Story*—a contemporary setting echoing a classic myth.

a modern-day Romeo and Juliet

The star-crossed lovers are now Tony, former leader of the Jets, and Maria, the sister of the leader of the Sharks and newly arrived from Puerto Rico. They meet at a dance, held not in a Renaissance palazzo but in a high school gym. Juliet's balcony is transformed into Maria's fire escape, and it is here that she and Tony sing the show-stopping duet "Tonight." Ultimately Tony, trying to make peace, causes the death of the leader of the Sharks and is himself killed, leaving Maria to grieve over his body.

West Side Story is a study in dramatic and musical opposites. Fast-paced dances for the gangs are set off against quiet duets for the lovers. The gangs' music is dissonant, syncopated, and percussive, much in the style of the musical avant-garde of the early twentieth century (see page 336). The lovers' music, on the other hand, is consonant and melodic, steady in its phrasing and beat. This contrast between the dissonant, syncopated modern style and the melodious Romantic style can be heard in two of the *Symphonic Dances* from *West Side Story*. Both "Mambo," a dance sequence for the gangs, and "Somewhere," a dream song envisioning a distant place of love and friendship, underscore the mood of the on-stage action. *West Side Story* is not a musical comedy but a musical tragedy in which competing forces race headlong toward destruction. By distilling the musical essences of these competing forces, Bernstein captures the energy and tenderness of this timeless tale.

modern dance, Romantic love songs

LISTENING GUIDE	Leonard Bernstein *Symphonic Dances* from *West Side Story* (1957) "Mambo" and "Somewhere"	6CD 6/14–15

Characters: The Jets and the Sharks, Tony and Maria

Situation: Friction between the Jets and the Sharks is felt at a high school dance, where gang members strut to the music of "Mambo"; Tony and Maria meet and express their hopes for love.

"Mambo" (6CD 6/14)

0:00	Introduction
0:10	Fast-moving, syncopated theme
0:37	Percussive blasts from percussion and brasses
1:05	Trumpet solo
2:02	Return of theme leads to climax and then fadeout

"Somewhere" (6CD 6/15)

0:00	Cellos tenderly play the melody of the song "Somewhere"
0:29	French horn plays "Somewhere" melody against counterpoint in oboe
0:55	Strings sweep forward with the theme
1:25	Middle strings play "Somewhere" melody against counterpoint in higher violins
1:50	Full orchestra carries melody to a climax and then fadeout

ROCK

Bursting on the scene in the mid-1950s, rock 'n' roll (and its later manifestation, rock) revolutionized popular music in America and indeed throughout the world. Its style is well known to all—the pounding beat, the heavy, amplified guitar sound, the driving bass, and the simple, repetitive harmonies. There is, to be sure, much harmonic repetition, noisy filler, and electronic distortion. But, of course, rock involves much more than just music. The style of dress of the rockers, their sometimes-outrageous behavior, both on and off stage, and their social and political beliefs are just as important to rock culture as is the music they produce. Rock was born as a music of protest and rebellion directed against the established musical and social orders.

The origins of rock can be found in a style of music called rhythm and blues that came out of the South around 1950. Like the blues, **rhythm and blues** makes use of the twelve-bar blues pattern, 4/4 meter, and an expressive style of singing. But here the usually slow tempo of the blues is changed to a faster 4/4,

rhythm and blues

❋ FIGURE 18–12
Little Richard (Richard Penniman, b. 1932), one of rock 'n' roll's early stars. Along with Chuck Berry and Bo Diddley, he transformed rhythm and blues into rock 'n' roll.

❋ FIGURE 18–13
The "King Is Dead, Long Live the King." The hysteria surrounding Elvis has diminished only slightly since his death in 1977. Elvis "sightings" are reported almost weekly in the tabloids. One recent television special had him alive and well, living under the F.B.I.'s witness protection program.

upbeats and downbeats are made stronger, a saxophone is added to the basic guitar sound, and the text is shouted as much as sung. All of this produces a raw, driving, highly danceable kind of music. At first rhythm and blues was created and played exclusively by black musicians for a black audience. But as many of these musicians and listeners moved to the urban centers of the North in the 1950s, a white audience began to hear and dance to this energized black music, mostly over the radio. Indeed, the term "rock 'n' roll" was first coined in 1951 by a white disk jockey in Cleveland, Alan Freed, who championed black rhythm and blues—that is the principal reason the new rock 'n' roll Hall of Fame was situated in Cleveland. Soon black artists like Chuck Berry ("Maybellene" and "Roll Over Beethoven"), Bo Diddley ("Bo Diddley"), Fats Domino ("Blueberry Hill"), and Little Richard ("Tutti Frutti" and "Lucille") found that there was a demand for their music in the white market. And white musicians like Bill Haley ("Rock Around the Clock"), Carl Perkins ("Blue Suede Shoes"), Jerry Lee Lewis ("Great Balls of Fire"), and Elvis Presley ("Jail House Rock") began to copy the black sound. Perkins, Lewis, and Presley had grown up in the South in the environment of black rhythm and blues. Presley's first manager said that he was simply "looking for a white boy who could sing colored."

Elvis Presley (1935–1977) became the "King of Rock 'n' Roll"; his singing electrified a white audience only then coming to know the sounds of black rhythm and blues. Presley's first national hit "Heartbreak Hotel" and subsequent "Love Me Tender" (both 1956) were in the tradition of the white country ballad, though sung in an expressive, throbbing style. But his "Hound Dog" (1956) and "Jail House Rock" (1957) continued the development of hard-driving rhythm and blues. Indeed, "Hound Dog" had been borrowed from blues singer Big Mama Thornton. Within two years of his first hit, Presley had become a national obsession, his every gyration the object of scrutiny by the media. But the public Elvis was very much a creation of the tabloids and Presley's clever managers. Though on stage he projected an image of the youthful rebel, the hard-guy rocker, exuding sexual confidence and suggestiveness, in reality he was very much a pampered mama's boy and timid about sexual matters. He died young, of drug abuse, a bloated caricature of himself. The sad part is that, in spite of the rhinestones, the Cadillacs, and all the other silliness that attended his life, he was highly musical and blessed with an exceptionally rich and wide-ranging baritone voice. His was by far the best voice of any of the male rock singers, then or now.

By the early 1960s much of the initial energy and freshness of early rock 'n' roll had been lost. Sentimental tunes directed at the hordes of teenagers of the postwar baby boom (*Teenager in Love* and *Teen Angel,* for example) began to dominate the market. But American rock soon received a shot in the arm from an unexpected source, Great Britain. The reason for this is clear. England had recently become infatuated with the sounds of American blues players like Muddy Waters as well as rhythm and blues singers like Chuck Berry and Bo Diddley, some of whom had toured there. As foreign imitators, British pop musicians embraced the new styles with greater fidelity to the original than did their American cousins. The pounding, swaggering style of Mick Jagger and his Rolling Stones is very much in the tradition of "shouting" rhythm and blues from Louisiana and Mississippi. And The Who, led by guitarist Pete Townshend, added more varied chord changes, notably in their two "rock operas" *Tommy* (1969) and *Quadrophenia* (1973). But of all the British groups, the most adaptive and most successful was the Beatles.

The Beatles were formed in Liverpool, England, in 1960 and achieved an almost overnight success in that country with their first single "Love Me Do" (1962) and the follow-up "Please Please Me" (1963). In 1964 they took America by storm, first with their best-selling single "I Want to Hold Your Hand" and then in person through their sensational appearance on the *Ed Sullivan Show* and a sold-out national tour. "Beatlemania" was born. But unlike the equally popular Elvis, a dynamic performer but not a composer, each of the Beatles was a songwriter in his own right. And two of them, bass guitarist Paul McCartney and rhythm guitarist John Lennon, were exceptionally creative. They wrote fresh lyrics and unpredictable tunes that the parents as well as the kids could enjoy. What is most remarkable about the Beatles is the variety of musical styles that they adopted and made their own: rhythm and blues ("Roll Over Beethoven" and "Twist and Shout"), country blues ("Oh, Darling"), gospel ("Let It Be"), Broadway show tunes ("The Long and Winding Road"), British music-hall songs ("When I'm Sixty-Four"), novelty songs ("The Yellow Submarine" and "Octopus's Garden"), Baroque instrumental styles ("Eleanor Rigby" and "Penny Lane"), Indian raga ("Love You To"), and psychadelic Rock ("Lucy in the Sky with Diamonds"). In 1970, after a decade of unprecedented popularity and financial gain, the Beatles disbanded, though each of them ultimately returned, with differing degrees of success, to the field of popular music with his own band.

While America was held captive to Beatlemania, a newer, softer style of rock music, called folk-rock, emerged on these shores. **Folk-rock** was a mixture of the steady beat of rock with the forms, topics, and styles of singing of the traditional Anglo-American folk ballad (see page 377). The folk ballad had survived in the South and West in the form of the country-western ballad. Folk music, in general, enjoyed a revival, beginning with the Kingston Trio's recording of the ballad "Tom Dooley" (1958) and with the work of Peter, Paul, and Mary and of Joan Baez. But the sources of the new folk-rock were more city than country, and the primary artists urban Jewish rather than Appalachian Protestant. The labor movement, the civil rights movement, and protests against the Vietnam War were supported by these artists. Bob Dylan, who sang accompanied only by his guitar and harmonica, inaugurated this urban folk style with protest songs such as "Blowin' in the Wind" (1963). Paul Simon, the creative force behind Simon and Garfunkel, started in the footsteps of Dylan

🔹 FIGURE 18–14
The Beatles's *Sergeant Pepper's Lonely Hearts Club Band* was one of the first to establish "album-oriented" rock, in which tunes in a variety of styles and performing media, from sitar to symphony, are selected and arranged to form a single, unified collection. This revolutionary album required seven hundred hours of recording time in a London studio.

folk-rock and protest rock

FIGURE 18–15
R.E.M. began in Athens, Georgia, in the tradition of Southern rhythm and blues, with a mule-kicking drumbeat, a tight ensemble of electric guitars, and regular chord changes. The group's more recent offerings are still hard-driving, but use more electrically synthesized sounds and electrically generated distortion.

but quickly developed his own folk-rock manner on such early singles as "The Sounds of Silence" (1966) and "Scarborough Fair" (1968). More recently, he has drawn on the indigenous folk and choral traditions of South Africa for his anti-apartheid album *Graceland* (1986). James Taylor, Judy Collins, and Joni Mitchell are three other folksingers who occasionally incorporate rock idioms in their music. The beat is there, but they sing accompanied by the sound of the acoustical guitar rather than the noisier, electrically amplified instrument.

Rock (and its progenitor rock 'n' roll) is now nearly fifty years old but shows no signs of losing its popular following. Each time one rock style gets stale, two others emerge to take its place. The last thirty years have seen the rise of acid rock (Jefferson Airplane and the Grateful Dead), progressive rock (Pink Floyd and Yes), glam rock (David Bowie and Kiss), Latin rock (Santana and Los Lobos), jazz rock (Steely Dan and Frank Zappa), heavy metal (Led Zeppelin and Metallica), disco (Chic and the Bee Gees), punk (Green Day and the Clash), new wave (the B-52s and the Talking Heads), dance pop (Michael Jackson and Madonna), blues rock (Stevie Ray Vaughan and Steve Winwood), working-class hard rock (Bruce Springsteen and John Mellencamp), rap/hip hop (Public Enemy and the Beastie Boys), techno (Kraftwerk and Prodigy), industrial (Ministry and Nine Inch Nails), goth (Bauhaus and Marilyn Manson), grunge (Pearl Jam and Nirvana), along with many others.

A half-century of hearing the "sinful" beat of rock 'n' roll has lessened its shock value. The "oldies but goodies" of the mid-1950s keep going strong as remakes. Mick Jagger, Pete Townshend, and Eric Clapton enjoy comeback tours even though they never really went away. Only a few extreme styles, like grunge and goth, exist today as countercultural protest. What began as a youthful rebellion is now the accepted mainstream of popular music, not only in America but also around the world.

 LISTENING EXERCISES

38 *Lost Your Head Blues* 6CD 6/10
sung by Bessie Smith (recorded in New York, 1926)

Lost Your Head Blues tells the tale of a "good old gal" who has "just been treated wrong." In a format typical of the blues, Bessie Smith belts out five stanzas of text, each with three lines. There are "classic" performances in every genre and style of music. With its blend of precision (changing chords in the blues harmony) and freedom (slides and "wah-wah's"), this rendition of *Lost Your Head Blues* is surely a classic.

1. How many performers are there in this recording? _____
2. Which two instruments play during the introduction? _____
3. Is the twelve-bar blues harmony heard during the introduction? _____
4. Which instrument always sets the harmony (the twelve-bar blues pattern) beneath the soloists? _____
5. Within each of the five stanzas of text, the twelve-bar blues harmony is heard how many times? _____
6. Including the introduction, how many times, then, is it heard during the course of the entire song? _____
7. Which instrument always plays the instrumental breaks? _____
8. Which two instruments engage in a dialogue throughout?
   a. voice and piano   b. voice and trumpet   c. piano and trumpet
9. Which two instruments continually slide into their pitches?
   a. voice and piano   b. voice and trumpet   c. piano and trumpet
10. Why does this recording last only three minutes?
   a. Because in the 1920s a single side of a 78 record could hold only three minutes of music.
   b. Because the twelve-bar blues pattern was never repeated.

---

39   Bebop-style Jazz   6CD 6/12
My Melancholy Baby
Charlie "Bird" Parker, saxophone; Dizzy Gillespie, trumpet
(recorded in New York, 1950)

Bebop is a highly complex style of progressive jazz with difficult chord changes and dizzying flights of instrumental virtuosity. What makes *My Melancholy Baby* easy to follow is the form: a short introduction, three sixteen-bar choruses, and a short coda. The form is made clear to the listener because there is a change to a new solo instrument at the beginning of each chorus. From one chorus to the next, however, the playing becomes progressively more complex and the tune more heavily disguised by ornamentation. The first five questions that follow help illuminate the musical form, while the second five concentrate on aspects of the bass line.

1. (0:00–0:12) Which instrument solos during the introduction?
   a. piano   b. trumpet   c. saxophone
2. (0:13–1:11) What does the piano do during Charlie Parker's solo in chorus 1?

   _____

3. (1:12–2:12) During the trumpet solo of chorus 2, is Parker's saxophone heard?
   a. yes   b. no
4. (2:13–3:04) During chorus 3, is Gillespie's trumpet heard?
   a. yes   b. no
5. Which of the forms that we have studied is embodied in this piece?
   a. sonata–allegro
   b. theme and variations
   c. rondo
6. Is the bass instrument that plays in this quintet the double bass of the symphony orchestra or the electric bass guitar? _____
7. Does the player use a bow or play pizzicato? _____

8. Which figure more accurately reflects the rhythm of the bass?

9. Which statement correctly describes the bass line?
   a. moves mainly in stepwise motion in regular, even notes
   b. moves by leaps in highly varied rhythms
10. This sort of bass line, then, can be said to be similar to which musical procedure of the Baroque era?
    a. the pedal point*
    b. the ostinato* bass
    c. the walking bass*

    Listening to Contemporary Rock

This book was written as a text for music courses in colleges and universities. Although the author played piano in a rock 'n'-roll band many years back, he is certain that you, the college student, are more familiar with the contemporary rock scene than he. This last listening exercise gives you the chance to demonstrate your expertise. Your task is to choose a piece of contemporary rock music, analyze it, and write a brief report. As you listen, you may wish to consider the following questions as a way of focusing your thoughts.

1. What instruments are playing?
2. Are they acoustical musical instruments or electronically amplified ones?
3. What do you think is the relationship between music and noise in your piece? Is there any "electronic filler"? If so, what purpose does it serve?
4. Is your piece an original composition by the artist, or is it a "cover" version (remake) of a pre-existing rock or pop song? If it is a cover, how does it compare to the original version?
5. What do you think is the single most important element in your piece? Is it the text, a catchy melody, a satisfying harmonic pattern, a driving rhythm, or something else?
6. What instrument is playing the bass line? Does the bass stand out in any special way? Is it, for example, played louder than the other parts? If so, why?
7. What about the form of your rock song: Is it through-composed* like Schubert's *Erlking* (page 248) or strophic* like *Lost Your Head Blues* (page 380)? Many pop tunes are strophic but each stanza ends with a text refrain. Is yours arranged in this fashion?
8. Is the mood and style of the music well suited to the text of your piece, or might this music be used just as well for another set of lyrics?
9. Has a music video been made to accompany your piece? If so, how do the visual images enhance the message conveyed by the music and lyrics?
10. Finally, how inventive is your work? Is it fresh and innovative, or is it simply a repackaging of the clichés of popular music? Do you think your selection will stand the test of time to become a classic? If so, why; if not, why not?

KEY WORDS

bebop	folk-rock	ragtime
big band	free jazz	rhythm and blues
blue note	instrumental break	rhythm section
blues	jazz	swing
blues scale	jazz-fusion	symphonic jazz
chorus	musical comedy	
cool jazz	operetta	

CONTRASTS: WESTERN MUSIC AND NON-WESTERN MUSIC

 Most of the music we have discussed in this book has been Western European classical music. It is a musical tradition that originated in Europe and spread both east and west, to Russia and gradually to North and South America. Western-style symphonies, concertos, and operas have become the standard currency of art music around the world. In Tokyo, for example, there are presently nine professional symphony orchestras, more than any other city in the world, and huge numbers of ordinary Japanese relax after school or work with a Western violin or piano. It is the Japanese market, in addition, that keeps classical recording companies, such as SONY/Columbia, in business. Young students from Korea, China, Taiwan, Singapore, and Japan flood the conservatories of London and New York to develop their considerable talents as performers on Western-style instruments. Some of the hottest young stars on the American classical stage, such as Midori Goto and Sarah Chang (Fig. 3–3), are from Asian countries or Asian-American parents.

But the music of the West, both classical and popular, is by no means the only music of the world. Great masses of people remain wholly or mostly unaffected by it. For example, China, with a quarter of the world's people, India, with 960 million citizens, and Indonesia, the fourth most populous nation on earth, with 250 million inhabitants, all retain their native musical traditions independent of the West, as do the tribes of sub-Saharan Africa. The sounds of each of these cultures are radically different from each other, just as they are all unrelated to the music of Bach, Mozart, and Beethoven. And while we cannot here enjoy anything more than a tantalizing taste of these foreign delights, they will be enough to demonstrate how the art music of the West is different—indeed unique—among the musics of the world.

GAMELAN MUSIC OF BALI

Bali is an island, about the size of Delaware, that belongs to a chain of islands forming the southeast Asian country of Indonesia (see Fig. 19–1). It is a place of swaying palm trees, fertile rice fields, and hundreds of small villages, each with its own vital and distinctive musical tradition. For the more than two million inhabitants of Bali, music is an integral part of their daily lives, for music is intimately bound up with religion and folklore. Hindu deities and local spirits must be honored daily in the temple and in the home. Larger ceremonies are invariably celebrated to the accompaniment of music performed by a gamelan.

A **gamelan** is a collection of as many as twenty-five musical instruments played together as an orchestra. The ensemble, however, sounds very unlike our Western orchestra, for the dominant family of the gamelan is not the strings, but percussion: metallophones (xylophone-like instruments with bronze keys and bamboo resonators), tuned gongs, gong-chimes, cymbals, and drums, along with an occasional flute. So, too, the gamelan employs a different approach to generating musical lines. In the Western orchestra a single instrument is responsible for providing a melody or countermelody, or creating a single instrumental color. In gamelan music, however, players of several instruments

the gamelan: an Indonesian orchestra of percussion instruments

continually contribute bits of music which, when taken together, form a composite line of distinctive color. In the example that follows, notice how the parts are interlocking and mutually interdependent. It is only their composite sound, not the individual parts, that is conveyed to the ear of the listener. In gamelan music, solos are rare. What sound like solos are actually passages played by small groups. There is a strong commitment to group interaction, with each performer doing his or her part for the benefit of the whole. The effect is that of a well-polished, well-disciplined musical machine—a source of pride for the local village. Indeed, most gamelans are organized as community or village clubs, and they draw heavily on the local populace for performers.

FIGURE 19–1
The subcontinent of Asia, South-East Asia, and the Pacific rim.

EXAMPLE 19–1

A striking example of Balinese gamelan music is the piece entitled *Jaya Semara (Victorious Goddess of Love)*. In a way similar to Britten's *The Young Person's Guide to the Orchestra, Jaya Semara* begins by exploring the colors and textures of the various instruments and instrumental families of the Balinese orchestra, all the while showing off the extraordinary virtuosity of the performers. Only midway through the piece (at 2:10) does a melody enter and a steady rhythmic pulse assert itself.

As with every piece of Balinese music, *Jaya Semara* was taught to the performers, a group from the town of Denpasar, by a master teacher, or guru. The teacher played and explained each part, bit by bit, until finally the entire composition was learned. Though the music is extraordinarily complex, no notation was used. On Bali, everything is taught, learned, and performed entirely by ear.

LISTENING GUIDE	*Jaya Semara (Victorious Goddess of Love)* a piece for Balinese gamelan (recorded in Denpasar, Bali, Indonesia in 1989 by Michael Tenzer)	6CD 6/16

0:00	Full gamelan, with "solos" by high gongs, drums, and then metallophones
0:26	High gongs dominate
0:41	Full gamelan
0:47	High metallophones dominate
1:00	High gongs return
1:24	Single deep gong
1:30	Tempo increases; full gamelan enters
1:37	Drum beat begins
1:47	Drum solo
2:10	Full gamelan with bamboo flute plays repeating melody and ostinato rhythmic patterns
3:17	Tempo increases; then rhythmic patterns break down
3:37	Final gong

MUSIC FOR A CHINESE STRING ORCHESTRA

China is arguably the oldest and richest continuing civilization in the world. Many of the inventions and products that altered the course of Western history—gunpowder, printing, paper, silk, the nautical compass, and the dictionary, for example—were first developed in China. China also has a musical his-

 FIGURE 19–2
A Balinese gamelan fronted by a set of gongs tuned to a pentatonic scale.

tory that extends back thousands of years. A mathematical theory for generating all musical pitches was known in the third century B.C.; orchestras with twenty and more performers played at court during the T'ang dynasty (618–907); and full-fledged opera developed during the Yuan period (1271–1368) and continues to be popular today.

In a country with many distinct ethnic groups and more than three hundred forms of regional theater, there is, naturally, no one uniform musical style. But a common denominator of all Chinese music is the importance given to the string instruments. They are played alone as solo instruments, and, as in the West, they form the nucleus of the Chinese orchestra. Traditionally the Chinese orchestra is much smaller than its Western counterpart, and the tones it produces are totally different. The **pipa** (a four-string lute), the **qin** (a seven-string zither), and the **erhu** (a two-string fiddle, pronounced "R-who") usually provide the dominant sound. While the strings of the pipa and qin are plucked, those of the erhu (see Fig. 19–3) are made of silk and are played with a bow. A vibrato-rich sound results, a strange, veiled tone of great beauty.

We hear the sound of the erhu prominently in the orchestral piece *The Moon Mirrored in the Pool,* composed by a poor, blind musician from the region of Shangai, Hua Yanjun (1890–1950). As with most Chinese music, here melody is paramount. The task of the player of the erhu and the other bowed instruments is to perform it with great subtlety of color and infinite gradations of pitch. There is little harmony in Chinese music. What there is usually results from two instruments playing different versions of the melody simultaneously. Sometimes the melody is simply doubled at the octave or in unison with tremolos*, a technique that produces a shimmering effect. Typical of Chinese music, the scale used in *The Moon Mirrored in the Pool* is a pentatonic* one (here G, A, B, D, E, [G]). But these five notes are merely a point of departure for the astonishingly beautiful erhu, which plays as much between pitches as on them.

❋ FIGURE 19–3

The erhu is played by passing a bow between the two strings and continually twisting the instrument so that the bow can move from one string to the other. Playing is Min Hui-Fen of Shanghai, China.

LISTENING GUIDE

Hua Yanjun (1890–1950)
The Moon Mirrored in the Pool
(performed by the Central Broadcasting Traditional Instruments Orchestra of China)

Phases of the Moon†
CBS CD MK 36705
track 1

0:00	Bamboo flute plays introduction
0:07	Full orchestra introduces melody
0:30	Erhu continues with melody
0:39	Pipa amplifies and extends melody
1:06	Erhu plays variation of melody against background of tremolos on the main notes of the melody
1:42	Crescendo
2:24	Bowed strings play melody with tremolo by plucked strings
2:45	Erhu and pipa play different versions of the melody together
3:16	Prominent "Western-style" bass emerges in low register
3:32	High bowed strings and plucked strings play melody in unison
3:52	Lower bowed strings and plucked strings play melody
4:15	Erhu returns with melody; duple meter accompaniment plucked in background
4:50	Erhu plays fragments of melody

†Although this piece appears in the CD set accompanying the first and second editions of the text, Sony Corporation was unable to extend permission for the third edition. Instructors wishing to obtain a copy should contact the music editor at Wadsworth.

FIGURE 19–4
Ravi Shankar performing on the sitar.

MUSIC FOR THE INDIAN SITAR

Stretching from the towering Himalayan mountains in the north to the tidal mud flats of the south, India is a vast land, full of contrasts: the beauty of the Taj Mahal and the squalor of the urban slums; the wealth of the maharajas and the abject poverty of the untouchables; the jewels on the neck of a prince who, for religious reasons, wears no shoes. It is also a land of many ethnic and religious groups, with the Moslems strong in the north and the Hindus dominating the south. Indian music, too, is divided somewhat along regional lines. What is called **Hindustani-style music** is heard in the north, while **Karnatak-style music** prevails in the south. Among the many differences between the two is the fact that Karnatak music is almost always sung, whereas Hindustani music frequently makes use of an instrument called the sitar.

the sitar and tabla

The **sitar** is a large lutelike instrument with as many as twenty strings, some of which are used to play a melody, some simply to vibrate sympathetically with the melody strings, and some to provide a drone*. At each end of the instrument is a large, semicircular gourd that serves as a resonator to amplify the sound of the strings. With this impressive array of strings, the sitar is capable of producing a variety of timbres, dynamic levels, and special effects when in the hands of a capable performer. A performance on the sitar is invariably accompanied by a **tabla,** a double drum (a drum with a skin stretched over each end). The right-hand end of the tabla is tuned to the tonic, dominant, or subdominant note of the sitar melody, while the left-hand end can produce almost any low pitch, depending on the amount of pressure the drummer applies. With these two instruments alone, gifted Indian musicians can create a performance that is stunning in its virtuosity and exhilarating in its effect.

the raga: a scale with a "mystic expressive force"

Every piece of traditional Indian music makes use of a raga. A **raga** is a basic scale and a general melodic pattern, but it is more. A raga expresses the feeling, the mood of the piece. It has been called "the mystical expressive force" at the

heart of every Indian composition. To the trained ear, *Raga Jogeshwari*, which we shall hear, has the mood of love and pathos. It makes use of a six-note scale that rises and falls as the melody descends and ascends.

EXAMPLE 19–2

From the scale of *Raga Jogeshwari* is derived a basic theme that is presented here at the beginning of the piece three times in quick succession. Thereafter the work unfolds in a series of presentations of the theme and increasingly elaborate improvisations on it. As you will hear, not only are the notes of the scale of the raga played but also the microtones between pitches, as the performer manipulates the strings of the sitar to "bend" the pitches. Bending the pitch adds subtlety and expressive power to the music. The texture becomes increasingly saturated with such ornaments, and, toward the end, the tempo increases to heighten the sense of progress.

a melody with microtones

Perhaps more than any other musical culture, Indian music relies exclusively on melody for musical expression. There are no contrapuntal lines and no harmony other than the constant drone on the tonic and dominant notes of the melody. For an Indian performer, chords are thought to create too much sound at once and to detract from what is truly important: the expressive nuances of the melody and the intricate rhythmic interplay between the sitar and the tabla.

The performance of *Raga Jogeshwari* that you will hear is by Ravi Shankar, one of India's finest sitar players. Shankar personifies the ideal of Indian music in which composer and performer are one and the same person. Indeed, *Raga Jogeshwari* is his own creation. Yet each new performance of this raga results in a new composition because so much of the performance is improvised. For an Indian musician, composition, improvisation, and performance are three simultaneous manifestations of the urge for creative expression.

LISTENING GUIDE	*Raga Jogeshwari* Gat II (Theme II) (performed by Ravi Shankar, sitar, and Alla Rakha, tabla)	6CD 6/17

0:00	Scale of raga played as quick arpeggio
0:08	Sitar presents theme three times against beat in the tabla
0:45	Alternation of the theme with free improvisations
1:17	Ascending and descending improvisations on the scale of the raga
2:11	A strong cadence for the tabla
2:40	More elaborate patterns repeated on successive degrees of the scale
4:18	Tempo increases
4:45	Strumming on the drone strings of the sitar
5:00	Sitar explores half steps that occur naturally in ascending version of the raga
5:50	Tabla mimics rhythmic patterns of the sitar

MUSIC IN SOUTHERN AFRICA

Africa, the second largest continent, is a vast land three times the size of the United States. The Sahara Desert divides it into two racially, culturally, and climatically different zones: Northern Africa, with its historical ties to the Mediterranean region, and Southern Africa (or sub-Saharan Africa), which includes the whole of tropical Africa. Today Africa is partitioned into no fewer than 53 countries. The boundaries of most of these nations are, however, more or less artificial lines drawn by nineteenth- and early twentieth-century European rulers. Real unity and loyalty in Africa rests within the structure of the tribe. And there are more than a thousand tribes, each possessing its own history and language. Every indigenous group has its particular music as well, and thus there are as many styles of music in Africa as there are peoples. Nevertheless, several commonly held principles can be pointed to as distinctive qualities in the music of Southern Africa.

many tribes, many musics

Music as Social Expression

Music permeates every aspect of African life. It is sung or played while chopping wood, pounding grain, paddling a canoe, harvesting crops, weeding a field, sweeping the house, burying a chief, or stamping letters at the post office. Music keeps the workers together and makes their tasks go faster. When people perform music in the West, others stop and listen. But in Africa something else is always going on when music is being made. Music is thus inseparable from social activity. Each situation, moreover, has its own music, which is heard only in that particular context. People do not sing about chopping wood just for the pleasure of it, outside of the context of chopping wood. In African society, music is part of a holistic experience in which, by means of song and dance, the history and traditions of the community are maintained and renewed.

music inseparable from social activity

Importance of Rhythm

If it is harmony that distinguishes European music, and subtle melodic gradations that characterize Indian music, it is rhythm that marks African music. Rhythms are built into the way Africans relate to one another. The creation and structure of these African rhythms are, however, very different from those of the West.

Western performers invariably start at some beginning point, an opening downbeat*, perhaps one given by a conductor, and are guided by the regular recurrence of downbeats and upbeats. All parts lock onto and play with or against a regulating pulse. In African music, by contrast, the individual parts are far more likely to start independently and to stay that way. There is usually no common downbeat around which the players gravitate. Each part has its own downbeat and its own pulse. In African music, therefore, rhythms are not interdependent and interlocking but truly independent. The performers "play apart" as much as they do together. What is more, not only do African musicians commonly play with independent rhythms and separate downbeats, they also play in different meters simultaneously. We have encountered polymeter* before, specifically in the music of the European avant-garde (see page 343). The difference between the European and African use of polymeter is, again, the absence of a shared downbeat in African music, as can be seen in Ex. 19–3.

many rhythms but no common downbeat

EXAMPLE 19–3
Two African drumming patterns, each with its own rhythm and meter

There are always at least two rhythms going on in African music, and this accounts for its complexity. We Westerners perceive it as complex, indeed are often baffled by it, because we can't find a unifying downbeat amid the conflicting meters. We can't find one pulse to which to tap our feet. Africans, on the other hand, rejoice in the dynamic power of a music created by such rhythmic clashes.

delight in rhythmic conflict

Importance of the Drums

Many musical instruments are indigenous to Africa—flutes, whistles, harps, bells, even trumpets—but it is the drum we immediately associate with African culture. Drums are at the heart of almost all group music-making and all dances. Some tribes believe that drums are magical, that they contain the spirits of ancestral drummers. Drum makers sometimes place charms within the drum— pebbles from the yard of the village gossip so as to make the drum talk freely, a bit of skin of a lion to make it roar. African drums come in a staggering variety of shapes and sizes. There are hand drums, stick drums, water drums, slit drums (a hollowed-out log with a long slit on top), drums that are squeezed, and drums that are scraped. Even the human body sometimes functions as a drum when a person slaps the stomach or thigh.

spirits within drums

Despite the many sizes and tone colors of African drums, we tend to think of each drum as producing one and only one sound. But there are many drums that can produce a spectrum of tones. Tension can be placed on the drum head to tighten the skin and thus elevate the pitch. How one strikes and dampens the drum head can also affect pitch. Because native African languages are "tonal" languages, drums have the capacity to imitate speech. In a **tonal language** the precise pitch of a word can determine its meaning; one and the same "sound" can have different meanings depending on the pitch at which it is spoken. By duplicating the speech patterns of the tribe, an African drummer can communicate the salient sounds of the tribal tongue. When such a "talking drum" is present, music and language are one.

"talking drums"

Call and Response

The structure of African music is governed in large measure by a principle of performance called "call and response" (see also page 378). In vocal music a lead singer will announce an opening phrase, and the chorus will utter a short, simple reply. The soloist returns, extending and varying the call, to which the chorus responds again in simple, stable fashion. The soloist may enter and depart according to his or her whim. The chorus, however, responds at regular and predictable intervals. Instrumentalists can also engage in call and response.

❧ FIGURE 19–5 AND 19–6
(left) The dondon is a pressure drum, so called because the player can pull on the leather thongs connecting the two heads to raise the pitch. (right) A group of dondon and gongon drummers from Dagomba, Ghana.

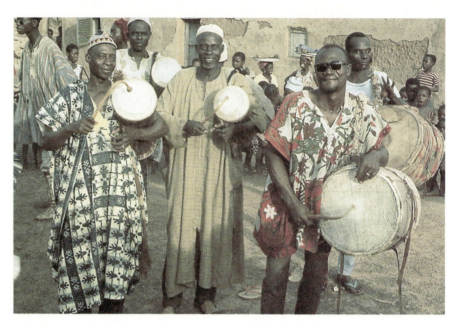

A master drummer, for example, can initiate a conversation with a chorus of subordinates. Sometimes the performing forces are mixed: A vocal soloist may engender a massed instrumental reply.

During the seventeenth and eighteenth centuries, the practice of call and response was carried to the Americas by slaves brought from West Africa. Today it remains an important structural feature of African-American spirituals, blues, gospel, and soul. When James Brown, the "godfather of soul," sings "Get up" and we then hear a collective "Get on up," we have a classic example of African call and response.

A PRAISE-SONG FROM GHANA

Ghana, in the western part of sub-Saharan Africa, is a country somewhat smaller than Texas, with a population of about fifteen million people (see Figs. 19–7 and 19–8). In its northeast corner, north of the Volta River, lies a territory called Dagomba, which supports a people called the Dagombas who speak a language called Dagbani, one of the forty-four official languages of Ghana. The primary musical instruments of the Dagombas are the drums, specifically the dondon and the gongon. The **dondon** (see Figs. 19–5 and 19–6)

a drum that changes pitch

is a "pressure" drum shaped like an hourglass, with heads at opposite ends. Leather thongs connect the two heads. Pulling on the thongs increases the pressure on the heads and raises the pitch. The **gongon** is a large, barrellike drum that produces a deep tone. By means of a single snare string stretched across the upper part of the face of the drum, it also emits the rattlelike sound of a snare drum*. Both the dondon and the gongon are struck with a stick in a wrist-flicking motion. Five or six dondons and one or two gongons typically constitute the "orchestra" for dance music and praise songs of this region of Ghana.

Kasuan Kura is a praise song of the Dagombas, a song that tells the history of an important member of the tribe. Its structure is call and response. The vocal soloist relates the history of the honored figure while the chorus repeats the name of this esteemed ancestor "Kasuan Kura" throughout. The piece begins with dondon drummers manipulating their instruments to make them speak.

✿ FIGURE 19–7 AND 19–8
(left) The continent of Africa and
(right) the country of Ghana situated
in the western portion of sub-Saharan
Africa.

Immediately thereafter at (0:02) the gongons enter, recognizable by their snare rattle and deeper sound. The gongons play throughout the song, while the higher-pitched dondons come and go. Whenever dondons and gongons are heard together, complex polyrhythms and polymeters result. When gongons merely support the choral response, a rather simple rhythm in a clear duple meter emerges. Thus two musical conversations develop: one between the solo singer and chorus, and a second between the complex dondon-gongon mixture and the simpler rhythmic texture of the gongons alone. In the course of this short piece the soloist's calls become more elaborate and exuberant, just as the drumming on the dondons grows more excited.

musical conversations

LISTENING GUIDE

The People of Dagomba, Ghana
Kasuan Kura
(recorded in Ghana by John Miller Chernoff)

6CD 6/18

0:00	Dondons begin
0:02	Gongons enter
0:12	Solo vocal call accompanied by dondons and gongons
0:16	Choral response accompanied by gongons alone
0:21	Solo call accompanied by dondons and gongons
0:25	Choral response accompanied by gongons alone
0:29	Call and response continues, accompanied as before
1:25	Dondon and gongon patterns become more complex
1:32	Call and response continues to the end

CONTRASTS

From this brief tour of four non-Western musical cultures, it is easy to hear the ways in which these four musical traditions sound different one from another. Yet they also have many things in common that separate them from the musical practices and traditions of the West. The following are among the more important contrasts between Western and non-Western music.

IMPORTANCE OF MELODY AND RHYTHM, AND THE ABSENCE OF HARMONY. Non-Western musics are marked by gradations and subtleties of pitch that are far more sophisticated than those in Western melodies, which tend to move directly from one well-defined pitch to the next. Rhythms, too, are generally more complex, and rhythmic interaction between the parts is more complicated. Yet at the same time, harmony as we in the West know it is virtually nonexistent. Of all the musical cultures of the world, only the West has emphasized the simultaneous sounding of several pitches, as for example, when chords are played on the piano. The harmony that results adds richness and depth to the sound, but often at the expense of melodic and rhythmic features.

IMPROVISATION. Spontaneous improvisation is a musical practice that occurs, to varying degree, in virtually all musical traditions except that of Western classical music. A singer of the Ashanti people in Ghana, Africa, is expected to vary a tribal song and add sections to it, just as the Indian sitar player is expected to ornament and extend a traditional raga, after years of patient study of the ornamental art. A performer's worth is measured in terms of his or her ability to create music that is new and imaginative within the confines of a traditional form. We in the West have a similar type of music, American jazz, but the strong emphasis on improvisation in jazz only serves to show that this style of music is African, not European, in its roots.

ORAL TEACHING AND LEARNING. Each of the musical cultures explored in this chapter relies exclusively on oral transmission, not written notation, as the means by which to communicate music. The Indian guru will teach the secrets of the ragas to the young student by rote. The same is true of the master drummer of Ghana. The master explains and plays, the student imitates and practices, year after year. Musical notation has no place in the process. There is musical notation in India, China, and Bali, but it is generally used in learned discussions of the theory of music, not in practical music-making. This is true everywhere throughout the non-Western world.

IMPORTANCE OF MUSICAL NOTATION IN THE WEST. Western musical culture is the only one to rely on notation as a means of preserving and passing on its musical heritage from one generation to the next. It is also the only culture in which performers play by reading written symbols. Working from notation has advantages and disadvantages. It allows the composer to prescribe in great detail exactly what he or she wishes to express. It is possible to have a very clear and unchanging notion of what a particular work of art is to be. Yet as a result each successive performance of that work tends to be rather similar to the last—there is little room for spontaneous creativity.

COMPOSER AND PERFORMER AS ONE. Musical notation in Western classical music has given extraordinary powers of control and authority to the composer. He or she can dictate every small detail of a composition, and it is up to the performer to carry out precisely these instructions. The performer is the servant of the composer. Non-Western cultures have a more balanced relationship between composer and performer. Indeed, the composer and performer, like Ravi Shankar, are usually one and the same person. A piece of music comes into being only at the time of performance. It has no life outside of performance. It is not thought out in advance in someone's head. It is not written down in musical notation. There is no composer and performer, only musician. Similarly, there is no conductor in non-Western cultures, no one who directs but does not produce sound. Even in the large Balinese gamelan, where many instrumental parts have to be coordinated, the leader is one of the performers, usually one of the drummers.

MUSIC AS COMMUNITY RITUAL. Just as we in the West compartmentalize music into producers (composers), middlemen (performers), and consumers (audience), so we tend to think of music as an abstraction. We view art generally as discrete objects divorced from other means of human expression. We speak of a painting or a musical composition as a "work of art." In other cultures music is not an abstract object. Most African languages have no word for the concept of "music," although there are words for poetry, dance, and song. "Music" is thus inseparably bound up with poetry, dance, gesture, pantomime, and other means of expression. As such it serves as a medium to reaffirm the values of the community in daily work and play, and in special rituals. The music for one type of activity or ritual is never heard in the context of another. Religious music, for example, is played only as part of a religious rite. We in the West, by contrast, will often take a sacred Mass of Palestrina, Bach, Mozart, or Beethoven, separate it from church and all religious associations, and perform it as a "work of art" in a concert hall.

CONCERTS AND AUDIENCE RESPONSE. Public performance of music in non-Western cultures occurs in a freer, more relaxed environment. In Africa it is not uncommon to see a group of expert musicians surrounded by people who join in by singing, clapping, playing rattles, and dancing with the music. Concerts in Bali usually occur in open-air pavilions where the audience crowds around, laughs, talks quietly, and encourages the performers. Interaction between the performers and the community is an important part of the music-making process. Prior to the nineteenth century, concerts in the West were similar to this freer, more interactive experience. Not until the Romantic era, when Western composers made a musical composition a revered "work of art," was the audience required to sit in respectful, meditative silence.

✿ CONCLUSION

The contrasts between Western and non-Western musical traditions have implications that extend far beyond the world of music, for music reflects the way a society thinks and what it values. From the preceding view of non-Western music, we can begin to see how much we have become a society of musical spectators rather than participants. We divorce the individual performers from the group experience. We value a single creator who determines all elements of the musical composition. We have turned away from improvisation and spontaneous creativity, preferring instead precise planning and faithful duplication at the moment of performance. The work of art is given an exalted position. It is fixed in notation and unalterable. It does not grow and evolve to reflect the changing needs and desires of the community. Finally, we have transformed what is at heart an oral and physical means of communication into one of visual relationships through a heavy reliance on musical notation. We have replaced sound with visual symbol, the ear and the body with the eye and the mind. We have also gradually replaced the musician with two individuals, the performer and the composer. More recently, with the advent of computer music in this century, we have replaced the composer with the computer programmer. Today, as arguments about "multiculturalism" swirl around us, even a cursory study of non-Western music suggests why such an experience is important. Not only do we learn something about the music of other people but we also find out even more about ourselves.

 KEY WORDS

call and response	Hindustani-style music	Ravi Shankar
erhu	Karnatak-style music	sitar
dondon	pipa	tabla
gamelan	qin	tonal language
gongon	raga	

SELECTED WEB RESOURCES

 This appendix consist of selected links to web sites covering a variety of musical topics. Students can use these web sites as a supplement to their course work, and as a stepping stone to further research. Links to web sites are organized by topic, and are accompanied by descriptions of each site's offerings. These selected web links will also be available on the web site for *Listening to Music*, accessible through Wadsworth's Music Lounge (http://music.wadsworth.com).

As is the nature of the World Wide Web, some of the links researched at the time of publication may now be inoperable. Though efforts have been made to select stable web sites for this appendix, the user should be aware that these site locations are subject to change.

The user must be careful when surfing the web for information. Anyone can post material regardless of its quality or accuracy. Numerous sites consist of undergraduate papers posted by students or class projects developed by high school or elementary students. While these efforts are laudable and can offer interesting perspectives, they do not qualify as good sources of information. The citations in this text consist of two types of listings: sites that include a wide range of composers and music topics and those that are specifically devoted to a single composer. It is an unfortunate fact that not all composers, for example Tchaikovsky and Liszt, have a site worthy of their musical importance. In cases where a prominent composer is not included in the chapter listings, then return to the general listings provided in this chapter. Finally, while the web is a good place to begin exploring the life and music of a favorite composer, don't neglect to use the library's print and CD sources.

GENERAL MUSIC WEBSITES

The sites listed below furnish introductory material and should be used when beginning a web search. Each of the four sites fulfills a unique niche that is not covered by the others, so it is worthwhile to examine all of them. If a composer, such as Tchaikovsky in Chapter 15, does not have a listing, look in these pages.

http://w3.rz-berlin.mpg.de/cmp/classmus.html

The strength of *Classical Music Pages* is its biographical information. Entries are extracted from *The New Grove Dictionary of Music and Musicians*, one of the foremost reference works on music in English. Even if a site is specifically highlighting a single composer, it is still a good idea to examine what is provided here. The entries under "Genre" and "Musical Epochs" are also valuable. Another excellent source is *Britannica Online*. The thorough composer biographies are geared toward the general reader and their links section is also good, if uneven at times (some sites have absolutely nothing to do with the topic). Many university libraries have this or similar sources available. Again, if the web version is not available, your library is sure to have the hard copy.

http://www.culturefinder.com

Culture Finder is useful for quick, basic information but is a little complicated to use. To access the information on classical composers, scroll down to the *Arts Resources and Community* section, click on *Classical & Opera*. In the left-hand column, click on either *CF Guide to Classics* or *CF Guide to Opera*. Select "All-Stars" and when the list of composers appears, select the desired individual. At the bottom of the brief sketch is a link to *Burkat Program Notes*, which offers a bit more biographical information as well as background material on selected compositions. This is perhaps the highlight of the site.

http://www.classical.net

If you are interested in purchasing CDs, finding a selected list of important works by a particular composer, or seeking links, turn to *Classical Net*. It advertises more than 4200 files and 2500 links. Select "Basic Repertoire," chose the desired period, and a host of composer names will appear. Each entry describes the composer in one or two paragraphs and includes a list of their most important works. Many composers have a links section and this is the highlight of the site, although many URL addresses are out of date. There are, however, enough current sites to make a visit worthwhile. The "Classical CD Buying Guide" offers good advice on building a music library.

www.mala.bc.ca/~mcneil

The *Malaspina Great Books Home Page* is a great place to locate the most current recordings and books about a composer. It is similar to Classical Net, but the list is more selective and the links are more current. There are more than 1,000 artists, musicians, authors, and other individuals of historical and cultural importance. This site does not have independent biographies, but includes an automatic link to the citation provided by *Classical Music Pages*. Click on the orange maple leaf to access the links.

ORGANIZATIONS

Most arts organizations now have performance schedules and ticket information posted on-line. Simply type the organization's name (e.g., Favorite City Symphony Orchestra) into a search engine and voilà. In most instances, student tickets are available at the door for reduced prices, just be sure to bring along your identification card. These sites are beneficial if you prefer to plan ahead and select the concert you really want to attend rather than look through the newspaper at the last minute.

OPERA

http://rick.stanford.edu/opera/main.html

The homepage for *Opera Glass* provides birth and death dates for numerous opera composers and synopses for selected operas. If you need to find this information on the web, this is a good place to start, but standard print material in any library will furnish better information.

MEDIEVAL MUSIC

Hildegard of Bingen

http://www.uni-mainz.de/~horst/hildegard

This German site is devoted to various aspects of Hildegard's life: religion, medicine, and music. Be sure to click on "English" to get the page in translation. Nancy Fierro's essay on Hildegard's music is quite good. "Internet resources" will direct the reader to numerous bibliographies, the best of which is the one by the *Catholic Encyclopedia*. The travel essay with pictures of Bingen on the Rhine is a nice addition for modern travelers.

BAROQUE

Farinelli

http://www.spe.sony.com/classics/farinelli/about/ffarinelli.html

This site provides a reasonably good biography of the greatest operatic star of the eighteenth century. Sony, the motion picture industrial giant, maintains it as background for their 1995 movie *Farinelli*, yet in spite of such dubious scholarly credentials, it is worth examining. The essay on the use, training, and popularity of the castrato voice is good. It mentions how many poor families regarded the anatomy of their sons as a lottery ticket, hoping to escape their grinding poverty and strike it rich.

Antonio Vivaldi

http://www.oasiskc.net/~bryanc/vivhome.htm

The *Antonio Vivaldi Homepage* provides a solid, if unusually organized biography. While the treatment is balanced, the author is unapologetic about starting with "the dirt." Those who are interested in purchasing a recording of *The Four Seasons* will find a helpful selection of record reviews as well as a translation of the Sonnets. Readers will find it worthwhile to look into the "Beginning CDs" section and the extensive links.

Johann Sebastian Bach

http://www.jsbach.org

This is one of the most outstanding sites available for any composer and an excellent source for high quality information. Of special interest is the "Tourist Guide" in the biography section. Photographs and accompanying commentary provide an interesting glimpse of where Bach lived and worked. The "Recommended Recordings" is another helpful section. While the reviews tend to be positive and only occasionally offer mild criticism, the reader soon gets a sense of each recording's performance characteristics and distinctions. The site also offers a revolving selection of recommended recordings and the links section can send an interested seeker into extensive labyrinths of material.

George Frideric Handel

http://www.npj.com/homepage/teritowe/welcome.html

While there is nothing currently available for Handel research that matches the Bach site, the Baroque scholar Teri Towe offers some interesting information, especially a variety of Handel portraits, a mid-nineteenth century history of *Messiah*, record reviews, and of course, links. Her homepage also has a section devoted to Bach.

CLASSICAL

Wolfgang Amadeus Mozart

http://www.geocities.com/vienna/strasse/2914/mozart

The highlights of this site include an interesting account of Mozart's last day, background on the movie *Amadeus*, and some pictures. While there are some nice photos of Salzburg, the images are lacking any commentary beyond identification. The section covering his compositions includes good historical background for many, but not all works.

http://www.frontiernet.net/~sboerner/mozart

The biography is superb, but currently in progress. Separate biographies are provided for Mozart's father, mother, and sister. The links section is outstanding.

http://www.artswire.org/~mrd/nozze

A good site devoted to Mozart's opera *The Marriage of Figaro*. It offers a readable discussion of the literary and historical background of the work and debunks the popular myth regarding the purpose of the *droit du seigneur*. Of course it is the incorrect version that inspired Beaumarchais, da Ponte, and Mozart.

Ludwig van Beethoven

http://www.geocities.com/Vienna/Strasse/3732

Currently the best web biography on the internet. Whereas most sites provide the equivalent of a two to three page summary of Beethoven's life and career, this one offers interesting detail. The only drawback is the poor quality of synthesized sound that cannot be silenced. The biography in *Britannica Online* is also an excellent resource.

http://www.music.sjsu.edu/Beethoven/index/home_page.html

This is the homepage for the Ira F. Brilliant Center for Beethoven Studies. An excellent source for doing serious research on any topic concerning the composer. Highlights include the bibliography database that provides citations for everything from books and scholarly articles to reviews of concerts, recordings, and publications. The Guide to Research summarizes the content of bibliographic tools. About the only concession to general interest is just that, an online concession stand where one can purchase mugs and tee shirts.

http://www.issay.com/bonn-beethoven-house/index.html

This is the homepage site for the Beethoven museum located in the house where Beethoven was born. As of writing, the entire site is under construction, but it should be worth a look. Unless you are fluent in German or Japanese, select the English button.

http://physics.usyd.edu.au/~simonj/lvb/ht.html
http://physics.usyd.edu.au/~simonj/lvb/ib.html
These two sites specialize in the Heiligenstadt Testament (ht.html) and Beethoven's letters to the Immortal Beloved (ib.html). The first provides English translations of the Heiligenstadt Testament and the letters along with appropriate commentary. The Immortal Beloved site summarizes the current thinking regarding the identity of this mystery woman. If you enjoy detective stories, examine this site.

http://members.tripod.com/~zzzed/beetho.html
A good specialty page on a favorite Beethoven quartet, Opus 59, No. 1. The interesting historical background and musical analysis are geared for general readers. The only drawback with this site is that the author employs British terminology for rhythmic notation, such as "crotchet" for "quarter-note."

http://www.ida.his.se/ida/
http://www.geocities.com/Vienna/Strasse/2914/beethoven/
The interesting aspect in these two sites is the various descriptions of individual compositions. The second site is by the same author of one of the Mozart sites listed above. The author began work on these sites when he was nineteen, so while much of the information is derivative, the perspective might be appealing to readers of the text.

ROMANTIC

Johann von Goethe (poet)

http://members.aol.com/KatharenaE/private/Pweek/Goethe/goethe.html
This site on the great German Romantic poet, *Penetrating Goethe,* is by Katharena Eiermann. It contains a good biographical sketch, numerous translations of his poems and interesting links. Although the site has a Java script error, just click OK and everything works fine. This location can also be accessed through the biographical link from the *Malaspina Great Books Home Page* (see General Web Sites for address).

Franz Schubert

http://dspace.dial.pipex.com/ramorris
Homepage of *The Schubert Institute.* A biography is in progress and a complete survey of his life written during the nineteenth century is also provided. A section is devoted to Schubert's friends and acquaintances and a few analyses of selected works can be found in the links section.

http://www.charm.net/~tomokoy/schubert.html
The highlight of this page is an excellent selection of photographs and commentary regarding Austrian locations associated with Schubert, including an attractive photo and information on the town where Schubert composed The "Trout" Quintet.

Hector Berlioz

http://www.standrews.u-net.com/BerliozSociety.html
http://www.standrews.u-net/BerliozLacote.html
http://www.ozemail.com.au/~phillijr/Berlioz.html

The first site is the homepage for the *Berlioz Society*. While there is little to interest the casual reader, the links section is worthwhile. The second listing, a sister page to the *Berlioz Society*, features great photographs and information about various spots of biographical interest in the city of his birth. The last entry, geared for the general reader, is a good site for biography and commentary about specific works.

Robert and Clara Schumann

http://www.uah.edu/clara/schumann.html
http://members.aol.com/abelard2/davidsbuendler.htm

The site devoted to Clara Schumann offers a modest biography, works list, midi file, and a good selection of pictures. The second site is really quite intriguing. The authors have decided to continue the aesthetic battle launched by Robert Schumann under the name of "The League of David" or "Davidsbünd." Read the "History of the Davidsbünd" section for an interesting account of Schumann's musical views and writing style. The site also has hilarious anecdotes by Mendelssohn and Clara Schumann concerning the music of Liszt and Wagner. A humorous satirical poem by Heine concludes with a jab at Liszt's libido.

Frédéric Chopin

http://www.geocities.com/Vienna/2217/

The Unofficial Frédéric Chopin Homepage. Highlights of this site include a biographical sketch that emphasizes the composer's influence and importance rather than the events of his life and a survey of different genres (look up *Mazurka*). There is also a section devoted to quotes by his contemporaries. George Sand: "Chopin has written two wonderful mazurkas which are worth more than forty novels and are more eloquent than the entire century's literature."

http://lonestar.texas.net/~gebbie/gsand/gs_home.html

The homepage for George Sand includes a modest biography, pictures, and timeline.

Richard Wagner

http://www-2.roughguides.com/opera

This site excerpts passages from the *Rough Guide to Opera*. Wagner's biography is concise, but excellent and the historical background for individual operas is well worth reading.

Guiseppe Verdi

http://www.edinboro.edu/CWIS/Music/Cordell/00hpverdi.html

The Giuseppe Verdi Homepage gives an interesting biography of the composer's early years. It describes his musical training, early setbacks, the tragic death of his family, and concludes with this first operatic triumph, *Nabucco*. The link to *La Scala,* Italy's premiere opera house, has a virtual tour with photographs and diagrams (the site is in Italian, so click on "Visita Virtuale" and explore).

Johannes Brahms

http://www.austria-tourism.at/personen/brahms
A good place to get acquainted with the life and music of Brahms. It offers a series of short biographical essays treating different periods of the composer's life and genres of composition. The section covering *A German Requiem* is of modest interest.

http://www.mjq.net/brahms
The Johannes Brahms WebSource offers extensive links to numerous sources, including most on-line encyclopedia articles. The biography is currently under construction.

http://members.aol.com/abelard2/brahms.htm
Another *Davidsbündler* site (see the Schumann citations above), this one commemorating the centennial of Brahms's death. The title page has a nice photograph of the composer's funeral monument. Two of the four articles are of significant interest: an essay on the fourth symphony by the great German conductor Wilhelm Furtwängler and a memoir by one of Brahms's composition students. The student submitted the same composition to Brahms and Tchaikovsky. Their critiques provide a unique comparison between the different styles of the two artists.

Gustav Mahler

http://www.netaxs.com/~jgreshes/mahler
A behemoth site devoted to the composer. While it advertises approximately 300 pages devoted to Mahler scholarship, the centerpiece is a 125-page biography. Written in 1932 and currently out of print, the site manager has thoughtfully included all the original page numbers to facilitate citation and has included numerous illustrations. For those who find the full biography intimidating, a short biographical sketch may be located at the bottom of the title page. The site also features a Mahler discography, recording guide (e.g., the best recordings of each symphony—worth checking out), and an overview of the first symphony. The links section is among the best to be found on any subject.

http://www.geocities.com/Vienna/Strasse/4133
The Mahlerite Home Page is managed by Paul Zukas. Two interesting features include his timed commentary on Symphony No. 5 (similar in structure to the text's Listening Guides) and a short reminiscence about his introduction to Mahler's music at the age of fifteen.

✤ TWENTIETH CENTURY

Béla Bartók

http://www.geocities.com/Vienna/2414/index.html
http://www.ultranet.com/~cwholl/bartok/bartok.html
The first address is for *Béla Bartók: his life, times, and music*. This site is currently under construction, but now offers a useful survey of his early life and career. The second site offers a decent, though brief, biography and a timeline. Some

anecdotal information regarding his life in the United States provides a glimpse into this composer's uncompromising character.

John Cage

http://charon.sfsu.edu/CAGE.HTML
http://www.io.com/~glenford/Cage.html
http://www.lcdf.org/indeterminacy

The first site is a short reminiscence of a performance of *4'33"*. The second provides a good introduction to Cage's music and aesthetic philosophy. Even though the author does not agree with the composer's philosophy of music, he gives a balanced presentation. There is also a brief section that covers five works, including *4'33"*. The last site contains a selection of Cage's writings.

Charles Ives

http://www.housatonic.org/ives.html
http://www.charlesives.org

The first site offers a short biography that emphasizes the composer's childhood experiences. It also has a photograph of Ives's birthplace in Danbury. The second listing is for the *Charles Ives Society*. It is currently under construction, but helpful material for the general reader will likely be included. At the moment, the best Web biographies are located in the General Sites.

Arnold Schoenberg

http://www.schoenberg.at/

The Arnold Schoenberg Center. One of the top music sites currently available. If it happens to come up in German, click on the words "English Version." A good biography and essay about his music as well as his importance to twentieth-century music is located under "Schoenberg" in the left-hand column (be sure to click on the arrows to get the subsequent pages). The site also has seven pages of photos, including one with Charlie Chaplin, a frequent tennis partner. The mammoth links section will keep an interested surfer going for a good week at least, but one needs to look under "Archive" to find it. An excellent bibliography is also provided under "Frequently Asked Questions" in "Archive." For a visual analog of twelve-tone music and its use (retrograde, inversion, etc.), click on "Logo Concept." Begin with "Symbol" and work your way through the section. If you are interested in visual form or mathematical symbolism, this will be fascinating.

Igor Stravinsky

http://www.geocities.com/vienna/1807/strav.html

The *Igor Stravinsky Homepage* offers an annotated list of the composer's works. The background material for many works, while not exhaustive, provides a good start. At the time of writing, the biography section was not accessible and other portions of the site were under construction.

http://www.geocities.com/WestHollywood/3660/Stravinsky.html

The site includes a biography of moderate length and some general historical background on his early ballets. It is a good source for links, although most of them are not particularly informative. One notable exception is a page devoted to his religious compositions (**http://www.cco.caltech.edu/~tan/Stravinsky/. index.html**). These late works are provided with historical background, a discussion of musical form, some helpful analysis for listening, and a bibliography.

John Tavener

http://easyweb.easynet.co.uk/~snc/tavener.htm
Provides an excellent biography of John Tavener. A sound clip where the composer discusses his thoughts on John Lennon is also available.

Edgard Varèse

http://csunix1.lvc.edu/~snyder/em/varese.html
http://csunix1.lvc.edu/~snyder/em/zappa.html
http://csunix1.lvc.edu/~snyder/em/mc.html
This is a good collection of interrelated sites offering solid information with a touch of humor. The biographical sketch is thorough but avoids becoming mired in detail. The description of *Ionization* is pungent: "with 37 percussion instruments and two sirens, it was likened to 'a sock in the Jaw.'" The second site, accessible by a link from the first, is an essay by Frank Zappa narrating his adolescent introduction to the music of Varèse. The third site is a brief introduction, with good illustrations, to *musique concrète*.

Ellen Taaffe Zwillich

http://www.presser.com/zwilich.html
This site offers a slim biography and a listing of her compositions. Be sure to check her listings in the General Web Sites.

 AMERICAN POPULAR MUSIC

Louis Armstrong

http://www.foppejohnson.com/armstrong
This is a useful discography in which each of his periods of recordings is provided with a brief historical and biographical perspective.

Leonard Bernstein

http://www.leonardbernstein.com
The *Official Leonard Bernstein Website* is organized in an unusual manner. It offers a good biography, copies of famous letters, telegrams, and photographs, and an annotated section of recommended recordings. Other sections are devoted to scholarships, etc.

http://www.users.globalnet.co.uk/~mcgoni
Leonard Bernstein Homepage. While the biography is minimal, the background on Bernstein's works for the theater is quite good (*West Side Story* is not currently included) and the links section is worthwhile.

Swing

http://www.anyswinggoes.com

A good source for background on this genre. This site provides a documented history of early swing and its current revival. Of special interest is a section that offers hints on how to get the right swing band for a wedding as well as how to prepare the reception—a site with relevant information!

GLOSSARY

absolute music: instrumental music free of a text or any pre-existing program

a cappella: a term applied to unaccompanied vocal music; originated in the expression *a cappella Sistina*, "in the Sistine Chapel" of the pope, where instruments were forbidden to accompany the singers

accelerando: a tempo mark indicating "getting faster"

accent: emphasis or stress placed on a musical tone or a chord

accidental: a sharp, flat, or natural sign that alters the pitch of a note a half step

accompagnato: see *recitativo accompagnato*

acoustical instruments: instruments that produce sounds naturally when strings are bowed or plucked, a tube has air passed through it, or percussion instruments are struck

acoustical music: music produced by acoustical instruments (see above)

adagio: a tempo mark indicating "slow"

Alberti bass: instead of having the pitches of a chord sound all together, the notes are played in succession to provide a continual stream of sound

aleatoric music: see *chance music*

allegretto: a tempo mark indicating "moderately fast"

allegro: a tempo mark indicating "fast"

allemande: a stately dance in 4/4 meter with gracefully interweaving lines

alto (contralto): the lower of the two female voice parts, the soprano being higher

andante: a tempo mark indicating "moderately moving"

andantino: a tempo mark indicating "moderately moving" yet slightly faster than *andante*

antecedent phrase: the opening, incomplete-sounding phrase of a melody; often followed by a consequent phrase that brings the melody to closure

anthem: a composition for chorus on a sacred subject; similar in design and function to a motet

aria: an elaborate lyrical song for solo voice

arpeggio: the notes of a triad or seventh chord played in direct succession and in a direct line up or down

arioso: a style of singing and a type of song midway between an aria and a recitative

art song: an accompanied song or ayre with artistic aspirations

atonal music: music without tonality, music without a key center; most often associated with the twentieth-century avant-garde style of Arnold Schoenberg

augmentation: the notes of a melody held for longer, usually double, their normal duration

ballad: a traditional song, or folk song, sung by a soloist that tells a tale and is organized by stanzas

ballet: an art form that uses dance and music, along with costumes and scenery, to tell a story and display emotions through expressive gestures and movement

Ballets russes: a Russian ballet company of the early twentieth century led by Sergei Diaghilev

banjo: a five-string plucked folk instrument of African-American origin

bar: see *measure*

baritone: a male voice part of a middle range, between the higher tenor and the lower bass

bas instruments: a class of soft musical instruments, including flute, recorder, fiddle, harp, and lute, popular during the late Middle Ages.

bass: the lowest male voice range

bass clef: a sign placed on a staff to indicate the notes below middle C

bass drum: a large, low-sounding drum struck with a soft-headed stick

bass viol: see *viola da gamba*

basso continuo: a small ensemble of at least two instrumentalists who provide a foundation for the melody or melodies above; heard almost exclusively in Baroque music

basso ostinato: a motive or phrase in the bass that is repeated again and again

bassoon: a low, double-reed instrument of the woodwind family

Bayreuth Festival House: an opera house in the town of Bayreuth, Germany, constructed exclusively for the music dramas of Richard Wagner

beat: an even pulse in music that divides the passing of time into equal segments

bebop: a complex, hard-driving style of jazz that emerged shortly after World War II; it is played without musical notation by a small ensemble

bel canto: (Italian for "beautiful singing") a style of singing and a type of Italian opera developed in the nineteenth century that features the beautiful tone and brilliant technique of the human voice

big band: a mid- to large-size dance band that emerged in the 1930s to play the style of jazz called swing

binary form: a musical form consisting of two units (**A** and **B**) constructed to balance and complement each other

blue note: the third, fifth, or seventh note of the blues scale that can be altered to be sharper or flatter; helps produce the wail of the blues

blues: an expressive, soulful style of singing that emerged from the African-American spiritual and work song at the end of the nineteenth century; its texts are strophic, its harmonies simple and repetitive

blues scale: a seven-note scale in which the third, fifth, and seventh pitches are sometimes flat, sometimes natural, and sometimes in between

bolero: a popular, suggestive Spanish dance for a soloist or couple often performed to the accompaniment of castanets

Brandenburg concertos: set of six concerti grossi composed by J. S. Bach between 1711 and 1720, and subsequently dedicated to Margrave Christian Ludwig of Brandenburg

brass family: a group of musical instruments traditionally made of brass and played with a mouthpiece; includes trumpet, trombone, French horn, and tuba

bridge: see *transition*

bugle: a simple brass instrument that evolved from the valveless military trumpet

cabaletta: the concluding fast aria of any two- or three-section operatic scene; a useful mechanism to get the principals off the stage

cadence: the concluding part of a musical phrase

cadenza: a showy passage for the soloist appearing near the end of the movement in a concerto; it usually incorporates rapid runs, arpeggios, and snippets of previously heard themes into a fantasylike improvisation

call and response: a method of performance in which a soloist sings and a group or another soloist answers; it is particularly favored in African music and genres of African-American music such as the blues

canon (round): a contrapuntal form in which the individual voices enter and each in turn duplicates exactly the melody that the first voice played or sang

cantata: a term originally meaning "something sung"; in its mature state it consists of several movements, including one or more arias, ariosos, and recitatives; cantatas can be on secular subjects, but those of J. S. Bach are primarily sacred in content

caprice: a light, whimsical character piece of the nineteenth century

castanets: percussion instruments (rattles) of indefinite pitch associated with Spanish music

castrato: a boy or adult singer who had been castrated to keep his voice from changing so that it would remain in the soprano register

celesta: a small percussive keyboard instrument using hammers to strike metal bars, thereby producing a bright, bell-like sound

cello (violoncello): an instrument of the violin family but more than twice the violin's size; it is played between the legs and produces a rich, lyrical tone

chamber music: music, usually instrumental music, performed in a small concert hall or private residence with just one performer on each part

chamber sonata: see *sonata da camera*

chance music (aleatory music): music that involves an element of chance (rolling dice, choosing cards, etc.) or whimsy on the part of the performers; especially popular with avant-garde composers

chanson: a French term used broadly to indicate a lyrical song from the Middle Ages into the twentieth century

character piece: a brief instrumental work seeking to capture a single mood; a genre much favored by composers of the Romantic era

chorale: the German word for the hymn of the Lutheran church; hence a simple religious melody to be sung by the congregation

chord: two or more simultaneously sounding pitches

chord progression: a succession of chords moving forward in a purposeful fashion

chorus: a group of singers, usually including sopranos, altos, tenors, and basses, with at least two and often many more singers on each vocal part; also, in jazz, a full statement of the tune around which the performers improvise

chromaticism: the frequent presence in melodies and chords of intervals only a half step apart; in a scale, the use of notes not part of the diatonic major or minor pattern

church sonata: see *sonata da chiesa*

clarinet: a single-reed instrument of the woodwind family with a large range and a wide variety of timbres within it

clavier: a general term for all keyboard instruments including harpsichord, organ, and piano

clef sign: a sign used to indicate the register, or range of pitches, in which an instrument is to play or a singer is to sing

coda: (Italian for "tail") a final and concluding section of a musical composition

col legno: (Italian for "with the wood") an instruction to string players to strike the strings of the instrument not with the horsehair of the bow, but with the wood of it

collegium musicum: a society of amateur musicians (usually associated with a university) dedicated to the performance of music, nowadays music of the Middle Ages, Renaissance, and Baroque era

color (timbre): the character or quality of a musical tone as determined by its harmonics and its attack and decay

comic opera: a genre of opera that originated in the eighteenth century, portraying everyday characters and situations, and using spoken dialogue and simple songs

computer music: the most recent development in electronic music; couples the computer with the electronic synthesizer to imitate the sounds of acoustical instruments and to produce new sounds

concert overture: an independent, one-movement work, usually of programmatic content, originally intended for the concert hall and not designed to precede an opera or play

concertino: the group of instruments that function as soloists in a concerto grosso

concerto: an instrumental genre in which one or more soloists play with and against a larger orchestra

concerto grosso: a three-movement concerto of the Baroque era that pits the sound of a small group of soloists (the concertino) against that of the full orchestra (the tutti)

conjunct motion: melodic motion that proceeds primarily by steps and without leaps

consequent phrase: the second phrase of a two-part melodic unit that brings a melody to a point of repose and closure

consonance: pitches sounding agreeable and stable

continuo: see *basso continuo*

contrabassoon: a larger, lower-sounding version of the bassoon

cool jazz: a style of jazz that emerged in the 1950s that is softer, more relaxed, and less frenzied than bebop

cornet: a brass instrument that looks like a short trumpet; it has a more mellow tone than the trumpet and is most often used in military bands

cornetto: a woodwind instrument that developed during the late Middle Ages and early Renaissance that sounds like a hybrid of a clarinet and trumpet

counterpoint: the harmonious opposition of two or more independent musical lines

courante: a lively dance in 6/4 with an upbeat and frequent changes of metrical accent

crescendo: a gradual increase in the volume of sound

cymbals: a percussion instrument of two metal disks; they are made to crash together to create emphasis and articulation in music

da capo aria: an aria in two sections, with an obligatory return to and repeat of the first; hence an aria in ternary (**ABA**) form

dance suite: a collection of instrumental dances, each with its own distinctive rhythm and character

development: the center-most portion of sonata-allegro form, in which the thematic material of the exposition is developed and extended, transformed, or reduced to its essence; it is often the most confrontational and unstable section of the movement

diatonic: pertaining to the seven notes that make up either the major or the minor scale

Dies irae: a Gregorian chant composed in the thirteenth century and used as the central portion of the Requiem Mass of the Catholic Church

diminished chord: a triad or seventh chord made up entirely of minor thirds and producing a tense, unstable sound

diminuendo: a gradual decrease in volume of sound

diminution: a reduction, usually by half, of all the rhythmic durations in a melody

disjunct motion: melodic motion that moves primarily by leaps rather than by steps

dissonance: a discordant mingling of sounds

diva: (Italian for "goddess") a celebrated female opera singer; a prima donna

dominant chord: the chord built on the fifth degree of the scale

dondon: a two-headed pressure drum indigenous to West Africa

dotted note: a note to which an additional duration of fifty percent has been added

double bass: the largest and lowest-pitched instrument in the string family

double counterpoint: counterpoint with two themes that can reverse position, the top theme moving to the bottom and the bottom to the top (also called *invertible counterpoint*)

double exposition form: a form, originating in the concerto of the Classical period, in which first the orchestra and then the soloist present the primary thematic material

double stops: a technique applied to string instruments in which two strings are pressed down and played simultaneously instead of just one

downbeat: the first beat of each measure; it is indicated by a downward motion of the conductor's hand and is usually stressed

drone: a continuous sound on one or more fixed pitches

dynamics: the various levels of volume, loud and soft, at which sounds are produced in a musical composition

electronic instruments: machines that produce musical sounds by electronic means, the most widespread instrument being the keyboard synthesizer

electronic music: sounds produced and manipulated by magnetic tape machines, synthesizers, and/or computers

eleventh chord: a chord comprised of five intervals of a third and spanning eleven different letter names of pitches

encore: French word meaning "again"; the repeat of a piece demanded by an appreciative audience; an extra piece added at the end of a concert

English horn: an alto oboe, pitched at the interval a fifth below the oboe, much favored by composers of the Romantic era

episode: a passage of free, nonimitative counterpoint found in a fugue

erhu: an ancient two-string Chinese fiddle

"Eroica" Symphony: Beethoven's Symphony No. 3 (1803) originally dedicated to Napoleon but published as the "Heroic Symphony"

etude: a short one-movement composition designed to improve one aspect of a performer's technique

exposition: in a fugue, the opening section, in which each voice in turn has the opportunity to present the subject; in sonata-allegro form, the principal section, in which all thematic material is presented

falsetto voice: a high, soprano-like voice produced by adult male singers when they sing in head voice and not in full chest voice

fantasy: a free improvisatory-like composition in which the composer follows his or her whims rather than an established musical form

fermata: in musical notation, a mark indicating that the performer(s) should hold a note or chord for an extended duration

fiddle: a popular term for the violin

figured bass: in musical notation, a numerical shorthand that tells the player which unwritten notes to fill in above the written bass note

finale: the last movement of a multimovement composition, one that usually works to a climax and conclusion

flat: in musical notation, a symbol that lowers a pitch by a half step

flute: a high-sounding member of the woodwind family; the instrument was initially made of wood but more recently, beginning in the nineteenth century, of silver or even platinum

folk-rock: a mixture of the steady beat of rock with the forms, topics, and styles of singing of the traditional Anglo-American folk ballad

folk song: a song originating from an ethnic group and passed from generation to generation by oral tradition rather than written notation

form: the purposeful organization of the artist's materials; in music, the general shape of a composition as perceived by the listener

forte (f): in musical notation, a dynamic mark indicating "loud"

fortepiano (pianoforte): the original name of the piano

fortissimo (ff): in musical notation, a dynamic mark indicating "very loud"

free counterpoint: counterpoint in which the voices do not all make use of some preexisting subject in imitation

free jazz: a style of jazz perfected during the 1960s in which a soloist indulges in flights of creative fancy without concern for the rhythm, melody, or harmony of the other performers

French horn: a brass instrument that plays in the middle range of the brass family; developed from the medieval hunting horn

French overture: a two-part musical form of the Baroque era consisting of a slow first section in duple meter with dotted rhythms and a fast second section with imitative counterpoint

fugato: a short fugue set in some other musical form like sonata-allegro or theme and variations

fugue: a composition for three, four, or five parts played or sung by voices or instruments, which begins with a presentation of a subject in imitation in each part and continues with modulating passages of free counterpoint and further appearances of the subject

full cadence: a cadence that sounds complete, in part because it usually ends on the tonic note

gamelan: the traditional orchestra of Indonesia consisting of as many as twenty-five instruments, mostly gongs, chimes, drums, and metallophones

genre of music: type of music; specifically, the quality of musical style, form, performing medium, and place of performance that characterize any one type of music

Gesamtkunstwerk: (German for "total art work") an art form that involves music, poetry, drama, and scenic design; often used in reference to Richard Wagner's music dramas

Gewandhaus Orchestra: the symphony orchestra that originated in the Clothiers' House in Leipzig, Germany, in the eighteenth century

gigue: a fast dance in 6/8 or 12/8 with a constant eighth-note pulse that produces a galloplike effect

glissando: a device of sliding up or down the scale very rapidly

glockenspiel: a percussion instrument made of tuned metal bars that are struck by mallets

gong: a circular, metal percussion instrument of Asian origin

gongon: a large barrel-like drum indigenous to West Africa

grave: a tempo mark indicating "very slow and grave"

great staff: a large musical staff that combines both the treble and the bass clefs

Gregorian chant (plainsong): a large body of unaccompanied monophonic vocal music, set to Latin texts, composed for the Western Church over the course of fifteen centuries, from the time of the earliest Fathers to the Council of Trent

ground bass: the English term for *basso ostinato*

guiro: a scraped percussion instrument originating in South America and the Caribbean

half cadence: a cadence at which the music does not come to a fully satisfying stop but stands as if suspended on a dominant chord

half step: the smallest musical interval in the Western major or minor scale; the distance between any two adjacent keys on the piano

harmonics: the secondary tones above a fundamental pitch that taken in sum help form the totality of that sound

harmony: the sounds that provide the support and enrichment—an accompaniment—for melody

harp: an ancient plucked-string instrument with a triangular shape

harpsichord: a keyboard instrument, especially popular during the Baroque era, that produces sound by depressing a key that drives a lever upward and forces a pick to pluck a string

hauts instruments: a class of loud musical instruments, including trumpet, sackbut, shawm, and drum, popular during the late Middle Ages

Hindustani-style music: the traditional, or classical, music of northern India

homophony: a texture in which all the voices, or lines, move to new pitches at roughly the same time; often referred to in contradistinction to polyphony

horn: a term generally used by musicians to refer to any brass instrument, but most often the French horn

hornpipe: an energetic dance, derived from the country jig, in either 3/2 or 2/4 time

idée fixe: literally a "fixed idea," but more specifically an obsessive musical theme as first used in Hector Berlioz's *Symphonie fantastique*

imitation: the process by which one or more musical voices, or parts, enter and duplicate exactly for a period of time the music presented by the previous voice

imitative counterpoint: a type of counterpoint in which the voices or lines frequently use imitation

incidental music: music to be inserted between the acts or during important scenes of a play to add an extra dimension to the drama

instrumental break: in the blues or in jazz, a short instrumental passage that interrupts and responds to the singing of a voice

intermezzo: (Italian for "between piece") a light musical interlude intended to separate and thus break the mood of two more serious, surrounding movements or operatic acts or scenes

interval: the distance between any two pitches on a musical scale

inversion: the process of inverting the musical intervals in a theme or melody; a melody that ascended by step, now descends by step, and so on

invertible counterpoint: see *double counterpoint*

jazz: a lively, energetic music with pulsating rhythms and scintillating syncopations, usually played by a small instrumental ensemble

jazz-fusion: a mixture of jazz and rock cultivated by American bands in the 1970s

Karnatak-style music: the traditional, or classical, music of southern India

key: a tonal center built on a tonic note and making use of a scale; also, on a keyboard instrument, one of a series of levers that can be depressed to generate sound

key signature: in musical notation, a preplaced set of sharps or flats used to indicate the scale and key

Kyrie: the first portion of the Ordinary of the Mass and hence usually the opening movement in a polyphonic setting of the Mass

La Scala: the principal opera house of the city of Milan, Italy, which opened in 1778

largo: a tempo mark indicating "slow and broad"

leading tone: the pitch a half step below the tonic, which pulls up and into it, especially at cadences

leap: melodic movement not by an interval of just a step but usually by a jump of at least a fourth

legato: in musical notation, an articulation mark indicating that the notes are to be smoothly connected; the opposite of staccato

Leitmotif: a brief, distinctive unit of music designed to represent a character, object, or idea; a term applied to the motives in the music dramas of Richard Wagner

lento: a tempo mark indicating "very slow"

libretto: the text of an opera

Liebestod: (German for "love death") the famous aria sung by the expiring Isolde at the end of Richard Wagner's opera *Tristan und Isolde*

Lied: (German for "song") the genre of art song, for voice and piano accompaniment, that originated in Germany ca. 1800

London symphonies: the twelve symphonies composed by Joseph Haydn for performance in London between 1791 and 1795; Haydn's last twelve symphonies (Nos. 93–104)

lute: a six-string instrument appearing in the West in the late Middle Ages

madrigal: a popular genre of secular vocal music that originated in Italy during the Renaissance, in which usually four or five voices sing love poems

madrigalism: a device, originating in the madrigal, by which key words in a text spark a particularly expressive musical setting

major scale: a seven-note scale that ascends in the following order of whole and half steps: 1-1-½-1-1-1-½

Mass: the central religious service of the Roman Catholic Church, one that incorporates singing for spiritual reflection or as accompaniment to sacred acts

mazurka: a fast dance of Polish origins in triple meter with an accent on the second beat

measure (bar): a group of beats, or musical pulses; usually the number of beats is fixed and constant so that the measure serves as a continual unit of measurement in music

melisma: in singing, one vowel luxuriously spread out over many notes

melodic sequence: the repetition of a musical motive at successively higher or lower degrees of the scale

melody: a series of notes arranged in order to form a distinctive, recognizable musical unit; it is most often placed in the treble

meter: the gathering of beats into regular groups

metronome: a mechanical device used by performers to keep a steady tempo

mezzo-soprano: a female vocal range between alto and soprano

middle C: the middle-most C on the modern piano

Minimalism: a style of modern music that takes a very small amount of musical material and repeats it over and over to form a composition

Minnesinger: a type of secular poet-musician that flourished in Germany during the twelfth through fourteenth centuries

minor scale: a seven-note scale that ascends in the following order of whole and half steps: 1-½-1-1-½-1-1

minuet: a moderate dance in 3/4, though actually danced in patterns of six steps, with no upbeat but with highly symmetrical phrasing

mode: a pattern of pitches forming a scale; the two primary modes in Western music are major and minor

moderato: a tempo marking indicating "moderately moving"

modified strophic form: strophic form in which the music is modified briefly to accommodate a particularly expressive word or phrase in the text

modulation: the process in music whereby the tonal center changes from one key to another, from G major to C major, for example

monophony: a musical texture involving only a single line of music with no accompaniment

motet: a composition for choir or larger chorus setting a religious, devotional, or solemn text; often sung *a cappella*

motive: a short, distinctive melodic figure that stands by itself

mouthpiece: a detachable portion of a brass instrument into which the player blows

movement: a large, independent section of a major instrumental work, such as a sonata, dance suite, symphony, quartet, or concerto

music: the rational organization of sounds and silences as they pass through time

music drama: a term used for the mature operas of Richard Wagner

musical comedy: a popular genre of musical theater designed to appeal to a general audience by means of spoken dialogue, songs, and energetic dances

musique concrète: music in which the composer works directly with sounds recorded on magnetic tape, not with musical notation and performers

mute: any device that muffles the sound of a musical instrument; on the trumpet, for example, it is a cup that is placed inside the bell of the instrument

nationalism: a movement in music in the nineteenth century in which composers sought to emphasize indigenous qualities in their music by incorporating folk songs, native scales, dance rhythms, and local instrumental sounds

natural: in musical notation, a symbol that cancels a pre-existing sharp or flat

Neo-classicism: a movement in twentieth-century music that seeks to return to the musical forms and aesthetics of the Baroque and Classical periods

ninth chord: a chord spanning nine letters of the scale and constructed by superimposing four intervals of a third

nocturne: a slow, introspective type of music, usually for piano, with rich harmonies and poignant dissonances intending to convey the mysteries of the night

nonimitative counterpoint: counterpoint with independent lines that do not imitate each other

oboe: an instrument of the woodwind family; the highest-pitched of the double-reed instruments

octave: the interval comprising the first and eighth tones of the major and minor diatonic scale; the sounds are quite similar because the frequency of vibration of the higher pitch is exactly twice that of the lower

octave displacement: a process used in constructing a melody whereby a simple, nearby interval is made more distant, and the melodic line more disjunct, by placing the next note up or down an octave

opera: a dramatic work in which the actors sing some or all of their parts; it usually makes use of elaborate stage sets and costumes

opera buffa: (Italian for "comic opera") an opera on a light, often domestic subject, with tuneful melodies, comic situations, and a happy ending

opera seria: a genre of opera that dominated the stage during the Baroque era, making use of serious historical or mythological subjects, *da capo* arias, and a lengthy overture

operetta: a light opera with spoken dialogue and numerous dances involving comedy and romance in equal measure

ophicleide: a low brass instrument originating in military bands about the time of the French Revolution; the precursor of the tuba

opus: (Latin for "work") the term adopted by composers to enumerate and identify their compositions

oral tradition: the process used in transmission of folk songs and other traditional music in which the material is passed from one generation to the next by singing, or playing, and hearing, without musical notation

oratorio: a large-scale genre of sacred music involving an overture, arias, recitatives, and choruses, but sung, whether in a theater or a church, without costumes or scenery

orchestra: see *symphony orchestra*

orchestral score: a composite of the musical lines of all of the instruments of the orchestra and from which a conductor conducts

orchestral song: a genre of music emerging in the nineteenth century in which the voice is accompanied not merely by a piano but by a full orchestra

orchestral suite: a dance suite written for orchestra

orchestration: the art of assigning to the various instruments of the orchestra, or of a chamber ensemble, the diverse melodies, accompaniments, and counterpoints of a musical composition

Ordinary of the Mass: the five sung portions of the Mass for which the texts are unvariable

organ: an ancient musical instrument constructed mainly of pipes and keys; the player depresses a key that allows air to rush into or over a pipe, thereby producing sound

organum: the name given to the early polyphony of the Western Church from the ninth through the thirteenth centuries

oscillator: a device that, when activated by an electronic current, pulses back and forth to produce an electronic signal that can be converted by a loudspeaker into sound

ostinato: (Italian for "obstinate") a musical figure, motive, melody, harmony, or rhythm that is repeated again and again

overtone: see *harmonics*

overture: an introductory movement, usually for orchestra, that precedes an opera, oratorio, or dance suite

parallel motion: a musical process in which all of the lines or parts move in the same direction, and at the same intervals, for a period of time; the opposite of counterpoint

part: an independent line or voice in a musical composition; also, a section of a composition

pedal point: a note, usually in the bass, sustained or continually repeated for a period of time while the harmonies change around it

pentatonic scale: a five-note scale found often in folk music and non-Western music

phrase: a self-contained portion of a melody, theme, or tune

pianissimo (*pp*): in musical notation, a dynamic mark indicating "very soft"

piano (*p*): in musical notation, a dynamic mark indicating "soft"

piano: a large keyboard instrument that creates sound at various dynamic levels when hammers are struck against strings

piano transcription: the transformation and reduction of an orchestral score, and a piece of orchestral music, onto the great staff for playing at the piano

pianoforte: see *fortepiano*

piccolo: a small flute; the smallest and highest-pitched woodwind instrument

pickup: a note or two coming before the first downbeat of a piece, intending to give a little extra push into that downbeat

pipa: an ancient four-string Chinese lute

pitch: the relative position, high or low, of a musical sound

pizzicato: the process whereby a performer plucks the strings of an instrument rather than bowing them

plainsong: see *Gregorian chant*

point of imitation: a distinctive motive that is sung or played in turn by each voice or instrumental line

polychords: the stacking of one triad or seventh chord on another so they sound simultaneously

polymeters: two or more meters sounding simultaneously

polyphony: a musical texture involving two or more simultaneously sounding lines; the lines are often independent and create counterpoint

polyrhythms: two or more rhythms sounding simultaneously

polytonality: the simultaneous sounding of two keys or tonalities

popular music: a broad category of music designed to please a large section of the general public; sometimes used in contradistinction to more "serious" or more "learned" classical music

prelude: an introductory, improvisatory-like movement that gives the performer a chance to warm up and sets the stage for a more substantive subsequent movement

prepared piano: a piano outfitted with screws, bolts, washers, erasers, and bits of felt and plastic to transform the instrument from a melodic one to a percussive one

prestissimo: in musical notation, a tempo mark indicating "as fast as possible"

presto: in musical notation, a tempo mark indicating "very fast"

prima donna: (Italian for "first lady") the leading female singer in an opera

program music: a piece of instrumental music, usually for symphony orchestra, that seeks to recreate in sound the events and emotions portrayed in some extramusical source: a story, a play, a historical event, an encounter with nature, or even a painting

program symphony: a symphony with the usual three, four or five movements in which the individual movements together tell a tale or depict a succession of specific events or scenes

Proper of the Mass: the sections of the Mass that are sung to texts that vary with each feast day

qin: an ancient seven-string Chinese zither

quadrivium: a curriculum of four scientific disciplines (arithmetic, geometry, astronomy, and music) taught in medieval schools and universities

quadruple meter: music with four beats per measure

quarter tone: the division of the whole tone, or whole step, into quarter tones, a division even smaller than the half tones, or half steps, on the piano

raga: an Indian scale and melodic pattern with a distinctive expressive mood

ragtime: an early type of jazz emerging in the 1890s and characterized by a steady bass and a syncopated, jazzy treble

rebec: a medieval fiddle

recapitulation: in sonata-allegro form, the return to the first theme and the tonic key following the development

recital: a concert of chamber music, usually for a solo performer

recitative: musically heightened speech, often used in an opera, oratorio, or cantata to report dramatic action and advance the plot

recitativo accompagnato: recitative accompanied by the orchestra instead of merely the harpsichord; the opposite of *secco* recitative

recorder: an end-blown wooden flute with seven finger holes played straight out instead of to one side

relative major: the major key in a pair of major and minor keys; relative keys have the same key signature, for example, E♭ major and C minor (both with three flats)

relative minor: the minor key in a pair of major and minor keys; see *relative major*

rest: a silence in music of a specific duration

retransition: the end of the development section where the tonality often becomes stabilized on the dominant in preparation for the return of the tonic (and first theme) at the beginning of the recapitulation

retrograde: a musical process in which a melody is played or sung, not from beginning to end, but starting with the last note and working backward to the first

rhythm: the organization of time in music, dividing up long spans of time into smaller, more easily comprehended units

rhythm and blues: a style of early rock 'n' roll ca. 1950 characterized by a pounding 4/4 beat and a raw, growling style of singing, all set within a twelve-bar blues harmony

rhythm section: the section within a jazz band, usually consisting of drums, double bass, piano, banjo, and/or guitar, that establishes the harmony and rhythm

Ring cycle: a cycle of four interconnected music dramas by Richard Wagner that collectively tell the tale of the Germanic legend *Der Ring des Nibelungen*

ritard: a gradual slowing down of the tempo

ritardando: in musical notation, a tempo mark indicating a slowing down of the tempo

ritornello: the Italian word for "return" or "refrain"; a short musical passage in a Baroque concerto grosso invariably played by the tutti

romance: a slow, lyrical piece, or movement within a larger work, for instruments, or instrument and voice, much favored by composers of the Romantic period

rondeau: see *rondo*

rondo: an ancient musical form (surviving into the twentieth century) in which a refrain alternates with contrasting material

rubato: (Italian for "robbed") in musical notation, a tempo mark indicating that the performer may take, or steal, great liberties with the tempo

Russian Five: a group of young composers (Borodin, Cui, Balakirev, Rimsky-Korsakov, and Musorgsky) centered in St. Petersburg, whose aim it was to write purely Russian music free of European influence

sackbut: a brass instrument of the late Middle Ages and Renaissance; the precursor of the trombone

Sanctus: the fourth section of the Ordinary of the Mass

sarabande: a slow, elegant dance in 3/4 with a strong accent on the second beat

scale: an arrangement of pitches that ascends and descends in a fixed and unvarying pattern

scherzo: (Italian for "joke") a rapid, jovial work in triple meter often used in place of the minuet as the third movement in a string quartet or symphony

Schubertiade: a social gathering for music and poetry that featured the songs and piano music of Franz Schubert

score: a volume of musical notation involving more than one staff

secco recitative: dry recitative accompanied only by the harpsichord

Sequence: a Gregorian chant, sung during the Proper of the Mass, in which a chorus and a soloist alternate; see also *melodic sequence*

serenade: an instrumental work for a small ensemble originally intended as a light entertainment in the evening

serial music: music in which some important component—pitch, dynamics, rhythm—comes in a continually repeating series; see also *twelve-tone composition*

seventh chord: a chord spanning seven letter names and constructed by superimposing three thirds

sforzando: a sudden, loud attack on one note or chord

sharp: a musical symbol that raises a pitch by a half step

shawm: a double-reed woodwind instrument of the late Middle Ages and Renaissance; the precursor of the oboe

sinfonia: (Italian for "symphony") a one-movement (later three- or four-movement) orchestral work that originated in Italy in the seventeenth century

Singspiel: (German for "singing play") a musical comedy originating in Germany with spoken dialogue, tuneful songs, and topical humor

sitar: a large lutelike instrument with as many as twenty strings, prominently used in the traditional music of northern India

snare drum: a small drum consisting of a metal cylinder covered with a skin or sheet of plastic that when played with sticks produces the "rat-ta-tat" sound familiar from marching bands

solo: a musical line sung or played by a single performer

solo concerto: a concerto in which an orchestra and a single performer in turn present and develop the musical material in the spirit of harmonious competition

solo sonata: a work, usually in three or four movements, for keyboard or other solo instrument; when a solo melodic instrument played a sonata in the Baroque era it was supported by the *basso continuo*

sonata: originally "something sounded" on an instrument as opposed to something sung (a "cantata"); later a multi-movement work for solo instrument, or instrument with keyboard accompaniment

sonata–allegro form: a dramatic musical form of the Classical and Romantic periods involving an exposition, development, and recapitulation, with optional introduction and coda

sonata da camera (chamber sonata): a suite for keyboard or small instrumental ensemble made up of individual dance movements

sonata da chiesa (church sonata): a suite for keyboard or small instrumental ensemble made up of movements indicated only by tempo marks such as *grave, vivace, adagio*; originally intended to be performed in church

song cycle: a collection of several songs united by a common textual theme or literary idea

soprano: the highest female vocal part

Sprechstimme: (German for "speech-voice") a singer declaims, rather than sings, a text at only approximate pitch levels

staccato: a manner of playing in which each note is held only for the shortest possible time

staff: a horizontal grid onto which are put the symbols of musical notation: notes, rests, accidentals, dynamic marks, etc.

stanza: a poetic unit of two or more lines with a consistent meter and rhyme scheme

step: the interval between adjacent pitches in the diatonic or chromatic scale; either a whole step or a half step

stomp: a piece of early jazz in which a distinctive rhythm, with syncopation, is established in the opening bars, as in the opening phrases of the "Charleston"

string bass: see *double bass*

string instruments: instruments that produce sound when strings are bowed or plucked; the harp, guitar, and the members of the violin family are all string instruments

string quartet: a standard instrumental ensemble for chamber music consisting of a first and second violin, a viola, and a

cello; also the genre of music, usually in three or four movements, composed for this ensemble

strophe: see *stanza*

strophic form: a musical form often used in setting a strophic, or stanzaic, text, such as a hymn or carol; the music is repeated anew for each successive strophe

style: the general surface sound produced by the interaction of the elements of music: melody, rhythm, harmony, color, texture, and form

subdominant chord: the chord built on the fourth, or subdominant, degree of the major or minor scale

subject: the term for the principal theme in a fugue

sustaining pedal: the right-most pedal on the piano; when it is depressed, all dampers are removed from the strings, allowing them to vibrate freely

swing: a mellow, bouncy, flowing style of jazz that originated in the 1930s

syllabic singing: a style of singing in which each syllable of text has one, and only one, note; the opposite of melismatic singing

symphonic poem (tone poem): a one-movement work for orchestra of the Romantic era that gives musical expression to the emotions and events associated with a story, play, political occurrence, personal experience, or encounter with nature

symphony: a genre of instrumental music for orchestra consisting of several movements; also the orchestral ensemble that plays this genre

symphony orchestra: the large instrumental ensemble that plays symphonies, overtures, concertos, and the like

syncopation: a rhythmic device in which the natural accent falling on a strong beat is displaced to a weak beat or between the beats

synthesizer: a machine that has the capacity to produce, transform, and combine (or synthesize) electronic sounds

tabla: a double drum used in the traditional music of northern India

tambourine: a small drum the head of which is hung with jangles; it can be struck or shaken to produce a tremolo effect

tam-tam: an unpitched gong used in Western orchestras

tempo: the speed at which the beats occur in music

tenor: the highest male vocal range

ternary form: a three-part musical form in which the third section is a repeat of the first, hence **ABA**

terraced dynamics: a term used to describe the sharp, abrupt dynamic contrasts found in the music of the Baroque era

texture: the density and disposition of the musical lines that make up a musical composition; monophonic, homophonic, and polyphonic are the primary musical textures

theme and variations: a musical form in which a theme continually returns but is varied by changing the notes of the melody, the harmony, the rhythm, or some other feature of the music

The Well-Tempered Clavier: two sets of twenty-four preludes and fugues compiled by J. S. Bach in 1720 and 1742

through composed: a term used to describe music that exhibits no obvious repetitions or overt musical form from beginning to end

timbre: see *color*

timpani (kettle drums): a percussion instrument consisting usually of two, sometimes four, large drums that can produce a specific pitch when struck with mallets

time signature (meter signature): two numbers, one on top of the other, usually placed at the beginning of the music to tell the performer what note value is carrying the beat and how the beats are to be grouped

toccata: a one-movement composition, free in form, originally for solo keyboard but later for instrumental ensemble as well

tonality: the organization of music around a central tone (the tonic) and the scale built on that tone

tonal language: any language in which the meaning of a word is expressed not only in its phonetic structure but also by the pitch at which it is spoken

tone: a sound with a definite, consistent pitch

tone cluster: a dissonant sounding of several pitches, each only a half step away from the other, in a densely packed chord

tone poem: see *symphonic poem*

tonic: the central pitch around which the melody and harmony gravitate

transition (bridge): in sonata-allegro form the unstable section in which the tonality changes from tonic to dominant (or relative major) in preparation for the appearance of the second theme

treble: the uppermost musical line, voice, or part; the part in which the melody is most often found

treble clef: the sign placed on a staff to indicate the notes above middle C

tremolo: a musical tremor produced on a string instrument by repeating the same pitch with quick up and down strokes of the bow

triad: a chord consisting of three pitches and two intervals of a third

trill: a rapid alternation of two neighboring pitches

trio: an ensemble, vocal or instrumental, with three performers; also, a brief, self-contained composition contrasting with a previous piece, such as a minuet or a polonaise; originally the trio was performed by only three instruments

trio sonata: an ensemble of the Baroque period consisting actually of four performers, two playing upper parts and two on the *basso continuo* instruments

triplet: a group of three notes inserted into the space of two

trivium: a literary curriculum of three disciplines (grammar, logic, and rhetoric) taught in medieval schools and universities

trombone: a brass instrument of medium to low range that is supplied with a slide, allowing a variety of pitches to sound

troubadour: a kind of secular poet-musician that flourished in southern France during the twelfth and thirteenth centuries

trouvère: a kind of secular poet-musician that flourished in northern France during the thirteenth and early fourteenth centuries

trumpet: a brass instrument of the soprano range

tuba: a brass instrument of the bass range

tune: a simple melody that is easy to sing

tutti: (Italian for "all") the full orchestra or full performing force

twelve-tone composition: a method of composing music, devised by Arnold Schoenberg, that has each of the twelve notes of the chromatic scale sound in a fixed, regularly recurring order

unison: two or more voices or instrumental parts singing or playing the same pitch

upbeat: the beat that occurs with the upward motion of the conductor's hand and immediately before the downbeat

verismo opera: "realism" opera; Italian term for a type of late nineteenth-century opera in which the subject matter concerns the unpleasant realities of everyday life

vibrato: a slight and continual wobbling of the pitch produced on a string instrument or by the human voice

viola: a string instrument; the alto member of the violin family

viola da gamba (bass viol): the lowest member of the viol family; a large six- or seven-string instrument played with a bow and heard primarily in the music of the late Renaissance and Baroque eras

violin: a string instrument; the soprano member of the violin family

virtuosity: extraordinary technical facility possessed by an instrumental performer or singer

vivace: in musical notation, a tempo mark indicating "fast and lively"

vocal ensemble: in opera, a group of four or more solo singers, usually the principals

voice: the vocal instrument of the human body; also a musical line or part

volume: the degree of softness or loudness of a sound

walking bass: a bass line that moves at a moderate pace, mostly in equal note values, and often stepwise up or down the scale

waltz: a popular, triple-meter dance of the late eighteenth and nineteenth centuries

whole step: the predominant interval in the Western major and minor scale; the interval made up of two half steps

whole-tone scale: a six-note scale each pitch of which is a whole tone away from the next

woodwind family: a group of instruments initially constructed of wood; most make their sound with the aid of a single or double reed; includes flute, piccolo, clarinet, oboe, English horn, and bassoon

word painting: the process of depicting the text in music, be it subtly, overtly, or even jokingly, by means of expressive musical devices

xylophone: a percussion instrument consisting of tuned wooden bars, with resonators below, that are struck with mallets

CREDITS

TEXT

80 Marsilio Ficino, "The Golden Age in Florence," in *The Portable Renaissance Reader*, ed. James Bruce Ross and Mary Martin McLaughlin, New York, The Viking Press, 1953, p. 79.

84 Edward Lowinsky, *Music in the Culture of the Renaissance and Other Essays*, ed. Bonnie J. Blackburn, Chicago, The University of Chicago Press, 1989, vol. I, p. 87.

89 Palestrina, *Pope Marcellus Mass*, ed. Lewis Lockwood, New York, W. W. Norton and Company, 1975, p. 12.

117 Walter Kolneder, *Antonio Vivaldi: Documents of his Life and Works*, New York, C. F. Peters Corporation, 1981, p. 43.

139 Christopher Hogwood, *Handel*, London, Thames and Hudson, 1984, p. 71.

156 *Music in the Western World: A History in Documents*, ed. Piero Weiss and Richard Taruskin, New York, Schirmer Books, 1984, p. 299.

156 "Haydn," in *The New Grove Dictionary of Music and Musicians*, ed. Stanley Sadie, London, Macmillan, 1980, vol. VIII, p. 344.

159 *The Letters of Mozart and his Family*, ed. Emily Anderson, London, Macmillan, 1938, vol. III, p. 1187.

179 A & M Records, SP-3735.

210 Conrad Fischer and Erich Koch, *Ludwig van Beethoven*, London, Macmillan, 1958, p. 28.

306 Neil Butterworth, *Dvořák*, London, Monibus Press, 1980, p. 105.

314 Alma Mahler Werfel, *And the Bridge was Love*, New York, Harcourt Brace, 1958, pp. 25–27.

341 Modris Eksteins, *Rites of Spring*, New York, Doubleday, 1989, p. 14.

346 Arnold Schoenberg, "The Composition with Twelve Tones," in *Composers on Music*, ed. Sam Morgenstern, New York, Pantheon Books, 1956, p. 380.

356 Charles Ives, *The Fourth of July*, ed. John Kirkpatrick, New York, Associated Music Publishers, 1974, p. 1.

ILLUSTRATIONS

2 Precision Graphics; **3** Precision Graphics; **4** CORBIS/Lynn Goldsmith; **5** CORBIS; **6** Novosti Information Agency, London; **7 (left and right)** SuperStock; **9 (left)** Rich Jew, one of the "Pictures at an Exhibition" by Gartman (hartman), Viktor Aleksandrovich/Novosti/Bridgeman Art Library, London/New York; **9 (right)** Poor Jew, one of the "Pictures at an Exhibition" by Gartman (hartman), Viktor Aleksandrovich/Novosti/Bridgeman Art Library, London/New York; **10 (bottom)** SuperStock; **10 (top)** Sketch of a Gate by Gartman (hartman), Viktor Aleksandrovich/Novosti/Bridgeman Art Library, London/New York; **14** © 1987 Garry D. McMichael, Photo Researchers, Inc.; **19** CORBIS/Hulton-Deutsch Collection; **22** Josef and Anni Albers Foundation; **23** Musée Nationale de l'Art Moderne, Paris; **27** The Granger Collection; **29** SuperStock; **30** The Waterlily Pond: Green Harmony, 1899 by Claud Monet, Musée d'Orsay, Paris, France/Bridgeman Art Library, London/New York; **32** Violinist at the Window, 1918 by Henri Matisse/Musée National de l'Art Moderne, Paris, France/Peter Willi/Bridgeman Art Library, London/New York; **38 (bottom)** CORBIS/David Lees; **38 (top)** Musée d'Orsay, Paris/SuperStock; **39** © Sheila Rock/ICM Artists, Ltd.; **40 (bottom)** Courtesy of Sony Classical; **40 (right)** © Ira Nozik 1987/Jane Davis Inc.; **40 (top)** Courtesy of ICM Artists, Ltd.; **41 (bottom)** Courtesy of the G. Leblanc Corporation, Kenosha, Wisconsin; **41 (top)** SuperStock; **42 (bottom)** Courtesy of the Yamaha Corporation; **42 (top)** © Martin Reichenthal; **43 (bottom)** Barrie-Kent Photographers; **43 (top)** The Minnesota Orchestral Association; **44 (left)** Yale University Collection of Musical Instruments; **44 (right)**

Improviso" in the Esterhazy Theatre, 29th August 1775 by German School/Deutsches Theatermuseum, Munich, Germany/Bridgeman Art Library, London/New York; **190** Kunsthistorisches Museum, Vienna; **191 (bottom)** Private Collection; **191 (top)** Mozart Memorial Collection, Prague; **192** Yale Center for British Art, Paul Mellon Collection; **195 (bottom)** Mozart Museum, Salzburg; **196** Mozart Museum, Salzburg; **200** Galerie Hlavniho, Prague; **201** The Granger Collection, N.Y.; **203** © Winnie Klotz; **210** Beethoven-Haus, Bonn; **214** Gesellschaft der Musikfreunde, Vienna; **215** CORBIS/Burstein Collection; **219** Museum der Stadt Wien, Vienna; **225** Deutsche Staats, Berlin; **226 (bottom)** Craig Wright, New Haven; **226 (top)** Beethovenhaus, Bonn; **231** The Wanderer over the Sea of Clouds, 1818 by Caspar-David Freidrich Kunsthalle, Hamburg, Germany/Bridgeman Art Library, London/ New York; **232** Giraudon/Art Resource, N.Y.; **233** National Portrait Gallery, London; **238 (bottom)** CORBIS; **240 (bottom)** Yale University; **240 (top)** The Bettmann Archive; **241 (right)** CORBIS; **247 (top and bottom)** Museum der Stadt Wien, Vienna; **248** Joachim Blauel-ARTOTHEK; **254 (bottom)** Bibliothèque Nationale; **254 (top)** Academie de France, Rome; **255** Yale Center for British Art, Paul Mellon Collection; **257** The Witches' Sabbath by Francisco Jose de Goya y Lucientes/Museo Lazaro Galdiano, Madrid, Spain/Index/Bridgeman Art Library, London/New York; **260 (bottom)** Mendelssohn Archiv, Staatsbibliothek, Berlin; **260 (top)** Musée du Louvre, Paris/ ET Archive, London/SuperStock; **261 (bottom)** Stadtgeschichtliches Museum, Leipzig; **261 (top)** Courtesy of the Library of Congress; **262** Tate Gallery/Art Resource; **264** Ernst Burger; **266** Culver Pictures; **267** Ernst Burger; **269 (bottom)** The Ordrupgaard Collection, Copenhagen; **269 (top)** CORBIS; **270** Bibliothèque Nationale; **272 (bottom)** Richard Wagner Museum, Bayreuth, Germany; **272 (top)** Conservatoire de Musique, Geneva; **273 (bottom)** Mary Evans Picture Library; **273 (top)** Märkisches Museum, Berlin; **279** Museo Teatrale alla Scala, Milan; **280 (bottom)** Museo Teatrale alla Scala, Milan; **280 (top)** Domenica del Corriere/ET Archive, London/SuperStock; **282** Portrait of Giuseppina Strepponi, celebrated soprano and wife of Giuseppe Verdi by Italian School/ Private Collection/Roger-Viollet, Paris/Bridgeman Art Library, London/New York; **283** Christiane Issartel; **285** © Beth Bergman 1987; **287** Richard Wagner Museum, Bayreuth; **288** Richard Wagner Museum, Bayreuth; **289** Richard Wagner Museum, Bayreuth; **290** Bayerisches National Museum, Munich; **294** The Bettmann Archive; **300** Museum der Stadt Wien, Vienna; **301** Museum der Stadt Wien, Vienna; **305 (bottom)** Antonin Dvořák Society, Prague; **305 (top)** Dvořák Museum, Prague, Czechoslovakia/ET Archive, London/SuperStock; **306 (bottom)** Antonin Dvořák Society, Prague; **306 (top)** The New York Public Library; **308 (bottom)** Novosti Information Agency, London; **308 (top)** Tretiakov Gallery, Moscow, Russia/SuperStock; **312** CORBIS/Bettmann; **313** Osterreichische Nationalbibliothek; **314** Otsterreichische Nationalbibliothek; **315** © Eric Shanes; **321 (bottom)** Peter Willi; **321 (top)** Musée Marmottan, Paris, France/SuperStock; **322** Visual Arts Library, London, UK; **323 (bottom)** Musée du Petit Palais, Paris; **323 (top)** Musée d'Orsay, Paris; **325 (bottom)** Bulloz; **325 (top)** The Bettmann Archive; **326** The Fine Arts Museums of San Francisco, Gift of Bruno and Sadie Adriani; **328** 1951 Purchase Fund, Museum of Fine Arts, Boston; **329 (bottom)** Photo collection Sirot; **329 (top)** Kunstmuseum, Basel/A.K.G., Berlin/ SuperStock; **330** Artephot/Trela/Bridgeman Art Library, London/SuperStock; **334 (bottom)** Peter Willi, Stadtische Galerie im Lenbachaus, Munich; **334 (top)** Picasso, Pablo. *Les Demoiselles d'Avignon*. Paris (begun May, reworked July 1907) Oil on canvas, 8' x 7'8". Collection, The Museum of Modern Art, New York. Acquired through the Lillie P. Bliss Bequest; **335 (bottom)** Galérie Daniel Malingue, Paris, France; **335 (top)** Magrette, Rene. Portrait. (1935) Oil on canvas, 28 7/8" x 19 7/8". Collection, The Museum of Modern Art, New York. Gift of Kay Sage Tanguy; **338** Museum of Modern Art; **339** CORBIS/Alexander Burkatowski; **340 (bottom)** Roger-Viollet; **341** CORBIS/Burstein Collection; **342** Hermitage Museum, St. Petersburg, Russia/AGE FotoStock/SuperStock; **344** Offenliche Kunstammlung, Kunstmuseum, Basel; **346 (bottom)** Graphische Sammlung Albertina, Vienna, Austria; **346 (top)** Private Collection; **347** Erich Lessing, Art Resource, NY; **350** Rijksdienst Beeldende Kunst, The Hague; **351** Haaga Gemeentemuseum; **352** CORBIS/Archivo Iconografico, S.A.; **355 (bottom)** Music Library, Yale University; **355 (top)** SuperStock; **356** The Metropolitan Museum of Art, New York; **358 (left)** CBS/Sony; **358 (right)** Alexander Calder, Lobster Trap and Fish Tail. (1939) Hanging mobile: painted steel wire and sheet aluminum, 8'6"h x 9'6"w. Photo © The Museum of Modern Art, New York; **359** Rex Rystedt; **360 (left)** CORBIS/ Neal Preston; **(right)** Courtesy of Skywalker Sound, Marin County, California; **361 (bottom)** Saatchi Collection, London/Bridgeman Art Library, London/Superstock; **361 (top)**

INDEX